CONWAY'S DIRECTORY OF
MODERN NAVAL POWER
1986

CONWAY'S DIRECTORY OF
MODERN NAVAL POWER
1986

HUGH W COWIN

CONWAY
MARITIME

Acknowledgements

The author wishes to thank the following navies and organisations for their generous assistance in providing photographic and, in many cases additional documentary support, without which this work would have been far less informative. My thanks go to the navies of Australia, Brazil, Canada, Chinese Peoples' Republic, Denmark, Finland, Federal Germany, France, Greece, India, Ireland, Israel, Italy, Japan, Netherlands, New Zealand, Norway, Pakistan, Portugal, South Africa, Spain, Sweden, United Kingdom, United States, and Yugoslavia. Similar invaluable aid was provided by ABMTM, Aerospatiale, Bath Iron Works, Bazan, Bell Aerospace, Bell Helicopters, Bethlehem Steel, Blohm und Voss, Boeing, Bofors Ordnance, Bremer Vulkan, British Aerospace, British Aerospace Dynamics, British Shipbuilders, Brooke Marine, Cantieri Navali Riuniti, Dassault Breguet, Direction Technique des Constructions Navales, Emerson Electric, Fokker, General Dynamics, Hall Russell, Halter Marine, Howaldtswerke-Deutsche Werft, Intermarine, Kaman Aerospace, Karlskronavarvet, Litton Industries, Lurssen Werft, Newport News Shipbuilding, National Steel & Shipbuilding, Oerlikon-Buhrle, OTO-Melara, Peterson Builders, Raytheon Company, Richards Shipbuilders, Rolls-Royce Limited, Royal Fleet Auxiliary, RSV, Scott Lithgow, Shorts, SNCF, St John's Shipbuilding, Swan Hunter, Swiftships, Tacoma Boat, Todd shipyards, Vickers Shipbuilding and Engineering, Vosper Group, Vosper Thornycroft, Wartsila, Westland Helicopters, Wilton-Fijenoord, YARD Limited, Yarrow Shipbuilders. From amongst the many individuals who have lent their support, special mention must be made of the assistance and advice rendered by Michael Hill, Lt Comm W R 'Bill' Harlow, US Navy and Capt A Flamigni, Italian Navy.

Published by Conway Maritime Press
24 Bride Lane
Fleet Street
London EC4Y 8DR

© Hugh W Cowin 1985

ISBN 0 85177 362 1

Typeset by C.R. Barber & Partners (Highland) Ltd, Fort William, Scotland.
Printed in Great Britain by R.J. Acford, Chichester

Designed by Jonathan Doney

Contents

During the spring of 1982, the waters around the Falklands and South Georgia saw the first major naval action to occur in almost 37 years. Far from being of only parochial and passing interest to the participating belligerents, the lessons and ramifications of this brief but bitter struggle are still being digested worldwide by naval operational planners, warship designers and naval systems developers, alike.

While countless hundreds of thousands of words have been written around the Falklands conflict, most have tended to sensationalise rather than analyse the frequently vexed questions that flowed out of these distant South Atlantic events. In fact, the naval/air contest that centred around the Falklands revealed little that was not, to a greater or lesser degree, foreseeable. For instance, the effectiveness of the modern anti-ship missile had been clearly demonstrated as early as October 1967, with the sinking of the Israeli destroyer *Eilat* by an Egyptian-launched SS-N-2 'Styx' missile. Similarly, severe superstructural damage, one by collision-induced friction and consequent fire damage, the other through ballistic fragmentation damage to the US Navy cruisers *Belknap* and *Worden*, respectively, during the latter 1960s, should have served to highlight the potential combat vulnerability of light alloys in warship construction. Indeed, even the absence of an effective close-in anti-air weapons system aboard most of the Royal Navy's South Atlantic task group vessels simply served to validate the much earlier Soviet and Italian Navies' decisions to equip all of their warships, from corvette size upwards, with such systems. This said, the one indisputable fact remains that the battle for the Falklands imparted operational perspectives on such a scale that they simply could not be ignored.

That the experience gained during the spring of 1982 will take a perceptible time to incorporate should be obvious, particularly when it is realised that the gestation time from original concept to initial operational deployment of a new warship class or even a close-in weapons system may well exceed eight years. These considerations notwithstanding, the one instantly visible aspect of the Falklands conflict that, hopefully, will not be lost on the politicians, was its implicit demonstration of the vital need to maintain an effective navy.

The purpose of *Conway's Naval Directory* is to provide the broadest possible informed and timely coverage of the global naval development scene post-spring 1982; all within the one set of more accessibly priced covers than have hitherto existed.

To achieve such an objective necessarily involved the systematic gathering together of many seemingly disparate threads, ranging from comprehending the fundamental economic and political considerations that shape the primary role and size of a particular navy, to forming some appreciation of the equipment available for use in today's potentially fully three-dimensional combat environment within which navies may well find themselves compelled to operate.

Unlike its more expensive rival naval references, *Conway's Naval Directory* sets out to illustrate, explain and, where needed, comment in plain English across a broad range of naval-related aspects. Further, wherever possible, the pitfall of viewing a development or piece of equipment in isolation has been avoided and, thus, the **Notes** sections of individual entries frequently cross-refer to other related aspects, not even, necessarily, in the same section of the book.

NOTES

Section 1: dealing with the world's navies, abandons the traditional method of calling up each service in national alphabetical order, preferring to group navies by size, expanding out into regional or ethnical groupings when dealing with the numerous smaller navies.

Section 2: dealing with warships, gathers together all vessels of similar generic function, regardless of nationality and then stratifies them in generally descending order of full displacement. Here, however, the author has deliberately introduced one or two anomalies to this rule, such as in the case of the Royal Navy's 'Broadsword' class frigate series, which are set out in chronological order of batch appearance, so as to gauge better the pace and pressure of the programme development.

Section 3: dealing with naval aircraft, is similarly grouped by generic function and sub-grouped by descending all-up weight of the aircraft. In general, the criteria for machines included in this section is that they must meet some operational naval role and, unlike the Royal Air Force-operated British Aerospace Nimrods, or Soviet Air Force Tupolev Tu-126 'Moss', be operated by a naval air arm.

Section 4: devoted to naval missiles and gun mounts, is subdivided by generic function of weapon. In the case of missiles, the generic subdivisions are exemplified by anti-ship, ship-launched, or anti-ship, air launched and, within these groups, follow a sub-ordering by maximum range. All naval gun mounts are straightforwardly ordered by descending order of calibre.

Terminology

In describing the roles undertaken by certain navies, two mission requirements are used that require basic amplication:

Power projection: this term is employed in the context of a navy's ability to mount an offensive thrust against opposing forces, usually at some distance from its nearest base support. The term can be used in the tactical context of operating an aircraft carrier-centred task group, screened by both submarine and surface combatants and possibly including an amphibious warfare element, such as deployed by the US Navy's Sixth Fleet to the Lebanon from 1982 onwards. Equally, the term can be used in the strategic sense to denote a navy's ability to strike a mortal nuclear blow at the very heartland of an enemy through the use of intercontinental ballistic missile-carrying submarine forces.

Sea control: a mission description covering the gaining and maintenance of control over a predetermined sea area for as long as is tactically necessary. The term can be used in the defensive context of guarding vital sea lanes of communication, or in the offensive connotation of clearing the seaward approaches for an amphibious assault.

Vessel pennant numbering

As aids to identification, warships not engaged in active service usually carry pennant numbers, consisting of either a single letter (descriptive of their primary function, such as D for destroyer), plus one, two, three or four number sequences that identify the individual ship. Alternatively, some navies, including the Soviet and US, simply display the numeric identifier only. To confuse matters, however, some navies, including the Soviet, follow the practice of frequently changing the pennant number of their ships. In such cases, all references to pennant numbers have been omitted in order to avoid subsequent confusion. In the case of those vessels carrying combined alphanumeric pennant numbers, the following table relates prefix letter to function:

A	Auxiliary (support)	M	Mine countermeasures
C	Cruiser	N	Minelayer
D	Destroyer	P	Patrol or fast attack
F	Frigate or corvette	R	Aircraft carrier
L	Landing (assault)	S	Submarine

Unfortunately, anomalies exist even in this area, exemplified by the Brazilian Navy's *Minas Gerais*, which despite its 'A' prefix is an aircraft carrier and not an auxiliary. To compound the problem, the US Navy and those of the North Atlantic Treaty Organisation (NATO) employ a more detailed system of functional prefixes, which while not reflected in the ships' pennant numbers, is used almost universally in verbal and written references and, indeed, is made use of in this work as an aid to defining more clearly specific mission capability. In this prefix system, the letter prefixes (with the exception of cruisers and patrol and fast attack craft) are expanded into two letter groups, exemplified by SS for submarine; CV for aircraft carrier; BB for battleship; CC for cruiser; DD for destroyer; FF for frigate, fleet (or ocean-going), as opposed to FL for frigate light, or corvette. To these basic groupings are added a further letter to provide additional mission-orientated qualifiers, such as N for nuclear-powered, G for guided missile-carrying, H for helicopter or VTOL aircraft-carrying, and B for ballistic missile-carrying. Thus the conventional aircraft-carrying, nuclear-powered USS

Nimitz is a CVN, whilst the VTOL aircraft and helicopter-carrying Soviet aircraft carrier *Kiev*, equipped as it is with a formidable missile armament, is a CVHG.

Ship categorisation

While most sectional headings used in Section 2 are self-explanatory, one or two areas of ambiguity do exist, as in the case of the Soviet Navy's 'Moskva' class helicopter-carrying ships. As these ships have no full-length flight deck, they have been grouped as Cruisers. By the same definition, both the Royal Navy's 'Invincible' class and the Soviet's 'Kiev' class ships have been included in the Aircraft Carrier section.

In the Support Ships section, the convention of sequencing the entries by descending order of displacement has not been followed. In fact, this section has been deliberately split into two sub-groupings, the first relating to operational ships (replenishment vessels), and the second grouping formed from largely statically-based types, such as submarine tenders and salvage tugs.

Within the section devoted to Submarines, the submariner's traditional practice of referring to his craft as a 'boat' has been followed.

Where only a sole example of a ship has been built, the word 'class' does not apply and the ship is more appropriately described in the entry heading as a 'type'.

Abbreviations

bhp	brake horsepower
CODAG	These terms refer to propulsive machinery
CODOG	arrangements with CO referring to COmbining
COGAG	power transmission systems, D for Diesel, G for
COSAG	Gas turbine, S for Steam, with the fourth letter, either A or O, standing for And or Or
ft	feet
IFF	Interrogation, Friend or Foe
m	metres
mm	millimetres
shp	shaft horsepower
VTOL	vertical take-off and landing (aircraft)
3-D	three-dimensional

Typifying the more visible tactical power projection capability of the US Navy is this Indian ocean battle group, centred on the carriers USS Eisenhower *and* Nimitz *with guided missile cruisers* California *and* South Carolina *in attendance (above).*

The Soviet 'Kiev' class aircraft carrier Minsk *and the guided missile destroyer* Kara.

Navies

Leading navies

United States Navy

The United States Navy is, by almost every yardstick, the largest and most capable naval force extant and, despite the impressive latterday growth of the Soviet Navy, should remain so well into the next century. To comprehend why such a prediction can be made with such confidence requires more than a direct comparison of current hull numbers, along with comparing projected build rates, and involves an analysis of the fundamental mission roles assigned to the two navies.

In the case of the US Navy, both the geography and the politics of the Western Hemisphere have tended to be longstanding spurs to its governmentally-perceived importance as an instrument of US foreign policy; a navy being the natural primary prerequisite in both defending or sortieing offensively from a large, isolated land mass. Historically, the Soviet Navy enjoyed neither of these intrinsic advantages until, in the wake of the 1962 Cuban missile crisis and the subsequent growth of distant Soviet client nations, the Soviet Government came to recognize the need to guard these new and suddenly politically important sea lanes of communication.

Unlike its Soviet counterpart, the US Navy has benefited not only from its massive exposure to World War II and the conduct of numerous more recent long-range campaigns, but has also been in a better position than the Soviet Navy to grow up with the sometimes rapidly evolving technology of the twentieth century, as evidenced by its relatively early recognition of the value of the aircraft carrier as a prime asset with which to wrest distant sea control. In more recent times, the US Navy has successfully pioneered a number of innovative naval developments, including the adapting of nuclear propulsion systems and the marriage of the intercontinental ballistic missile to the submarine endowed with an underwater launch capability.

Today, the US Navy has both the capability and means to meet virtually all of the mission requirements set for it, ranging from strategic power projection, with its fleet of ballistic missile-carrying submarines, to securing distant tactical sea control with its large, carrier-centred inventory of surface combatants and hunter/killer submarines. Thanks to its subordinate US Marine Corps, the US Navy is far better equipped than any other navy to meet the need for tactical power projection, involving the securing of a distant beach-head, thanks to its large amphibious warfare assets; an operational area, incidentally, where the US Navy maintains a demonstrable ascendancy over the Soviet Navy.

Personnel: Total 571,300 active US Navy personnel, plus 134,400 US Navy Reserves, along with 198,300 active US Marine Corps personnel, and 40,200 US Marine Corps reservists as of the beginning of January 1985.

Composition of forces: The US Navy is organized into four major fleets comprising the Third and Seventh Fleets, with responsibility for the Pacific and Indian Oceans; the Second Fleet, which covers the Atlantic; and the Sixth Fleet, whose primary responsibility lies in the Mediterranean Sea. Where additional logistic support is needed, the fleets can call upon the US Navy-controlled,

civilian-operated Military Sealift Command. US naval aviation comprises both long-range, shore-based operational patrol elements as well as seagoing tactical air groups and is subordinated to the operational fleets. All are sustained by largely US continental-based US Navy aviation logistics, support and training units.

Order of battle, naval forces

Nuclear-powered submarines, ballistic missile equipped	36*
hunter/killer	99*
diesel-electric powered	4
Large nuclear-powered aircraft carriers	4*
Large aircraft carriers	9
Aircraft carrier (training duties only)	1
Battleships (2 refitted, plus 2 planned refits)	4
Nuclear-powered cruisers, missile equipped	9
Cruisers, missile equipped	20*
Destroyers, missile equipped	68
Frigates, missile equipped	97*
Fast attack craft, missile equipped	6
Patrol vessels (all light craft)	80*
Minesweepers	3*
Amphibious assault ships	61*
Auxiliaries, replenishers (including Military Sealift Command)	14*
other support type (with MSC vessels included)	79*

Order of battle, US Navy and US Marine aviation

Fighters	878*
Strike fighters	134*
Bombers (seagoing)	1284*
Anti-submarine (both fixed and rotary winged)	783*
Airborne warning and control	148*
Electronic warfare	46*
Observation	94
Tankers	60*
Transport and training types	1254*
Utility (both fixed and rotary winged)	1402

Notes: Ship and aircraft strengths are as of end 1984. Asterisks denote ongoing procurement.

Soviet Navy

While virtually all of the world's navies have undergone a radical transformation in terms of equipment and capabilities over the past quarter of a century, nowhere has such change been more manifest than within the Soviet Navy. Whereas most navies have shrunk, the Soviet Navy has flourished in both quantitative and qualitative measure, becoming in the process not only the world's second largest naval force, but also one of the most balanced in terms of accomplishing its primary task of establishing a credible global presence.

Two readily definable factors have played a prime role in the transformation of the Soviet Navy from being an essentially coastal-waters-only force into the omnipresent entity of today. Initially, there necessarily had to be the political will of successive Soviet administrations, coupled to which there had to be a Soviet Naval staff with sufficient tenacity and vision to translate the politicians' desires into a manifestly capable navy. In terms of the latter objective, the Soviet Navy has much to thank one man, its Commander-in-Chief for the past 28 years. Admiral of the Fleet Sergi Georgiyevich Gorschkov, the long-acknowledged chief architect of its awesome development.

While both technical and operational comparisons will continue to be made between the rival capabilities of the two super-power navies, it is as well initially to recognize both the recent historical interplay in the development directions taken by these two services, along with the differing primary role priorities that exist. Fundamentally, over the past 30 years or so, the Soviet Navy's primary concern has been to build an essentially defensive naval force, capable of countering the US Navy's tactical sea/air power projection abilities. The Soviet's pioneering development of both ship and air-launched anti-ship cruise missiles reflect their need to combat the potent threat posed from a carrier-centred task group. Similarly, the everpresent threat of air attack clearly acted as the spur for the innovative Soviet Navy development of shipboard anti-air close-in weapons systems for the early 1960s onwards. While the Soviet Navy has felt it necessary to emulate US Navy submarine-launched strategic missile developments, it is of interest to note that the Soviet Navy's amphibious warfare capability falls far short of that available to the United States.

Personnel: Total 185,000 sea going, 68,000 naval aviation, 8000 coastal defence, 14,500 naval infantry, 54,000 training and 127,000 shore support, as of the end of June 1983.

Composition of forces: The Soviet navy is organised into four fleets, plus a Caspian Sea Flotilla. These fleets in descending order of size comprise Northern Fleet (with responsibility for the Atlantic), Pacific Fleet (with responsibility for the Indian ocean also), Black Sea Fleet (with prime responsibility for the Mediterranean Sea) and the Baltic Fleet. Soviet naval aviation, which consists of long-range, land-based elements as well as tactical seagoing elements, is operationally subordinated within the structures of the individual fleets. Training of Soviet naval aviation personnel is undertaken by the Soviet Air Force, with whom naval personnel share the same rank structure.

Order of battle, naval forces

Nuclear-powered submarines ballistic missile equipped	70*
cruise missile equipped	50*
hunter/killer	55*
Diesel-electric submarines: ballistic missile equipped	17
cruise missile equipped	20
hunter/killer	160*
Large aircraft carriers for conventional aircraft	1 in build
VSTOL aircraft carriers	3 + 1 in build
Helicopter-carrying carriers	2
Nuclear-powered cruisers	1 + 1 in build
Cruisers equipped with anti-air or anti-ship missiles	27*
Light cruisers	9
Destroyers, equipped with anti-air or anti-ship missiles	38*
Destroyers, gun equipped	30
Frigates equipped with missiles	28*
Light frigates or corvettes	143*
Small surface combat vessels: missile equipped	147*
patrol and anti-submarine	395*
Minesweepers of all categories	400*
Amphibious assault ships: 'Rogov' class 'Alligator' and 'Ropuchka' classes	25
1000 medium landing ships	60
Auxiliaries: replenishment ships	150*
light auxiliaries	610*

Note: The auxiliary elements are primarily supplied by the Mercantile Marine.

Order of battle, naval aviation *(asterisks denote ongoing procurement).*

Bombers ('Backfire', 'Blinder' and 'Badger')	370*
Strike aircraft ('Forger' and 'Fitter')	
Reconnaissance and electronic warfare ('Blinder', 'Badger' and 'Bear')	170
Anti-submarine warfare (both fixed and rotary winged)	390*
Tanker aircraft 'Badger'	70
Transport and training types	340

Notes: Ship and aircraft strengths are as of end June 1983. Asterisks denote ongoing procurement.

Chinese Peoples' Republic's Navy

The Chinese Peoples' Republic Navy presents a number of major anomalies to the casual observer intent on making comparisons between it and other major navies. In terms of active naval manpower, the Chinese hold third place in the global rankings, while, if the number of deployable hulls is taken as the criterion, then China has the largest navy extant. Even in terms of total tonnage deployable, China's navy ranks among the three largest navies. However, unlike both the US and Soviet navies with their highly visible offensive capabilities, the Chinese Navy's composition predicates an almost entirely defensive force, with an extremely limited ability to operate at any significant distance beyond its own coastal waters. On a subtler level of equipment comparisons, the Chinese Navy can be seen to be still largely dependant upon largely obsolete Soviet naval vessel, weapons and sensor technology dating back to the mid-1950s.

This said, the expansion of the Chinese Navy from its virtually non-existent state in the late 1930s to its current size has been little short of incredible. Looking to the future, while the past unparalleled growth cannot be expected to continue, there is every indication that China has already embarked on a policy of consolidating its home-grown technological base. In naval terms, this is likely to manifest itself in a gradual diminution of deployable vessels in favour of developing more capable hulls, sensors and weapons, along with associated systems, more and more of which will be of Chinese design and construction. The emergence of potentially vast offshore oil reserves in the South China Sea, with its natural consequent need to ensure adequate protection for these assets, is likely to further Chinese Government support for its navy.

Personnel: Total of approximately 360,000, including around 38,000 naval aviation and 38,000 marines. In addition, China maintains approximately 1,000,000 naval militia.

Composition of forces: The Chinese Peoples' Republic's naval arm is organized into three operating fleets. These comprise the North China Sea Fleet, the East China Sea Fleet and the South China Sea Fleet. Chinese naval aviation, which is entirely shore-based, is operationally subordinated to the fleet. However, its large, if elderly fighter forces form an integral part of the homeland air defence system, central control of which is vested with the Chinese Peoples' Republic's Air Force.

Order of battle, naval forces

Nuclear-powered submarines, ballistic missile equipped	3*
Diesel-electric submarines, ballistic missile equipped	1

Typifying the essentially geographically limited, defensive role of the Chinese Peoples' Republic's Navy is this dramatic photograph of three Chinese-built fast torpedo patrol boats, based on the Soviet Navy's 'P-4' class design.

Diesel-electric submarines	97
Destroyers, missile equipped	12*
Frigates, missile equipped	18*
gun equipped	5
Corvettes (all very elderly)	probably less than 8
Fast attack craft, missile equipped	210*
torpedo equipped	285
Patrol vessels	510*
Amphibious assault ships	17
Auxiliaries, replenishers	2
armed trawlers	around 245
other support types	126*

Order of battle, naval aviation

Fighters	600*
Bombers	210*
Anti-submarine (both fixed and rotary winged)	22*
Transport and training types	60

Notes: Ship and aircraft strengths are as of end 1984.
Asterisks denote ongoing procurement.

The Royal Navy's HMS Birmingham (D86), RFA Olmeda (A124), RFA Fort Austin (A386).

Royal Navy

No longer in the dominant position it once enjoyed, the Royal Navy has, arguably, borne more of the brunt in terms of UK Government defence budgetary cuts over the past 20 years or so than either of the other two UK services, largely as a result of the growth of European-centred policy on the part of successive British governments.

Regrettably, this succession of cutbacks has wrought profound changes both on the size and capability of today's Royal Navy, whose tactical and strategic power projection capabilities are quite sparse outside the sphere of specialized anti-submarine warfare.

Indeed, nowhere better than in its conduct of the recent Falklands campaign can the growing material impoverishment of the Royal Navy's assets be highlighted. While in no way attempting to disparage either the competence or courage of Britain's sailors, the Falklands War, when viewed objectively, spotlighted a number of significant naval deficiencies, perhaps primarily among which was the Royal Navy's inability to mount the necessary logistics support without recourse to drawing upon a large number of merchant ships. In operational terms, despite the favourable outcome, the vulnerability of British warships to air attack ought to engender anxiety,

11

particularly when the number of unexploded bomb hits are considered. That such enemy air strikes could have been reduced had the Royal Navy retained a force of larger aircraft carriers, capable of operating supersonic fighters and early-warning aircraft, can be of little solace to Royal Navy planning staff. To conclude this somewhat depressing analysis of the Falklands campaign, it must also be recalled that following the initial naval skirmish in which the Argentinian cruiser *General Belgrano* was lost, the Argentinian Navy's surface elements played no further effective part in the conflict; an aspect, which by its absence, may well have had a crucial impact on the hostilities' outcome.

This said, the Royal Navy is still the fourth largest navy, whether gauged in terms of major warship hulls, total tonnage or manpower. With most of its assets committed to the North Atlantic Treaty Organisation defensive pact, the Royal Navy contributes the largest single national element of that grouping's naval forces.

Personnel Total 70,600, comprising 29,500 seagoing, 7500 Royal Marines and approximately 13,000 naval aviation personnel. Not included in the above figures are 2870 civilians operating with the Royal Fleet Auxiliary: all figures pertaining to end March 1985.

Composition of forces: The Royal Navy comprises three major surface ship flotillas: the 1st and 2nd being made up of destroyer and frigate elements, while the 3rd consists of carriers and assault ships. The remaining flotillas comprise submarines, mine-countermeasures and survey. Vessels from each flotilla are drawn as required to meet operational commitments, normally predicated by NATO, in such areas as the North Eastern Atlantic, North Sea, Channel and Western Approaches. Additional logistics support is provided by the Royal Fleet Auxiliary. The Royal Navy maintains and operates all of its own aircraft, with the exception of Hunter GA11s drawn from Royal Air Force inventory.

Order of battle, naval forces

Nuclear-powered submarines, ballistic missile	
equipped	4
hunter/killer	12*
Diesel-electric submarines	15*
VSTOL aircraft carriers	3*
Destroyers, missile equipped	15*
Frigates, missile equipped	38*
gun equipped only	4
Patrol vessels	27
Minesweepers and hunters of all categories	36*
Amphibious assault ships (including Royal Fleet Auxiliary)	8
Coastal training craft	15*
Auxiliaries, replenishers (Royal Fleet Auxiliary operated)	14
other support types	20*

Order of battle, naval aviation

Strike fighters and reconnaissance types	34
Anti-submarine (helicopters entirely)	147*
Transport and training types	69*

Notes: Ships and aircraft strengths are as of end March 1985. Asterisks denote ongoing procurement.

French Navy

Only marginally smaller when measured in terms of tonnage than the Royal Navy, the French Navy has managed to retain a more balanced total capability, thanks largely to its retention of a conventional aircraft-operating carrier force. Based on projected new builds scheduled to commence during the current four-year French Defence Plan, the tonnage comparison is likely to

narrow as France receives two more large replenishers and starts construction of its 36,000-ton full displacement, nuclear-powered aircraft carrier. In the sphere of strategic power projection, France has already overtaken Britain in deployable ballistic missile-carrying submarines, with more either in build or planned. Similarly, while the Royal Navy were first into the field of glass-reinforced plastic mine countermeasures vessel construction, it is notable that the French Navy has not only initiated its own construction programme for glass-reinforced plastic minehunters, but has succeeded, where the British failed, in attracting the work and cost-sharing support of the Dutch and Belgian navies in their vessel.

Significantly, while the French Navy's tactical surface, air and submarine elements are nominally considered a part of the North Atlantic Treaty Organization's forces, the French ballistic missile-carrying submarine force, along with France's other strategic nuclear forces, remains exclusively under the control of the French Government.

Personnel: Total 68,400 including 8840 reservists and comprising approximately 27,000 seagoing personnel, 13,000 naval aviation, 21,000 shore support and 7000 training, as of end 1984.

Composition of forces: The French Navy is organized around three major commands based at Cherbourg, to cover the Channel and northern waters; Brest, with responsibility for the Atlantic and Toulon, supervising Mediterranean operations. Four smaller overseas commands control operations in the French territories within the Pacific, the Indian Ocean, Caribbean and South Atlantic.

Order of battle, naval forces

Nuclear-powered submarines, ballistic missile	
equipped	5*
hunter/killer	2*
Diesel-electric submarines	18
Nuclear-powered aircraft carriers	1 planned
Aircraft carriers	2
Helicopter cruisers	1
Cruisers, missile equipped	1
Destroyers, missile equipped	15*
Destroyers, gun equipped	2
Frigates, missile equipped	8
Frigates, gun equipped	1
Corvettes, missile equipped	17*
Patrol vessels	19*
Minesweepers/hunters	23*
Amphibious assault ships	11*
Auxiliaries: replenishers	3*
other support types	9*

Order of battle, naval aviation

Fighters	15
Strike aircraft	36
Anti-submarine (both fixed and rotary winged)	118*
Reconnaissance aircraft	20*
Transport and training types	91*

Notes: Ship and aircraft strengths are as of end 1984. Asterisks denote ongoing procurement.

Other navies

Argentina Along with Brazil, the Argentinian Navy is significantly larger than any of the other Latin American countries. Interestingly, while relatively limited in terms of its maximum operational range, the Argentinian Navy has a more offensive orientation than that of other Latin American navies, as evidenced by their retention of a carrier-borne tactical air strike capability, coupled with an ongoing emphasis on building both surface and

An impressive array of French naval power exercising in the Mediterranean during 1982. Visible are both French carriers and five destroyers comprising two 'Georges Leygues' class, two 'Suffren' class and a 'D'Estrees' class.

submarine sea-control capable vessels. Currently, the Argentinian Navy is undergoing a programme of major modernisation, ranging from the offshore procurement of West German TR 1700 submarines and 'Almirante Brown' class destroyers, to the building in their own yards of the Blohm und Voss-designed 'Espora' class corvettes. While the Argentinian Navy may not overtake that of Brazil within the next decade in terms of deployable hulls or manpower, there can be little question that, under their current impetus, Argentina will enter the 1990s with the most modern and offensively equipped navy within the region.

Australia Recently deprived of its sole aircraft carrier, the Australian Navy currently appears to be concentrating its resources on the specific areas of regional anti-submarine warfare and coastal water policing. In terms of the anti-submarine role, the Australians are in the course of procuring four US-built 'Perry' class frigates with a fifth and sixth example being locally built. To increase the range of these frigates, Australia is buying a 'Durance' class replenisher from France. To help counter illegal immigrant traffic, Australia maintains a relatively large patrol boat force, of which the essentially locally-built 'Fremantle' class will remain the mainstay through the year 2000.

Brazil Currently the largest of the Latin American navies, the Brazilian Navy's primary tasks fall under three headings, all essentially defensive in posture. To guard their vital sea lanes of communications, the Brazilians maintain a small but modern regional anti-submarine force, currently being supplemented with locally-built Type 209 class submarines and the Brazilian-developed 'V28' corvette programme, along with the modified 'Niteroi' class training frigate *Brasil*. Closer inshore, the Brazilian Navy operates a small force of seagoing patrol vessels to guard its significant offshore oil and gas assets. The third significant task undertaken by the Brazilian Navy is that of providing border policing and civil community support services along the many hundreds of miles of waterways that form the Amazon basin to the north and the Paraguay River to the south-west of the country.

Canada A two-ocean navy with bases bordering the Atlantic and Pacific coasts, the Canadian Navy may be much smaller in size today than during World War II, but has lost nothing of its reputation as a pioneer of long-range, rough water anti-submarine warfare. With its Atlantic-based forces committed to the North Atlantic Treaty Organization, the Canadian Navy's existing destroyer and frigate forces are nearing the completion of life extension programmes. In addition, work is now underway on the first of the six 'Halifax' class frigates, destined to replace the elderly 'St Laurent' class ships from 1987 onwards.

Federal German Republic As only to be expected of a navy that did much to pioneer the operational use of submarines in both world wars, the Federal German Navy retains a large submarine force, backed essentially by a surface force largely of many small displacement vessels. Backing both surface and submarine elements is a formidably modern navy-controlled land-based air strike force, currently in the process of converting from Lockheed F-104 Starfighters to Panavia Tornado all-weather aircraft, each capable of carrying four air-launched medium-range Kormoran anti-ship missiles. Similarly, the Federal German Navy is in the process of replacing its six ageing 'Koln' class vessels with the new 'Bremen' class frigates. Federal Germany is a member of the North Atlantic Treaty Organization (NATO).

Greece The Hellenic Navy, charged with the task of protecting a coastline characterized by its many inlets and offshore islands, understandably favours the missile-equipped fast attack craft as its primary surface combat element, backed by a relatively small number of destroyers and frigates for longer range operations. Greece is a member of the North Atlantic Treaty Organization (NATO).

India One of the major so-called non-aligned navies, that of India maintains a relatively long-range, deep water surface force of frigates and corvettes, backed by one aircraft carrier and two replenishers, and being supplemented with delivery of the last of three Soviet-designed Modified 'Kashin' class destroyers. Indian Navy air strength is currently being bolstered by the acquisition of British Aerospace Sea Harriers, to be equipped with Sea Eagle anti-ship missiles.

Italy A major element in the North Atlantic Treaty Organization's Mediterranean-based naval forces, the

13

Italian Navy is built around a relatively small number of cruisers, destroyers and frigates, all of which are fast and most of which pack the optimum weapons punch for their size and role. These Italian surface forces are being further enhanced with the delivery of the last of the new 'Maestrale' class frigates and will soon be augmented with the delivery of the carrier *Garibaldi*. The Italian Government actively supports its national shipbuilding and naval equipment industries, with the result that Italian warships have been exported extensively, along with Italian-developed ordnance.

Japan Since the reformation of the Japanese Maritime Self-Defence Force in 1954, the service has been primarily anti-submarine warfare orientated and is supported by its own long-range, land-based force of Lockheed P-3 Orions and shipboard Sea King anti-submarine helicopters. Currently, the Japanese service is in the middle of a major modernization programme involving the construction of 'Yushio' class submarines, 'Hatsuyuki' class destroyers, a final 'Tachikaze' class ship, 'Ishikara' class frigates and 'Hatsushima' class minehunters.

Netherlands A member of the North Atlantic Treaty Organization (NATO), the Royal Netherlands Navy maintains a relatively compact fleet of replenisher-supported, modern rough water frigates for anti-submarine and anti-ship missions, backed by corvettes for offshore patrol, along with a relatively large standing force of minesweepers/hunters. Currently, the Netherlands are replacing the elderly 'Dokkum' class mine counter-measures vessels with the new 'Alkmar' class Tripartite minehunters. The Dutch Navy controls its own small air arm, whose front-line equipment comprises land-based Lockheed P-3 Orions and shipboard Westland Lynx helicopters.

Spain The relatively large Spanish Navy clearly intends to preserve its tactical seagoing air power and is currently awaiting the completion of its new *Principe de Asturias* aircraft carrier to replace the venerated *Dedalo*.

Turkey Formerly a largely US-supplied navy operating mostly ex-World War II vessels, the Turkish Navy has, in recent years, turned towards Europe and, in particular Federal Germany for its new build submarines, frigates and fast attack craft. Of these newer vessels, a significant number have been or are being locally constructed in Turkish shipyards.

Asia and the Pacific

Bangladesh A recently-formed navy employing a mix of elderly British frigates, along with Chinese and Yugoslavian patrol vessels. No air arm.

Brunei A pocket-sized naval force spearheaded by no less than three Exocet missile-armed 'Waspada' class fast attack craft for localized operations.

Burma A small, rather elderly equipped navy, whose tactical operations are centred on patrolling the country's inland waterways.

Fiji A small, very localized patrol force that operates without air support.

Indonesia The Indonesian Navy is one of the largest navies in this region and is currently in the process of modernizing its missile-equipped fast attack forces with additional destroyers and corvettes. In recent years, Indonesia has turned away from being a naval equipment client of first the US, and later of the Soviets, and now buys its warships from The Netherlands, South Korea and Yugoslavia, its Exocet missiles from France, and its naval ordnance from Bofors of Sweden. Indonesia has ordered two 'Lerici' class minehunters from Italy, along with 26 Aerospatiale AS 322F Super Puma helicopters, each capable of lifting two air-launched AM 39 Exocet missiles.

Laos The Laotian Navy is a small coastal force operating with Soviet-supplied equipment.

Malaysia The Royal Malaysian Navy is currently undergoing a programme of modernization and growth. In terms of warship procurement, Malaysia is in the process of receiving two Howaldtswerke FS 1500 frigates and additional 'Handalan' class fast attack craft, along with two 'Lerici' class minehunters, plus one 'Sri Indera' class multi-purpose support ship delivered.

	Argentina	Australia	Brazil	Canada	Federal Germany	Greece	India	Italy	Japan	Netherlands	Spain	Turkey
Total personnel:	36,000	16,990	46,000	24,600	36,200	19,500	47,000	44,500	44,000	16,870	57,000	46,000
Naval forces:												
Diesel-electric submarines	3*	6	8*	3	24	10	8*	10*	14*	6*	5*	16*
Aircraft carriers	1	–	1	–	–	–	1	0*	–	–	1*	–
Cruisers, missile equipped	–	–	–	–	–	–	–	3	–	–	–	–
gun only	–	–	–	–	1	–	1	–	–	–	–	–
Destroyers, missile equipped	5*	3	2	4	7	5	2*	4	20*	–	1	9
gun only	4	1	8	–	–	9	–	–	8	–	7	6
Frigates, missile equipped	–	9*	6*	16*	3	2	8	8*	16*	17*	11*	0*
gun only	–	–	–	3	4*	5	13	4	4	–	–	2
Corvettes, missile equipped	3*	–	0*	–	–	–	3	–	–	–	–	–
gun only	4	4	10	–	6	–	–	8*	–	6	4	–
Fast attack craft, missile	–	–	–	–	33*	16	14	7	–	–	–	13*
gun only	2	–	–	–	5	11	2	4	5	–	12	8
Patrol vessel/craft	6	8*	26	7	–	8	–	–	12*	5	93	25
Assault ships	2	1	3	–	–	21	10*	3*	6	–	6	2
Landing craft	18	6	47	–	50	61	–	50	37	10	91	77*
Minesweepers/hunters	6	3	6	–	88	14	14*	25*	31*	17	9	34
Auxiliaries, replenishers	1	1*	2	3	8	2	2	2	2	2	1	6
other support	67	27	81*	53*	106	36	29	82	34*	46	108*	75*
Naval aviation:												
Strike aircraft	14	6	–	–	106*	–	16*	–	–	–	15	–
Anti-submarine (all types)	27*	23	–	47	48	14	31	93*	148*	23*	36	24
Utility helicopters	3	23	–	3	–	–	10	–	39*	6	11	3
Transport and training types	87*	10	–	12	25	–	36*	–	117*	–	6	–

Notes: Ship and aircraft strengths are as of end of June 1984. Asterisks denote ongoing procurement.

New Zealand The Royal New Zealand Navy maintains a small, rough water force of Westland Wasp-carrying ex-Royal Navy frigates for anti-submarine duties, along with small numbers of coastal and inshore patrol craft: all of British origin. Primary naval air cover is provided by Royal New Zealand Air Force Lockheed P-3 Orions and Douglas A-4 Skyhawks.

North Korea Essentially a quantitatively large coastal force, the North Korean Navy operates a mix of Soviet and Chinese built vessels and equipment.

Pakistan The Pakistani Navy is a relatively small force centred on a rough water nucleus of one ex-Royal Navy 'County' class and a number of ex-US 'Gearing' class destroyers, the latter of which is destined to reach 14 in number. A small naval air arm operates three Breguet Atlantics, six Sea King and four Aerospatiale Alouette III helicopters.

Papua New Guinea A small, currently exclusively ex-Australian equipped Papuan New Guinea Navy has been formed to undertake coastal patrols, along with providing internal policing and civil community support functions. Any air cover is supplied by the country's small air force operating eight GAF Nomad maritime surveillance aircraft, plus four Douglas C-47 transports.

Philippines An essentially coastal force primarily concerned with guarding this island chain nation. Currently, the Philippine Navy is acquiring additional PSMM Mk 5 class fast attack craft and tank landing ships of South Korean construction, along with locally-built patrol craft. The small, primarily search and rescue orientated naval air arm operates nine Britten-Norman Islander aircraft and five MBB Bo 105 helicopters.

Sabah A small, launch-equipped force operated by the country's police.

Singapore A small but powerfully armed navy, larger than most other navies in this region, particularly when viewed in relation to the size and population of this island state. Singapore's gun-equipped fast attack force strength is currently being augmented with the delivery of an additional three 'Lurssen TNC 45' class built locally. If required, the Singapore Navy can call upon fairly

formidable air force-provided air cover, whose primary strike elements comprise a roughly equal mix of Northrop f-5E Tiger IIs, Douglas A-4 Skyhawks and Hawker Hunters totalling almost 100 jets in all.

South Korea Although the largest of this region's navies in terms of manpower and larger tonnage warships, the South Korean Navy lacks any submarines, while its surface combatant forces largely comprise of very elderly ex-US destroyers, frigates and corvettes that are in the process of being supplemented by the addition of a second locally-built 'Ulsan' class missile frigate. The South Korean Navy, which operates largely under air cover provided by the country's air force employs a small force of ship-going Hughes Model 500 helicopters.

Sri Lanka A small coastal patrol force, the Sri Lankan Navy employs Chinese-built patrol vessels.

Taiwan The Taiwanese Navy is unquestionably the largest of the region's navies when measured in deployable hull tonnage terms. This said, it must be noted that this navy's submarine and destroyer elements all comprise elderly ex-US vessels. On order are two additional 'Lung Chiang' class fast attack craft, plus up to four more locally-built 'Tzu Chiang' missile-carrying light strike craft. The Taiwanese Navy operates 12 ship-going Hughes Model 500 anti-submarine helicopters.

Thailand The Royal Thai Navy is centred on a small but relatively potent force of anti-ship missile armed fast attack craft, backed by a larger force of gun-equipped patrol craft, the latest of which comprise three Italian built 'Chonburi' class patrol vessels, delivery of which should have been completed prior to the end of 1984. The Royal Thai Navy operates its own, largely land-based air arm which includes 10 Grumman S-2 Trackers, three Fokker F27M and two Canadair CL-215.

Tonga A light craft force operated as part of the country's small army.

Vietnam An essentially coastal and riverine force, the Vietnamese Navy operates with Soviet-supplied surface combatants, such as two 'Petya' class frigates and eight 'Osa II', plus eight 'Shershen' class fast attack craft, plus a legacy of ex-US vessels, ranging from two elderly frigates

	Bangladesh	Brunei	Burma	Fiji	Indonesia	Laos	Malaysia	New Zealand	North Korea	Pakistan	Papua New Guinea	Philippines	Singapore	Sri Lanka	South Korea	Taiwan	Thailand	Vietnam
Total personnel:	5300	420	10,000	160	42,000	1700	11,000	2830	33,500	11,000	300	28,000	4500	49,000	2960	38,000	32,200	12,000
Naval forces:																		
Diesel-electric submarines	–	–	–	–	3	–	–	–	21	6	–	–	–	–	–	2	–	–
Aircraft carriers	–	–	–	–	–	–	–	–	–	–	–	–	–	–	–	–	–	–
Cruisers, missile equipped	–	–	–	–	–	–	–	–	–	–	–	–	–	–	–	–	–	–
gun only	–	–	–	–	–	–	–	–	–	–	–	–	–	–	–	–	–	–
Destroyers, missile equipped	–	–	–	–	–	–	–	–	–	9*	–	–	–	–	7	9	–	–
gun only	–	–	–	–	–	–	–	–	–	–	–	–	–	–	4	15	–	–
Frigates, missile equipped	–	–	–	–	1	–	0*	–	–	–	–	–	–	–	1*	–	–	–
gun only	3	–	1	–	6*	–	2	3*	–	–	–	7	–	–	7	9	6	6
Corvettes, missile equipped	–	–	–	–	3	–	–	–	–	–	–	–	–	–	–	–	–	–
gun only	–	–	2	–	–	–	–	–	6	–	–	10	–	3	–	3	–	–
Fast attack craft, missiles	–	3	–	–	5*	6	8*	–	18	4	6	2*	6	–	11	28*	6*	8
gun only	8	3	–	–	–	–	8	–	161	4	–	–	8*	–	1	–	–	18
Patrol vessel/craft	10	3	28	–	17	8	22*	8	146	31	4*	127*	2	48	32*	–	89	162
Assault ships	–	–	–	–	11	–	2	–	–	–	–	24*	6	20	–	29	7	10
Landing craft	6	26	9	–	13	7	29	–	99	–	11	90	6	20	–	400	42*	255
Minesweepers/hunters	–	–	–	3	2*	–	2*	–	–	6	–	–	2	9	–	14	9	30
Auxiliaries, replenishers	–	–	–	–	1	–	–	–	–	1	–	2	–	–	–	3	1	6
other support	1	–	46	3	10*	8	13*	6*	–	7*	2	40	–	15	1	30	19	14
Naval aviation																		
Strike aircraft	–	–	–	–	–	–	–	–	–	–	–	–	–	–	–	–	–	–
Anti-submarine (all types)	–	–	–	–	10	–	–	6	–	13	–	–	–	18	–	12	10	–
Utility helicoptors	–	–	–	–	9*	–	–	–	–	–	–	5	–	–	–	–	11	10
Transport and training types	–	–	–	–	17	–	–	–	–	–	–	9	–	–	–	–	44	–

Notes: Ship and aircraft strengths are as of end June 1984. Asterisks denote ongoing procurement.

	Albania	Belgium	Bulgaria	Denmark	Finland	German Democratic Republic	Ireland	Norway	Poland	Portugal	Romania	Sweden	Yugoslavia
Total personnel:	3200	4550	8500	5900	2700	14,000	1180	7500	22,000	15,000	7500	9650	12,000
Naval forces													
Diesel-electric submarines	3	–	2	5*	–	–	–	13*	4	3	–	12*	7
Aircraft carriers	–	–	–	–	–	–	–	–	–	–	–	–	–
Cruisers, missile equipped	–	–	–	–	–	–	–	–	–	–	–	–	–
gun only	–	–	–	–	–	–	–	–	–	–	–	–	–
Destroyers, missile equipped	–	–	–	–	–	–	–	–	1	–	–	–	–
gun only	–	–	–	–	–	–	–	–	–	–	–	2	–
Frigates, missile equipped	–	4	–	2	–	–	–	5	–	–	–	–	2*
gun only	–	–	2	–	1	2	–	–	–	17	–	–	
Corvettes, missile equipped	–	–	–	3	–	–	–	–	–	–	–	–	–
gun only	–	–	3	–	3	15*	–	2	–	–	3	–	3
Fast attack craft, missiles	–	–	4	10	6*	15	–	40	13	–	5	28*	16*
gun only	–	–	13	6	14	18	–	–	18	–	35*	6	15
Patrol vessel/craft	51	8	–	85	5	16	4	1	66	23	48	17	20*
Assault ships	–	–	–	–	–	14	–	–	23	–	–	–	–
Landing craft	–	–	–	–	14	–	–	7	19	12	–	–	24
Minesweepers/hunters	8	29*	7	6	6*	47	2	10	49*	4	16	28*	31
Auxiliaries, replenishers	1	–	–	2	–	6	–	–	6	1	3	1	–
other support	11	9	28	16	76	41	8	19	43	10*	9	45*	42
Naval aviation:													
Strike aircraft	–	–	–	–	–	–	–	–	49	–	–	–	–
Anti-submarine (all types)	–	3*	3*	8	–	5	0*	6	–	–	–	10*	8
Utility helicopters	–	–	8	2	–	13	–	–	25	–	4	13	6
Transport and training types	–	–	–	–	–	–	–	–	–	–	–	–	–

Notes: Ship and aircraft strengths are as of end June 1984. Asterisks denote ongoing procurement.

to numerous utility craft. The Vietnamese Navy operates a land-based force of 10 Soviet-built Mil-4 helicopters.

Europe

Albania A small coastal navy largely operating Chinese-built submarines and vessels of mixed Soviet and Chinese design.

Belgium The Royal Belgian Navy, a member of the North Atlantic Treaty Organization (NATO), maintains a small standing force comprising a quartet of missile-equipped 'Wielingen' class frigates, plus a flotilla of mixed ex-US minesweepers, some of which will shortly start to be replaced by 10 Tripartite-built 'Eridan' class minehunters. The naval air arm operates three elderly Aerospatiale Alouettes, used primarily in the search and rescue role.

Bulgaria A member of the Warsaw Pact's southern naval forces, the relatively small Bulgarian Navy is totally Soviet-equipped. The major units of the Bulgarian Navy comprise two 'Riga' class frigates and three 'Poti' class corvettes, supported by 'Osa' and 'Shershen' class fast attack craft. The small naval air arm includes three Mil-14 anti-submarine helicopters, plus eight more elderly Soviet helicopters for utility work.

Cyprus Two patrol craft are operated as part of the Greek enclave's police.

Denmark The Royal Danish Navy contributes to the North Atlantic Treaty Organization's standing naval forces. A small but relatively potent force, the Royal Danish Navy has two primary operational tasks; coastal defence, along with frequently far-ranging patrol and policing of Danish waters, including those around Greenland. The major Danish naval combat forces consist of two 'Peder Skram' frigates, plus three 'Niels Juel' corvettes and 10 'Willemoes' class Harpoon-equipped fast attack craft, supported by five patrol submarines and six 'Soloven' class fast torpedo craft. Five large helicopter-carrying and gun-equipped, rough water patrol vessels

head up the naval offshore protection elements. Four new Type 210 class submarines have been ordered to replace the existing 'Delfinen' class boats. The Royal Danish Navy's small air arm employs eight Westland Lynx.

Finland As with the other arms of Finland's defence forces, the size of the country's naval elements is limited under a 1948 treaty signed with the USSR. Notwithstanding these limitations, Finland manages to maintain a small but quite powerfully-armed surface combatant force led by two 'Turunmaa' class corvettes, backed up by four 'Osa II' class fast attack craft. The Finnish 'Osa II' class is in the process of being replaced by the Finnish-designed and built 'Helsinki' class craft, armed with the Swedish-developed SAAB-Bofors RBS-15 anti-ship missile.

German Democratic Republic A relatively small navy operated as part of the Warsaw Pact's Baltic naval forces. The flagships of the fleet consist of two 'Koni' class frigates, backed by 'Parchim' and 'Hai' class corvettes, the latter class reportedly being phased out as replaced by additional 'Parchims'. The small East German naval air arm operates five Mil-14 and 13 Mil-8 helicopters, all of which are land-based.

Iceland Iceland has no navy, but operates a rough water Coast Guard.

Ireland A small coastal navy primarily centred on fishery protection duties. A new helicopter-carrying patrol vessel along with two Aerospatiale AS 365 Dauphins have recently entered service.

Malta Malta operates a small Coast Guard made up of light craft.

Norway A part of the North Atlantic Treaty Organization's naval forces, the Royal Norwegian Navy operates a relatively large submarine force, along with an 'Oslo' class frigate-led surface fleet, largely made up of missile-carrying fast attack craft of Norwegian design and build. The six naval Westland Lynx helicopters are operated from the three Norwegian Coast Guard 'Nordkapp' class patrol vessels.

Poland The Polish Navy, a Warsaw Pact member, operates a fleet of Soviet developed and elderly 'Whisky' class submarines, a Soviet designed 'Kotlin' class

	Bolivia	Chile	Columbia	Costa Rica	Cuba	Dominican Republic	Ecuador	El Salvador	Guatemala	Guyana	Honduras	Mexico	Nicaragua	Paraguay	Peru	Surinam	Uraguay	Venezuela
Total personnel:	3600	28,000	8500	260	12,000	4500	20,000	300	1000	300	500	20,000	300	2500	20,500	160	4500	12,000
Naval forces:																		
Diesel-electric submarines	–	2*	2	–	2	–	2	–	–	–	–	–	–	–	12	–	–	3*
Aircraft carriers	–	–	–	–	–	–	–	–	–	–	–	–	–	–	–	–	–	–
Cruisers, missile equipped	–	–	–	–	–	–	–	–	–	–	–	–	–	–	1	–	–	–
gun only	–	3	–	–	–	–	–	–	–	–	–	–	–	–	1	–	–	–
Destroyers, missile equipped	–	2*	–	–	–	–	–	–	–	–	–	–	–	–	2	–	–	–
gun only	–	2	3	–	–	–	1	–	–	–	–	4	–	–	8	–	0*	–
Frigates, missile equipped	–	2	1*	–	–	–	–	–	–	–	–	–	–	–	2*	–	–	6
gun only	–	–	1	–	1	1	1	–	–	–	–	4	–	–	–	–	3	–
Corvettes, missile equipped	–	–	–	–	–	–	3*	–	–	–	–	–	–	–	6	–	–	–
gun only	–	–	–	–	–	5	–	–	–	–	–	18	–	–	–	–	1	–
Fast attack craft, missile	–	2	–	–	27	–	6	–	–	–	–	–	–	–	–	–	–	3
gun only	–	4	6	7	6	–	–	–	–	–	–	–	–	–	–	–	3	3
Patrol vessel/craft	10	22	13	1	14	8*	8	29	37	9	11	68	13	0*	23	10	4	–
Assault ships	–	8	–	–	1	–	3	–	–	–	–	3	–	8	5	–	–	3*
Landing craft	–	–	–	–	7	1	6	–	3	–	–	–	–	2	–	–	5	12
Minesweepers/hunters	–	–	–	–	10*	–	–	–	–	–	–	3	–	–	–	–	–	–
Auxiliaries, replenishers	–	2	1	–	–	–	–	–	–	–	–	–	–	–	5	–	–	–
other support	27	11	18	–	17	19	11	1	1	–	6	28	–	8	22	–	9	14
Naval aviation:																		
Strike aircraft	–	–	–	–	–	–	–	–	–	–	–	–	–	–	–	–	–	–
Anti-submarine (all types)	–	18	–	–	–	–	16	–	–	–	–	13	–	–	17	–	10	18
Utility helicoptors	–	14	–	–	–	–	7	–	–	–	–	7	–	4	5	–	2	–
Transport and training types	–	16	–	–	–	–	38	–	–	–	–	44	–	6	18	–	7	3

Notes: Ship and aircraft strengths are as of end of June 1984. Asterisks denote ongoing procurement.

destroyer, supported by 'Osa' class missile fast attack craft and 10 locally developed 'Wilga' class high speed craft. Virtually all other patrol and support surface craft operated are of Polish origin, and Polish shipyards are kept busy producing surface support and amphibious warfare vessels for use with the Soviet Navy. Poland operates a naval air arm of Mig-17 fighters and a mix of other elderly Soviet types, mainly formed from various models of Mil helicopters.

Portugal A North Atlantic Treaty Organization (NATO) member, the Portuguese Navy operates a compact force of three 'Daphne' class submarines, along with 17 frigates of the 'Baptista de Andrade', 'João Coutinho' and 'Dealey' classes. Reported Portuguese interest in procuring three 'Kortenaer' class frigates had not translated into an order by the end of 1984. Portugal has no naval air arm, relying on its air force for air support.

Romania A Warsaw Pact member, the Romanian Navy is a Soviet equipment client, operating three 'Poti' class corvettes and five 'Osa' class missile-armed fast attack craft as its primary combatant force. The small naval air arm operates four Mil-4 land-based, search and rescue helicopters.

Sweden The Royal Swedish Navy has, in recent years, shifted its stance with regard to its operational equipment, discarding destroyers in favour of the speedier and more agile fast attack craft, epitomized by their 'Spica' I and II classes. Current Royal Swedish Navy shipbuilding programmes include the construction of the 'Stockholm' (or 'Spica' III) class craft, along with the new 'Landsort' class minehunters and four new 'A-17' class submarines. The naval air arm operates a fleet of Boeing Vertol HKP tandem-rotored helicopters, of which four additional anti-submarine versions are on order.

Yugoslavia The Yugoslavian Navy is a small, coastal defence orientated service that, nonetheless, manages to support its national shipbuilding industry in a much more material fashion than many much larger navies. In terms of equipment, Yugoslavia operates three classes of patrol submarines, all of local design and construction, along with surface elements comprising two 'Koni' class frigates supported by a mixture of six locally-developed 'Rade Koncar', 10 'Osa II' class and 15 'Shershen' class fast attack craft. Virtually all other patrol and support vessels employed are of local origin. Yugoslavia is currently building two new locally-developed frigates for its navy, based on the earlier Yugoslavian Training Frigate exported to Iraq and Indonesia. A number of other small Yugoslavian naval vessels have also proved exportable. The front line equipment for the country's small naval air arm comprises eight Kamov Ka-25 anti-submarine helicopters.

Latin America

Bahamas This island chain nation operates a Coast Guard force only.

Barbados This Windward Islands nation operates a Coast Guard service only.

Belize Belize operates a small patrol craft service run by the police.

Bolivia Despite the landlocked nature of this country, a small naval service exists, primarily to police the country's lakes and rivers.

Chile As predicated by the nation's long coastline, and the bad weather encountered in the south, the Chilean Navy necessarily favours the larger, rough water warship. Thus, the surface elements of the fleet comprise mainly destroyers and frigates led by an elderly ex-Swedish cruiser/command ship. Supplementing these forces are three 'Oberon' class submarines of British origin, two Israeli-built 'Reshel' class missile craft and four torpedo-carrying 'Lurssen TB 36' class fast attack craft. Recently, Chile acquired an ex-Royal Navy 'County' class destroyer and have taken delivery of a second prior to the close of 1984. The Chilean naval arm is made up of five Embraer Bandeirantes, four Bell Model 206 and nine Aerospatiale Alouette helicopters, supported by 10 Pilatus Porter utility transports.

Colombia The small Colombian Navy is currently modernizing its major surface combatant elements through the replacement of its elderly ex-US destroyers and frigate with four new Howaldtswerke FS 1500 missile frigates. The Colombian Navy relies on its air force for air cover.

Costa Rica A small naval force centred around US-built lightly armed craft.

Cuba An exclusively Soviet-supplied force, the Cuban Navy is spearheaded by two operational submarines and a 'Koni' class frigate, supported by numerous missile and torpedo-carrying fast attack craft. Naval air cover and support is the responsibility of the Cuban Air Force.

Dominican Republic The Dominican Republic's Navy is a small coastal force operating almost exclusively with ex-US Navy equipment, including the three patrol boats currently being delivered. No naval air arm.

Ecuador A middle-sized navy by regional standards, the Ecuadoran Navy operates two Type 209 submarines and is in the course of replacing its elderly US frigate with four new Italian-built 'Esmeraldas' class corvettes. The small naval air arm includes three Beech T-34C light strike/trainers and two Aerospatiale Alouette III helicopters.

El Salvador Another small coastal naval force built around US light craft.

Grenada Any maritime protection is provided by police launches.

Guatemala A small coastal naval force firmly committed to US purchases.

Guyana Guyana maintains a very small coastal naval force.

Honduras Another pocket-sized coastal naval force that buys US craft.

Mexico One of the larger regional navies, the Mexican Navy had until relatively recently operated largely elderly US-supplied vessels. However, latterly, Mexico has turned more to European designers and suppliers, as evidenced by their selection of the British-designed 'Azteca' class patrol craft and the larger Spanish-built 'Halcon' class vessels. The Mexican Navy's small air arm includes four Beech T-34C light strike/ trainers, plus six MMB Bo 105 anti-submarine helicopters.

Nicaragua A small coastal naval force employing US, Isreali and French patrol craft. Air support is provided by the air force's elderly US types.

Panama Maritime patrol and policing provided by Coast Guard only.

Paraguay Although landlocked, the Paraguayan Navy patrols a lengthy network of river waterways. During 1983, Paraguay ordered a 'Roraima' class patrol vessel from Brazil, scheduled for early 1986 delivery. The small Paraguayan naval air arm operates a mix of elderly US fixed winged and rotary winged types.

Peru One of the region's larger navies, the Peruvian Navy has a dozen submarines, including six Type 209 class. Currently, its larger surface unit elements are being added to with two locally-built 'Lupo' class frigates and its fast strike capability was recently enhanced with the acquisition of six French-built PR72 missile-carrying corvettes. The naval air arm employs seven Grumman S-2 Trackers, backed by four Sikorsky SH-3 Sea Kings and six Agusta-Bell AB212s for anti-submarine duties. Maritime surveillance is conducted with Fokker F27Ms and some coastal tactical air support can be furnished by the six Beech T-34C turboprop light strike/trainer aircraft bought in the mid-1970s.

Surinam A small coastal naval defence force employing Dutch-built craft.

Trinidad and Tobago No navy, but operates a large Coast Guard headed by two large and relatively well armed Swedish-built 'CG 40' class vessels.

Uruguay A comparatively small coastal naval force largely equipped with elderly US-provided vessels, recently supplemented by the addition of an ex-US Navy 'Gearing' class destroyer. The small naval air arm is headed up by six Grumman S-2 Tracker anti-submarine machines.

	Bahrain	Iran	Iraq	Israel	Kuwait	Lebanon	Oman	Qutar	Saudi Arabia	Syria	United Arab Emirates	Yemen Arab Republic (North)	Yemen Democratic Republic (South)
Total personnel:	300	20,000	4800	9000	800	250	2000	700	2500	2500	1500	550	1000
Naval forces:													
Diesel-electric submarines	–	–	–	3	–	–	–	–	–	–	–	–	–
Aircraft carriers	–	–	–	–	–	–	–	–	–	–	–	–	–
Cruisers, missile equipped	–	–	–	–	–	–	–	–	–	–	–	–	–
gun only	–	–	–	–	–	–	–	–	–	–	–	–	–
Destroyers, missile equipped	–	3	–	–	–	–	–	–	–	–	–	–	–
gun only	–	3	–	–	–	–	–	–	–	–	–	–	–
Frigates, missile equipped	–	4	1*	–	–	–	–	–	0*	–	–	–	–
gun only	–	2	–	–	–	–	–	–	–	2	–	–	–
Corvettes, missile equipped	–	–	0*	–	–	–	–	–	4	0*	–	–	–
gun only	–	–	–	–	–	–	–	–	–	–	–	–	1
Fast attack craft, missile	3*	10	9	24*	5*	–	3*	2*	9	18	6	4	6
gun only	–	–	7	1	–	–	–	6	3	8	6	4	4
Patrol vessel/craft	13	2	8	55	37	9	10*	36	–	4	3	5	8
Assault ships	–	2*	3	4	–	–	1*	–	–	–	–	–	1
Landing craft	1	15	–	–	3*	–	6	–	12	–	–	2	3
Minehunters/sweepers	–	1	10	–	–	–	–	–	4	3	–	–	–
Auxiliaries, replenishers	–	2	–	–	–	–	–	–	0*	–	–	–	–
	–	5*	1	2	2	–							5
Naval aviation:													
Strike aircraft	–	–	–	–	–	–	–	–	–	–	–	–	–
Anti-submarine (all types)	–	12	–	–	–	–	–	–	0*	–	–	–	–
Utility helicopters	–	13	–	3	–	–	–	–	–	–	–	–	–
Transport and training types	–	9	–	41*	–	–	–	–	–	–	–	–	–

Notes: Ship and aircraft strengths are as of June 1984. Asterisks denote ongoing procurement.

Venezuela A small, but powerfully-armed naval force, the Venezuelan Navy is made up of surface, sub-surface and air elements. The submarine force comprises four Type 209 class boats, two of which are in course of delivery. The service's primary surface combatants consists of six recently delivered 'Lupo' class missile frigates, backed by British- built 'Constitucion' class fast attack craft. The major anti-submarine elements of the naval air arm comprise Agusta-Bell AB-212 helicopters, of which all 12 should now have been delivered, backed by a land-based force of six Grumman S-2 Tracker aircraft.

Middle East

Bahrain A growing coastal naval force, whose primary, gun-equipped fast attack craft are purchased from Lurssen Werft of West Germany.

Iran Following the initiation of hostilities with Iraq in late 1980, it is difficult to ascertain the current operational status of the Iranian Navy, which is known to have incurred some losses and which is said to be experiencing difficulties in procuring vital spares.

Iraq During the late 1970's, the Iraqi Navy embarked on a major programme of growth and modernization, ordering four 'Lupo' class frigates and six Modified 'Esmeraldas' class corvettes from Italian yards; deliveries of which should have commenced by late 1984. Prior to these purchases, the Iraqi Navy had largely relied on Soviet-supplied vessels, some of which are known to have been lost to Iranian action.

Israel Israel maintains a relatively large navy in relation to the country's overall size. The Israeli Navy's sub-surface forces consist of three Vickers-built Type 206 submarines, supporting a relatively large surface force of both conventional-hulled and hydrofoiled, missile- carrying fast attack craft of mostly local origin. A very small naval air arm is headed up with three ship-going Bell Model 206 helicopters, used to direct naval gun and missile fire.

Kuwait One of the region's smaller navies, that of Kuwait is centred on a compact, fast reaction surface strike force, the primary elements of which have been or are being supplied by Lurssen of West Germany. Air support is the responsibility of the Kuwaiti Air Force.

Lebanon Following more than two years of intensive external and internally induced conflict, the precise status of this small coastal naval patrol force is uncertain. Minimum Lebanese Air Force support can be expected in the light of known aircraft destruction.

Oman The Omani Navy appears set on a path of growth, centred on an expansion of their potently-armed fast attack craft forces; all of which are British in origin, as is the 93-metre logistic support ship course of completion. Air force support would come primarily from the three recently delivered squadrons of Jaguar strike aircraft.

Qatar A small coastal naval force spearheaded by French-built 'La Combattante' fast attack craft, delivery of the third and final vessel being made in 1984. Most other Qatar Navy vessels are of British origin. Naval air cover would be provided by air force Alpha Jets and Hunters.

Saudi Arabia Currently in the throes of a major expansion programme, the Royal Saudi Arabian Navy had previously been viewed as a client for US naval vessels, but has recently turned to France as its major supplier. Currently, the Royal Saudi Arabian Navy is in the process of receiving three 'Medina' class missile frigates, two 'Boraida' class replenishers; all from France, to supplement the four missile corvettes and nine missile-carrying fast attack craft bought from the US. Although the Royal Saudi Arabian Navy had previously relied totally upon the air force for air cover, a naval air arm has recently been established and will commence taking delivery of 24 Aerospatiale AS 365 Dauphin helicopters during 1984; 20 will be anti-ship missile equipped.

Syria The Syrian Navy is a relatively small coastal naval force tasked with guarding a comparatively narrow coastline. The force is a client for Soviet vessels and equipment and is in the process of acquiring four 'Nanuchka' class missile corvettes. The air force provides cover.

United Arab Emirates A small but growing force, the United Arab Emirates' Navy comprises Lurssen-supplied fast attack craft, supported by British patrol and support craft. No naval air arm.

Yemen Arab Republic A small coastal naval force of fast attack and patrol craft is maintained to guard the North Yemen shoreline.

Yemeni Democratic Republic Somewhat larger than its

	Algeria	Egypt	Libya	Mauritania	Morocco	Tunisia
Total personnel:	8000	33,000	6500	320	6000	2500
Naval forces:						
Diesel-electric submarines	1*	12	6	–	–	–
Aircraft carriers	–	–	–	–	–	–
Cruisers, missile equipped	–	–	–	–	–	–
gun only	–	–	–	–	–	–
Destroyers, missile equipped	–	1	–	–	–	–
gun only	–	4	–	–	–	–
Frigates, missile equipped	2	2	1	–	1	–
gun only	2	3	–	–	–	1
Corvettes, missile equipped	3	–	6*	–	–	–
gun only	–	–	1	–	–	–
Fast attack craft, missile	18*	24*	25*	–	4	3
gun only	10*	26	–	–	2*	–
Patrol vessel/craft	6	12*	9*	10	19	20
Assault ships	0*	12	5	–	4	–
Landing craft	–	18*	5*	–	–	0*
Minesweepers/hunters	2	10	4	–	1	–
Auxiliaries, replenishers	–	–	–	–	–	–
other support	7	15	11	1	4	1
Naval aviation:						
Strike aircraft	–	–	–	–	–	–
Anti-submarine (all types)	–	6	–	–	–	–
Utility helicoptors	–	–	–	–	–	–
Transport and training types	–	–	–	–	–	–

Notes: Ships and aircraft strengths are as of end June 1984. Asterisks denote ongoing procurement.

	Angola	Benin	Cameroon	Cape Verde	Comoros Islands	Congo	Ethiopia	Equatorial Guinea	Gabon	Ghana	Guinea
Total personnel:	1500	200	350	75	70	200	2500	100	180	1200	600
Naval forces:											
Diesel-electric submarines	–	–	–	–	–	–	–	–	–	–	–
Aircraft carriers	–	–	–	–	–	–	–	–	–	–	–
Cruisers, missile equipped	–	–	–	–	–	–	–	–	–	–	–
gun only	–	–	–	–	–	–	–	–	–	–	–
Destroyers, missile equipped	–	–	–	–	–	–	–	–	–	–	–
gun only	–	–	–	–	–	–	–	–	–	–	–
Frigates, missile equipped	–	–	–	–	–	–	1	–	–	–	–
gun only	–	–	–	–	–	–	–	–	–	–	–
Corvettes, missile equipped	–	–	–	–	–	–	–	–	–	–	–
gun only	–	–	–	–	–	–	–	–	–	2	–
Fast attack craft, missile	2	–	2*	–	–	–	7	–	1	–	–
gun only	6	–	–	2	–	1	–	1	1	4	6
Patrol vessel/craft	14	2	10*	2	–	10*	10	4	3	6	9
Assault ships	4	–	–	–	1	–	1	–	–	–	–
Landing craft	5	–	12	–	–	–	10	–	1	2	2
Minesweepers/hunters	–	–	–	–	–	–	–	–	–	–	1
Auxiliaries, replenishers	–	–	–	–	–	–	–	–	–	–	–
other support	4	–	2	–	–	6	1	–	–	–	–
Naval aviation:											
Strike aircraft	–	–	–	–	–	–	–	–	–	–	–
Anti-submarine (all types)	–	–	–	–	–	–	–	–	–	–	–
Utility helicoptors	–	–	–	–	–	–	–	–	–	–	–
Transport and training types	–	–	–	–	–	–	–	–	–	–	–

Notes: *Ships and aircraft strengths are as of end June 1984. Asterisks denote ongoing procurement.*

near neighbour, the navy is a client for Soviet vessels and equipment. No naval air arm.

North Africa

Algeria Currently the second largest naval force in the region, the Algerian Navy was until very recently almost exclusively Soviet-equipped, but of late has placed two major contracts for four fast attack craft and two 93-metre logistic support ships with the UK yard of Brooke Marine; these vessels being in course of delivery. Naval air cover is provided by the Algerian Air Force.

Egypt By far the largest naval force in this region, the Egyptian Navy has undergone a fairly major transformation within recent years, largely as a result of its decision to buy a growing percentage of its surface vessels and their equipment from Western European sources and submarines from China, rather than from its former Soviet suppliers. While the Egyptian Navy still employs many Soviet-supplied vessels, its fast attack elements have been recently boosted by the addition of six Vosper Thornycroft-built 'Ramadan' class vessels, while its larger naval units are being added to with the delivery of two Spanish-built missile frigates of the 'Descubierta' class. The naval air arm operates six Westland-built Sea King helicopters for land-based anti-submarine duties.

Libya The Libyan Navy is built around a compact force of six missile-equipped Italian-built 'Wadi' class corvettes, backed by a relatively large force of missile-armed fast attack craft and patrol boats. The existing surface force elements are currently being bolstered by the addition of two more corvettes and three 'La Combattante' fast attack craft. Air cover is provided by the Libyan Air Force.

Mauritania This Northwest African Islamic nation maintains a very small naval coastal force of mixed French and Spanish craft and relies on a handful of air force-operated light aircraft for naval cover.

Morocco The Royal Moroccan Navy has been set on a path of expansion since the late 1970s. It recently took delivery of a new flagship in the shape of a Spanish-built 'Descubierta' class frigate, along with four Bazan-built Lurssen PB 57 fast attack craft. Currently, the Royal Moroccan Navy is in the process of taking two French-built PR 72 patrol vessels. The country's air force provides naval air cover.

Tunisia The Tunisian Navy is a comparatively small coastal defence force led with one elderly US frigate, backed by French-built 'La Combattante' fast attack craft in course of delivery, supported by British-built patrol craft. The Tunisian Air Force provides naval air cover.

Sub-Saharan Africa

Angola The Angolan Navy's vessels are largely Soviet-supplied and are headed by two 'Osa' class and six 'Shershen' class fast attack craft. A few ex-Portuguese craft are still operated. No naval air arm exists.

Benin A pocket-sized coastal force operating Soviet-supplied craft.

Cameroon A small service, the Cameroon Navy operates two 'La Combattante'class fast attack craft, backed by Chinese-supplied 'Shanghai' class patrol craft, with additional French-built patrol vessels in build.

Cape Verde Operates two 'Shershen' class and two 'Zhuk' class patrol craft.

Comoros Islands Operates one ex-British tank landing ship.

Congo Another tiny navy that operates one Soviet-built 'Shershen' class and two Chinese-supplied 'Shanghai' class vessels, plus assorted smaller patrol craft, currently being supplemented with five new launches.

Ethiopia A coastal defence-orientated service, the Ethiopian Navy's main elements comprise one 'Petya'

	Guinea Bissau	Ivory Coast	Kenya	Madagascar	Mozambique	Nigeria	Senegal	Somalia	South Africa	Sudan	Tanzania	Zaire
Total personnel:	275	700	650	600	650	4000	700	550	6000	2000	1500	1500
Naval forces:												
Diesel-electric submarines	–	–	–	–	–	–	–	–	3	–	–	–
Aircraft carriers	–	–	–	–	–	–	–	–	–	–	–	–
Cruisers, missile equipped	–	–	–	–	–	–	–	–	–	–	–	–
gun only	–	–	–	–	–	–	–	–	–	–	–	–
Destroyers, missile equipped	–	–	–	–	–	–	–	–	–	–	–	–
gun only	–	–	–	–	–	1	–	–	–	–	–	–
Frigates, missile equipped	–	–	–	–	–	1	–	–	2	–	–	–
gun only	–	–	–	–	–	2	–	–	–	–	–	–
Corvettes, missile equipped	–	–	–	–	–	2	–	–	–	–	–	–
gun only	–	–	3	–	–	6	–	2	12	–	–	–
Fast attack craft, missile	2	–	1	–	–	–	1	8	1	7	14	–
gun only	7	16	3*	5	14	9*	6	5	37	8	9	7
Patrol vessel/craft	–	1	–	1	–	2	–	1	–	–	–	25
Assault ships	2	10	–	–	3	1*	2	4	–	2	1	–
Landing craft	–	–	–	–	–	0*	–	–	10	–	–	–
Minesweepers/hunters	–	–	–	–	–	–	–	–	1	1	–	–
Auxiliaries, replenishers	1	1	3	6	–	4	2	–	9	2	2	–
other support	–	–	–	–	–	–	–	–	–	–	–	–
Naval aviation:												
Strike aircraft	–	–	–	–	–	–	–	–	–	–	–	–
Anti-submarine (all types)	–	–	–	–	–	0*	–	–	5	–	–	–
Utility helicopters	–	–	–	–	–	–	–	–	–	–	–	–
Transport and training types	–	–	–	–	–	–	–	–	–	•	–	–

Notes: Ship and aircraft strengths are as of end June 1984. Asterisks denote ongoing procurement.

class frigate, plus 'Osa' class craft.

Equatorial Guinea A small, exclusively Soviet-supplied coastal force.

Djibouti Three inshore patrol boats are operated by the police force.

Gabon The small Gabonese Navy operates mainly French-built vessels, with a handful of locally-built patrol craft.

Ghana One of the relatively larger navies operating in this region, the Ghanaian Navy operates two British-built 'Kromantse' class corvettes supported by a mix of West German-built Lurssen fast attack craft and French or British-built patrol craft. Air cover is air force supplied.

Guinea A small coastal naval force operating Soviet or Chinese supplied vessels. No naval air arm.

Guinea Bissau This small coastal force operates a mix of Soviet and French-built vessels. No separate naval air arm.

Ivory Coast The small Ivory Coast naval force employs exclusively French-provisioned vessels and equipment. No naval air arm.

Kenya A relatively small coastal naval force that operates a compact element of British-built fast attack craft, at least three of which are now armed with Israeli-built Gabriel anti-ship missiles. Air cover for naval operations is provided by the country's air force.

Liberia A small coastal patrol is mounted by the Coast Guard.

Madagascar This island state off the coast of East Africa operates a small naval contingent of patrol craft of French or North Korean origin. Air cover is provided by the largely Soviet-equipped air force.

Mozambique A small naval force operating primarily Soviet-supplied vessels. Has no naval air arm.

Nigeria The Nigerian Navy's growth during the 1970's was not only quantative, but equally qualitative in terms of its new ships and weapons. The second largest navy in the region, the Nigerian fleet is headed by NNS *Arudu*, a modern, missile-equipped MEKO 360 type frigate. Supporting the *Arudu* is a small force of British-built Mk 9 and Mk 3 corvettes, backed by six large missile-equipped fast attack craft of the Lurssen FPB 57 and 'La Combattante' III classes, in turn, supported by a number of British and West German-built patrol craft. Currently, Nigeria operates two West German-built 'Ambe' class assault ships and is acquiring additional landing craft to augment its amphibious warfare capabilities. The Nigerian Navy will be taking delivery of three Westland Lynx anti- submarine helicopters in early 1985.

Senegal A small naval force of French-built patrol craft.

Seychelles A small coastal patrol is mounted by the army.

Sierra Leone Coastal patrol is the responsibility of the Coast Guard.

Somalia A small coastal patrol force employing Soviet-supplied craft, including two 'Osa II' class missile-equipped fast attack types.

South Africa While diminished in size from yesteryear, the South African Navy is still the largest and most potent naval force in the southern region of the African continent. The South African Navy operates three 'Daphne' class patrol submarines, plus one, possibly two 'Whitby' class frigates, supported by a still growing number of 'Reshef/Minister' class large missile-carrying strike craft; their major tactical surface element. The South African Navy maintains six British-built 'Coniston' class mine warfare vessels, plus a further four of the same class now employed as offshore patrol vessels. Although most air cover is provided by the South African Air Force, five Westland Wasps are maintained by the navy for shipboard anti-submarine duty.

Sudan A small coastal naval force that operates a fleet of mixed origin vessels and craft, including a significant number of hulls designed and built in Yugoslavian yards. No naval air arm.

Tanzania A small coastal naval force operating Soviet and Chinese-built vessels. The Tanzanian Air Force provides a naval air cover.

Togo A small coastal force is maintained by the army.

Zaire Operates a relatively large number of small patrol craft, the largest of which were Chinese-supplied. No naval air arm exists.

21

Warships

Submarines

Typhoon Class Submarines

Role: Strategic power projection.
Builder: Severodvinsk, USSR.
User: Soviet Navy.
Basic data: 25,000 tons estimated dived displacement: 557.7ft (170m) overall length: 82.0ft (25m) maximum beam.
Crew: around 150.
Propulsion: 2 nuclear reactors/steam turbines (estimated total 120,000shp): 2 propellers.
Sensors: 1 surface search radar: undesignated multiple passive and active sonars; undesignated inertial navigation and fire control systems; automated action information data-processing system.
Armament: 20 SS-N-18 or SS-N-20 intercontinental submarine-launched ballistic missiles; 6 heavyweight anti-submarine torpedo tubes.
Top speed: 30 knots dived.
Range: Unlimited.
Programme: The first published Western World reports of the existence of this class were released in early October 1981, well over a year after the launching of the lead boat in August 1980. A second of class was launched in September 1982 and a third had been built by early 1985. According to US intelligence reports, the lead of class

The Soviet Navy's gigantic 'Typhoon' class ballistic missile-carrying submarine.

entered Soviet Navy service trials in late February 1983 and was fully operational before the end of 1983. These three known boats are to replace the existing 'Delta' class submarine.
Notes: The world's biggest submarine, the 'Typhoon' class represents the Soviet's response to the US Navy's 'Trident/Ohio' class programme. The massive dimensions and weight of the 'Typhoon' class appear to be tied directly to the much larger-than-Trident I-sized SS-N-18 or SS-N-20 missiles that they carry rather than as a result of inferior constructional practices. As with the US Navy's 'Trident/Ohio' class submarine combination, the SS-N-18 or SS-N-20/'Typhoon' class submarines' capability is awesome, particularly in the Soviet case, where the 'Typhoon' class can strike almost all US targets without ever leaving home waters, thanks to the up to 4479 nautical mile (8300km) range of the six to nine re-entry vehicle-headed SS-N-20 nuclear missiles. Using the rules set out under the US-Soviet Arms Limitation Talks (SALT) Phase I agreement, with each 'Typhoon' class accepted into service, one 'Yankee' and one 'Hotel' class submarine should be dismantled in order to maintain the mutually agreed number of 950 launchers in 62 strategic submarines. Unfortunately, this does not limit the numbers of re-entry vehicles/warheads installed; each 'Typhoon' carrying up to 200, compared with a total of 54 carried by both earlier submarines.

Ohio Class Submarines

Role: Strategic power projection.
Builder: General Dynamics, USA.
User: US Navy.
Basic data: 18,700 tons dived displacement, 560ft (170.7m) overall length; 42ft (12.8m) maximum beam.
Crew: 157.
Propulsion: 1 General Electric S8G pressurised water nuclear reactor/1 General Electric geared steam turbine (60,000shp); 1 propeller.
Sensors: BQQ-6 bow-mounted and towed array sonar

This view of USS Ohio (SSBN726) emphasises its great length, only marginally shorter than that of the 'Ticonderoga' class cruiser.

system: 1 surface search radar; 2 SINS shipboard inertial navigational systems; Mk 98 missile fire control system; automated action information data processor.

Armament: 24 Trident submarine-launched intercontinental ballistic missiles; 4 heavyweight anti-submarine torpedo tubes.

Top speed: Over 25 knots dived.

Range: Unlimited.

Programme: Currently a planned 17-boat class, of which 11 had been ordered by the end of 1984. The class, along with their completion dates or projected deliveries, comprise: USS *Ohio* (SSBN726), October 1981; USS *Michigan* (SSBN727), September 1982, USS *Florida* (SSBN728), June 1983; USS *Georgia* (SSBN729), February 1984; USS *Henry M Jackson* (SSBN730), October 1984; USS *Alabama* (SSBN731), June 1985; USS *Alaska* (SSBN732), February 1986; SSBN733, October 1986 and SSBN734, early 1987. SSBNs 735, 736 and 737 should be delivered during the 1988 through 1990 period.

Notes: Initially authorised in May 1972 as part of the US Navy's Trident System, the development phase of the 'Ohio' class programme proved more protracted than anticipated, but now appears to be over the mass of problems. The overall Trident System comprises not only the Lockheed-built Trident missiles and the 'Ohio' class submarines, but their two purpose-built bases (one each for the US Atlantic and Pacific coasts), along with a host of other specific-to-Trident support equipment. Much longer than their 'Lafayette/Franklin' class predecessors, the 'Ohio' class boats carry not only half as many again missiles, but also employ a more refined and quieter running propulsive system, itself some four times more powerful than that of the 'Lafayettes'. Thanks to this propulsive machinery, the 'Ohio' class operate at a significantly higher normal speed than the 'Lafayettes', which, in turn, permits them to deploy over between ten and twenty times as much sea area in a given time compared with their precursors, making them a far more elusive target to both track and counter. Currently, the 'Ohio' class carry the multiple, independently-targeted nuclear warheaded Trident strategic missile with a range in excess of 4000 nautical miles (7413km), but will be used to deploy the improved Trident II missiles as they become available in the late 1980s. Initially envisaged as being a ten submarine, plus 369 missile and support package costing a total of just under $11.3 billion in 1974 values, the programme was expanded to encompass 15 submarines and 636 missiles, which with inflation took overall Trident System costs to $30.3 billion in 1981 terms. Currently, the British Government plans to procure four or five British-built examples of the basic 'Ohio' class design modified to carry 16 Trident II missiles in place of the 'Ohio's 24. The unit cost of each boat would be just over £656 million, exclusive of weapons system equipment content, in 1981 values.

Delta II and III Classes Submarines

Role: Strategic power projection.

Builder: Severodvinsk, USSR.

User: Soviet Navy.

Basic data: 11,300 tons ('Delta' II), 13,250 tons ('Delta' III) dived displacement; 508ft (155m) overall length; 39.4ft (12m) maximum beam.

Crew: 100 ('Delta' II), 120 ('Delta' III).

Propulsion: 1 nuclear reactor/steam turbines; 2 propellers.

Sensors: 1 surface search radar; undesignated sonars and fire control systems.

Armament: 16 SS-N-8 ('Delta' II) or 16 SS-N-18 ('Delta' III) intercontinental, submarine-launched ballistic missiles; 6 heavyweight anti-submarine torpedo tubes with 18 torpedoes ('Delta' II) or 12 torpedoes ('Delta' III).

A Soviet Navy 'Delta' running on the surface.

Top speed: 24 knots dived.

Range: Unlimited.

Programme: The 'Delta' IIs were an interim two-ship class built in the 1974/5 period immediately followed by the 'Delta' IIIs, the first of which entered service in 1975. At least 17 'Delta' IIIs are known to have been built by the close of 1984, at which time the construction of the first 2 'Delta' IVs had been completed according to intelligence sources.

Notes: Just under 50 feet longer than the 'Delta' I, the saddle tapers down in an unbroken fashion to meet the main pressure hull. The only external difference between the 'Delta' II and III lies in the increased height of the III's saddle structure.

Delta I Class Submarines

Role: Strategic power projection.

Builders: Severodvinsk & Komsomolsk, USSR.

User: Soviet Navy.

Basic data: 9700 tons dived displacement; 460ft (140m) overall length; 39.4ft (12m) maximum beam.

Crew: 100.

Propulsion: 1 nuclear reactor/steam turbines; 2 propellers.

Sensors: 1 surface search radar; undesignated sonars and fire control systems.

Armament: 12 SS-N-88 intercontinental, submarine-launched ballistic missiles; 6 heavyweight anti-submarine torpedo tubes with 18 torpedoes.

A 'Delta' I class with its 'stepped' aft saddle deck.

The ballistic missile-equipped Le Redoutable *(S611).*

Top speed: 25 knots dived.
Range: Unlimited.
Programme: A 16-ship class, the 'Delta' Is all entered service between 1971 and 1977.
Notes: In 1968, the Soviet Navy deployed the first of 34 'Yankee' class ballistic missile-carrying submarines. The 9500 ton dived 'Yankees' represented the first credible Soviet attempt to produce a strategic submarine comparable to the 'US George Washington' class of nearly a decade earlier. However, despite the large numbers of 'Yankees' built, these submarines suffered from the very real limitations imposed by the modest 1600 nautical mile range of their SS-N-6 missiles, 16 of which are carried by the 'Yankee' class. Logical developments of the 'Yankee' design, the 'Delta' Is are larger and heavier, being built to carry 12 of the 4000 nautical mile ranged SS-N-88 missiles which, in range terms at least, eclipsed the US's Poseidon by around 800 nautical miles.

Le Redoutable Class Submarines

Role: Strategic power projection.
Builder: Cherbourg, France.
User: French Navy.
Basic data: 9000 tons dived displacement; 419.95ft (128m) overall length; 34.8ft (10.6m) maximum beam.
Crew: 135.
Propulsion: 1 nuclear reactor/2 geared steam turbines; 1 propeller.
Sensors: 1DUUV23 and DUUX2 active and passive sonar systems. 1 sea search and navigational radar; automated fire control systems.
Armament: 16 M20 thermo-nuclear ballistic missiles; 4 lightweight anti-submarine torpedo tubes (18 torpedoes).
Top speed: 20 knots dived.
Range: Unlimited.
Programme: Ordered on an incremental basis, the first two of this seven-boat class were authorised in 1963. The class comprises: *Le Redoutable* (S611), *Le Terrible* (S612), *Le Foudroyant* (S610), *L'Indomptable* (S613) and *Le Tonnant* (S614) plus two improved vessels *L'Inflexible* (S615) and S617. All of the first five were laid down between 1964 and 1973 and respectively entered service in December 1971, January 1973, June 1974, December 1976 and May 1980. *L'Inflexible* should enter service in

1985, followed by S615 in 1994.
Notes: Unlike the Royal Navy's 'Resolution' class ballistic missile-carrying submarines, which lean heavily on both US nuclear reactor and hull design, the 'Le Redoutable' class boats are the result of the French Government's 1960 decision to develop their own nuclear-powered submarine and parallel ballistic missile programmes. As with other nuclear-powered submarines, this class of boat employs a hybrid propulsion system, using the nuclear reactor as its main power source, but backed by a diesel-electric auxiliary system, capable of a range of 5000 nautical miles.

Resolution Class Submarines

Role: Strategic power projection.
Builders: Various, UK.
User: Royal Navy.
Basic data: 8400 tons dived displacement; 425ft (129.5m) overall length, 33ft (10.1m) maximum beam.
Crew: 143.
Propulsion: 1 Rolls-Royce pressurised water nuclear reactor; 1 English Electric geared steam turbine (c20,000shp); 1 propeller.
Sensors: 1 Type 1003 surface search radar; 1 Type 2001 and 1 Type 2007 bow-mounted sonars; automated fire control system.
Armament: 16 Polaris A3 thermo-nuclear ballistic missiles; 6 tubes for heavyweight anti-submarine torpedoes.
Top speed: 25 knots dived.
Range: Unlimited.
Programme: The first of this four-boat class was laid down at Vickers' Barrow-in-Furness yards in February 1964 and the last completed in late 1969. The class comprises: HMS *Resolution* (S22), HMS *Repulse* (S23), HMS *Renown* (S26) and HMS *Revenge* (S27), the first pair being built by Vickers and the second two being constructed by Cammell Laird of Birkenhead. The respective commissioning dates for the boats were October 1967, September 1968, November 1968 and December 1969.
Notes: Although differing considerably in detail, the overall design of the 'Resolution' class is based on that of the US Navy's 'Lafayette' class submarine, both in terms of their nuclear reactor and hull technology; the major

HMS Resolution *(S22), July 1982.*

external difference being that the 'Resolution' class are fitted with bow section hydroplanes.

Lafayette/Franklin Class Submarines

Role: Strategic power projection.
Builders: Various, USA.
User: US Navy.
Basic data: 8250 tons dived displacement; 425ft (129.5m) overall length; 33ft (10.1m) maximum beam.
Crew: 141.
Propulsion: 1 Westinghouse S5W pressurised water nuclear reactor/2 geared steam turbines (total 15,000shp); 1 propeller.
Sensors: 1 BQR-7, plus BQR-19 and 1 BQS-4 bow-mounted sonars; 1 BQR-15 towed array sonar; automated launch control systems.
Armament: 16 Poseidon or Trident submarine-launched intercontinental ballistic missiles; 4 heavyweight anti-submarine torpedo tubes.
Top speed: Over 25 knots dived.
Range: Unlimited.
Programme: USS *Lafayette* (SSBN616), the lead boat of this 31 vessel class, was laid down in January 1961 at the Groton, Connecticut, yards of General Dynamics' Electric Boat Division, launched in May 1962 and commissioned in April 1963. *Lafayette* was followed by an additional 30 boats, the full list of which comprises; *Lafayette* (SSBN616), *Alexander Hamilton* (617), *Andrew Jackson* (619), *John Adams* (620), *James Monroe* (622), *Nathan Hale* (623), *Woodrow Wilson* (624), *Henry Clay* (625), *Daniel Webster* (626), *James Madison* (627), *Tecumseh* (628), *Daniel Boone* (629), *John C Calhoun* (630), *Ulysses S Grant* (631), *Von Steuben* (632), *Casimir Pulaski* (633), *Stonewall Jackson* (634), *Sam Rayburn* (635), *Nathanael Greene* (636), *Benjamin Franklin* (640), *Simon Bolivar* (641), *Kamehameha* (642), *George Bancroft* (643), *Lewis and Clark*

USS Francis Scott Key *(SSBN657), the first submarine to deploy with Trident I missiles.*

(644), *James K Polk* (645), *George C Marshall* (654), *Henry L Stimson* (655), *George Washington Carver* (656), *Francis Scott Key* (657), *Mariano G Vallejo* (658), and *Will Rogers* (659), the last of which was commissioned in April 1967. Besides General Dynamics, other shipbuilders participating in the programmes were two US Navy dockyards and Newport News. The final 12 boats, starting with the USS *Benjamin Franklin* (SSBN640), incorporated numerous detail design changes and are thus sometimes referred to as a separate class. The 'Franklin' class were the first to be retrofitted to operate with the Trident missile, the initial deployment being carried out by USS *Francis Scott Key* (SSBN657) in October 1979.
Notes: The 'Lafayettes' are a direct development of the 'Ethan Allens'.

Los Angeles Class Submarines

Role: Anti-submarine.
Builder: Newport News & General Dynamics, USA.
User: US Navy.
Basic data: 6900 tons dived displacement; 360ft (109.7m) overall length; 33ft (10.1m) maximum beam.

USS La Jolla (SSN701) during 1981 sea trials.

Crew: 127.
Propulsion: 1 General Electric S6G pressurised water nuclear reactor/2 geared steam turbines (total 30,000shp); 1 propeller.
Sensors: 1 BPS-15 surface search radar; 1 BQQ-5 bow-mounted sonar; 1 BQS-13 sonar; 1 BQS-15 sonar; 1 passive towed array sonar.
Armament: 4 amidships torpedo tubes for Harpoon anti-ship missiles or heavyweight anti-submarine torpedoes or Tomahawk cruise missiles in boats up to SSN719, with SSN719 and onwards carrying additional Tomahawks in vertical launch tubes.
Top speed: Over 30 knots dived.
Range: Unlimited.
Programme: Currently a 48-boat class, the first keel, that of USS *Los Angeles* (SSN688), was laid down in January 1972 and this ship commissioned in November 1976, followed by the boats comprising: *Baton Rouge* (689), *Philadelphia* (690), *Memphis* (691), *Omaha* (692), *Cincinnati* (693), *Groton* (694), *Birmingham* (695), *New York City* (696), *Indianapolis* (697), *Bremerton* (698), *Jacksonville* (699), *Dallas* (700), *La Jolla* (701), *Phoenix* (702), *Boston* (703), *Baltimore* (704), *City of Corpus Christie* (705), *Albuquerque* (706), *Portsmouth* (707), *Minneapolis-St Paul* (708), *Hyman G Rickover* (709), *Augusta* (710), *San Francisco* (711), *Atlanta* (712), *Houston* (713), *Norfolk* (714), *Buffalo* (715), *Salt Lake City* (716), *Olympia* (717), *Honolulu* (718), *Providence* (719), *Pittsburg* (720), *Chicago* (721), (722), (723), (724), (725), *Newport News* (750), (751), (752), (753), (754), (755), (756), (757), (758), (759). Some 28 boats were known to have been delivered by the end of 1984, comprising ten built by Newport News (SSNs 688, 689, 691, 693, 695 and 711 to 715) and with General Dynamics having completed 18 (SSNs 690, 692, 694 and 696 to 710). The first of the vertically-launched Tomahawk carriers, SSN719, should now have been delivered by General Dynamics.
Notes: Designed to counter the Soviet Navy's 'Charlie' and 'Victor' classes, the mission capability of these hunter/killer submarines, already expanded by Harpoon, will be further enhanced by Tomahawk.

Victor I, II and III Classes Submarines

Role: Anti-submarine.
Builder: Leningrad, USSR.
User: Soviet Navy.
Basic data: 5100 tons, ('Victor' 1), 5700 tons ('Victor' II) dived displacement; 311ft (95m) ('Victor' I), 328.1ft (100m) ('Victor' II) overall length; 32.8ft (10m) maximum beam. No data available on 'Victor' III class vessels.
Crew: 80 ('Victor' II).
Propulsion: 1 nuclear reactor/steam turbines; 1 propeller.
Sensors: Advanced passive sonar and other electronics systems.
Armament: 8 heavyweight anti-submarine torpedo tubes; unknown number of SS-N-15 anti-submarine, submarine-launched missiles.
Top speed: More than 30 knots dived.
Range: Unlimited.
Programme: The first of the 14 ship 'Victor' I class was completed in 1967 and the last was delivered in 1974. These ships were to be followed by at least eight 'Victor' IIs and the programme is continuing with construction of the even larger 'Victor' IIIs.
Notes: Designed to replace the earlier 'November' class nuclear-powered attack submarines, the 'Victors' despite their bulbously gross appearance, are amongst the fastest warships extant, having a sustained submerged speed greater than that of the briefly sustainable 'dash' speed of most surface combatants.

Trafalgar Class Submarines

Role: Anti-submarine.
Builder: Vickers, UK.
User: Royal Navy.
Basic data: 5050 tons dived displacement; 208.2ft (85.4m) overall length; 32.25ft (9.83m) maximum beam.
Crew: 111.
Propulsion: 1 Rolls-Royce nuclear pressurised water reactor/1 steam turbine (20,000shp) or 1 standby diesel-electric generator/electric motor; 1 propeller.
Sensors: 1 sea search and navigational radar; advanced passive and active sonar systems; automated action information and fire control data-processing system.
Armament: 5 heavyweight anti-submarine torpedo tubes for launching either Mk 24 Tigerfish torpedoes or Sub-Harpoon anti-ship missiles.
Top speed; Over 30 knots dived.
Range; Unlimited.
Programme: A planned seven-boat class, of which six had been ordered on an incremental basis by September 1984. Initially ordered in September 1977, the lead boat, HMS *Trafalgar* (S113) was followed by HMS *Turbulent* (S114), HMS *Tireless* (S115), HMS *Torbay* (S116) and HMS *Trenchant* (S91) and a sixth boat. The lead boat, *Trafalgar*, was laid down in April 1979, launched in July 1981 and commissioned in late May 1983. *Turbulent* was commissioned in April 1984 and all of these boats are expected to be in service by the end of 1989.
Notes: The 'Trafalgar' class design is an improved and slightly stretched derivative of the 'Swiftsure' class, but equipped with a new design of longer life nuclear reactor core and other improvements to quieten the boats' noise whilst running submerged. The 'Trafalgar' class also incorporates an improved weapons fire control system. The crew complement of 111 is likely to be increased to around 115 as the class enters operational service.

Valiant Class Submarines

Role: Anti-submarine.
Builders: Vickers and Cammell Laird, UK.
User: Royal Navy.
Basic Data: 4900 tons dived displacement; 285.0ft (86.9m) overall length; 33.2ft (10.1m) maximum beam.
Crew: 108.
Propulsion: 1 Rolls-Royce nuclear pressurised water reactor/1 geared steam turbine (15,000shp); 1 propeller.
Sensors: 1 Type 1003 sea search and navigational radar; 1 each of Type 2001 active/passive and Type 2007 passive sonars; inertial navigation and position fixing system; automated action information data-processing system.
Armament: 6 heavyweight anti-submarine torpedo tubes with 26 torpedoes or Sub-Harpoon submarine-launched anti-ship missiles.
Top Speed: Around 30 knots.
Range: Unlimited.
Programme: This five-boat class comprises: HMS *Valiant* (S102), HMS *Warspite* (S103), HMS *Churchill* (S46), HMS *Conqueror* (S48) and HMS *Courageous* (S50). *Valiant*, laid down at Vickers' Barrow shipyards in January 1962 was commissioned in mid-July 1966; the remaining four entering service in April 1967, July 1970, October 1971 and November 1971, respectively. All but the Cammell Laird-built *Conqueror* were constructed by Vickers at Barrow-in-Furness.
Notes: Successors to the Royal Navy's first nuclear-powered submarine, HMS *Dreadnought*, the 'Valiant' class, while employing US propulsive technology, was equipped with a fully British-designed and built system of nuclear reactor, turbine equipment and heat exchangers. The

A 'Victor' I class hunter/killer submarine.

HMS *Trafalgar* (S113) on sea trials, April 1983.

HMS *Warspite* (S103), second of this Royal Navy five-boat class.

USS Seahorse (SSN669) 'Sturgeon' class hunter/killer.

boats vary in detail between the first two and latter three vessels, resulting in some Royal Navy submariners referring to the three later boats as 'C' class submarines. HMS *Valiant, Conqueror* and *Courageous* all participated in the Falklands campaign, with HMS *Conqueror* being responsible for the sinking of the Argentinian cruiser *General Belgrano.*

Sturgeon Class Submarines

Role: Anti-submarine.
Builders: Various, USA.
User: US Navy.
Basic data: 4650 tons dived displacement; 292.2ft (89m) overall length; 31.7ft (9.7m) maximum beam.
Crew: 130.
Propulsion; 1 Westinghouse S5W pressurised water nuclear reactor/1 General Electric or De Laval geared steam turbine (15,000shp); 1 propeller.
Sensors: 1 BPS-15 surface search radar; 1 of various bow-mounted sonars, coupled with towed array sonar system.
Armament: Tomahawk cruise missiles; Harpoon anti-ship missiles; 4 heavyweight anti-submarine torpedo tubes.
Top Speed: 30 knots dived.
Range: Unlimited.
Programme: This 37-boat class, commissioned between March 1967 through August 1975 and involving construction in six separate shipyards, comprises: USS *Sturgeon* (SSN637), *Whale* (638), *Tautog* (639), *Grayling* (646), *Pogy* (647), *Aspro* (648), *Sunfish* (649), *Pargo*

(650), *Queenfish* (651), *Puffer* (652), *Ray* (653), *Sand Lance* (660), *Lapon* (661), *Gurnard* (662), *Hammerhead* (663), *Sea Devil* (664), *Guitarro* (665), *Hawkbill* (666), *Bergall* (667), *Spadefish* (668), *Seahorse* (669), *Finback* (670), *Pintado* (672), *Flying Fish* (673), *Trepang* (674), *Bluefish* (675), *Billfish* (676), *Drum* (677), *Archerfish* (678), *Silverside* (679), *William H Bates* (680), *Batfish* (681), *Tunny* (682), *Parche* (683), *Cavalla* (684), *L Mendel Rivers* (686) and *Richard R Russel* (687).
Notes: A development of the earlier 13 boat 'Permit' class design.

Swiftsure Class Submarines

Role: Anti-submarine.
Builder: Vickers, UK.
User: Royal Navy.
Basic data: 4500 tons dived displacement; 272ft (82.9m) overall length; 33.2ft (10.12m) maximum beam.
Crew: 97.
Propulsion: 1 nuclear pressurised water reactor/1 steam turbine (20,000shp); 1 propeller.
Sensors: 1 surface search and navigational radar; 4 sonars (including 3 active-passive systems).
Armament: 5 heavyweight, anti-submarine torpedo tubes with 20 torpedoes or submarine-launched Harpoon long-range anti-ship missiles.
Top speed: 30 knots dived.
Range: Unlimited.
Programme: The construction of this six-boat class was initiated in June 1969 and completed in early 1981. The vessels and their commissioning dates are: HMS *Swiftsure* (S126), April 1973; HMS *Sovereign* (S108), July 1974; HMS *Superb* (S109), November 1976; HMS *Sceptre* (S104), February 1978; HMS *Spartan* (S111), September 1979 and HMS *Splendid* (S112), May 1981.
Notes: As with the Soviet Navy's 'Victor' class submarines, the 'Swiftsures' were designed to provide a forward anti-submarine screen to an advancing naval task force. However, the 'Swiftsure's' mission compatibility is currently being expanded to include a useful secondary anti-shipping function as the vessels are progressively equipped with Sub-Harpoon missiles.

Charlie I and II Classes Submarines

Role: Anti-shipping.
Builder: Gorki, USSR.
User: Soviet Navy.

HMS Superb (S109) hunter/killer submarine, September 1981.

Basic data: 4200 tons ('Charlie' I), 5100 tons ('Charlie' II) dived displacement; 311ft (95m) ('Charlie' I), 338ft (103m) ('Charlie' II) overall length; 32.8ft (10m) maximum beam.
Crew: 80.
Propulsion: 1 nuclear reactor/steam turbines; 1 propeller.
Sensors: Advanced passive sonar and electronic systems.
Armament: 6 heavyweight anti-submarine torpedo tubes; 8 SS-N-7 ('Charlie' I) or 8 SS-N-15 or SS-N-9 submarine-launched, anti-ship cruise missiles. Some if not all 'Charlie' class are equipped to carry 8 SS-N-9 'Siren' submarine-launched, anti-ship missiles.
Top speed: 27 knots dived.
Range: Unlimited.
Programme: Initially deployed in 1968, about 12 'Charlie' Is were built before the type was superseded in 1973 by the larger and heavier 'Charlie' II, of which four had been delivered by 1979 and construction of the class was reported to be continuing during 1981, but appeared to have ceased by the end of 1982.
Notes: Built as successors to the 50 or so earlier diesel-powered 'Juliett' class and nuclear-powered 'Echo' class cruise missile-carrying submarines, the primary task of the 'Charlie' classes is to engage an oncoming enemy task force from a range of around 30 nautical miles when using SS-N-7s, or 60 nautical miles if equipped with SS-N-9s. All missiles can be fired from underwater.

Tango Class Submarines

Role: Anti-submarine.
Builder: Gorky, USSR.
User: Soviet Navy.
Basic data: 3700 tons dived displacement; 300.2ft (91.5m) overall length; 29.5ft (9.0m) maximum beam.
Crew: 72.
Propulsion: 3 diesels/batteries/3 electric motors (6000shp); 3 propellers.
Sensors: 1 surface search radar; unidentified passive and active sonar systems; echo sounder; automated launch control system.
Armament: 6 forward-firing and 4 aft-firing heavyweight anti-submarine torpedo tubes for conventional or nuclear warhead-tipped torpedoes and SS-N-15 submarine-launched anti-ship missiles.
Top speed: 16 knots dived; 20 knots running on surface.
Range: 4000 nautical miles dived at 8 knots with periodic snorkel.
Programme: Reported to have entered service with the Soviet Fleet during 1972, 14 of this class were believed to be operational by the end of 1981, at which time construction of around two 'Tango' class boats per year was continuing. Despite the emergence of the later 'Kilo' class diesel-electric submarines, 'Tango' class building is likely to continue for some years, particularly as these boats could well find export outlets to Soviet client states as a replacement for the ageing 'Foxtrot' class submarines.
Notes: According to US naval technical intelligence assessments, the 'Tango' class reflects some of the most modern diesel-electric submarine technology available, including having the hull coated in a sonar-absorbing rubber compound. While not as deep-diving as their stronger-hulled nuclear- powered contemporaries, the 'Tango' class submarines, with their long endurance, make admirable boats for operation in waters such as the Mediterranean and Baltic.

Kilo Class Submarines

Role: Patrol.
Builder: (lead yard): Komsomolsk, USSR.

A 'Charlie' I anti-ship cruise missile carrier.

User: Soviet Navy.
Basic data: Estimated 3200 tons dived displacement; 219.8ft (67.0m) overall length; 29.5ft (9.0m) maximum beam.
Crew: around 90.
Propulsion: Diesel-electric drive; no further data.
Sensors: Undesignated passive and active sonar systems.
Armament: Includes both nuclear warheaded and conventional 533mm heavyweight anti-submarine torpedoes.
Top speed: Around 20 knots dived.
Range: No available data.
Programme: Believed to be a replacement for the ageing 'Foxtrot' class diesel-electric submarines, the 'Kilo' class will probably be built in fairly large numbers during the 1980s.

A Soviet Navy diesel-powered 'Tango' class photographed in 1977.

One of the first views of the lead 'Kilo' class submarine, reveals the boat to have a relatively short hull, topped by an elongated and rectangular conning tower or 'sail'.

Notes: Built to fulfil the same requirements as set down for the Royal Navy's Vickers Type 2400 diesel-electric design, the emergence of the 'Kilo' class was first noted in 1981, the first photographic evidence being published in the West towards the close of 1982. Of interest is the generally close similar external appearance of the 'Kilo' class hull design to that of the earlier Dutch-developed 'Zwaardis' class submarine. While clearly not as capable as the deep-diving, dedicated hunter/killer 'Alfa' class submarines employed by the Soviets, the 'Kilo' class programme is likely to cost considerably less, or, alternatively, provide many more 'Kilos' than 'Alfas' for the same outlay. Despite the extensive development effort placed on producing advanced, nuclear-powered Soviet submarines, the debut of the 'Kilo' class simply serves to vindicate the many senior Soviet submariners' massive support for the silent-running diesel-electric submarine, evidenced in much of their writing. Certainly, the 'Kilo' class should provide Soviet sub-surface forces with some very useful additional anti-surface ship capability, along with added anti-submarine strength against potential hostiles, operating within relatively shallow waters.

Walrus Class Submarines

Role: Patrol.
Builder: RDM, Netherlands.
User: Royal Netherlands Navy.
Basic data: 2800 tons dived displacement; 219.8ft (67.0m) overall length; 27.9ft (8.5m) maximum beam.
Crew: 49.
Propulsion: 3 SEMT-Pielstick 12PA4-V200 diesel-electric generators/ batteries/1 electric motor (5500shp); 1 propeller.
Sensors: 1 Thomson-CSF Octopus sonar suite; 1 type 2026 passive towed array sonar; 1 Racal-Decca Type 1001 surface search radar and IFF; SATNAV satellite-fed precision position fixing system; Hollandse Gipsy III automated action information data processing.
Armament: 6 heavyweight torpedo tubes (16 heavyweight anti-submarine torpedoes or Sub-Harpoon submarine-launched anti-ship missiles.
Top speed: 20 knots dived.
Range: 10,000 nautical miles at 9 knots dived with snorkel.
Programme: The lead of this two-boat class, HNLMS *Walrus* (S801), was ordered in June 1978 and her sister, HNLMS *Zeeleeuw* (S802) was contracted in December 1979. The boats were to be launched in early 1984 and 1985, respectively, followed by entry into service in 1986 and 1987.
Notes: Built to replace HNLMS *Dolfijn* and HNLMS *Zeehund*, the 'Walrus' class are slightly physically larger than the earlier Dutch- developed 'Zwaardvis' class, from which they differ externally in embodying 'X' configured rudders. The extensive use of modern automated systems have reduced the crew number needed to man each of the 'Walrus' class by nearly 27 per cent in comparison with the 'Zwaardvis' class.

A cut-away view of this new Dutch two-boat class currently under construction in Rotterdam.

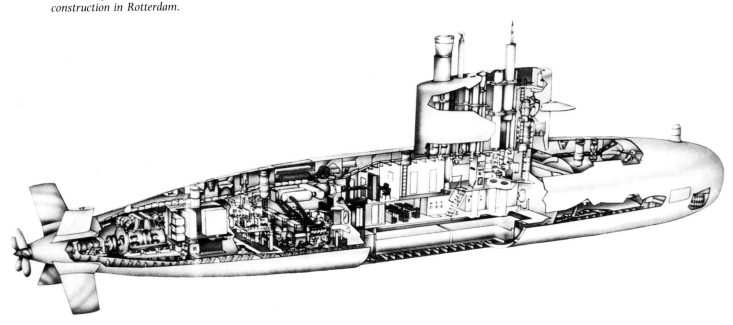

An 'Alfa' class running on the surface, July 1981.

Alfa Class Submarines

Role: Anti-submarine.
Builder: Leningrad, USSR.
User: Soviet Navy.
Basic data: 2760 tons dived displacement; 262ft (80m) overall length; 32.8ft (10m) maximum beam.
Crew: 60.
Propulsion: 1 nuclear reactor/steam turbines; 1 propeller.
Sensors: 1 surface search radar; comprehensive suite of advanced sonars and other electronic detection systems.
Armament: 6 heavyweight anti-submarine torpedo tubes with 20 torpedoes, or SS-NX-16 submarine-launched, rocket-propelled anti- submarine missiles.
Top speed: Over 40 knots dived.
Range: Unlimited.
Programme: Believed to have been initiated during 1972, eight were known to have been built by the end of 1983, at which time US intelligence reports indicated that series production of the class had been completed.
Notes: Believed to be the fastest and deepest diving operational submarine yet built, the small, extremely clean, titanium-hulled 'Alfa' class hunter/killers have a submerged top speed significantly faster than that of a number of torpedoes currently in service with navies in the West. This intrinsic advantage of being able to outrun most torpedoes is further complemented by the boat's ability to dive to depths of around 4425 feet for short periods, or loiter at nearly 3000 feet. While titanium is a very expensive material, it is extremely strong and is also non magnetic, making the task of detecting these boats all the more difficult.

Yushio Class Submarines

Role: Patrol.
Builders: Mitsubishi and Kawasaki, Japan.
User: Japanese Maritime Self-defence Force.
Basic data: 2700 tons full displacement dived; 249.3ft (76.0m) overall length; 32.5ft (9.9m) maximum beam.
Crew: 80.
Propulsion: 2 Kawasaki-MAN V8V 24/30 AMIL diesel-electric generators (total 3400bhp)/batteries/electric drive (7200shp); 1 propeller.
Sensors: 1 surface search radar; active and passive sonar systems; inertial navigational and precision position fixing system.
Armament; 6 heavyweight anti-submarine torpedo tubes; mines.

Top speed: 20 knots dived.
Endurance: No published data available.
Programme: A planned nine-boat class, with the final vessel set to be ordered in early 1984. The known class comprises: *Yushio* (S573), *Mochishio* (S574), *Setoshio* (S575), *Okishio* (S576), *Nadashio* (S577), *Hamashio* S578, *Akishio* S579, S580 and S581. Mitsubishi was given responsibility for building the lead boat, along with the 3rd, 5th, 7th and 9th, leaving Kawasaki constructing the 2nd, 4th, 6th, and 8th. *Yushio* was laid down in December 1976, launched in March 1979 and entered service in February 1980. With *Okishio* delivered by March 1983 and subsequent acceptances taking place at a rate of one per year, the last of the nine boats should be handed over around March 1988.
Notes: The 'Yushio' class as with its slightly smaller forebears in the shape of the 'Uzushio' class, employ the US-developed teardrop-shaped hull, with amidships torpedo tubes and bow-mounted sonar installation. Again, as with the 'Uzushio' design, the 'Yushio' class boats reflect the US practice of mounting the boat's attitude-controlling hydroplanes on the sail or conning tower, rather than on the forward section of the hull.

Rubis Class Submarines

Role: Anti-submarine.
Builder: DCAN, Cherbourg, France.
User: French Navy.
Basic data: 2670 tons dived displacement; 236.2ft (72m) overall length; 24.9ft (7.6m) maximum beam.

A starboard beam aspect of the lead of class, Yushio (S573).

Rubis (S601), lead boat of this French Navy Class, 1981.

HNLMS Tijgerhaai *(S807) patrol submarine.*

Crew: 66.
Propulsion: 1 pressurised water nuclear reactor; 1 electric motor; 1 propeller.
Sensors: 1 DRUA 33 surface search radar; passive and active sonar and underwater telephone systems including 1 DSUV 22, 1 DUUA 2B and 1 DUUX 2 equipment; echo sounder.
Armament: 4 forward-firing heavyweight anti-submarine torpedo tubes for 14 torpedoes or SM 39 Exocet submarine-launched anti-ship missiles or 533mm (21 inch) mines.
Top speed: Over 25 knots dived.
Range: Unlimited.
Programme: This five-boat class comprises; *Rubis* (S601), *Saphir* (S602), *Casabianca (S603), S604* and *S605. The lead boat, Rubis,* was laid down in December 1976, launched in July 1979 and entered service in July 1982. Programme schedules call for the delivery of the *Saphir* in July 1984, followed by the remaining boats in July 1986, September 1987 and December 1988.
Notes: Powered by a 48-megawatt pressurised water reactor, driving two turbo-alternators, the 'Rubis' class hunter/killer submarines represent the French equivalent of the US Navy's 'Los Angeles' class and the Royal Navy's 'Trafalgar' and 'Swiftsure' class boats.

Zwaardvis Class Submarines

Role: patrol.
Builder: RDM, Netherlands.
Users: Royal Netherlands Navy (2) and Taiwan (2).
Basic data: 2640 tons dived displacement; 219.6ft (66.92m) overall length; 27.6ft (8.4m) maximum beam.
Crew: 67.
Propulsion: 3 diesel generators (total 4200bhp)/ batteries/1 electric motor, 1 propeller.
Sensors: 1 surface search radar; comprehensive sonar equipment.
Armament: 6 heavyweight anti-submarine torpedo tubes (20 torpedoes).
Top speed: 20 knots dived.
Range: Not known, but boats have snorkel.
Programme: This two-boat class, consisting of HNLMS *Zwaardvis* (S806) and HNLMS *Tijgerhaai* (S807), were both laid down in July 1967 and entered service with the Royal Netherlands Navy in August 1972 and October 1972, respectively. Two modified versions are under construction for Taiwan.

Notes: The design of the 'Zwaardvis' boats is based on that of the US Navy's 'Barbel' class diesel-electric submarine, but incorporates Dutch equipment, which, in turn, necessitates both internal and external modification. Most noticeable differences between the US and Dutch submarines is visible in the faired appendage halfway up the trailing edge of the Dutch boat's 'sail' or conning tower. Another external difference lies in the raised aft upper coaming of the 'Zwaardvis' boats' hulls, which starts approximately halfway back along the 'sail'. All noise-producing machinery is mounted on anti-vibration attachments for maximum shock/noise absorption.

Guppy I/II/III Classes Submarines

Role: Patrol.
Builders: Various, USA.
Users: Navies of Argentina (1 x III), Brazil (2 x III, 3 x II), Greece (1 x III, 1 x II), Spain (3 x II), Taiwan (2 x II), Turkey (2 x III, 7 x II, 1 x I) and Venezuela (1 x II).
Basic data: 2540 tons (III) or 2440 tons (II) or 2400 tons (I) dived displacement; 326.5ft/99.5m (III) or 306.3ft/93.4m (II, I) overall length; 27.0ft/8.2m maximum beam.
Crew: 85.
Propulsion: 4 General Motors 16-278A or Fairbank-Morse 38D diesels (total 6400bhp) batteries/2 electric motor; 2 propellers.
Sensors: 1 SS-2A sea search and navigational radar; 1 BQC-4 sonar (in III only); 1 BQR-2B sonar.
Armament: 6 forward and 4 aft heavyweight anti-submarine torpedo tubes; 24 torpedoes.
Top speed: 14 knots dived.
Range: 11,000 nautical miles at 10 knots.
Programme: The 'Guppy' class boats are refurbished and, in the case of the II and III sub-classes, progressively modernised examples of the World War II US Navy's 'Tench' class submarines. All of the 24 boats remaining in service at the end of 1982 were built during the 1943 through 1946 period and comprise: Argentina's S22 (III); Brazil's S10, S12, S14 (IIs) and S15, S16 (IIIs); Greece's S114 (II) and S115 (III); Spain's S32, S34, S35 (IIs); Taiwan's 736, 794 (IIs); Turkey's S333, S341 (IIIs) and S335, S336, S337, S338, S340, S345, S346 (IIs) and S339; (I) Venezuela's S22 (II).
Notes: Despite the obvious age of these boats, which it

The Hellenic Navy's 'Guppy' III class boat, L Katsonis (S115).

should be remembered have been virtually rebuilt from the keel up on more than one occasion, many of the surviving boats are likely to remain in service through to the end of the 1980s, largely as a result of the ongoing economic constraints and the ever rising cost of new submarine acquisition.

Porpoise/Oberon Classes Submarines

Role: Patrol.
Builders: Various, UK.
Users: Navies of Australia, Brazil, Canada, Chile and UK.
Basic data: 2410 tons dived displacement; 295ft (89.9m) overall length; 26ft (7.9m) maximum beam.
Crew: c70.

Propulsion: 2 Admiralty SR 16-cylinder diesels/batteries/2 electric motors (to-tal 6000shp); 2 propellers.
Sensors: 1 Type 1002 or 1 Type 1006 surface search and nav radar; 1 Type 186 and 1 Type 187 bow-mounted sonars.
Armament: 6 bow tubes for 20 heavyweight anti-submarine torpedoes; 2 stern tubes for 4 heavyweight anti-submarine torpedoes.
Top speed: 16 knots dived.
Range: Submerged endurance quoted as being in excess of six weeks with periodic use of snorkel.
Programme: Two 'Porpoise' class and 27 out of the original 33 'Oberons' remain in service. Both classes, which are virtually identical, were built between 1954 and 1967 and are currently distributed thus: Australia six, Brazil three, Canada three (modified and known as 'Objibwa' class). Chile two and UK 13 'Oberon' and two 'Porpoise' class.

HMAS Oxley (S57), one of six Australian operated 'Oberons'.

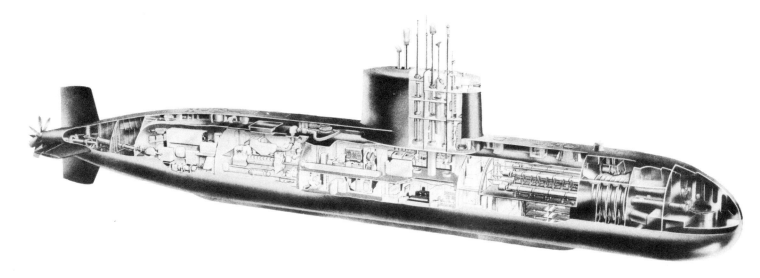

An artist's cut-away impression of the Type 2400.

Notes: Generally considered excellent submarines, the 'Oberons' are especially liked by their crews for their relatively superior habitability and living quarters. Maximum diving depth has been quoted as around 655 feet (200m); a depth well surpassed by more modern diesel-electric powered submarines. Although to be replaced by the 'Upholder' class in Royal Navy service, the 'Oberon' class will remain in service for some years yet.

Upholder Class Submarines

Role: Patrol.
Builder: Vickers (lead yard), UK.
User: On order for the Royal Navy.
Basic data: 2400 tons dived displacement; 230.5ft (70.25m) overall length; 24.9ft (7.6m) maximum beam.
Crew: 46.
Propulsion: 2 Paxman Ventura diesel generators (total 2015bhp)/batteries/ 1 GEC electric motor (5400shp); 1 propeller.
Sensors: 1 Kelvin Hughes Type 1006 surface search and navigational radar; 1 Thomson-CSF Type 2040 passive sonar; Thomson-CSF Type 2019 passive/active sonar; Type 2026 towed array sonar; Omega very low frequency underway navigational system; automated action information data processing and launch control system; 1 echo sounder.
Armament: 6 forward-firing heavyweight torpedo tubes for 18 torpedoes/mines or Sub-Harpoon anti-ship missiles.
Top speed: 20 knots dived.
Endurance: Over 28 days on station, after a dived transit of 2500 nautical miles and the same on return.
Programme: With preliminary design work completed during the late 1970s and referred to in the UK Defence Estimates paper of April 1980, the lead of class contract was awarded to Vickers at the beginning of November 1983. Early 1980s reports that the Type 2400 built for the Royal Navy could amount to an 18-boat class may well prove optimistic, but could well run to an ultimate 14 boats. The lead of class, HMS *Upholder* (S40),should be delivered during the late 1987/early 1988 period.
Notes: Designed as a replacement for the Royal Navy's 'Oberon' class submarines, the protracted nature of this diesel-electric follow-on to the 'Oberons' has done nothing for its export prospects, already eroded by recent year Federal German and French encroachment into the world's medium displacement submarine markets. Of conventional two-decked, single pressure-hull design, the Type 2400 can dive to depths in excess of 656ft (200m).

Foxtrot Class Submarines

Role: Patrol.
Builder: Leningrad, USSR.
Users: Navies of USSR, India, Libya and Cuba.
Basic data: 2400 tons dived displacement; 315ft (96m) overall length; 24.6ft (7.5m) maximum beam.
Crew: 78.
Propulsion: Diesels (total 6000bhp)/batteries/electric motors; 3 propellers.
Sensors: 1 surface search radar; 1 passive sonar.
Armament: 10 heavyweight anti-submarine torpedo tubes (6 forward 4 aft) with 22 torpedoes or 44 mines.
Top speed: 16 knots dived.
Range: 11,000 nautical miles at 8 knots dived using snorkel.
Programme: 60 of these vessels were built between 1957 and 1974.
Notes: In many respects directly comparable to the Royal Navy's 'Porpoise/Oberon' class contemporaries, the 'Foxtrot' class remains in front line with Mediterranean and Indian Ocean-based units of the Soviet fleet. While these ageing diesel-electric driven 'Foxtrots' may be significantly slower than the subsequent generations of nuclear-powered submarines, their retention in service reflects the respect many senior submariners have for these very silent-when-running submersed hunter/killers. Here it should be remembered that one of the biggest problems facing nuclear-powered submarine designers is how effectively to muffle all the heat-exchanging steam plumbing. Eight 'Foxtrots' have been transferred to the Indian Navy, three to Libya and several to Cuba.

Santa Cruz Class Submarines

Role: Patrol.
Builder: Thyssen Nordseewerke (lead). Federal Germany.
User: Argentinian Navy.
Basic data: 2300 tons dived displacement; 216.5ft (66.0m) overall length; 24.0ft (7.3m) maximum beam.
Crew: 30.
Propulsion: 4 MTU diesel-generators/batteries/1 Siemens electric motor (4950shp); 1 propeller.

A Soviet 'Foxtrot' class photographed off Sicily, 1975.

Sensors: 1 Hollandse surface search radar; Hollandse passive and active sonar system; Hollandse launch control system.
Armament: 6 forward-firing heavyweight torpedo tubes for 22 to 24 torpedoes or 533mm mines.
Top speed: 24 knots dived.
Endurance: Over 8000 nautical miles.
Programme: Argentina placed an order for four of this class in November 1977, the lead of which, *Santa Cruz* (S33), was laid down in December 1980, launched at the beginning of 1983 and delivered in late 1983. The 2nd of class, *San Juan* (S34), was laid down in early 1982; this vessel, along with S33, was built by Thyssen Nordseewerke. Under the original contract the third and fourth boats were to be locally built by Astilleres Domecq Garcia, but whether Garcia will build these boats from the keel up or simply complete the assembly of pre-manufactured main elements produced by Thyssen Nordseewerke remains uncertain at press time. All four boats should be in service by the close of 1985.
Notes: Designed for long-range patrol missions, the TR-

1700 is impressively fast for a diesel-electric submarine and is capable of operating at depths in excess of 886ft (270m). The design employs a conventional three-compartmented, single pressure-hull layout, terminating in four cruciform fins.

Asashio Class Submarines

Role: Patrol.
Builders: Kawasaki and Mitsubishi, Japan.
User: Japanese Maritime Self-Defence Force.
Basic data: 2300 tons full displacement dived; 288.7ft (88.0m) overall length; 26.9ft (8.2m) maximum beam.
Crew: 80.
Propulsion: 2 Kawasaki diesels (total 5800bhp)/batteries/2 electric motors (total 6300shp); 2 propellers.
Sensors: 1 surface search radar; active and passive sonar systems.

An artist's impression of the TR-1700 boat ordered by Argentina.

This aerial aspect of an 'Asashio' class emphasises the forward location and 'stepped' profile of the boat's sail, or conning tower.

Armament: 6 forward and 2 aft heavyweight anti-submarine torpedo tubes.
Top speed: 18 knots dived.
Range: Up to 8 days dived with snorkel.
Programme: This four-boat class comprises: *Asashio* (S562), *Harushio* (S563), *Michishio* (S564) and *Arashio* (S565). Kawasaki built the lead of class and third boat, with Mitsubishi responsible for the construction of the second and fourth boats. All laid down between October 1964 and July 1967, the four submarines were launched between November 1965 and October 1968, the class entering service between October 1966 and July 1979.
Notes: The 'Asashio' class, derived from the prototype *Oshio* boat, represents Japan's first post-World War II submarine construction programme; the design's elderly technology tending to reflect the curtailment of Japanese submarine development and construction during the latter 1940s and almost the entirety of the 1950s. The *Oshio*, from which the 'Asashio' class stemmed, was withdrawn from service in March 1982.

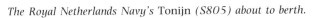

The Royal Netherlands Navy's Tonijn (S805) about to berth.

Dolfijn/Potvis Classes Submarines

Role: Patrol.
Builders: Wilton-Fijenoord and Rotterdam, Netherlands.
User: Royal Netherlands Navy.
Basic data: 1830 tons dived displacement; 260.8ft (79.5m) overall length; 25.7ft (7.84m) maximum beam.
Crew: 64.
Propulsion: 2 SEMT-Pielstick 12 PA4V185 diesels (total 2800bhp)/batteries/2 electric motors (total 4400shp); 2 propellers.
Sensors: 1 Type 1001 surface search radar; passive and active sonar systems; bottom depth echo sounder; automated torpedo launch control.
Armament: 4 forward and 2 aft heavyweight anti-submarine torpedo tubes; mines.
Top speed: 17 knots.
Endurance: Over 4000 nautical miles dived with snorkel.
Programme: The first two boats of these closely related classes were ordered during 1949, the vessels *Dolfijn* (S808) and *Zeehund* (S809) both being laid down in December 1954, launched in May 1959 and February 1960, the boats entering service in December 1960 and March 1961, respectively. The second pair, ordered in 1962, comprise *Potvis* (S804) and *Tonijn* (S805), the submarines being laid down in September and November 1962, entering service in November 1965 and February 1966, respectively. The latter pair of 'Potvis' class boats underwent a major refit during the 1978/79 period. The earlier pair of 'Dolfijn' class are scheduled to be retired in the 1985/6 period, replaced by the two new Dutch-built 'Walrus' class boats. Responsibility for the construction of S808 and S809 was vested with Rotterdam DDM, while S804 and S805 were built by Wilton-Fijenoord BV.
Notes: Although the 'Dolfijn' class bore a close external likeness to the US-developed 'Guppy' class, the innards of these Dutch boats, along with the later 'Potvis' class vessels, employ a novel triple inner pressure-hull system, with the crew and armament occupying the shorter, upper cylinder, while the twin independent propulsion machinery packages each fit into one of the two lower inner hulls.

Agosta Class Submarines

Role: Ocean patrol.
Builders: DCAN Cherbourg and Dubigeon, France; Bazan, Spain.

Agosta *(S620) lead boat of this French diesel-electric powered submarine class.*

Users: Navies of France, Pakistan and Spain.
Basic data: 1740 tons dived displacement; 221.7ft (67.97m) overall length; 22.3ft (6.8m) maximum beam.
Crew: 54.
Propulsion: 2 SEMT-Pielstick 320-16PA 4 185 diesel-generators/batteries/1 electric motor (4600shp); 1 propeller.
Sensors: 1 DRUA 33 surface search radar; passive and active sonar and underwater telephone systems, including 1 DUUA 1 D, 1 each DUUA 2A and 2D, 1 DSUV 22; 1 DUUX 2A.
Armament: 4 forward-firing heavyweight torpedo tubes for 20L5 or F17 torpedoes.
Top speed: 20.5 knots dived; 12.5 knots running on surface.
Range: 10,000 nautical miles at 10 knots employing periodic snorkel.
Programme: Ten of these boats had been built or were on order by mid-1985 consisting of four for the French Navy, two Pakistani vessels and four in course of construction by Bazan for the Spanish Navy. The French vessels comprise: *Agosta* (S620), *Beveziers* (S621), *La Praya* (S622) and *Ouessant* (S623): all entering service between July 1977 and July 1978. The two Pakistani boats, built at the Dubigeon yards comprise: *Hashmat* (S135) and *Hurmat* (S136) and entered service in February 1979 and February 1980, respectively. The four Bazan-built boats for Spain comprise: *Galera* (S71), *Sciroco* (S72), *Mistral* (S73) and *Tramontana* (S74). The lead boat of the Spanish vessels was delivered in January 1983 and all should have entered service by the close of 1985.
Notes: The 'Agosta' class represents a follow-on for the earlier French-developed 'Daphne' class submarines and, as such, has already penetrated some of the Francophone export markets.

Sauro Class Submarines

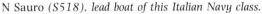

Role: Patrol.
Builder: CRDA Malfoncone, Italy.
User: Italian Navy.
Basic data: 1641 tons dived displacement; 209.5ft (63.85m) overall length; 22.4ft (6.83m) maximum beam.
Crew: 45.
Propulsion: 3 GMT A210 16M diesel generators (total 2935shp)/batteries/electric motor; 1 propeller.

N Sauro *(S518), lead boat of this Italian Navy class.*

Sensors: 1 SMG RM-20 radar; Selenia USEA IPD-70 sonar system; 1 Velox M5 sonar.
Armament: 6 tubes for heavyweight torpedoes (6 reloads carried).
Top speed: 20 knots dived.
Range: 12,500 nautical miles dived at 4 knots using snorkel.
Programme: The initial Italian Government contracts covered two boats, *Nazario Sauro* (S518) and *Carlo Fecia di Cossato* (S519), ordered in 1974 and 1975 respectively, and which entered service in 1979 and 1980. Two more of this class, *Leonardo Da Vinci* (S520) and *Guglielmo Marconi* (S521), were ordered in 1977 and both entered service during the latter half of 1981. Two more boats, S522 and S523 were ordered in August 1983, bringing the class total to six submarines.
Notes: Designed with the export market very much in mind, the 'Sauro' class boats employ Italian equipment exclusively in their construction. Capable of diving to a sustained depth of around 820 feet, the 'Sauro' class can travel submerged at top speed for up to one hour, or up to 100 hours at 4 knots which necessitates approaching the surface to 'snorkel'.

The lead of class Sjoormen *showing its distinctive sail or conning tower.*

Sjoormen Class Submarines

Role: Coastal patrol.
Builders: Kockums and Karlskrona. Sweden.
User: Royal Swedish Navy.
Basic data: 1400 tons dived displacement; 167.3ft (51.0m) overall length; 20.0ft (6.1m) maximum beam.
Crew: 28.
Propulsion: 4 Hedemora-Pielstick 12.PA-4 diesel-generator/batteries/ 1 ASEA electric motor (1500shp); 1 propeller.
Sensors: 1 Philips (Sweden) surface search radar; passive and active sonar systems; echo sounder.
Armament: 4 forward-firing heavyweight torpedo tubes and 2 forward-firing medium anti-submarine torpedo tubes for wire-guided torpedoes and 533mm (21in) mines.
Top speed: 20 knots dived; 15 knots running on surface.
Endurance: Up to 21 days.
Programme: This five-boat class comprises: *Sjoormen, Sjolejonet, Sjohunden, Sjobjornen* and *Sjohasten* (as is Swedish practice, each boat carries the first three letters of its name on its sail in place of a pennant number). Kockums built the first three boats, while Karlskronavarvet built the latter two; all entering service between July 1967 and September 1969.
Notes: The 'Sjoormen' class is reported to have a relatively shallow maximum diving depth of around 492ft (150m); quite adequate for operations in Baltic waters.

Heroj *(S821), lead boat of this Yugoslavian Navy class.*

Heroj Class Submarines

Role: Patrol.
Builder: Uljanik, Yugoslavia.
User: Yugoslavian Navy.
Basic data: 1350 tons dived displacement; 210.2ft (64.0m) overall length; 23.6ft (7.2m) maximum beam.
Crew: 36.
Propulsion: 2 diesel-electric generators/batteries/2 electric motors (total 2400shp); 1 propeller.
Sensors: 1 surface search radar; active and passive sonar systems.
Armament: 6 heavyweight anti-submarine torpedo tubes.
Top speed: 10 knots dived.
Range: 9700 nautical miles at 8 knots with snorkel.
Programme: This three-boat class comprises: *Heroj* (S821), *Junak* (S822) and *Uskok* (S823). These boats entered service in the 1968 through 1970 period.
Notes: The 'Heroj' class represents a relatively conventional design for a submarine of this size and mission. However, unlike the majority of their contemporaries, the 'Heroj' class boats mount all of their torpedo tubes at the forward end, an aspect that must reduce their operational flexibility by preventing them from launching the sometimes useful frigate-scaring torpedo on a reciprocal track from a stern tube.

Whiskey Class Submarines

Role: Patrol.
Builders: Various USSR and China.
Users: Navies of Albania (3), China (21), Egypt (6), Indonesia (1), North Korea (4), Poland (4), and USSR (60).
Basic data: 1350 tons dived displacement; 246.0ft (75.0m) overall length; 24.6ft (7.5m) maximum beam.
Crew: 70.
Propulsion: 2 Type 37D diesels (total 4000bhp)/batteries/2 electric motors (total 2500shp); 2 propellers.
Sensors: 1 surface search radar; passive and active sonar systems.
Armament: 4 forward and 2 aft-firing heavyweight anti-submarine torpedo tubes for 12 torpedoes or 24 mines. *Note:* 12 Soviet boats have been converted to carry 2 SS-N-3 'Shaddrock' anti-ship missile launchers, mounted outside the hull.
Top speed: 13.5 knots dived.
Range: 6000 nautical miles at 5 knots with periodic snorkel.
Programme: Around 235 examples of this class were built in Soviet yards between 1949 and 1957, with at least a further 18 built in Chinese shipyards during the latter half of the 1950s. Currently, around 99 remain operational as listed in the Users' section above.
Notes: The 'Whiskey' class design was clearly greatly influenced by later World War II German U-boat

A Polish Navy 'Whiskey' class boat photographed from a Royal Air Force BAe Nimrod, August 1983.

technology, particularly that of the German Type XXI boat. All deck-mounted gun armament fitted to early 'Whiskey' class submarines has long since been removed. Four of these boats were converted as radar pickets during the early 1960s, being equipped with a folding long-range air search radar, which, when not in use, was stowed in the upper rear section of the boat's sail or conning tower.

Type 209 Classes Submarines

Role: Patrol.
Builders: Howaldtswerke, Federal Germany.
Users: Navies of Argentina, Chile, Ecuador, Greece, India, Indonesia, Peru, Turkey and Venezuela.
Basic data: 1230 tons dived displacement; 180.4ft (55m) overall length; 21.65ft (6.6m) maximum beam.
Crew: 31.
Propulsion: 4 MTU Type 12-V-492-TB-90 diesels/bat-

teries/1 Siemens electric motor (3600shp); 1 propeller.
Sensors: 1 Omega navigational system; 1 of various surface search radars; 1 of various bow-mounted sonars.
Armament: 8 heavyweight anti-submarine torpedo tubes (14 torpedoes).
Top speed: 22 knots dived.
Endurance: In excess of 50 days.
Programme: Greece placed the first order for the Type 209s in 1967, for six boats, since increased to eight the first of the Greek submarines, *Glavkos* (S110), being accepted in September 1971 and the last during 1980. Further orders for the Type 209 followed quickly, with Argentina ordering two operated as 'Salta' class boats, the first *Salta* (S31) being accepted in May 1974. Peru contracted for three, the first of which, *Islay* (S45), was commissioned in January 1975, and has subsequently ordered a further three. Turkey, with orders for five, took delivery of their first boat, *Atilay* (S347), in July 1975. Venezuela has four, their first, *Sabalo* (S31), being accepted into service in August 1976. Ecuador has also

The Peruvian Navy's Casma *(S31).*

Nacken, *lead ship of this three-boat Royal Swedish Navy class.*

ordered two boats, the first being *Shyri*. Indonesia ordered two Type 209s in 1977. More recently, Chile has ordered two of the type, along with India, who have ordered the first two of a planned six- boat procurement, bringing total known Type 209 orders to 37 boats.

Notes: The Type 209s can reach a depth in excess of 655ft (200m), some later deliveries are 9.8ft longer and 70 tons heavier dived. Characterised by the turtle deck section.

Nacken Class Submarines

Role: Patrol.
Builder: Kockums, Sweden.
User: Royal Swedish Navy.
Basic data: 1125 tons dived displacement; 162.4ft (49.5m) overall length; 20ft (6.1m) maximum beam.
Crew: 19.
Propulsion: 2 Hedemora-Pielstick diesels/batteries/1 electric motor (1500shp); 1 propeller.
Sensors: 1 Philips (Sweden) surface search radar; 1 bow-mounted active/passive sonar system.
Armament: 6 heavyweight and 2 lightweight anti-submarine torpedo tubes; mines.
Top speed: 20 knots dived.
Endurance: In excess of 2000 nautical miles.
Programme: Ordered in 1972, this three-boat class comprises *Nacken* (Nak), *Najad* (Naj) and *Neptun* (Nep). Laid down between November 1972 and March 1974, *Nacken*, the first of the Type A 14 boats, entered service during 1979, followed by the other two boats in 1980.
Notes: An extremely compact design, the 'Nacken' class submarines have an almost full-length turtle deck structure above the main cylindrical pressure hull and it is only the turtle decking that is visible when the craft is running on the surface, adding appreciably to the boat's apparent short overall length. The small crew complement is as much a reflection of the high degree of automation used in these boats, as it is a function of their relatively short design, tailored to meet Sweden's overall defensive, as opposed to offensive, military equipment procurement policies.

Daphne Class Submarines

Role: Patrol.
Builders: Various French; Bazan, Spain.
Users: Navies of France, Portugal, Pakistan, South Africa, Spain.
Basic data: 1043 tons dived displacement; 198.5ft (57.75m) overall length; 22.2ft (6.76m) maximum beam.
Crew: 45.
Propulsion: 2 SEMT-Pielstick 450 KW diesel generators/batteries/ electric motors; 2 propellers.
Sensors: 1 Calypso II radar; 1 DUUA 2 passive sonar (French fit).
Armament: 12 tubes for 12 heavyweight torpedoes (no reserves).
Top speed: 16 knots dived.
Range: 4500 nautical miles dived at 5 knots using snorkel.
Programme: Nine boats were built for the French Navy, all entering service between June 1964 and March 1970: *Daphne* (S641), *Diane* (S642), *Doris* (S643), *Flore* (S645), *Galatee* (S646), *Junon* (S648), *Venus* (S649), *Psyche* (S650) and *Sirene* (S651). Portugal operates three: *Albacora* (S163), *Barracuda* (S164) and *Delfim* (S166). South Africa employs three: *Maria Van Riebeeck* (S97), *Emily Hobhouse* (S98), and *Johanna Van der Merwe* (S99). Four more currently in service with Pakistan are: *Hangor* (S131), *Shushuk* (S132), *Mangro* (S133) and *Ghazi* (S134). The final four 'Daphnes' to be built were constructed under licence by Bazan of Spain: *Delfin* (S61), *Tonina* (S62), *Marsopa* (S63) and *Narval* (S64); all entering into service between May 1973 and November 1975.
Notes: Capable of very quiet submerged running, this class of submarine can dive to depths of around 985 feet (300m).

Delfinen Class Submarines

Role: Patrol.
Builder: Danish Naval Dockyards, Denmark.
User: Royal Danish Navy.
Basic data: 643 tons dived displacement; 177.2ft (54.0m) overall length; 15.4ft (4.7m) maximum beam.
Crew: 33.
Propulsion: 2 Burmeister & Wain diesels/batteries/2

The Portuguese Navy's Albacora *(S163).*

The Royal Danish submarine Tumleren *(S328), with radio antenna extended above the boat's sail or conning tower.*

electric motors (1200shp); 2 propellers.
Sensors: 1 Philips (Sweden) surface search radar; passive and active systems; echo sounder.
Armament: 4 forward-firing heavyweight anti-submarine torpedo tubes.
Top Speed: 12 knots dived; 13 knots running on surface.
Range dived: 4500 nautical miles at 8.5 knots with periodic snorkel.
Programme: This four-boat class comprises: *Delfinen* (S326), *Spaekhuggeren* (S327), *Tumleren* (S328) and *Springeren* (S329). All were laid down between July 1954 and January 1961, launched between May 1956 and April 1963; the boats entering service between September 1958 and October 1964.
Notes: Although elderly by any standard, these boats have a good endurance, being capable of crossing the Atlantic to take up patrol in Greenland waters. In appearance, the 'Delfinen' class boats could easily be confused with a number of larger patrol submarine classes, particularly where few visual aids to scale exist.

Type 206 Class Submarines

Role: Patrol.
Builders: Howaldtswerke and Nordseewerke, Federal Germany; Vickers, UK.
Users: Navies of Federal Germany (18) and Israel (3).
Basic data: 825 tons full displacement dived; 160.8ft (49.0m) overall length; 15.75ft (4.8m) maximum beam.
Crew: 22.
Propulsion: 2 MTU 820Db diesels (total 1200bhp)/batteries/1 electric motor (2300shp); 1 propeller.
Sensors: 1 sea search and navigational radar; 1 long-range passive and 1 trainable active/passive sonars; 1 echo sounder.
Armament: 8 heavyweight anti-submarine torpedo tubes (16 torpedoes). (*Note:* neither navy has adopted the offered SLAM missile system).
Top speed: 17 knots dived.
Endurance: Over 19 days at 12 knots.
Programme: A total of 21 Type 206 boats have been constructed comprising 18 for Federal Germany (*U 13* through *U 30*) and three for Israel (*Gal*, *Tanin* and *Rahav*). Howaldtswerke built the lead of class, plus seven

41

U17 *of the Federal German Navy.*

subsequent boats, while Nordseewerke constructed the other ten vessels, all of which were delivered between April 1973 and March 1975. The three Vickers-built boats for Israel were delivered between December 1976 and December 1977.

Notes: A somewhat larger development of the earlier Type 205 boats, incorporting many valuable metalurgical lessons learnt from the early problems that dogged the Type 205s. The submerged range of the Type 206 is reported to be 200 nautical miles (371km) at a speed of 5 knots without recourse to snorkeling. The TIOS torpedo launch control system fitted to the Federal German boats is to be replaced by improved equipment during the next few years.

Enrico Toti Class Submarines

Role: Patrol.
Builder: CRDA Monfalcone, Italy.
User: Italian Navy.
Basic data: 591 tons dived displacement; 151.6ft (46.2m) overall length; 15.4ft (4.7m) maximum beam.
Crew: 26.

Propulsion: 2 Fiat MB 820 diesels/batteries/1 electric motor (2200shp); 1 propeller.
Sensors: 1 SMA 3RM30/SMG surface search radar; passive and active sonar systems and echo sounder.
Armament: 4 heavyweight anti-submarine torpedo tubes for 6 torpedoes.
Top speed: 20 knots dived.
Range: 7500 nautical miles at 4.5 knots with periodic snorkel.
Programme: This four-boat class comprises: *Attilio Bagnolini* (S505), *Enrico Toti* (S506), *Enrico Dandolo* (S513) and *Lazzaro Nocenigo* (S514). Although laid down in two separate two-boat batches in 1965 and 1967, all four submarines entered service within a 12-month period, spanning January 1968 through January 1969.
Notes: The 'Enrico Toti' class, like their contemporaries in the shape of the Federal German Navy's Type 205 class, are relatively compact boats built for fairly shallow water operations.

Kobben Class (Type 207) Submarines.

Role: Patrol.
Builder: Rheinmetall-Nordseewerke, Federal Germany.
User: Royal Norwegian Navy.
Basic data: 482 tons dived displacement; 149.0ft (45.41m) overall length; 15.1ft (4.6m) maximum beam.
Crew: 17.
Propulsion: 2 Mercedes-Benz MB 820Db diesels (total 1200bhp)/batteries/ 1 electric motor (1700shp); 1 propeller.
Sensors: 1 sea search radar; hull-mounted active and passive sonar systems; automated action information and torpedo launch system.
Armament: 8 heavyweight anti-submarine torpedo tubes.
Top speed: 17 knots dived.
Endurance: Over 400 nautical miles dived.

The Italian Navy's Attilio Bagnolini *(S505) in company with another of her class.*

Programme: Norway ordered 15 Type 207, or 'Kobben' class boats in the early 1960s, but the lead vessels, *Kya* (S317), was written off in 1981, leaving 14 in current service. These remaining boats comprise: *Ula* (S300), *Utsira* (S301), *Utstein* (S302), *Utvaer* (S303), *Uthaug* (S304), *Sklinna* (S305), *Skolpen* (S306), *Stadt* (S307), *Stord* (S308), *Svenner* (S309), *Kaura* (S315), *Kinn* (S316), *Kobben* (S318) and *Kunna* (S319). All entered service between mid-June 1964 and the beginning of July 1967; *Kobben*, despite its late pennant number being the earliest surviving delivery.

Notes: The design of the Type 207 or 'Kobben' class boat is based on that of the Federal German Navy's Type 205, but has a strengthened hull to permit operations at a greater depth than its forebear. The 'Kobben' class boats are scheduled to be replaced by the Federal German-designed Type 210 submarine, with deliveries commencing in 1989. Currently, Norway has ordered six of the around 950-ton displacement Type 210s and holds options on two more.

The Royal Norwegian Navy's Svenner *(S309) passing another 'Kobben' class at its berth.*

Aircraft carriers

Nimitz Class Aircraft Carriers

Role: Air power projection.
Builder: Newport News, USA.
User: US Navy.
Basic data: 93,405 tons full displacement; 1092ft (332.8m) overall length; 252ft (76.8m) maximum beam.
Crew: 6280.
Propulsion: 2 Westinghouse A4W pressurised water nuclear reactors powering steam turbines (total 280,000shp); 4 propellers.
Sensors: Comprehensive suite of SPS-10 (surface) and SPS-43A or SPS-48 (air) long-range radars; 3 Mk 115 fire control radars (Mk 91 systems substituted in CVN 70 onwards); all integrated and managed by highly automated tactical action control systemry. 1 URN-20 or -25 TACAN aircraft homer.
Armament: 1 air group of around 95 aircraft; 3 octuple Sea Sparrow point defence surface-to-air missile launchers; 3 Phalanx 20mm rapid-fire gun close-in weapons systems (a 4th Phalanx is fitted to CVN 70 onwards).
Top speed: 32 knots.
Range: Unlimited.
Programme: Originally conceived during the mid-1960s as a three-ship class to replace the 'Midway' carriers, the contract for the lead ship, USS *Nimitz* (CVN68), was placed in 1967, the next two ships, USS *Dwight D Eisenhower* (CVN69) and USS *Carl Vinson* (CVN70), being ordered in 1970 and 1974, respectively. *Nimitz* entered service in May 1975, followed by CVN69 in late 1977 and CVN70 in 1982. An order for a fourth 'Nimitz' class ship, USS *Theodore Roosevelt* (CVN71), was placed in late 1980, with delivery planned for 1987. Two more carriers, *Abraham Lincoln* (CVN72) and *George Washington*

(CVN73), were ordered in December 1982, bringing the current class total to six carriers.
Notes: The largest aircraft carriers extant, the 'Nimitz' class carriers embody a 4.5 acre flightdeck layout based on that of the earlier, conventionally-powered 'Kitty Hawk' class, while the 'Nimitz' class's nuclear reactor system is a much refined development of the eight reactor installation used to power the USS *Enterprise* (CVN65), America's first nuclear-powered carrier. The nominal 13-year useful life of the 'Nimitz' class's nuclear fuel rods provides the energy equivalent to 11 million barrels of fuel oil, giving the ships the ability to sail unrefuelled for between 800,000 and one million nautical miles. Of the total crew complement, 2620, or just over 40 per cent, are aviation personnel. A typical air group embarked aboard these 'Nimitz' class carriers comprise two squadrons of Grumman F-14 Tomcat all-weather fighters, two squadrons of Vought A-7 Corsair II attack types, one squadron of Grumman A-6E Intruder all-weather attack machines, four to six Grumman EA-6B Prowler electronic warfare types, four Grumman KA-6D Intruder tanker aircraft, along with one squadron of Lockheed S-3A Viking and one squadron of Sikorsky SH-3 Sea King helicopters for anti-submarine missions. For tactical airborne control and early warning, each of these carriers always operates with four Grumman E-2C Hawkeyes aboard.

Enterprise Type Aircraft Carrier

Role: Air power projection.
Builder: Newport News, USA.
User: US Navy.

Two complementary views of USS Dwight D Eisenhower (CVN69) taken during a visit to Portsmouth, September 1981. Aircraft visible in the bow-on photograph are mainly Vought A-7s and Grumman A-6s with the nose of a Lockheed S-3 and the fins of a Grumman E-2 and EA-6B also visible. Clearly discernible in the stern-on picture are at least 11 Grumman F-14As mostly parked aft, plus two Sikorsky SH-3s, three Grumman EA-6B and a gaggle of Vought A-7s on the port bow section of the flight deck.

Basic data: 89,600 tons full displacement; 1123ft (342.3m) overall length; 248.3ft (75.7m) maximum beam.

Crew: 5785.

Propulsion: 8 pressurised water A2W nuclear reactors/4 geared steam turbines (all by Westinghouse) providing a total of 280,000shp and driving 4 propellers.

Sensors: 1 SPS-49 long-range air search; 1 SPS-48 height finder (3-D) radar; 1 SPS-10 surface search and navigational radar; 1 SPS-65 low-level air threat warning radar; 3 Mk 91 fire control radar systems for Sea Sparrow missiles; 1 URN-20 TACAN aircraft homer; 1 NTDS automated action information data processor.

Armament: 1 air group of around 90 aircraft; 3 octuple Mk 29 Sea Sparrow point air defence missile launchers; 3 Phalanx 20mm close-in weapons systems.

Top speed: 31 knots.

Range: Unlimited.

Programme: The USS *Enterprise* (CVN65) is the sole example of her type, being ordered in 1958, launched in September 1960 and commissioned in November 1961. *Enterprise's* latest refit was completed in 1981, involving major refurbishment including the replacement of the earlier SPS-32 and SPS-33 fixed array radars.

Notes: Essentially a 'Kitty Hawk' class hull modified to serve as an operational prototype for the 'Nimitz' class nuclear-powered carriers, the 'Big E' as the ship is known by her crew carries 2628 people especially associated with aircraft operations. The ship carries the same aircraft type mix as that described in the preceding 'Nimitz' class entry.

Kitty Hawk Class Aircraft Carriers

Role: Air power projection.

Builders: Various, USA.

User: US Navy.

Basic data: 80,800 tons full displacement; 1062.5ft (323.9m) overall length; 250ft (76.2m) maximum beam.

Crew: 5380.

Propulsion: 4 Westinghouse geared steam turbines (total 280,000shp); 4 propellers.

Sensors: 1 SPS-49 long-range air search radar; 1 SPS-48 height finder (3-D) radar; 1 SPS-10B surface search and navigational radar; 2 Mk 91 missile fire control systems; 1 URN-22 TACAN aircraft homer; 1 SQS-23 bow-mounted sonar (in CV66 only); 1 NTDS automated action information data processing system.

Armament: 1 air group of around 85 aircraft; 2 octuple Mk 29 launchers for Sea Sparrow point air defence missiles in CV63, CV66 and CV67, while CV64 has twin Mk 10 launchers for Terrier area air defence missiles; 3 Phalanx 20mm close-in weapons systems.

Top speed: 33 knots.

Range: 8000 nautical miles at 20 knots.

Programme: A four-ship class comprising: USS *Kitty Hawk* (CV63), USS *Constellation* (CV64), USS *America* (CV66) and USS *John F Kennedy* (CV67); commissioned in April 1961, October 1961, January 1965 and September 1968, respectively.

The builders involved were: New York Shipbuilding (CV63), Brooklyn Navy Shipyards (CV64) and Newport News Shipbuilding (CV66 and 67).

Notes: Developed from the 'Forrestal' class, the 'Kitty Hawk's' air group includes a squadron of S-3A Viking anti-submarine aircraft and requires 2500 aviation personnel. The *John F Kennedy* incorporates certain improvements, including a fourth aircraft elevator and has an increased full displacement of 82,560 tons.

USS Enterprise *(CVN65) steaming in the Pacific, 1976.*

USS John F Kennedy *(CV67) at sea in July 1968.*

USS Constellation *(CV64) with a mix of A-7Es, S-3As and F-14As forward, July 1977.*

USS Forrestal *(CV59) at sea in December 1975.*

Forrestal Class Aircraft Carriers

Role: Air power projection.
Builders: Various, USA.
User: US Navy.
Basic data: 78,000 tons full displacement; 1039ft (316.7m) overall length; 238ft (72.5m) maximum beam.
Crew: 5390.
Propulsion: 4 Westinghouse geared steam turbines (total 280,000shp); 4 propellers.
Sensors: 1 SP3-43A (SPS-49 to be retrofitted) long-range air search radar; 1 SPS-48 height finder (3-D) radar; 1 SPS-58 low-level air threat warning radar; 1 SPS-10 surface search and navigational radar; 2 Mk 91 fire control radar systems for Sea Sparrow; 1 URN-22 TACAN aircraft homer; NTDS automated action information data processor.
Armament: 1 air group of up to 85 aircraft. Ships have or are being fitted with 2 octuple Mk 25 or 29 launchers for Sea Sparrow point air defence missiles; 3 Phalanx 20mm close-in weapons systems are being fitted as they become available.
Top speed: 32 knots.
Range: 8000 nautical miles at 20 knots.
Programme: This four-ship class comprises: USS *Forrestal* (CV59), USS *Saratoga* (CV60), USS *Ranger* (CV61) and USS *Independence* (CV62); the first and third ships being built by Newport News, while the second and fourth being constructed by the New York Naval Dockyard, Commissioning dates: October 1955, April 1956, August 1957 and January 1959, respectively. All are to undergo Service Life Extension Programme (SLEP) during the 1980s to provide an extra 15 years of useful service, work having started on *Saratoga*.
Notes: These were the first post-World War II US carriers and are in the process of being modernised under the US Navy's Service Life Extension Programme (SLEP).

Midway Class Aircraft Carriers

Role: Air power projection.
Builder: Newport News, USA.

USS Midway *(CV41) with A-6E, EA-6B, A-7 and F-4s on flight deck, in the western Pacific, May 1982.*

User: US Navy.
Basic data: 64,000 tons full displacement; 979ft (298.4m) overall length; 258.5ft (78.8m) maximum beam.
Crew: 4560.
Propulsion: 4 Westinghouse geared steam turbines (total 212,000shp); 4 propellers.
Sensors: 1 SPS-49 long-range air search radar; 1 SPS-48 height finder (3-D) radar; 1 SPS-10 surface search radar and navigational radar; 2 Mk 115 missile fire control system radars; NTDS automated action information data-processing.
Armament: 1 air group of up to 72 aircraft; 2 octuple Mk 25 Sea Sparrow point air defence missile launchers; 2 Phalanx 20mm close-in weapons systems.
Top speed: 32 knots.
Endurance: In excess of 12,000 nautical miles.
Programme: Originally a three-ship class comprising USS *Midway* (CV41), USS *Franklin D Roosevelt* (CV42) and USS *Coral Sea* (CV43), of which only *Midway* and *Coral Sea* remain in service. Commissioned in September 1945 and October 1947, respectively, the ships have undergone major modernisation during the late 1950s and, in the case of the *Midway*, again in the late 1960s. Both ships will stay in service through the 1980s.
Notes: Too late to see service in World War II, these ships were the largest aircraft carriers of their time. Although their flight deck is not sufficiently stressed to operate the heavy Grumman F-14 Tomcat, they can and do operate McDonnell F-4 Phantoms.

Kiev Class Aircraft Carriers

Kiev in the Mediterranean, July 1976, an aspect of Kiev *that highlights the angled flight deck and sensor/weapons fit.*

Role: Fleet air defence.
Builder: Nikolayev, USSR.
User: Soviet Navy.
Basic data: 37,000 tons full displacement; 900ft (270m) overall length; 164ft (50m) maximum beam.
Crew: 1700.
Propulsion: 4 geared steam turbines (total 140,000shp); 4 propellers.

Sensors: 1 long-range air search radar; 2 separate height finder (3-D) radars (one probably for ship-controlled interception); 2 surface search and navigational radars; 2 fire control radars each for the SA-N-3 and SA-N-4 missile systems; 1 fire control radar for the SS-N-12 missile system; 2 fire control radars for the 76mm guns; 4 fire control radars for the 30mm Gatling guns; 1 hull-mounted and 1 towed variable depth sonar.

Armament: Typically 12 Yakolev Yak-36 VTOL strike fighters and 24 Kamov Ka 25 helicopters; 4 twin SS-N-12 anti-ship cruise missile launchers; 2 twin SA-N-3 area air defence missile launchers; 2 twin SA-N-4 short-range air defence missile launchers; 1 twin SUW-N-1 short-range anti-submarine missile launcher; 2 twin 76mm dual-purpose guns; 8 single 30mm Gatling anti-aircraft guns.

Top speed: 32 knots.

Range: 13,500 nautical miles at 18 knots.

Programme: The first of this four-known ship class, *Kiev* was laid down in September 1970 and accepted into service in May 1975; a second ship, *Minsk*, followed on to the stocks in December 1972 and was accepted in February 1978. The third ship, *Kharkov*, laid down in October 1975, entered service early in 1982, while the fourth vessel, *Novorossiysk*, joined the Soviet Fleet in the late spring of 1983.

Notes: The 'Kiev' class ships are not only the largest Soviet warships yet to enter service, but with their complement of vertical take-off and landing (VTOL) Yakolev Yak-36 'Forger' strike fighters, these ships provide the Soviet Navy with a quantum jump in seagoing air capability. Unlike the earlier 'Moskva' class helicopter cruisers, the 'Kiev' class must be seen as real aircraft carriers, particularly when viewed in the light of recent successful operational deployment of the smaller HMS *Invincible* in the South Atlantic. Considering the previous total lack of Soviet navy fixed winged, carrier-going aircraft operating experience, the apparently trouble-free deployment of the just-supersonic Yakolev Yak-36 is particularly notable, as is the exceptionally heavy and well-balanced sensors/weapons fit installed aboard these ships. Indeed, in terms of both offensive and defensive armament, the 'Kiev' class ships not only have much more capability than all but the much larger US carriers, but the 'Kiev' class actually carries more onboard weaponry than just about any US warship, including the 'Virginia' class nuclear-powered cruisers. Range of the 'Kiev's' SS-N-12 anti-ship cruise missiles is quoted as being around 300 nautical miles, while the 'Kiev' class carry no less than a five-tier air defence capability built around the 'Forger' the 30 nautical mile ranged SA-N-3 and 8 nautical mile ranged SA-N-4 missiles, backed by 76mm and rapid fire 30mm gun systems; all radar directed.

Charles De Gaulle Class Aircraft Carriers

Role: Air power projection.

Builder: DCAN Brest, France.

User: French Navy.

Basic data: 36,000 tons full displacement; 853.0ft (260.0m) overall length; 200.1ft (61.0m) maximum beam.

Crew: 1700.

Propulsion: 2 pressurised water nuclear reactors (total 120,000shp estimated); 2 propellers.

Sensors: 1 DRBJ11B long-range air search 3-D radar; 1 DRBV 27 air search radar; 1 DRBV 15 low-level air and sea search radar; 1 Vampir infra red optronic fire control system for air defence missiles; SENIT 6 automated action information data-processing.

Armament: 1 air group of 40 aircraft; 2 octuple Crotale Navale point air defence missile launchers; 3 sextuple Sadrale point air defence missile launchers.

Top speed: 28 knots.

Tank testing the models of the 'Charles de Gaulle' aircraft carriers and proposed deck layout.

Range: Unlimited.

Programme: A larger development of the earlier nuclear-powered PH-75 or 'Provence' class studies of the latter 1970s, design work on the definitive *Charles de Gaulle* (R??) was initiated during 1980. Authorisation for full-scale development on the lead carrier was provided in the French 1984/88 defence budget plan. Scheduled to be laid down during 1986, *Charles de Gaulle* should enter service in 1995. An as yet unnamed second of class carrier is expected to be authorized in the 1988/92 French defence budget plan.

Notes: Designed to replace the existing pair of 'Clemenceau' class aircraft carriers, the projected 'Charles de Gaulle' class are physically larger than their forebears, particularly in terms of both flight deck length and area. Besides the normal ship's complement of 1150, a further 550 aviation personnel are needed to operate and maintain the 40-unit air group, consisting of Dassault Super Etendard fixed winged strike aircraft and anti-submarine helicopters (most probably Aerospatiale's navalised Super Puma).

Clemenceau Class Aircraft Carriers

Foch (R99) showing her side-mounted gun armament, 1982.

Role: Air power projection.
Builders: Various, France.
User: French Navy.
Basic data: 32,780 tons full displacement; 869.4ft (265m) overall length; 168ft (51.2m) maximum beam.
Crew: 1338.
Propulsion: 2 Parsons geared steam turbines (total 126,000shp); 2 propellers.
Sensors: 1 DRBV 20C long-range air search radar; 1 DRBV 23B air search radar; 2 DRBI 10 height finder (3-D) radars; 1 DRBV 50 low-level air and sea search radar; 1 Decca sea search and navigational radar; 3 DRBC 31 and 2 DRBC 32 fire control radars for the 100mm guns; 1 URN 6 TACAN aircraft homer; 1 SQS 505 hull-mounted sonar; SENIT II automated action information data-processing system.
Armament: 1 air group of around 40 aircraft; 8 single 100mm Model 1953 dual-purpose guns.
Top speed: 32 knots.
Range: 7500 nautical miles at 18 knots.
Programme: This two-ship class, made up of Clemenceau (R98) and Foch (R99), were authorised under the 1953 and 1955 French defence budgets and were accepted into service in November 1961 and July 1963, respectively. Clemenceau underwent a major refit between late 1977 and late 1978, while Foch underwent a similarly extensive refit during 1980.
Notes: The normal air group embarked comprises 16 Super Etendards (strike), three Etendard IVP (reconnaissance), ten F-8 Crusaders (fighters), seven Alizes (anti-submarine) and two or three Alouette helicopters.

Improved Centaur Type Aircraft Carrier

Role: Fleet anti-air/anti-submarine defence.
Builder: Vickers, UK.
User: Royal Navy.

Basic data: 28,700 tons full displacement; 744.3ft (226.85m) overall length; 160.0ft (48.78m) maximum beam.
Crew: 1170.
Propulsion: 2 Parsons geared steam turbines (total 76,000shp); 2 propellers.
Sensors: 1 Type 965 long-range air search and height finder (3-D) radar; 1 Type 993 combined low-level air and sea search radar; 1 Type 978 navigational radar; 2 Type 903 Seacat missile fire control radars; 1 Type 184 hull-mounted sonar; 1 TACAN aircraft homer; Ferranti automated action information data-processing system; satellite-fed data links.
Armament: Peacetime complement of 5 Sea Harriers and 12 Sea King helicopters; 2 quadruple Seacat point air defence missile launchers.

HMS Hermes (R12), flagship of the Royal Navy's Falklands' Task Force, showing her bow ski-jump and complement of Sea Harriers plus Sea King helicopters, May 1983.

Top speed: 28 knots.
Range: Over 4000 nautical miles at 18 knots.
Programme: One of four 'Centaur' class carriers laid down for the Royal Navy during 1944, HMS Hermes (R12) became a casualty of the post-World War II defence cutbacks and was not launched until February 1958, entering service in November 1959. Hermes, along with her sister ship HMS Bulwark, underwent major modernisation during the early 1970s. Hermes has subsequently undergone two further major refits, the most recent during 1980/81, during which the bow ski-jump was fitted to enable Sea Harrier operations from her decks. Planned to have been decommissioned in 1983, Hermes was given a new lease of life as a result of the Falklands crisis. Stood down in the spring of 1985, the carrier is reportedly being offered for sale to India.
Notes: The last remaining example of her class, HMS Hermes was the first Royal Navy carrier to operate the Sea Harrier, with which she deployed in June 1981. In April 1982, HMS Hermes was chosen to act as flagship for the Falklands' Task Force, primarily because of her ample accommodation and data links. During much of the Falklands campaign, Hermes operated with a mix of more than 20 Harrier GR 3s and Sea Harrier FRS 1s, plus 15 Sea Kings, a figure approaching the 42 aircraft complement she was originally envisaged as carrying when designed in the early 1940s. Besides her aircraft complement, Hermes retains the ability to accommodate up to 750 Royal Marines, plus four landing craft slung from her deckside davits.

Minas Gerais Type Aircraft Carrier

Role: Anti-submarine.
Builder: Swan Hunter, UK.

User: Brazilian Navy.
Basic data: 19,800 tons full displacement; 693ft (211.25m) overall length; 119.5ft (36.4m) maximum beam.
Crew: 1300.
Propulsion: 2 Parsons geared steam turbines (total 42,000shp); 2 propellers.
Sensors: 1 SPS-12 air search radar; 1 SPS-8B height finder radar; 1 SPS-4 surface search radar; 1 Type 1402 sea search and navigational radar; 2 SPG-34 gun fire control radar; data link facilities.
Armament: 1 anti-submarine air group of 21 aircraft; 4 twin and 2 single 40mm anti-aircraft guns.
Top speed: 24 knots.
Range: 12,000 nautical miles at 14 knots.
Programme: Laid down in November 1942 as HMS *Vengeance*, a 'Colossus' class carrier, the ship was bought by Brazil in November 1956 and entered service with the Brazilian Navy as the *Minas Gerais* (A11) in 1960, following a major modernisation carried out by a Dutch shipyard. The ship underwent refit between 1976 and 1979.

A recent view of Minas Gerais *(A11), showing her new mast-mounted data-link sensors.*

Notes: Unlike the Argentinian *25 de Mayo* (R81), another former 'Colossus' class carrier, the *Minas Gerais* is now being operated in a dedicated anti-submarine role working closely with other naval units led by the 'Niteroi' class frigates, with whom the carrier has data links. In its current role, the *Minas Gerais* operates seven fixed winged Grumman S-2 Trackers and up to 13 Sikorsky SH-3 Sea King helicopters.

Invincible Class Aircraft Carriers

Role: Multi-purpose.
Builders: Various, UK.
User: Royal Navy.
Basic data: 19,500 tons full displacement; 677.8ft (206.6m) overall length; 90.2ft (27.5m) maximum beam.
Crew: 903.
Propulsion: 4 Rolls-Royce TM3B Olympus gas turbines (total derated 79,200shp); COGAG; 2 controllable-pitch propellers.
Sensors: 1 Type 1022 long-range air search radar; 1 Type 922 low-level air and sea search radar; 1 Type 1006 sea search and navigational radar; 2 type 909 missile fire control radars; 1 Type 184 hull-mounted sonar; ADAWS 5 automated action information data processing.
Armament: 1 air group of, typically, 14 aircraft; 1 twin Mk 30 launcher for Sea Dart area air defence missiles;

being equipped with 2 Phalanx 20mm close-in weapons systems.
Top speed: 28 knots.
Range: 5000 nautical miles at 18 knots.
Programme: This three-ship class consists of HMS *Invincible* (R05), HMS *Illustrious* (R06) and HMS *Ark Royal* (R09). Ordered incrementally in April 1973, May 1976 and December 1978, the lead ship was constructed at Vickers' Barrow-in-Furness yards, while the second and third ships were built at Swan Hunter on the Tyne. *Invincible* was commissioned in March 1980, followed by *Illustrious* in June 1982 and *Ark Royal* in July 1985.
Notes: The history of these large, rather stark ships is one of extremely chequered fortunes right up until 1982 when the existence of the lead ship, *Invincible*, alone made the mounting of a British task force to the Falklands feasible. Prior to that point, these rather modestly sized VSTOL aircraft carriers had come in for a lot of criticism, particularly on grounds of cost (the first ship cost £175 million). Indeed, in March 1982, the UK Minister of Defence announced that *Invincible* was to be sold to the Royal Australian Navy in late 1983 as part of a general reduction in Royal Navy force levels. Within a space of less than two months *Invincible* was providing the initial vital air cover for the Falklands-bound force, as well as supplying an equally essential contribution by providing a major share of the Sea King anti-submarine helicopter force. Unlike the highly specialised functional solutions provided by the 'Sheffield' and 'Broadsword' class ships, the 'Invincibles' were always intended to fill a multiplicity of roles. These range from fleet air defence to providing anti-submarine helicopter support, as well as acting as task group command ships.

A helicopter pilot's eye view of HMS Illustrious *(R06) and* Ark Royal *(R09).*

Dedalo Type Aircraft Carrier

Role: VTOL aircraft platform.
Builder: New York Shipbuilders, USA.
User: Spanish Navy.
Basic data: 16,415 tons full displacement; 622.5ft (189.75m) overall length; 109.25ft (33.3m) maximum beam.
Crew: c1500.
Propulsion: Geared steam turbines (total 100,000shp); 4 propellers.
Sensors: 1 SPS-40A long-range air search radar; 1 SPS-6 air search radar; 1 SPS-8 height finder radar; 4 Mk 34 gun fire control systems; 1 URN-22 TACAN.
Armament: Around 20 aircraft, comprising a mix of 6 Matadors (Harriers), 3 or 4 Sikorsky SH-3 Sea Kings and around 10 light helicopters; 2 quadruple and 9 twin 40mm anti-aircraft guns.
Top speed: 30 knots.
Range: 7200 nautical miles at 15 knots.

Dedalo (PA01) with Hughes 300s forward and SH.3s aft.

Principe de Asturias seen during its 22 May 1982 launching.

Garibaldi (R551) under tow and showing its forward flight deck ski-jump to advantage.

Programme: The *Dedalo* (PA01) started life as a light cruiser (CL79), ordered 1940. During 1942, CL79 was one of several hulls converted into 'Independence' class light carriers, being redesignated as USS *Cabot* (CVL28), which entered service with the US Navy in July 1943. The ship was transferred to the Spanish Navy in August 1967.
Notes: Old enough to have been damaged by a *Kamikaze* attack off Luzon in late 1944, it became one of the first aircraft carriers, second only to the USS *Guam* (LPH9), to deploy the AV-8A Harrier (Matador in Spanish service) operationally.

Principe de Asturias Type Aircraft Carrier

Role: Tactical air and anti-submarine.
Builder: Bazan, Spain.
User: Royal Spanish Navy.
Basic data: 15,000 tons full displacement; 640.0ft (195.1m) overall length; 80.0ft (24.4m) maximum beam.
Crew: 774.
Propulsion: 2 General Electric LM2500 gas turbines (total derated to 40,000shp); 1 controllable-pitch propeller.
Sensors: 1 SPS-52C air search and height finder (3-D) radar; 1 SPS-55 surface search and navigational radar; 1 SPN-35A aircraft precision approach control radar; 1 URN-22 TACAN aircraft homing radar.
Armament: 3 Matadors (Harriers); 14 Sikorsky SH-3D Sea King helicopters; 2 lighter anti-submarine helicopters; 4 Meroka 20mm close-in anti-air weapons systems; mines.
Top speed: 26 knots.
Range: 7500 nautical miles at 20 knots.
Programme: The *Principe de Asturias* (R11) was ordered in June 1977, laid down in October 1979, launched in May 1982 and is scheduled to enter service during 1985. Construction of a second vessel is planned.
Notes: Designed by the US naval architects Gibbs and Cox for the now cancelled US Navy's Sea Control Ship requirement, this ship is one of the new breed of compact, through-deck VSTOL aircraft carriers initiated by the Royal Navy's 'Invincible' class. Lighter than the 'Invincibles', but heavier than Italy's 'Garibaldi' design, the Spanish carrier has two aircraft elevators, one on the starboard side immediately forward of the ship's bridge, while the other, when elevated, forms a centreline extension to the aft end of the flight deck. Steel is the basic material employed throughout both hull and superstructure, in an effort to minimise the effects of combat damage. The ship's four Meroka 20mm gun mounts are installed high on the superstructure, the forward pair being set side by side just forward and below the wheelhouse, while the aft guns are mounted in staggered tandem (one above the other) at the aft end of the 'island', as a carrier's superstructure is generally referred to by the crew.

Garibaldi Type Aircraft Carrier

Role: Anti-submarine and amphibious assault.
Builder: Italcantieri, Italy.
User: Italian Navy.
Basic data: 13,370 tons full displacement; 591.2ft (180.2m) overall length; 99.7ft (30.4m) maximum beam.
Crew: 560.
Propulsion: 4 Fiat-built General Electric LM2500 gas turbines (total derated to 80,000shp); COGAG; 2 controllable-pitch propellers.
Sensors: 1 Selenia RAN-3L long-range air search and height finder (3-D) radar; 1 Selenia RAN-106 medium-range air/sea search radar; 1 Selenia RAN-205 surface search and navigational radar; 2 Selenia/SMA RTN-30X Albatros system fire control radars; 3 Selenia/SMA RTN-

20X 40mm close-in weapons fire control radars; 1 Raytheon DE 1160 bow-mounted sonar; 1 TACAN aircraft homing radar; Selenia IPN-10 automated action information data processing system.
Armament: 18 Agosta-Sikorsky SH-3D Sea King helicopters; 4 single OTO-Melara Otomat Mk 2 anti-ship missile launchers; 2 octuple Albatros point air defence missile launchers; 3 twin 40mm Breda/Bofors close-in anti-air weapons; 2 triple Mk 32 lightweight anti-submarine torpedo tubes.
Top speed: 29.5 knots.
Range: Over 7000 nautical miles at 20 knots.
Programme: Ordered in November 1980, the *Giuseppe Garibaldi* (R551) was laid down in March 1981. Scheduled for launching during 1983, the ship should enter service in 1985.

Notes: The *Garibaldi* is the latest of the compact, through-deck VTOL aircraft carriers to be built and will serve as the flag ship of the Italian Navy once in service. Unlike the 'Invincibles' and Spain's *Principe de Asturias*, the *Garibaldi's* design, in mission terms, is much closer to the Soviet's 'Kiev' class than that of either of its British or Spanish contemporaries; an aspect underscored by *Garibaldi's* respectable anti-ship missile fit and two-tier shipboard anti-air capability. The ship also has space to accommodate up to 265 marine commandos. Although the Italian Navy has no current plans to operate Harrier-type aircraft off the ship, it has been recently decided to equip the carrier with a forward ski-jump in order to meet NATO forces' inter-operability requirements.

Battleships

Iowa Class Battleships

Role: Power projection.
Builder: Navy Dockyards, USA.
User: US Navy.
Basic data: 57,500 tons full displacement; 887.6ft (270.5m) overall length; 108.2ft (33m) maximum beam.
Crew: Around 1620.
Propulsion: 4 geared steam turbines (total 212,000shp); 4 propellers.
Sensors: 1 SPS-49 long-range air search radar; 1 SLQ-32 electronics warfare suite; NTDS automated action information processing system.
Armament: Facilities for up to 4 Sikorsky SH-60 Seahawk helicopters; 8 quadruple Tomahawk cruise missile launchers; 4 quadruple Harpoon anti-ship missile launchers; 3 triple 16 inch guns; 6 twin 5 in Mk 28 dual-purpose guns; 4 Phalanx 20mm close-in weapons systems, as currently being installed.
Top speed: 33 knots.
Range: 16,000 nautical miles at 15 knots.
Programme: Planned as a six-ship class, only four were completed: USS *Iowa* (BB61), USS *New Jersey* (BB62), USS *Missouri* (BB63) and USS *Wisconsin* (BB64); all four being commissioned between February 1943 and April 1944. All four ships are being refurbished, with USS *New Jersey* recommissioning in January 1983, *Iowa* (BB61) in April 1984, with the remaining two ships scheduled for 1987.
Notes: Being rebuilt as true multi-purpose ships, the 'Iowa' class will serve as something of a cross between the tactical aircraft carrier and the strategic missile-carrying submarine, while retaining their big guns for long range shore bombardment. These guns can deliver a 2 ton shell to a maximum range of around 20 nautical miles (37km) against surface targets. The current modernisation programme is only a partial portion of that initially envisaged by the US Navy. As foreseen in the mid-1970s, each ship would have had its aft-mounted 16 inch gun turret removed and aft-section modified to house and operate more anti-submarine helicopters. While there has been some US Congressional resistance to such a move, the prospect of seeing this type of subsequent major refit cannot be discounted.

This frontal aspect emphasises New Jersey's *aggressive lines.*

Cruisers

Kirov Class Cruisers

This high aerial of Kirov *reveals the two sets of missile silo banks forward of the bridge, those on the slightly raised plinth closest to the bridge being for the anti-ship SS-N-19s.*

Role: General-purpose.
Builder: Baltic Yard, Leningrad, USSR.
User: Soviet Navy.
Basic data: 23,400 tons full displacement; 810ft (245m) overall length; 91.9ft (28m) maximum beam.
Crew: Around 800.
Propulsion: 2 sets of nuclear reactors plus oil-fired superheat booster boilers, each powering a geared steam turbine and propeller shaft (estimated total 150,000shp); 2 propellers.
Sensors: 1 long-range air search radar; 1 height finder (3-D) radar; 1 each fire control radar for SS-N-19, SS-N-6 and SS-N-14 missiles; 2 fire control radars for SA-N-4 missiles; 1 fire control radar for 100mm guns; 2 fire control radars for 30mm guns; 1 hull-mounted sonar; 1 towed variable depth sonar; automated action information data processing system and long-range (satellite) data links.
Armament: 3 Kamov Ka-26 'Hormone' or Ka-27 'Helix' helicopters; 20 SS-N-19 anti-ship cruise missiles in individual launch silos; 12 SA-N-6 area air defence missiles in individual vertical-launch silos; 1 twin SS-N-14 anti-submarine missile launcher; 2 fore and 2 aft quadruple vertical launchers for SA-N-8 short-range air defence missiles on *Frunze*; 2 twin SA-N-4 point air defence missile launchers; 2 single 100mm dual-purpose guns on *Kirov*, replaced by 1 twin 130mm dual-purpose gun on *Frunze*; 8 single 30mm Gatling-type anti-aircraft guns; 2 twelve-barrel 250mm anti-submarine rocket launchers.
Top speed: Over 33 knots.
Range: Unlimited.
Programme: *Kirov*, the lead ship of this as yet indeterminate-sized class was reported to have been laid down in 1973, launched in 1977 and entered trials in September 1980. A second ship of this class, *Frunze*, laid down in January 1978, was launched in June 1981 and entered service during 1984. US naval intelligence report that a third ship was started in 1983 and anticipate the completion of a fourth of this class prior to the end of the 1980s.
Notes: Certainly the largest and most powerful ship built to meet the conventional heavy cruiser role anywhere in the world since the end of World War II, the *Kirov's* finely proportioned lines and weight indicate an extremely efficient hull design, married to a form of construction capable of withstanding far more combat damage than any of its Western World contemporaries. Turning to the operational requirement aspect, *Kirov's* primary role appears precisely to parallel that of the US Navy's 'California/Virginia' classes of cruiser, namely that of

acting as the main defensive screen for a carrier-centred task force, particularly in the light of the noticeable shift towards a primary anti-air defence weapon/sensor fit adopted for *Frunze*. However, as with their US rivals, these ships carry the necessary mass of communications equipment to enable them to act as command ships for a non-carrier group. *Kirov's* sensor/weapons fit is extremely impressive, being both heavy and well balanced to meet the demands of the modern naval need to fight a potentially fully three-dimensional threat. The anti-ship SS-N-19 has an effective range out to around 300 nautical miles (556km), whilst the SA-N-6 area air defence missiles are reported to be effective out to a range of 40 nautical miles (74km) and up to an altitude of 100,000 feet (30,480m).

Long Beach Type Cruiser

Role: Area air defence.
Builder: Bethlehem Steel, USA.
User: US Navy.
Basic data: 17,350 tons full displacement; 721.25ft (219.8m) overall length; 73.25ft (22.3m) maximum beam.
Crew: 983.
Propulsion: 2 Westinghouse pressurised water nuclear reactors; 2 General Electric geared steam turbines (total 80,000shp); 2 propellers.
Sensors: 1 SPS-48 long-range air search and height finder (3-D) radar; 1 SPS-49 long-range air search radar; 1 SPS-10 sea search and navigational radar; 2 Mk 76 missile fire control radars; 4 SPG-55A gun fire control radars; 1 URN-25 TACAN aircraft homer; 1 SQS-23 bow-mounted sonar; NTDS automated action information data processing system. *Note:* sensor fit is post-1980 refit standard.
Armament: 2 twin Mk 10 launchers for 120 Standard MR and ER area air defence missiles; 2 quadruple Harpoon anti-ship missile launchers; 1 octuple ASROC anti-submarine missile launchers; 2 single 5in Mk 30 dual-purpose guns; 2 Mk 15 Phalanx 20mm close-in weapons systems; 2 triple lightweight anti-submarine torpedo tubes. *Note:* fit is post-1980 refit standard.
Top speed: 31 knots.
Range: Unlimited.
Programme: Ordered in October 1956, the USS *Long Beach* (CGN9) was laid down in early December 1957, launched

USS Long Beach *(CGN9) prior to its 1980 refit that adds a prominent lattice mast in place of the aft pole-type shown.*

in mid-July 1959 and commissioned in early September 1961. *Long Beach's* latest major refit was in 1980/81.
Notes: Not only the US Navy's first nuclear-powered cruiser, but also the first post-World War II US cruiser to be laid down, this ship can still pack a formidable air-aircraft punch and, thanks to the advent of such missiles as the Harpoon, now carries a far greater ranging anti-ship strike capability than when she was first commissioned.

Sverdlov Class Cruisers

One of the nine remaining standard 'Sverdlov' class cruisers, seen steaming through the English Channel in March 1974.

Role: General-purpose.
Builders: Various, USSR.
User: Soviet Navy.
Basic data: 17,200 tons full displacement; 689ft (210m) overall length; 70.85ft (21.6ft) maximum beam.
Crew: 1010.
Propulsion: 2 geared steam turbines (total 100,000shp); 2 propellers.
Sensors: 3 separate long-range air search radars; 1 sea search and navigational radar; 16 fire control radars consisting of 4 differing types.
Armament: 4 triple 152mm guns; 6 twin 100mm dual-purpose guns; 16 twin 37mm anti-aircraft (5 of this class also carry 8 twin 30mm anti-aircraft guns in addition to 37mm guns); mines. *Note:* 2 Modified 'Sverdlovs' carry 1 twin SA-N-4 point air defence missile launcher in place of either one or both of the aft 152mm turrets. Another Modified 'Sverdlov' carries 1 twin SA-N-2 area air defence missile launcher in place of third, or 'X' turret.
Top speed: 32 knots.
Range: 8400 nautical miles at 15 knots.
Programme: An original 14-ship class built in three separate shipyards during the early 1950s. Nine standard and three Modified 'Sverdlovs' to remain in use at the end of 1984 and the ships appear destined to remain in service for some years yet.
Notes: Rather handsome, twin-funnelled cruisers of conventional World War II-period appearance, two of the 'Sverdlovs' were converted to command cruisers, and one into a guided missile cruiser, but all retain at least six big guns for use in shore bombardment, while nine retain all 12 big guns.

Moskva Class Cruisers

Role: Anti-submarine.
Builder: Nikolayev, USSR.
User: Soviet Navy.
Basic data: 17,000 tons full displacement; 623ft (190m) overall length; 111.5ft (34m) maximum beam.
Crew: 850.

Moskva, *viewed from abeam, displaying her somewhat stark, angular appearance.*

Propulsion: 2 geared steam turbines (total 100,000shp); 2 propellers.
Sensors: 1 long-range air search radar; 1 height finder (3-D) radar; 3 sea search and navigational radars; 2 fire control radars (missile); 2 fire control radars (57mm guns); 1 hull-mounted sonar; 1 towed, variable depth sonar; IFF and aircraft homing aids; automated action information data-processing system.
Armament: 18 Kamov Ka-25 helicopters; 2 twin SA-N-3 area air defence missile launchers; 1 twin SUW-N-1 short-range anti-submarine missile launcher; 2 twin 57mm anti-aircraft guns; 2 RBU 6000 twelve-barrel 250mm anti-submarine rocket launchers.
Top speed: 30 knots.
Range: 7000 nautical miles at 15 knots.
Programme: This two-ship class, the initial unit of which was laid down in 1962, comprises *Moskva* and *Leningrad*, which entered service with the Soviet fleet in 1967 and 1968, respectively.
Notes: Although not the first post-World War II hybrid ship (half cruiser, half helicopter carrier) to emerge (that honour must go to the French Navy's *Jeanne d'Arc*), the 'Moskva' class display a typically aggressive Russian design approach to meeting a stated operational requirement. Both in terms of onboard weaponry and deployed airborne anti-submarine capability, these ships compare very favourably with the Italian's later *Vittorio Veneto* helicopter cruiser.

Jeanne d'Arc Type Cruiser

The French Navy's Jeanne d'Arc *(R97) entering port in 1975.*

Slava, *the lead ship of this new Soviet cruiser class, whose primary armament is the around 300-nautical-mile (556km) ranging SS-N-12 anti-ship cruise missile.*

Role: Multi-purpose.
Builder: DCAN Brest, France.
User: French Navy.
Basic data: 12,365 tons full displacement; 597.1ft (182.0m) overall length; 78.7ft (24.0m) maximum beam.
Crew: 627.
Propulsion: 2 Rateau-Bretagne geared steam turbine (total 40,000bhp); 2 propellers.
Sensors: 1 DRBI 10 air search and height finder (3-D) radar; 1DRBV 22D air search radar; 1 DRBV 50 combined low-level air and sea search radar; 1 DRBN 32 sea search and navigational radar; 3 DRBC 32A gunfire control radars; 1 TACAN aircraft homer; 1 SQS 503-2 hull-mounted sonar system; SENIT II automated action information data-processing system.
Armament: Up to 8 Aerospatiale Puma helicopters; 6 MM38 Exocet anti-ship missile launchers; 4 single 100mm Model 1953 dual-purpose guns.
Top speed: 28 knots.
Range: 6800 nautical miles at 16 knots.
Programme: Authorised in 1957, *Jeanne d'Arc* (R97) was laid down in July 1960, launched in September 1961 and entered service at the end of June 1964. The ship underwent its latest refit in 1982/83 and is scheduled to remain in service until the year 2004.
Notes: *Jeanne d'Arc* was the first of the post-World War II generation of hybrid cruiser/helicopter carriers that currently culminate in the Soviet Navy's 'Moskva' class ships. *Jeanne d'Arc* is primarily employed in peacetime as a training ship, but in operational terms can be readily used as an anti-submarine helicopter platform, a helicopter-equipped amphibious assault ship, or a fairly major troop and equipment transport asset. Her complement of Exocet missiles give the vessel a useful long-range anti-ship capability, while her dual-purpose guns could prove effective in countering air attack, particularly by manned aircraft, along with providing onshore bombardment support during the establishment of a beachhead.

Colbert Type Cruiser

Role: Anti-aircraft.
Builder: DCAN Brest, France.
User: French Navy.
Basic data: 11,300 tons full displacement; 590.5ft (190m) overall length; 66.25ft (20.2m) maximum beam.
Crew: 562.
Propulsion: CEM Parsons geared steam turbines (total 86,000shp); 2 propellers.
Sensors: 1 DRBV 51 and 1 DRBV 23C air search radars; 1 DRB1 10D height finder (3-D) radar; DRBV 50 surface search and navigational radar; 2 DRBR 51 Masurca fire control radars; 2 DRBC 31 fire control radar (57mm guns); 1 DRBC 32C 100mm gun fire control radar; 1

Colbert (C611) seen at speed. Note the twin Masurca area air defence missile launcher mounted at the forward end of the ship's quarter deck, most of which serves as a helipad.

TACAN aircraft homer; SENIT automated action information data processor.
Armament: 4 Exocet anti-ship missile launchers; 1 twin Masurca area air defence missile launcher (48 missiles); 2 single 100mm dual-purpose guns; 6 twin 57mm anti-aircraft guns.
Top speed: 32 knots.
Range: 4000 nautical miles at 25 knots.
Programme: Originally ordered in 1953, the sole *Colbert* (C611) was laid down in December 1953, launched in March 1956 and joined the fleet in May 1959. Underwent a major modernisation between 1970 and 1972.
Notes: *Colbert* was always envisaged as primarily filling the anti-aircraft role, but initially mounted no less than 16 127mm dual-purpose guns that have now been replaced by the 30 nautical mile ranged, near Mach 3 Masurca missiles and the two mounted forward 100mm guns. During the ship's most recent refit, racking to carry four Exocet container/launchers have been added, two each flanking the structure just forward of the bridge, very much in the same position as that adopted on the Royal Navy's 'Broadsword' class frigates. The ship can accept helicopter operations, but carries no hangars.

Slava Class Cruisers

Role: Anti-ship.
Builder: Nikolayev (lead yard), USSR.
User: Soviet Navy.
Basic data: 11,250 tons full displacement; 603.7ft (184.0m) overall length; 63.2ft (19.25m) maximum beam.
Crew: Around 650.
Propulsion: 4 gas turbines (total 120,000shp); 2 propellers.
Sensors: 1 each of 2 separate types of long-range air search and height finder (3-D) radars; 1 IFF radar; 3 sea search and navigational radars; 4 separate types of fire control radar and optronic fire control radar/director systems for the ship's missiles and guns; 2 TACAN type aircraft homers; bow-mounted and variable depth sonar systems; automated action information data-processing and satellite-fed data link systems.
Armament: 1 Kamov Ka-27 'Helix' helicopter; 8 twin SS-N-12 anti-ship cruise missile launchers; 1 octuple SA-N-6 vertically launched area air defence missile silo; 2 twin SA-N-4 point air defence missile launchers; 1 twin 130mm dual-purpose gun; 6 multi-barrelled 30mm Gatling-type close-in weapons systems; 2 twelve-barrelled 250mm RBU-6000 anti-submarine rocket launchers; 10 heavyweight anti-submarine torpedo tubes.
Top speed: 31 knots.
Range: 10,000 nautical miles at 15 knots.
Programme: *Slava*, the lead of class ship was reported to have been laid down in 1976, launched in 1979 and entered service in late 1982, with the Soviet's Black Sea Fleet. Two more of this class were said to have been laid down in 1978 and in 1979, reportedly to enter service in 1983 and 1984, respectively. Just how many of these

cruisers will be built remains a matter of some conjecture, but could total up to eight ships.

Notes: The 'Slava' class is seen as something of an enigma in Western naval intelligence circles, who view the design as being a curious mixture of something old, something new and certainly much borrowed from the preceeding 'Kara' class cruisers. Previously referred to as the BLK-COM-1, or Black Sea Combatant-1 class, these ships were clearly designed as dedicated anti-ship counters to surface elements of the US Navy's Mediterranean-based 6th Fleet; a conclusion borne out by the not inconsiderable, but essentially defensive anti-submarine sensor/weapons fit installed. The hull design of the 'Slava' class appears to be a simply scaled-up duplicate of that of the 'Kara' class vessel, with the 'Slava' class probably employing a common-to-'Kara' propulsion machinery package. Unlike the 'Kara' class, however, the 'Slava' design has a taller, much more conventional looking superstructure that appears far less bedecked with radar aerials.

Virginia Class Cruisers

Role: General-purpose.
Builder: Newport News, USA.
User: US Navy.
Basic data: 11,000 tons full displacement; 585ft (178.3m) overall length; 63ft (19.2m) maximum beam.
Crew: 519.
Propulsion: 2 pressurised water D2G nuclear reactors/steam turbines (total 60,000shp); 2 propellers.
Sensors: 1 SPS-40B long-range air search radar; 1 SPS-48C height finder (3-D) radar; 1 SPS-55 sea search and navigational radar; 2 SPG-51D and 1 SPG-60 fire control radars (missiles); 1 SPQ-9A fire control radar (guns and ASROC); 1 SQS-53 bow-mounted sonar; NTDS automated action information data processing system.
Armament: 1 Kaman SH-2 Seasprite helicopter; 2 twin Mk 26 launchers for Standard area air defence missiles (the forward Mk 26 launcher also handles ASROC anti-submarine missiles); 2 single 5in Mk 45 dual-purpose guns; 2 triple lightweight anti-submarine torpedo tubes. (Tomahawk cruise missiles and Harpoon anti-ship missiles are scheduled to be fitted to these cruisers during the early 1980s, as will be 2 Phalanx 20mm close-in weapons systems.)
Top speed: 30 knots.
Range: Unlimited.
Programme: Like the preceding 'California' class cruisers, the four-ship 'Virginia' class programme started life with much larger envisaged numbers than were actually achieved; the real constraint proving to be the eco-politically induced reduced fleet strength plans that emerged during the latter half of the 1970s. All four ships, USS *Virginia* (CGN38), USS *Texas* (CGN39), USS *Mississippi* (CGN40) and USS *Arkansas* (CGN41), were laid down between August 1972 and January 1977 and their

USS Arkansas *(CGN41), in late 1980.*

respective commissioning dates were: September 1976, September 1977, August 1978 and October 1980.

Notes: Designed to act as large, high capability escorts for nuclear-powered carriers, the 'Virginia' class ships are larger improved versions of the 'California' class nuclear-powered cruisers. Although not immediately apparent, one of the 'Virginia' class's major advances is the incorporation of a helicopter hangar under the stern flight pad, similar to that employed in the earlier Italian cruiser, *Vittorio Veneto*. While acting as a carrier escort, the 'Virginia' class's primary role is to provide area air defence, and to this end the ships are equipped with Standard missiles which have a 30 nautical mile, or 56km range (improvements to the Standard should extend its effective range out to 65 nautical miles, or 121km). Having said this, it is interesting to compare the anti-air weaponry of these US ships with that to be found aboard the Soviet's smaller 'Kara' and 'Kresta' classes of cruiser.

California Class Cruisers

Role: General-purpose.
Builder: Newport News, USA.
User: US Navy.
Basic data: 10,150 tons full displacement; 596ft (181.7m) overall length; 61ft (18.6m) maximum beam.
Crew: 533.
Propulsion: 2 General Electric D2G pressurised water nuclear reactors/geared steam turbines (total 60,000shp); 2 propellers.
Sensors: 1 SPS-40B long-range air search radar; 1 SPS-48C height finder (3-D) radar; 1 SPS-55 sea search and navigational radar; 1 SPG-51D and 1 SPG-60 missile fire control radars; 1 SPQ-9A surface target fire control radar; 1 SQS-26CX bow-mounted sonar; NTDS automated action information data processing system.
Armament: 2 single Mk 13 launchers for Tartar/Standard MR area air defence missiles; 1 octuple ASROC anti-

USS South Carolina *(CGN37) nuclear-powered cruiser.*

submarine missile launcher; 2 single 5in Mk 45 dual-purpose guns; 2 Phalanx 20mm close-in weapons systems; 4 lightweight anti-submarine torpedo tubes; Tomahawk cruise missiles and Harpoon anti-ship missiles are scheduled to be fitted to this class.

Top speed: 31 knots.

Range: Unlimited.

Programme: Authorised under US fiscal year 1967 and 1968 budgets, this two-ship class comprises USS *California* (CGN36) and USS *South Carolina* (CGN37). Both laid down during 1970, the ships entered service 11 months apart, in February 1974 and January 1975, respectively.

Notes: These ships, designed essentially as aircraft carrier escorts, were the first US nuclear-powered cruisers to be series built. They have helicopter pad but no hangar.

Tre Kronor Class Cruisers

The rakishly-lined Chilean cruiser Almirante Latorre *(C04).*

Role: Anti-aircraft.

Builder: Eriksberg, Sweden.

User: Chilean Navy.

Basic data: 10,000 tons full displacement; 597.1ft (182m) overall length; 54.1ft (16.5m) maximum beam.

Crew: 455.

Propulsion: 2 De Laval geared steam turbines (total 100,000shp); 2 propellers.

Sensors: 1 Hollandse LWO-3 long-range air search radar; 1 Type 277 height finder radar; 1 Type 293 gun fire control radar; 1 Type 903. Seacat fire control radar; 4 SQR-102 fire control radars for 40mm guns.

Armament: 1 triple and 2 twin 152mm dual-purpose guns; 4 single 57mm and 11 single 40mm anti-aircraft guns; 2 quadruple Seacat point air defence missile launchers; 2 triple heavyweight anti-submarine torpedo tubes; 2 depth charge racks; up to 120 mines.

Top speed: 33 knots.

Endurance: Over 8000 nautical miles.

Programme: The *Almirante Latorre* (C04) started life as the Royal Swedish Navy's *Gota Lejon*. Launched in November 1945 and initially commissioned in December 1947, the ship was bought by Chile in July 1971. The *Almirante Latorre* is known to have undergone a major refit in the post-1972 period.

Notes: A handsome looking ship, which, like France's *Colbert* and most of the later World War II US cruisers, was designed specifically to act as an anti-aircraft screen for accompanying ships. Although elderly and relatively ineffectual against both stand-off launched air-to-surface and sea skimming missiles, the *Almirante Latorre* can still pack a healthy punch against manned air attacks.

Kara Class Cruisers

Role: Anti-submarine.

Builder: Nikolayev, USSR.

User: Soviet Navy.

Basic data: 9700 tons full displacement; 574ft (175.0m) overall length; 60ft (18.3m) maximum beam.

Crew: 520.

Propulsion: 4 gas turbines (total 120,000shp); 2 propellers.

Sensors: 1 long-range air search radar; 1 height finder (3-D) radar; 2 surface search and navigational radars; 2 surface-to-air missile fire control radars; 2 each fire control radars for 76mm and 30mm gun systems; 1 hull-mounted sonar; 1 towed variable depth sonar.

Armament: 1 Kamov Ka-26 'Hormone' helicopter; 2 quadruple SS-N-14 anti-submarine missile launchers; 2 twin SA-N-3 surface-to-air missile launchers; 2 twin 76mm dual-purpose guns; 4 single 30mm Gatling anti-aircraft guns; 2 twelve-barrel 250mm RBU-6000 anti-submarine rocket launchers; 2 five-tube heavyweight anti-submarine launchers.

Top speed: 32 knots.

Range: 8000 nautical miles at 15 knots.

Programme: The first of this seven-ship class was laid down during 1969 and joined the Soviet fleet in 1973. Delivery of this ship, *Nikolayev*, was followed by *Ochakov* (1974), *Kerch* (1975), *Azov* (1976), *Petropavlovsk* (1977), *Taskent* (1978) and *Tallin* (1979). The fourth ship, *Azov*, has undergone extensive modification to its aft sections, reportedly to act as trials ship for a new, vertically-stowed surface-to-air missile system being developed for the new classes of Soviet cruisers and heavy destroyers now under construction.

A 'Kara' class cruiser of the Soviet Navy's Black Sea Fleet.

Vittorio Veneto (C550), showing her heavy forward and beam armaments and expansive helipad aft.

Notes: The 'Kara' class represents a larger and heavier follow-on to the Soviet first-generation 'Kresta II' anti-submarine cruisers and carries the same primary armament of 8 SS-N-14 'Silex' 25 nautical mile (46km) ranged missiles. Where the 'Karas' differ from their forebears is in the adoption of gas turbine propulsion (the first application to a Soviet cruiser) and the incorporation of a SA-N-4 short-range (out to around 8 nautical miles/15km) surface-to-air missile system to back up the ships' primary defensive armament of out to 30 nautical mile (55.5km) SA-N-3 missiles. Any aircraft or missile penetrating these two outer defensive zones would still have to contend with the ships' not inconsiderable gun armament combination of out to around 5 nautical mile (8.25km) ranging 76mm fire and the very high rate 30mm Gatling gun close-in weapons systems, reported to be highly effective out to around 2 nautical miles (3.7km). Although marginally lighter and smaller than the contemporary US Navy 'California' class nuclear-powered cruisers, the 'Kara' class's heavy armament provides an interesting comparison between the two generally similar sized ships, particularly in terms of the broader spectrum of weapons system fitted to the Soviet cruisers.

Vittorio Veneto Type Cruiser

Role: Anti-submarine.
Builder: CNR Castellammare, Italy.
User: Italian Navy.
Basic data: 9500 tons full displacement; 589.2ft (179.6m) overall length; 63.6ft (19.4m) maximum beam.
Crew: 547.
Propulsion: 2 Tosi geared steam turbines (total 73,000shp); 2 propellers.
Sensors: 1 SPS-40 long-range air search radar; 1 SPS-52 height finder (3-D) radar; 1 SPQ-2B sea search and navigational radar; 1 SRM-7 navigational radar; 2 SPG-55B fire control radars (missile); 4 Selenia RTN-10X fire

control radars (guns); 1 URN-20A TACAN aircraft homer; 1 SQS-23 hull-mounted sonar.
Armament: Up to 9 Bell 204/212 sized, or 4 SH-3 Sea King sized helicopters; 1 twin Mk 20 Aster missile launcher for both Standard area air defence missiles or ASROC anti-submarine missiles; 8 single OTO-Melara 76mm anti-aircraft guns; 3 single 40mm Breda-Bofors 40/70 DARDO-directed close-in weapon systems; 2 triple lightweight anti-submarine torpedo tubes.
Top speed: 30.5 knots.
Range: 6000 nautical miles at 20 knots.
Programme: The sole type, *Vittorio Veneto* (C550), was laid down in June 1965, launched in February 1967 and entered into service in July 1969. It completed a major refit in 1982.
Notes: Flagship of the Italian Navy, the handsome lines of this powerfully-armed cruiser are further enhanced by the expansive aft helicopter deck, with its below-deck hangar (which cannot accept the larger-sized helicopters). Note the heavy secondary anti-aircraft gun armament flanking the ship.

Ticonderoga Class Cruisers

Role: Area air defence.
Builders: Ingalls Shipbuilding and Bath Iron Works, USA.
User: US Navy.
Basic data: 9400 tons full displacement; 567.0ft (172.8m) overall length, 55ft (16.8m) maximum beam.
Crew: 360.
Propulsion: 4 General Electric LM2500 gas turbines (total 80,000shp); COGAG; 2 controllable-pitch propellers.
Sensors: 1 SPS-49 long-range air search radar; 1 SPS-55 surface search radar; 1 SPY-1A multi-function radar; 1 SQS-53A bow-mounted sonar; Mk 1 command and decision action data processing system.
Armament: 2 Sikorsky SH-60B Seahawk helicopters; 2 twin Mk 26 (early ships) or 2 octuple Ex Mk 41 vertical

USS Ticonderoga *(CG47) showing to advantage the blend of 'Spruance' class hull lines and 'Kidd' class forward gun and missile launcher armament.*

An informative view of USS Vincennes *(CG49) during fitting out.*

missile launchers compatible with Standard MR and ER area air defence missiles, Harpoon anti-ship missiles or ASROC anti-submarine missiles (CG52 onwards); 2 single 5in Mk 45 dual-purpose guns; 2 Mk 15 Phalanx 20mm close-in weapons systems; 2 triple lightweight anti-submarine torpedo tubes.

Top speed: 32 knots.

Range: 6000 nautical miles at 20 knots.

Programme: Studied in conceptual form since the late 1960s under the US Navy's Aegis sea-going air defence requirement, early studies centred on a derivative of the 'Virginia' class nuclear-powered cruiser, but this was ultimately dropped in favour of the CG47, or 'Ticonderoga' class ship, itself a development of the existing 'Spruance' and 'Kidd' class destroyers. The first of this possibly 18-ship class, USS *Ticonderoga* (CG47) was initially contracted in September 1978, laid down in January 1980, launched in May 1981 and commissioned in January 1983. The second of class, USS *Yorktown* (CG48), was ordered in April 1980 and should commission in mid-1984. By end 1984, a total of 16 of this class had been authorised, with USS *Vincennes* (CG49), *Valley Forge* (CG50), *Bunker Hill* (CG52), 53, 54, 55 and 56 to be built by Ingalls, while Bath Iron Works,

The nuclear-powered cruiser USS Truxton *(CGN35).*

selected as the second source contractor, will be responsible for CG51, 58, 59 and 60. All first 16 ships should have been delivered by October 1989.

Notes: The 'Ticonderoga' class cruisers employ the same basic hull and propulsive machinery package as that of the 'Spruance' class destroyers, along with the same basic armament as that of the earlier 'Kidd' class ships, married to a very advanced sensor, command and control system. Heavier than either of its forebears, the CG47 design represents about the ultimate in development stretch of the basically modular structured 'Spruance/Kidd' solutions. A fast and, for its size, agile ship, the *Ticonderoga* and its sisters embody a lot of the latest composite material armour that should help ensure that the ships can accept more combat damage and still continue to function than many earlier generation US Navy surface combatants. The shipboard Aegis system, which embraces the range of shipborne anti-air sensors, air defence missiles and highly automated data processing systems, enables each 'Ticonderoga' class ship to detect, track and destroy an unprecedent number of enemy targets simultaneously. The latest quoted price for the three-ship package covering CG54, 55 and 56, cited by Ingalls in June 1983, was $926.129 million, or $308.7 million per fully-equipped ship.

Truxton Type Cruiser

Role: General-purpose.

Builder: NY Shipbuilding, USA.

User: US Navy.

Basic data: 9200 tons full displacement; 564ft (171.91m) overall length; 58ft (17.67m) maximum beam.

Crew: 538.

Propulsion: 2 General Electric D2G nuclear reactors/2 geared steam turbines (total 60,000shp); 2 propellers.

Sensors: 1 SPS-40 long-range air search radar; 1 SPS-48 height finder (3-D) radar; 1 SPS-10 sea search and navigational radar; 1 SPG-53 and 1 SPG-55 fire control radars; 1 SQS-26 bow-mounted sonar; NTDS automated action information data-processing system.

Armament: 1 Kaman SH-2 Seasprite helicopter; 1 twin MK 10 launcher for Terrier/Standard SM-1-ER area air defence missiles, or ASROC anti-submarine missiles; 2 quadruple Harpoon anti-ship missile launchers; 1 single 5in Mk 42 gun; 4 single, fixed lightweight anti-submarine torpedo tubes.

Top speed: 32 knots.

Range: Unlimited.

Programme: Originally planned as the tenth of the oil-burning 'Belknap' class cruisers, the US Congress directed that the ship be converted to nuclear propulsion. USS *Truxton* (CGN35) commissioned in May 1967.

Notes: This modified 'Belknap' design adopts a juxtaposed

USS Bainbridge *(CGN25) with the US Pacific Fleet, 1978.*

USS Belknap *(CG26) with multi-type missile launchers forward.*

primary armament layout relative to its oil-burning sister ships. As built, USS *Truxton* had one twin 3in anti-aircraft gun, but this has been replaced by Harpoon. Two Phalanx 20mm close-in weapons systems are to be fitted.

Bainbridge Type Cruiser

Role: General-purpose.
Builder; Bethlehem Steel, USA.
User: US Navy.
Basic data: 8580 tons full displacement; 565ft (172.5m) overall length; 58ft (17.7m) maximum beam.
Crew: 499.
Propulsion: 2 pressurised water D2G nuclear reactors/steam turbines (total 60,000shp); 2 propellers.
Sensors: 1 SPS-37 long-range air search radar; 1 SPS-39 height finder (3-D) radar; 1 SPS-10D sea search and navigational radar; 4 SPG-55B fire control radars (missiles); 1 Mk 111 fire control system (anti-submarine); 1 SQS-23 bow-mounted sonar.
Armament: 1 quadruple Harpoon anti-ship missile launcher; 2 twin Mk 10 Terrier/Standard ER area air defence missile launchers; 1 octuple cell Mk 16 ASROC anti-submarine missile launcher; 2 single 20mm Mk 67 anti-aircraft guns being replaced by 2 Phalanx 20mm close-in weapons systems; 2 triple lightweight anti-submarine torpedo tubes.
Top speed: 32 knots.
Range: Unlimited.
Programme: Approved under US fiscal year 1956 authority, the USS *Bainbridge* (CGN25) was laid down in May 1959, launched in April 1961, and joined the US fleet in October 1962.
Notes: The sole of type, USS *Bainbridge* (CGN25) was the second US Navy nuclear-powered cruiser to be built, her hull and weapons layout closely resembling those of the near contemporary 'Leahy' class conventionally-powered guided missile-carrying cruisers.

Belknap Class Cruisers

Role: General-purpose.
Builders: Various, USA.
User: US Navy.
Basic data: 7930 tons full displacement; 547ft (166.7m) overall length; 54.75ft (16.7m) maximum beam.
Crew: 450.
Propulsion: 2 geared steam turbines (total 85,000shp); 2 propellers.
Sensors: 1 SPS-49 long-range air search radar; 1 SPS-48 height finder (3-D) radar; 1 SPS-10F surface search radar; 1 LN66 navigational radar; 1 SPG-53 (gun) and 1 SPG-55 (missile) fire control radar systems; 1 SQS-26BX hull-mounted (bow) sonar; NDTS automated action

information data processing system.
Armament: 1 Kaman SH-2 Seasprite helicopter; 2 quadruple Harpoon anti-ship missile launchers; 1 twin Mk 10 launcher for either Standard ER area air defence missiles or ASROC anti-submarine missiles; 1 single 5in Mk 42 dual-purpose gun; 1 Phalanx 20mm air defence close-in weapons system; 6 torpedo tubes now removed.
Top speed: 33 knots.
Range: 7100 nautical miles at 20 knots.
Programme: This nine-ship class comprises: USS *Belknap* (CG26), USS *Josephus Daniels* (CG27), USS *Wainwright* (CG28), USS *Jouett* (CG29), USS *Horne* (CG30), USS *Sterett* (CG31), USS *William P Standley* (CG32), USS *Fox* (CG33) and USS *Biddle* (CG34). All vessels were laid down between February 1962 and December 1963, entering into service between November 1964 and January 1967.
Notes: Designed as primary carrier escorts, the 'Belknaps' are a more potently armed development of the slightly smaller 'Leahy' class.

Leahy Class Cruisers

Role: General-purpose.
Builders: Various, USA.
User: US Navy.
Basic data: 7880 tons full displacement; 533ft (162.5m) overall length; 55ft (16.8m) maximum beam.
Crew: 405.
Propulsion: 2 geared steam turbines (total 85,000shp); 2 propellers.
Sensors: 1 SPS-49 long-range air search radar; 1 SPS-48 height finder (3-D) radar; 1 SPS-10 surface search and navigational radar; 1 SPG-55B missile fire control radar; 1 SQS-23 bow-mounted sonar; NTDS automated action information data processing system.
Armament: 2 twin Mk 10 launchers for Terrier/Standard ER area air defence missiles; Harpoon anti-ship being fitted in place of original 2 twin 3in guns amidships; 1

USS Reeves *(CG24) seen in the Indian Ocean, 1975.*

octuple ASROC anti-submarine missile launcher; 2 triple lightweight anti-submarine torpedo tubes. Helicopter pad only.
Top speed: 32 knots.
Range: 8000 nautical miles at 14 knots.
Programme: This nine-ship class comprises: USS *Leahy* (CG16), USS *Harry E Yarnell* (CG17), USS *Worden* (CG18), USS *Dale* (CG19), USS *Richmond K Turner* (CG20), USS *Gridley* (CG21), USS *England* (CG22), USS *Halsey* (CG23) and USS *Reeves* (CG24). All were commissioned between August 1962 and June 1964. Last major refit commenced during 1976.
Notes: The smallest of the US cruiser classes, the 'Leahys', as with other US warships, are being equipped with two Phalanx 20mm close-in weapons systems to help fend off air attack.

Kresta II Class Cruisers

'Kresta' II with Ka-25 helicopter aft, April 1975.

Role: Anti-submarine.
Builder: Zhdanov, USSR.
User: Soviet Navy.
Basic data: 7600 tons full displacement; 524ft (160m) overall length; 55.75ft (17m) maximum beam.
Crew: 380.
Propulsion: Steam turbines (total 100,000shp); 2 propellers.
Sensors: 1 long-range air search radar; 1 height finder radar; 2 sea search and navigational radars; 4 fire control radars (2 each for missile and gun systems); 1 hull-mounted sonar.
Armament: 1 Kamov Ka-25 helicopter; 2 quadruple SS-N-14 anti-submarine missile launchers; 2 twin SA-N-3 surface-to-air missile launchers; 2 twin 57mm and 4 Gatling 30mm anti-aircraft guns; 2 multi-barrel anti-submarine rocket launchers; 10 torpedo tubes.
Top speed: 35 knots.
Range: 7000 nautical miles at 14 knots.
Programme: All 10 ships of this class were delivered between 1970 and 1978, comprising; *Kronshtadt* (1970), *Admiral Isakov* (1971), *Admiral Nakimov* (1972), *Admiral Marakov* (1973), *Marshal Voroshilov* (1973), *Admiral Oktyabr'skiy* (1974), *Admiral Isachenkov* (1975), *Marshal Timosenko* (1976), *Vasiliy Chapaev* (1977), and *Admiral Yumashev* (1978).
Notes: Marginally longer and heavier than the 'Kresta' Is, these ships are the first of the recent Soviet cruisers to be primarily armed for anti-submarine duties. Note the heavy SA-N-3 area air defence capability effective out to 30 nautical miles.

Kresta I Class Cruisers

Role: Anti-ship.
Builder: Zhdanov, USSR.
User: Soviet Navy.
Basic data: 7500 tons full displacement; 508.5ft (155.0m)

overall length; 55.8ft (17.0m) maximum beam.
Crew: 380.
Propulsion: 2 geared steam turbines (total 100,000shp); 2 propellers.
Sensors: 1 each of 2 separate long-range air search radars; 2 sea search and navigational radars; 2 and 1 of two separate fire control radars for SS-N-3 missiles; 2 fire control radars for SA-N-1 missiles; 2 fire control radars for 57mm guns; 1 IFF radar; 1 hull-mounted sonar; automated action information data-processing; satellite-fed data links.
Armament: 1 Kamov Ka-26 helicopter; 2 twin SS-N-3 'Shaddrock' anti-ship missile launchers; 2 twin SA-N-1 'Goa' area air defence missile launchers; 2 twin 57mm anti-aircraft guns; 2 twelve-barrelled 250mm RBU-6000 and 2 six-barrelled 450mm RBU-1000 anti-submarine rocket launchers; 2 quintuple heavyweight anti-submarine torpedo tubes.
Top speed: 32 knots.
Range: 7000 nautical miles at 14 knots.
Programme: This four-ship class comprises; *Vitse Admiral Drozd*, *Sevastopol*, *Admiral Zozulya* and *Vladivostok*. Two ships each were launched in 1965 and 1966, with two each entering service in 1966 and 1967, respectively.
Notes: Still primarily orientated towards the anti-ship mission as was the preceding 'Kynda' class of cruisers, the 'Kresta' I class ships were heavier than their forebears, reflecting their heavier and better balanced weapons fit. The 'Kresta' I class were the first Soviet cruisers to be fitted with a helicopter hangar and are reported to be refitted with 4 single 30mm Gatling type close-in weapons systems.

A Soviet Navy 'Kresta' I class cruising in the Mediterranean.

Andrea Doria Class Cruisers

Role: Anti-aircraft.
Builder: CNR, Italy.
User: Italian Navy.
Basic data: 6412 tons full displacement; 489.8ft (149.3m) overall length; 56.4ft (17.2m) maximum beam.
Crew: 514.
Propulsion: 2 CNR-built De Laval geared steam turbines (60,000shp); 2 propellers.
Sensors: 1 SPS-52B air search/height finder (3-D) radar; 1 Selenia/Elsag RAN-20S low-level air search and tracking radar; 1 SMA SPQ-2D surface search and navigational radar; 2 SPG-55C missile fire control radars; 4 Selenia/Elsag RTN-10X missile/gun fire control radars; 1 SQS-23 hull-mounted sonar. Selenia automated action information data-processing.
Armament: 4 Agusta-Bell AB 212ASW helicopters (2 only on C554); 1 twin Mk 10 launcher for Standard area air defence missiles; 8 single 76mm OTO-Melara anti-aircraft guns (6 only on C554); 2 triple Elsag Mk 32 lightweight anti-submarine torpedo tubes.
Top speed: 32 knots.
Range: 5210 nautical miles at 20 knots.
Programme: This two-ship class comprises: *Andrea Doria*

Caio Duilio (C554) seen prior to its conversion as a training ship.

(C553) and *Caio Duilio* (C554). Built in separate CNR yards, both ships were laid down in May 1958, with the *Andrea Doria* entering service in February 1964, followed by its sister ship in November 1964. Both cruisers underwent major refits during the latter 1970s, having their Terrier missiles replaced by Standard SM-1ER, along with the updating of the ships' electronics. During this refit, *Caio Duilio* was converted into a training cruiser, having its aft pair of pedestal-mounted 76mm guns removed in order to lengthen and heighten the former hangar, now used as a school and living quarters for trainees.

Notes: Designed from the outset to serve as task force command ships. Besides shipping a powerful anti-air capability, the spacious helipad aft ensures that the ships can make a material contribution when operating against a submarine threat. Although a twin-funnelled design, the forward funnel is barely visible, being merged into the aft end of the bridge superstructure.

Kynda Class Cruisers

Role: Anti-ship.
Builder: Zhdanov, USSR.
User: Soviet Navy.

Looking for all the world like two huge waterbeds, the quadruple 'Shaddrock' missile launchers, positioned at either end of the 'Kynda' class's main superstructure tend to dominate the ship's profile from abeam. Note the forward mounted 'Goa' missile launcher.

Basic data: 5600 tons displacement; 459ft (140m) overall length; 51.8ft (15.8m) maximum beam.
Crew: 375.
Propulsion: 2 geared steam turbines (total 100,000shp); 2 propellers.
Sensors: 2 long-range air search radars; 2 sea search and navigational radars; 2 tracking radars (SS-N-3); 1 tracking radar (both missile systems); 2 tracking radars (SA-N-1); 1 hull-mounted sonar.
Armament: 2 quadruple SS-N-3 'Shaddrock' anti-ship cruise missile launchers; 1 twin SA-N-1 'Goa' medium-range anti-aircraft missile launcher; 2 twin 76mm dual-purpose guns; 2 triple heavyweight anti-submarine torpedo tubes; 2 twelve-barrel 250mm RBU 6000 anti-submarine rocket launchers. Helicopter pad aft, but no onboard facilities.
Top speed: 34 knots.
Range: 6800 nautical miles at 15 knots.
Programme: The first of this four-ship class was laid down in June 1960, with the first two, *Groznyy* and *Admiral Fukin*, entering service with the Soviet fleet in 1962, followed by *Admiral Golovko* and *Varyag* in 1965.
Notes: The first of the modern breed of Soviet guided missile-carrying cruisers, these relatively light ships pack a potent primary armament of 16 'Shaddrock' anti-ship cruise missiles (including reloads), capable of delivering a nuclear or conventional warhead over a range of around 250 nautical miles (463km). Besides the area air defence missiles, the 'Kynda' class carries a fairly heavy onboard sub-surface punch in the form of its anti-submarine torpedoes and the complement of up to 3.2 nautical mile (6km) ranging anti-submarine rockets.

Destroyers

Arleigh Burke Class Destroyers

Role: General-purpose.
Builder: Bath Iron Works, US (Lead Yard).
User: Under development for the US Navy.
Basic data: 8500 tons full displacement; 466.0ft (142.0m) overall length; 62.0ft (18.9m) maximum beam.
Crew: 336.
Propulsion: 4 General Electric LM2500 gas turbines (total 80,000shp); 2 propellers.

Sensors: 1 SPY-1D multi-function, long-range air search/tracking and height finder (3-D) radar; 1 SPS-67 sea search and navigational radar; 3 SPG-62 missile/gun fire control radars; 1 SQS-53C hull-mounted sonar; 1 SQR-19 towed array sonar; 1 URN-25 TACAN aircraft homer; new model NTDS automated action information data-processing system.
Armament: Helipad and support facilities, but no hangarage for 1 Sikorsky SH-60B Sea Hawk helicopter; 90 siloes (61 forward, 29 aft) for vertically-launched

A US Navy artist's impression of the lead of class, DDG51.

Standard area air defence missiles/Tomahawk anti-ship missiles/ASROC anti-submarine missiles (mix as desired); 2 quadruple Harpoon anti-ship missile launchers; 1 single 5in Mk 45 dual-purpose gun; 2 Mk 15 Phalanx 20mm close-in weapons systems; 2 Mk 32 triple lightweight anti-submarine torpedo tubes.

Top speed: 30 knots.

Range: 5000 nautical miles at 20 knots.

Programme: Three US shipyards, Bath Ironworks, Ingalls Shipbuilding and Todd Shipyards were competing for the lead yard contract for the DDG51 *Arleigh Burke* and subsequent ships of this class. Selection of the winning tender was announced in March 1985, with the contract for the first ship following shortly thereafter under Fiscal Year 1985 funding. Completion date for the lead ship is scheduled for October 1989. On current scheduling, the second, third and fourth ships should be ordered during Fiscal Year 1987, followed by five per fiscal period through 1992.

Notes: US Navy studies aimed at defining this new, important destroyer class, then referred to as the DDGX, commenced during the latter half of the 1970s, aimed at providing a more general-purpose replacement for the existing 'Coontz' and 'Charles F Adams' class destroyers and, to a lesser degree, the 'Belknap' and 'Leahy' class cruisers. Now crystallised around the DDG51 'Arleigh Burke' class design, the ship is shorter and lighter than the CG47 'Ticonderoga' class cruiser class, with which it will share a common propulsion machinery package, some major sensor systems and similar weaponry. Critics of the ship's limited anti-submarine helicopter operating ability may need to take greater account of the envisaged 1990s task group composition that could well include specialised helicopter support ship capability, similar to that fitted aboard RFA *Reliant*.

Udaloy Class Destroyers

Role: Anti-submarine.

Builders: Various, USSR.

User: Soviet Navy.

Basic data: 8200 tons full displacement; 531ft (162.0m) overall length; 63.3ft (19.3m) maximum beam.

Crew: Around 300.

Propulsion: 4 gas turbines (total 120,000shp); COGAG; 2 propellers.

Sensors: 2 air search and height finder (3-D) radars; 3 low-level air/sea search radars; 2 each fire control radars for anti-submarine missile and air defence missile systems; 1 fire control radar for 100mm guns; 2 fire control radars for 30mm guns; 1 bow-mounted sonar; 1 towed variable depth sonar; automated action information data-processing system and long-range (satellite) data links.

Udaloy *showing the ship's highly raked clipper bow and generally 'busy' upper profile surmounting a clean, seaworthy-looking hull.*

Armament: 2 Kamov Ka-26 'Hormone' or Ka-27 'Helix' helicopters; 2 quadruple SS-N-14 anti-submarine missile launchers; 8 vertically-launched SA-NX-8 air defence missiles; 2 single 100mm dual-purpose guns; 4 single 30mm Gatling-type anti-aircraft guns; 2 twelve-barrel 250mm RBU-6000 anti-submarine rocket launchers; 2 quadruple heavyweight anti-submarine torpedo tubes; mines.

Top speed: 33 knots.

Range: 6000 nautical miles at 20 knots (estimated).

Programme: Believed to be the precursor of a large class, the first two ships, *Udaloy* and *Vitse Admiral Kulikov* were laid down during 1978 in the Kaliningrad and Zhdanov shipyards, respectively, followed by two more in 1979. *Udaloy*, the lead ship, commenced sea trials in the Baltic in November 1980 and the *Vitse Admiral Kulikov* went to sea in 1982.

Notes: Designed as a replacement for the earlier 'Krivak' class anti-submarine frigates, the 'Udaloy' class consists of much larger and heavier ships, being in many ways directly comparable to the US Navy's 'Spruance' class destroyers. As with the 'Spruance' class, the 'Udaloys' carry a very respectable secondary anti-air sensor/weapons fit. The ship's primary armament of eight 25 nautical mile ranging SS-N-14 anti-submarine missiles are mounted, as with the 'Kara' and 'Kresta' II classes, in two quadruple 'bin' launchers immediately below the ship's bridge. The eight siloes for the new, vertically-launched SA-NX-8 air defence missiles are reported to be dispersed about the ship; four being housed under a large hatch in the bow section; the other two twin missile siloes being mounted in tandem immediately forward of the helicopter hangar structure. The ship's two single 100mm guns are fully automatic and are reported to have an 80 rounds per minute maximum rate of fire. The four 30mm Gatling-type rapid-fire anti-aircraft guns are placed above the corners of the raised main hull section amidships, from where each has a totally unobstructed hemispherical arc of fire. The 'Udaloys'' two 12-barrelled RBU-6000 anti-submarine rocket launchers are mounted on either side of the forward part of the helicopter hangar superstructure; the quadruple 533mm anti-submarine torpedo launchers each being mounted at the sides of the forward end of the low deck. As with other Soviet warships, the 'Udaloys'' upper hull sections are pockmarked with readily openable portholes; a practice frowned upon in the West for many years now, as part of the steps deemed necessary to 'close the ship down' so as to minimise inward seepages when operating in a chemical/bacteriological/nuclear warfare environment.

Kidd Class Destroyers

Role: Anti-aircraft.

Builder: Ingalls Shipbuilding, USA.

User: US Navy.

Basic data: 8140 tons full displacement; 563.3ft (171.7m) overall length; 55.0ft (16.8m) maximum beam.

Crew: 338.
Propulsion: 4 General Electric LM2500 gas turbines (total derated to 80,000shp); COGAG; 2 controllable-pitch propellers.
Sensors: 1 SPG-48 air search/height finder (3-D) radar; 1 SPS-55 surface search radar; 2 SPG-51 and 1 SPG-60 fire control radars (for missiles); 1 SPQ-9A gun fire control radar; 1 SQS-53 bow-mounted sonar; NTDS automated action information data-processing system.
Armament: 2 Kaman SH-2F Seasprite or Sikorsky SH-60B Seahawk helicopters; 2 twin Mk 26 launchers for Standard MR area defence missiles; 2 quadruple Harpoon anti-ship missile launchers; 2 single 5in Mk 45 dual-purpose guns; 2 Phalanx 20mm close-in weapons systems; ASROC anti-submarine missiles (launched from forward Mk 26 launcher); 2 triple lightweight anti-submarine torpedo tubes.
Top speed: 31 knots.
Range: 6000 nautical miles at 20 knots.
Programme: Originally envisaged as a six-ship programme for the Iranian Navy, the actual contract, when placed in early 1978, called for four. Within a year this contract was to become a casualty of the Iranian revolution, the ships being taken over by the US Navy in July 1979. Named USS *Kidd* (DDG993), USS *Callaghan* (DDG994), USS *Scott* (DDG995) and USS *Chandler* (DDG996), all were laid down between June 1978 and May 1979, the ships being commissioned in June 1981, August 1981, October 1981 and March 1982, respectively.
Notes: Heavier, but externally very similar to the earlier 'Spruance' class design, of which the 'Kidd' class is a more anti-air capable variant. Salient visible differences are confined to the 'Kidd' class's less 'boxy' fore-and-aft-mounted missile launchers and the mast-carried sensor complement. Internally, quite marked differences exist, centred on the widespread embodiment of high strength, low weight materials aboard the 'Kidd' class, aimed at minimising the effects of battle damage.

Sovremennyy Class Destroyers

Role: General-purpose.
Builder: Zhdanov, Leningrad, USSR.
User: Soviet Navy.
Basic data: 8075 tons full displacement; 510.5ft (155.6m) overall length; 57.1 ft (17.4m) maximum beam.
Crew: 330.
Propulsion: 2 geared steam turbines (total 110,000shp); 2 propellers.
Sensors: 1 long-range air search and height finder (3-D) radar; 3 sea search and navigational radars; 6 fire control radars for SA-N-7 missiles; 1 fire control radar for 130mm guns; 2 fire control radars for 30mm guns; 1 bow-mounted sonar; automated action information system and long-range (satellite) data link.
Armament: 1 Kamov Ka-26 'Hormone B' helicopter; 2 quadruple SS-N-9 'Siren' anti-ship cruise missile launchers; 2 single SA-N-7 medium-ranged air defence missile launchers; 2 twin 130mm dual-purpose guns; 4 single 30mm Gatling-type anti-aircraft guns; 2 twin 533mm heavyweight anti-submarine torpedo tubes; 2 six-barrel 450mm RBU-1000 anti-submarine rocket launchers; mines.
Top speed: 33 knots.
Range: 6500 nautical miles at 18 knots.
Programme: Believed to be at least a five-ship class, the lead ship, *Sovremennyy*, is reported to have been laid down during 1976 and entered sea trials in the summer of 1980 before joining the Northern Fleet in late 1981. The second of class, *Otchavanij*, laid down in 1977, entered trials in May 1982. A third and fourth of class are reported to have been laid down in 1978 and 1979, respectively. In all, five

USS Callaghan *(DDG994) undergoing sea trials.*

This deck-high view of Sovremennyy *shows the still unarmed vessel during early sea trials in October 1980.*

of these ships had been launched by the end of 1983.
Notes: The 'Sovremennyy' class design employs the same basic hull and propulsion machinery as the 'Kresta' I and II classes but incorporates a more up-to-date armament fit on a radically altered superstructure. The 'Sovremmenyy' class carries the SS-N-9 'Siren' anti-ship cruise missile with a range of up to 60 nautical miles (111km), the missiles being housed in large canister-type quadruple launchers mounted on the main deck on either side of the bridge structure. The two single SA-N-7 air defence missile launchers are mounted on the raised deck areas immediately aft of the forward 130mm gun and the helipad, respectively. With a range of up to 15.1 nautical miles (28km), the SA-N-7 installations with their nearby missile reload magazines give the ship a healthy anti-air capability, supported by the new, water-cooled 130mm guns and 30mm rapid-fire close-in anti-sea skimmer missile weapons. As with the other most recent classes of Soviet warships, this class carries four of these six-barrelled 30mm close-in weapons positioned on either flank of the ship immediately forward of the bridge and just aft of the retracted telescopic hangar (quite clearly the Soviets had respect for the incoming low-level air threat long before the Falklands experience brought the lesson home). The fully automatic 130mm guns, with their effective range of 8.1 nautical miles (15km) should provide the ship with not only a useful secondary anti-ship punch, but be useful in terms of ship-to-shore bombardment.

Spruance Class Destroyers

Role: Anti-submarine.
Builder: Ingalls Shipbuilding, USA.
User: US Navy.
Basic data: 7800 tons full displacement; 563.3ft (171.7m) overall length; 55ft (16.8m) maximum beam.
Crew: 302.

USS John Hancock *(DDG 981) in the Caribbean Sea, June 1984.*

Propulsion: 4 General Electric LM2500 gas turbines (total 80,000shp); COGAG; 2 controllable-pitch propellers.
Sensors: 1 SPS-40B air search radar; 1 SPS-55 surface search radar; 1 SPG-60 STIR missile fire control radar; 1 SPQ-9A surface target fire control radar; 1 SQS-53 bow-mounted sonar; NTDS automated action information data-processing system.
Armament: 1 Sikorsky SH-3 Sea King or 2 Sikorsky SH-60 Seahawk helicopters; 1 octuple Mk 29 launcher for Sea Sparrow point air defence missiles; 2 quadruple Harpoon anti-ship missile launchers; 2 single 5in Mk 45 dual-purpose guns; 2 Phalanx 20mm close-in weapons systems; 1 octuple Mk 16 launcher for ASROC anti-submarine missiles.
Top speed: 32 knots.
Range: 6000 nautical miles at 20 knots.
Programme: The 31-ship 'Spruance' class destroyers were subject of a sole source contract placed with the Ingalls Shipbuilding Division of Litton Industries in June 1970 (for 30 ships, one being added in September 1979). The class comprises: USS *Spruance* (DD963), USS *Paul F Foster* (DD964), USS *Kinkaid* (DD965), USS *Hewitt* (DD966), USS *Elliott* (DD967), USS *Arthur W Radford* (DD968), USS *Peterson* (DD969), USS *Caron* (DD970), USS *David R Ray* (DD971), USS *Oldendorf* (DD972), USS *John Young* (DD973), USS *Comte de Grasse* (DD974), USS *O'Brien* (DD975), USS *Merrill* (DD976), USS *Briscoe* (DD977), USS *Stump* (DD978), USS *Conolly* (DD979), USS *Moosbrugger* (DD980), USS *John Hancock* (DD981), USS *Nicholson* (DD982), USS *John Rodgers* (DD983), USS *Leftwich* (DD984), USS *Cushing* (DD985), USS *Harry W Hill* (DD986), USS *O'Bannon* (DD987), USS *Thorn* (DD988), USS *Deyo* (DD989), USS *Ingersoll* (DD990), USS *Fife* (DD991), USS *Fletcher* (DD992) and USS *Hayler* (DD997). With the exception of the lately ordered 31st ship, all 'Spruances' were laid down between November 1972 and April 1978 and all 30 were commissioned between September 1975 and July 1980; with the 31st ship *Hayler*, commissioning in March 1983. (The four ships, DD993 through DD996, were anti-air versions of the 'Spruance' ordered by Iran, but subsequently brought into US Navy service as the 'Kidd' class).
Notes: Large and very angular of line, the 'Spruance' class ships were built as replacements for the World War II destroyers of the 'Allen M Sumner' and 'Gearing' classes. Designed using modular construction techniques, the 'Spruance' class ships employ a Combined Gas and Gas (COGAG) machinery arrangement in which the vessel can be propelled by one, two, three or all four LM2500 engines. In the 'Spruances', the ship's main machinery of four gas turbines is grouped into two physically separated engine rooms (to minimise potential battle damage) and this, in turn, leads to the rather unusual asymmetric

staggering of the ship's funnels, or stacks, as they are called, the forward one being set to port, aft to starboard. All are being retrofitted with two Phalanx 20mm systems.

Shirane Class Destroyers

Role: Anti-submarine.
Builder: Ishikawajima Heavy Industries, Japan.
User: Japanese Maritime Self-Defence Force.
Basic data: 6800 tons full displacement; 521.0ft (158.8m) overall length; 57.4ft (17.5m) maximum beam.
Crew: 370.
Propulsion: 2 geared steam turbines (total 70,000shp); 2 propellers.
Sensors: 1 OPS 12 long-range air search and height finder (3-D) radar; 1 OPS 28 sea search and navigational radar; 1 Hollandse WM 25 fire control radar (for Sea Sparrow); 2 GFCS 1A gun fire control radars; 1 TACAN aircraft homer; 1 OQS 100 bow-mounted sonar; 1 SQS-35 variable depth sonar; 1 SQS-18A passive towed array sonar; naval tactical information data-processing system.
Armament: 3 Kawasaki-built SH-3 Sea King helicopters; 2 single 5in Mk 42 dual-purpose guns; 1 octuple Mk 20 launcher for Sea Sparrow point air defence missiles; 1 octuple launcher for ASROC anti-submarine missiles; 2 triple lightweight anti-submarine torpedo tubes; 2 Phalanx 20mm close-in weapons systems.
Top speed: 32 knots.
Endurance: Over 6000 nautical miles.
Programme: Authorised for construction in 1976, this two-ship class comprises: *Shirane* (DDG143) and *Kurama* (DDG144). The *Shirane* was laid down in February 1977, launched in September 1978 and entered service in March 1980. *Kurama* was laid down in February 1978, was launched in September 1979 and joined the Japanese fleet in March 1981.
Notes: The 'Shirane' class design is based on that of the earlier 'Haruna' class, using the same propulsive machinery married to a slightly longer hull. Better armed than the 'Haruna' class, these 'Shirane' class destroyers have a very impressive anti-submarine capability and once fitted with Harpoon anti-ship missiles, as is planned, will pack a useful anti-ship punch too. Unlike many earlier Japanese destroyer designs, the 'Shirane' class vessels were designed from the outset to incorporate a useful, if somewhat localised anti-air sensor/weapon fit. The *Shirane* and her sister ship both incorporate the Masker bubble-generating system on their hulls; a technique adopted in order to reduce the amount of externally radiated ship-generated noise and, hence, enhance the detection capability of the ships' sonar equipment.

Japan's Shirane *(DDH143) with Sea King on helipad aft.*

HMS Bristol *(D23); note the unusual side-by-side positioning of the ship's two aft funnels.*

Bristol Type Destroyer

Role: Area air defence.
Builder: Swan Hunter, UK.
User: Royal Navy.
Basic data: 6750 tons displacement; 507.0ft (154.5m) overall length; 55.0ft (16.8m) maximum beam.
Crew: 407.
Propulsion: 2 Rolls-Royce TM-1A Olympus gas turbines (total 44,000shp); 2 GEC geared steam turbines (total 30,000shp); COSAG; 2 propellers.
Sensors: 1 Type 965M long-range air search radar with IFF; 1 Type 992Q low-altitude air search radar; 2 Type 909 fire control radars for Sea Dart; 2 fire control radars for Ikara; 1 Type 1006 navigational radar; 1 each of Types 162, 170, 182, 184 and 189 hull-mounted sonars; Ferranti ADAWS 2 automated action information data-processing system.
Armament: 1 twin Sea Dart area air defence missile launcher; 1 single 4.5in Vickers Mk 8 dual-purpose gun; 1 single Ikara anti-submarine launcher; 1 triple-barrel Mk 10 Limbo anti-submarine mortar; 2 single 20mm anti-aircraft guns; aft helipad for up to Lynx-sized helicopter but no hangar.
Top speed: 32 knots.
Range: 5000 nautical miles at 18 knots.
Programme: Initially planned as a four-ship class of which only HMS *Bristol* (D23) was authorised for building in 1966 (the other three being cancelled in Mid-1967). Laid down in November 1967 and launched in June 1969, HMS *Bristol* commissioned in March 1973.
Notes: Designed as a successor to the 'County' class destroyers, the primary function of the 'Bristol', or Type 82 ships was to have given air defence screening for the Royal Navy's planned 50,000 ton CVA aircraft carrier; a secondary function of the Type 82 being to act as command ship for a surface-only task force. Unfortunately, with the cancellation of the CVA programme in early 1966, much of the reason for the Type 82's existence evaporated and helped lend impetus to the development of the existing Type 42 'Sheffield' class design. Since entering service in March 1973 HMS *Bristol* has largely served in the unglamorous, if necessary role of trials ship right up to the Falklands conflict, when the ship was pressed into service with the South Atlantic Force.

'Haruna' class Hiei (DDH142) with Sea King.

Haruna Class Destroyers

Role: Anti-submarine.
Builders: Mitsubishi and IHI, Japan.
User: Japanese Maritime Self-Defence Force.
Basic data: 6300 tons full displacement; 502ft (153m) overall length; 57.4ft (17.5m) maximum beam.
Crew: 340.
Propulsion: 2 geared steam turbines (total 70,000shp); 2 propellers.
Sensors: 1 OPS 11 long-range air search radar; 1 OPS 17 sea search and navigational radar; 2 GFCS 1 fire control radars; 1 OQS 3 hull-mounted sonar; 1 URN-20A TACAN aircraft homer; automated naval tactical information data-processing system.
Armament: 3 Kawasaki-built SH-3 Sea King helicopters; 2 single 5in Mk 42 dual-purpose guns; 1 octuple Mk 16 launcher for ASROC anti-submarine missiles (1 Mk 25 launcher for Sea Sparrow point air defence missiles being retrofitted to both ships during early 1980s refits, along with the requisite fire control radar system).
Top speed: 32 knots.
Endurance: Over 7000 nautical miles.
Programme: *Haruna* (DDH141), the lead destroyer of this two-ship class was built by Mitsubishi, while *Hiei* (DDH142) was constructed at the yards of Ishikawajima Heavy Industries. Laid down in March 1970 and March 1972, the ships entered service in March 1973 and December 1974, respectively.
Notes: Large, fast ships, the 'Haruna' class design, with its capability to deploy no less than three Sea King submarine-hunting helicopters clearly added a broader dimension to Japan's naval anti-submarine forces; the choice of the larger sized Sea King reflecting the influence of the Royal Canadian Navy's pioneering developments with these aircraft. As originally built, this class appeared to be distinctly lacking in anti-air capability, but this is, at least, being partially rectified by the retrofitting of Sea Sparrow and these vessels appear to be logical candidates to mount the Phalanx 20mm close-in weapons systems that Japan is buying.

County Class Destroyers

Role: Anti-aircraft.
Builders: Various, UK.
Users: Royal Navy, Chilean Navy, Pakistan Navy.
Basic data: 6200 tons full displacement; 520ft (158.5m) overall length; 54ft (16.5m) maximum beam.
Crew: 486.
Propulsion: 2 AEI geared steam turbines (total 30,000shp) plus 4 Metrovick G.6 gas turbines (total 30,000shp); COSAG; 2 propellers.
Sensors: 1 Type 965 long-range air search radar; 1 Type 992Q low-level air and surface search radar, 1 Type 278 height finder (3-D) radar, 1 Type 901 Seaslug fire control radar; 1 Type 903 gun fire control radar; 2 Type 904 Seacat fire control radars; 1 Type 1006 sea search and navigational radar; 1 Type 184 hull-mounted sonars, ADAWS 1 automated action information data-processing system.
Armament: 2 Westland Wessex helicopters; 1 twin Mk II launcher for Seaslug area air defence missiles; 4 Exocet anti-ship missiles on D18, D19, D20 and D21, which replaces the 'B' or 2nd gun turret, other ships carrying 2 twin 4.5in Mk 6 dual-purpose guns; 2 quadruple Seacat point air defence missile launchers.
Top speed: 30 knots.
Range: 3500 nautical miles at 28 knots.
Programme: Originally an eight-ship class built between March 1959 and October 1970, HMS *Antrim* (D18) and HMS *Glamorgan* (D19) and HMS *Fife* (D20) remained in service with the Royal Navy, while the former HMS *Norfolk* (D21) have been sold to the Chilean Navy where they serve as the *Capitan Prat* and *Almirante Cochrane*. Another ship, the former HMS *London* (D16), has been sold to Pakistan, where it serves as the *Babur*.
Notes: Sturdy ships, HMS *Glamorgan* survived an Exocet strike on 11 June 1982, while operating with the Falklands task force along with her sister, HMS *Antrim*.

Suffren Class Destroyers

Role: General purpose.
Builders: DCAN (various), France.
User: French Navy.
Basic data: 6090 tons full displacement 517ft (157.6m)

HMS Antrim *(D18) with Wessex on helipad.*

overall length; 50.85ft (15.5m) maximum beam.
Crew: 355.
Propulsion: 2 Rateau geared steam turbines (total 72,500shp); 2 propellers.
Sensors: 1 DRBI 23 air search and height finder (3-D) radar, 1 DRBV 50 surface search radar; 1 Decca/DRBN 32 sea search and navigational radar, 2 DRBR 51 fire control radars (Masurca); 1 DRBC 32A fire control radar (100mm guns); 1 DUBV 23 hull-mounted sonar; 1 DUBV 43 towed variable depth sonar, SENIT automated action information data-processor.
Armament: 4 Exocet anti-ship missile launchers; 1 twin Masurca area air defence missile launcher (reloadable); 1 Malafon anti-submarine missile launcher (13 missiles); 2 100mm Model 1968 dual-purpose guns; 4 single 20mm Oerlikon anti-aircraft guns; 2 heavyweight anti-submarine torpedo catapults (10 torpedoes).
Top speed: 34 knots.
Range: 5100 nautical miles at 18 knots.
Programme: A two-ship class, the first, *Suffren* (D602), was laid down in December 1962, launched in May 1965 and accepted in July 1967. *Duquesne* (D603) was laid down in November 1964, launched in February 1966 and accepted in April 1970.
Notes: One of the first generation guided missile destroyers, the two 'Suffren' class ships were the first post-World War II French warships to be designed from the start as general-purpose vessels.

Coontz Class Destroyers

Role: Anti-aircraft.
Builders: Various, USA.
User: US Navy.
Basic data: 5800 tons full displacement; 512.5ft (152.6m) overall length; 52.5ft (15.9m) maximum beam.
Crew: 398.
Propulsion: 2 geared steam turbines (total 85,000shp); 2 propellers.

Duquesne (D603) underway in the Atlantic, 1977.

USS Coontz *(DDG40) in the Caribbean, October 1978.*

Tourville (D610), with her massive towed, variable-depth sonar equipment clearly visible immediately aft of the stern.

Sensors: 1 SPS-29 or 1 SPS-37 air search radar; 1 SPS-48 height finder (3-D) radar; 1 SPS-10B sea search and navigational radar; 1 SPG-53A gun fire control radar; 2 SPG-55B missile fire control radar; 1 SQS-23 hull-mounted sonar; NTDS automated action information data-processing system.

Armament: 1 twin Mk 10 launcher for Terrier/Standard ER area air defence missiles; 2 quadruple Harpoon anti-ship missile launchers; 1 single 5in Mk 42 dual-purpose gun; 1 octuple Mk 16 launcher for ASROC anti-submarine missiles; 2 triple lightweight anti-submarine torpedo tubes; 2 Phalanx 20mm close-in weapons systems in process of being fitted.

Top speed: 33 knots.

Range: 6000 nautical miles at 14 knots.

Programme: This ten-ship class comprises: USS *Farragut* (DDG37), USS *Luce* (DDG38), USS *MacDonough* (DDG39), USS *Coontz* (DDG40), USS *King* (DDG41), USS *Mahan* (DDG42), USS *Dahlgren* (DDG43), USS *Wm V Pratt* (DDG44), USS *Dewey* (DDG45) and USS *Preble* (DDG46); all commissioned between late 1959 and late 1961.

Notes: The 'Coontz' class vessels were the first of the US Navy's series production surface combatants to be missile equipped. The 'Coontz' class design was to serve as the basis for both the somewhat larger 'Leahy' class cruiser and the small 'Charles F Adams' class destroyers. These ships have a helicopter pad aft, but no facilities.

Tourville Class Destroyers

Role: Anti-submarine.

Builder: DCAN Lorient, France.

User: French Navy.

Basic data: 5700 tons full displacement; 500.3ft (152.5m) overall length; 50.2ft (15.3m) maximum beam.

Crew: 282.

Propulsion: 2 Rateau geared steam turbines (total 57,300shp); 2 propellers.

Sensors: 1 DRBV 26 long-range air search radar; 1 DRBV 51 B low-level air and surface search radar; 1 DRBC 32D gun fire control radar; 2 Decca 1226 sea search and navigational radars; 1 DUBV 23 bow-mounted sonar, used in conjunction with 1 DUBV 43 towed, variable depth sonar; SENIT 3 automated action information data-processing system.

Armament: 2 Westland Lynx helicopters; 6 Exocet anti-ship missile launchers; 2 single 100mm Model 1968 dual-purpose guns; 1 Crotale point air defence missile launcher system; 2 single 20mm Oerlikon anti-aircraft guns; 1 single Malafon anti-submarine missile launcher; 2 heavyweight anti-submarine torpedo catapults.

Top speed: 31 knots.

Endurance: In excess of 6000 nautical miles.

Programme: This three-ship class comprises *Tourville* (D610), *Duguay Trouin* (D611) and *De Grasse* (D612). Laid down between 1970 and 1972, the ships entered service in June 1974, September 1975 and October 1977, respectively. The rapid-response Crotale was recently installed in place of the aft (third) 100mm gun shown in the photograph. All three ships are planned to remain in service, until the year 2000.

Notes: This class is a more compact, well armed development of the earlier 'Suffren' class.

Modified Kashin/Kashin Class Destroyers

Role: General-purpose.

Builders: Various, USSR.

Users: Soviet and Indian Navies.

Basic data: Around 4850 tons full displacement; 479ft (146m) overall length; 51.85ft (15.8m) maximum beam.

Crew: 280.

Propulsion: 4 gas turbines (total 96,000shp); 2 propellers.

Sensors: 1 long-range air search radar; 2 height finder (3-D) radars; 2 sea search and navigational radars; 4 fire control radars consisting of 2 separate systems; 1 hull-mounted sonar; 1 towed variable depth sonar (on Modified 'Kashins' only).

Armament: 4 single SS-N-2 anti-ship missile launchers (Modified 'Kashins' only); 2 twin SA-N-1 point air defence missile launchers; 2 twin 76mm anti-aircraft guns; 4 single Gatling-type 30mm anti-aircraft guns (Modified 'Kashins' only); 5 heavyweight anti-submarine torpedo tubes; 2 twelve-barrel RB 6000 anti-submarine 250mm rocket launchers (on all 'Kashins' and on at least 1 Modified 'Kashin'.

Top speed: 36 knots.

Range: 5000 nautical miles at 18 knots.

Programme: Twenty 'Kashin' class ships were constructed between 1962 and 1972 and five of these

A Modified 'Kashin' operating in the Mediterranean, May 1979.

ships were known to have been converted to Modified 'Kashins' commencing 1973. One 'Kashin' sank in the Black Sea in August 1974 following an internal explosion. The Indian Government has ordered three Modified 'Kashins' for early 1980s delivery; the ships' names and pennant numbers being: *Rajput* (D51), *Rana* (D52) and *Ranjit* (D53).

Notes: The 'Kashin' class guided missile destroyers were the first large gas-turbine powered ships to emerge anywhere in the world. Modified 'Kashins' have an enlarged and elevated helicopter pad aft capable of operating a Kamov Ka-25.

Tachikaze Class Destroyers

Role: Anti-aircraft.
Builder: Mitsubishi, Japan.
User: Japanese Maritime Self-Defence Force.
Basic data: 4800 tons full displacement; 469.2ft (143m) overall length; 46.9ft (14.3m) maximum beam.
Crew: 277.
Propulsion: 2 geared steam turbines (total 70,000shp); 2 propellers.
Sensors: 1 OPS-17 sea search and navigational radar; 1 SPS-52B height finder (3-D) radar; 2 SPG-51 missile fire control radars; 1 GFCS 1 gun fire control radar; 1 OQS-3 hull-mounted sonar, automated action information data-processing system.
Armament: 1 single Mk 13 launcher for Standard SM-1 MR area air defence missiles; 2 single 5in Mk 42 dual-purpose guns; 1 octuple ASROC anti-submarine missile launcher; 2 triple lightweight anti-submarine torpedo tubes.
Top speed: 32 knots.
Endurance: In excess of 4000 nautical miles.
Programme: This three-ship class comprises *Tachikaze* (D168), *Asakaze* (D169) and *Sawakaze* (D170). Laid down in 1973, 1976 and 1979. The three ships entered service in March 1976, March 1979 and March 1983.
Notes: Employing the same propulsive machinery as the somewhat heavier 'Haruna' class destroyers, the 'Tachikaze' class, along with the single 'Amatsukaze' type destroyer, were the first Japanese warships to carry an area air defence capability. No helicopter is carried.

Tachikaze (D168) photographed at speed in 1976.

Sheffield Class Destroyers

Role: Area air defence.
Builders: Various, UK and Argentina.
Users: Royal Navy and Argentinian Navy.

Basic data:

	Batch I and II	Batch III
Full displacement:	4250 tons	4700 tons
Overall length:	410ft (125m)	463ft (141.1m)
Maximum beam:	47ft (14.3m)	49ft (14.9m)
Crew:	280	301

Propulsion: 2 Rolls-Royce TM3B Olympus gas turbines (total 54,400shp); 2 Rolls-Royce RM1A in Batch 1 or RM1C in Batches II and III (total 7600 or 10,680shp); COGOG; 2 controllable-pitch propellers.
Sensors: 1 Type 965M (Batch 1) or 1 Type 1022 (Batches II and III) long-range air search radar and IFF; 1 Type 992Q low-altitude air search radar; 1 Type 1006 sea search and navigational radar; 2 Type 909 fire control radars for Sea Dart; Types 162, 170B, 174 and 184 hull-mounted sonars; Ferranti ADAWS 4 automated action information data-processing system; long-range (satellite) data links.
Armament: 1 Westland Lynx helicopter; 1 twin Mk 30

Sea Dart area air defence missile launcher; 1 single 4.5in Vickers Mk 8 dual-purpose gun; 2 twin 30mm Oerlikon and 2 single 20mm Mk 7 Oerlikon anti-aircraft guns; 2 triple lightweight anti-submarine torpedo tubes.

Top speed: 28 knots (Batch I and II) or 30 knots (Batch III).

Range: 4500 (Batch I and II) or 4750 nautical miles (Batch III) at 18 knots.

Programme: Originally destined to be a 16-ship class, of which two have been lost, the Type 42 or 'Sheffield' class comprises eight Batch 1 vessels, four Batch II and four Batch III examples of the Stretched Type 42. The Royal Navy Batch I ships, along with their commissioning dates are: HMS *Sheffield* (D80), February 1975; HMS *Birmingham* (D86), December 1976; HMS *Coventry* (D118), November 1978; HMS *Cardiff* (D108), October 1979; HMS *Newcastle* (D87), March 1978 and HMS *Glasgow* (D88), May 1979. The two Argentinian ships (also Batch I) are *Hercules* (D28), July 1976 and *Santisima Trinidad* (D29), 1981. The Batch IIs are: HMS *Exeter* (D89), September 1980; HMS *Southampton* (D90), July 1981; HMS *Nottingham* (D91), April 1983 and HMS *Liverpool* (D92), July 1982. The Batch III Stretched Type 42s comprise: HMS *Manchester* (D95), December 1982, along with HMS *Gloucester* (D96), HMS *Edinburgh* (D97) and HMS *York* (D98), all of which should be completed by late 1985. Vickers acted as the lead yard for both Batch I and III ships with the building programme spread over five yards comprising: Vickers—D80, D28, D108 and D95; Cammell Laird—D86, D118, D92 and D97; Swan Hunter—D87, D88, D89 and D98; Vosper Thornycroft—D90, D91 and D96, with the Argentinian AFNE naval yard responsible for D29. Both HMS *Sheffield* and HMS *Coventry* were lost to enemy action in May 1982.

Notes: Designed as replacement for the 'County' class destroyers, the 'Sheffield' class, or Type 42s are much more compact and austere than their forebears. The primary role of the Type 42s is to provide area air defence for the ships that they are accompanying. Because of their long-range sensor fit, the 'Sheffield' class are also a logical choice to act as radar pickets, sailing ahead of a task group to act as its eyes and ears. Regrettably, as the loss of HMS *Sheffield* and HMS *Coventry* demonstrated, this latter role isolated these ships from the supporting fire of their fellow warships and highlighted their vulnerability to low-level air attack from sea-skimming missiles in the case of HMS *Sheffield*, or streamed manned aircraft, as in the case of the sinking of HMS *Coventry* by Argentinian A-4 Skyhawks, two of which were downed by the ship's Sea Darts before the third aircraft released its lethal bombload. Her Majesty's ships *Cardiff*, *Glasgow* and *Exeter* also saw action in the Falklands theatre, *Glasgow* surviving a direct hit in its main engine space by a bomb that, fortunately, failed to explode.

A frontal aspect of HMS Glasgow (D88) executing a high speed turn.

HMS Manchester (D95), the first of the Batch III Stretched Type 42s.

Kanin Class Destroyers

Role: Anti-aircraft.
Builders: Zhdanov, Severodvinsk and Kommuna, USSR.
User: Soviet Navy.
Basic data: 4700 tons full displacement; 462.6ft (141.0m) overall length; 47.9ft (14.6m) maximum beam.
Crew: 300.
Propulsion: 2 geared steam turbines (total 80,000shp); 2 propellers.
Sensors: 1 long-range air search radar; 1 IFF radar; 2 sea search and navigational radars; 3 separate types of fire control radars (1 each for missiles, 57mm and 30mm guns); 1 hull-mounted sonar; naval tactical information system.
Armament: 1 twin SA-N-1 'Goa' area air defence missile launcher; 2 quadruple 57mm and 4 twin 30mm anti-aircraft guns; 3 twelve-barrelled 250mm RBU-6000 anti-submarine rocket launchers; 2 quintuple heavyweight anti-submarine torpedo tubes.
Top speed: 34 knots.
Range: 4500 nautical miles at 18 knots.
Programme: The 'Kanin' class comprises eight converted 'Krupnyy' class destroyers, these modernised missile-carrying convertions entering service between 1958 and 1960. The 'Kanin' class ship names are: *Boykiy, Derzkiy, Gnevnyy, Gordyy, Gremyashchiy, Upornyy, Zhguchiy* and *Zorkiy*.
Notes: Almost direct contemporaries of the US Navy's 'Charles F Adams' class, the 'Kanin' class was slightly faster despite its greater weight, but lacked the bigger gunned anti-ship punch of their US rivals. This Soviet class will probably be retired before the close of the 1980s.

Audace Class Destroyers

Role: Anti-submarine.
Builders: Various, Italy.
Basic data: 4554 tons full displacement; 469.2ft (143.0m) overall length; 47.9ft (14.6m) maximum beam.
Crew: 380.
Propulsion: 2 CNR or Ansoldo geared steam turbines (total 73,000shp); 2 propellers.
Sensors: 1 SPS-12 long-range air search radar; 1 SPQ-2 combined air/sea search radar; 1 SPS-52 height finder (3-D) radar, 1 sea search and navigational radar; 2 SPG-51B fire control radars (missile); 3 Selenia RNT-10X fire control radars (guns); 1 CWE 610 hull-mounted sonar; naval tactical data system.
Armament: 3 AB204/212-sized or 2 SH-3-sized helicopters; 1 single launcher for Standard SM-1 area air defence missiles; 2 single OTO-Melara 127mm dual-purpose guns; 4 single OTO-Melara 76mm anti-aircraft guns; 2 triple and 4 single lightweight anti-submarine torpedo tubes.
Top speed: 35.2 knots.
Range: 4000 nautical miles at 25 knots.
Programme: A two-ship class, *Ardito* (D550) and *Audace* (D551), were ordered in 1968. Both entered service in 1972.
Notes: Extremely fast and efficient ships, the 'Audace' class carry a well-balanced weapons fit. The hulls of these destroyers are built of steel, while their superstructure is built largely of light alloy. Besides having a high top speed, the 'Audace' class cruise at around 25 knots.

Charles F Adams Class Destroyers

Role: Anti-aircraft.
Builders: Various, USA.

A 'Kanin' class revealing much of her generally low profile.

Italy's Audace *(D551) guided missile destroyer.*

Users: US Navy, Royal Australian Navy, Federal German Navy.
Basic data: 4550 tons full displacement; 437ft (133.2m) overall length; 47ft (14.3m) maximum beam.
Crew: Around 330.
Propulsion: 2 General Electric or Westinghouse geared steam turbines (total 70,000shp); 2 propellers.
Sensors: 1 SPS-29, -37 or -40 air search radar; 1 SPS-39 height finder (3-D) radar; 1 SPS-10 sea search and navigational radar; 2 SPG-51C fire control radars (Standard); 1 SPG-53 fire control radar (gun); 1 SPS-23 hull-mounted sonar.
Armament: 1 twin Mk 11 or 13 launcher for Standard area air defence or Harpoon anti-ship missiles; 2 single 5in Mk 42 guns (aft gun removed on the 3 Federal German ships to make way for 2 twin Harpoon anti-ship missile launchers); 1 octuple ASROC anti-submarine rocket launcher (replaced by 2 Ikara anti-missile launchers on the 3 Australian ships); 2 triple lightweight anti-submarine torpedo tubes.
Top speed: 31 knots.
Range: 4500 nautical miles at 20 knots.
Programme: The 23-ship 'Charles F Adams' class was ordered for the US Navy between mid-1957 and mid-

USS Charles F Adams *(DDG2), November 1978.*

1961, all ships being laid down between 1958 and 1962. The lead ship, USS *Charles F Adams* (DDG2), built by Bath Iron Works, was followed by: USS *John King* (3), *Lawrence* (4), *Claude V Ricketts* (5), *Barney* (6), *Henry B Wilson* (7), *Lynde McCormick* (8), *Towers* (9), *Sampson* (10), *Sellers* (11), *Robison* (12), *Hoel* (13), *Buchanan* (14), *Berkeley* (15), *Joseph Strauss* (16), *Conyngham* (17), *Semmes* (18), *Tattnal* (19), *Goldsborough* (20), *Cochrane* (21), *Benjamin Stoddert* (22), *Richard E Byrd* (23), and *Waddel* (24). All of this class entered service between September 1960 and September 1964. Australia bought three additional ships, HMAS *Perth* (DDG38), HMAS *Hobart* (DDG39) and HMAS *Brisbane* (DDG41), all three being accepted between July 1965 and December 1967. In service with the Royal Australian Navy, these vessels are referred to as 'Perth' class ships. During 1964, the Federal German Government placed orders for a further three ships of this class, *Lutjens* (D185), *Molders* (D186) and *Rommel* (D187), all of which were accepted between March 1969 and May 1970 and are operated as 'Lutjens' class destroyers.

Notes: Slightly smaller and lighter than the 'Coontz' class guided missile destroyers that preceded the 'Adams' into service with the US Navy, the 'Adams' class ships still provide around a quarter of the US Navy's total task force anti-aircraft screening capability. Currently, the US

vessels are undergoing an extensive modernisation of their shipboard electronics and action information systems, along with the installation of Harpoon missile systems. Similar electronics modernisation is being carried out on the three 'Lutjens' class destroyers, while within the short term, the 'Perth' class are scheduled to be retrofitted to take Harpoon missiles. It should be noted that while the external appearance of the US and Australian ships is generally similar, the additional aft funnel-mounted mast, with its aerial arrays, helps disguise the 'Lutjens' class ships' ancestry quite markedly. All 29 ships of this generic class carry 40 Standard SM-1 MR area air defence missiles as their primary armament, this missile being capable of ranging out to 30 nautical miles, or reaching an altitude of 60,000 feet.

Takatsuki Class Destroyers

Role: Anti-submarine.
Builders: Various, Japan.
User: Japanese Maritime Self-Defence Force.
Basic data: 4500 tons full displacement; 446.8ft (136m) overall length; 44ft (13.4m) maximum beam.
Crew: 270.
Propulsion: 2 Mitsubishi geared steam turbines (total 60,000shp); 2 propellers.
Sensors: 1 OPS 11 long-range air search radar; 1 OPS 17 sea search and navigational radar; 2 Mk 35 gun fire control radars; 1 OQS 3 or 1 SQS-23 hull-mounted sonar; 1 SQS 35 towed variable depth sonar.
Armament: 2 quadruple Harpoon anti-ship missile launchers; 1 octuple Sea Sparrow point air defence missile launcher; 1 Mk 15 Phalanx close-in weapons system; 1 single 5in Mk 42 dual-purpose gun on DD164 and 165; 2 single 5in Mk 42 dual-purpose guns on DD166 and 167; 1 octuple Mk 16 launcher for ASROC anti-submarine missiles; 1 quadruple-barrelled Bofors 375mm anti-submarine rocket launcher; 2 triple lightweight anti-submarine torpedo tubes.
Top speed: 32 knots.
Range: 7000 nautical miles at 20 knots.
Programme: A four-ship class comprising *Takatsuki* (DD164), *Kikizuki* (DD165), *Mochizuki* (DD166) and

Takatsuki (DD164) *of the Japanese Maritime Self-Defence Force.*

Schleswig-Holstein (D182) after modernisation.

Nagatsuki (DD167), with all but the Mitsubishi-built DD165 being produced in the yards of Ishakawajima. Laid down between October 1965 and March 1968, the class entered service between March 1967 and February 1970.
Notes: A relatively large ship, the *Takatsuki* and her sisters started life with a formidable anti-submarine weapons fit, a modest, gun-only, anti-ship capability and almost no effective anti-air defences. However, *Takatsuki* and *Kikizuki* have undergone modernisation during the first half of the 1980s. No helicopters are carried.

Modified Hamburg Class Destroyers

Role: General-purpose.
Builder: Blohm und Voss, Federal Germany.
User: Federal German Navy.
Basic data: 4400 tons full displacement; 439.6ft (134m) overall length; 44ft (13.4m) maximum beam.
Crew: 280.
Propulsion: 2 geared steam turbines (total 68,000shp); 2 fixed-pitch propellers.
Sensors: 1 Hollandse DA 08 long-range air search radar; 1 Hollandse SGR 103 low-level air and sea search radar; 1 Hollandse SGR 105 sea search and navigational radar, 3 Hollandse M45 fire control radars; 1 Atlas hull-mounted sonar; naval tactical data system.
Armament: 4 Exocet anti-ship missile launchers; 3 single 100mm dual-purpose guns; 4 twin Breda 40mm anti-aircraft guns; 4 single heavyweight anti-submarine torpedo tubes; 2 quadruple-barrelled Bofors 375mm anti-submarine rocket launchers; mines.
Top speed: 35 knots.
Range: 5000 nautical miles at 18 knots.
Programme: Laid down between January 1959 and February 1961, this four-ship class comprises *Hamburg* (D181), *Schleswig-Holstein* (D182), *Bayern* (D183) and *Hassen* (D184). The ships entered service in March 1964, October 1964, July 1965 and October 1968, respectively. All four destroyers underwent major modernisation between November 1974 and December 1976, during which Exocets replaced what had been the third, or 'X' positioned gun turret.
Notes: Despite their inability to operate helicopters, these ships pack a considerable anti-ship punch out to about 30 miles.

Iroquois Class Destroyers

Role: Anti-submarine.
Builders: Marine Industries & Davie, Canada.
User: Canadian Navy.
Basic data: 4200 tons full displacement; 425ft (129.5m) overall length; 50ft (15.2m) maximum beam.
Crew: 285.
Propulsion: 2 Pratt & Whitney FT4 gas turbines (total 50,000shp) or 2 Pratt & Whitney FT12 gas turbines (total 7400shp); COGOG; 2 controllable-pitch propellers.
Sensors: 1 SPS-502 long-range air search radar; 1 SPQ-2D air and sea search radar; 2 Hollandse WM22 fire control radars; 3 sonars, comprising SQS-501 and SQS-505 hull-mounted and SQS-505 towed variable depth sonar; Litton automated action data-processing.
Armament: 2 Sikorsky Sea King helicopters; 1 OTO-Melara 127mm dual-purpose gun; 2 quadruple Sea Sparrow point air defence missile launchers; 1 Mk 10 Limbo anti-submarine mortar; 2 triple lightweight anti-submarine torpedo tubes.

Canada's HMCS Athabaskan *(DDH282).*

Top speed: 29 knots.

Range: 4500 nautical miles at 20 knots.

Programme: A four-ship class, the first two ships, HMCS *Iroquois* (DDH280) and HMCS *Huron* (DDH281), were both built by Marine Industries, being both laid down in January 1969. The other pair, HMCS *Athabascan* (DDH282) and HMCS *Algonquin* (DDH283), were laid down by Davie Shipbuilders in June and September 1969, respectively. The acceptance dates of all four ships were: July 1972, December 1972, November 1972 and September 1973.

Notes: The ship's 'boxy' superstructure sports V-shaped funnels; a configuration which, like so many other features of this class, including their large size relative to earlier Canadian frigates, was predicated by the need to operate two large helicopters in rough seas, day or night.

Georges Leygues Class Destroyers

Role: Anti-submarine.

Builder: DCAN Brest, France.

User: French Navy.

Basic data: 4170 tons full displacement; 456ft (139m) overall length; 45.9ft (14m) maximum beam.

Crew: 216.

Propulsion: 2 Rolls-Royce TM3B Olympus gas turbines (total 56,000shp) or 2 SEMT-Pielstick 16 PA 6 CV diesels (10,400bhp); CODOG; 2 controllable-pitch propellers.

Sensors: 1 DRBV 51 long-range air search radar; 1 DRBV 26 low-level air search radar; 1 DRBC 32 fire control radar; 2 Decca 1226 sea search and navigational radars; 1 DUBV 23 hull-mounted sonar; 1 DUBV 43 variable depth sonar; SENIT 4 automated action information data-processing system.

Armament: 2 Westland Lynx helicopters; 4 Exocet anti-ship missile launchers; 1 single 100mm Model 1968 dual-purpose gun; 1 octuple Crotale point air defence missile launcher; 2 single 20mm anti-aircraft guns; 2 heavyweight anti-submarine torpedo catapults.

Top speed: 30 knots.

Range: 9500 nautical miles at 17 knots.

Programme: Currently a seven-ship class comprising: *Georges Leygues* (D640), *Dupleix* (D641), *Montcalm* (D642), *Jean de Vienne* (D643), *Primauget* (D644), *La Motte Pequet* (D645) and D646. Launched in December 1976, December 1978 and May 1983, respectively, the first three of this class entered service in December 1979, June 1981 and May 1982. *Jean de Vienne* entered service in

USS Decatur *(DDG31) off San Diego, June 1976.*

1983, with the fifth, sixth and seventh destroyers planned for delivery in 1986, 1987 and 1988. The first of two much modified anti-aircraft derivatives of this class, referred to as C 70AAs and built by DCAN Lorient, was ordered in September 1981 and should enter service in 1988.

Notes: Very much contemporaries of the Royal Netherlands Navy's 'Kortenear' class and the Royal Navy's 'Broadword' class frigates, the 'Georges Leygues' class, or Type C 70 destroyers carry a potent-looking anti-

Georges Leygues (D640), *showing the ship's generally low profile.*

Top speed: 32.5 knots.
Range: 4500 nautical miles at 20 knots.
Programme: Originally laid down between 1954 and 1957 as 'Forrest Sherman' class ships, these destroyers, sometimes referred to as 'Decatur' class, comprise USS *Decatur* (DDG31), USS *John Paul Jones* (DDG32), USS *Parsons* (DDG33) and USS *Somers* (DDG34). These ships entered service in their current guise between April 1967 and February 1968.
Notes: While converting existing destroyers is clearly much more economic that building new ones, the deployment of these elderly, largely aluminium superstructured ships to the US Pacific Fleet (until 1980 considered the less demanding in operational terms) tends to indicate that they are considered of limited usefulness.

Amatsukaze Type Destroyer

Japanese Maritime Self-Defence Force's Amatsukaze *(D163).*

submarine sensor/weapons fit, particularly for the more distant from ship type of subsurface operations. Further, the ability to carry a second helicopter is not only of material advantage to the ship's primary anti-submarine role, but could well prove valuable in the anti-shipping environment relating to both over-the-horizon missile targeting and for providing an additional airborne strike capability against hostile fast attack craft. The combination of the 100mm dual-purpose gun and Crotale point air defence missile (26 rounds carried) provides the ship with a useful anti-air capability.

Converted Sherman Class Destroyers

Role: Anti-aircraft.
Builders: Various USA.
User: US Navy.
Basic data: 4150 tons full displacement; 418ft (127.4m) overall length; 45ft (13.7m) maximum beam.
Crew: 340.
Propulsion: 2 General Electric (Westinghouse in DDG32) geared steam turbines (total 70,000shp); 2 propellers.
Sensors: 1 SPS-29E (1 SPS-40 in DDG34) air search radar, 1 SPS-48 height finder (3-D) radar; 1 SPS-10B sea search and navigational radar; 1 SPG-51C missile fire control radar; 1 SPG-53B gun fire control radar; 1 SQS-23 hull-mounted sonar. NTDS automated action information system.
Armament: 1 single Mk 13 launcher for Tartar/Standard MR area defence missiles; 1 single 5in Mk 42 dual-purpose gun; 1 octuple Mk 16 ASROC anti-submarine missile launcher; 2 triple lightweight anti-submarine torpedo tubes.

Role: Anti-aircraft.
Builder: Mitsubishi, Japan.
User: Japanese Maritime Self-Defence Force.
Basic data: 4000 tons full displacement; 429.8ft (131m) overall length; 44ft (13.4m) maximum beam.
Crew: 290.
Propulsion: 2 Ishikawajima-General Electric geared steam turbines (total 60,000shp); 2 propellers.
Sensors: 1 SPS-29 air search radar; 1 SPS-52 height finder (3-D) radar; 1 OPS-17 sea search and navigational radar; 2 SPG-51 missile fire control radars; 2 SPG-34 gun fire control radars; 1 SQS-23 hull-mounted sonar; naval tactical data system.
Armament: 1 single Mk 13 launcher for Standard SM-1 MR area air defence missiles; 2 twin 76mm dual-purpose guns; 1 octuple ASROC anti-submarine missile launcher; 2 triple lightweight anti-submarine torpedo tubes; 2 Mk 15 Hedgehog anti-submarine launchers.
Top speed: 33 knots.
Range: 7000 nautical miles at 18 knots.
Programme: This sole example, the *Amatsukaze* (D163), was laid down in November 1962, launched in October 1963 and entered service in February 1965. The ship underwent a major refit in 1967 when it was equipped with its SPS-52 height finding radar and its torpedo tubes.
Notes: The first guided missile destroyer to be designed in Japan, the twin-funnelled *Amatsukaze* bears a strong resemblance to the classic Japanese destroyers of World War II. Despite the clear deck area aft, the ship cannot operate helicopters.

'Luta' class 163 with its two sets of upward tilted and swivelling anti-ship missile launchers clearly visible, each being located immediately aft of the ship's raked twin funnels.

A frontal aspect of Aconit *(D609) of the French Navy.*

Luta Class Destroyers

Role: General-purpose.
Builders: Various, Chinese Peoples' Republic.
User: Navy of the Chinese Peoples' Republic.
Basic data: 3960 tons full displacement; 418.3ft (127.5m) overall length; 42.3ft (12.9m) maximum beam.
Crew: Around 300.
Propulsion: 2 geared steam turbines (total 60,000shp); 2 propellers.
Sensors: 1 long-range air search radar; 1 short-range combined air/sea search radar; 1 navigational radar; 2 separate types of fire control radars (not fitted to all ships); 1 or more hull-mounted sonars.
Armament: 2 triple SS-N-2 Styx-type anti-ship missile launchers; 2 twin 130mm dual-purpose guns; 4 twin 57mm or 37mm anti-aircraft guns; 2 twin 25mm anti-aircraft guns; 2 twelve-barrelled 250mm anti-submarine rocket launchers; 2 depth charge racks; mines.
Top speed: 32 knots.
Range: 4000 nautical miles at 15 knots.
Programme: Believed to be at least a ten-ship class, the lead ship was constructed at the Luta Shipyards in Kuangchou, with others known to have been built in Shanghai shipyard. The first of class is reported to have entered service during 1972. One of this class is known to have exploded and sunk in August 1978. Known pennant numbers given to these ships include: 105, 106, 107, 131, 132, 160 and 163.
Notes: Although very similar in layout and general appearance to the Soviet Navy's 'Kotlin' class destroyers, the 'Luta' design is somewhat heavier, in part attributable to the installation of the two large triple-tubed anti-ship missile launchers which the 'Kotlins' lack. While the 'Luta' class pack a potentially potent anti-ship weapons punch, the effectiveness of this primary armament could well be diluted in a modern combat environment as a result of the seeming lack of current technology shipboard sensors.

Aconit Type Destroyer

Role: Anti-submarine.
Builder: DCAN Lorient, France.
User: French Navy.
Basic data: 3840 tons full displacement; 416.7ft (127.0m) overall length; 44.0ft (13.4m) maximum beam.
Crew: 232.
Propulsion: 1 Rateau double reduction geared steam turbine (31,500shp); 1 propeller.
Sensors: 1 DRBV 22A air search and height finder (3-D) radar; 1 DRBN 32 sea search and navigational radar; 1 DRBV 13 fire control radar (Malafon); 1 DRBC 32B gun fire control radar; 1 DUBV 23 bow-mounted sonar; 1

DUBV 43 variable depth sonar; SENIT III automated action information data-processing system.
Armament: 1 Malafon anti-submarine missile launcher; 2 single 100mm Model 1968 dual-purpose guns; 1 quadruple 305mm anti-submarine rocket mortar; 2 heavyweight anti-submarine torpedo catapults. *Note:* 4 MM 40 Exocets are being fitted during current refit, replacing the originally fitted 305mm anti-submarine rocket mortar.
Top speed: 27 knots.
Range: 5000 nautical miles at 18 knots.
Programme: The sole *Aconit* (F609), or Type C 65 design, was laid down in 1967, launched in March 1970 and entered service in March 1973. Scheduled to undergo modernisation refit in the 1983/4 period.
Notes: All the evidence points to the *Aconit* being something of an unfruitful excursion in meeting its operational design aims; the mission requirement of which is now being met by the 'Georges Leygues' class destroyers. Unlike these later destroyers, *Aconit* carries no pad or facilities from which to operate anti-submarine helicopters, little effective anti-air capability from aft attack and seems potentially more vulnerable to mechanical failure than most warships, thanks to its single propeller shaft propulsion.

D'Estrees Class Destroyers

Role: Anti-submarine.
Builder: DCAN (Various), France.
User: French Navy.
Basic data: 3740 tons full displacement; 434.7ft (132.5m) overall length; 41.7ft (12.72m) maximum beam.

The 'D'Estrees' class destroyer Vauquelin *(D628), 1978.*

La Galissoniere (D638) seen here flag bedecked and with her crew standing at their review stations.

Crew: 269.

Propulsion: 2 Rateau geared steam turbines (total 63,000shp); 2 propellers.

Sensors: 1 DRBV 22A air search radar; 1 DRBV 50 surface search radar; 1 Decca/DRBN 32 sea search and navigational radar; 2 SPG-51C fire control radars (Malafon); 2 DRBC 32A fire control radars (100mm guns); 1 DUBV 23 hull-mounted sonar; 1 DUBV 43 towed variable depth sonar; SENIT automated action information data processing system.

Armament: 2 single 100mm Model 1968 dual-purpose guns; 1 Malafon anti-submarine missile launcher (13 missiles); 1 twin Oerlikon 20mm anti-aircraft gun; 1 sextuple Bofors 375mm anti-submarine rocket launcher; 2 triple heavyweight anti-submarine torpedo tubes.

Top speed: 32 knots.

Range: 5000 nautical miles at 18 knots.

Programme: Five Type 47 destroyers completed in 1956/7 were converted and modernised to undertake anti-submarine duties between the beginning of 1968 and 1971. These 'D'Estrees' class vessels as they are known comprise: *Maille Breze* (D627), *Vauquelin* (D628), *D'Estrees* (D629), *Casabianca* (D631) and *Guepratte* (D632). All should be phased out of service by 1989.

Notes: Embodying the traditionally handsome lines of the heavy twin-funnelled French destroyers of the inter-war years, the 'D'Estrees' class's primary anti-submarine armament consists of the Latecoere-designed Malafon missile with a range of up to 6.5 nautical miles and a speed of around 500mph.

La Galissoniere Class Destroyers

Role: Anti-submarine.

Builder: DCAN Lorient, France.

User: French Navy.

Basic data: 3740 tons full displacement; 435.7ft (132.8m) overall length; 41.7ft (12.7m) maximum beam.

Crew: 272.

Propulsion: 2 Rateau geared steam turbines (total 63,000shp); 2 propellers.

Sensors: 1 DRBV 22A air search radar; 1 DRBV low-level air and sea search radar; 1 DRBN 32 sea search and navigational radar; 1 DRBC 32A fire control radar; 1 URN 20 TACAN aircraft homer; 1 DUBV 23 bow-mounted sonar; 1 DUBV 43 variable depth sonar.

Armament: Aerospatiale Alouette III helicopter; 1 Malafon anti-submarine missile launcher; 2 single 100mm Model 1953 dual-purpose guns; 2 triple heavyweight torpedo launchers.

Top speed: 34 knots.

Range: 5000 nautical miles at 18 knots.

Programme: The sole T-56 destroyer *La Galissoniere* (D638) was laid down in November 1958, launched in March 1960 and entered service in July 1962. Scheduled for disposal during 1990.

Notes: Initially employed as an anti-submarine warfare and sonar trials ship, *La Galissoniere*, or sole Type 56 destroyer represents the final variant of the basic French Type 47 design. The Latecoere Malafon missile launcher is positioned forward of the stern-mounted variable depth sonar and aft of the elevated helipad, the base of which serves as the magazine for the 13 Malafon reloads. The helipad sides fold up to form a weatherproof hangar for the helicopter when the machine is not in use.

Hatsuyuki Class Destroyers

Role: General-purpose.

Builders: Various, Japan.

User: Japanese Maritime Self-Defence Force.

Basic data; 3700 tons full displacement; 432.1ft (131.7m) overall length; 44.9ft (13.7m) maximum beam.

Crew: 190.

Propulsion: 2 Kawasaki-built Rolls-Royce Olympus TM3B gas turbines (total 56,780shp) or 2 Rolls-Royce Type RM1C gas turbines (total 10,680shp); COGOG; 2 controllable-pitch propellers. *Note:* later ships will employ a Rolls-Royce Spey-Tyne COGAG arrangement similar to that fitted to 'Broadsword' Batch II and III class Royal Navy frigates.

Sensors: 1 OPS-18 long-range air search radar; 1 OPS-14B sea search and navigational radar; 1 FCS-2 (missile) and 1 GFCS-2 (gun) fire control radars; 1 OQS-4 hull-mounted sonar; automated action information data-processing system.

Armament: 1 Kawasaki-built SH-3 Sea King helicopter; 2 quadruple Harpoon anti-ship missile launchers; 1 octuple Sea Sparrow point air defence missile launcher; 1 octuple ASROC anti-submarine missile launcher; 1 single 76mm, OTO-Melara compact dual-purpose gun; 2 Phalanx 20mm close-in weapons systems; 2 triple lightweight anti-submarine torpedo tubes.

Top speed: 30 knots.

Range: Over 4500 nautical miles at 18 knots.

Programme: A planned 12-ship class, of which all had been ordered on an incremental basis by the spring of 1984. The lead ship, *Hatsuyuki* (DDG122) was ordered in 1977, laid down in March 1979, launched in November 1980 and delivered in March 1983, following extended lead of class trials. *Shirayuki* (123), *Mireyuki* (124), *Sawuyuki* (125) and *Hamayuki* (126) *Isokuki* (127), *Haruyuki* (128), *Yamayuki* (129), *Matsuyuki* (130), along with 131, 132 and 133 had all been laid down between December 1979 and May 1984; the first 7 having been completed by the end of 1984. Five shipyards are involved in the programme: Sumitomo as the lead yard, along with Hitachi, Mitsubishi, Ishikawajima and Mitsui.

Japan's Hatsuyuki *(DDG122), lead of this 12-ship class. Note the tall mainmast, bulky funnel and aft superstructure.*

Notes: While the weapons fit of the 'Hatsuyuki' class is still biased towards the anti-submarine warfare role, these destroyers carry a good secondary anti-ship and defensive anti-air armament capability: aspects that reflect both the quantitative and qualitative growth of the Soviet naval presence around the Japanese islands within the past 15 or more years. Of equal technical interest is the Japanese Maritime Self-Defence Force's selection of British rather than US propulsive machinery for these ships; a choice that ran counter to the previous Japanese naval preference either to buy or build adaptations of US systems and equipment. The construction of the 'Hatsuyuki' class represents the largest single Japanese naval programme to be put underway since World War II and will add considerably to the stature of this already respectably-sized navy.

Daring Class Destroyers

Role: General-purpose.
Builders: Various UK and Australian.
Users: Navies of Australia and Peru.
Basic data: 3700 tons full displacement; 390ft (118.9m) overall length; 43ft (13.1m) maximum beam.
Crew: 321.
Propulsion: 2 Parsons geared steam turbines (total 54,000shp); 2 propellers.
Sensors: 1 Hollandse LWO2 long-range air search radar; 1 Hollandse sea search and navigational radar; 2 Hollandse M22 fire control radars; 3 sonars (Types 162, 170 and 174). *Note:* sensors as for Australian ship.
Armament: 3 twin 4.5in dual-purpose Mk 6 guns; 2 twin and 2 single Bofors 40mm anti-aircraft guns; 1 triple-barrel Limbo anti-submarine mortar.
Top speed: 32 knots.
Range: 3700 nautical miles at 20 knots.
Programme: In the late 1940s, the Australian Government decided to procure two locally-built examples of the Royal Navy's 'Daring' class destroyer. The lead Australian ship, HMAS *Vendetta* (D08), was laid down at the Naval Dockyard, Williamstown, in July 1949 and commissioned in November 1958. The second Australian ship, HMAS *Vampire* (D11), was laid down at the Cockatoo Island yards, Sydney, in July 1952 and was commissioned in June 1959. Both of these vessels went through a major modernisation programme in 1972. A third 'Daring' class destroyer, HMAS *Duchess* (D154), was purchased from the Royal Navy in 1972 for use as a training ship. Peru bought two ex-Royal Navy 'Darings' in 1969, comprising *Palacios* (D74) and *Ferre* (D75). Delivered in 1973, following refitting, both ships had aft-

The Royal Australian Navy's HMAS Vampire *(D11).*

mounted helipads fitted in 1975. HMAS *Vendetta* was paid off and taken out of service in October 1979.
Notes: The largest destroyers to enter service with the Royal Navy up to the advent of the missile-carrying 'County' class, the 'Daring' class ships were commissioned between 1949 and 1952.

Gearing Class Destroyers

Role: Anti-submarine.
Builders: Various, USA.
Users: Navies of Argentina, Brazil, Ecuador, Greece, Mexico, Pakistan, South Korea, Spain and Taiwan.
Basic data: 3520 tons full displacement; 390.5ft (119m) overall length; 40.85ft (12.45m) maximum beam.
Crew: Around 275.
Propulsion: 2 geared steam turbines (total 60,000shp); 2 propellers.
Sensors: 1 SPS-40 long-range air search radar; 1 SPS-10 sea search and navigational radar; 1 SQS-23 hull-mounted sonar.
Armament: The original weapons fit comprised: 3 twin 5in guns; 12 single 40mm anti-aircraft guns; 10 heavyweight anti-submarine torpedo tubes (some ships had 16 anti-aircraft guns, no torpedoes). Most ships currently operate with only 2 twin 5in guns and 2 triple

Sachtouris (D214) serves with the Greek Navy.

A Modified 'Kildin' class Soviet destroyer.

The Royal Swedish Navy's Halland *(J18), now in reserve.*

lightweight anti-submarine torpedo tubes. Argentine ships carry 2 twin Exocet anti-ship missile launchers, while South Korean ships carry 2 quadruple Harpoon anti-ship missile launchers; 1 octuple ASROC anti-submarine missile launcher is fitted to ships of the Brazilian, Pakistani and Spanish navies. Argentinian, Greek and Spanish vessels have a helicopter pad immediately aft the rear superstructure.

Top speed: 33 knots.
Range: 4000 nautical miles at 20 knots.
Programme: A 98-ship class built between 1945 and 1952.
Notes: Essentially the 'Allen M Sumner' class design stretched by 14 feet (4.27m) amid ships. Around 45 remain in service.

Modified Kildin/Kildin Class Destroyers

Role: Anti-ship.
Builders: Various, USSR.
User: Soviet Navy.
Basic data: 3500 tons full displacement; 413ft (126m) overall length; 42.3ft (12.9m) maximum beam.
Crew: 300.
Propulsion: 2 geared steam turbines (total 72,000shp); 2 propellers.
Sensors: 1 long-range air search radar; 1 sea search and navigational radar; 3 fire control radars; 1 hull-mounted sonar.
Armament: 4 single SS-N-2C anti-ship missile launchers on Modified ships only (1 single SS-N-1 anti-ship cruise missile launcher on sole Kildin); 2 twin 76mm anti-aircraft guns on Modified ships only, 4 quadruple 57mm anti-aircraft guns; 2 RB6000 twelve-barrel 250mm anti-submarine rocket launchers; 2 twin heavyweight anti-submarine torpedo tubes.
Top speed: 34 knots.
Range: 4000 nautical miles at 18 knots.
Programme: This four-ship class completed at the close of the 1950s comprises: *Bedovy, Neuderzhimyy, Prozorlivyy* and *Neulovimyy*. All but the latter ship were converted to Modified 'Kildins' between 1973 and 1975. It is doubtful if the remaining vessel, which serves with the Soviet Pacific fleet, will be converted.
Notes: A development of the earlier 'Kotlin' class anti-submarine destroyers, the 'Kildins' represent an interim design solution to the anti-carrier centred task group ship requirement, aimed at supplementing the 'Kashin' class destroyers already in service.

Halland Class Destroyers

Role: General-purpose.
Builders: Gotaverkin, Eriksberg and Kockums, Sweden.
Users: Navies of Sweden and Colombia.

Basic data: 3450 tons full displacement; 397.1ft (121.05m) overall length; 41.3ft (12.6m) maximum beam.
Crew: 290 (Sweden), 248 (Colombia).
Propulsion: 2 De Laval geared steam turbines (total 57,000shp); 2 propellers.
Sensors: 1 Scanter 009 (Swedish) or Hollandse LWO 3 (Colombian) air search radar; 1 Thomson-CSF (Swedish) or Hollandse (Colombian) low-level air/sea search and navigational radar; 1 each Hollandse M22 and Philips (Swedish) 9LV200 fire control radars on Swedish ships or 6 SGR-102 fire control radars on Colombian ships; 1 hull-mounted passive active sonar system (Swedish ships only).
Armament: 1 single SAAB RBO8A anti-ship missile launcher (Swedish ships only); 2 twin (Swedish) or 3 twin (Colombian) 120mm Bofors dual-purpose guns; 1 twin 57mm Bofors dual-purpose gun (Swedish only); 6 single (Swedish) or 4 (Colombian) 40mm Bofors anti-aircraft guns; 2 quadruple 375mm Bofors anti-submarine rocket launchers; 8 (Swedish) or 4 (Colombian) heavyweight anti-submarine torpedo tubes; mines (Swedish ships only).
Top speed: 35 knots.
Range: 3000 nautical miles at 20 knots.
Programme: Originally planned as a four-ship Royal Swedish Navy class, initially authorised in 1948, only two ships, *Halland* (J18) and *Smaland* (J19), were to enter Swedish service in June 1955 and January 1956, respectively. When Sweden cancelled the mid-1950s-placed order for its second pair, Colombia stepped in to acquire them as *Veinte de Julio* (D05) and *Siete de Agosto* (D06), these ships entering service in June and October of 1958, respectively. *Halland* is now in reserve, but *Smaland* remains in service, as do the Colombian destroyers.
Notes: Big ships by European destroyer design standards of the period, the 'Halland' class ships were also technically advanced for their day, particularly in terms of their fully automatic, high-rate-of-fire 120mm primary gun armament. The two Colombian destroyers are reported to have a reduced top speed of around 25 knots.

Almirante Brown Class Destroyers

Role: General-purpose.
Builder: Blohm und Voss, Federal Germany.
User: Argentinian Navy.
Basic data: 3360 tons full displacement; 412.1ft (126.6m) overall length; 43.1ft (15.0m) maximum beam.
Crew: 230.
Propulsion: 2 Rolls-Royce TM3B Olympus gas turbines (total 56,800shp) or 2 Rolls-Royce Tyne RM1C gas turbines (total 10,800shp); COGOG; 2 controllable-pitch propellers.
Sensors: 1 Hollandse DA 08A air search radar; 1 Decca 1226 sea search and navigational radar; 1 each Hollandse STIR (for missiles) and WM25 (for guns) fire

Almirante Brown *(D10) and* La Argentina *(D11) sailing in company.*

Espirito Santo *(D38) of the Brazilian Navy.*

control radars; 1 Hollandse LIROD optronic fire control system; 1 Krupp Atlas 80 hull-mounted sonar; SATIR automated action information data-processing system.
Armament: 2 Lynx-sized helicopters; 8 MM 40 Exocet anti-ship missile launchers; 1 octuple Aspide point air defence missile launcher; 1 single 127mm OTO-Melara compact dual-purpose gun; 4 twin 40mm Breda/Bofors close-in weapons systems; 2 triple lightweight anti-submarine torpedo tubes.
Top speed: 30.5 knots.
Range: 4500 nautical miles at 18 knots.
Programme: Ordered by the Argentinian Government in December 1978, the original contract was for six ships, four of which were to be built in Argentina. However, by July 1979, the contract was ratified around four ships, all to be built by Blohm und Voss, while Argentina was to build six of the smaller Blohm und Voss MEKO 140 corvettes in its own shipyards. The four Argentinian destroyers are a variant of the basic Blohm und Voss MEKO 360 design and comprise; *Almirante Brown* (D10), *La Argentina* (D11), *Heroina* (D12) and *Sarandi* (D13). All launched between the close of March 1981 and the end of August 1982, *Almirante Brown* was accepted by the Argentinian Navy in February 1983, with the remaining three ships completed by mid-1984.
Notes: The class differs from the initial MEKO 360 design (see the Nigerian Navy's *Arudu* frigate) in that it employs an all gas turbine propulsive arrangement, supplied by Rolls-Royce and saving some 320 tons in terms of the ships' full displacement. In terms of sensors and weapons fit, these four destroyers add a new and formidable element to the Argentinian Navy's overall capability, particularly in terms of its short-range and close-in anti-air defence. In this respect, the ships radar-directed four-barrels-per side 40mm gun system could well prove a useful counter against both the manned aircraft and current generation high subsonic sea-skimming missile threat. Two other design aspects of these ships are of interest, namely, the MEKO building block system for the various weapons and electronics shipboard packages employed, along with the choice of construction materials used. In the case of the MEKO building block philosophy, which involves pre-packaging virtually everything from gun mountings to prime propulsive machinery, even if it may be costly in compelling the operator to hold a larger inventory of onshore spares than would otherwise be needed, the system significantly reduces the amount of time that the ship has to spend in dock, non-operational. Turning to the materials employed within both hull and superstructure, it is interesting to note that the builders have elected to use steel throughout; a choice that cannot but enhance the ship's survivability in terms of tolerance to battle damage.

Allen M Sumner Class Destroyers

Role: Anti-submarine.
Builders: Various, USA.
Users: Navies of Argentina, Brazil, Colombia, Greece, Iran, South Korea, Taiwan, Turkey and Venezuela.
Basic data: 3320 tons full displacement; 376.5ft (114.8m) overall length; 41ft (12.5m) maximum beam.
Crew: Around 265.
Propulsion: 2 geared steam turbines (total 60,000shp); 2 propellers.
Sensors: 1 SPS-40 long-range air search radar; 1 SPS-10 sea search and navigational radar; Mk 25 fire control radar; 1 SQS-29 hull-mounted sonar (some ships have SQA-10 variable depth sonar).
Armament: Originally comprised: 3 twin 5in guns; 12 single 40mm anti-aircraft guns; 10 heavyweight anti-submarine torpedo tubes. Currently, all but the ships of Argentina and Iran retain the full 5in gun fit. All ships now carry 6 lightweight anti-submarine torpedo tubes in place of the heavyweight originals. In terms of anti-ship missiles, the Argentinians carry 2 twin Exocet, while the Iranian ships have 2 quadruple Harpoon launchers plus 1 quadruple Standard area air defence missile launcher. The Brazilian ships carry 1 quadruple Seacat point air defence missile launcher. Virtually all ships can operate 1 helicopter.
Top speed: 33 knots.
Range: 4400 nautical miles at 15 knots.
Programme: Originally a 58-ship class built between 1942 and 1943, four were lost during World War II, with a fifth scrapped in 1947.
Notes: 24 remain in service at the time of going to press.

Almirante Williams Class Destroyers

Role: General-purpose.
Builder: Vickers, UK.
User: Chilean Navy.
Basic data: 3300 tons full displacement; 402ft (122.5m) overall length; 43ft (13.1m) maximum beam.
Crew: 266.
Propulsion: 2 Parsons-Paramtreda geared steam turbines (50,000shp); 2 propellers.
Sensors: 1 Plessey AWS-1 long-range air search radar; 1 SGR 102 height finder (3-D) radar; 1 Marconi sea search and navigational radar; 2 Hollandse M-4 missile fire control radars; 1 Type 164B hull-mounted sonar.
Armament: 2 twin Exocet anti-ship missile launchers; 4 single 4in dual-purpose guns; 2 quadruple Seacat point air defence missile launchers; 4 single Bofors 40mm anti-aircraft guns; 2 triple lightweight anti-submarine torpedo tubes; 2 Squid anti-submarine mortars.
Top speed: 34.5 knots.

Almirante Riveros, *(D18) at speed.*

Range: 7800 nautical miles at 18 knots.
Programme: This two-ship class comprises *Almirante Riveros* (D18) and *Almirante Williams* (D19). Laid down by Vickers at Barrow-in-Furness between June 1956 and April 1957, the ships joined the Chilean Navy in December 1960 and March 1960, respectively.
Notes: Designed very much in the mould established by the British destroyers of World War II, the 'Almirante Williams' class carry a respectable anti-ship capability. Both ships were refitted by Vickers during the first half of the 1970s.

Skoryy and Modified Skoryy Classes Destroyers

Role: General-purpose.
Builders: Various, USSR.
Users: Navies of USSR and Egypt.
Basic data: 3200 tons full displacement; 397.6ft (121.1m) overall length; 39.4ft (12.0m) maximum beam.
Crew: From 218 to 272.
Propulsion: 2 geared steam turbines (total 60,000shp); 2 propellers.
Sensors: 1 long-range air search radar; 2 or 3 sea search and navigational radars; 2 to 4 gun fire control radars; 1 hull-mounted sonar; naval tactical information system.
Armament: 2 SS-N-2A 'Styx' anti-ship missile launchers (1 Egyptian ship only); 2 twin 130mm dual-purpose guns; 1 twin 85mm and 7 or 8 twin and single mounted 37mm (plus 2 or 3 twin 25mm on Modified Skoryy) anti-aircraft guns; 2 sixteen-barrelled 250mm RBU-2500 anti-submarine rocket launchers (on Modified Skoryy only); 1 or 2 quintuple heavyweight anti-submarine torpedo tubes; 2 depth charge racks; 50 mines.
Top speed: 33 knots.
Range: 3000 nautical miles at 18 knots.
Programme: Originally a 72-ship class delivered to the Soviet Navy between 1949 and 1953, only 16 were

A standard 'Skoryy' class destroyer of the Soviet Navy.

thought to be still in Soviet service, along with four Egyptian operated vessels at the end of 1982. About eight of these destroyers were converted into Modified 'Skoryy' class ships at the beginning of the 1960s; the conversion adding more anti-air firepower and the RBU-2500 anti-submarine rocket launchers. The Egyptian ships, transferred in pairs during 1956 and 1967, comprise: 6 *October, Al Zaffer, Damiet* and *Suez; Al Zaffer* being the sole 'Styx' equipped example.
Notes: The 'Skoryy' class represents the first post-World War II Soviet destroyer production programme and marked something of a break with former Soviet destroyer design practice that had displayed the effects of strong German influences during the late 1930s and early 1940s.

Akizuki Class Destroyers

Role: Anti-submarine.
Builder: Mitsubishi, Japan.
User: Japanese Maritime Self-Defence Force.
Basic data: 3100 tons full displacement; 387.1ft (118.0m) overall length; 39.4ft (12.0m) maximum beam.
Crew: 330.
Propulsion: 2 geared steam turbines (total 45,000shp); 2 propellers.
Sensors: 1 OPS 1 long-range air search radar; 1 OPS-15 sea search and navigational radar; 3 Mk 34 gun fire control radars; 1 SQS-23 hull-mounted sonar; 1 OQA 1 variable depth sonar; naval tactical information system.
Armament: 3 single 5in Mk 39 dual-purpose guns; 2 twin 3in Mk 33 anti-aircraft guns; 1 quadruple heavyweight anti-submarine torpedo tube; 2 triple Mk 32 lightweight anti-submarine torpedo tubes; 1 quadruple 375mm Bofors anti-submarine rocket launcher; 2 trainable Mk 15 anti-submarine mortars.
Top speed: 32 knots.
Range: 5600 nautical miles at 18 knots.
Programme: This two-ship class comprises: *Akizuki* (DD161) and *Teruzuki* (DD162). Both laid down in mid-1958, the ships were launched in June 1959 and entered service in February 1960.
Notes: Twin-funnelled, low-profiled destroyers, these ships carried a fairly powerful anti-air gun armament for their day in order to fulfil their secondary role of providing anti-air protection for accompanying ships. These 'Akizuki' class vessels are scheduled for early retirement from front-line service, but may be retained in some auxiliary role.

Akizuki (DD161), lead of this two-ship class.

The former Dutch destroyer Overijssel, *now serving as the Peruvian Navy's* Bolognesi (D70).

The Hellenic (Greek) Navy's Aspic (D06).

Friesland Class Destroyers

Role: General-purpose.
Builders: Various, Netherlands.
User: Peruvian Navy.
Basic data: 3100 tons full displacement; 380.6ft (116m) overall length; 38.6ft (11.8m) maximum beam.
Crew: 280.
Propulsion: 2 Parsons geared steam turbines (total 60,000shp), 2 propellers.
Sensors: 1 Hollandse LWO 2 long-range air search radar; 1 Decca 1229 sea search and navigational radar; 1 Hollandse DA 05 low-level air and sea search radar; 1 Hollandse M 45 fire control radar; 1 Hollandse CWE 610 hull-mounted sonar.
Armament: 2 twin 120mm dual-purpose guns; 4 single 40mm Bofors anti-aircraft guns; 2 quadruple Bofors 375mm anti-submarine mortars; 1 depth charge rack.
Top speed: 36 knots.
Range: 4000 nautical miles at 18 knots.
Programme: This eight-ship class comprised HNLMS *Friesland* (D812), HNLMS *Groningen* (D813), HNLMS *Limburg* (D814), HNLMS *Overijssel* (D815), HNLMS *Drenthe* (D816), HNLMS *Utrecht* (D817), HNLMS *Rotterdam* (D818) and HNLMS *Amsterdam* (D819). All were sold to Peru between 1980 and 1982 and seven were known to have entered service as: *Galvez* (D78), *Capitan Quinones* (D76), *Bolognesi* (D70), *Guise* (D72), *Castilla* (D71), *Diez Canseco* (D79) and *Villar* (D77). *Note:* These Peruvian ships are listed in the same order as the Dutch, starting with the former D813.
Notes: Commissioned between 1956 and 1958, these robustly-built two-funnelled destroyers are still useful workhorses and will probably remain in service beyond the year 2000.

Fletcher Class Destroyers

Role: General-purpose.
Builders: Various, USA.
Users: Navies of Argentina, Brazil, Chile, Greece, Mexico, Peru, South Korea, Spain, Taiwan and Turkey.
Basic data: 2850 tons full displacement; 376.8ft (114.85m) overall length; 39.5ft (12.0m) maximum beam.
Crew: around 265.
Propulsion: 2 geared steam turbines (total 60,000shp); 2 propellers.
Sensors: All ships carry 1 SPS-6 air search radar and 1 SPS-10 sea search and navigational radar. All ships fitted with sonar, mainly SQS-4 or -29. Various fire control radars equip the ships of Brazil, Greece, Spain, Taiwan and Turkey.
Armament: Original fit comprised: 5 single 5in guns; 6 or 10 single 40mm anti-aircraft guns; 10 heavyweight torpedo tubes and depth charges. Some ships still carry the full primary gun complement, but most now only carry 4. Similarly, only the navies of Brazil, South Korea and Spain retain the 40mm guns, the rest having switched to 6 single 76mm guns. Anti-submarine torpedoes are still carried, but current installations consist of either 5 heavyweight or 6 lightweight torpedo tubes. All ships still mount a Hedgehog depth charge mortar.
Top speed: 32-36 knots.
Range: 5000 nautical miles at 15 knots.
Programme: In all, 180 'Fletcher' class destroyers were built in numerous US shipyards between 1942 and 1944.
Notes: Over 40 of these elderly ships still serve in mid-1985.

Minegumo Class Destroyers

Role: Anti-submarine.
Builders: Various, Japan.
User: Japanese Maritime Self-Defence Force.
Basic data: 2750 tons full displacement; 377ft (114.9m) overall length; 37.7ft (11.8m) maximum beam.
Crew: 215.
Propulsion: 6 Mitsubishi 12UEV 30/40 diesels (total 26,500bhp); 2 propellers.
Sensors: 1 OPS 11 long-range air search radar; 1 OPS 17 surface search and navigational radar; 1 SPG-34 gun fire control radar; 1 OQS 3 hull-mounted sonar; 1 SQS-35 towed variable depth sonar on F118.
Armament: 2 twin 76mm dual-purpose guns; 1 Bofors 375mm anti-submarine rocket launcher; 2 triple lightweight anti-submarine torpedo tubes. *Note:* F118

Minegumo (D116) of the Japanese Maritime Self-Defence Force.

carries 1 octuple Mk 16 launcher for ASROC anti-submarine missile aft and has had aft twin gun turret replaced by 1 single 76mm OTO-Melara gun. All 3 ships will be fitted with ASROC and all 3 will end up with OTO-Melara guns.

Top speed: 27 knots.

Range: 7000 nautical miles at 20 knots.

Programme: This three-ship class comprises *Minegumo* (D116), *Natsugumo* (D117) and *Murakumo* (D118), built by Mitsui, Uraga and Maizuru, respectively. Laid down between March 1967 and October 1968, all three ships entered service between August 1968 and August 1970.

Notes: Finely proportioned, handsome ships, the 'Minegumo' class are a development of the 'Yamagumo' class vessels. The 'Minegumos' may be most economic vessels to operate but appear generally under-armed, particularly in terms of anti-air capability.

Yamagumo (D113) exhibits its very clean lines.

Yamagumo Class Destroyers

Role: Anti-submarine.

Builders: Various, Japan.

User: Japanese Maritime Self-Defence Force.

Basic data: 2700 tons full displacement; 377ft (114.9m) overall length; 38.7ft (11.8m) maximum beam.

Crew: 237.

Propulsion: 6 Mitsubishi 12UEV diesels (total 26,500bhp); 2 propellers.

Sensors: 1 OPS-11 air search radar; 1 OPS-17 sea search and navigational radar; 2 GFCS 2 gun fire control radars; 1 SQS-23 hull-mounted sonar; 1 SQS-35J variable depth sonar.

Armament: 2 twin 76mm dual-purpose guns; 1 octuple ASROC anti-submarine missile launcher; 1 quadruple 375mm Bofors anti-submarine rocket launcher; 2 triple lightweight anti-submarine torpedo tubes.

Top speed: 27 knots.

Range: 7000 nautical miles at 20 knots.

Programme: This six-ship class comprises; *Yamagumo* (D113), *Makigumo* (D114), *Asagumo* (D115), *Aokumo* (D119), *Akigumo* (D120) and *Yugumo* (D121). Constructed in four separate shipyards, the class was laid down between March 1964 and February 1976, the ships entering service between January 1966 and March 1978. The ships are scheduled to undergo major refits during the earlier part of the 1980s.

Notes: Based on the 'Minegumo' class destroyers, the 'Yamagumo' class, as with other Japanese surface combatants, carry a very heavy anti-submarine armament at the expense of anti-air capability. The class carries no facilities for helicopter operation.

Murasame Class Destroyers

Role: Anti-submarine.

Builders: Various, Japan.

User: Japanese Maritime Self-Defence Force.

Basic data: 2400 tons full displacement; 360ft (109.7m) overall length; 36ft (11m) maximum beam.

Crew: 250.

Propulsion: 2 geared steam turbines (total 35,000shp); 2 propellers.

Sensors: 1 OPS-15 long-range air search radar; 1 OPS-1 sea search and navigational search radar; 3 Mk 34 gun fire control radars; 1 OQA-1 variable depth sonar.

Armament: 3 single 5in Mk 39 dual-purpose guns; 2 twin 76mm dual-purpose guns; 1 Mk 15 Hedgehog anti-submarine mortar; 2 triple lightweight anti-submarine torpedo tubes.

Top speed: 30 knots.

Range: 6000 nautical miles at 18 knots.

Programme: This three-ship class comprises *Murasame* (D107), *Yudachi* (D108) and *Harusame* (D109); all laid down between December 1957 and June 1958. Respective commissioning dates for the three-ships were February 1959, March 1959 and December 1959.

Notes: Similar in hull form and machinery layout to the smaller 'Ayanami' class destroyers, the 'Murasame' class must now be considered obsolescent, particularly in the context of modern air and surface threats. The primary 5in gun armament fitted to this class were removed from the US Navy's 'Midway' class aircraft carriers.

Ayanami Class Destroyers

Role: Anti-submarine.

Builders: Various, Japan.

User: Japanese Maritime Self-Defence Force.

Basic data: 2400 tons full displacement; 357.6ft (109.0m) overall length; 35.1ft (10.7m) maximum beam.

Crew: 230.

Propulsion: 2 geared steam turbines (total 35,000shp); 2 propellers.

Sensors: 1 OPS 15 long-range air search radar; 1 OPS 1 or 2 sea search and navigational radar; 2 Mk 34 gun fire control radars; 1 OQS 12 or 14 hull-mounted sonar; 1 OQA 1 variable depth sonar (on DD103, 104, 110 only); naval tactical information system.

Armament: 3 twin 3in Mk 33 anti-aircraft guns; 1 quadruple heavyweight anti-submarine torpedo tube (not

Murasame (D107), the Mitsubishi-built lead of class.

Ayanami *(DD103), the Mitsubishi-built lead of class.*

on DD104, 106); 2 triple lightweight anti-submarine torpedo tubes (not on DD110, 111); 2 Mk 15 trainable anti-submarine mortars.

Top speed: 32 knots.
Range: 6000 nautical miles at 18 knots.
Programme: This seven-ship class comprises: *Ayanami* (DD103), *Isonami* (DD104), *Uranami* (DD105), *Shikinami* (DD106), *Takanami* (DD110), *Onami* (DD111) and *Makinami* (DD112). Responsibility for construction lay with Mitsubishi for DD103 and 104, Kawasaki for DD105, Mitsui for DD106 and 110, Ishikawajima Heavy Industries for DD111, along with Iino for DD112. All were launched between June 1957 and April 1960, and all entered service between February 1958 and October 1960. DD104 and 106 were converted to the training ship role during 1975/76 period by having their amidships quadruple heavyweight torpedo tubes removed and replaced by a classroom.
Notes: The ageing, low-profile twin-funnelled destroyers will be replaced by the 'Hatsuyuki' class destroyers in front line service, with a few of the 'Ayanami' class retained in the training role.

Frigates

Broadsword Class Batch II and III Frigates

Role: Anti-submarine.
Builders: Yarrow and Swan Hunter, UK.
User: Royal Navy.
Basic data: 4350 tons (early Batch II) to 5000 tons (Batch III) full displacement; 479.25ft (146.1m) overall length; 48.5ft (14.75m) maximum beam.
Crew: 250 (Batch II); around 270 (Batch III).
Propulsion: 2 Rolls-Royce Olympus TM3B gas turbines (total 54,400shp) or 2 Rolls-Royce Tyne RM1C gas turbines (total 10,680shp); COGOG on F92, F93, and F95; others have 2 Rolls-Royce Spey Sm1A gas turbines (total 36,000shp) and 2 Rolls-Royce Tyne RM1C gas turbines (total 10,680shp); COGAG. All ships have 2 controllable-pitch propellers.
Sensors: 1 Type 968 air search radar; 1 Type 967 (back-to-back) sea search radar; 1 Type 1006 navigational radar; 2 Type 911 Sea Wolf fire control radars; 1 Type 2016 hull-mounted sonar; Ferranti CAAIS automated action information data-processing system. **Armament:** 2

A model of the gun-equipped 'Broadsword' Batch III frigate with EH-101 helicopter aft.

Westland Lynx helicopters; 4 MM38 Exocet anti-ship missile launchers; 2 sextuple Sea Wolf point air defence missile launchers; 2 triple lightweight anti-submarine torpedo tubes; 2 single 40mm Bofors anti-aircraft guns (to be supplemented by 2 multi-barrelled 30mm Hollandse/General Electric Goalkeeper close-in weapons systems on all ships); 1 single 4.5in Mk 8 dual-purpose gun to be fitted to Batch III ships.
Top speed: 30 knots (early Batch II) or 28 knots (all others).
Range: 4500 nautical miles at 18 knots.
Programme: Ordered between April 1979 and December 1982, the six ships of Batch II comprises: HMS *Boxer* (F92), HMS *Beaver* (F93), HMS *Brave* (F94), HMS *London* (F95), HMS *Sheffield* (F96) and HMS *Coventry* (F98); all but the latter two Swan Hunter-built ships, being constructed by Yarrow, the lead yard. The initial order for two of the reported planned three Batch III procurement was placed with Yarrow in December 1982, followed by two further ships in January 1985. The Batch III vessels so far identified are the lead, HMS *Cornwall* (F99) and the second ship, HMS *Cumberland* (F85). A fifth Batch III is planned.
Notes: With the design of the Batch II finalised long before

This sea trials view of HMS Boxer *(F92) emphasises the newly adopted, highly raked 'clipper' bow.*

the Falklands War could be foreseen, the new elongated hull and combined gas and gas (COGAG) propulsion arrangement promise to give these later 'Broadsword' ships more fuel space, more fuel ecomony and, hence, more actual autonomy through reducing their reliance on frequent refuelling. The Batch III ships clearly reflect some of the Falklands War lessons in terms of weapons fit.

Broadsword Class Batch I Frigates

Role: Anti-submarine.
Builder: Yarrow, UK.
User: Royal Navy.
Basic data: 4000 tons full displacement; 430ft (131m) overall length; 48.5ft (14.75m) maximum beam.
Crew: 248.
Propulsion: 2 Rolls-Royce TM3B Olympus gas turbines (total 56,000shp) or 2 Rolls-Royce RM1A Tyne gas turbines (total 8500shp); COGOG; 2 controllable-pitch propellers.
Sensors: 1 Marconi Type 968 air search radar; Marconi Type 967 (back-to-back) surface search radar; 1 Kelvin Hughes Type 1006 sea search and navigational radar; 2 Marconi Type 910 Seawolf fire control radars; 1 Plessey Type 2016 hull-mounted sonar; Ferranti CAAIS automated action data-processing system.
Armament: 2 Westland Lynx helicopters, 2 twin Exocet anti-ship missile launchers; 2 sextuple Seawolf close-in air defence missile launchers; 2 Bofors 40mm anti-aircraft guns; 2 Plessey STWS triple lightweight anti-submarine torpedo tubes.
Top speed: 30 knots.
Range: 4500 nautical miles at 19 knots.
Programme: Yarrow received an initial contract to support Ministry of Defence Navy by providing lead yard services for the Type 22 'Broadsword' class frigate development in July 1972. Orders for the first batch of four ships, HMS *Broadsword* (F88), HMS *Battleaxe* (F89), HMS *Brilliant* (F90) and HMS *Brazen* (F91), followed at intervals of roughly a year between February 1974 and October 1977, these ships being accepted in February 1979, December 1979, April 1981 and September 1982, respectively.
Notes: The Type 22 'Broadswords' are the first Royal Navy ships to be built to metric measurements and are also the first not to embody any primary gun armament from design inception. Probably the most expensive and complex part solution to the anti-submarine problem yet devised (around £90 million fully equipped unit price in 1981 values), the 'Broadswords' were designed as a major element of an all-weather anti-submarine task group using air, surface and sub-surface units in the hostile waters of the Greenland/Faroes Gap. Indeed, even in the latter 1970s, there were powerful critics within the Royal Navy who were arguing that there really was no future for the frigate, especially ones as expensive as the 'Broadswords'. Ironically, as the Falklands conflict was to highlight dramatically, HMS *Broadsword* and HMS *Brilliant* were to place a vital role, albeit in the context of employing their highly effective radar-guided Seawolf point air defence missile systems.

Tromp Class Frigates

Role: General-purpose.
Builder: De Schelde, Netherlands.
User: Royal Netherlands Navy.
Basic data: 4308 tons full displacement; 452.75ft (138m) overall length; 48.9ft (14.9m) maximum beam.
Crew: 306.
Propulsion: 2 Rolls-Royce TM3B Olympus gas turbines

HMS Brilliant *(F90) transiting the Clyde, October 1981.*

HNLMS De Ruyter *(F806) showing her V-shaped funnels and enclosed primary radar housing.*

(derated to total 44,000shp) or 2 Rolls-Royce Tyne RM1C gas turbine (total 8200shp); COGOG; 2 controllable-pitch propellers.
Sensors: 1 Hollandse SPS-01 long-range (3-D) air search radar; 1 Hollandse ZW05 sea search and navigational radar; 1 Hollandse WM25 fire control radar; 2 Hollandse SPG-51C fire control radar; 1 Hollandse CWE 610 hull-mounted sonar; Hollandse SEWACO automated data processing system.
Armament: 1 Westland Lynx helicopter; 2 quadruple Harpoon anti-ship missile launchers; 1 Standard area air defence launcher system with 40 missiles; 1 octuple Sea Sparrow short-range air defence missile launcher; 1 twin 120mm Bofors dual-purpose gun; 2 triple anti-submarine lightweight torpedo tubes.
Top speed: 28 knots.
Range: 5000 nautical miles at 18 knots.
Programme: This two-ship class comprises HNLMS *Tromp* (F801) and HNLMS *De Ruyter* (F806), laid down in August and December 1971, respectively. *Tromp* was launched in June 1973 and entered service in October 1975, while *De Ruyter* was launched in March 1974 and joined the fleet in June 1976.
Notes: These two large frigates exemplify the enormous strides made in shipborne armaments brought about by the introduction of the guided missile, ilustrated by the fact that these ships pack considerably more firepower with greater strike range than that carried aboard the two nearly 12,000 ton cruisers that they replaced. Characterised by the massive bulbous radome that covers the ship's powerful 3-D surveillance radar, the two 'Tromp' class frigates serve as the flagships of the Royal Netherlands Navy, being used as the respective leaders of the two Netherlands Navy long-range, deep water task groups. Comparable in size to the Royal Navy's 'Sheffield' class destroyers and the 'Broadsword' class frigates, the 'Tromps' carry a more balanced armament than either of their British counterparts, particularly in terms of the

An artist's impression of HMCS Halifax (FFH330) in service.

'Tromp's' two tier surface-to-air missile defences and the retention of twin dual-purpose gun as a back up to both the air defence and anti-ship missiles. In terms of weapons fit, itself a function of the ship's envisaged primary role, the 'Tromp's' armament mix seems to follow that of the Soviet's 'Kashin' class destroyer that first appeared in 1962, as does that of Italy's 'Audace' class destroyer, a near contemporary of the 'Tromp' frigates.

Halifax Class Frigates

Role: Anti-submarine.
Builders: St John Shipbuilding (lead), Canada.
User: Royal Canadian Navy.
Basic data: 4200 tons full displacement; 488.0ft (133.5m) overall length; 53.8ft (16.4m) maximum beam.
Crew: 250.
Propulsion: 2 General Electric LM2500 gas turbines (total 40,000shp); 1 Pielstick diesel; CODOG; 2 propellers.
Sensors: 1 SPS-49 long-range air search radar; 1 LM Ericsson Sea Giraffe low-level air and sea search radar; 1 sea search and navigational radar; 2 Raytheon fire control radars for Sea Sparrow; 1 hull-mounted and 1 towed array sonar systems; automated action information data-processing system.
Armament: 1 Sikorsky Sea King helicopter; 2 quadruple Harpoon anti-ship missile launchers; 2 octuple siloes for vertically launched Sea Sparrow point air defence missiles; 1 single 57mm Bofors SAK 57 Mk 2 dual-purpose gun; 1 Mk 15 Phalanx 20mm close-in weapons system; 2 triple lightweight anti-submarine torpedo tubes.
Top speed: 28 knots.
Range: 4500 nautical miles at 18 knots.
Programme: In late December 1977, the Canadian

The Spanish Navy's Baleares (F71) with Standard area air defence missile launcher aft.

Federal Government announced its decision to proceed with the design and development of a new six-ship class, then known as the Canadian Patrol Frigate (CPF). Initially five companies presented bids in response to the August 1978 request for tenders, subsequently being whittled down to two by July 1981; St John Shipbuilding and Drydock being announced as the prime contractor and lead yard in June 1983. In order to spread the employment impact of the programme, three ships will be built by St John Shipbuilding and Drydock, while three others will be built by Marine Industries. The class comprises: HMCS *Halifax* (FFH330), HMSC *Vancouver* (FFH331), HMCS *Ville de Quebec* (FFH332), HMCS *Toronto* (FFH333), HMCS *Regina* (FFH334) and HMCS *Calgary* (FFH335). HMCS *Halifax* is scheduled to be laid down in July 1985, launched in July 1986, commence trials in September 1988 and enter service in February 1989. The 2nd ship, HMCS *Vancouver*, is scheduled to enter service in March 1990, with the third through sixth frigate joining the fleet at six-monthly intervals finishing in March 1992.
Notes: Designed as a replacement for the elderly 'St Laurent' class frigates, the 'Halifax' class continues the strong Canadian tradition of producing large, rough water, dedicated anti-submarine vessels. The installation of a three-tier air defence capability in the shape of the point air defence missiles, the rapid-fire 57mm Bofors gun and the close-in Phalanx system are a great improvement on that found on earlier Canadian warships, including the larger 'Iroquois' class destroyers, and shows a somewhat belated recognition of the need to defend against incoming missile attack. The low-profiled 'Halifax' class employs a steel hull and light alloy superstructure. The targeted overall cost of this six-ship programme was quoted as Canadian $3.414 billion in 1983/4 values.

Baleares Class Frigates

Role: Area air defence.
Builder: Bazan, Spain.
User: Spanish Navy.
Basic data: 4177 tons full displacement; 438.0ft (133.8m) overall length; 46.75ft (14.25m) maximum beam.
Crew: 256.
Propulsion: 1 Westinghouse geared steam turbine (35,000shp); 1 propeller.
Sensors: 1 SPS-52A long-range air search and height finder (3-D) radar; 1 SPS-10 sea search radar; 1 Decca TM1226 sea search and navigational radar; 1 SPG-51C and 1 SPG-53B fire control radars for Standard missiles; 1 SQS-23 hull-mounted sonar; 1 SQS-35 variable depth sonar; NTDS automated action information data processing system.
Armament: 1 Hughes 500 helicopter; 1 single Mk 22 launcher for 16 Standard area air defence missiles; 1 single 5in Mk 42 dual-purpose gun; 1 octuple ASROC anti-submarine missile launcher; 2 middleweight anti-submarine torpedo tubes; 1 quadruple lightweight anti-submarine torpedo tube.
Top speed: 27 knots.
Range: 4500 nautical miles at 20 knots.
Programme: This five-ship class comprises: *Baleares* (F71), *Andalucia* (F72), *Cataluña* (F73), *Asturias* (F74) and *Extremedura* (F75). All were laid down between October 1968 and November 1971 and entered service between September 1973 and November 1976.
Notes: A Spanish-built variant of the US Navy's 'Knox' class frigates, the 'Baleares' class trades off the facilities to operate a shipboard helicopter against the installation of the Standard area air defence missile launcher. The 'Baleares' class ships are being retrofitted with the Spanish-developed 20mm Meroka close-in weapons system and are scheduled to have Harpoon anti-ship missiles added during the early-to-mid 1980s.

Knox Class Frigates

Role: General-purpose.
Builders: Various, USA and Bazan, Spain.
Users: US and Spanish Navies.
Basic data: 4100 tons full displacement; 438ft (133.8m) overall length; 46.75ft (14.25m) maximum beam.
Crew: 266.
Propulsion: 1 Westinghouse geared steam turbine (35,000shp); 1 propeller.
Sensors: 1 SPS-40 air search radar; 1 SPS-10 sea search and navigational radar; 1 SPS-58 low-level air threat warning radar; 1 Mk 115 missile fire control radar; 1 Mk 68 gun fire control radar; 1 SPG-53 surface target fire control radar; 1SQS-26CX bow-mounted sonar; 1 SQS-18 towed array sonar; NTDS automated action information data-processing.
Armament: 1 Kaman SH-2 Seasprite (US) or Hughes 500 (Spanish) helicopter; 1 octuple Mk 25 launcher for Sea Sparrow point air defence missiles in US ships or 1 single Mk 22 launcher for Standard MR area air defence missiles on Spanish ships; 1 octuple Mk 16 launcher for ASROC anti-submarine missiles or Harpoon anti-ship missiles; 1 single 5in Mk 42 dual-purpose gun; 4 lightweight anti-submarine torpedo tubes.
Top speed: 28 knots.
Range: 4000 nautical miles at 20 knots.
Programme: The first of the US Navy's 46 'Knox' class vessels was laid down in October 1965 and the first of Spain's five 'Baleares' class ships in October 1968. Builders involved in the US programme were Todd Shipyards, Lockheed and Avondale Shipyards (the latter building most), while all five Spanish frigates were built in Bazan's el Ferrol yards. The US class comprises: USS *Knox* (FF1052), USS *Roark* (FF1053), USS *Gray* (FF1054), USS *Hepburn* (FF1055), USS *Connole* (FF1056), USS *Rathburne* (FF1057), USS *Meyerkord* (FF1058), USS *W S Sims* (FF1059), USS *Lang* (FF1060), USS *Patterson* (FF1061), USS *Whipple* (FF1062), USS *Reasoner* (FF1063), USS *Lockwood* (FF1064), USS *Stein* (FF1065), USS *Marvin Shields* (FF1066), USS *Francis Hammond* (FF1067), USS *Vreeland* (FF1068), USS *Bagley* (FF1069), USS *Downes* (FF1070), USS *Badger* (FF1071), USS *Blakely* (FF1072), USS *Robert E Peary* (FF1073), USS *Harold E Holt* (FF1074), USS *Trippe* (FF1075), USS *Fanning* (FF1076), USS *Quellet* (FF1077), USS *Joseph Hewes* (FF1078), USS *Bowen* (FF1079), USS *Paul* (FF1080), USS *Alwin* (FF1081), USS *Elmer Montgomery* (FF1082), USS *Cook* (FF1083), USS *McCandless* (FF1084), USS *Donald B Beary* (FF1085), USS *Brewton* (FF1086), USS *Kirk* (FF1087), USS *Barbey* (FF1088), USS *Jesse L Brown* (FF1089), USS *Ainsworth* (FF1090), USS *Miller* (FF1091), USS *Thomas C Hart* (FF1092), USS *Capodanno* (FF1093), USS *Pharris* (FF1094), USS *Truett* (FF1095), USS *Valdez* (FF1096), and USS *Moinester* (FF1097), all of these ships being commissioned between April 1969 and November 1974. The five Spanish ships comprise: *Baleares* (F71), *Andalucia* (F72), *Cataluna* (F73), *Asturias* (F74) and *Extremadura* (F75), all commissioned between September 1973 and November 1976.
Notes: The 'Knox' class form the backbone of the US Navy's frigate strength and are readily identified by the large centrally-mounted combined mast and stack (funnel), referred to as a 'mack'.

Krivak I/II Classes Frigates

Role: Anti-submarine.
Builder: Zhdanov, Kaliningrad, etc., USSR.
User: Soviet Navy.
Basic data: Around 4000 tons full displacement; 410ft (125m) overall length; 47ft (14.3m) maximum beam.

USS Blakely *(FF1072) operating with the US Atlantic Fleet.*

Crew: 200.
Propulsion: 2 gas turbines (total 50,000shp); 2 propellers.
Sensors: 1 long-range air search radar; 1 sea search and navigational radar; 5 fire control radars; 1 hull-mounted sonar; 1 towed variable depth sonar; naval tactical information system and satellite-fed data links.
Armament: 4 SS-N-14 anti-submarine missile launchers; 2 twin SA-N-4 surface-to-air missile launchers; 2 twin 76mm anti-aircraft guns in Krivak Is, or 2 single 100mm dual-purpose guns in Krivak IIs; 2 anti-submarine rocket launchers; 2 quadruple 21 inch anti-submarine torpedo tubes; mines.
Top speed: 31 knots.
Range: 700 nautical miles at 30 knots.
Programme: The first 'Krivak' class frigate put to sea during 1970 and construction of the class continues, with a known 32 ships having entered Soviet service by the end of 1983, reportedly completing the build programme. At least five Soviet shipyards were reported to have been involved in the construction of the known 17 ship 'Krivak' I programme, with Kaliningrad delivering the first of the 'Krivak' IIs in 1976. The differences between the 'Krivak' Is and IIs lie in the substitution of heavier calibre guns in the aft turrets of the 'Krivak' IIs, along with the incorporation of an improved variable depth sonar.
Notes: The 'Krivak' class frigates exemplify the Soviet Navy's philosophy of packing as much weaponry into their vessels as possible. Indeed, even despite the 'Krivak' class's lack of a helicopter, the class still carries more anti-

Krivak II Razitel'nyj *October 1979.*

Bremen (F207) in initial sea trials, May 1981.

submarine weaponry than any other ship of comparable size, such as the Royal Navy's 'Broadsword' class. In comparison with the contemporary 'Kresta' II cruiser, it is interesting to note that the 'Krivaks' mount identical primary armament and only fall short in terms of lacking an area air defence missile system of the larger Soviet ship. Along with the 'Kresta' IIs, the emergence of the 'Krivak' class frigates marked a major shift in Soviet naval mission emphasis, in which the role of the ships was clearly dedicated towards killing submarines, unlike the previous practice of equipping vessels with the kind of cruise missiles best suited to conducting long-range engagements against carrier-centred task groups. The SS-N-14 'Silex' anti-submarine missiles that form the 'Krivak' class's primary armament are reported to have a maximum effective range of around 25 nautical miles, which they cover at a high subsonic speed of around Mach 0.95, or around 645mph.

Bremen Class Frigates

Role: General-purpose.
Builders: Various, Federal Germany.
User: Federal German Navy.
Basic data: 3800 tons full displacement; 426.5ft (130m) overall length; 47.25ft (14.4m) maximum beam.
Crew: 200.
Propulsion: 2 General Electric LM2500 gas turbines (total 50,000shp) or 2 MTU Type 20V 956 TB 92 diesels (total 10,400bhp); CODOG; 2 controllable-pitch propellers.
Sensors: 1 Hollandse DA 08 air and sea search radar; 1 SMA 3 RM 20 sea search and navigational radar; 1 Hollandse WM25 and 1 Hollandse STIR fire control radars; 1 Krupp Atlas DSQS-21BZ hull-mounted sonar; SATIR automated action information data-processing.
Armament: 2 Westland Lynx helicopters; 2 quadruple Harpoon long-range anti-ship missile launchers; 1 single 76mm OTO-Melara dual-purpose gun; 1 octuple Sea Sparrow point air defence missile launcher; 2 twin lightweight anti-submarine torpedo tubes; provision for twin 24-cell RAM close-in air defence missile launchers.
Top speed: 30 knots.
Range: 4000 nautical miles at 18 knots.
Programme: The first six of what was to be a 12-ship class were ordered in July 1977. The ninth through twelfth ships were cancelled in mid-1980, while plans to build a seventh and eighth vessels have been dropped. The six frigates currently completed are *Bremen* (F207), *Niedersachen* (F208), *Rheinland-Pfalz* (F209), *Emden* (F210), *Koln* (F211) and *Karlsruhe* (F212). The construction programme has been spread widely around the West German naval shipbuilders, with Bremer Vulkan acting as lead yard and responsible for the building of F207 and sensor/weapon system fitment to all vessels. Blohm und Voss, the large Hamburg-based yard, built

HNLMS Kortenaer *(F807), 1978.*

F209 and F211, while AG Weser built F208 and Thyssen Nordseewerke built F210 and Howaldtswerke-Deutsche Werft built F212. All six frigates were launched between September 1979 and January 1982, at which time the lead ship *Bremen* (F207) was undergoing extended sea trials and was accepted in May 1982. All six ships had been completed by the end of 1984.
Notes: Conceived as replacement for the existing Type 120 or 'Koln' class frigates, the Type 122 or 'Bremen' class design is based on the Dutch-developed 'Standard' or 'Kortenaer' class hull, but breaks with the Dutch design in adopting a combined diesel or gas turbine machinery solution. While the primary anti-ship and air defence missile complement of the Dutch and West German ships is the same, the 'Bremens' carry only 1 OTO-Melara 76mm gun, deleting the Dutch vessel's aft-mounted 76mm for space provision in which to fit the General Dynamics-developed RAM rapid response, close-in air defence missile system. The 'Bremen' class frigates' DA 08 medium-range radar is quoted as being able to detect an incoming combat aircraft at around 45 nautical miles, while the Sea Sparrow missiles are effective out to around 8 nautical miles and altitudes up to around 20,000 feet.

Kortenaer Class Frigates

Role: Anti-submarine.
Builder: De Schelde and Wilton-Fijenoord (F823, F824 only), Netherlands.
Users: Royal Netherlands Navy, Hellenic (Greek) Navy.
Basic data: 3750 tons full displacement; 420ft (128m) overall length; 47.3ft (14.4m) maximum beam.
Crew: 200.
Propulsion: 2 Rolls-Royce TM3B Olympus gas turbines (total 56,800shp) or 2 Rolls-Royce Tyne RM1C gas turbines (total 10,800shp); COGOG; 2 controllable-pitch propellers.
Sensors: 1 Hollandse LW 08 long-range 3-D air search radar; 1 Hollandse DA 06 sea search and navigational radar; 1 Hollandse M45 fire control radar (76mm gun); 1 Hollandse fire control radar (Sea Sparrow); 1 Hollandse SQS 505 hull-mounted sonar; Hollandse SEWACO automated action information data-processor. *Note:*F812 and F813 carry an additional Hollandse DA06 air search 3.D radar.

A Yarrow model of the Royal Navy's latest Type 23 frigate as completed. Note the forward deck silo for the ship's 32 vertically launched Sea Wolf point air defence missiles.

Armament: 2 Westland Lynx helicopters; 2 quadruple Harpoon anti-ship missile launchers; 1 octuple Sea Sparrow close-in air defence missile launcher; 2 single 76mm OTO-Melara dual-purpose guns; 2 twin lightweight anti-submarine torpedo tubes. *Note:* F812 and F813 have 1 single Mk 13 launcher for Standard area air defence missiles in place of helicopter hangar.
Top speed: 30 knots.
Range: 4700 nautical miles at 16 knots.
Programme: Currently a 14-ship class, the original 12 Dutch vessels were ordered in three batches (four each) between August 1974 and December 1976, the first keel being laid in April 1975. In September 1980, Greece placed an order for one of this class and took options to buy two more (one to be built in Greece). The Greek need for early delivery led the Dutch to reallocate what should have been their sixth ship to Greece and the same procedure was followed with the planned seventh Dutch vessel, when Greece took up its first option in July 1981. The Dutch ships, along with the year of their completion, are: *Kortenaer* (F807) 1978, *Callenburgh* (F808) 1979, *Van Kinsbergen* (F809) 1980, *Banckert* (F810) 1980, *Piet Heyn* (F811) 1981, *Abraham Crijnssen* (F816) 1982, *Philips van Almonde* (F823) 1981, *Bloys van Treslong* (F824) 1982, *Jan van Brakel* (F825) 1982 and *Peter Florisz* (F826) 1983. The two modified ships, *Jacob Van Heemskerck* (F812) 1984 and *Witte de With* (F813) 1985, are referred to as 'Pieter Florisz' class frigates. The two Greek vessels, so far ordered are *Elli* (F450) 1981 and *Lemnos* (F451) 1982.
Notes: Initially referred to as Standard or S frigates (relating to the Standard NATO Frigate concept around which they were designed), the 'Kortenaer' class, display functional, relatively compact lines. In functional terms, the 'Kortenaers' primary role is the same as that of the Royal Navy's 'Broadswords', US Navy's 'Perry' class and French Navy's 'Georges Leygues' vessels. While of the four rival designs, the French vessels would appear to carry the most comprehensive anti-submarine package of sensors and weapons, the 'Kortenaers' embody the most balanced sensor/weapons fit in terms of offensive and defensive armament. Under a collaborative agreement signed in 1975 between the West German and Dutch Governments, the hull and much of the 'Kortenaer's' internal design layout has been adopted as the basis for West Germany's Type 122 'Bremen' class frigate.

Duke Class Frigates

Role: Anti-submarine.
Builder: Yarrow (Lead Yard), UK.
User: Royal Navy.
Basic data: 3700 tons full displacement; 436.4ft (133.0m) overall length; 51.8ft (15.8m) maximum beam.
Crew: 177.
Propulsion: 2 Rolls-Royce Spey SM1A gas turbines (total 36,000shp) or/and 4 Paxman Valenta diesel generators (total 12,700bhp) used to drive 2 electric propulsion motors; CODLAG; 2 propellers.
Sensors: 1 undesignated combined low-level air/sea search and navigational radar; 2 Type 911 Sea Wolf fire control radars; 1 optronic fire control system; 1 Type 2050 hull-mounted and 1 towed array sonar; Ferranti automated action information data-processing system.
Armament: 1 Sea King or EH-101 sized anti-submarine helicopter; 2 quadruple Harpoon anti-ship missile launchers; silo for 32 vertically launched Sea Wolf point air defence missiles; 1 single 4.5in Vickers Mk 8 dual-purpose gun; 2 single 30mm Oerlikon anti-aircraft guns; 4 fixed tubes for lightweight anti-submarine torpedoes.
Top speed: Around 28 knots.
Endurance: Over 7000 nautical miles.
Programme: As lead yard for the projected Royal Navy Type 23 frigate Yarrow received their first design contract for this vessel during the latter half of 1982, followed by a contract, to proceed with the construction of the lead ship, HMS *Norfolk* (F...) in October 1984. Contracts for the building of a second and third of class were being negotiated during the spring of 1985. The 'Duke' class should form the backbone of the Royal Navy's anti-submarine surface force by the year 2000.
Notes: Marginally longer and broader than a Batch I 'Broadsword' class frigate, the Type 23 design incorporates a number of innovations for a British warship in terms of both weapons fit and propulsive machinery arrangement. In the context of weaponry the Type 23 will be the first Royal Navy operational ship to deploy the vertically launched Sea Wolf system; an advance that promises to both extend the range of this highly agile point air defence missile and permit more missiles to be instantly available for launch in the case of a saturation attack from multiple threats. Turning to the novel-for-frigate propulsive machinery arrangement, the Type 23's system has been described as Combined Diesel electric And Gas, or CODLAG; a combination that is claimed will enhance the performance of the ship's anti-submarine sensors by reducing ship's machinery-generated noise levels fairly significantly. Another aspect

A trio of 'Perry' class, comprising USS Jack Williams *(FFG24), USS* Antrim *(FFG20) and USS* Oliver Hazard Perry *(FFG7), July 1982.*

of more than passing interest to naval manpower planners is the Type 23's much reduced crew complement: more than a third down on that required to man a Batch II 'Broadsword'; a factor that reflects very favourably in the context of overall ship operating costs. Somewhat more austerely armed and equipped versions of the Type 23 are planned to meet export market needs. The unit cost of £110 million is quoted for the Type 23 frigate in 1984/5 values, exclusive of development costs.

Oliver Hazard Perry Class Frigates

Role: General-purpose.
Builders: Bath Iron Works & Todd Shipyards, USA; Bazan, Spain and Williamstown Dockyards, Australia.
Users: Navies of the USA, Australia and Spain.
Basic data: 3700 tons full displacement; 445ft (135.6m) overall length; 45ft (13.7m) maximum beam.
Crew: 180.
Propulsion: 2 General Electric LM2500 gas turbines (total 40,000shp); COGAG; 1 controllable-pitch propeller.
Sensors: 1 SPS-49 long-range air search radar; 1 SPS-55 sea search and navigational search radar; 1 SPG-60 STIR fire control radar (missile); 1 Mk 92 fire control radar (gun); 1 SQS-56 hull-mounted sonar; NTDS automated action information data-processing.
Armament: 2 up to Sikorsky SH-60 Seahawk sized helicopters; 1 single Mk 13 launcher for either Standard MR area air defence missiles or Harpoon anti-ship missiles; 1 single 76mm Mk 75 anti-aircraft gun; 1 Phalanx 20mm close-in weapons system; 2 triple lightweight anti-submarine torpedo tubes.
Top speed: 28 knots.
Range: 4000 nautical miles at 20 knots.
Programme: With design work on this class initiated in January 1971, an order for the lead ship, USS *Oliver Hazard Perry* (FFG7), was placed in October 1973. Laid down by the Bath Iron Works in June 1975, the *Perry* was launched in September 1976 and formally entered service in December 1977. From inception, construction of the class was split roughly half-and-half, between the lead yard, East Coast-based Bath Iron Works, and the West Coast-based Todd Shipyards. By late 1983, the US Navy had ordered 50 of this class but a further ten planned to be contracted between 1984 and 1987 failed to materialise. The US Navy's so far identified ships comprise: *Oliver Hazard Perry* (7), *McInerney* (8), *Wadsworth* (9), *Duncan* (10), *Clark*(11), *George Philip* (12), *Samuel E Morison* (13), *John H Sides* (14), *Estocin* (15), *Clifton Sprague* (16), *John A Moore* (19), *Antrim* (20), *Flatley* (21), *Fahrion* (22), *Lewis B Puller* (23), *Jack Williams* (24), *Copeland* (25), *Gallery* (26), *Mahlon S Tisdale* (27), *Boone* (28), *Stephen W Groves* (29), *Reid* (30), *Stark* (31), *John L Hall* (32), *Jarrett* (33), *Aubrey Fitch* (34), *Underwood* (36), *Crommelin* (37),*Curts* (38), *Doyle* (39), *Halyburton* (40), *McCluskey* (41), *Klakring* (42), *Thach* (43), *De Wert* (45), *Rentz* (46), *Nicholas* (47), *Vandergrift* (48), *Robert G Bradley* (49), *Gary* (51), *Carr* (52), *Hawes* (53), *Ford* (54), *Elrod* (55), *Simpson* (56), *Reuben James* (57), *Samuel B Roberts* (58), (59), *Rodney M Davis* (60). The first export customer for the 'Perry' class was the Royal Australian Navy, who have ordered four ships from Todd Shipyards, comprising HMAS *Adelaide* (FFG01), commissioned in November 1980; HMAS *Canberra* (FFG02), commissioned in March 1982; HMAS *Sydney* (FFG03), commissioned in January 1983 and HMAS *Darwin* (FFG04) joining in 1984. Two additional Australian frigates were ordered in late 1983, both to be built locally by Williamstown Dockyards. Spain is building five vessels of this class in their own yards, the first of these Bazan-built ships being laid in mid-1981. The Spanish ships comprise: *Navarra* (FFG81), *Murcia* (FFG82) *Leon* (FFG83), plus FFG84 and FFG85.
Notes: Unlovely-looking ships, the 'Perry' class were designed for modular assembly to facilitate high-rate series production. In operational terms, the 'Perry' class has been produced to provide oceangoing escort for merchantmen or a naval amphibious task force. As a

result of the potential combat damage vulnerability of the single shaft/propeller arrangement adopted for the ship (itself an economy measure allowing the use of a standard 'Spruance' class propulsion cell to be employed), the 'Perry' class frigates are equipped with two diesel-driven retractable thrusters that can propel the ship through the water at up to 5 knots, should the main propulsion be lost. The position of the 76mm OTO-Melara gun, between mast and funnel, significantly limits its arcs of fire.

Aradu Type Frigate

Role: General-purpose.
Builder: Blohm und Voss, Federal Germany.
User: Nigerian Navy.
Basic data: 3680 tons full displacement; 412.1ft (125.6m) overall length; 43.1ft (15.0m) maximum beam.
Crew: 230.
Propulsion: 2 Rolls-Royce TM3B Olympus gas turbines (56,800shp) or 2 MTU 20V956 TB92 diesels (total 11,070bhp); CODOG; 2 controllable-pitch propellers.
Sensors: 1 Plessey AWS 5D long-range air search and height finder (3-D) radar; 1 Decca TM1226 sea search and navigational radar; 1 Hollandse WM 25 fire control radar and automated action information data-processing system; 1 Hollandse STIR fire control radar (missiles); 1 Hollandse PHS 32 hull-mounted sonar.
Armament: 1 Lynx helicopter; 8 MM 40 Exocet anti-ship missile launchers; 1 octuple Albatros (Sea Sparrow) point air defence missile launcher; 1 single 127mm OTO-Melara dual-purpose gun; 4 twin 40mm Breda/Bofors L70/40 anti-aircraft guns; 2 triple lightweight anti-submarine torpedo tubes.
Top speed: 29 knots.
Range: 4500 nautical miles at 18 knots.
Programme: The sole Nigerian ship, NNS *Aradu* (F89) was ordered in November 1977, launched in January 1980 and entered service in July 1981.
Notes: NNS *Aradu* represents the first of the Blohm und Voss designed and developed MEKO 360 family to be sold. NNS *Aradu* is a MEKO 360H-1 design, signifying that it carries only one helicopter, unlike the subsequent Argentinian 'Almirante Brown' class MEKO 360H-2 destroyers that can accommodate two machines. The Nigerian ship also differs from the later Argentinian vessels in employing a gas turbine/diesel propulsion arrangement, as opposed to the all gas turbine system adopted by the Argentinian Navy.

Niteroi Class Frigates

Roles: Anti-submarine (AS) version: F40, F41, F44 and F45. General-purpose (GP) versions: F42 and F43.
Builders: Vosper Thornycroft, UK: F40, F41, F42 and F43. Brazilian Naval Dockyards, Brazil: F44 and F45.
User: Brazilian Navy.
Basic data: 3645 tons full displacement; 424ft (129.2m) overall length; 44.25ft (13.5m) maximum beam.
Crew: 201.
Propulsion: 2 Rolls-Royce TM3B Olympus gas turbines (total 56,000shp) or 4 MTU MA 16V 956 diesels (total 14,560bhp); CODOG; 2 controllable-pitch propellers.
Sensors: 1 Plessey AWS-2 air search radar/IFF; Hollandse ZW06 sea search and navigational radar; 2 Selenia Orion fire control radars; 1 Edo 610E hull-mounted sonar (plus Edo 700E variable depth towed sonar in AS versions); Ferranti CAAIS automated data-processing.
Armament: 1 Westland Lynx helicopter; 4 Exocet anti-ship missile launchers (GP version only); 1 Vickers 4.5in Mk 8 gun (a second Mk 8 gun is fitted at the stern of GP version); 1 Ikara anti-submarine missile launcher (fitted

NNS Aradu *(F89), flagship of the Nigerian Navy.*

to AS version only); 2 triple Seacat short range air defence missile launchers; 1 twin Bofors 375mm anti-submarine rocket launcher; 2 Bofors 40mm L70 guns; 2 Plessey triple anti-submarine lightweight torpedo tubes.
Top speed: 30 knots.
Range: 5300 nautical miles at 17.5 knots.
Programme: Early in 1970, the Brazilian Government invited tenders for a new six-ship class of large frigate, the contract for which was won by Vosper Thornycroft in September 1971. Under the terms of the contract, Vosper Thornycroft would build the first four ships, while two more would be built in Brazil. All laid down between June 1972 and June 1975, the four Vosper-built ships, *Niteroi* (F40), *Defensora* (F41), *Constituicao* (F42) and *Liberal* (F43), were all accepted between November 1976 and November 1978, while the two Brazilian-built vessels, *Independencia* (F44) and *Unico* (F45), entered service in November 1979 and September 1980, respectively, after having both been laid down in June 1972.
Notes: These Mark 10 frigates, to use the builder's designation, clearly carry the stamp of Vosper Thornycroft in almost every line of their beautifully proportioned hull and superstructure. Larger and heavier than Vosper Thornycroft's 'Amazon' class that immediately preceded them through the company's yards, the 'Niteroi' class provide yet another example of the growth in size of the modern frigate, being considerably heavier and more powerfully armed than the ex-US World War II 'Gearing', 'Sumner' and 'Fletcher' class destroyers that had formed the backbone of the Brazilian Navy's fleet during the latter 1960s and early 1970s. In comparison with the elder US vessels, the 'Niteroi' class not only sail significantly further, but

Niteroi (F40) anti-submarine frigate with Westland Wasp on helipad.

The 'Garcia' class frigate, USS Brumby *(FF1044).*

thanks to the Ferranti-developed computer assisted action data-processing system can fight more efficiently and operate with a crew complement reduced by around 25 per cent compared with the older US destroyers.

Garcia Class Frigates

Role: Anti-submarine.
Builder: Various, USA.
User: US Navy.
Basic data: 3400 tons full displacement; 414.5ft (126.3m) overall length; 44.2ft (13.5m) maximum beam.
Crew: 270.
Propulsion: 1 Westinghouse geared steam turbine (35,000shp); 1 propeller.
Sensors: 1 SPS-40 long-range air search radar; 1 SPS-10 sea search and navigational radar; 1 Mk 35 fire control radar; 1 SQS-26 bow-mounted sonar; 1 SQR-15 towed array sonar system; NTDS automated action information processing system.
Armament: 1 Kaman SH-2 Seasprite helicopter (except FF1048 and FF1050); 2 single 5in Mk 30 dual-purpose guns; 1 octuple MI 16 ASROC anti-submarine missile launcher; 2 triple lightweight anti-submarine torpedo tubes.
Top speed: 27 knots.
Range: 4000 nautical miles at 20 knots.
Programme: A 10-ship class, the first keel was laid in October 1962 and the last ship completed by July 1968. Shipyards were Bethlehem Steel, being responsible for the first and second, Avondale Shipyards built the third, fourth and fifth, Defoe Shipbuilding completed the sixth, eighth and tenth, and Lockheed Shipbuilding delivered the seventh and ninth. The class consists of USS *Garcia* (FF1040), USS *Bradley* (FF1041), USS *Edward McDonnell* (FF1043), USS *Brumby* (FF1044), USS *Davidson* (FF1045), USS *Voge* (FF1047), USS *Sample* (FF1048), USS *Koelsck* (FF1049), USS *Albert David* (FF1050), and USS *O'Callahan* (FF1051).
Notes: Contemporaries of the 'Brooke' class but lacking effective air defence capability.

Amazon Class Frigates

Role: General-purpose.
Builder: Vosper Thornycroft and Yarrow, UK.
User: Royal Navy.
Basic data: 3250 tons full displacement; 385ft (117.0m) overall length; 41.75ft (12.7m) maximum beam.
Crew: 171.
Propulsion: 2 Rolls-Royce TN3B Olympus gas turbines (total 56,000shp) or 2 Rolls-Royce Tyne RMIA gas turbines (total 8000shp); COGOG; 2 controllable-pitch propellers.
Sensors: 1 Type 992Q air search radar; 1 Decca Type 978 sea search and navigational radar; 2 Selenia Orion missile/gun fire control radars; 4 hull-mounted sonars (Types 162M, 170B, 174 and 184).
Armament: A Westland Lynx helicopter; 4 Exocet anti-ship missile launchers; 1 Vickers 4.5in Mk 8 gun; 1 quadruple Seacat surface-to-air missile launcher; 2 Oerlikon 20mm guns; 2 triple anti-submarine lightweight-torpedo tubes.
Top speed: 32 knots.
Range: 4300 nautical miles at 17 knots.
Programme: All eight of these Type 21 frigates, as the ships were first known, were ordered within a 20-month period commencing late March 1969, the first three as set out below being ordered from Vosper Thornycroft, the lead yard, while the last five were contracted from Yarrow. The ships and their commissioning dates are: HMS *Amazon* (F169), May 1974; HMS *Antelope* (F170), July 1975; HMS *Active* (F171), June 1977; HMS *Ambuscade* (F172), September 1975; HMS *Arrow* (F173), July 1976; HMS *Alacrity* (F174), July 1977; HMS *Ardent* (F184), October 1977; and HMS *Avenger* (F185), May 1978. Two of the class, F170 and F184 were lost in action during May 1982.
Notes: Sleek, fast and agile, the Type 21 or 'Amazon' class ships established a number of precedents when they came into service, being the first Royal Navy warships of modern times not to have been designed by that service, along with which, they were the first Royal Navy warship to be designed around all gas turbine propulsion from the outset. The fruit of a collaborative design effort between Vosper Thornycroft and Yarrow, in which the former were to lead, the 'Amazons' made extensive use of aluminium within the ship's superstructure, saving some

HMS Ardent *(F184) lost to enemy air action in Falklands Sound, 21 May 1982.*

60 tons of above deck weight. Unfortunately aluminium burns much more readily than steel, resulting in a retrofit programme of replacing former aluminium companion-ways (ladders) and other fittings with items built of less combustible steel. In terms of handling and sea-keeping, the 'Amazon' class have proven to be fine ships, but sadly, as the loss of HMS *Ardent* and HMS *Antelope* to Argentinian air strikes in Falkland Sound during the latter part of May 1982 demonstrated, these ships' weakest link could well lie in their elderly anti-air weapons systems. Ironically, during the first half of the 1970s, a much more air defence capable version of the 'Amazon' had been proposed, equipped with the demonstrably effective Seawolf missile. Unfortunately, plans to develop this so-called broad-beamed version were shelved when, in 1977, the Argentine government elected to purchase the Blohm und Voss MEKO 360 frigates in preference to the modified 'Amazons'.

Brooke Class Frigates

Role: Anti-submarine.
Builders: Lockheed & Bath Iron Works, USA.
User: US Navy.
Basic data: 3245 tons full displacement; 414.5ft (126.3m) overall length; 44.2ft (13.5m) maximum beam.
Crew: 255.
Propulsion: 1 geared steam turbine (35,000shp); 1 propeller.
Sensors: 1 SPS-52D combined air search and height finder (3-D) radar; 1 SPS-10F sea search and navigational radar; 1 SPG-51C missile fire control radar; 1 Mk 35 gun fire control radar; 1 SQS-26AX bow-mounted sonar; NTDS automated action information data-processing system.
Armament: 1 Kaman SH-2 Seasprite helicopter; 1 single Mk 22 Tartar/Standard MR area air defence missile launcher; 1 single 5in Mk 30 dual-purpose gun; 1 octuple Mk 16 ASROC anti-submarine missile launcher; 2 triple lightweight anti-submarine torpedo tubes.
Top speed: 27 knots.
Range: 4000 nautical miles at 20 knots.
Programme: Ordered in two batches of three ships during the 1962/3 period this six-ship class comprises; USS *Brooke* (FFG1), USS *Ramsey* (LFFG2), USS *Schofield* (FFG3), USS *Talbot* (FFG4), USS *Richard L Page* (FFG5) and USS *Julius A Furer* (FFG6). Lockheed Shipbuilding built the first three ships, with Bath Iron Works responsible for the others. Built between December 1962 and November 1967, all ships entered service between March 1966 and November 1967.
Notes: Employing the same hull design and layout as that of the 'Garcia' class, the 'Brookes' differ only in replacing the aft 5in gun with the Tartar/Standard missile launcher.

De Zeven Provincien Class Frigates

Role: General-purpose.
Builder: KMS, Netherlands.
Users: Planned for the Royal Netherlands Navy.
Basic data: 3200 tons full displacement; 374.3ft (114.1m) overall length; 47.2ft (14.4m) maximum beam.
Crew: 137.
Propulsion: 2 Rolls-Royce Spey SM 1A gas turbines (36,000shp) or 2 SEMT-Pielstick diesels (total 8500bhp); CODOG; 2 controllable-pitch propellers.
Sensors: 1 Hollandse DA 08 long-range air search radar; 1 Hollandse ZW 06 sea search and navigational radar; 1 Hollandse WM 25 missile and gunfire control radar/optronics system; 1 PHS 36 bow-mounted and variable depth sonar system; SEWACO automated action

USS Richard L Page *(FFG5), part of the US Atlantic Fleet.*

An impression of the Dutch-developed 'M' class frigate as it will be on completion.

information data-processing system.

Armament: 1 Westland Lynx helicopter; 2 quadruple Harpoon anti-ship launchers; 1 octuple Sea Sparrow point air defence missile launcher; 1 single 57mm Bofors SAK 57 Mk 2 compact dual-purpose gun; 1 multi-barrelled 30mm Hollandse/General Electric Goalkeeper close-in weapons system; 2 twin lightweight anti-submarine torpedo tubes.

Top speed: 30 knots.

Range: 5000 nautical miles at 18 knots.

Programme: A planned eight-ship class, design of which was initiated in late 1970s. The lead ship, HNLMS *De Zeven Provincien* (F827); plus three further vessels were ordered in February 1984; the contract including options on four more frigates. The lead ship, laid down in late February 1985, should complete sea trials and be handed over in 1988.

Notes: A well-armed, seaworthy-looking design, the 'M', or 'De Zeven Provincien' class ships were meant to replace the 'Wolf' class frigates operated by the Royal Netherlands Navy from the mid-1980s onwards. Unfortunately, the 'M' class programme fell victim, in early 1982, to various economically-driven factors, ranging from the collapse of the Dutch shipbuilding group, RSV, to considerations of maximising the content of locally-built equipment content; factors leading to an almost two year slippage in deliveries.

Maestrale Class Frigates

Role: Anti-submarine.
Builder: CNR, Italy.
User: Italian Navy.
Basic data: 3040 tons full displacement; 402.65ft (122.73m) overall length; 42.25ft (12.88m) maximum beam.
Crew: 232.

Maestrale (F570) with Agusta-Bell AB212 ASW on helipad.

Propulsion: 2 General Electric LM2500 gas turbines (total 50,000shp) or 2 GMT B230-20DVM diesels (total 14.160bhp); CODOG; 2 controllable-pitch propellers.

Sensors: 1 Selenia RAN 10S primary air/sea search radar; 1 SMA MM/SPS-702 close-in air/sea search radar; 1 SMA 3RM20 navigational radar; 1 ELSAG NA-30 fire control radar (guns); 2 Selenia RTN-30X fire control radars (missiles); 1 Raytheon DE 1164 integrated hull and variable depth sonars; Selenia IPN-10 automated action information data-processing.

Armament: 2 Agusta-Bell 212 helicopters; 4 Otomat Mk 2 anti-ship missile launchers; 1 OTO-Melara 127mm gun; 1 octuple Aspide short-range air defence missile launcher; 2 Breda/Bofors 40mm anti-aircraft guns; 2 each heavyweight and lightweight anti-submarine torpedo tubes.

Top speed: 33 knots.

Range: 6000 nautical miles at 15 knots.

Programme: Subject of a special piece of Italian Government legislation passed in 1975 approving the construction of eight 'Maestrale' class frigates, two ships were deleted from the planned programme in 1977, but restored in October 1980. The class comprises: *Maestrale* (F570), *Grecale* (F571), *Libeccio* (F572), *Scirocco* (F573), *Aliseo* (F574), *Euro* (F575), *Espero* (F576) and *Zeffiro* (F577). The first of class, *Maestrale* (F570), was laid down in March 1978, launched in February 1981 and commissioned in March 1982. The second through fifth vessels commissioned during 1983 and all should be in service by 1985.

Notes: Although exhibiting a strong family resemblance to the smaller 'Lupo' class frigates that came from the same drawing boards, the 'Maestrale' class is, in mission terms, more readily related to the 'Kortenaer/Bremen' class of open ocean submarine hunters. Of well proportioned, if somewhat angular lines the 'Maestrale' class, along with the 'Lupos', are the first of the modern, gas turbine boosted European or US frigates to reverse the downward trend in terms of top speed, the former being designed to achieve 32.5 knots with six months of hull exposure to marine encrustation. Already well-armed by Western-world standards, provision exists to equip these ships with a hangar roof located close-in weapons system at some future date. The Mk 2 Otomat anti-ship missiles with which the 'Maestrales' are equipped have demonstrated a range capability in excess of 97 nautical miles, while the Mach 2.0 Aspide (Italian version of the Sea Sparrow) air defence missile has a range of around 5.4 nautical miles.

Annapolis Class Frigates

Role: Anti-submarine.
Builder: Various, Canada.
User: Royal Canadian Navy.
Basic data: 3000 tons full displacement; 371ft (113.1m) overall length; 42ft (12.8m) maximum beam.
Crew: 228.

Propulsion: 2 English Electric geared steam turbines (total 30,000shp); 2 propellers.

Sensors: 1 SPS-12 air search radar; 1 SPS-10 sea search and navigational radar; 1 Sperry Mk 2 fire control radar; 1 TACAN aircraft homer; 1 SQS-501, 1 SQS-503 and 1 SQS-505 hull-mounted and variable depth sonar system; automated action information data-processing system.

Armament: 1 Sikorsky SH-3 Sea King helicopter; 1 twin 3in Mk 22 dual-purpose gun; 1 Mk 10 Limbo anti-submarine mortar; 2 triple lightweight anti-submarine torpedo tubes.

Top speed: 28 knots.

Range: 4750 nautical miles at 14 knots.

Programme: This two-ship class comprises HMCS *Annapolis* (FFH265) and HMCS *Nipigon* (FFH266). Built in Halifax Shipyards and Marine Industries, respectively,

HMCS Annapolis *(FFH265) steaming in Atlantic waters.*

these ships both entered service during 1964, having been laid down in 1960. The 'Annapolis' class ships, along with the four-ship Improved 'Restigouche' class destroyers in service with the Canadian Armed Forces, will undergo a major programme of modernisation during the next few years.

Notes: Functional, if rather unbeautiful ships, the 'Annapolis' class are characterised by their small, side by side-mounted funnels that project from the forward end of the helicopter hangar. Air defence capability is limited for a ship of this size.

Tribal Class (UK) Frigates

Role: General-purpose.
Builders: Various, UK.
User: Indonesian Navy.

Basic data: 3000 tons full displacement; 360.0ft (109.7m) overall length; 42.0ft (12.8m) maximum beam.
Crew: 295.
Propulsion: 1 Metrovick geared steam turbine (15,000shp); 1 Metrovick G.6 gas turbine (7500shp); COSAG; 1 propeller.
Sensors: 1 Type 965 long-range air search radar; 1 Type 993 low-level air and sea search radar; 1 Type 978 navigational radar; 2 Type 262 and 1 Type 963 fire control radars; 1 Type 162, 1 Type 170B and 1 Type 177 hull-mounted sonars; 1 Type 199 towed variable depth sonar (F117 and F122 only).
Armament: 1 Westland Wasp helicopter; 2 single 4.5in Mk 5 dual-purpose guns; 2 quadruple Sea Cat point air defence missile launchers; 2 single 20mm anti-aircraft guns; 1 triple-barrel Limbo Mk 10 anti-submarine mortar.
Top speed: 24 knots.
Range: 4500 nautical miles at 12 knots.
Programme: Originally a seven-ship class, the Type 81

KRI Martha Kristina Tiyahuhu *(F331), the former HMS* Zulu.

The Federal German Navy's Braunschwig *(F225).*

frigates were completed between November 1961 and April 1964, with Yarrow completing the lead ship. The class comprised:

HMS *Ashanti* (F117), HMS *Eskimo* (F119), HMS *Gurkha* (F122), HMS *Mohawk* (F125), HMS *Nubian* (F131), HMS *Tartar* (F133) and HMS *Zulu* (F124). All were modernised, including the incorporation of helipad and hangar, between 1967 and 1974. All ships had been planned to be decommissioned by 1982, but as a result of the Falklands conflict HMS *Gurkah*, HMS *Tartar* and HMS *Zulu* remained in Royal Navy service through 1983, when all three were sold to Indonesia. Vosper Thornycroft are refitting the ships, the work being scheduled for completion in late 1985.

Notes: Of deceptively, conventional appearance, the 'Tribal' class was, in fact, made up of the first series-built warship to employ a combined steam and gas turbine (COSAG) propulsion arrangement. Based on the development work undertaken by Yarrow-Admiralty Research Department, the 'Tribal' frigates' COSAG system was actually an adaptation of that already being designed for the later 'County' class destroyers. The Wasp helicopter is stowed in its below helipad hangar at a right angle to the ship's fore-and-aft axis.

Koln Class Frigates

Role: Anti-submarine.
Builder: Blohm und Voss, Federal Germany.
Users: Federal German Navy; Turkish Navy.
Basic data: 2970 tons full displacement; 360.3ft (109.83m) overall length; 34.4ft (10.5m) maximum beam.
Crew: 210.
Propulsion: 2 Brown Boveri gas turbines (total 26,000shp) and 4 MAN V16 diesels (total 12,000bhp); CODAG; 2 controllable-pitch propellers.
Sensors: 1 Hollandse DA 02 air search radar; 1 SGR-103 low-level air/sea search radar; 1 Kelvin Hughes 14/9 sea search and navigational radar; 2 Hollandse M44 fire control radars; tactical data-processing.
Armament: 2 single 100mm Model 1963 dual-purpose guns; 2 twin and 2 single 40mm anti-aircraft guns; 2 quadruple 375mm Bofors anti-submarine rocket launchers; 4 heavy-weight anti-submarine torpedo tubes; 2 depth charge racks for 12 depth charges; 82 mines.
Top speed: 30 knots.
Range: 900 nautical miles at 30 knots.

Programme: A six-ship class comprising: *Koln* (F220), *Emden* (F221), *Augburg* (F222), *Karlsruhe* (F223), *Lubeck* (F224) and *Braunschwig* (F225). All laid down between December 1957 and July 1960, the ships entered service between April 1961 and June 1964. These frigates were to be taken out of service and replaced by 'Bremen' class vessels during the first half of the 1980s, but mid-1983 reports indicate that the rate of retirement of some of the class may well be extended.
Notes: Amongst the first gas turbine warships to appear, the 'Koln' class demonstrated a top speed of 33 knots during trials. *Karlsruhe* was transferred to the Turkish Navy in March 1983 as *Gazi Osman Pasa* (D360), while *Emden* became *Gemlik* (P361).

Improved Restagouche Class Frigates

Role: Anti-submarine.
Builders: Various, Canada.
User: Royal Canadian Navy.
Basic date: 2900 tons full displacement; 371.0ft (113.1m) overall length; 42.0ft (12.8m) maximum beam.
Crew: 214.
Propulsion: 2 English Electric geared steam turbines (total 30,000shp); 2 propellers.
Sensors: 1 SPS-12 long-range air search radar; 1 SPS-10 low-level air and sea search radar; 1 Sperry Mk 2 sea search and navigational radar; 1 SPG-48 fire control radar; 1 SQS-501 and SQS-503 hull-mounted sonar and 1 SQS-505 variable depth sonar; naval tactical information system.
Armament: 1 twin 3in Mk 6 dual-purpose gun; 1 octuple ASROC anti-submarine missile launcher; 1 triple-barrelled Mk 10 Limbo anti-submarine rocket launcher.
Top speed: 28 knots.
Range: 4750 nautical miles at 14 knots.
Programme: Originally a seven-ship class, four remain in operational use comprising: HMCS *Gatineau* (FF236), HMCS *Restagouche* (FF257); HMCS *Kootenay* (FF258) and HMCS *Terra Nova* (FF259); all of these entering service between June 1958 and June 1959. An additional unmodified member of the class, HMCS *Columbia* (FF260) is still in use as a stationery training vessel. All four improved 'Restagouche' frigates are currently undergoing a major life extension refurbishment.
Notes: Retrofitted with SQS-505 variable depth sonar systems between 1968 and 1973, involving modifying and lengthening the vessels' sterns, all four of these ships currently serve with the Royal Canadian Navy's Pacific coast-based Second Canadian Destroyer Squadron. The current destroyer life extension (DELEX) programme on these frigates is scheduled for completion by 1986.

McKenzie Class Frigates

Role: Anti-submarine.
Builders: Various, Canada.
User: Royal Canadian Navy.
Basic data: 2890 tons full displacement; 366.0ft (111.6m) overall length; 42.0ft (12.8m) maximum beam.
Crew: 210.
Propulsion: 2 English Electric geared steam turbines (total 30,000shp); 2 propellers.
Sensors: 1 SPS-12 long-range air search radar; 1 SPS-10 low-level air and sea search radar; 1 Sperry Mk 2 sea search and navigational radar; 1 SPG-34 and 1 SPG-48 fire control radars; 1 SQS-501 and 1 SQS-503 hull-mounted sonars; naval tactical information system.
Armament: 2 twin 3in Mk 34 dual-purpose guns; 2 triple-barrelled Mk 10 Limbo anti-submarine mortars; 2 triple Mk 32 lightweight anti-submarine torpedo tubes.

Top speed: 28 knots.

Range: 4750 nautical miles at 14 knots.

Programme: This four-ship class comprises : HMCS *McKenzie* (FF261), HMCS *Saskatchewan* (FF262), HMCS *Yukon* (FF263) and HMCS *Qu'Appelle* (FF264). Built by four different shipbuilders, this class were laid down between December 1958 and January 1960, launched between February 1961 and May 1962 and all entered service between October 1962 and September 1963. Currently undergoing major modernisation.

Notes: Although relegated to serve with the Royal Canadian Navy's Pacific coast Training Group, all four ships of this class are currently undergoing a life extension refurbishment programme, including the retrofitting of new SQS-505 in place of the existing SQS-503 sonar systems.

Leander Class Frigates

Role: Anti-submarine.

Builders: Various UK, Indian and Dutch.

Users: Navies of India, Netherlands, New Zealand and UK.

Basic data: 2860 tons full displacement; 373ft (113.7m) overall length; 41ft (12.5m) or 43ft (13.1m) maximum beam on last 10 UK and 6 Indian ships.

Crew: 260.

Propulsion: 2 White E-E geared steam turbines (total 30,000shp); 2 propellers.

Sensors: 1 Type 965 long-range air search radar on gun and Exocet-equipped ships or 1 Type 993 low-altitude air search radar on Ikara ships; 2 Type 903 Seacat fire control radars; 1 Type 975 or 978 sea search and navigational radar; 1 Type 177 or 184 hull-mounted and 1 Type 162, 170B or 199 towed variable depth sonar (deleted from some ships); Ferranti CAAIS automated action information data-processing.

Armament: 1 Westland Wasp or Lynx helicopter; 1 twin 4.5in Mk 6 dual-purpose gun, or 4 Exocet anti-ship missile launchers, or 1 Ikara anti-submarine missile launcher, or 1 sextuple Sea Wolf rapid response close-in air defence missile launcher and 4 Exocet (with the exception of the Sea Wolf ships, all carry 6 cell Seacat point air defence missile launchers, gun-equipped ships having 1, Ikara ships having 2 and Exocet ships carrying 3; Ikara and Exocet ships have 2 single 40mm anti-aircraft guns, while gun equipped ships have 2 single 20mm anti-aircraft guns; 1 treble barrelled Limbo Mk 10 anti-submarine mortar (deleted from Exocet ships, which carry 2 triple lightweight anti-submarine torpedo tubes).

Top speed: 28.5 knots.

Range: Up to 5500 nautical miles at 12 knots.

Programme: All 26 Royal Navy ships were commissioned between March 1963 and February 1973. Having undergone extensive refits, the ships fall into three categories; the Ikara group, comprising HMS *Leander* (F109). HMS *Ajax* (F114), HMS *Aurora* (F10), HMS *Euryalus* (F15), HMS *Galatea* (F18), HMS *Arethusa* (F38), HMS *Naiad* (F39) and HMS *Dido* (F104); the Exocet group, comprising HMS *Cleopatra* (F28), HMS *Minerva* (F45), HMS *Phoebe* (F42), HMS *Sirius* (F40), HMS *Argonaut* (F56), HMS *Juno* (F52), HMS *Danae* (F47) and HMS *Penelope* (F127); and the Broad-Beamed group, originally gun-equipped being converted into Sea Wolf ships, comprising HMS *Andromeda* (F57), HMS *Scylla* (F71), HMS *Hermione* (F58), HMS *Achilles* (F12), HMS *Jupiter* (F60), HMS *Diomede* (F16), HMS *Bacchante* (F69). HMS *Apollo* (F70), HMS *Charybdis* (F75) and HMS *Ariadne* (F72). The two British-built New Zealand vessels, HMNZS *Waikato* (F55) and HMNZS *Canterbury* (F421), were

HMS Andromeda *(F57) one of the much modified refitted Batch III Exocet and Sea Wolf-equipped ships.*

An aft aspect of HMCS Terra Nova *(FF259), showing the ASROC missile-launcher and stern variable depth sonar.*

The Royal Canadian Navy's lead of class HMCS McKenzie *(FF261).*

New Zealand's HMNZS Canterbury *(F421) retains her twin 4.5in forward gun turret.*

accepted 1966 and 1971, respectively. Two Dutch shipyards built six ships known as 'Van Speijk' class, all accepted into service between 1967 and 1968. Six more were locally built in India between 1972 and 1980, while two British-built ships were delivered to Chile in December 1973 and May 1974 (see Modified 'Leander').

Notes: A development of the 'Rothesay' class frigates. All of the Royal Netherlands Navy's 'Van Speijk' class ships have had their twin 4.5in gun turret removed and replaced by the rounded single 76mm OTO-Melara gun turret. HMS *Andromeda* (F57) has been equipped with a six cell Sea Wolf launcher in place of her gun turret and is fitted with Type 967/968 search radar and GWS 25 tracking radar. The former Royal Navy ships, HMS *Dido* and *Bacchante* have been transferred to the Royal New Zealand Navy, where they will operate as HMNZS *Southland* and *Wellington*, respectively,; HMNZS *Waikato* having been withdrawn from service.

Modified Leander Class Frigates

Role: General-purpose.
Builder: Yarrow, UK.
User: Chilean Navy.
Basic data: 3200 tons full displacement; 372ft (113.4m) overall length; 43ft (13.1m) maximum beam.
Crew: 253.
Propulsion: 2 White E-E geared steam turbines (total 30,000shp); 2 propellers.

The Chilean Navy frigate Condell *(F06), 1977.*

Sensors: 1 Type 965 long-range air search radar; 1 Type 992 low-level air search radar; 1 Type 978 sea search and navigational radar; 1 Type 903 Seacat fire control radar; 1 Type 162, 1 Type 170B and 1 Type 177 hull-mounted sonars.
Armament: 1 Aerospatiale Alouette helicopter; 4 Exocet anti-ship missile launchers; 1 twin 4.5in Mk 6 dual-purpose guns; 1 quadruple Seacat point air defence missile launcher; 2 single 20mm Oerlikon anti-aircraft guns; 2 triple lightweight anti-submarine torpedo tubes.
Top speed: 28.5 knots.
Range: 5500 nautical miles at 12 knots.
Programme: Ordered in January 1970, this two-ship class comprises *Condell* (F06) and *Lynch* (F07). Laid down in June 1971 and December 1972, the ships were launched in December 1972 and June 1973, entering service in December 1973 and May 1974, respectively.
Notes: Based on the hull and machinery of the existing broad-beam 'Leanders', the design of these ships was modified to meet the specific needs of the Chilean Navy, which included additional fuel oil tankage endurance and the stern Exocet launcher installation, which permits retention of the forward gun.

Van Speijk Class Frigates

Role: General purpose.
Builders: Various, Netherlands.
User: Royal Netherlands Navy.
Basic data: 2835 tons full displacement; 372.0ft (113.4m) overall length; 41.0ft (12.5m) maximum beam.
Crew: 180.
Propulsion: 2 Werkspoor-built English Electric geared steam turbines (total 30,000shp); 2 propellers.
Sensors: 1 Hollandse LW 08 long-range air search radar; 1 Hollandse DA 05/2 combined low-level air and sea search radar; 1 Decca 1226 sea search and navigational radar; 2 Hollandse M 44 fire control radars for Seacat and 1 Hollandse M 45 gunfire control radar; 2 separate Hollandse hull-mounted sonar systems; Hollandse SEWACO automated action information data-processing.
Armament: 1 Westland Lynx helicopter; 2 twin Harpoon anti-ship missile launchers; 2 quadruple Seacat point air defence missile launchers; 1 single 76mm OTO-Melara compact dual-purpose gun; 2 triple Mk 32 lightweight anti-submarine torpedo tubes.
Top speed: 28 knots.
Range: 4500 nautical miles at 12 knots.
Programme: This six-ship class comprises: HMNLS *Van Speijk* (F802), HMNLS *Van Galen* (F803), HMNS *Tjerk Hiddes* (F804), HMNLS *Van Nes* (F805), HMNLS *Isacc Sweers* (F814) and HMNLS *Evertsen* (F815). All were laid down between July 1963 and July 1965 and entered service between February 1967 and August 1968. The ships were modernised between 1977 and 1981.
Notes: The 'Van Speijk' class started life as Dutch-built and sensored versions of the broad-beamed or Group III 'Leander' class frigates, carrying an extra Seacat missile launcher compared to their Royal Navy contemporaries. As originally built, the ships carried the standard Royal Navy twin 4.5in Mk 6 dual-purpose gun, removed during modernisation, to be replaced by the single 76mm OTO-Melara mount and provision for Harpoon missiles.

Rothesay Class Frigates

Role: Anti-submarine.
Builders: Various, UK.
Users: Royal Navy; Royal New Zealand Navy.
Basic data: 2800 tons full displacement; 370ft (112.8m) overall length; 41ft (12.5m) maximum beam.

Crew: 251.

Propulsion: 2 English Electric geared steam turbines (total 30,000shp); 2 propellers.

Sensors: 1 Type 993 low-level air and surface search radar; 1 Type 978 navigational radar; 1 Type 903 gun fire control radar; 1 each of Types 162, 190 and 174 hull-mounted sonars.

Armament: 1 Westland Wasp helicopter; 1 twin 4.5in Mk 6 dual-purpose gun; 1 quadruple Seacat point air defence missile launcher; 2 single 20mm Oerlikon anti-aircraft guns; 1 triple-barrel Limbo Mk 10 anti-submarine mortar.

Top speed: 30 knots.

Range: 4500 nautical miles at 12 knots.

Programme: Eleven of the 'Rothesay' class were built in all between March 1960 and October 1961 comprising: HMS *Yarmouth* (F101), HMS *Rothesay* (F107), HMS *Londonderry* (F108), HMS *Rhyl* (F129), HMS *Plymouth* (F126), HMS *Berwick* (F115), HMS *Falmouth* (F113), HMS *Brighton* (F106) and HMS *Lowestoft* (F103). In addition, another two vessels; HMNZS *Otago* (F111) and HMNZS *Taranaki* (F148), were built in British yards for the Royal New Zealand Navy. The Royal Navy ships *Rhyl*, *Berwick*, *Brighton* and *Falmouth* were all planned to be withdrawn from service during 1982, but in the light of the Falklands conflict, all but *Brighton* will now remain in service through the mid-1980s. *Taranaki* was decommissioned in 1981, with *Otago* being withdrawn during 1983. All Royal Navy ships were modernised between 1966 and 1972.

Notes: The 'Rothesay' class is an improved variant of the Royal Navy's 'Whitby' class (both being referred to as Type 12 frigates). All have been modernised to embody a helipad and hangar. Visually, the 'Rothesay' class ships are characterised by the very close proximity of their largely enclosed mast and tall funnel. Two of this class, HMS *Yarmouth* and HMS *Plymouth* formed part of the Royal Navy's anti-aircraft 'gunline' defensive screen in Falklands Sound, *Plymouth* surviving a direct bomb hit.

Whitby and River Classes Frigates

Role: Anti-submarine.

Builders: Various, UK and Australian.

Users: Navies of Australia (4), India (2) and South Africa (2).

Basic data: 2800 tons full displacement; 370.0ft (112.8m) overall length; 41.0ft (12.5m) maximum beam.

Crew: around 210.

Propulsion: 2 geared steam turbines (total 30,000shp); 2 propellers.

Sensors: 1 Hollandse LWO-2 (Australian) or Thomson-CSF Jupiter (South African) long-range air search radar; 1 Type 298 height finder radar; 1 Type 978 sea search and navigational radar; 1 Hollandse M 22 (Australian) or ELSAG NA 9 C (South African) gunfire control radar; 1 each of various British hull-mounted and variable depth sonars as original fit.

Armament: 1 Wasp helicopter (South African only); 1 twin 4.5in Mk 6 dual-purpose gun; 1 quadruple Seacat point air defence missile launcher (Australian only); 2 single 40mm Bofors anti-aircraft guns (South African only); 1 Ikara anti-submarine missile launcher (Australian only) or 1 triple Mk 10 Limbo anti-submarine mortar (South African only); 1 triple lightweight anti-submarine torpedo tube (South African) or 2 triple torpedo tubes being refitted to Australian, except F45.

Top speed: 29 knots.

Range: 4500 nautical miles at 12 knots.

Programme: A total of fourteen ships of this basic Type 12 AS class were built; four for the Royal Navy, four locally-built for Australia, plus six British-built for export to India, New Zealand and South Africa. All delivered between 1956 and 1964, the eight ships remaining in service

The lead of class HMNLS Van Speijk *(F802), photographed in 1981 following the installation of its forward OTO-Melara gun.*

HMS Plymouth *(F126), one of the Falklands Task Force ships.*

South African Navy's President Steyn *(F147) Modified 'Whitby' class frigate.*

comprise: the Royal Australian Navy's *Yarra* (F45), *Parramatta* (F46), *Stuart* (F48) and *Derwent* (F49), India's *Talwar* (F40) and *Trishul* (F43), along with the South African Navy's *President Pretorius* (F145) and *President Steyn* (F147); the latter having been brought out of reserve, following the loss of the *President Kruger* in early 1982.

Notes: The 'Whitby' class, or Type 12 AS as the Royal Navy referred to them, were the first of the post-World War II, British-developed frigates that evolved through the 'Rothesays' into the 'Leander' class. Interestingly, all remaining examples are much modified variants of the original 'Whitby' design, which totally lacked effective aircraft detection capability.

Improved River Class Frigates

HMAS Torrens *(F53), one of two improved 'River' class ships.*

Role: Anti-submarine.
Builder: Various, Australia.
User: Royal Australian Navy.
Basic data: 2750 tons full displacement; 370ft (112.8m) overall length; 41ft (12.5m) maximum beam.
Crew: 250.
Propulsion: 2 geared steam turbines (total 30,400shp); 2 propellers.
Sensors: 1 Hollandse LWO2 long-range air search radar; 1 sea search and navigational radar; 2 Hollandse M22 fire control radars; 3 sonars (Type 162, 170 and 177).
Armament: 1 twin 4.5in Mk 6 dual-purpose gun; 1 Ikara anti-submarine missile launcher; 1 twin Seacat point air defence missile launcher; 1 Limbo anti-submarine mortar; 6 lightweight anti-submarine torpedo tubes.
Top speed: 27 knots.
Range: 4500 nautical miles at 12 knots.
Programme: During the early 1960s four 'River' class frigates were built by the naval Dockyard at Williamstown and the Cockatoo Island yard at Sydney. These ships, HMAS *Yarra* (F45), HMAS *Parramatta* (F46), HMAS *Stuart* (F48) and HMAS *Derwent* (F49), were based on the Royal Navy's 'Rothesay' class. This quartet was followed some six years on by HMAS *Swan* (F50) and HMAS *Torrens* (F53), built by the Naval Dockyard and Cockatoo and commissioned in January 1970 and January 1971, respectively.
Notes: The Improved 'River' class ships, although marginally shorter, closely resemble the Royal Navy's 'Leander' class ships.

St Laurent Class Frigates

Role: Anti-submarine.
Builders: Various, Canada.
User: Royal Canadian Navy.
Basic data: 2850 tons full displacement; 366ft (111.5m) overall length; 42.0ft (12.8m) maximum beam.

Crew: 218.
Propulsion: 2 English Electric steam turbines (total 30,000shp); 2 propellers.
Sensors: 1 SPS-12 air search radar; 1 SPS-10 sea search and navigational radar; 1 SPG-48 gun fire control radar; 1 TACAN aircraft homer; SQS-501, -503 and -505 hull-mounted and variable depth sonar system; naval tactical information data-processing.
Armament: 1 Sea King helicopter; 1 twin 3in Mk 33 anti-aircraft gun; 2 triple lightweight anti-submarine torpedo tubes; 1 triple-barrelled Mk 10 Limbo depth charge launcher.

HMCS Saquenay *(F206) with Sea King on helipad. Note the stern-mounted variable depth sonar installation.*

Top speed: 28 knots.
Range: 4750 nautical miles at 14 knots.
Programme: Originally a seven-ship class comprising HMCS *St Laurent* (F205), HMCS *Sanquenay* (F206), HMCS *Ottawa* (F229), HMCS *Margaree* (F230), HMCS *Fraser* (F233), and HMCS *Assiniboine* (F234). All were laid down between April 1951 and May 1952, the class entering service between November 1956 and October 1957. The lead ship, St Laurent, was withdrawn from service during 1974, but the remaining six ships should remain in service until the late 1980s when they will be replaced by the six new build Canadian Patrol Frigates.
Notes: An innovative enough design when it first appeared in the early 1950s, the 'St Laurent' class continued the Royal Canadian Navy's pioneering developments in anti-submarine warfare, when, in the 1963 to 1966 period, all seven ships underwent a major modernisation to add the elevated helipad/hangar complex and variable depth sonar.

Pedar Skram Class Frigates

Role: General-purpose.
Builder: Helsinger Vaerft, Denmark.
User: Royal Danish Navy.
Basic data: 2720 tons full displacement; 369.1ft (112.5m) overall length; 39.4ft (12.0m) maximum beam.
Crew: 200.
Propulsion: 2 Pratt & Whitney GG4A-3 gas turbines (total 44,000shp) or 2 General Motors 16-567D diesels (total 4800bhp); CODOG; 2 controllable-pitch propellers.
Sensors: 1 CWS-2 long-range air search radar; 1 CWS-3 combined low-level air/sea search radar; 1 Scantar 009 sea search and navigational radar; 3 M 40 gun fire control radars; 2 Mk 91 fire control radars (Sea Sparrow); 1 Plessey MS 26 hull-mounted sonar; CEPLO automated action information data-processing system.
Armament: 8 Harpoon anti-ship missile launchers; 1

octuple Sea Sparrow point air defence missile launcher; 1 twin 5in Mk 12 dual-purpose gun; 4 single 40mm Bofors anti-aircraft guns; 4 heavyweight anti-submarine torpedo tubes; 1 depth charge rack.

Top speed: 28 knots.

Range: 3900 nautical miles at 14 knots.

Programme: This two-ship class comprises: *Pedar Skram* (F352) and *Herlaf Trolle* (F353). These sister ships were laid down in September and December of 1964, launched in May and September of 1965, with service entry dates of June 1966 and April 1967, respectively. The ships underwent a modernisation refit during the 1977–79 period.

Notes: Comparable in displacement to the Royal Navy's 'Leander' class frigates, the 'Pedar Skram' design has an extremely seaworthy hull, a relatively capable and balanced weapons fit and a massive twin funnel-dominated superstructure that looks as if it belongs to a much larger destroyer or light cruiser.

Alpino Class Frigates

Role: General-purpose.

Builder: CNR, Italy.

User: Italian Navy.

Basic data: 2698 tons full displacement; 371.6ft (113.25m) overall length; 43.6ft (13.3m) maximum beam.

Crew: 254.

Propulsion: 2 CNR-built Metrovick G6 gas turbines (total 15,400shp) and 4 Tosi OTV-320 diesels (total 16,800bhp); CODAG; 2 propellers.

Sensors: 1 SPS-12 air search radar; 1 SPQ-2 low-level air/sea search and navigational radar; 2 Selenia/Elsag RTN-10X fire control radars; 1 SQS-43 hull-mounted sonar; 1 SQA-10 towed variable depth sonar.

Armament: 2 Agusta-Bell AB 204 or 212 helicopters; 6 single 76mm dual-purpose guns; 1 single 305mm Menon anti-submarine mortar; 2 triple Elsag-built Mk 32 lightweight anti-submarine torpedo tubes.

Top speed: 29 knots.

Range: 5070 nautical miles at 18 knots.

Programme: This two-ship class comprises: *Alpino* (F580) and *Caribiniere* (F581). The frigates were laid down in February 1963 and January 1965, entering service in January and April 1968, respectively.

Notes: The first warships anywhere in the world to be designed around a combined diesel and gas, (CODAG) propulsion machinery arrangement, the 'Alpino' class can achieve speeds of up to 20 knots under diesel power alone. Although the elevated helipad provides insufficient space to operate both helicopters simultaneously, it and the associated hangar, whose forward end terminates immediately aft of the relatively massive funnel, eat up so much space that the designers were compelled to adopt a most unusual main armament arrangement. In this, while the two forward main guns follow the normal 'A' and 'B' tandem turret positioning, the four after turrets flank the funnel and aft end of the helicopter hangar.

Bronstein Class Frigates

Role: Anti-submarine.

Builder: Avondale, USA.

User: US Navy.

Basic data: 2650 tons full displacement; 350ft (106.7m) overall length; 40.5ft (12.3m) maximum beam.

Crew: 208.

Propulsion: 1 De Laval geared steam turbine (20,000sph); 1 propeller.

Sensors: 1 SPS-40 air search radar; 1 SPS-10 surface

The Royal Danish Navy ship Herlaf Trolle *(F353) with Harpoon missiles just forward of the bridge.*

Carabiniere *(F581) with AB212 ASW on helipad.*

USS Bronstein *(FF1037) in the South China Sea, 1975.*

search and navigational radar; 1 Mk 35 gun control radar; 1 SQS-26 bow-mounted sonar; 1 SQR-15 towed array sonar system.

Armament: 1 twin 3in Mk 33 anti-aircraft gun; 1 octuple Mk 16 launcher for ASROC anti-submarine missiles; 2 triple lightweight anti-submarine torpedo tubes.

Top speed: 24 knots.

Range: 2300 nautical miles at 20 knots.

Programme: Ordered during the US Fiscal Year 1960, this two-ship class comprises USS *Bronstein* (FF1037) and USS *McCloy* (FF1038). Laid down in May 1961 and September 1961, the ships were commissioned in June 1963 and October 1963, respectively.

Notes: The smallest of the US Navy's deep water-going combatants, the 'Bronsteins' were to be the lead ship of a new class of escorts, but were to prove the victims of advancing naval operational needs, such as the ability to operate manned helicopters. Perhaps the most surprising omission during subsequent refits was the decision not to fit a Sea Sparrow launcher immediately aft of the superstructure to cover the blind spot of the forward mounted anti-aircraft guns.

Madina Class Frigates

Role: General-purpose.

Builders: DCAN and CNIM, France.

User: Royal Saudi Arabian Navy.

Basic data: 2610 tons full displacement; 377.3ft (115.0m) overall length; 41.0ft (12.5m) maximum beam.

Crew: 179.

Propulsion: 4 SEMT-Pielstick 16 PA 6BTC diesels (total 35,200bhp); 2 propellers.

Sensors: 1 Thomson-CSF Sea Tiger (DRBV 15) air search radar with IFF; 2 Racal-Decca 1226 sea search and navigational radars; 1 Thomson-CSF Castor II primary missile/gun fire control radar; 1 Thomson-CSF DRBC 32E fire control radar for Crotale; 1 Thomson-CSF Diodin hull-mounted sonar; 1 Thomson-CSF Sorel variable depth sonar; 3 CSEE Naja optronic fire direction systems; Thomson-CSF SENIT VI automated action information data-processing system; 1 CSEE Sylosat precision position fixing system.

Armament: 1 Aerospatiale AS 365F Dauphin 2 helicopter; 8 Otomat Mk 2 anti-ship missile launchers; 1 single 100mm Creusot Loire compact dual-purpose gun; 1 octuple Naval Crotale point air defence missile launcher; 2 twin 40mm Breda/Bofors anti-aircraft guns; 4 heavyweight anti-submarine torpedo tubes.

Top speed: 30 knots.

Range: 6500 nautical miles at 15 knots.

Madina (F702) showing her Naval Crotale missile launcher, flank-mounted twin 40mm turrets and helipad.

Programme: The Saudi Arabian Government ordered four of these F2000S design ships as part of the multi-system Sawari Contract ratified in early October 1980. The lead vessel, *Madina* (F702), was laid down in the yards of DCAN, Lorient in mid-October 1981, launched in April 1982 and was delivered during March 1984. The remaining three frigates, *Hofouf* (F704), *Abha* (F706) and *Taif* (F708), are currently being fitted out in CNIM, La Seyne yards where they were built, and should all be delivered by the latter half of 1985.

Notes: Although undoubtedly expensive ships, the 'Madina' class frigates are amongst the best sensored and armed ships of their size, certainly in terms of anti-ship and anti-submarine capability. Much more significantly, the total weapons systems concept, that is the vessel, its equipment and support programme in terms of logistics and training, are all attuned to the specific user's requirements, which is, perhaps one of the underlying reasons why the Saudi Arabians selected this particular Thomson-CSF-managed programme instead of the rival Italian submission. In terms of the 'Madina' class vessels' armament, it is of interest to make a direct comparison between these ships and the larger 'Georges Leygues' destroyers, for, with the exception of a second onboard helicopter, the 'Madina' design can muster more throw-weight than their larger brethren, particularly in the area of close-in anti-air firepower, thanks largely to their fire-directed pair of Breda/Bofors twin gun mounts.

Lupo Class Frigates

Role: General-purpose.

Builder: CNR, Italy.

Users: Navies of Italy, Iraq, Peru and Venezuela.

Basic data: 2525 tons full displacement; 371.4ft (113.2m) overall length; 37.1ft (11.8m) maximum beam.

Crew: 185.

Propulsion: 2 General Electric LM2500 gas turbines (total 50,000shp) or 2 GMT A320-20M diesels (total 8490bhp); CODOG; 2 controllable-pitch propellers.

Sensors: 1 Selenia RAN-10S primary air/sea search radar; 1 Selenia RAN-11XL close-in air/sea search and navigational radar; 2 Selenia RTN-10X fire control radars (missile); 2 ELSAG NA-10 fire control radars (guns); 1 Raytheon 1160B hull-mounted sonar; Selenia IPN-10 automated action information data processing.

Armament: 1 Agusta-Bell 212 helicopter; 8 Otomat MK 2 anti-ship missile launchers; 1 OTO-Melara 127mm dual-purpose gun; 1 octuple Aspide short-range air defence missile launcher; 2 twin Breda/Bofors 40mm anti-aircraft guns; 2 triple lightweight anti-submarine tubes.

Venezuela's General Soublette *(F24) on sea trials.*

Top speed: 35 knots.

Range: 4350 nautical miles at 16 knots.

Programme: Ordered between 1974 and 1977, the four Italian frigates comprise: *Lupo* (F564), *Sagittario* (F565), *Perseo* (F566) and *Orsa* (F567), the ships entering service in September 1977, November 1978, February 1979 and March 1980 respectively. In 1974, Peru ordered four examples of this class, comprising: *Meliton Carvajal* (F51), *Villavicencio* (F52), both built by CNR and delivered in mid-1979, while SIMA in Peru were responsible for the building of *Montero* (F53) and F54, the former being launched in 1982. In October 1975, the Venezuelan Government placed contracts for six, all to be built in Italy. *Mariscal Sucre* (F21), the first of the Venezuelan ships, entered service in November 1979, followed by *Almirante Brion* (F22) in 1980 and *General Urdaneta* (F23) in 1981. All three remaining ships, *General Soublette* (F24), *General Salom* (F25) and *Jose Felix Ribas* (F26) (re-named *Almirante de Garcia*), had been delivered by the close of 1982. In February 1981, Iraq contracted for four of these ships, *Hittin* (F   ), *Thi Qar* (F   ), *Alqadisyya* (F   ) and *Alyrmook* (F   ), the first of which entered trials in April 1984.

Notes: While the primary armament of the 'Lupo' class vessels remains the same in all cases, there are a number of layout variations that help to distinguish the ships of each navy. In the case of both Peruvian and Venezuelan vessels there is an open quarter deck below the stern-mounted helicopter flight pad, while the Peruvian vessels employ a fixed as opposed to the telescoping hangar of the parent 'Lupo' class.

Hang Tuah Type Frigate

Role: General-purpose.

Builder: Yarrow, UK.

User: Royal Malaysian Navy.

Basic data: 2500 tons full displacement; 344.8ft (105.1m) overall length; 40.0ft (12.2m) maximum beam.

Crew: 227.

Propulsion: 8 Admiralty ASR 1 diesels (total 16,000bhp); 2 controllable-pitch propellers.

Sensors: 1 Plessey AWS 1 long range air search radar; 1 Type 978 sea search and navigational radar; 1 Mk 10 IFF radar; 1 each Type 170 and 176 hull-mounted sonars.

Armament: 1 MBB Bo-105 helicopter (no hangar); 1 single 100mm compact dual-purpose gun (replacing original twin 4in Vickers Mk 19 gun); 2 twin 30mm Emerlec and 2 single 40mm Bofors anti-aircraft guns; 1 triple-barrelled Mk 10 Limbo anti-submarine mortar. *Note*: the 2 twin Emerlecs were added during 1980/81 refit, during which two of the original four Bofors 40mm guns were deleted.

Top speed: 24.5 knots.

Range: 4800 nautical miles at 15 knots.

Programme: Originally ordered by Ghana in 1964, this contract was to lapse as a result of the then existing policital situation. The vessel was then bought by the Royal Navy as HMS *Mermaid*, commissioned in 1972. Subsequently sold to the Royal Malaysian Navy in 1977 as KD *Hang Tuah* (F76), the frigate underwent a major refit in Singapore during 1981/82.

The Royal Malaysian Navy's Hang Tuah *(F76).*

HMS Salisbury, now scrapped but identical to the Bangladeshi Navy's Umar Farooq (F16).

Notes: The *Hang Tuah* is described by its builders as a modified Type 41 or 'Leopard' class frigate. Besides the normal crew complement, this vessel carries accommodation for up to 16 senior staff officers, enabling it to act as a command ship for a task group.

Salisbury Class Frigates

Role: Aircraft direction.
Builders: Various, UK.
User: Bangladeshi Navy.
Basic data: 2410 tons full displacement; 340.0ft (103.6m) overall length; 40.0ft (122.2m) maximum beam.
Crew: 224.
Propulsion: 8 Admiralty diesels (total 12,400bhp); 2 propellers.
Sensors: 1 Type 985 long-range air search radar; 1 each of Types 277Q and 982 height finding radars; 1 Type 993 low-level air/sea search radar; 1 Type 975 sea search and navigational radar; 1 Type 275 gun fire control radar; 1 each of Types 170B and 174 hull-mounted sonars.
Armament: 1 twin 4.5in Mk 6 dual-purpose gun; 1 quadruple Seacat point air defence missile launcher or 1 twin 40mm Bofors anti-aircraft gun; 1 triple-barrelled Mk 4 Squid anti-submarine mortar.
Top speed: 24 knots.
Range: 7500 nautical miles at 16 knots.
Programme: Originally a four-ship Royal Navy class

The Vosper Thornycroft-built Iranian frigate Faramarz.

completed between February 1957 and July 1960 as HMS *Salisbury*, HMS *Chichester*, HMS *Lincoln* and HMS *Llandaff*, these ships were phased out of Royal Navy service during the latter part of the 1970s. Only one remains in service today, the former HMS *Llandaff*, transferred to Bangladesh in December 1976, where it now operates as *Umar Farooq* (F16).
Notes: The 'Salisbury' class, or Type 61 air direction frigates, were, in essence, floating fighter control stations,

User: Iranian Navy.
Basic data: 2350 tons full displacement; 310ft (94.5m) overall length; 36.3ft (11.1m) maximum beam.
Crew: 139.
Propulsion: 2 Rolls-Royce TM3A Olympus gas turbines (total 44,600shp) or 2 Paxman 16 YJMC diesels (total 3800bhp); CODOG; 2 controllable-pitch propellers.
Sensors: 1 Plessy AWS-1 long-range air search radar; 1 Decca 626 sea search and navigational radar; 2 Contraves Sea Hunter fire control radars; 1 Type 170 and 1 Type 174 hull-mounted sonars.
Armament: 1 quintuple Sea Killer anti-ship missile launcher; 1 single 4.5in Vickers Mk 6 dual-purpose gun; 1 triple Seacat point air defence missile launcher; 1 twin 35mm Oerlikon anti-aircraft gun; 1 Mk 10 anti-submarine mortar.
Top speed: 39 knots.
Range: 3220 nautical miles at 17.5 knots.
Programme: Ordered in early 1967, this four-ship class comprises the Saam (F71), Zaal (F72), Rostam (F73) and Faramarz (F74). F71 and F74 were built by Vosper Thornycroft, the lead yard, who delivered the ships between March and May 1972. F72 and F73, built by Vickers, were handed over simultaneously at the end of February 1972.
Notes: Extremely compact, handsomely proportioned ships, the 'Saam' class are the fastest frigates extant. The Sea Killer anti-ship missile system employed on the 'Saam' is of Italian origin and the Mk 2 version carries a 155lb (70kg) warhead out to a range of about 13.5 nautical miles (25km).

Wielingen Class Frigates

Role: General-purpose.
Builder: Boelwerf & Cockerill, Belgium.
User: Royal Belgium Navy.
Basic data: 2283 tons full displacement; 349ft (106.4m) overall length; 40.4ft (12.3m) maximum beam.
Crew: 160.
Propulsion: 1 Rolls-Royce TM3B Olympus gas turbine (28,000shp) or 2 Cockerill CO-240V-12 diesels (total 6000bhp); CODOG; 2 controllable-pitch propellers.
Sensors: 1 Hollandse DA 05 combined air and sea search radar; 1 Raytheon TM 1645/9X sea search and navigational radar; 1 Hollandse WM-25 fire control radar; 1 Canadian SQS-505A hull and towed variable

The Royal Belgian Navy ship Westdiep *(F911).*

their extensive sensor fit reflecting the technological limitations of being designed in the late 1940s.

Saam Class (Mk 5) Frigates

Role: General-purpose.
Builders: Vosper Thornycroft & Vickers, UK.

depth sonar; Hollandse SEWACO automated action information data-processor.
Armament: 4 Exocet anti-ship missile launchers; 1 single 10mm dual-purpose gun; 1 octuple Sea Sparrow point air defence missile launcher; 2 single 20mm anti-aircraft guns; 2 single heavyweight anti-submarine torpedo launchers; 1 sextuple 375mm Bofors anti-submarine rocket launcher.
Top speed: 28 knots.

Range: 5000 nautical miles at 14 knots.
Programme: This four-ship class comprises *Wielingen* (F910), *Westdiep* (F911), *Wandelaar* (F912) and *Westhinder* (F913). Laid down between March 1974 and December 1975, the respective dates of entry into service are: March 1976, June 1977 and October 1978 for the last 2 frigates.
Notes: These vessels have no helicopter facilities and are externally characterised by their low superstructure and massive funnel.

Commandant Riviere Class Frigates

The Portuguese Navy's Comandante Joao Belo *(F480).*

Role: General-purpose.
Builders: Various, France.
Users: Navies of France and Portugal.
Basic data: 2250 tons full displacement; 337.9ft (103m) overall length; 38.7ft (11.8m) maximum beam.
Crew: c200.
Propulsion: 4 SEMT-Pielstick PCV16 diesels (total 16,000bhp); 2 propellers.
Sensors: 1 DRBV 22A long-range air search radar; 1 DRBV 50 level air and surface search radar (Portuguese ships only); 1 DRBV 31D (Portuguese) or 32C (French) gun fire control radar; 1 Decca sea search and navigational radar; 1 DUBA 3 and 1 SQS-17A hull-mounted sonars.
Armament: 4 Exocet anti-ship missile launchers (French ships only); 2 single 100mm dual-purpose guns (3 in Portuguese ships); 2 single 40mm anti-aircraft guns; 1 305mm anti-submarine mortar; 2 triple heavyweight anti-submarine torpedo tubes.
Top speed: 26 knots.
Range: 4500 nautical miles at 15 knots.
Programme: Ordered incrementally between 1955 and 1957, the French Navy operate eight ships of this class. All Lorient-built, these ships and the entry into service dates are: *Commandant Riviere* (F733), *Victor Schoelcher* (F725) and *Admiral Charner* F727 in 1962; *Doudart de Lagree* (F728) and *Commandant Bourdais* (F740) in 1963; *Commandant Bory* (F740) and *Protet* (F748) in 1964; concluded by *Enseigne de Vaisseau Henry* (F749) in 1965. Ordered in early 1965, the four Portuguese ships commissioned between 1967 and 1968 are: *Comandante Joao Belo* (F480), *Comandante Hermegildo Capelo* (F481), *Comandante Roberto Ivens* (F482) and *Comandante Sacadura Cabral* (F483), these being built by AC de Bretagne.
Notes: Designed for load-carrying capability, rather than speed.

Yugoslavian Frigates

The Iraqi Navy's Ibn Khaldum *(F507) prior to delivery.*

Role: General-purpose/training.
Builder: Uljanic, Yugoslavia.
Users: Navies of Iraq and Indonesia.
Basic data: 2050 tons full displacement; 317.3ft (96.7m) overall length; 36.7ft (11.2m) maximum beam.
Crew: 76.
Propulsion: 1 Rolls-Royce TM3B Olympus (28,400shp) or 2 MTU 16V956 TB91 diesels (total 750bhp); CODOG; 2 controllable-pitch propellers.
Sensors: 1 Philips (Sweden) 9GR 600 combined low-level air/sea search radar; 2 Kelvin Hughes sea search and navigational radars; 1 Philips (Sweden) 9LV200 Mk II gun fire control and automated action information data-processing system; 1 hull-mounted sonar.
Armament: 4 MM 40 Exocet anti-ship missile launchers (Iraqi only) or 1 aft helipad (Indonesian only); 1 single 57mm Bofors SAK 57 Mk 1 dual-purpose gun; 1 single 40mm Bofors D70 and 4 quadruple 20mm M75 anti-aircraft guns; 1 depth charge mortar and depth charge rail.
Top speed: 26 knots.
Range: 4000 nautical miles at 18 knots.
Programme: Iraq was the first country to place a contract for these vessels, ordering the *Ibn Khaldum* (F507) in early 1977, the ship being launched in 1978 and entering service in March 1980. A second ship was ordered by Indonesia in March 1978 as the *Hadjar Bewantoro* (F364), which was launched in 1980 and entered service in October 1981. A second vessel for Indonesia was ordered in July 1983. Yugoslavia laid down the first of two frigates during 1981, using the same basic hull design but employing different propulsive machinery and weapons fit.
Notes: Promoted as a training ship, this Yugoslavian-designed and constructed vessel can accommodate up to 193 men, including up to 100 cadets and 17 instructors. However, as the Iraqi Navy has demonstrated, the ship can also be employed in a more aggressive role as both a missile-equipped multi-role frigate and troop transport. The hull is of welded mild steel, while the ship has a light alloy superstructure. The related pair of Yugoslavian frigates are reported to use a Soviet-developed gas turbine and to employ a CODAG arrangement, driving three propellers.

Koni Class Frigates

The Yugoslavian-operated Split *(F31) seen from abeam as delivered.*

Role: General-purpose.
Builder: Zelenodolsk, USSR.
Users: Navies of USSR, Algeria, Cuba, East Germany and Yugoslavia.
Basic data: 1980 tons full displacement; 315.0ft (96.0m) overall length; 38.4ft (12.0m) maximum beam.
Crew: c130.
Propulsion: 1 gas turbine (15,000shp) and 2 diesels (total 15,000bhp); CODAG; 3 propellers.
Sensors: 1 air search radar; 1 sea search and navigational radar; 1 missile fire control radar; 1 each fire control radars for 76.2mm and 30mm weapons; 1 hull-mounted sonar; automated action information system.
Armament: 4 SS-N-2B 'Styx' anti-ship missile launchers (on Yugoslavian ships only); 1 twin SA-N-4 point air defence missile launcher; 2 twin 76.2mm dual-purpose guns; 2 twin 30mm anti-aircraft guns; 2 twelve-barrelled 250mm RBU-6000 anti-submarine rocket launchers; depth charges; mines.
Top speed: 28 knots.
Range: In excess of 2000 nautical miles at 20 knots.
Programme: Apparently developed specifically for export to Soviet client nations, seven 'Koni' class vessels had been positively identified by mid-1983, comprising: the sole Soviet *Timofey Ul'yantsev*, the East German pair *Rostock* (F141) and *Berlin* (F142), Algeria's *Mourad Rais* (901), Cuba's *Mariel* and the Yugoslavian *Split* (F31) and as yet to be identified F32. Initial deliveries of the 'Koni' class commenced in 1978, with construction of these vessels continuing in the early 1980s at around one ship per year.
Notes: Sized somewhat larger than the current generation of 'Petya', 'Grisha' or 'Mirka' classes of light frigates operated by the Soviet Navy, the 'Koni' class design has a reasonably sound looking set of hull lines, combined with relatively little capsize-inducing superstructure, or 'top hamper'. With the exception of the 'Styx'-equipped Yugoslavian pair, the 'Koni' class appears to be positively under-armed in terms of modern day anti-surface ship fighting capability. Similarly, lacking a helipad, it is difficult to see how the ships' sensors could much extend the target detection range of any fast attack craft force that they might be leading.

Dealey Class Frigates

Role: Anti-submarine.
Builders: Various, USA and Portuguese Naval SY.

Users: Navies of Portugal and Uruguay.
Basic data: 1950 tons full displacement; 315.0ft (95.9m) overall length; 36.4ft (11.2m) maximum beam.
Crew: 165.
Propulsion: 1 De Laval geared steam turbine (20,000shp); 1 propeller.
Sensors: 1 SPS-5D (Uruguay) or MLA-1B (Portugal) air search radar; 1 SPS-6C (Uruguay) or Type 978 (Portugal) sea search and navigational radar; 2 Mk 34 gun fire control radars; 1 SQS-29 (Uruguay) or 1 each SQS-30, 31 and 32 hull-mounted and 1 SQA-10 variable depth sonar (Portugal).
Armament: 2 twin 3in Mk 33 anti-aircraft guns; 2 quadruple 375mm Bofors anti-submarine rocket launchers (Portugal) or 1 depth charge rack (Uruguay); 2 triple lightweight anti-submarine torpedo tubes.
Top speed: 26 knots.
Range: 1600 nautical miles at 25 knots.
Programme: Originally a 13-ship class for the US Navy built during the early 1950s, plus three more constructed in Portuguese naval shipyards between June 1962 and November 1968. Of these 17 vessels only four were still in service by mid-1983 comprising: Portugal's *Almirante Pereira da Silva* (F472), *Almirante Gago Coutinho* (F473) and *Almirante Magalhaes Correa* (F474), along with Uruguay's *18 de Julio* (FF3), the lead of class and former USS *Dealey*.
Notes: Designed as a fairly simple, readily producible replacement for the US Navy's family of World War II anti-submarine escort vessels, the 'Dealey' class first became something of a victim to changes in internal US Navy ship design thinking during the first half of the 1950s and then to advancing anti-submarine warfare ship technology that led to the development of the US Navy's 'Bronstein' class frigates. The Norwegian-built 'Oslo' class is a close derivative of the 'Dealey' design.

The Portuguese Navy's Almirante Pereira da Silva *(F472).*

514, a 'Jianghu' class missile frigate showing its low profile.

Jianghu Class Frigates

Role: General-purpose.
Builder: Jiangnan Shipyards, China.
Users: Chinese Peoples' Republic Navy and Egypt.
Basic data: 1900 tons full displacement; 338.6ft (103.2m) overall length; 33.5ft (10.2m) maximum beam.
Crew: 195.
Propulsion: 2 Pielstick diesels (total 16,000bhp); 2 propellers.
Sensors: 1 combined low-level air and sea search radar; 1 sea search and missile fire control radar; 1 sea search and navigational radar; 1 hull-mounted sonar; tactical information system.
Armament: 2 twin SS-N-2 'Styx' anti-ship missile launchers; 2 single 100mm dual-purpose guns; 4 twin 37mm anti-aircraft guns; 2 five-barrelled 250mm RBU-1200 anti-submarine rocket launchers; 2 depth charge projectors; 2 depth charge racks; mines.
Top speed: 26 knots.
Range: 4000 nautical miles at 20 knots.
Programme: Reported as having been initially deployed in 1975, at least 11 of this class were thought to be in service by early 1982 with two more being built.
Notes: A very workmanlike design that appears to employ steel construction throughout both hull and superstructure. The primary anti-ship armament of SS-N-2 'Styx' missiles is mounted on swivelling launchers similar to those fitted to the larger 'Luta' class destroyers operated by the Chinese. The ships' sensibly positioned secondary 37mm anti-aircraft armament appears to be manually laid, rather than radar-directed. At least one of this class, *533*, sports an oval-sectioned funnel in place of the rectangular-sectioned type depicted in the accompanying photograph. Egypt recently took two.

Makut Rajakumarn Type Frigate

Role: General-purpose.
Builder: Yarrow, UK.
User: Royal Thai Navy.
Basic data: 1900 tons full displacement; 320.0ft (97.56m) overall length; 36.0ft (10.97m) maximum beam.
Crew: 140.
Propulsion: 1 Rolls-Royce Olympus gas turbine (28,000shp) or 1 Crossley SEMT Pielstick 12PC2 diesel (6000bhp); CODOG; 2 controllable-pitch propellers.
Sensors: 1 Hollandse WM22 search/fire control radar; 1 Hollandse WM44 fire control radar; 1 Hollandse LWO4 search radar; Decca 625 sea search and navigational radar; 1 IFF; Plessey MS27 sonar; 1 Type 162 bottom

HTMS Makut Rajakumarn *(F7) of Royal Thai Navy, 1973.*

search sonar (both hull-mounted).
Armament: 2 single Vickers 4.5in Mk 8 guns; 1 quadruple Seacat surface-to-air missile launcher; 2 single Bofors 40mm guns; 1 Limbo anti-submarine mortar; depth charges.
Top speed: 26 knots.
Range: 4000 nautical miles at 17 knots.
Programme: The HTMS *Makut Rajakumarn* (F7) was ordered in 1969 and entered service with the Royal Thai Navy in May 1973.
Notes: The *Makut Rajakumarn*, which serves as the flagship of the Royal Thai Navy, is the second of the Yarrow Frigates to be built, the first being the slightly smaller and less heavily armed KD *Rahmat* (F24) for the Royal Malaysian Navy. Unlike the Malaysian ship, the *Makut Rajakumarn* carries a second Vickers 4.5in Mk 8 gun aft, in place of the helicopter platform installed aboard the *Rahmat* that was commissioned in March 1971. Both frigates employ a CODOG arrangement for their propulsion, where the ship can be propelled by either gas turbine or diesel, but not by both at once.

Howaldtswerke FS 1500 Classes Frigates

Role: General-purpose.
Builder: Howaldtswerke, Federal Germany.
Users: Navies of Colombia (4) and Malaysia (2).
Basic data: 1700 tons full displacement; 312.75ft (95.3m) overall length; 37.0ft (11.3m) maximum beam. (Colombian ships). 1900 tons full displacement; 319.2ft (97.3m) overall length; 37.0ft (11.3m) maximum beam. (Malaysian ships).
Crew: Around 88.
Propulsion: 4 MTU 20V1163 diesels (total 23,000bhp); 2 controllable-pitch propellers.
Sensors: 1 of various unidentified combined low-level air/sea search radar; 1 unidentified sea search and navigational radar; 1 unidentified fire control radar; 1 unidentified hull-mounted sonar; unidentified automated action information data-processing system.
Armament: 1 Lynx-sized helicopter; 8 (Colombian) or 4 (Malaysian) MM 40 Exocet anti-ship missile launchers; 1 single 100mm model 1968 Creusot-Loire (Malaysian) or 76mm OTO-Melara Compact (Colombian) dual-purpose gun; 1 twin 40mm Breda/Bofors anti-aircraft (Colombian) gun; 2 twin 30mm Emerlec anti-aircraft guns (Malaysian ships only); 2 triple lightweight anti-submarine torpedo tubes.
Top speed: 26.5 knots.
Range: 5000 nautical miles at 18 knots.
Programme: Six examples of this light frigate had been ordered by mid-1985, the initial Colombian order for four ships having been placed in May 1980, followed by the July 1981 Malaysian order for two vessels. The Colombian ships comprise: *Almirante Padilla* (F51), *Caldas* (F52), *Antioquia* (F53) and *Independiente* (F54). Launched in January 1982, F51, the lead ship, commenced sea trials in July 1982 and all of the Colombian vessels were delivered before the close of 1984. The Royal Malaysian Navy frigates comprise: *Kasturi* (F25) and *Lekir* (F26).
Notes: Designed for their weapons load-carrying ability, coupled to long mission endurance, rather than against a requirement calling for a high speed vessel, the forward superstructure of the two nation's ships varies considerably, as do their weapons fit. The sale of these frigates represents a major commercial success for Howaldtswerke-Deutsche Werft, well established as the supplier of the Type 209 classes of submarine, but previously totally unknown in the highly competitive market for frigate designs. The quite different weapons fits selected by the two customer navies reflect Colombia's primary anti-shipping priorities, versus Malaysia's interest in naval bombardment and anti-air missions.

The lead ship Almirante Padilla *(F51) during its 1982 sea trials.*

Malaysia's Kasturi *(F26), note the 100mm Creusot-Loire compact gun forward.*

Oslo Class Frigates

Role: General-purpose.
Builder: Royal Norwegian Naval Dockyards.
User: Royal Norwegian Navy.
Basic data: 1850 tons full displacement; 317.0ft (96.62m) overall length; 36.65ft (11.17m) maximum beam.
Crew: 150.
Propulsion: 1 STAL-Laval PN 20 geared steam turbine (20,000shp); 1 propeller.
Sensors: 1 DRBV 22 air search radar; 1 Decca TM 1226 sea search and navigational radar; 1 Hollandse M 22 fire control radar; 1 Mk 91 Sea Sparrow fire control radar; 1 SQS-36 hull-mounted sonar; 1 each search and attack hull-mounted sonars for Terne system; automated action information data-processing system.
Armament: 1 octuple Sea Sparrow point air defence missile launcher; 6 Penguin anti-ship missile launchers; 2 twin 3in Mk 33 anti-aircraft guns; 1 single 200mm Terne anti-submarine rocket launcher; 2 single lightweight anti-submarine torpedo tubes.
Top speed: 25 knots.
Range: 4500 nautical miles at 15 knots.
Programme: This five-ship class comprises: *Oslo* (F300), *Bergen* (F301), *Trondheim* (F302), *Stavanger* (F303) and *Narvik* (F304). All laid down in the 1963/64 period, the ships were completed between January 1966 and December 1967.

KNM Bergen (F301), with three of its six Penguin anti-ship missile launchers visible beneath the stern flagpole.

Notes: Although employing the hull, propulsive machinery and basic weapons fit of the US Navy's 'Dealey' class design, the 'Oslo' class incorporate a number of significant improvements in terms of their sensors and weapons fit, particularly in relation to localised anti-air capability, thanks to the embodiment of the Sea Sparrow system. The installation of the Norwegian-developed Terne anti-submarine rocket launcher enables the 'Oslo' class vessels to lob a 106lb (48kg) warhead out to a range of around 0.5 nautical miles (900m). Because of their differences from 'Dealey' class sensor fit, the 'Oslo' class ships are readily identifiable from the Portuguese Navy's three 'da Silva' class frigates that vary little from the original 'Dealey' design. One prominent identifying feature of the 'Oslo' class centres on their highly raked, single-stemmed mainmast.

Dat Assawari Type (Mk 7) Frigate

Role: General-purpose.
Builder: Vosper Thornycroft, UK.
User: Libyan Navy.

Dat Assawari (F211) prior to recent modernisation.

Basic data: 1800 tons full displacement; 333ft (101.6m) overall length; 38.3ft (11.7m) maximum beam.
Crew: 128.
Propulsion: 2 Rolls-Royce T3MA gas turbines (total 48,000shp) or 2 Paxman 16 YJCM diesels (total 3800bhp); CODOG; controllable-pitch propellers.
Sensors: 1 Plessey AWS-1 long-range air search radar; 1 Decca 629 sea search and navigational radar; 2 Contraves Sea Hunter fire control radars; 1 Type 162, 1 Type 170 and 1 Type 174 hull-mounted sonars. (*Note:* this is the original sensor fit as installed by the builders, see **Notes**.)
Armament: 1 single 4.5in Vickers Mk 8 dual-purpose gun; 1 triple Seacat point air defence missile launcher; 1 twin 35mm Oerlikon anti-aircraft gun; 2 single 40mm Bofors anti-aircraft guns; 1 triple Mk 10 Limbo anti-submarine mortar. (Original fit equipment. See **Notes** below.)
Top speed: 36 knots.
Range: 6000 nautical miles at 16 knots.
Programme: This single ship was ordered in 1968, laid down in September of that year, launched in September 1969 and accepted into service in February 1973. *Dat Assawari* carried the original pennant number of F01, but this had been changed to F211.

Notes: This ship's fighting capabilities have been significantly increased during its 1979/83 refit carried out in Italy, which involved replacement of Seacat and Limbo by quadruple Aspide and two triple torpedo tubes, plus the addition of four Otomat point air defence missiles. New Italian search and fire control radars have been fitted. Despite the changes, the ship's appearance has not been altered significantly.

Chikugo Class Frigates

Role: Anti-submarine.
Builders: Various, Japan.
User: Japanese Maritime Self-Defence Force.
Basic data: 1800 tons full displacement; 305.5ft (93.1m) overall length; 35.5ft (10.8m) maximum beam.
Crew: 165.
Propulsion: 4 Mitsui diesels (total 16,000bhp); 2 propellers.
Sensors: OPS-14 air search radar; 1 OPS-17 sea search and navigational radar; 1 GFCS-1 fire control radar; 1 OQS-3 hull-mounted sonar; 1 SPS-35J variable depth sonar.
Armament: 1 twin 76mm dual-purpose gun; 1 twin 40mm anti-aircraft gun; 1 octuple ASROC anti-submarine missile launcher; 2 triple lightweight anti-submarine torpedo tubes.
Top speed: 25 knots.
Endurance: Over 4000 nautical miles.
Programme: Mitsui acted as lead yard for this 11 ship class, all of which were delivered between July 1970 and August 1977. The ships and their acceptance dates comprise: *Chikugo* (F215), July 1970; *Ayase* (F216), July 1971; *Mikumo* (F217), August 1971; *Tokachi* (F218), May 1972; *Iwase* (F219), December 1972; *Chitose* (F220), August 1973; *Niyodo* (F221), February 1974; *Teshio* (F222), January 1975; *Yoshino* (F223), February 1975; *Kumano* (F224), November 1975; and *Noshiro* (F225), August 1977. F215, F217, F218, F219, F223 and F225 were built by Mitsui; F220, F222 and F224 by Hitachi, while F216 was constructed by Ishikawajima.
Notes: Speed and endurance are clearly subordinated to sensors and weaponry in these clean, uncluttered light frigates.

Rahmat Type Frigate

Role: General-purpose.
Builder: Yarrow, UK.
User: Royal Malaysian Navy.
Basic data: 1800 tons full displacement; 308.1ft (93.9m) overall length; 34.1ft (10.4m) maximum beam.
Crew: 142.
Propulsion: 1 Rolls-Royce TM1B Olympus gas turbine (19,500shp) or 1 Crossley Pielstick 12 PC 2VT diesel (3850bhp); CODOG; 2 controllable-pitch propellers.
Sensors: 1 Hollandse LW/2 long-range air search radar; 1 Decca TM 626 sea search and navigational radar; 1 Hollandse WM 22 search/fire control radar; 1 Hollandse WM 44 fire control radar (for Seacat); 1 each Type 170, 174 and 162 hull-mounted sonars; Hollandse M 22 automated action information data-processing system.
Armament: 1 MBB Bo-105 helicopter; 1 single 100m dual-purpose gun (replacing original 4.5in Vickers Mk 8); 1 quadruple Seacat point air defence missile launcher; 1 triple-barrelled Mk 10 Limbo anti-submarine mortar; 2 single 40mm Bofors anti-aircraft guns.
Top speed: 26 knots.
Range: 5200 nautical miles at 16 knots.
Programme: Ordered in February 1966, KD *Rahmat* (F24) was launched in December 1967 and entered service with

Chikugo *(F215) with ASROC launcher aft of funnel.*

The Yarrow-built Royal Malaysian ship, KD Rahmat *(F24).*

the Royal Malaysian Navy in March 1971. Refitted in Singapore during 1980/81.
Notes: The 'Rahmat' type design is a slightly scaled-down derivative of the Yarrow-designed Modified Type 41 frigate originally laid down in 1965 for Ghana, but subsequently sold to the Royal Navy in 1972 as HMS *Mermaid* before being resold to Malaysia in 1977 as KD *Hang Tuah* (F76). However, unlike the diesel-powered *Hang Tuah*, the 'Rahmat' employs a combined diesel or gas turbine (CODOG) propulsive machinery arrangement.

Isuzu Class Frigates

Role: Anti-submarine.
Builders Various, Japan.
User: Japanese Maritime Self-Defence Force.
Basic data: 1790 tons full displacement; 308.4ft (94m) overall length; 34.1ft (10.4m) maximum beam.
Crew: 180.
Propulsion: 2 or 4 diesels of various make (total 16,000bhp); 2 propellers.
Sensors: 1 OPS-16 combined low-level air/sea search and navigational radar; 1 OPS-1 surface search radar 2 Mk 34 gun fire control radars; 1 OQS 12 or 14 hull-mounted sonar. *Note:* F212 and F213 have 1 OQA1 variable depth sonar.
Armament: 2 twin 76mm dual-purpose guns; 1 quadruple .375mm Bofors anti-submarine rocket launcher. *Note:* F213 and F214 have 2 triple lightweight anti-submarine torpedo tubes; 1 depth charge projector (not fitted to F212 and F213).
Top speed: 25 knots.
Endurance: In excess of 6000 nautical miles.
Programme: This four-ship class was laid down between April 1960 and June 1962 in four separate shipyards and comprises *Isuzu* (F211), *Mogami* (F212), *Kitakami* (F213)

Mogami (F212), an 'Isuzu' class anti-submarine frigate.

and *Ohi* (F214). The respective dates for the ships' entry into service were July 1961, October 1961, February 1964 and January 1964. This class is scheduled to be phased out within the next few years.

Notes: Designed as economic light escorts, the armament of this class is weak even in modern day anti-submarine terms.

L'Alsacien Class Frigates

Role: Anti-submarine.
Builders: Lorient & F.C.M., France.
User: French Navy.
Basic data: 1700 tons full displacement; 327.4ft (99.8m) overall length; 33.8ft (10.3m) maximum beam.
Crew: 171.
Propulsion: 2 Parsons or Rateau geared steam turbines (total 20,000shp); 2 propellers.
Sensors: 1 DRBV 22A long-range air search radar; 1 DRBV 31 sea search and navigational radar; 1 DRBC 32 gun fire control radar; 1 DUBV 24 hull-mounted sonar; 1 DUBV 1 hull-mounted sonar.
Armament: 2 twin 57mm anti-aircraft guns; 1 twin 20mm anti-aircraft gun; 4 triple heavyweight anti-submarine torpedo tubes; 1 quadruple 305mm anti-submarine mortar.
Top speed: 27 knots.
Range: 4500 nautical miles at 15 knots.
Programme: *L'Alsacien* (F776), *Le Provençal* (F777) and *Le Vendeen* (F778), sometimes referred to as Type E 52B, along with two remaining Type E 52As, are all that still serve of what was an original 12-ship class built around the mid-1950s. The three existing 'L'Alsaciens' entered service between November 1959 and October 1960, with F776 and F777 being built by Lorient and F778 by F C de la Mediterranee.
Notes: Typifying the French Navy former preference for ships designed to meet a specific role, these elderly frigates are in the process of being retired, to be replaced by more truly multi-purpose vessels, such as the 'D'Estienne D'Orves' class corvettes.

Riga Class Frigates

Role: Anti-submarine.
Builders: Various, USSR and Chinese People's Republic.
Users: Navies of USSR, Bulgaria, Chinese People's Republic and Finland.
Basic data: 1480 tons full displacement; 298.6ft (91.0m)

L'Alsacien (F776) in the Mediterranean.

overall length; 36.1ft (11.0m) maximum beam.
Crew: Around 175.
Propulsion: 2 geared steam turbines (total 20,000shp); 2 propellers.
Sensors: 1 combined low-level air/sea search and navigational radar; 3 IFF; 2 separate fire control radars for 100mm and anti-aircraft guns; 1 hull-mounted sonar.
Armament: 3 single 100mm dual-purpose guns; 2 twin 37mm and 2 twin 25mm anti-aircraft guns (2 single 40mm; 1 twin 30mm Gatling type and 2 single 20mm anti-aircraft guns on Finnish ship); 2 sixteen-barrelled 150mm RBU 2500 anti-submarine rocket launchers; 2 or 3 heavyweight anti-submarine torpedo tubes; 2 racks of depth charges (Finnish ship has had all anti-submarine weaponry deleted since 1980 refit); mines.
Top speed: 30 knots.
Range: 550 nautical miles at 28 knots.
Programme: Around 64 'Riga' class ships were built in Soviet shipyards between 1952 and 1958, while another four were built in China between 1954 and 1957. Currently, around 35 still remain in service with the Soviet Navy including approximately ten in reserve. Other 'Riga' class ships still in service are the two Bulgarian vessels *Druzkiy* and *Smely*, the four Chinese ships, along with *Hameemaa* (F02), the remaining example of a pair transferred to Finland in 1964.
Notes: Built as light escort/anti-submarine vessels during the 1950s, the 'Riga' class, while long obsolete in terms of countering a modern day deep water submarine threat, could still prove relatively effective against sub-surface attackers in coastal waters. Many ships of the remaining 'Riga' class have undergone extensive modernisation, including the incorporation of the up to 1.3 nautical mile range RBU 2500 system with its 46lb (21kg) warhead anti-submarine rockets.

Finland's Hameemaa (F02) differs from others of her class in embodying a bow-mounted Soviet-developed 30mm close-in weapons system.

A 'Petya' II class Soviet anti-submarine frigate.

Petya I and II Classes Frigates

Role: Anti-submarine.
Builders: Kaliningrad and Komsomolsk, USSR.
Users: Navies of USSR, Ethiopia, India, Syria and Vietnam.
Basic data: 1140 tons full displacement; 270.0ft (82.3m) overall length; 29.85ft (9.1m) maximu beam.
Crew: 80 to 90.
Propulsion: 2 gas turbines (total 30,000shp) and 1 diesel (6000bhp); CODAG; 3 propellers.
Sensors: 1 combined air/sea search radar; 1 sea search and navigational radar; 1 gun fire control radar; 1 IFF radar; 1 dipping sonar; automated action information data-processing and data links.
Armament: 2 twin 76.2mm dual-purpose guns; 2 twelve-barrelled 250mm RBU-6000 ('Petya' II) or 4 sixteen-barrelled 250mm RBU-2500 anti-submarine rocket launchers; 2 quintuple ('Petya' II) or 1 quintuple ('Petya' I) medium anti-submarine torpedo tubes ; 2 depth charge racks; mines. *Note:* the 1 modified 'Petya' II vessel carries the same weapons fit as the 'Petya' I class ships).
Top speed: 29 knots.
Range: 4000 nautical miles at 10 knots.
Programme: This 45-ship programme consists of eight 'Petya' Is, 26 'Petya' IIs, 10 Modified 'Petya' Is and 1 Modified 'Petya' II. Deliveries of the 'Petya' Is occurred between 1961 and 1964, followed by the 'Petya' IIs from

1964 through 1969. The ten Modified 'Petya' II were converted in the 1973/74 period, while the sole Modified 'Petya' I was converted during 1978. Ten 'Petya' IIs comprising: *Arnala* (P68), *Androth* (P69), *Anjadie* (P73), *Andaman* (P74), *Amini* (P75), *Kamorta* (P77), *Kadmath* (P78), *Kiltan* (P79), *Kavaratti* (P80) and *Katchal* (P81) were sold to the Indian Navy between 1969 and 1975. Two 'Petya' IIs were transferred to Syria in 1975. A further four 'Petya' IIs were transferred to Vietnam's Navy in pairs during 1978 and 1981. Two 'Petya' IIs entered service with Ethopia during 1984.
Notes: The various 'Petya' classes follow the established Soviet formula for submarine chaser vessels, having a generally low profile superstructure mounted on a relatively low hull. The 11 Modified 'Petya' class vessels carry an additional variable depth sonar deployed from a stern-mounted housing, so built as to permit the retention of the ship's two mine dispensing rails.

Ishikari Class Frigates

Role: General-purpose.
Builders: Various, Japan.
User: Japanese Maritime Self-Defence Force.
Basic data: 1450 tons (F226) or 1690 tons (F227, F228) full displacement; 277.2ft (84.5m) for F226 or 298.6ft

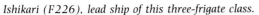

Ishikari (F226), lead ship of this three-frigate class.

(91.0m) for F227, F228 overall length; 32.8ft (10.0m) for F226 or 35.4ft (10.8m) for F227, F228 maximum beam.
Crew: 90 (F226); 98 (others).
Propulsion: 1 Kawasaki-built Rolls-Royce TM3B Olympus gas turbine (28,400shp); or 1 Mitsubishi 6DRV 35/44 diesel (4650bhp); CODOG; 2 controllable-pitch propellers.
Sensors: 1 OPS-28 sea search and navigational radar; 1 GFCS-2 gun and missile fire control radar; 1 unidentified hull-mounted sonar.
Armament: 2 quadruple Harpoon anti-ship missile launchers; 1 single 76mm OTO-Melara compact dual-purpose gun; 1 Phalanx 20mm close-in weapons system (F227, F228 only); 1 quadruple 375mm Bofors anti-submarine rocket launcher; 2 triple lightweight anti-submarine torpedo tubes.
Top speed: 25 knots.
Range: 4500 nautical miles at 18 knots.
Programme: Ordered in 1977, this three-ship class comprises: the semi-definitive *Ishikari* (F226) and the larger *Yubari* (F227) and *Yubbetsu* (F228). Laid down in May 1979, February 1981 and January 1982, the ships were launched in March 1980, March 1982 and February 1983, respectively. The lead frigate was accepted into service at the end of March 1981, F227 being completed in March 1983 and F228 at the start of 1984. Construction of the lead ship was undertaken by Mitsui, while Sumitomo and Hitachi were responsible for F227 and F228, respectively.
Notes: Designed as a replacement for the 'Chikugo' class frigates, the 'Ishikari' class carries a much more potent anti-ship weapons fit than its forebears. Equally significant is the fact that the much higher degree of systems automation incorporated in the 'Ishakari' design leads to a much lower manning requirement, and that, in turn, permits an overall reduction in the ship's size.

Corvettes

Brazilian V28 Class Corvettes

Role: Multi-role.
Builder: Rio de Janeiro Navy Shipyards, Brazil.
User: Brazilian Navy.
Basic data: 1900 tons full displacement; 314.2ft (95.77m) overall length; 37.4ft (11.4m) maximum beam.
Crew: 112.
Propulsion: 1 General Electric LM2500 gas turbine (25,000shp) or 2 MTU 16V956 TB91 diesels (total 9000bhp); CODOG; 2 propellers.
Sensors: 1 Plessey AWS4 air search radar; 1 Racal Decca 1229 sea search and navigational radar; 2 separate fire control radars including Selenia-Elsag RTN-10X; 1 optronic fire control system; 1 TACAN aircraft homer; 1 hull-mounted sonar; automated action information data processing system.
Note: information on some equipment manufacturer selection was still awaited at the time of going to press.
Armament: 1 Westland Lynx or Wasp helicopter; 4 MM 40 Exocet anti-ship missile launchers; 1 single 4.5in Vickers Mk 8 dual-purpose gun; 2 single 40mm Bofors L40/70 anti-aircraft guns; 2 triple lightweight anti-submarine torpedo tubes.
Top speed: 26 knots.
Endurance: Over 3500 nautical miles.
Programme: A planned 12-ship class, the first four of which were ordered at the beginning of October 1982. The lead of class is reported to be scheduled to enter constructors' trials during the spring of 1986.
Notes: One of the recent family of ships to be both designed and built in Brazil, this corvette design almost begs comparison with the Argentinian-built, if slightly smaller 'Espora' class vessels. Generally more lightly armed than their Argentinian MEKO 140 contemporaries, the Brazilian vessels appear to be particularly weak in terms of their anti-air weaponry and it will be interesting to see if these corvettes do not emerge with some form of close-in weapons system.

An artist's impression of this indigenously designed Brazilian warship, 12 of which are planned to be built.

Espora Class Corvettes

Role: General-purpose.
Builder: AFNE, Argentina.
User: Argentinian Navy.
Basic data: 1800 tons full displacement; 299.2ft (91.2m) overall length; 36.0ft (11.0m) maximum beam.
Crew: 90.
Propulsion: 2 SEMT-Pielstick 16 PC2-5V400 diesels (total 22,600bhp); 2 propellers.
Sensors: 1 Hollandse DA 05/2 combined air/sea search radar; 1 Decca TM 1226 sea search and navigational radar; 1 Hollandse WM 22 fire control radar (for Exocet and 76mm gun); 1 Hollandse LIROD optronic fire control system (for 40mm guns); 1 Krupp Atlas AS04 hull-mounted sonar system; EASY automated action information data-processing system.
Armament: 1 Lynx-sized helicopter; 8 MM 40 Exocet anti-ship missile launchers; 1 single 76mm OTO-Melara compact dual-purpose gun; 2 twin 40mm Breda/Bofors anti-aircraft guns; 2 triple lightweight anti-submarine

This Blohm und Voss model shows the variant without telescopic helicopter hangar.

torpedo tubes; 2 machine guns.
Top speed: 28 knots.
Range: 4000 nautical miles at 18 knots.
Programme: Designated MEKO 140 (without hangar) and 140H (with helicopter hangar) by Blohm und Voss, the West German company received an August 1979 contract to provide design and lead yard services to Argentina, who are building three examples each of both variants in their own naval shipyards. The first of these Argentinian vessels, ARA *Espora* (P4) was laid down in April 1981, launched in January 1982 and entered sea trials during early 1984. *Espora* was commissioned in early July 1985 and all six corvettes had been launched by this time. All ships were planned to be complete by the close of 1986, but some slippage must now be expected, resulting from budgetary cut-backs. The remaining ships comprise ARA *Rosales* (P5), ARA *Spiro* (P6), ARA *Parker* (P7), ARA *Robinson* (P8) and ARA *Seaver* (P9).
Notes: Larger and heavier than the three 'Drummond' class corvettes that the Argentinians procured from France in the mid-1970s, these Blohm und Voss-designed ships each packs far more anti-ship and anti-submarine weapons punch than that carried by the 13,480 ton Argentinian cruiser *General Belgrano*, lost to enemy action on 2 May 1982. Employing the same MEKO system of readily-exchangeable weapons packages as the Argentinian Navy's 'Almirante Brown' destroyers, the 'Espora' class corvettes can, therefore, benefit from a higher degree of fleet logistic support than could have been previously attained. As with their larger sisters, the 'Almirante Browns', the 'Espora' class vessels pack a considerable close-in anti-air capability, thanks to their fire directed 40mm gun system, known to be highly effective between 0.65 and 1.3 nautical miles (1.2 to 2.5km). As with other members of the MEKO family of vessels, the 'Espora' class utilises steel as the basic construction material for both hull and superstructure. Notably, while being formidable enough adversaries in terms of shipboard weapons punch relative to ship size, the addition of these six vessels must be seen in the broader context of other recent Argentinian naval procurement programmes.

Descubierta Class Corvettes

Role: General-purpose.
Builder: Bazan, Spain.
Users: Spanish, Moroccan and Egyptian Navies.
Basic data: 1520 tons full displacement; 291.6ft (88.88m) overall length; 34.1ft (10.4m) maximum beam.
Crew: 148.
Propulsion: 4 MTU-Bazan 16V956 TB91 diesels (total 16,000bhp); 2 controllable-pitch propellers.
Sensors: 1 Hollandse DA-05/2 air/sea search radar; 1 Hollandse ZW.06 sea search and navigational radar; 1 Hollandse WM-22 fire control radar; 1 Raytheon 1160B hull-mounted sonar; 1 Raytheon 1167 towed variable depth sonar.
Armament: 2 quadruple Harpoon anti-ship missile launchers; 1 octuple Sea Sparrow point air defence missile launcher; 1 OTO-Melara 76mm dual-purpose gun; 2 single 40mm anti-aircraft guns (to be replaced by 1 Meroka multiple-barrelled 20mm close-in air defence system); 1 twin 375mm Bofors anti-submarine rocket launcher; 2 triple lightweight anti-submarine torpedo tubes.

The Royal Moroccan Navy's Colonel Errhamani *(F501).*

Nala *(F363), unique in having a helicopter hangar aft.*

Top speed: 26 knots.
Range: 6100 nautical miles at 18 knots.
Programme: Currently a nine-ship class ordered in two batches of four Spanish ships each in 1973 and 1976, respectively, comprising *Descubierta* (F31), *Diana* (F32), *Infanta Elena* (F33), *Infanta Cristina* (F34), *Cazadora* (F35), *Vencedora* (F36), *Centinela* (F37) and *Serviola* (F38). Launched between 1975-80 they entered service between 1978-82, to be followed by four Improved 'Descubierta' class. In June 1977, Morocco ordered one ship, *Colonel Errhamani* (F501), which was launched in February 1982 and completed at the end of February 1983. An Egyptian order for two ships was placed in September 1982, the former Spanish Navy's F37 and F38 being earmarked for transfer to Egypt to facilitate their need for early delivery where they will operate as *El Suez* (F941) and *Abuqir* (F946), respectively.
Notes: The design of this class was influenced by Blohm und Voss's 'Joao Coutinho' class which Bazan helped to build. Characterised by the vee-shaped funnel, topped by thick aerials, these ships have a heavy, well-balanced armament, supported by a very able-looking sensor fit.

Fatahillah Class Corvettes

Role: General-purpose.
Builder: Wilton-Fijennoord, Netherlands.
User: Indonesian Navy.
Basic data: 1450 tons full displacement; 275.1ft (83.85m) overall length; 36.4ft (11.1m) maximum beam.
Crew: 82.
Propulsion: 1 Rolls-Royce TM3B Olympus (28,000shp) or 2 MTU 16V 956 TB91 diesels (total 4400bhp); CODOG; 2 controllable-pitch propellers.
Sensors: 1 Hollandse DA-05 search radar; 1 Decca AC

KRI Fatahillah *(F361), the lead of class during spring 1979 sea trials.*

1229 navigational radar; 1 Hollandse WM25 fire control radar; 1 Van der Heem PHS-32 hull-mounted sonar; Hollandse automated action information.
Armament: 4 Exocet anti-ship missile launchers; 1 Bofors 120mm gun; 1 Bofors 20mm anti-aircraft gun; 1 Bofors twin-barrel 375mm anti-submarine rocket launcher; 2 triple lightweight anti-submarine torpedo tubes. Only *Nala* has facilities and hangar for helicopter.
Top speed: 30 knots.
Range: 4250 nautical miles at 15 knots.
Programme: Ordered in August 1975, this three-ship class comprises *Fatahillah* (F361), *Malahayati* (F362) and *Nala* (F363), all laid down between January 1977 through January 1978 and commissioned between July 1979 and summer 1980.
Notes: Effectively the flagships of the Indonesian Navy, these modern, compact, well-armed corvettes demonstrate, once more, the recent strides made in cramming more weaponry into the minimum hull size. To illustrate this point it is interesting to compare the weaponry/sensor package of these ships with that of the Royal Navy's 3250 ton 'Amazons'.

Joao Coutinho Class Corvettes

Role: Anti-submarine.
Builders: Blohm und Voss, Federal Germany, and Bazan, Spain.
User: Portuguese Navy.
Basic data: 1400 tons full displacement; 277.6ft (84.6m) overall length; 33.8ft (10.3m) maximum beam.
Crew: 100.
Propulsion: 2 OEW-Pielstick 12PC2V diesels (total 10,560bhp); 2 propellers.
Sensors: 1 MLA air and sea search radar; 1 Decca TM 625 navigational radar; 1 SPG-50 fire control radar; 1 QCU 2 hull-mounted sonar.
Armament: 1 twin 76mm Mk 33 dual-purpose gun; 1 twin Bofors 40mm anti-aircraft gun; 1 Mk 10 Hedgehog and 2 Mk 6 depth charge projectors; aft helicopter pad, but no onboard facilities.
Top speed: 24 knots.
Range: 5900 nautical miles at 18 knots.
Programme: This six-ship class, ordered in 1967, consisted of two batches of three each, the lead batch being Blohm und Voss built, while the last three were constructed in the Spanish shipyards of Bazan. Blohm und Voss built *Joao Coutinho* (F475), *Jacinto Candido* (F476) and *General Pereira D'eca* (F477) and Bazan completed *Augusto Castilho* (F484), *Honorio Barreto* (F485) and *Antonio Enes* (F471). The respective service entry dates for these corvettes were: March 1970, June 1970, October 1970, November 1970, April 1971 and June 1971.

Joao Coutinho *(F475) with elevated helicopter pad aft.*

Notes: Designed to operate across the range of climatic conditions, their rather poor armament was quite adequate for Portugal's then colonial needs. These were West Germany's first post-World War II warships to be exported.

Baptista De Andrada Class Corvettes

Role: Anti-submarine.
Builder: Bazan, Spain.
User: Portuguese Navy.
Basic data: 1348 tons full displacement; 277.5ft (59.6m) overall length; 33.8ft (10.3m) maximum beam.
Crew: 113.
Propulsion: 2 OEW-Pielstick 12 PC2V400 diesels (total 10,560bhp); 2 propellers.
Sensors: 1 Plessey AWS-2 long range air search radar; 1 Decca TM 625 sea search and navigational radar; 1 Thomson-CSF Pollux gun fire control radar; 1 Thomson-CSF Diodon hull-mounted sonar.
Armament: Helipad, but no facilities to stow helicopter aboard; 1 single 100mm Model 1968 dual-purpose gun; 2 single 40mm Bofors anti-aircraft guns; 2 triple lightweight anti-submarine torpedo tubes; 1 depth charge rack.
Top speed: 21 knots.
Range: 5900 nautical miles at 18 knots.
Programme: This four-ship class comprises: *Baptista de Andrade* (F486), *Joao Roby* (F487), *Afonso Cerqueira* (F488) and *Oliveira E. Carmo* (F489). Built in Spain, all four corvettes were laid down during 1972/73 period, launched between March 1973 and February 1974, with service entry dates of November 1974, March 1975, June 1975 and February 1976, respectively.
Notes: Although modestly armed, this class, a development of the earlier 'Joao Coutinho' class vessels designed by Blohm und Voss, have a good endurance for ships of their size, coupled to a relatively high cruising speed.

Niels Juel Class Corvettes

Role: Anti-shipping.
Builder: Aaoborg Vaerft, Denmark.
User: Royal Danish Navy.
Basic data: 1320 tons full displacement; 273.55ft (84m) overall length; 32.85ft (10.3m) maximum beam.
Crew: 90.

Afonso Cerqueira *(F488), the third of this four-ship class.*

Niels Juel *(F354), with its solid, enclosed mainmast dominating.*

Propulsion: 1 General Electric LM2500 gas turbine (27,400shp) or 1 MTU 20V-956 diesel (4800bhp); CODOG; 2 propellers.
Sensors: 1 Plessey AWS5 search radar; 1 Philips (Sweden) 9LV200 fire control radar; 1 B & W Scanter navigational radar; 2 Raytheon EX-77 fire control radars; 1 Plessey PMS-26 hull-mounted sonar; DATA-SAAB automated action information data-processor.
Armament: 2 quadruple Harpoon anti-ship missile launchers; 1 OTO-Melara 76mm dual-purpose gun; single octuple Sea Sparrow short-range air defence missile launcher.
Top speed: 28 knots.
Range: 2500 nautical miles at 18 knots.
Programme: These three Yard of Glasgow-designed KV72 corvettes were ordered in 1975. The lead ship, *Niels Juel*

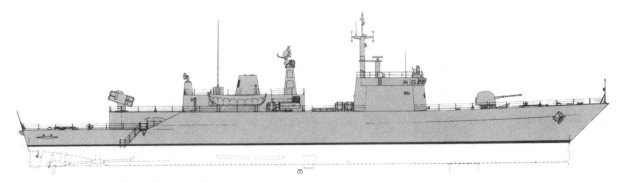

The Constructors's side elevation of the new 'Minerva' class.

(F354), was laid down in October 1976, launched in September 1978 and commissioned into service in August 1980. Both laid down during 1977, the other two of the class, *Olfert Fischer* (F355) and *Peter Tordenskjold* (F356), were commissioned simultaneously on 7 September 1981.

Notes: Built to replace four gun-only equipped 'Triton' class (Danish name for the Italian-designed 800 tons 'Albatros' class corvettes), these 'Niels Juel' class vessels, although not yet so equipped, were designed from the outset to accept internally launched anti-submarine torpedoes and to mount the General Dynamics RAM point air defence missile system.

Minerva Class Corvettes

Role: General-purpose/escort.
Builders: CNR Riva Trogoso (first and second) CNR Muggiano (third and fourth) Italy.
Builder: Italian Navy.
Basic data: 1285 tons full displacement; 288.7ft (88.0m) overall length; 33.8ft (10.3m) maximum beam.
Crew: 121.
Propulsion: 2 GMT 230.20DVM diesels (total 14,160bhp); 2 controllable-pitch propellers.
Sensors: 1 Selenia RAN 105 air search radar; 1 sea search and navitational radar; 1 Elsag Dardo E fire control radar; 1 optronic control system; 1 hull-mounted sonar; Selenia IPN 10 automated action information data processing.
Armament: 1 single 76mm OTO-Melara compact dual-purpose gun; 1 octuple Selenia Aspide point air defence missile launcher; 2 triple KAS 3 lightweight anti-submarine torpedo tubes.
Top speed: 24 knots.
Range: 3500 nautical miles at 18 knots.
Programme: Ordered in November 1983, this four-ship class comprises: *Minerva* (F551), *Urania* (F552), *Dandaide* (F553) and *Sfinge* (F554). The first and second corvettes were laid down during February 1984, while the third and fourth were laid down in August 1984.
Notes: Being built to replace the Italian Navy's elderly 'Albatros' class corvettes, the 'Minerva' class design incorporates a reasonably balanced anti-air, anti-surface and anti-submarine weapons/sensor fit. The 'Minerva' class design's seaworthiness has been enhanced by the use of anti-roll stabilizers. As these corvettes have been optimized around a high endurance mission, crew habitability has been given a relatively high priority.

D'Estienne D'Orves Class Corvettes

Role: Anti-submarine.
Builder: DCAN Lorient, France.
Users: French and Argentinian Navies.

The French Navy's Commandant Duching (F795) with her Exocet container/launchers yet to be fitted, mid-1983.

Basic data: 1250 tons full displacement; 262.5ft (80m) overall length; 33.8ft (10.3m) maximum beam.
Crew: 75.
Propulsion: 2 SEMT-Pielstick 12 PC2 diesels (total 12,000bhp); 2 controllable-pitch propellers.
Sensors: 1 DRBV 51 search radar; 1 DRBC fire control radar; 1 Decca 1228 (DBBN 32) navigational radar; 1 DUBA 25 sonar (Diodin in Argentinian vessels).
Armament: 2 Exocet anti-ship missile launchers; 1 single 100mm Model 1968 dual-purpose gun; 1 sextuple Bofors 375mm anti-submarine rocket launcher (1 Bofors 40mm anti-aircraft gun on Argentinian ships only); 1 twin Oerlikon 20mm anti-aircraft gun; 2 triple lightweight anti-submarine torpedo tubes.
Top speed: 23.5 knots.
Range: 4500 nautical miles at 15 knots.
Programme: Originally envisaged as a 14-ship class, 20 of these vessels were in service or nearing completion by mid-1983, with 17 ordered for the French Navy and three in service with Argentina. Ordered between 1972 and 1980, the French Navy class, also known as the A69 (A signifying Aviso, or corvette) comprises: *D'Estienne d'Orves* (F781), *Amyot d'Inville* (F782), *Drogou* (F783), *Détroyat* (F784), *Jean Moulin* (F785), *Quartier-Maitre Anquiel* (F786), *Commandant de Pimodan* (F787), *Second Maitre Le Bihan* (F788), *Lieutenant de Vaisseau Le Henaff* (F789), *Lieutenant de Vaisseau Lavallee* (F790), *Commandant l'Herminier* (F791), *Premier Maitre l'Her* (F792), *Commandant Blaison* (F793), *Enseigne de Vaisseau Jacoubet* (F794), *Commandant Ducuing* (F795), *Commandant Birot* (F796) and *Commandant Bouan* (F797). All of these corvettes were laid down between September 1972 and October 1981 and all have entered service by mid-1984. The three Argentinian vessels comprise:*Drummond* (F701), *Guerrico* (F702) and *Granville* (F703). Known as 'Drummond' class ships in Argentinian service, all three vessels entered service between October 1978 and June 1981.
Notes: Although designed primarily for anti-submarine escort work, these corvettes carry a useful anti-ship weapons fit. Low profiled warships, these Type A69 vessels were designed to be rugged, seaworthy ships,

Quezon *(PS70) patrol corvette of the Philippines Navy at anchor.*

specifically pitched at being economic on fuel and with good overall endurance, rather than high dash-speed.

Auk Class Corvettes

Role: Former ocean-going minesweepers now employed on coastal patrol or anti-submarine duties.
Builders: Various, US.
Users: Navies of Mexico (19), Philippines (2), Taiwan (3) and Uruguay (1).
Basic data: 1250 tons full displacement; 221.25ft (67.4m) overall length; 32.0ft (9.8m) maximum beam.
Crew: 100.
Propulsion: 2 General Motors diesels/electric drive (total 3532shp); 2 propellers.
Sensors: 1 SPS-5 air search radar; 1 SQS-17 hull-mounted sonar (on Philippine and Taiwanese ships only).
Armament: 2 single 3in dual-purpose guns on Taiwanese ships, all others having 1 single mount only; 2 twin 40mm anti-aircraft guns (all ships); 1 triple lightweight anti-submarine Torpedo tube; 1 Hedgehog depth charge mortar; 2 depth charge racks on Philippine and Taiwanese ships only, the rest carrying no anti-submarine weapons fit.
Top speed: 18 knots.
Range: 3750 nautical miles at 14 knots.
Programme: Originally a 74-ship class completed between August 1941 and November 1944 in 11 separate US shipyards of which 25 remain in service. Mexico operates 18 as corvettes *IG-01* through *IG19*, plus a 19th, *H-1* as a

survey ship. The Philippine Navy operates *Rizal* (PS69) and *Quezon* (PS70), while the Taiwanese Navy has *Chu Yung* (896), *Ping Jin* (897) and *Wu Sheng* (884), along with the sole Uruguayan Navy's *Commandante Pedro Campbell* (4).
Notes: Robust, steel-hulled vessels, the Philippine ship *Quezon* has had her aft section cleared to make way for an elevated helipad, capable of accepting an MMB Bo-105 helicopter.

Parchim Class Corvettes

Role: Anti-submarine.
Builder: Peenewerft, East Germany.
User: East German Navy.
Basic data: 1200 tons full displacement; 237.9ft (72.5m) overall length; 30.8ft (9.4m) maximum beam.
Crew: 60.
Propulsion: 2 diesels (total 12,000bhp); 2 propellers.
Sensors: 1 air search radar; 1 sea search and navigational radar; 1 IFF radar; 1 fire control radar (57mm guns); 1 hull-mounted sonar.
Armament: 1 twin 57mm and 1 twin 30mm anti-aircraft guns; 2 quadruple SA-N-5 point air defence missile launchers; 4 medium weight anti-submarine torpedo tubes; 2 twelve-barrelled 250mm RBU-6000 anti-submarine rocket launchers; 2 depth charge racks for 24 depth charges; mines.
Top speed: 25 knots.
Endurance: Over 2000 nautical miles.

119

The East German Navy's 'Parchim' class bears a strong resemblance to a scaled-down Soviet-developed 'Koni' class frigate.

Programme: The lead of class *Parchim* (FL17) is reported to have entered service during April 1981, at which time a second vessel, *FL45*, was nearing or had completed sea trials. Western intelligence reports indicate that up to 12 'Parchim' class corvettes could be constructed to supplement and ultimately replace the earlier 'Hai' class anti-submarine corvettes operated by the East German navy.

Notes: Although smaller and lighter than the Soviet's 'Koni' class frigate, the two vessels resemble each other closely in general outline. At close quarters, the 'Parchim' class vessels can be differentiated by their lack of forward-mounted twin 76mm gun turret and their two-tier hull-reinforcing strakes which periodically project slightly beyond the main hull plating.

Grisha I/II/III Classes Corvettes

Role: anti-submarine.
Builder: Unidentified, USSR.
User: Soviet Navy.
Basic data: 1200 tons full displacement; 239.5ft (73.0m) overall length; 31.8ft (9.7m) maximum beam.
Crew: 60.
Propulsion: 1 gas turbine (15,000shp) and 4 diesels (total 16,000bhp); CODAG; 3 propellers.
Sensors: 1 long-range air search radar; 1 sea search and navigational radar; 1 fire control radar for SA-N-4 missiles ('Grisha' I and III only); 1 fire control radar for 57mm guns; 1 fire control radar for 30mm gun ('Grisha' III only); 1 hull-mounted and 1 dipping sonars; automated action information data-processing system.
Armament: 1 twin SA-N-4 short-range air defence missile-launcher ('Grisha' I and III only); 1 twin 57mm dual-purpose gun; 1 six-barrelled 30mm Gatling- type close-in weapons system ('Grisha' III only); 2 twelve-

barrelled 250mm RBU-6000 anti-submarine rocket launchers; 2 twin heavyweight anti-submarine torpedo tubes; 2 depth charge racks for up to 12 depth charges.
Top speed: 34 knots.
Range: 450 nautical miles at 30 knots.
Programme: The first of 16 'Grisha' Is entered service in 1968, with deliveries continuing into 1974. These vessels were followed by seven 'Grisha' IIs, delivered between 1974 and 1976. The first of more than 20 'Grisha' IIIs entered service during 1975 and construction of this sub-class was reported to be continuing as of mid-1983.
Notes: Light and fast, these vessels can and frequently do operate beyond the Soviet coastal waters to provide an outer surface anti-submarine screen for Soviet Navy squadrons. A favourite tactic of these 'Grisha' class ships when seeking their submarine prey is to sprint into the target area, then, having stopped all engines, drift along while deploying their sonars, prior to once more sprinting to a new location, there to take more sonar fixes.

Pietro De Cristofaro Class Corvettes

Role: Anti-submarine.
Builders: Various, Italy.
User: Italian navy.
Basic data: 1020 tons full displacement; 263.3ft (80.25m) overall length; 33.6ft (10.25m) maximum beam.
Crew: 120.
Propulsion: 2 FIAT 3012 RSS or Tosi (on F546) diesels (total 8400bhp); 2 propellers.
Sensors: 1 SMA SPQ-2 combined low-level air/sea search and navigational radar; 1 Selenia-Elsag RTN 10X fire control radar; 1 SQS-36 sonar employing both hull-mounted and variable depth elements.
Armament: 2 single 76mm OTO-Melara dual-purpose guns; 2 triple lightweight anti-submarine torpedo tubes; 1 single 305mm Motofides anti-submarine mortar.
Top speed: 23.5 knots.
Range: 3900 nautical miles at 18 knots.
Programme: This four-ship class comprises: *Pietro de Cristofaro* (F540), *Umberto Grosso* (F541), *Licio Visintini* (F546) and *Salvatore Todaro* (F550). All were laid down between October 1962 and September 1963, all entering service between December 1965 and August 1966.
Notes: Steel hulled with light alloy superstructures, these medium-range vessels have a relatively modest top speed, but a good cruising speed of 22.2 knots. The 'Pietro de Cristofaro' class has a useful local anti-submarine capability both in terms of sensors and weapons, while their two 76mm guns enable the ships to take on secondary roles either as coastal convoy escorts or patrol vessels for maritime policing duties.

A Soviet Navy's 'Grisha III' coastal anti-submarine corvette.

The lead of class Pietro de Cristofaro *(F540).*

Nanuchka I/II/III Classes Corvettes

Role: Anti-shipping.
Builder: Petrovskiy, USSR.
Users: Soviet and Indian Navies.
Basic data: 950 tons full displacement; 229ft (69.8m) overall length; 40ft (12.2m) maximum beam.
Crew: 60.
Propulsion: 6 diesels (total 30,000bhp); 3 propellers.
Sensors: 1 air search radar; 1 surface search and navigational radar; 1 IFF; 3 separate fire control radar systems.
Armament: 2 triple SS-N-9 anti-ship missile launchers; 1 twin SA-N-4 point air defence missile launcher; 1 twin 57mm anti-aircraft guns in 'Nanuchka' I and IIs, or 1 single 76mm and 1 multi-barrelled 30mm Gatling-type anti-aircraft guns on 'Nanuchka' IIIs. Export 'Nanuchka' IIs carry only 4 SS-N-2C STYX missiles.
Top speed: 34 knots.
Range: 4500 nautical miles at 15 knots.
Programme: Building of the 'Nanuchka' class commenced in 1968, leading to the construction of a known 18 'Nanuchka' Is, delivered between 1969 and 1976. This phase of the programme was followed by the delivery of three 'Nanuchka' IIs to the Indian Navy, comprising: *Vijaydurg* (K71), *Sindhurdurg* (K72) and *Hosdurg* (K73) between 1976 and 1978. The first of a known four 'Nanuchka' IIIs were delivered to the Soviet Navy commencing in 1977.
Notes: Broad-beamed vessels, the 'Nanuchka' class craft were designed for greater endurance and improved sea-keeping qualities when compared with earlier generation Soviet missile boats, such as the 'Osa' class. Besides the weapons fit, which varies between the three sub-classes, the major difference between the 'Nanuchka' Is and IIs, compared with the later III series, lies in the IIIs having a taller bridge structure with the large radome now above it rather than immediately aft and just forward of the mainmast.

Imperial Marinheiro Class Corvettes

Role: Patrol.
Builders: Various, Netherlands.
User: Brazilian Navy.
Basic data: 915 tons full displacement; 182.8ft (55.7m) overall length; 31.3ft (9.6m) maximum beam.
Crew: 60.
Propulsion: 2 Sulzer diesels (total 2160bhp); 2 propellers.
Sensors: 1 unidentified sea search and navigational radar.
Armament: 1 single 3in dual-purpose gun; 4 single 20mm anti-aircraft guns.
Top speed: 15 knots.

A 'Nanuchka' I of the Soviet Navy.

Range: 3200 nautical miles at 12 knots.
Programme: This ten-ship class comprises: *Imperial Marinheiro* (V15), *Iguatemi* (V16), *Ipiranga* (V17), *Forte de Coimbra* (V18), *Caboclo* (V19), *Angostura* (V20), *Bahiana* (V21), *Mearim* (V22), *Purus* (V23) and *Solimoes* (V24). The class entered service during the 1954/55 period.
Notes: These Dutch-built ships are conversions of an ocean-going tug design and, as such, are admirably suited to longer ranging coastal patrol work, along with policing Brazilian offshore interests out to the 200 mile limit of their Exclusive Economic Zone (EEZ).

Hippo Class (Mk9) Corvettes

Role: General-purpose.
Builder: Vosper Thornycroft, UK.
User: Nigerian Navy.
Basic data: 850 tons full displacement; 226ft (69m) overall length; 31.5ft (9.6m) maximum beam.
Crew: 90.
Propulsion: 4 MTU 20V 956 diesels (total 20,512bhp); 2 controllable-pitch propellers.
Sensors: 1 Plessey AWS2 air search radar; 1 Decca TM1226 sea search and navigational radar; 1 Hollandse WM24 fire control radar; 1 Plessey PMS 26 sonar.
Armament: 1 OTO-Melara 76mm dual-purpose gun; 1 Bofors 40mm gun; 2 Oerlikon 20mm anti-aircraft guns; 1 triple Seacat short-range air defence missile launcher; 1 Bofors twin 375mm anti-submarine rocket launcher.
Top speed: 27 knots.
Range: 2200 nautical miles at 14 knots.
Programme: The two Mark 9 'Hippo' class corvettes, NNS *Erinomi* (F83) and NNS *Emyimiri* (F84), were ordered by the Nigerian Government in April 1975 as heavier, more powerful follow-ons to the erlier Mk 3s. Laid down in

The Brazilian Navy Ship Coimbra *(V18) fourth of a ten-ship class.*

NNS Enyimiri (F84), July 1980.

Badr (PCG612) lead ship of the Royal Saudi Arabian Navy class.

October 1975, *Erinomi* was launched in January 1977 and entered service in December 1979, while the *Enyimiri* was commenced in February 1977, launched in February 1978 and accepted in May 1980.

Notes: somewhat confusingly grouped along with the earlier Mark 3s under the one 'Hippo' class designation, the two Mark 9s provide yet another instance of the operational pressures acting on shipbuilders to design ever larger vessels to meet expanding mission needs, in this case an added anti-submarine capability. Compare with the Mark 3 in a later entry.

PCG612/BADR Class Corvettes

Role: Anti-shipping.
Builder: Tacoma Boat, USA.
User: Royal Saudi Arabian Navy.
Basic data: 815 tons full displacement; 245.0ft (74.7m) overall length; 31.5ft (9.6m) maximum beam.
Crew: 53.
Propulsion: 1 General Electric LM2500 gas turbine (23,000shp); 2 MTU 12V652 diesels (total 3058bhp); CODOG; 2 controllable-pitch propellers.
Sensors: 1 SPS-40B air search radar; 1 SPS-55 sea search and navigational radar; 1 Mk 92 fire control radar for 76mm gun; 1 SQS-56 hull-mounted sonar; automated action information data-processing system.
Armament: 8 Harpoon anti-ship missile launchers; 1 single 76mm Mk 75 (OTO-Melara) compact dual-purpose gun; 1 Phalanx 20mm close-in weapons system; 2 single 20mm anti-aircraft guns; 1 single 81mm mortar; 2 single 40mm mortars; 2 triple Mk 32 lightweight anti-submarine torpedo tubes.
Top speed: 30 knots.
Range: Over 500 nautical miles at 28 knots.
Programme: This four-ship class was ordered by Saudi Arabia in August 1977 and comprises: *Badr* (PCG612), *Al Yarmook* (PCG614), *Hitten* (PCG616) and *Tabuk* (PCG618). All laid down between May 1979 and September 1980, the ships were launched between

January 1980 and June 1981 and all were accepted into service between September 1981 and December 1982.
Notes: Much larger vessels than either the 'Ashville' class or the Patrol Ship, Multi-Mission (PSMM) designs by Tacoma, the 'Badr' class missile corvettes carry a heavier, longer ranged anti-ship missile armament than some warships five or six times their size. In terms of defensive capability, the ships' three-tier anti-air guns ought to prove effective even against incoming sea-skimming missiles. The three mortars with which the ships are equipped are intended to be used primarily for ship-to-shore bombardment. The four 'Badr' class corvettes served as the flagships of the fast growing Royal Saudi Arabian Navy until delivery of the first of the French designed and built 'Madina' class missile frigates.

Wolf Class Corvettes

Role: Anti-submarine.
Builders: Various, USA.
User: Royal Netherlands Navy.
Basic data: 808 tons full displacement; 184.7ft (56.27m) overall length; 33.8ft (10.3m) maximum beam.
Crew: 80.
Propulsion: 2 General Motors 12-567 ATL diesels (total 1800bhp); 2 propellers.
Sensors: 1 Decca 1226 sea search and navigational radar; 1 OCU 2 hull-mounted sonar.
Armament: 1 single 76mm Mk 22 dual-purpose gun; 3 twin 40mm anti-aircraft guns; 1 Mk 10 Hedgehog submarine mortar; 4 anti-submarine depth charge launchers; 2 depth charge racks.
Top speed: 15 knots.
Range: 9000 nautical miles at 10 knots.
Programme: Previously known as the 'Roofdier' class, these six ships all entered service during 1954 and comprise: HNLMS *Wolf* (F817), HNLMS *Fret* (F818), HNLMS *Hermelijn* (F819), HNLMS *Vos* (F820), HNLMS *Panter* (F821) and HNLMS *Jaguar* (F822). The 'Wolf' class is to be replaced during the late 1980s by the new and

larger Dutch 'M' type or 'De Zeven Provincien' class frigates.

Notes: Designed as convoy escorts, the primary current task of these elderly vessels is to provide fishery protection.

Turunmaa Class Corvettes

Role: General-purpose.
Builder: Wartsila, Finland.
User: Finnish Naval Forces.
Basic data: 770 tons full displacement; 243.1ft (74.1m) overall length; 25.6ft (7.8m) maximum beam.
Crew: 70.
Propulsion: 1 Rolls-Royce TM3B Olympus gas turbine (derated to 22,000shp) or 3 MTU diesels (total 8790bhp); CODOG; 3 propellers.
Sensors: 1 Decca 1226 sea search and navigational radar; 1 Hollandse WM 22 combined air/sea fire control radar and automated action information data-processing system.
Armament: 1 Bofors 120mm automatic dual-purpose gun; 2 single Bofors 40mm anti-aircraft guns; 1 twin 30mm anti-aircraft gun; 2 RBU-1200 five-barrel 250mm anti-submarine rocket launchers (internally-mounted behind amidships main-deck doors); 2 depth charge racks.
Top speed: 35 knots.
Range: 2500 nautical miles at 14 knots.
Programme: The two-ship 'Turunmaa' class were both laid down in March 1967. The *Turunmaa* (F03) and *Karjala* (F04) were launched in July and August 1967, the ships subsequently entering service in August and October of 1968, respectively.
Notes: Long, low-profiled, angular boats, the 'Turunmaa' class's 120mm primary armament can fire up to 80 rounds per minute and elevate its barrel up to angles of 80 degrees. The gun can fire its 77.5lbs (35kg) shells at surface targets out to an effective maximum range of around 9.7 nautical miles (18km). The ships have a well-balanced anti-ship, anti-air and anti-submarine capability.

Esmeraldas Class Corvettes

Role: General-purpose.
Builder: CNR, Italy.
Users: Navies of Ecuador and Iraq.
Basic data: 700 tons full displacement; 204.4ft (62.3m) overall length; 30.5ft (9.3m) maximum beam.
Crew: 62.
Propulsion: 4 MTU 20V 956 TB92 diesels (total 24,400bhp); 4 propellers.
Sensors: 1 Selenia/SMA RAN-10S air/sea search radar; 1 Decca TM 1226 navigational radar; 1 Selenia/Elsag Orion 20X fire control radar for Albatros missile system; 1 Thomson-CSF Diodon hull-mounted sonar; Selenia IPN-10 automated action information data-processing system.
Armament: Helipad for Agusta-Bell AB-212 ASW helicopter; six Exocet anti-ship missile launchers; 1 single 76mm OTO-Melara compact dual-purpose gun; 1 twin 40mm Breda/Bofors rapid fire anti-aircraft gun; 2 triple ILAS 3 lightweight anti-submarine torpedo tubes.
Top speed: 38 knots.
Range: Over 4000 nautical miles at 18 knots.
Programme: A total of eight of this class had been ordered by the end of 1982, consisting of six for Ecuador and two for Iraq. Ordered in 1978, the Ecuadorian vessels comprise: *Esmeraldas* (CM11), *Manabi* (CM12), *Los Ríos* (CM13), *El Oro* (CM14), *Galápagos* (CN15) and *Luja* (CM16). All were laid down between September 1979 and February 1981, with *Esmeraldas* being handed over to the Ecuadorian Navy in July 1982, with all of the class

The 'Wolf' class corvette HNLMS Jaguar *(F822).*

Karjala *(F04), the second of this two-ship class, at speed.*

Esmeraldas *(CM11), lead of class, seen during sea trials.*

Thetis (P6052) anti-submarine corvette, 1978.

delivered by May 1984. The two Iraqi ships of this class, *Mussa El Hassar* and *Tariq Ibn Ziad*, were ordered in early 1981 along with a later order for four non-helicopter-carrying corvettes from the same builder, comprising *Abdula Ibn Abiserbh*, *Kalid Ibn Alwaldi*, *Saad Ibn Abi Waqqas* and *Salah Aldin Alayoobi*.

Notes: The 'Esmeraldas' class is a development of CNR's 'Wadi' class corvette and as such is one of the latest of the new generation of truly multi-purpose compact corvettes. Packing as much or more weaponry punch as that fitted to a typical World War II cruiser, these veritable mini-frigates carry an impressive anti-air capability, not only against aircraft, but also against sea-skimming missiles. The Iraqi vessels substitute Otomat anti-ship missiles in place of the Exocets employed aboard the Ecuadorian ships.

Thetis Class Corvettes

Role: Anti-submarine.
Builder: Roland Werft, Federal Germany.
User: Federal German Navy.
Basic data: 660 tons full displacement; 229ft (69.8m) except *Thetis* which is 223.75ft (68.21m) overall length; 26.9ft (8.2m) maximum beam.
Crew: 48.
Propulsion: 2 MAN diesels (total 6800bhp); 2 propellers.
Sensors: TRS-N combined air and sea search radar; 1 Kelvin Hughes Type 149 navigational radar; 1 ELAC 1BV sonar.
Armament: 1 quadruple-barrelled Bofors 375mm anti-submarine rocket launcher (forward of bridge); 4 single heavyweight anti-submarine torpedo tubes (port and starboard pairs aft of funnel); 1 twin Bofors 40mm anti-aircraft gun (on elevated platform aft).
Top speed: 23.5 knots.
Range: 2800 nautical miles at 16 knots.
Programme: A five-ship class, these vessels and their service entry dates are: *Thetis* (P6052), March 1960; *Hermes* (P6053), August 1960; *Najade* (P6054), December 1960; *Triton* (P6055), August 1961; and *Theseus* (P6056), March 1962.

Notes: Designed as torpedo recovery boats, a role in which they provide a useful peacetime service, the 'Thetis' class corvettes make ideal submarine chasers in the in-shore waters of the Baltic and its multi-channelled mouth. Besides the variation in overall length between the lead boat and the other four mentioned above, *Najade* (P6054) embodies a larger forward superstructure, while the aft superstructures vary considerably between the vessels.

Wadi Class Corvettes

Role: General-purpose.
Builder: CNR Riva Trigoso, Italy.
User: Libyan Navy.
Basic data: 650 tons full displacement; 202.4ft (61.7m) overall length; 30.5ft (9.3m) maximum beam.
Crew: 58.
Propulsion: 4 MTU 16V956 TB91 diesels (total 16,400bhp); 4 controllable-pitch propellers.
Sensors: 1 Selena RAN 11 L/X combined low-level air/sea search radar; 1 Decca TM1226 sea search and navigational radar; 1 ELSAG NA 10/2 fire control radar and optronic director; Selenia IPN 10 automated action information data-processing; 1 Thomson-CSF Dioden hull-mounted sonar.
Armament: 4 Otomat Mk 1 anti-ship missile launchers; 1 single 76mm OTO-Melara Compact dual-purpose gun; 1 twin 35mm Breda/Oerlikon anti-aircraft gun; 2 triple ILAS 3 lightweight anti-submarine torpedo tubes; 2 mine rails for up to 16 mines.
Top speed: 34 knots.
Range: 4000 nautical miles at 18 knots.
Programme: Ordered in 1974, this four-ship class comprises: *Assad Al Tadjer* (FL412), *Assad Al Tougour* (FL413), *Assad Al Khali* (FL414) and *Assad Al Hudud* (FL415). Launch dates for the four corvettes spanned the period between the end of April 1977 and June 1979, the vessels entering service in September 1979, February 1980, along with the simultaneous acceptance of the latter two at the close of March 1981.

Notes: The Italian-developed 'Wadi' class corvettes represent the first of a series of design thrusts aimed at capturing a dominant position for the Italian naval

The lead of class Libyan Navy vessel during 1979 sea trials.

constructors in what can best be described as the smaller navies' market for mini-frigates. While the weapons fit of the 'Wadi' class is no better and, in some cases, is poorer than that to be found in some examples at the bigger end of the fast attack craft range, what the 'Wadi' class offered was a larger hull, which, in turn, affords the opportunities to mount more sensors, coupled to enhancing the general level of crew comfort. This class, still referred to as 'Wadis', despite the 1981 Libyan name change decision, served as the precursors of the slightly larger and much better armed and helicopter-carrying 'Esmeraldas' class corvettes.

Hippo Class (Mk 3) Corvettes

Role: Anti-shipping.
Builder: Vosper Thornycroft, UK.
User: Nigerian Navy.
Basic data: 650 tons full displacement; 200ft (61.57m) overall length; 30.85ft (9.4m) maximum beam.
Crew: 67.
Propulsion: 2 MAN V8V 24/30B diesels (total 8860bhp); 2 propellers.
Sensors: 1 Plessey AWS1 air search radar; 1 Decca TM 626 navigational radar; 1 Hollandse M22 fire control radar; 1 Plessey sonar.
Armament: 1 twin 4 in Mk 19 dual-purpose gun; 2 Bofors 40mm anti-aircraft guns; 2 Oerlikon 20mm anti-aircraft guns and provision for Seacat short-range air defence missile launcher.
Top speed: 22 knots.
Range: 3000 nautical miles at 14 knots.
Programme: In 1968, the Nigerian Government ordered two Mark 3 corvettes from Vosper Thornycroft, the vessels being NNS *Dorina* (F81) and NNS *Otobo* (F82). *Dorina* was laid down in January 1970, launched in September 1970 and accepted in June 1972, while *Otobo*'s keel was laid in September 1970, launched in May 1971 and joined the Nigerian Navy in November 1972. Refitted by Vosper Thornycroft in 1976/7.
Notes: A larger-hulled derivative of Vosper Thornycroft's Mk 1 corvettes sold to Ghana and Libya, the Mk 3's greater size permitted the incorporation of a heavier weapons fit.

The Nigerian Navy's NNS Otobo *(F82).*

The Plessey sonar was fitted during Vosper Thornycroft's refit of the two vessels, carried out during 1976/7.

Pauk Class Corvettes

Role: Anti-submarine.
Builder: As yet unidentified, USSR.
User: Soviet Navy.
Basic data: 600 tons full displacement; 191.9ft (58.5m) overall length; 34.4ft (10.5m) maximum beam.
Crew: 40.
Propulsion: 2 diesels (total 20,000bhp); 2 propellers.
Sensors: 1 combined air/sea search radar; 1 sea search and navigational radar; 1 fire control radar (for both 76.2 and 30mm guns); 1 each hull-mounted and stern-mounted dipping sonars; automated naval tactical information processing system.
Armament: 1 single 76.2mm dual-purpose gun; 1 quintuple SA-N-5 'Grail' point air defence missile launcher; 1 multi-barrel 30mm Gatling type close-in weapons system; 2 quintuple 250mm anti-submarine rocket launchers; 4 medium weight anti-submarine

A 'Pauk' class corvette of the Soviet Navy at speed, 1981.

torpedo tubes; 2 depth charge racks for 12 depth charges.
Top speed: 35 knots.
Endurance: Over 3000 nautical miles.
Programme: Three of this class were known to exist by the end of 1981; the vessels being first deployed during 1980. This class could be built in large numbers, if, as seems probable, these ships have been developed as a replacement for the Soviet Navy's now ageing 62-vessel 'Poti' class anti-submarine corvettes built in the 1960s.
Notes: The 'Pauk' class employs the same hull and has the same full load displacement as that of the anti-ship weapons-equipped 'Tarantul' class corvette, which first appeared in 1979. However, unlike the 'Tarantul' design, which employs a combined diesel and gas turbine (CODAG) propulsive arrangement driving three propellers, the 'Pauk' class employs a twin diesel arrangement driving two propellers. The 'Pauk' class is equipped with a dipping sonar system that is installed inside a sizable housing standing on and extending aft of the vessel's stern.

SFCN PR 72 Class Corvettes

Role: Anti-shipping.
Builders: DCAN Lorient and SFCN, France.
Users: Peruvian Navy.
Basic data: 590 tons full displacement; 210.0ft (64.0m) overall length; 29.5ft (9.0m) maximum beam.
Crew: 36.
Propulsion: 4 SACM AGO 240 diesels (total 22,000bhp); 4 propellers.
Sensors: 1 Thomson-CSF Triton combined air/sea search radar; 1 Decca TM1226 sea search and navigational radar; 1 Thomson-CSF Castor fire control radar/optronics system; 1 IFF radar.
Armament: 4 MM 38 Exocet anti-ship missile launchers; 1 single 76mm OTO-Melara compact dual-purpose gun; 1 twin 40mm Breda/Bofors L40/70 anti-aircraft gun; 2 single 20mm anti-aircraft guns; 2 heavyweight torpedo tubes.
Top speed: 38 knots.
Range: 2800 nautical miles at 16 knots.
Programme: Peru placed the order for this six-vessel class in 1978, the ships comprising: *Velarde* (P101), *Santillana* (P102), *De los Heroes* (P103), *Herrera* (P104), *Larrea* (P105) and *Sanchez Carrion* (P106). The lead craft, along with the third and fifth examples were built by DCAN Lorient, while SFCN constructed the second, fourth and sixth vessels. All launched between September 1978 and June 1979, the sixth craft entered service between July 1980 and September 1981. A slightly smaller PR 72 MS has been supplied to Senegal and is dealt with separately within the fast attack craft section.
Notes: Designed for all-weather, long range, ocean-going patrol, this class employs a steel hull and light alloy superstructure. The hull is sheathed in steel plating never less than 8mm thick. Although the Peruvian vessels only carry four Exocets, the design is capable of carrying twice this number. Amongst the fastest missile-carrying corvettes extant, the PR 72 carries the option of having the Crotale Naval point air defence missile system fitted if desired.

Poti Class Corvettes

Role: Anti-submarine.
Builders: Various, USSR.
Users: Navies of USSR, Bulgaria and Romania.
Basic data: 580 tons full displacement; 200.1ft (61.0m) overall length; 25.9ft (7.9m) maximum beam.

The Peruvian Navy's Herrera (P104), as P24 during trials.

A Soviet Navy coastal submarine-chasing 'Poti' class vessel.

Crew: 46.
Propulsion: 2 gas turbines (total 40,000shp) and 2 M503A diesels (total 8000bhp); CODAG; 2 propellers.
Sensors: 1 long-range air search radar; 1 sea search and navigational radar; 1 gun fire control radar; 1 IFF radar; 1 dipping sonar.
Armament: 1 twin 57mm anti-aircraft gun; 2 twelve-barrelled 250mm RBU-6000 anti-submarine rocket launchers; 4 medium anti-submarine torpedo tubes.
Top speed: 36 knots.
Range: 320 nautical miles at 32 knots.
Programme: 68 of this class are believed to have been built between 1961 and 1967. Although considered obsolete, at least 40 of these vessels were reported to be in service with the Soviet Navy's coastal forces in mid-1983, at which time three each of this class served with the navies of Bulgaria and Romania.
Notes: Classified as 'Malyy Protivolodochnyy Korabl', or small anti-submarine ships by the Soviet Navy, the 'Poti' class and their heirs apparent in the shape of the 'Pauk' class have no real equivalent in service with the major Western world navies and, as such, help to highlight the Soviet Navy's doctrine of, where applicable, opting to go for quantity rather than quality. However, while the 'Poti' class design was built around an adaptation of a Soviet-developed helicopter dipping sonar system and a fairly modest anti-submarine weapons fit, it should be remembered that the efficacy of sonar detection, particularly in shallow coastal waters, can be related directly to quantity as well as to the quality of sensors employed. In fact, it can be argued that, in such

circumstances, better results can be achieved by using many inexpensive systems rather than a few very much more costly ones.

Kromantse Class Corvettes

Role: General-purpose.
Builders: Vosper Thornycroft and Vickers, UK.
Users: Navies of Ghana and Libya.
Basic data: 500 tons full displacement; 177.0ft (53.95m) overall length; 28.5ft (8.7m) maximum beam.
Crew: 51.
Propulsion: 2 Bristol Siddeley-Maybach MD827 diesels (total 6700bhp) on Ghanaian ships or 2 Paxman Ventura 16 YJCM diesels (total 4800bhp); 2 propellers.
Sensors: 1 Plessey AWS1 combined air/sea search radar; 1 Type 978 sea search and navigational radar; 1 Type 164 hull-mounted sonar (not fitted to Libyan ship).
Armament: 1 single 4in Mk 52 dual-purpose gun; 1 single on Ghanaian ships or 2 single (Libyan) 40mm Bofors Mk 9 anti-aircraft guns; 1 triple-barrelled Squid Mk 4 anti-submarine mortar (not fitted to Libyan ship).
Top speed: 20 knots.
Range: 2000 nautical miles at 16 knots.
Programme: This three-ship class programme comprises: GNS *Kromantse* (F17) and GNS *Keta* (F18), along with the Libyan Navy's LNS *Tobruk* (FL411). Designed jointly by Vosper Thornycroft and Vickers, the first order for these Mark 1 corvettes came from Ghana in 1962, with Vosper

The Ghanaian Navy's GNS Kromantse *(F17) at speed.*

Borac (FL552), the second of this Yugoslavian two-ship class.

building the lead vessel and Vickers building *Keta*; these ships entering service in September 1964 and August 1965, respectively. The Vosper-built *Tobruk*, ordered in early 1964, entered service in April 1966. The two Ghanaian ships underwent refits in 1974/5.

Notes: These sleek-lined Mark 1 corvette designs represent a deliberate attempt to reverse the existing trend of producing even larger and more complex ships to meet a given task. Timely as this design goal may have been, coinciding as it did with the emergence of many new African countries, subsequent developments in the shape of growth pressures manifest in the later Vosper Thornycroft Mark 3 and 9 corvettes, taken together with the limited sales of Mark 1 corvettes, show this design philosophy to be far from an unalloyed success. The lower-powered Libyan ship has a top speed of 18 knots.

Mornar Class Corvettes

Role: Anti-submarine.
Builder: Tito Shipyard, Yugoslavia.
User: Yugoslavian Navy.
Basic data: 430 tons full displacement; 169.9ft (51.8m)

overall length; 22.9ft (6.97m) maximum beam.
Crew: 60.
Propulsion: 3 Werkspoor diesels (total 7500bhp); 3 propellers.
Sensors: 1 Decca 45 sea search and navigational radar; 1 Tamir hull-mounted sonar.
Armament: 2 single 40mm Bofors anti-aircraft guns; 4 five-barrelled 250mm RBU-1200 anti-submarine rocket launchers; 2 Mk 6 depth charge mortars; 2 Mk 9 depth charge racks.
Top speed: 24 knots.
Range: 3000 nautical miles at 12 knots.
Programme: This two-ship class comprises: *Mornar* (FL551) and *Borac* (FL552). Launched in 1958 and 1965, respectively, the ships entered service during 1959 and 1965; both being modernised in the 1970 through 1973 period.
Notes: Originally designed to carry two 76.2mm dual-purpose guns with which the ships were equipped up to their modernisation, the 'Mornar' class units have emerged as dedicated anti-submarine vessels. The Soviet-developed RBU-1200 anti-submarine rocket launcher delivers a 154lb (70kg) warhead to a range of 0.65 nautical miles (1.2km); these weapons being installed during the ship's modernisation.

Fast attack craft

Aliyah Class Fast Attack Craft

Role: Anti-shipping.
Builder: Israeli Shipyards.
User: Israeli Navy.
Basic data: 500 tons full displacement 202.4ft (61.7m) overall length; 24.9ft (7.6m) maximum beam.
Crew: Up to 83.
Propulsion: 4 MTU MD871 diesels (total 14,000bhp); 4 propellers.

Sensors: 1 Thomson-CSF TH-D 1040 Neptune combined air/sea search radar; 1 Selenia-ELSAG RTN-10X missile and gunfire control radar; 1 TACAN air craft homer; 1 IFF radar; 1 Israeli-developed variable depth sonar (on at least one missile-carrying craft); Israeli-developed automated action information system supplementing that provided by the RTN-10X Orion capability.
Armament: 1 Bell H-58 Kiowa helicopter (hangared craft only); 4 Harpoon (all craft) and 3 (hangared craft) or 6 Gabriel Mk 2 anti-ship missile launchers (non-hangared

A most informative view of three berthed 'Aliyah' class craft, the furthermost mounting Harpoon and Gabriel anti-ship missiles, while the middle vessel has a helicopter hangar. The nearest boat carries no / *Harpoons forward of the Gabriels, but has a variable depth sonar system over its stern.*

craft); 1 single 76mm OTO-Melara compact dual-purpose gun (all craft), plus 2 single 20mm anti-aircraft guns; 2 single 12.7mm machine guns.

Top speed: 31 knots.

Range: 4000 nautical miles at 17 knots.

Programme: A planned six-craft class of which four are known to have been delivered by mid-1983 and comprise: *Aliyah, Geoula, Romach* and *Keshet*. Of these the earlier two carry hangars and helipad aft, while the latter two are missile-carriers. The lead craft entered service in the summer of 1980, the second and third in mid- and late-1981, with the fourth following in mid-1982.

Notes: Built in two versions, one of which trades some of its missile firepower for a hangar-stowed helicopter, these very large fast attack craft can all act as group leaders for a fast attack flotilla. The onboard helicopter is carried to facilitate mid-course missile guidance data in situations where the target remains obscured from the launch vessel. The 'Aliyah' class is sometimes referred to as, the 'Saar 4.5' class, while, their smaller brethren, the 'Rashef' class are known as 'Saar 4' class vessels.

Chonburi Class Fast Attack Craft

Role: Anti-shipping.

Builder: CN Breda, Italy.

User: Royal Thai Navy.

Basic data: 450 tons full displacement; 198.2ft (60.4m) overall length; 28.9ft (8.8m) maximum beam.

Crew: 45.

Propulsion: 3 MTU 20V538 TB92 diesels (total 15,000bhp); 3 controllable-pitch propellers.

Sensors: 1 Hollandse combined air/sea search radar; 1 SMA 3RM sea search and navigational radar; 1 Hollandse WM 22/61 radar/optronic fire control and automated action information data-processing system.

Armament: 2 single 76mm OTO-Melara Compact dual-purpose guns; 1 twin 40mm Breda/Bofors L40/70.

Top speed: 30 knots.

Range: 2500 nautical miles at 18 knots.

Programme: This three-craft Royal Thai Navy class comprise: *Chonburi* (P1), *Song-Khla* (P2) and *Phuket* (P3). Ordered in November 1979, the three craft were laid down between August and December 1981, the lead craft being completed by November 1982 and delivered in February 1983, with the remaining vessels both being delivered prior to the end of 1983.

Notes: Designed more for patrol endurance than maximum strike capability, the 'Chonburi' class, or MV 400TH to quote its design designation, can also act as command ship for a group of fast attack craft or minehunters.

Chonburi (P1), lead craft of this Royal Thai Navy class.

A South African 'Minister' class with four locally-developed missiles.

Rashef/Minister Class Fast Attack Craft

Role: Anti-shipping.
Builders: Israel Shipyards, Israel and Durban, South Africa.
Users: Chile (2), Israel (8) and South Africa (12).
Basic data: 450 tons full displacement; 190.5ft (58m) overall length; 25ft (7.8m) maximum beam.
Crew: 45.
Propulsion: 4 MTU MD671 diesels (total 10,680bhp); 2 propellers.
Sensors: 1 Thomson/CSF Neptune combined air and sea search and navigational radar; 1 Selenia Orion fire control radar (Thomson/CSF Vega air/sea search radars reported fitted in South African craft).
Armament: 2 twin Harpoon plus 9 single Gabriel anti-ship missile launchers (South African boats carry no Harpoon, but carry up to 7 Gabriel or 4 indigenously-designed anti-ship missiles); 2 single OTO-Melara 76mm dual-purpose guns; 2 (Israeli) or 4 (South African) single Oerlikon 20mm anti-aircraft guns.
Top speed: 32 knots.
Range: 4000 nautical miles at 17.5 knots.
Programme: The Israeli Navy currently operate four 'Rashef' class, comprising *Rashef*, *Kidon*, *Tarshish* and *Yafo*, all delivered between 1973 and 1980; two more having been transferred to Chile as *Chasma* and *Chipana*. South Africa has ordered 12 of these craft, the last nine being built in South Africa. Named after South African Ministers of Defence, all entering service between September 1977 and late 1984. 'Minister' class craft carry the pennant numbers *P1561* to *P1572*.
Notes: Big, seaworthy craft combining endurance with speed, as demonstrated by the goodwill visit paid to New York by a number of Israeli Navy 'Rashef' or 'Saar 4' class vessels during the latter 1970s.

Lurssen FPB 57 Classes Fast Attack Craft

Role: Anti-shipping.
Builders: Lurssen, Federal Germany and Turkish Naval Dockyards.
Users: Navies of Turkey (6), Nigeria (3) and Kuwait (2).
Basic data: 444 tons full displacement; 190.6ft (58.1m) overall length; 25.0ft (7.62m) maximum beam.
Crew: 54.
Propulsion: 4 MTU 16V956 TB91 diesels (total 19,940bhp); 4 propellers.
Sensors: 1 Decca 1226 sea search and navigational radar; 1 Hollandse WM 28 fire control radar and automated action information data-processing system.
Armament: 8 Harpoon (Turkish craft) or 4 Otomat Mk 2 (Nigerian craft) or 4 MM 40 Exocet (Kuwaiti craft) anti-ship missile launchers; 1 single 76mm OTO-Melara compact dual-purpose gun; 1 twin 40mm Breda/Bofors anti-aircraft gun or 1 twin 35mm Oerlikon anti-aircraft gun (Kuwaiti craft); 2 single 7.62mm machine guns.
Top speed: 40 knots.

The Nigerian Navy's Damisa *(P179) at speed, 1980.*

Range: 2000 nautical miles at 16 knots.
Programme: A total of 11 of these craft had been ordered by mid-1983, of which ten had been completed, with one Turkish craft outstanding. The initial contract placed with Lurssen came from Turkey in August 1973; this order being for four craft, with Lurssen to build the lead boat, while the rest were to be constructed in Turkey, this Turkish build being subsequently increased to five boats comprising: *P340*, the Lurssen-built lead craft, plus *P341* through *P345*. The next export contract, for three craft came from Nigeria, whose *P178* through *P180* had all been delivered by April 1981. The Kuwaiti order for two craft was fulfilled around the middle of 1983.
Notes: Fast, very seaworthy craft, the Lurssen FPB 57 design is essentially an export version of the Lurssen-designed Federal German Navy's Type 'S143' class missile attack craft (dealt with under a separate entry). However, unlike the Type S143A, which employs a composite form of construction using a light alloy hull sheathed in mahogany, the FPB 57 craft use an all-steel hull structure, married to a light alloy superstructure.

SFCN PR 72 MS Type Fast Attack Craft

Role: Anti-shipping.
Builder: SFCN, France.
User: Senegalese Navy.
Basic data: 420 tons full displacement; 192.6ft (58.7m) overall length; 28.9ft (8.2m) maximum beam.
Crew: 45.
Propulsion: 4 SACM AGO 195V16 RVR diesels (total 12,800bhp); 4 propellers.
Sensors: 1 Thomson-CSF Castor fire control radar/optronics system; 1 Decca TM1226 sea search and navigational radar.

Armament: 4 MM 40 Exocet anti-ship missile launchers; 2 single 76mm OTO-Melara compact dual-purpose guns; 2 single 40mm anti-aircraft guns.
Top speed: 31 knots.
Range: 2500 nautical miles at 16 knots.
Programme: Ordered in early 1980, the sole example to date of this design, the Senegalese *Niambur* (P773) was laid down in May 1980, launched in December 1980 and entered service in June 1981.
Notes: A smaller and lighter variant of the DTCN-designed PR 72 580-ton PR 72 corvette (see separate entry in corvette section). Interestingly, this sole missile-carrying craft packs far more powerful anti-ship weapons punch than all three SFCN-built PR 48 patrol craft delivered to Senegal between 1971 and 1977. As with the larger PR 72 corvettes, the PR 72 MS design has provision to retrofit Crotale Naval point air defence missiles if required.

La Combattante III Class Fast Attack Craft

The Hellenic Navy's Simairforos Kavalanthis *(P24).*

Role: Anti-shipping.
Builder: CNM Normandy, France.
Users: Navies of Greece (10), Nigeria (3), Tunisia (3).
Basic data: 400 tons (Greek) or 425 tons (Nigerian) full displacement; 183.7ft (56m) overall length; 25.9ft (7.9m) maximum beam.
Crew: 42.
Propulsion: 4 MTU 20V538 TB92 diesels (total 18,000bhp) on first four Greek, or TB91 (total 15,000bhp) on the latter six Greek, or MTU 16V956 TB92 diesels (total 20.840bhp) on Nigerian craft; 4 propellers.
Sensors: 1 Thomson-CSF Triton combined air/sea search radar; 1 Decca TM1226 sea search and navigational radar; 1 Thomson CSF Castor fire control radar; Thomson-CSF automated action information data-processing system.
Armament: 4 Exocet anti-ship missile launchers; 2 single 76mm OTO-Melara purpose guns (aft 76mm gun replaced by 1 twin Breda 40mm anti-aircraft gun on Nigerian craft); 2 twin Emerlec 30mm anti-aircraft guns; 2 single lightweight anti-submarine torpedo tubes.
Top speed: 37 knots (Nigerian) or 33 knots (Greek).
Range: 2000 nautical miles at 15 knots.
Programme: Greece was the first nation to place orders for this class, contracting for four craft, all delivered during 1977 and comprising *Antipliarchos Lascos* (P50), *Antipliarchos Blessas* (P51), *Antipliarchos Troupakis* (P52) and *Antipliarchos Mukonios* (P53). The follow-on Greek order for six additional craft comprise: *Simaiforos Kavalanthis* (P24), *Antipliarchos Kostakos* (P25), *Ipopliarchos Deyiannis* (P26), *Simaiforos Xenos* (P27), *Simaiforos Simitzopoulos* (P28) and *Simaiforos Starakis* (P29); all delivered between July 1980 and October 1982. In 1977, Nigeria placed orders for three of the slightly heavier 'La Combattante' IIIB class comprising:*Siri* (P181), *Ayam* (P182) and *Ekun* (P183); all delivered in 1981. The three Tunisian craft, ordered in mid-1981,

The Senegalese Navy's PR72 MS Niambur *(P773) seen on trials.*

comprise: *La Galite, Tunis* and *Carthage.*
Notes: The 'La Combattante' family is based on the Lurssen Type 148 and 143 designs, the 'La Combattante' IIIs being the equivalent of the Lurssen Type 143/FPB57 series. These large fast attack craft can cover up to 700 nautical miles at maximum sustainable speed.

Lurssen PB 57 Classes Fast Attack Craft

Lazaga *(P-01) with its original Mk 22 gun forward.*

Role: Patrol.
Builders: Lurssen, W Germany and Bazan, Spain.
Users: Navies of Ghana (2), Spain (6), Turkey (7).
Basic data: 400 tons full displacement; 190.6ft (58.1m) overall length; 24.9ft (7.6m) maximum beam.
Crew: 39.
Propulsion: 2 MTU MA-16V956 TB91 diesels (total 7780bhp); 2 propellers.
Sensors: 1 Raytheon 1620/6 or Racal-Decca 1229 sea search and navigational radar; 1 Hollandse M22 fire control radar; provision for sonar equipment.

Armament: 1 single OTO-Melara 76mm dual-purpose gun (1 single 76mm Mk 22 gun in *Lazaga*); 1 single Breda-Bofors 40mm anti-aircraft gun; 2 single 20mm anti-aircraft guns. Provision has been made for mounting anti-ship missiles.

Top speed: 29.5 knots.

Range: 4200 nautical miles at 17 knots.

Programme: A six-ship class for the Spanish Navy comprising the Lurssen-built lead craft, *Lazaga* (P-01), along with the Bazan-built P-02 through P-06. Service entry dates for these craft were July 1975 (P-01), February (P-02), July 1976 (P-03), April 1977 (P-04), July 1977 (P-05) and December 1977 (P-06). The two Ghanaian craft, *Achimota* (P28) and *Yogaga* (P29) were ordered in 1977, both being delivered at the end of March 1981. Turkey operates a single example *Girne* (P140) accepted in mid-1976.

Notes: Lurssen have optimised the design of these large, seaworthy boats around a high speed cruise capability, the craft being able to cover 2260 nautical miles at 27 knots.

Type 143 and 143A Class Fast Attack Craft

The Federal German Navy's second of Type 143, Falke

Role: Anti-shipping.

Builders: Lurssen and Kroger, Federal Germany.

User: Federal German Navy (10 × T143 and 10 × T143A).

Basic data: 393 tons full displacement; 189.0ft (57.6m) overall length; 25.5ft (7.76m) maximum beam.

Crew: 39 (143); 34 (143A).

Propulsion: 4 MTU 16V956 TB91 diesels (total 16,000bhp); 4 propellers.

Sensors: 1 SMA 3RM 20 sea search and navigational radar; 1 Hollandse WM 27 fire control radar; AGIS automated action information data-processing system.

Armament: 4 MM 38 Exocet anti-ship missile launchers; 2 single 76mm OTO-Melara Compact dual-purpose guns on Type 143s or aft mount deleted from Type 143As in order to install single 24-cell General Dynamics RAM point air defence missile launcher when available; 2 heavyweight anti-submarine torpedo tubes (Type 143 only); mines.

Top speed: 36 knots.

Range: 2000 nautical miles.

Programme: These classes consist of ten craft each for a total of 20 vessels. Launched between October 1973 and April 1976, the Type 143s comprise: P6111/S61 through P6120/S70; all entering service between April 1976 and December 1977. The first of the Type 143As was launched in September 1981 with the last of this ten boat class scheduled for delivery in November 1984. The Type 143As comprise: P6121/S71 through P6130/S80. In each case Lurssen acted as lead year for the ships, three of each class being under sub-contract by Kroger.

Notes: Unlike the closely related Lurssen FPB 57 design, both the Type 143 and 143A craft employ a steel-framed hull sheathed with wood planking married to a light alloy superstructure. Interestingly, the prime motivation behind the procurement of the Type 143A class lay in the Federal Germany Government's doubts concerning the US Navy's resolve to pursue adequately the development of their 'Pegasus' class hydrofoil programme in which the Germans had initially participated.

PGG511/AS Siddiq Class Fast Attack Craft

Role: Anti-shipping.

Builder: Peterson Builders, USA.

User: Royal Saudi Arabian Navy.

Basic data: 390 tons full displacement; 190.0ft (57.9m) overall length; 26.5ft (8.1m) maximum beam.

Crew: 38.

Propulsion: 1 General Electric LM2500 gas turbine (23,000shp); 2 MTU 12V652 diesels (total 3058bhp); CODOG; 2 controllable-pitch propellers.

Abu Obaidah (PGG527), the last of the class, seen at speed.

Sensors: 1 SPS-55 sea search and navigational radar; 1 Mk 92 fire control radar for 76mm gun.

Armament: 4 Harpoon anti-ship missile launchers; 1 single 76mm Mk 75 (OTO-Melara) compact dual-purpose gun; 1 Phalanx 20mm close-in weapons system; 2 single 20mm anti-aircraft guns; 1 single 81mm mortar; 2 single 40mm mortars.

Top speed: 38 knots.

Range: Over 500 nautical miles at 32 knots.

Programme: Saudi Arabia ordered this nine-ship class in February 1977, the vessels comprising: *As Siddiq* (PGG511), *Al Farouq* (PGG513), *Abdul Aziz* (PGG515), *Faisal* (PGG517), *Khalid* (PGG519), *Amr* (PGG521), *Tariq* (PGG523), *Oqbah* (PGG525) and *Abu Obaidah* (PGG527). Laid down between September 1978 and September 1981, all were launched between September 1979 and April 1982, with deliveries taking place from December 1980 to December 1982.

Notes: Almost directly comparable to the larger Lurssen designs (including the French-built 'La Combattante' family), the Peterson-built PGG511 class places greater emphasis on the 'dash' speed capability of the gas turbine, whose fuel hunger at high power settings relative to the modern diesel engine is offset by the loiter ability associated with the choice of two low-powered diesels. The large funnel, necessitated by the air intake and exhaust needs of the gas turbine, gives this class of patrol craft a distinctly corvette-like appearance. The total commonality of both the sensors and weapons fitted to this class and the larger PCG612/'Badr' class corvettes

The 'Province' class SNV Al Bat'Nar (B11), operated by Oman, 1983.

should help considerably in reducing the support costs incurred by the Saudi Arabians in the operations of these two classes.

Province Class Fast Attack Craft

Role: Anti-shipping.
Builder: Vosper Thornycroft, UK.
Users: Omani Navy (3), Kenyan Navy (2).
Basic data: 370 tons full displacement; 186ft (56.7m) overall length; 26.9ft (8.2m) maximum beam.
Crew: 65.
Propulsion: 4 Paxman Valenta 18GM diesels (total 15,200bhp); 4 propellers.
Sensors: 1 Decca AC 1226 sea search and navigational radar; 1 Sperry Sea Archer optronic fire control system; IFF facilities.
Armament: 4 Exocet (or 8 Sea Killer optional fit) anti-ship missile launchers; 1 single 76mm OTO-Melara compact dual-purpose gun; 1 twin Breda/Bofors 40mm anti-aircraft gun.
Top speed: 38 knots.
Range: 2000 nautical miles at 16 knots.
Programme: The first of this three-craft class was ordered late in 1979, to be followed by a further two craft order in January 1981. The class comprises SNV *Dhofar* (B10), *Al Bat'Nar* (B11) and *Al Sharqiyah* (B12). All three were laid down between September 1980 and December 1981 and were completed in July 1982, November 1983 and January 1984, respectively. Two additional craft of the same basic design for an African nation, reportedly Kenya, were in build by early 1985.
Notes: The 'Province' class craft are the largest fast attack craft yet to be built in Vosper Thornycroft's Porchester yards. Their high speed, agility, relatively small size and powerful anti-ship armament provide this class with a potent strike capability against much larger, well-armed warships. The total cost of the three-craft Omani programme was put at around £75 million in 1981.

SFCN PR48 Type Fast Attack Craft

Role: Anti-shipping.
Builder: SFCN, France.
User: Cameroon Navy.
Basic data: 324 tons full displacement; 171.3ft (52.2m) overall length; 25.1ft (7.65m) maximum beam.

Bakassi (P104) of the Cameroon Navy, seen on late 1983 sea trials carrying eight MM40 Exocet launchers.

Crew: 39.
Propulsion: 2 SACM AGO 16 RVR diesels (total 6400bhp); 2 controllable-pitch propellers.
Sensors: 1 Racal Decca 1230 low-level air and sea search radar; 1 Racal Decca TM 1229C sea search and navigational radar; 2 CSEE Naja optronic fire directors; Radop 30 automated action information data-processing.
Armament: 8 MM40 Exocet anti-ship missile launchers; 2 single 40mm Bofors L70 anti-aircraft guns. *Note:* as fitted to Cameroon craft.
Top speed: 30 knots.
Range: 2000 nautical miles at 16 knots.
Programme: The first order, for one craft, came from the Cameroon in December 1980. This craft, *Bakassi* (P104) was laid down in late 1981, launched in October 1983 and was delivered in January 1984.
Notes: The steel hulled SFCN PR48 design started life as a 164ft (50.0m) craft, pitched primarily at the 200 nautical mile offshore asset protection role, but has emerged as a larger and quite potent missile craft. The PR48 is being offered with a number of optional weapons fits. The peacetime crew complement is 35.

Ramadan Class Fast Attack Craft

Role: Anti-shipping.
Builder: Vosper Thornycroft, UK.

The Egyptian ARES Hettein *(P680). Note the anti-ship missile installation aft of the craft's mainmast.*

User: Egyptian Navy.
Basic data: 324 tons full displacement; 170.6ft (52m) overall length; 24.9ft (7.6m) maximum beam.
Crew: 37.
Propulsion: 4 MTU 20V 538 diesels (total 17.150bhp); 4 propellers.
Sensors: 1 Marconi S820 combined air/sea short-range search radar; 1 Marconi ST802 tracking radar; 1 Marconi/Sperry optronic gun fire control system; 1 Decca RM1226 sea search and navigational radar.
Armament: 2 twin Otomat anti-ship missile launchers; 1 OTO-Melara 76mm compact dual-purpose gun; 1 twin Breda/Bofors 40mm anti-aircraft gun.
Top speed: Over 35 knots.
Range: 1600 nautical miles at 18 knots.
Programme: The Egyptian Government order for this six-boat class was placed in September 1977 and was valued by the builders as being in excess of £150 million. All six hulls were laid down between September 1979 and February 1980 and all launches took place in the period September 1979 and November 1980. The first two vessels, ARES *Ramadan* (P670) and ARES *Khyber* (P672), were accepted during July and September 1981, respectively, while the remaining four, ARES *El Kadessaya* (P674), ARES *Yarmouk* (P676), ARES *Hettein* (P680) and ARES *Badr* (P678), were accepted during 1982.
Notes: With a hull design based on that of Vosper Thornycroft's earlier 'Tenacity' class boats, the larger, heavier 'Ramadan' class carry an impressive armament of 32 nautical mile ranging Otomat anti-ship missiles, backed by a two-tier anti-air gun capability.

Stockholm Class Fast Attack Craft

Role: Anti-shipping.
Builder: Karlskronavarvet, Sweden.
User: Royal Swedish Navy.
Basic data: 300 tons full displacement; 164.0ft (50.0m) overall length; 24.6ft (7.5m) maximum beam.
Crew: 26.
Propulsion: 1 Allison 570-KF gas turbine (15,000shp) and 2 MTU 16V396 diesels (total 7200bhp); CODAG; 2 controllable-pitch propellers.
Sensors: 1 Ericson Sea Giraffe pulse doppler air search radar; 1 Racal Decca 1229 sea search and navigational radar; 1 Philips (Sweden) 9LV200 fire control radar and automated action information data processing system.
Armament: 6 SAAB-Bofors RBS 15 anti-ship missile launchers; 1 single 57mm SAK 57 Mk 2 compact dual-purpose gun; 1 single 40mm Bofors L 40/70 anti-aircraft gun; 2 single heavyweight anti-submarine torpedo tubes.
Top speed: 38 knots.
Range: 2000 nautical miles at 18 knots.
Programme: The first two of this six-craft class were ordered by the Swedish Government in September 1981. The lead of class, *Stockholm* (K11) was laid down in August 1982, followed by *Malmo* (K12) in March 1983. Initial deployment of this class occurred in March 1985 with the commissioning of *Stockholm*.
Notes: This latest Karlskronavarvet-developed missile-carrying fast attack craft represents an amalgam of experience gained from three previous generations of the 'Spica', 'Spica' II and 'Handalan' strike craft. Interestingly, the 'Stockholm' class sometimes referred to as the 'Spica' III, utilises a composite gas turbine/diesel propulsive machinery arrangement rather than the all gas turbine or all diesel of the 'Spica' I/II and 'Handalan' craft. The 'Stockholm' class carries a heavy and well balanced armament, backed by effective sensors, particularly in the shape of the new Ericson pulse dopplar search radar, which has improved performance in both adverse weather and electronic countermeasures environments.

Helsinki Class Fast Attack Craft

Role: Anti-shipping.
Builder: Wartsila, Finland.
User: Finnish Defence Force.
Basic data: 300 tons full displacement; 147.6ft (45.0m) overall length; 29.2ft (8.9m) maximum beam.
Crew: 30.
Propulsion: 3 MTU 16V 538 diesels (total 12,000bhp); 3 controllable-pitch propellers.
Sensors: 1 combined low-level air/sea search radar; 1 navigational radar; 1 Philips (Sweden) 9LV225 electro-optronic fire control and automated action information processing system.
Armament: 4 SAAB RBS 15 anti-ship missile launchers; 1 single 57mm Bofors SAK-57 Mk 1 dual-purpose gun; 2 single 23mm anti-aircraft guns.

Top speed: 33 knots.
Endurance: In excess of 2000 nautical miles.
Programme: The first of this planned eight-craft class was ordered in October 1978, launched in September 1980 and delivered to the Finnish Defence Force in January 1981. This prototype vessel, *Helsinki* (P60), has now been joined in build by the as yet unnamed P61, P62 and P63, all of which were ordered in January 1983.
Notes: This Finnish-design fast attack craft class breaks with convention in terms of its hull proportions, being much broader of beam in relation to its length than any of its contemporaries from the drawing boards of Lurssen or Vosper Thornycroft. The choice is 4 SAAB-Bofors RBS 15 sea-skimming anti-ship missiles is interesting when it is remembered that the Finnish selection of this missile represents not only its first export contract, but must have been made prior to the completion of Royal Swedish Navy development trials with this 43 nautical mile (80km) or more ranging weapon.

Racharit Class Fast Attack Craft

Role: Anti-shipping.
Builder: CN Breda, Italy.
User: Thai Navy.
Basic data: 270 tons full displacement; 163.4ft (49.8m) overall length; 24.6ft (7.5m) maximum beam.
Crew: 45.
Propulsion: 3 MTU 20V538 TB91 diesels (total 13,500bhp); 3 controllable pitch propellers.
Sensors: 1 Decca TM 1226 sea search/navigational radar; 1 Hallandse M 25 fire control radar.
Armament: 4 Exocet anti-ship missile launchers; 1 single 76mm OTO-Melara compact dual-purpose gun; 1 single 40mm Breda/Bofors anti-aircraft gun.
Top speed: 36 knots.
Range: 2000 nautical miles at 15 knots.
Programme: Thailand ordered this three-craft class in July 1976, the vessels comprising: *Racharit* (4), *Witthayakom* (5) and *Udomet* (6). All launched between July and September of 1978, the three respectively entered service in August 1979, November 1979 and February 1980.
Notes: A sturdy-looking design in many ways directly comparable to the near contemporary, if heavier Vosper Thornycroft-developed 'Ramadan' class. While the 'Racharits' appear to haul the same kind of sensor/weapons fit over similar range at comparable speeds, all on the power of three rather than four diesels, the lower crew complement of the 'Ramadan' class suggests a higher degree of automation.

PSMM-1/Paek Ku Class Fast Attack Craft

Role: Anti-shipping.
Builders: Tacoma Boat, USA and Tacoma Korea.
User: South Korean Navy.
Basic data: 268 tons full displacement; 176.1ft (53.7m) overall length; 26.25ft (8.0m) maximum beam.
Crew: 32.
Propulsion: 6 Avco-Lycoming TF35 gas turbines (total derated to 16,800shp); COGAG; 2 controllable-pitch propellers.
Sensors: 1 Litton LN-66 HP combined air/sea search and navigational radar; 1 Mk 63 (first 3 craft) or 1 Westinghouse M-1200 (last 5 craft) fire control radar.
Armament: 2 quadruple Harpoon anti-ship missile launchers; 1 single 3in Mk 34 dual-purpose gun; 1 single 40mm anti-aircraft gun; 2 single 12.7mm machine guns.

The Tacoma-built lead of the PSMM-1 class, wearing its old pennant number.

An artist's impression of the Royal Swedish Navy's new 'Stockholm' class, or 'Spica' III missile craft.

Helsinki (P60), the lead craft of this Finnish class in mid-1983, as yet to be equipped with its four Swedish-developed anti-ship missiles.

Thailand's Racharit (4), lead craft of a three-vessel class.

135

Norby *(P545) with Harpoons mounted aft.*

Top speed: Over 40 knots.
Range: 2400 nautical miles at 18 knots.
Programme: An eight-craft class that entered service between 1975 and 1978, the first three were built by the parent US company, while the rest were built by Tacoma's Korean subsidiary, based in Chinhae. Known as 'Paek Ku' (seagull) class craft in South Korean Navy service, the vessels' most recent pennant numbers were: 52, 53, 55, 56, 57, 58, 59 and 61 (to complicate matters these are no longer displayed on the hulls).
Notes: A larger and more powerful derivative of Tacoma's 'Ashville' class fast patrol craft, the PSMM-1s (PSMM signifies patrol ship, Multi-Mission) are powered by two clusters, each of three TF35 gas turbines driving its own propeller shaft, via a speed-reducing gearbox. In operation, one, two or three engines can be engaged to drive each shaft in order to achieve the desired power output.

Willemoes Class Fast Attack Craft

Role: Anti-shipping.
Builder: Frederikshavn, Denmark.
User: Royal Danish Navy.
Basic data: 265 tons full displacement; 151.25ft (46.1m) overall length; 24.25ft (7.4m) maximum beam.
Crew: 25.
Propulsion: 3 Rolls-Royce Proteus gas turbines (total 12.750shp) or 2 General Motors 8V-71 diesels (total 960bhp) arranged in CODOG; 3 controllable-pitch propellers.
Sensors: 1 Philips (Sweden) 9GA208 combined air/sea search radar; 1 Hollandse NWS 3 sea search and navigational radar; 1 Philips (Sweden) LV200 fire control radar and naval tactical data-processing system.
Armament: 1 OTO-Melara 76mm gun; 34 torpedo tubes or 2 twin Harpoon anti-ship missile launchers or 20 mines.
Top speed: 40 knots.
Range: 400 nautical miles at 36 knots.

Programme: Deliveries of this ten-craft class were *Willemoes* (P549) and *Bille* (P540) in 1976; *Bredal* (P541), *Hammer* (P542), *Huitfeldt* (P543) and *Krieger* (P544) in 1977; plus the *Norby* (P545), *Rodsteen* (P546), *Sehested* (P547) and *Suenson* (P548) in 1978.
Notes: Lursen designed, the 'Willemoes' structure and layout closely follows that of the 'Spica' class fast attack craft operated by the Swedish Navy. As with the 'Spica', the 'Willemoes' class were designed around a primary armament of four heavyweight, wire-guided 21in, Swedish Type 61 anti-submarine torpedoes with a reported range of 10.85 nautical miles. In service the 'Willemoes' class boats have demonstrated an impressive versatility of weapons fitment, including the carriage of four Harpoons, with their 60 nautical mile range, while retaining the ability to mount two of the heavyweight torpedoes.

Matka Class Fast Attack Craft

Role: Anti-shipping.
Builder: Izhora Shipyard, USSR.
User: Soviet Navy.
Basic data: 260 tons full displacement; 131.2ft (40.0m) overall length; 25.25ft (7.7m) maximum beam of hull.
Crew: 30.
Propulsion: 3 M504 diesels (total 15,000bhp); 3 propellers.
Sensors: 1 combined low-level air/sea search and navigational radar; 1 fire control radar (for SS-N-2C missiles); 1 fire control radar (for 76.2mm and 30mm guns); 2 separate IFF radars; naval tactical information processing system.
Armament: 2 single SS-N-2C anti-ship missile launchers; 1 single 76.2mm dual-purpose gun; 1 multi-barrel 30mm Gatling type close-in weapons system.
Top speed: 40 knots.
Range: 400 nautical miles at 36 knots.
Programme: A known eight-craft class, this hydrofoil was reported to have initially deployed with the Soviet Fleet during 1978.

Notes: The 'Matka' class design is a missile equipped derivative of the Soviet Navy's 'Turya' class torpedo-carrying hydrofoil. Judging from the 'Matka' craft's relatively modest performance and weapons carrying capability, compared with the much lighter 'Sparviero' class hydrofoil, it would appear that the 'Matka' design is less than adequately powered for its task. If, indeed, the craft is as underpowered and overloaded as some photographs would suggest, then it would seem that the 'Matka' design will never be built in large numbers; a point that tends to coincide with Western intelligence reports that the Soviets are developing a new class of missile-carrying hydrofoil, based on the gas turbine-powered 'Sarancka' type design.

Lurssen TNC-45 Classes Fast Attack Craft

Role: Anti-shipping.
Builder: Lurssen, Federal Germany.
Users: Navies of Argentina (2), Bahrain (2) and Kuwait (6).
Basic data: 259 tons full displacement; 147.3ft (44.9m) overall length; 23.0ft (7.0m) maximum beam.
Crew: 33.
Propulsion: 4 MTU 16V538 TB92 diesels (total 15,600bhp); 4 propellers.
Sensors: 1 Philips (Sweden) 9LV223 fire control radar and automated action information data-processing system; 1 IFF Mk 10 radar; CSEE Panda optical fire director.
Armament: 2 twin MM 40 Exocet anti-ship missile launchers; 1 single 76mm OTO-Melara compact dual-purpose gun; 1 single 40mm Breda/Bofors L70B anti-aircraft gun; 2 single MG-3 machine guns.
Top speed: 41.5 knots.
Range: 1500 nautical miles at 16 knots.
Programme: Argentina was the first customer for this export version of the Lurssen-developed Federal German Navy's Type 148, placing a contract for two craft, *Intrépida* (ELPR1) and *Indómita* (ELPR2) in 1974; the vessels being delivered in July and December 1975. More recently both Bahrain and Kuwait have ordered two and six craft, respectively; the two Bahrain vessels being scheduled for 1982 and 1983 delivery, while Kuwaiti deliveries commenced in late 1982.
Notes: Steel-hulled with aluminium superstructures, the TNC in the designation is an abbreviation of Top speed Navy Craft. Faster, but shorter ranged than the UK-

This high-angle view looking down on a foilborne 'Matka' class hydrofoil helps to convey the lack of free deck space and general sense of above deck clutter associated with this design.

developed 'Ramadan' class 52 metre craft, the Lurssen TNC-45 carries almost as much weaponry, but lacks the sensor fit capability of its somewhat larger British rival.

PSMM-5/Lung Chiang Class Fast Attack Craft

Role: Anti-shipping.
Builders: Tacoma Boat, USA, and China Shipbuilding, Taiwan.
User: Taiwanese Navy.
Basic data: 250 tons full displacement; 165.0ft (50.2m) overall length; 23.8ft (7.25m) maximum beam.
Crew: 35.
Propulsion: 3 Avco-Lycoming TF40A gas turbines (total 12,000shp); 3 General Motors 12V149 TI diesels (total 3600bhp); CODOG; 3 controllable pitch propellers.
Sensors: 1 Selenia/SMA RAN-11LX combined air/sea search and navigational radar; 1 DSN NA-10 fire control radar; Selenia IPN-10 automated action information data-processing system.
Armament: 4 Taiwanese-built IAI Gabriel anti-ship missile launchers; 1 single 76mm OTO-Melara compact dual-purpose gun; 1 twin 30mm Emerlec anti-aircraft gun; 2 single 12.7mm machine guns.
Top speed: 40 knots.
Range: 2700 nautical miles at 12 knots.

Lurssen TNC-45 on trials.

The lead PSMM-5 craft minus armament prior to delivery.

The former USS Crockett *(PG88), 'Ashville' class.*

Programme: This two-craft class entered service in 1978 and 1979, the lead craft being constructed by Tacoma Boat. Neither the lead craft, *Lung Chiang* (581) nor its sister (582) carries any external identification.

Notes: While generally similar to the earlier, all gas turbine powered PSMM-1 vessels, these Taiwanese craft embody a lower wheelhouse, a lowered centre-section to their superstructure and a more massively girdered mast. A slightly larger derivative, weighing in at 290 tons full displacement, has been adopted by Indonesia, who have eight of these PSK (Patrol Ship, Korean-built) in service or on order. The PSKs employ a CODOG propulsion arrangement as do the PSMM-5s, but use a single Fiat-built General Electric LM2500 gas turbine (25,000shp) and 3 MTU 12V331 TC81 diesels (total 2240bhp). Armament of the Indonesian craft comprises: four Exocet anti-ship missile launchers; one single 57mm Bofors gun; one single 40mm Bofors anti-aircraft gun and two single 20mm Bofors anti-aircraft guns.

Rade Koncar Class Fast Attack Craft

Role: Anti-shipping.
Builder: Tito Shipyards, Yugoslavia.
User: Yugoslavian Navy.
Basic data: 250 tons full displacement; 147.6ft (45.0m) overall length; 26.2ft (8.0m) maximum beam.
Crew: 30.
Propulsion: 2 Rolls-Royce Proteus gas turbines (total 9000shp) and 2 MTU diesels (total 7200bhp); CODAG; 4 controllable-pitch propellers.
Sensors: 1 Philips (Sweden) 9LV 200 missile and gun fire control radar system, 1 IFF; 1 Decca 1226 sea search and navigational radar; Philips (Sweden) automated action data-processing system.
Armament: 2 single SS-N-2B 'Styx' anti-ship missile launchers; 2 single 57mm Bofors D70 dual-purpose guns.
Top speed: 37 knots.

The lead of class, Rade Koncar *(PGG401), of the Yugoslavian Navy at speed. Powered by British gas turbines and German diesels, these craft are armed with Soviet missiles and Swedish guns.*

Range: 1650 nautical miles at 15 knots.
Programme: This six-craft class comprises: *Rade Koncar* (PGG401), *Vlado Cetkovic* (402), *Ramiz Sadiku* (403), *Hasan Zahirovic Lase* (404), *Jordan Nikolov Orce* (405) and *Ante Banina* (406). All entered service between April 1977 and December 1979.
Notes: This extremely compact Yugoslavian-designed craft carries an interesting weapons balance of missiles and high capability guns; the two 57mm Bofors guns providing a respectable anti-air capability of considerable range against both aircraft and sea-skimming missiles, thanks to their proximity, pre-fragmented warheaded ammunition. Although primarily designed for coastal operations, this class has a deep water, rough weather capability extending up to seven days without need for any kind of replenishment. These craft can cover 880 nautical miles at 23 knots under the power of their twin diesels alone.

Ashville Class Fast Attack Craft

Role: Anti-shipping.
Builders: Tacoma Boat and Peterson Builders, USA.
Users: Navies of Colombia (2), South Korea (1) and Turkey (2).
Basic data: 245 tons full displacement; 164.5ft (50.1m) overall length; 23.9ft (7.3m) maximum beam.
Crew: 28.
Propulsion: 1 General Electric LM1500 gas turbine (13,300shp); 2 Cummins VT12-S75M diesels (total 3300bhp); CODOG; 2 controllable-pitch propellers.
Sensors: 1 Raytheon Pathfinder combined low-level air/sea search and navigational radar; 1 SPG-50 fire control radar.
Armament: 1 single 3in Mk 34 anti-aircraft gun; 1 single 40mm Mk 3 anti-aircraft gun; 2 twin 0.5in machine guns. *Note:* Four of the former US Navy craft were equipped with two Standard anti-radiation missile bin launchers at the stern, which involved the deletion of the 40mm Mk 3 gun.
Top speed: Over 40 knots.
Range: 1700 nautical miles at 16 knots.
Programme: A total of 17 craft of this class were built for the US Navy; all being delivered between 1966 and 1971. The first transfer of this class to US allied navies commenced with the delivery of *Paek Ku 51* to South Korea in October 1971. Within the next two years, four more 'Ashvilles' were transferred in pairs to Greece, which no longer operates them, and Turkey which continues to operate *Yildirim* (P338) and *Bora* (P339). More recently, the last two US Navy craft, *Tacoma* and *Welch* were transferred on lease in 1982 to Colombia.
Notes: The 'Ashville' class requirement was brought into focus by the Cuban crisis of 1962 and the subsequent US Navy realisation that it lacked modern, high speed interdiction craft. However, by the time the 'Ashvilles'

began to enter service, the climate of US Navy planning opinion had already swung away from conventional hulled design solutions in favour of the even faster, missile-armed hydrofoil: a decision that, in turn, was to prove transitory, as evidenced by the massive cut-back to the originally planned number of Boeing-built 'Pegasus' class craft to be procured. The 'Ashville' class design and development effort was not, however, to be totally wasted; much of their technology serving as the basis for Tacoma Boat's subsequent Patrol Ship Multi-Mission (PSMM) family and Peterson Builders' PGG511/As 'Siddiq' class.

Handalan Class (Spica M) Fast Attack Craft

Role: Anti-shipping.
Builder: Karlskronavarvet, Sweden.
User: Royal Malaysian Navy.
Basic data: 240 tons full displacement; 143.0ft (43.6m) overall length; 23.3ft 7.1m) maximum beam.
Crew: 40.
Propulsion: 3 MTU 16V538 TB91 diesels (total 10,800bhp); 3 propellers.
Sensors: 1 Philips (Sweden) 9LV 200 combined air/sea search and tracking radar and fire control system with automated action information data-processing.
Armament: 2 twin MM40 Exocet anti-ship missile launchers; 1 single 57mm Bofors SAK Bofors SAK 57 Mk 1 dual-purpose gun; 1 single 40mm Bofors anti-aircraft gun; provision to carry 2 heavyweight anti-submarine, wire-guided homing torpedoes.
Top speed: 34.5 knots.
Range: 1850 nautical miles at 14 knots.
Programme: An eight-craft class, the first four of which were ordered by Malaysia in August 1976 comprising: *Handalan* (P3511), *Perkasa* (P3512), *Pendikar* (P3513) and *Gempita* (P3514). All of this first batch were laid down between May 1977 and October 1977; the four being accepted simultaneously in late October 1979. Malaysia placed a repeat order for a further four of these craft in December 1982.
Notes: The 'Handalan' class, or 'Spica' M design, is a more heavily anti-ship armed derivative of the Royal Swedish Navy's 'Spica' II class craft and are the first new-built Swedish vessels to be exported in the post-World War II period. The 'Handalan' class differs physically from the 'Spica' II in having a more forward positioned bridge and superstructure, giving them a generally similar appearance to the Malaysian operated 'Combattant' II class, when viewed from abeam, the most ready 'Handalan' class identifying feature being their forward-raked bridge windscreens.

Pegasus Class Fast Attack Craft

Role: Anti-shipping.
Builder: Boeing Marine, USA.
User: US Navy.
Basic data: 231 tons full displacement; 131.5ft (40.1m) overall length (on foils); 28.2ft (8.6m) maximum beam.
Crew: 21.
Propulsion: 1 General Electric LM2500 gas turbine (18,000shp) or 2 MTU 8V331 diesels (total 1600bhp). The gas turbine drives 1 Aerojet General waterjet when foilborne. When hullborne, the 2 diesels provide power to 2 waterjets and bow thruster.
Sensors: 1 Raytheon Pathfinder sea search and navigational radar; 1 Mk 94 (Hollandse WM 28) fire control radar.
Armament: 2 quadruple Harpoon anti-ship missile launchers; 1 single 76mm Mk 75 anti-aircraft gun.
Top speed: Over 40 knots.

Handalan *(P3511) lead craft of the Royal Malaysian Navy class.*

Aquila *(PHM-4), fourth of the 'Pegasus' class, foilborne.*

Endurance: Over 500 nautical miles on foils.
Programme: Boeing received the design contract for this craft in November 1971 and was given go-ahead to build the lead craft in April 1973, at which time it was envisaged as the first of a 30-vessel class, but when the series production contract was placed in November 1977, the number had been reduced to five craft, which form the six hydrofoil class comprising: *Pegasus* (PHM-1), *Hercules* (PHM-2), *Taurus* (PHM-3), *Aquila* (PHM-4), *Aries* (PHM-5) and *Gemini* (PHM-6). All were delivered by 1982.
Notes: These six hydrofoils are based in Key West, Florida, where their high sustained speed and agility could prove useful in the Caribbean and Gulf of Mexico.

Fremantle Class Fast Attack Craft

Role: Offshore patrol.
Builders: Brooke Marine, UK, and NQE, Australia.
User: Royal Australian Navy.
Basic data: 230 tons full displacement; 137.8ft (42m) overall length; 23.45ft (7.15m) maximum beam.
Crew: 22.
Propulsion: 2 MTU 16V 538 TB91 diesels (total 7200bhp); 2 propellers.
Sensors: 1 Decca Type 1006 sea search and navigational radar. **Armament:** 1 Bofors 40mm Mk VII; 2 single 12.6mm machine guns; 1 aft-mounted 81mm mortar.
Top speed: 29 knots.
Range: 2450 nautical miles at 15 knots.

HMAS Bendigo *(P211) departing for a patrol.*

Programme: In September 1977, Brooke Marine received an Australian Government order calling for the construction of the lead boat, HMAS *Fremantle* (P203), of a 15-craft class, along with the provision of lead yard services to the Australian Navy and North Queensland Engineers of Cairn, who have responsibility for the building of the remaining 14 'Fremantles', P204 through P217. Laid down in December 1977 and launched in February 1979, HMAS *Fremantle* (P203) was commissioned on 17 March 1980. By the end of 1984 *Fremantle* had been joined by all remaining craft comprising HMAS *Warrnambool* (P204), HMAS *Townsville* (P205) and HMAS *Wollongong* (P206), HMAS *Launceston* (P207), HMAS *Whyalla* (P208), HMAS *Ipswich* (P209), HMAS *Cessnock* (P210), HMAS *Bendigo* (P211), HMAS *Gawler* (P212), HMAS *Geraldton* (P213), HMAS *Dibbo* (P214), HMAS *Geelong* (P215), HMAS *Gladstone* (P216) and HMAS *Bunbury* (P217).

Notes: Ordered as a replacement for the Royal Australian Navy's 'Attack' class patrol boats, the primary role of the 'Fremantles' is to act as long-range coastal pickets against illegal immigrant landing, hence the lack of heavier armament.

Osa I/II Classes Fast Attack Craft

Role: Anti-shipping.
Builders: Various, USSR and China.
Users: Navies of Algeria (8), Bulgaria (1), China (around 90), Cuba (13), East Germany (15), Egypt (6), Finland (4), India (8), Iraq (4), Libya (12), North Korea (8), Poland

(13), Romania (5), Somalia (2), Syria (6) and Yugoslavia (10).
Basic data: 240 tons full displacement; 127.95ft (39.0m) overall length; 25.25ft (7.7m) maximum beam.
Crew: 30.
Propulsion: 3 M504 diesels (15,000bhp); 3 propellers in 'Osa' IIs, 'Osa' I have 3 M503A diesels (12,000bhp); 3 propellers.
Sensors: 1 combined low-level air/sea search and navigational radar; 1 fire control radar (for 30mm guns); 3 separate IFF radars.
Armament: 4 single SS-N-2 'Styx' anti-ship missile launchers; 2 twin 30mm Gatling type close-in weapons systems. *Note:* 'Osa' IIs carry the improved model SS-N-2 'Styx' with a range of around 40 nautical miles, rather than the 'Osa' Is 25 nautical mile ranged earlier version missiles.
Top speed: 36 knots.
Range: 700 nautical miles at 20 knots.
Programme: The USSR built approximately 240 'Osa' I and IIs comprising 120 for the Soviet Navy (70 'Osa' Is and 50 'Osa' IIs), plus a known 118 for export to friendly navies (70 'Osa Is and 48 'Osa' IIs); the Soviet-built 'Osa' I deliveries being completed between 1959 and 1966, with 'Osa' IIs following between 1966 and 1970. In addition to the Soviet-built craft, approximately 90 'Osa' Is have been built in the Chinese People's Republic, with deliveries commenced in 1960. Currently around 105 'Osa' class boats remain in service with the Soviet Navy, consisting of 65 'Osa' Is and 40 'Osa' IIs.
Notes: With a total of around 330 'Osa' I and IIs built, this steel-hulled design can rightfully lay claim to being not only the largest post-World War II warship programme, but also to being the most widely used fast attack craft extant. Unlike many contemporary fast attack craft, the 'Osa' classes have been put to the test under actual combat conditions; the Egyptians having operated them during the 1967 and 1973 wars with Israel (two having been lost), while Indian Navy 'Osa' IIs saw action in the 1971/72 war with Pakistan, sinking a Pakistani destroyer and severely damaging another as well as sinking or damaging several Pakistani merchant ships.

Spica Class Fast Attack Craft

Role: Anti-shipping.
User: Royal Swedish Navy.
Basic data: 235 tons full displacement; 139.4ft (42.5m) overall length; 24ft (7.3m) maximum beam.
Crew: 28.
Propulsion: 3 Rolls-Royce Proteus 1274 gas turbines (total 12,720shp); 3 controllable-pitch propellers.
Sensors: 1 Decca 1226 sea search and navigational radar; 1 Hollandse M22 fire control radar.
Armament: 1 single 57mm Bofors dual-purpose gun; 6

Tuuli (P14), one of four Finnish operated 'Osa' II boats.

Virgo (T126), a 'Spica' class boat of the Royal Swedish Navy.

Halmstad (R140) 'Norrkoping' class, with Saab-Bofors RBS15 missiles aft.

heavyweight anti-submarine torpedo tubes or mines. *Note*: Prior to 1985, the boats are to be refitted to carry 8 RBS-15 anti-ship missiles at the expense of four torpedo tubes.
Top speed: 40 knots.
Range: 400 nautical miles at 36 knots.
Programme: This six-boat class comprises *Spica* (T121), *Sirius* (T122), *Capella* (T123), *Castor* (T124), *Vega* (T125) and *Virgo* (T126). All six boats entered service between 1966 and 1967 and are scheduled to undergo modernisation during the first half of the 1980s.
Notes: Extremely fast, seaworthy boats, the Lurssen designed 'Spica' class, along with the improved 12-boat 'Spica' II class are visually characterised by their aft-mounted superstructure and large, forward-mounted gun turret. With their shallow draft of just under 5.25ft (1.6m) at full load, these very fast, agile craft are ideal for operations in the frequently shallow waters of the Baltic, offering a very low radar signature to an enemy by virtue of their small size.

Norrkoping (Spica II) Class Fast Attack Craft

Role: Anti-shipping.
Builder: Karlskronavarvet, Sweden.
User: Royal Swedish Navy.
Basic data: 230 tons full displacement; 143.0ft (43.6m) overall length; 23.3ft (7.1m) maximum beam.
Crew: 27.
Propulsion: 3 Rolls-Royce Proteus gas turbines (total 12,900shp); 3 propellers.
Sensors: 1 Scanter 009 sea search and navigational radar (to be replaced by Ericson Sea Giraffe combined air/sea and navigational radar); 1 Philips (Sweden) 9LV200 fire control radar and automated action information data-processing system.
Armament: 8RBS-15 anti-ship missile launchers (from 1984) or 6 heavyweight anti-submarine torpedo tubes; 1 single 57mm Bofors SAK 57 Mk 1 dual-purpose gun; mines (in place of torpedo tubes).
Top speed: 40 knots.
Range: Over 700 nautical miles at 35 knots.
Programme: This 12-craft class comprises: *Norrkoping* (R131), *Nynashamn* (R132), *Nortalje* (R133), *Varberg* (R134), *Vasteras* (R135), *Vastervik* (R136), *Umea* (R137), *Pitea* (R138), *Lulea* (R139), *Halmstad* (R140), *Stromstad* (R141) and *Ystad* (R142). All boats of this class were laid

down between November 1972 and September 1976, entering service between September 1973 and December 1976. *Note*: this class had T (for Torpedo) pennant number prefixes, changed to R (for Rocket) to denote their retrofitted missile-carrying capability.
Notes: Although slightly longer than the 'Spica' class, the 'Spica' II design is marginally lighter and faster for the same total installed propulsive power. The 'Spica' II hull, married to an all diesel propulsion arrangement and different weapons fit, served as the basis for the 'Handalan' class craft exported to Malaysia.

Freccia Class Fast Attack Craft

Role: Anti-shipping.
Builders: Various CNR yards, Italy.
User: Italian Navy.
Basic data: 217 tons full displacement; 150.8ft (45.96m) overall length; 23.95ft (7.3m) maximum beam.
Crew: 37.
Propulsion: 1 Rolls-Royce Proteus gas turbine (4300shp); 2 FIAT 1832 diesels (total 6600bhp); CODAG; 3 controllable-pitch propellers.
Sensors: 1 SMA 3ST7-250 combined low-level air/sea search and navigational radar; 1 Selenia-Elsag RTN 150 fire control radar; naval tactical information processing system.
Armament: 2 heavyweight anti-submarine torpedo tubes; 2 single 40mm anti-aircraft guns (as torpedo craft), or 3 single 40mm anti-aircraft guns (as patrol craft), or 1 single 40mm anti-aircraft gun; 8 mines (as minelayer). *Note*: Role change can be carried out within a day.
Top speed: 41 knots.
Range: 695 nautical miles at 27 knots.
Programme: This two-craft class comprises: *Freccia* (P493) and *Saetta* (P494), the vessels being built by CNR Taranto and Monfalcone, respectively. Laid down in April and June of 1963, both craft entered service in July 1966. During the latter half of the 1970s, *Saetta* acted as trials craft for the Sistel Sea Killer anti-ship missile system, but has now reverted to her original role.
Notes: The 'Freccia' class design follows the 1960s and 1970s Italian practice of employing a steel hull, married to a light alloy superstructure. Along with the Italian Navy's 'Alpino' class frigates, the 'Freccia' class reflects Italy's early interest in the naval application of aircraft gas turbine technology.

Freccia (P493) as configured for the patrol mission and, thus, carrying all three 40mm Breda/Bofors gun mounts.

Lurssen FPB 38 Class Fast Attack Craft

Role: Patrol.
Builder: Lurssen, Federal Germany and Malaysia.
Users: Bahrain Navy (2), Federal German Coast Guard (8) and Royal Malaysian Marine Police (12).
Basic data: 186 tons full displacement; 126.3ft (38.5m) overall length; 23.0ft (7.0m) maximum beam.
Crew: 21 (Bahrain).
Propulsion: 2 MTU 20V539 TB91 diesels (total 7800bhp); 2 propellers.
Sensors: 1 Racal Decca TM1226 sea search and navigational radar; 1 Philips (Sweden) 9LV100 fire control radar and automated action information data-processing system; 1 CSEE Lynx optical fire control system (Bahraini craft).
Armament: 1 twin 40mm Breda/Bofors 40 L70B anti-aircraft gun; 2 single 7.62mm MG 3 machine guns; 14 mines (Bahraini craft fit).
Top speed: 33 knots.
Range: 1150 nautical miles at 16 knots.
Programme: Designed as a coast guard patrol craft during the latter half of the 1960s, eight of this basic design were delivered to the Federal German Coast Guard during 1969 and 1970 as their 'Neustadt' class. More recently, 12 more were ordered by the Royal Malaysian Marine Police, the first of these PZ class craft being delivered during 1980, all being built in Lurssen's Malaysian yards. In

The lead of this two-craft Bahraini Navy FPB38 class, P10 1981.

1979, the Bahraini Government placed an order for the first two more powerfully armed and sensored naval craft version; these vessels, *P10* and *P11*, being delivered during 1981.
Notes: Built around a standard hull design made of steel, all of the FPB 38 vessels employ an aluminium superstructure that differs markedly between the earlier para-military version and that of the more recently produced naval craft. The somewhat heavier coast guard/police version has a full load displacement of 221 tons and can accommodate up to 38 officers and ratings.

Al Mansur Class Fast Attack Craft

Role: Anti-shipping.
Builders: Brooke Marine, UK and Algeria.
Users: Navies of Oman (6) and Algeria (5).
Basic data: 180 tons full displacement; 123ft (37.5m) overall length; 20ft (6.1m) maximum beam.
Crew: 27.
Propulsion: 2 Paxman Ventura YJCM diesels (total 4800bhp); 2 propellers.
Sensors: 1 Decca TM916 sea search and navigational radar; 1 Sperry Sea Archer optronic fire control system.
Armament: 2 Exocet anti-ship missile launchers (on B2 and B3 only); 1 single 76mm OTO-Melara dual-purpose gun; 2 single 12.7mm machine guns.
Top speed: 26 knots.
Range: 2800 nautical miles at 12 knots.
Programme: Originally a seven-craft class comprising *Al Bushra* (B-1), *Al Mansur* (B-2), *Al Nejah* (B-3), *Al Wafi* (B-4), *Al Fulk* (B-5), *Al Meujahid* (B-6) and *Al Jasbbar* (B-7). Delivered between March 1973 and August 1977, the first three craft were modified to carry Exocet between 1977 and 1979, but B-1 was it was swept overboard from a freighter in the Bay of Biscay and sunk. Algeria ordered six of these craft in late 1980, the first of which was in sea trials by mid 1982. Comprising *P341* through *P346*, the first two being built by Brooke Marine, while the last four were built locally in Algeria's Mer-el-Kebir yards.
Notes: Developed from Brooke Marine's smaller 108 feet (32.9mm) Standard Patrol Craft, the 'Al Mansur' class have a somewhat similar appearance to that of the comparably sized Vosper Thornycroft 110 feet standard craft (see 'Barzan' class), the main visual difference centring on the 'Al Mansur' class's larger forward-mounted 76mm gun mount.

P342, second of the two British-built craft constructed for Algeria.

Constitucion Class Fast Attack Craft

Role: Anti-shipping.
Builder: Vosper Thornycroft, UK.
User: Venezuelan Navy.
Basic data: 170 tons full displacement; 121ft (36.9m) overall length; 23.45ft (7.2m) maximum beam.
Crew: 18.
Propulsion: 2 MTU MD16V538 diesels (total 7080bhp); 2 propellers.
Sensors: 1 SMA SPQ-2D combined air/sea search and navigational radar; 1 ELSAG NA 10 fire control radar; 1 Kelvin Hughes MS 45 echo sounder; 1 Navamatic direction finder.
Armament: 1 OTO-Melara 76mm dual-purpose gun (P11, P13 and P15) or 2 Otomat anti-ship missile launchers; 1 single Bofors 40mm anti-aircraft gun (P12, P14 and P16).
Top speed: 31 knots.
Range: 1350 nautical miles at 16 knots.
Programme: Ordered in April 1972 for a sum in excess of £6 million, this six-craft class and their delivery dates were: *Constitucion* (P11) August 1974, *Federacion* (P12) March 1975, *Independencia* (P13) September 1974, *Libertad* (P14) June 1975, *Patria* (P15) January 1975 and *Victoria* (P16) September 1975.
Notes: With a hull based on that of the earlier 'Tenacity' craft, the 'Constitucion' class boats departed from the latter 1960s trend of going for speed, relatively short-ranged, gas turbine-powered craft in the adoption of more fuel-economic diesels in order to provide the longer operational ranges needed.

ARV Constitucion (P11) of the Venezuelan Navy.

President El Hadj Omar Bongo (GC05) of the Gabonese Navy.

President Bongo Type Fast Attack Craft

Role: Patrol.
Builder: CN de l'Esterel, France.
User: Gabonese Navy.
Basic data: 160 tons full displacement; 138.2ft (42.13m) overall length; 23.5ft (7.15m) maximum beam.
Crew: 23.
Propulsion: 3 MTU 16V538TB91 diesels (total 12,240bhp); 2 propellers.
Sensors: 1 Decca RM 1226 sea search and navigational radar.
Armament: 1 single 40mm Bofors anti-aircraft gun; 1 single 20mm Oerlikon anti-aircraft gun; 1 quadruple SS-12M wire-guided, light anti-ship missile launcher.
Top speed: 40 knots.
Range: 1500 nautical miles at 15 knots.
Programme: Known by its builders as the 'Type 42', the sole example to enter naval service was delivered to Gabon in 1977, where it operates as the *President El Hadj Omar Bongo* (GC05).
Notes: A fast, light design employing a combination of mahogany for the hull, which is protected by epoxy resin, and marine plywood for the craft's deck and superstructure.

Biokovak (P221), the 11th of a 14-craft Yugoslavian 'Shershen'.

Shershen Class Fast Attack Craft

Role: Anti-shipping.
Builders: Various, USSR and Tito SY, Yugoslavia.
Users: Navies of USSR (30), Yugoslavia (14), Angola (6), Cape Verde Islands (3), Egypt (6), East Germany (18), Guinea (3), North Korea (4) and Vietnam (8).
Basic data: 160 tons full displacement; 111.5ft (34.0m) overall length; 23.6ft (7.2m) maximum beam.
Crew: 21.
Propulsion: 3 M503A diesels (total 12,000bhp); 3 propellers.
Sensors: 1 combined low-level air/sea search and navigational radar; 1 fire control radar (for 30mm guns); 2 separate IFF radars.
Armament: 4 heavyweight anti-submarine torpedo tubes; 2 twin 30mm Gatling type close-in weapons systems; 2 depth charge racks with a total of up to 12 depth charges. *Note:* a number of these craft, including the Cape Verde, three Egyptian and some East German vessels have had their torpedo tubes removed. The three non torpedo-carrying Egyptian craft have been modified to carry twin 20-cell 122mm artillery rocket launchers. Most craft can

be expected to carry SA-N-5 'Grail' light point air defence missile launchers.
Top speed: 45 knots.
Range: 700 nautical miles at 20 knots.
Programme: Approximately 80 of this class were built in Soviet shipyards between 1963 and 1970, plus a further ten built in Yugoslavia between 1966 and 1971. Ex-Soviet navy craft commenced being transferred to eastern Bloc client navies in 1967, the first going to Egypt, followed in 1968 by the first to East Germany; the body of remaining transfers being made during the latter half of the 1970s.
Notes: The 'Shershen' class has a wooden hull and was designed in parallel with the missile-carrying 'Osa' I class. Compared with the 'Osa' class, the 'Shershen' design employs the same propulsive machinery married to a smaller hull, hence the latter's higher top speed.

Hauk Class Fast Attack Craft

Role: Anti-shipping/submarine.
Builders: Bergens MV and Westermoen, Norway.
User: Royal Norwegian Navy.
Basic data: 155 tons full displacement; 119.8ft (36.53m) overall length; 20.7ft (6.3m) maximum beam.
Crew: 22.
Propulsion: 2 MTU 16V538 TB92 diesels (total 7340bhp); 2 propellers.
Sensors: 2 Decca TM 1226 sea search and navigational radars; 1 Kongsberg Vf MSI-80 fire control radar.
Armament: 2 to 6 Penguin Mk 2 anti-ship missile launchers; 2 heavyweight anti-ship torpedo tubes; 1 single 40mm Bofors anti-aircraft gun; 1 single 20mm Rheinmetall anti-aircraft gun.
Top speed: 35 knots.
Range: 440 nautical miles at 34 knots.
Programme: This 14-craft class comprises: *Hauk* (P986), *Orn* (P987), *Terne* (P988), *Tjeld* (P989), *Skarv* (P990), *Teist* (P991), *Jo* (P992), *Lom* (P993), *Stegg* (P994), *Falk* (P995), *Ravn* (P996), *Gribb* (P997), *Geir* (P998) and *Erle* (P999). All but P996 through P999 were built in the yards of Bergens MV and all this class entered service between August 1978 and December 1980.
Notes: The 'Hauk' class is the latest derivative of the highly successful 'Storm' class design. The 'Hauk' class design is

KNM Terne (P988) of the Royal Norwegian Navy loosing off one of its Penguin anti-ship missiles.

somewhat heavier than either the preceding 'Storm' or 'Snogg' classes, deliberately trading a modest degree of dash speed capability against the ability to carry a more effective and balanced fit of sensors and weapons.

Hugin Class Fast Attack Craft

Role: Anti-shipping.
Builders: Bergens and Westermoens, Norway.
User: Royal Swedish Navy.
Basic data: 150 tons full displacement; 119.85ft (36.53m) overall length; 20.3ft (6.2m) maximum beam.
Crew: 22.
Propulsion: 2 MTU 20V672 TB90 diesels (total 7200bhp); 2 propellers.
Sensors: 1 Scanter 009 sea search and navigational radar; 1 Philips (Sweden) 9LV200 Mk 2 fire control radar and automated action information data-processing system; 1 Simrad SQ3D/SF hull-mounted sonar.
Armament: 6 Penguin Mk 2 anti-ship missile launchers or 24 mines or 2 depth charge racks; 1 single 57mm Bofors SAK 57 Mk 1 dual-purpose gun. *Note:* scheduled to have Penguin missiles replaced by RBS-15s.
Top speed: 35 knots.
Range: 550 nautical miles at 35 knots.
Programme: Impressed by the Norwegian-developed 'Storm' class design, the Royal Swedish Navy ordered a prototype of a more anti-air capable derivative of the 'Storm' class design from Bergens in the early 1970s. This craft, *Jagaren* (P150) was delivered in 1972 and underwent extensive evaluation during 1973 and 1974. These trials led to a contract for a further 16 craft being placed with Bergens in 1975 and covering: *Hugin* (P151), *Munin* (P152), *Magne* (P153), *Mode* (P154), *Vale* (P155), *Vidar* (P156), *Mjolner* (P157), *Mysing* (P158), *Kaparen* (P159), *Vaktaren* (P160), *Snapphanen* (P161), *Spejaren* (P162), *Styrbjorn* (P163), *Starkodder* (P164), *Tordon* (P165) and *Tirfing* (P166). All were launched between June 1977 and July 1981; the craft entering service between July 1978 and 1982. All but P154 through P158 were constructed by Bergens, the lead yard.
Notes: The hull and decking of the 'Hugin' class employs welded steel construction, married to a superstructure built entirely from glass reinforced plastic.

Waspada Class Fast Attack Craft

Role: Anti-shipping.
Builder: Vosper Group, Singapore.
User: Royal Brunei Defence Force.
Basic data: 150 tons full displacement; 124.0ft (37.8m) overall length; 23.5ft (7.16m) maximum beam.
Crew: 24.
Propulsion: 2 MTU 20V 538 TB91 diesels (total 9000bhp); 2 propellers.
Sensors: 1 Decca 1226 sea search and navigational radar; 1 Sperry Sea Archer radar ranging and optronic fire control system.
Armament: 2 MM 38 Exocet anti-ship missile launchers; 1 twin 30mm Oerlikon GCM-BO1 anti-aircraft gun.
Top speed: 32 knots.
Range: 2000 nautical miles at 14 knots.
Programme: This three-craft class comprises: *Waspada* (PO2), *Pejuang* (PO3) and *Seteria* (PO4). Ordered in early 1976, all three were launched between August 1977 and August 1978 and entered service in the latter half of 1978 and 1979 period.
Notes: These relatively small craft employ a welded steel hull and light alloy superstructure. The unusual weapons fit of two Exocets, backed by a relatively light twin cannon tends to reflect the specific user's needs, which essentially

Hugin (P151), *lead craft of this Royal Swedish Navy class.*

centre on the rapid-fire gun mount, useful in the interception of contraband and pirate surface traffic. The upper superstructure of the lead craft differs from the other two in having an enclosed bridge.

Patra Class Fast Attack Craft

Role: Patrol picket.
Builders: Various, France.
Users: Navies of France, Ivory Coast and Mauritania.
Basic data: 148 tons full displacement; 133.5ft (40.7m) overall length; 19.4ft (5.9m) maximum beam.
Crew: 19.
Propulsion: 2 AGO 195 V12 CZSHR diesels (total 5000bhp); 2 controllable-pitch propellers.
Sensors: 1 Decca TM 1226 sea search and navigation radar.
Armament: 4 Exocet anti-ship missile launchers (on Ivory Coast craft only); 1 single 40mm anti-aircraft gun; 6 wire-guided SS12 anti-ship missiles (French craft only); 1 single 20mm anti-aircraft gun (Ivory Coast craft only); 2 light machine guns (1 only on French craft).
Top speed: 28 knots.
Range: 1500 nautical miles at 15 knots.

Waspada (PO2), *the lead of this three-craft class at speed.*

The French Navy's Pertuisane *(P673) seen at speed, January 1977.*

Programme: Currently a seven-craft class, the French Navy originally planned to buy a far greater number, but ultimately ordered only four, comprising: *Trident* (P670), *Glaive* (P671), *Epée* (P672) and *Pertuisane* (P673). Service entry dates for these French craft were December 1976, March 1977, October 1976 and January 1977, respectively. The two Ivory Coast vessels, *L'Ardent* and *L'Intrepide*, both entered service in October 1978. Another of this class, the Mauritanian *Le Dix Juillet* (P411) was delivered in May 1982. The lead yard for this class was Auroux, which built all but P672 and P673, the latter being built by CNM Cherbourg.

Notes: Handsomely proportioned craft, the 'Patra' class was designed to meet the same policing role as that of the Royal Australian Navy's 'Fremantle' class, hence the relatively light armament fitted to the four French craft. The two Ivory Coast vessels had their Exocet missiles retrofitted during 1981. Range at 10 knots is quoted as being 1750 nautical miles.

Barzan Class Fast Attack Craft

Role: Patrol.
Builder: Vosper Thornycroft, UK.
Users: Qatar (6), Abu Dhabi (6), Singapore (6) and Peru (6).
Basic data: 140 tons full displacement; 110ft (33.5m) overall length; 21ft (6.4m) maximum beam.
Crew: 27.
Propulsion: 2 Paxman Valente 16RP 200M diesels (total 6350bhp); 2 propellers.
Sensors: 1 Decca 1226 sea search and navigation radar.
Armament: 2 twin Oerlikon 30mm GCM guns.
Top speed: 30 knots.
Range: 1400 nautical miles at 14 knots.
Programme: This six-craft class was ordered in 1973, laid down in 1974/5 and delivered between January 1975 and March 1976. The six craft comprise *Barzan* (Q11), *Hwar* (Q12), *That Assuari* (Q13), *Al Wussail* (Q14), *Al Khatab* (Q15) and *Tariq* (Q16). These six craft were the last of 24 Vosper Thornycroft vessels built around a standard 110ft hull, equipped with engines and armament of the customer's choice. The first six of these hulls were ordered by the Peruvian Coast Guard and delivered during 1965. The next order was from Singapore for two batches of three, which differed in armament fit and which were delivered in 1971 and 1972. Six more of these craft, the 'Ardhana' class, P1101 to P1106, were delivered to Abu Dhabi between 1974 and 1975.
Notes: The presence of the attractively raked funnel gives these relatively small warships a distinctly corvette-like appearance, except in the case of the six Singapore vessels that lack funnels.

The Qatar 'Barzan' class with HMS Amazon *in background, 1982.*

Isku Type Fast Attack Craft

Role: Fast attack craft training/trials.
Builder: Reposaaron Konepaja, Finland.
User: Finnish Defence Force.
Basic data: 140 tons full displacement; 86.45ft (26.35m) overall length; 28.54ft (8.7m) maximum beam.
Crew: 25.
Propulsion: 4 Soviet-built M-50 diesels (total 4000bhp); 4 propellers.
Sensors: 1 Soviet-developed sea search and navigational radar.
Armament: 4 SS-N-2A 'Styx' anti-ship missile launchers; 1 twin-barrelled 30mm anti-aircraft gun.
Top speed: 15 knots.
Range: In excess of 800 nautical miles at 12 knots.
Programme: *Isku* (P16) was laid down in November 1968, launched in December 1969 and entered service during 1970.
Notes: Developed specifically to meet the 'Osa' II crew training requirement, the *Isku* was originally to be driven by a more powerful diesel propulsive arrangement, capable of giving the craft a top speed of between 25 and 26 knots. Sometimes referred to as having a sea sled hull, *Isku* actually employs that of a former landing craft. *Isku* has, on occasion, served a useful secondary function as a trials craft for Finnish-developed sensors and shipboard electronics.

Snogg Class Fast Attack Craft

Role: Anti-shipping.
Builder: Batservice Verft, Norway.
User: Royal Norwegian Navy.

Basic data: 140 tons full displacement; 119.8ft (36.53m) overall length; 20.7ft (6.3m) maximum beam.

Crew: 20.

Propulsion: 2 MTU 16V538 TB92 diesels (total 7200bhp); 2 propellers.

Sensors: 1 Decca TM 1226 sea search and navigational radar; 1 Philips (Sweden) TORI fire control radar.

Armament: 4 heavyweight anti-ship torpedo tubes; 4 Penguin anti-ship missile launchers; 1 single 40mm Bofors anti-aircraft gun.

Top speed: 36 knots.

Range: 550 nautical miles at 35 knots.

Programme: This six-craft class comprises: *Snogg* (P980), *Rapp* (P981), *Snarr* (P982), *Rask* (P983), *Kvir* (P984) and *Kjapp* (P985). All six of this class entered service in the 1970/71 period.

Notes: Designed to carry four of the very effective Swedish-developed TP-61 wire-guided 21in heavyweight torpedoes, the 'Snogg' class are also equipped to carry the Penguin anti-ship missile system. Although slightly heavier than their forebears, the 'Snogg' class design derives directly from that of the Norwegian-developed 'Storm' class craft.

Used primarily for training Finnish 'Osa' II class crews, the Isku *(P16) employs a landing craft, or barge-like hull, married to a superstructure and 'Styx' missile launchers akin to that of the Soviet fast attack craft.*

Lurssen FPB 36 Classes Fast Attack Craft

Role: Coastal patrol.

Builders: Lurssen, Federal Germany and Bazán, Spain.

Users: Navies of Spain (6), Mauritania (3) and Congo People's Republic (3).

Basic data: 134 tons full displacement; 118.8ft (36.2m) overall length; 19.0ft (5.8m) maximum beam.

KNM Rapp *(P981) with its four deck-mounted heavyweight torpedo tubes. When fitted, the Penguin missiles are carried aft.*

Marien Nguoabi (P601), lead craft of this three-vessel FPB36 class operated by the Congolese People's Republic.

Crew: 19.
Propulsion: 2 MTU 16V538 TB90 diesels (total 7320bhp); 2 propellers.
Sensors: 1 Raytheon 1620 sea search and navigational radar.
Armament: 1 single 40mm Bofors anti-aircraft gun and 1 single 20mm Oerlikon anti-aircraft gun (on Spanish craft) or 1 single 40mm and 1 twin 20mm anti-aircraft guns (on Mauritania-vessels) or 2 single 40mm anti-aircraft guns (on Congolese craft); 2 single 12.7mm machine guns (all craft).
Top speed: 36.5 knots.
Range: 1200 nautical miles at 16 knots.
Programme: Spain ordered six of these craft in late 1974, comprising the Lurssen-built lead vessel *Barcelo* (PC11) and the Bazan-built *Laya* (PC12), *Javier Quiroga* (PC13), *Ordoñez* (PC14), *Acevedo* (PC15) and *Cándido Pérez* (PC16); all entering service between March 1976 and November 1977. The Mauritanian order for three Bazan-built craft was placed in late 1976, the trio comprising: *El Vaiz* (P362), *El Beg* (P363) and *El Kenz* (P364) being delivered between May 1979 and 1981. The Congolese craft, again all Bazan-built, were ordered in 1980 and comprise: *Marien Nguoabi* (P601), *Les Trois Glorieuses* (P602) and *Les Maloango* (P603), all of which were in service by March 1983.
Notes: These relatively small and lightly armed craft offer an inexpensive solution to the coastal patrol and policing requirement. Known as 'Barcelo' class craft in Spanish service, Bazán refers to this design as the 'Piraña' class as sold to the Congolese People's Republic.

Fresia (P81), one of a four craft Chilean-operated TB36 class.

Lurssen TB 36 Classes Fast Attack Craft

Role: Anti-shipping.
Builders: Lurssen, Federal Germany and Bazan, Spain.
Users: Navies of Ecuador (3) and Chile (4).
Basic data: 134 tons full displacement; 118.8ft (36.2m) overall length; 19.0ft (5.8m) maximum beam.
Crew: 20.
Propulsion: 3 Mercedes-Benz diesels (total 9000bhp); 3 propellers on Ecuadorian craft or 2 Mercedes-Benz diesels (total 4800bhp); 2 propellers on Chilean craft.
Sensors: 1 Decca 505 sea search and navigational radar; 1 Selenia Orion 10X fire control radar (on Ecuadorian craft only).
Armament: 4 Gabriel anti-ship missile launchers (replacing torpedo tubes on Ecuadorian craft since 1980/81); 4 heavyweight anti-submarine torpedo tubes; 2 single 40mm Bofors (Chilean craft) or 1 twin 30mm Emerlec (Ecuadorian craft since 1979) anti-aircraft guns.
Top speed: 35 knots (Ecuadorian) or 32 knots (Chilean).
Range: 700 nautical miles at 30 knots.
Programme: This seven-craft programme was initiated with a Chilean order for four craft, built under licence by Bazan, comprising: *Fresia* (P81), *Guacolda* (P82), *Quidora* (P83) and *Tegualda* (P84); these craft entering service during the 1965/1966 period. The three Ecuadorian craft comprising: *Manta* (P24), *Tulcan* (P25) and *Nuevo Rocafuerte* (P26) were built by Lürssen and delivered between April and June of 1971.
Notes: Smaller derivatives of Lurssen's Type 142 design for the Federal German Navy, the Chilean craft are referred to as 'Guacolda' class torpedo boats, while the Ecuadorian Navy's class have now been converted into missile-carriers.

Mirna Class Fast Attack Craft

Role: Anti-submarine/patrol.
Builder: Yugoslavia.
User: Yugoslavian Navy.
Basic data: 131 tons full displacement; 105.0ft (32.0m) overall length; 21.9ft (6.68m) maximum beam.
Crew: 19.
Propulsion: 2 SEMT-Pielstick 12PA4 200GDS diesels (total 6000bhp).
Sensors: 1 unidentified sea search and navigational radar; 1 unidentified hull-mounted sonar; 1 unidentified echo sounder.
Armament: 1 single 40mm Bofors L70 and 1 single 20mm M71 anti-aircraft guns; rails for 8 depth charges.

Top speed: 30 knots.

Range: 400 nautical miles at 20 knots.

Programme: Reported as being a six or more craft class for the Yugoslavian Navy, comprising *Biokovo* (P171), *Pohorse* (P172), *Koprivnik* (P173), *Ucka* (P174), *Brmec* (P175) and *Mukos* (P176); all of these craft reportedly entering service during the 1981-1982 period.

Notes: Steel hulled, light alloy superstructured craft, the 'Mirna' class design, or Type 140 as it is referred to by its Yugoslavian constructors, is a multi-role craft, whose primary function is that of submarine chaser. Under wartime conditions, these vessels can operate for up to eight days without recourse to any form of replenishment. An electrically driven outboard propeller is used for quiet running operations and can give a speed of up to 6 knots in smooth sea conditions.

Storm Class Fast Attack Craft

Role: Anti-shipping.

Builders: Bergens MV and Westermoen, Norway.

User: Royal Norwegian Navy.

Basic data: 125 tons full displacement; 119.8ft (36.53m) overall length; 20.7ft (6.3m) maximum beam.

Crew: 26.

Propulsion: 2 Maybach (MTU) MB 872A diesels (total 7200bhp); 2 propellers.

Sensors: 1 Decca TM 1226 sea search and navigational radar; 1 Hollandse WM 26 fire control radar.

Armament: 4 or 6 Penguin anti-ship missile launchers, replaceable by 2 depth charge racks; 1 single 76mm Bofors gun; 1 single 40mm Bofors anti-aircraft gun.

Top speed: 37 knots.

Range: 550 nautical miles at 36 knots.

Programme: Originally a 20-craft class comprising: *Storm* (P960), *Blink* (P961), *Glint* (P962), *Skjold* (P963), *Trygg* (P964), *Kjekk* (P965), *Djerv* (P966), *Skudd* (P967), *Arg* (P968), *Steil* (P969), *Brann* (P970), *Tross* (P971), *Hvass* (P972), *Traust* (P973), *Brott* (P974), *Odd* (P975), *Pil* (P976), *Brask* (P977), *Rokk* (P978) and *Gnist* (P979). Bergens were responsible for the construction of P960, 961, 962, 964, 965, 967, 968, 970, 971, 973, 974, 976, 977 and 979, while Westermoen built the remainder of this class. All entered service between mid-1965 and late 1967. *Note: Pil* (P967) is no longer in service, having been damaged beyond repair.

Notes: Designed in the early 1960s as gun-equipped fast patrol boats, the 'Storm' class was modernised during the early 1970s to carry the Norwegian-developed Penguin anti-ship missile system. The 'Storm' class hull and basic propulsive machinery layout have subsequently provided the basis for both the 'Snogg' and 'Hauk' class of Norwegian fast attack craft.

Boeing Jetfoil Class Fast Attack Craft

Role: Offshore patrol and rapid intervention.

Builder: Boeing Marine Systems, USA.

User: Indonesian Navy.

Basic data: 117 tons full displacement; 90.0ft (27.4m) overall length (foilborne); 31.0ft (9.5m) maximum beam.

Crew: 4.

Propulsion: 2 Allison 501-K20A gas turbines (total 7560shp) driving 2 Rocketdyne R-20 waterjet pumps for both foilborne or hullborne operation.

Sensors: 1 Raytheon Pathfinder sea search and navigational radar.

Armament: Nil fitted to first 5 craft, 1 single 57mm Bofors SAK 57 Mk 2 dual-purpose gun mounted forward on subsequent vessels. (Maker's artwork also shows aft-mounted anti-ship missile launchers).

The lead craft of this Yugoslavian Navy 'Mirna' class seen at speed during sea trials.

The Norwegian KNM Tross (P971) seen fitted with depth charge racks aft in place of its Penguin missiles.

An artist's impression of the navalised Boeing Model 929-119 Jetfoil.

Top speed: 48 knots.

Range: 600 nautical miles at 43 knots.

Programme: Indonesia purchased a single commercial Boeing Model 929-115 Jetfoil, *Bima Sumudera I* for evaluation in both naval and commercial applications in 1981. Subsequently, in October 1983, Indonesia ordered four Model 929-119 Jetfoils with modified

Soridderen (P511) undergoing sea trials, 1964.

superstructures, but still unarmed, plus placing options on a further six craft. The first two Model 929-119s were delivered during 1984, the third in 1985, with the fourth set for 1986 delivery. In the longer term, the Indonesian Navy foresee a need for up to 47 Jetfoils, exclusive of additional commercial needs. The Indonesian national shipbuilder, PT Pabrik Kapal will participate on a progressively mounting basis in the construction of these craft.

Notes: Based on the proven 260 passenger-carrying Boeing Model 929-115 Jetfoil, the navalised -119 models feature a revised superstructure, lacking the upper passenger deck aft of the wheelhouse. The value of the four craft ordered in 1983 was quoted as US$150 million, indicating a programme unit cost of US$37.5 million.

Soloven Class Fast Attack Craft

Role: Anti-shipping.
Builders: Vosper, UK, and Royal Danish Dockyards.
User: Royal Danish Navy.
Basic data: 114 tons full displacement; 99.1ft (30.26m) overall length; 26.35ft (8.0m) maximum beam.
Crew: 29.
Propulsion: 2 Rolls-Royce Proteus gas turbines (total 12,600shp) or 2 General Motors 6V-71 diesels (total 300bhp); 3 propellers.
Sensors: 1 Decca 1226 sea search and navigational radar.
Armament: 2 single Bofors 40mm guns; 2 single torpedo tubes.
Top speed: 54 knots.
Range: 1800 nautical miles at 9 knots.
Programme: The 1962 Danish Government order for two Vosper-built craft carried provision for the building of a further four boats under licence by the Royal Danish Dockyards. Completion dates for the six boats were: *Soloven* (P510) and *Soridderen* (P511), June 1964; *Sobjornen* (P512), September 1965; *Sohesten* (P513), June 1966; *Sohunden* (P514), December 1966; and *Soulven* (P515), March 1967.
Notes: Amongst the fastest conventional-hulled craft ever built, the 'Soloven' class boats are an improved version of Vosper's 'Brave' design with the diesel facility for economic cruising added (this feature being first tested aboard Vosper's slightly smaller *Ferocity* built in 1960 as a private venture demonstrator). The armament combination of the 'Soloven' class boats can be varied to delete one of the guns, allowing the carriage of two additional Swedish Tp-61 wire-guided torpedoes. These wooden-hulled craft are not scheduled to be withdrawn from Danish service until the mid-1980s.

Shimrit Class Fast Attack Craft

Shimrit's primary weapons consist of Harpoons astern, supplemented by Gabriels in their box launchers further forward.

Role: Anti-shipping.
Builders: Grumman, USA, and Israeli Shipyards.
User: Israeli Navy.
Basic data: 104 tons full displacement; 84.0ft (25.6m) overall length; 24.0ft (7.32m) maximum beam.
Crew: 15.
Propulsion: 1 Allison 501KF gas turbine (5400shp) driving 1 controllable-pitch propeller when foilborne; 2 Pratt & Whitney ST6 gas turbines (total 1100shp) driving twin stern-mounted hydraulic water pumps when hullborne.
Sensors: 1 combined air/sea search radar with IFF; 1 navigational radar; 1 fire control radar (all reported to be Israeli developed).
Armament: 4 Harpoon anti-ship missile launchers; 2 Gabriel anti-ship missile launchers; 1 twin 30mm anti-aircraft gun.
Top speed: 50 knots.
Range: 700 nautical miles at 45 knots.
Programme: A two-craft class ordered by Israel in late 1977, the lead craft, *Shimrit*, was launched in May 1981 and was delivered in July 1982. A second craft is nearing completion in Israel.
Notes: The 'Shimrit' class, or Grumman 'Flagstaff' Mk 2/M 161 design is a development of the earlier *Flagstaff* (PGH1) delivered to the US Navy in 1968. In contrast with both the US Navy's 'Pegasus' class and Italian Navy's 'Sparviero' class hydrofoils, the Grumman craft employs a two-forward-and-one-aft foil configuration, allowing the after foil to house a transmission shaft to drive the single

super-cavitating propeller. The craft has a specific range of over 50 nautical miles per ton of fuel used. The Israeli choice of armament for their hydrofoils is interesting, placing far more emphasis on strike missiles and, consequently, relatively less on gun armament than either of its operational rival hydrofoils. This class can maintain speeds of 45 knots in sea state 5 conditions.

Athos Class Fast Attack Craft

Role: Coastal patrol.
Builder: CN de l'Esterel, France.
User: French Navy.
Basic data: 96 tons full displacement; 105.3ft (32.1m) overall length; 21.2ft (6.45m) maximum beam.
Crew: 18.
Propulsion: 2 SACM diesels (total 4640bhp); 2 propellers.
Sensors: 1 Decca 1216 sea search and navigational radar; provision for 1 undesignated fire control system.
Armament: Provision for 1 single 40mm Bofors anti-aircraft gun (aft) and 1 single 20mm Oerlikon anti-aircraft gun (forward). *Note:* no armament is carried by the two French vessels.
Top speed: 32 knots.
Range: 1500 nautical miles at 15 knots.
Programme: Ordered in 1978, *Athos* (A712) and *Aramis* (A713) entered service with the French Navy in November 1979 and September 1980, respectively.
Notes: A development of the 80-ton full displacement 32-metre CN de l'Esterel design, four being sold to Tunisia in the late 1950s, plus two of which were supplied to Mauritania in 1969 and are operated as 'Tichitt' class craft, along with one for Gabon. As with other CN de l'Esterel craft, these Type 32L vessels employ an all-wooden construction of mahogany for the hull and marine plywood for the decking and superstructure.

Broadsword Type Fast Attack Craft

Role: Coastal patrol.
Builder: Halter Marine, USA.
User: Guatemalan Navy.

The French Navy's Aramis *(A713); the 'A' for Auxiliary prefix denoting the class's employment as weapons range safety patrol craft.*

Basic data: 92.1 tons full displacement; 105ft (32.0m) overall length; 20.4ft (6.2m) maximum beam.
Crew: 20.
Propulsion: 2 General Motors 16V149T1 diesels (total 3200bhp); 2 propellers.
Sensors: 1 Decca sea search navigational radar.
Armament: Single 75mm gun; 1 mortar; up to 3 light machine guns.
Top speed: 32 knots.
Range: 1150 nautical miles at 20 knots.
Programme: Delivery of the sole example purchased, *Kukulkan* (P1051), was made in 1976, the craft entering service in August of that year as the flagship of the small Guatemalan Navy.
Notes: Typical of the many more lightly armed patrol craft operated by the navies of the so-called Third World nations, the armament of this boat was fitted after delivery to Guatemala. The craft's seemingly large electrical generating capacity, provided by twin 30KW generators, becomes more understandable in the light of the installation of 8 tons of heating and air-conditioning equipment.

Guatemala's Kukulkan *(P1051), 1976.*

An improved 'October' class without Otomat launchers, photographed during Vosper Thornycroft sea trials, 1980.

Improved October Class Fast Attack Craft

Role: Anti-shipping.
Builder: Egypt/Vosper Thornycroft, UK.
User: Egyptian Navy.
Basic data: 88 tons full displacement; 83.0ft (25.3m) overall length; 23.6ft (7.2m) maximum beam.
Crew: 22.
Propulsion: 4 CRM 18V-12D/55 YE diesels (total 5400 bhp); 4 propellers.
Sensors: 1 Marconi S810 Sapphire fire control radar and ST802 optronic fire director with associated automated action information system (retrofitted by Vosper Thornycroft).
Armament: 2 Otomat Mk 1 anti-ship missile launchers; 2 twin 30mm Oerlikon Type A32 anti-aircraft guns.
Top speed: 37 knots.
Range: 400 nautical miles at 30 knots.
Programme: Eight of these Egyptian-built craft were completed between 1969 and the mid-1970s, with two believed to have been lost during the 1973 Yom Kippur War. In August 1976, the Egyptian Government placed a £50 million contract with Vosper Thornycroft to modernise the remaining six vessels, the first of which arrived in Britain during early 1978. Following what amounted to a virtual rebuild, these six craft were redelivered to Egypt during the 1980/1 period.
Notes: The 'October' class, named thus to commemorate the October 1967 sinking of the Israeli destroyer *Eilat* by 'Styx'-equipped 'Komar' class fast attack craft, were, prior to modernisation, Egyptian-built, Italian-engined versions of the Soviet-developed 'Komar' class boats. The modernisation work involved fitting a completely new sensor/weapons fit, reworking the superstructure and building walkway sponsons onto the hull mid-section to allow fore-and-aft access past Otomat cannister/-launchers.

Sparviero Class Fast Attack Craft

Role: Anti-shipping.
Builder: C N R La Spezia, Italy.
User: Italian Navy.
Basic data: 60.5 tons full displacement; 75.3ft (23.0m) overall length (foilborne); 23.0ft (7.0m) maximum beam.
Crew: 10.
Propulsion: 1 Rolls-Royce Proteus 15 gas turbine (5000shp) or 1 General Motors 6V-53N diesel (160bhp). The gas turbine drives 1 Byron Jackson waterjet when foilborne, while the diesel drives a single propeller when the craft is hullborne.
Sensors: 1 Selenia 3RM7-250B (P420 only) or 1 SMA SPQ-701 combined air/sea search and navigational radar; 1 Selenia/Elsag RTN-10X fire control radar; IFF (on all but P420).
Armament: 2 single OTO-Melara OTOMAT Mk 2 anti-ship missile launchers; 1 single 76mm OTO-Melara compact dual-purpose gun.
Top speed: 50 knots.
Range: 400 nautical miles at 45 knots.
Programme: This seven-craft class comprises: *Sparviero* (P420), *Nibbio* (P421), *Falcone* (P422), *Astore* (P423), *Grifone* (P424), *Greppio* (P425) and *Condore* (P426). Following the ordering of the prototype craft, *Sparviero* in 1971, which entered service in July 1974, the other six of this class (an eighth had been planned) were ordered in 1977. All of the series-built craft were laid down between

mid-1977 and 1980 and all were accepted into service between November 1980 and early 1982.

Notes: The fruit of a collaborative US-Italian industry study group's efforts, the 'Sparviero' class design owes much to Boeing's *Tucumcari* development fast attack hydrofoil, but is marginally larger in order to accommodate the craft's potent sensor/weapons fit. When operated in the conventional hullborne mode, these hydrofoils have a range of up to 1050 nautical miles at 8 knots. When foilborne, the craft can operate in sea states in excess of 4.

Periwa Class Fast Attack Craft

Role: Coastal patrol.
Builder: Vosper Group, Singapore.
User: Royal Brunei Defence Force.
Basic data: 38.5 tons full displacement; 70.7ft (21.54m) overall length; 20.0ft (6.1m) maximum beam.
Crew: 12.
Propulsion: 2 MTU 12V 331 TC81 diesels (total 2700bhp); 2 propellers.
Sensors: 1 Decca 916 or 1216A sea search and navigational radar; 1 Kelvin Hughes MS45 echo sounder.
Armament: 2 single 20mm Oerlikon anti-aircraft guns; 2 single 7.62mm light machine guns.
Top speed: 31 knots.
Range: 400 nautical miles at 14 knots.
Programme: A three-craft class comprising: *Periwa* (P14), *Pemburu* (P15) and *Penyarang* (P16). The craft were launched between May 1974 and March 1975; all entering service between September 1974 and June 1975.
Notes: Used for intercepting contraband runners, the design of these craft is similar to that of the 23-metre Keith Nelson plastic-hulled vessels, but employs a laminated wood hull with aluminium alloy bulkheads and superstructure. The 'Periwa' class is capable of 29 knots sustained high speed cruise.

Periwa (P14) accompanied by the somewhat larger 'Brave' class Pahlawan (P01), which is no longer in service.

Nibbio *(P421), the first of the series-built 'Sparviero' craft. Note the mast-mounted sensor fit.*

Patrol vessels

Endurance Type Patrol Vessel

Role: Ice patrol.
Builder: Krogerwerft, Federal Germany.
User: Royal Navy.
Basic data: 4000 tons full displacement; 305.0ft (92.96m) overall length; 45.9ft (14.0m) maximum beam.
Crew: 127.
Propulsion: 1 Burmeister & Wain 550VTBF (3220bhp); 1 propeller, plus 1 bow thruster.
Sensors: 1 Type 978 sea search and navigational radar; 1 Kelvin Hughes MS45 echo sounder; satellite data link, backed by low frequency radio systems for position fixing; active vertical and sidescan sonars.
Armament: 2 Westland Wasp helicopters; 2 single 20mm Oerlikon anti-aircraft guns.

Top speed: 14.5 knots.
Range: 12,000 nautical miles at 14 knots.
Programme: Completed as the ice-going Danish motor vessel *Anita Dan* in 1956, the ship was purchased by the Royal Navy in February 1967 and modified for Antarctic patrol duties by Harland & Wolff. The ship had been scheduled to have been withdrawn from service during 1982, but will now remain in use following the Falklands War.
Notes: Acquired to support British interests in the Antarctic region, HMS *Endurance* is equipped to carry out detailed hydrographic survey work, along with other scientific research. In this content the ship carries accommodation for up to 12 scientists in addition to her normal crew. HMS *Endurance* and her Wasp helicopters participated in the retaking of South Georgia in late April 1982.

153

HMS Endurance *(A171) prior to fitment of her satellite data link aerial dome atop the centre rear of the helicopter hangar.*

Piloto Pardo Type Patrol Vessel

Role: Antarctic patrol.
Builder: Haaremsche, Netherlands.
User: Chilean Navy.
Basic data: 2545 tons full displacement; 272.3ft (83.0m) overall length; 39.0ft (11.9m) maximum beam.
Crew: 44, plus 24 others.
Propulsion: Diesel-electric (2000shp); 1 propeller.
Sensors: 1 Decca 707 sea search and navigational radar; 1 TACAN aircraft homer.
Armament: 2 Bell 47 helicopters. *Note:* shipboard armament removed.
Top speed: 14 knots.
Range: 6000 nautical miles at 10 knots.
Programme: Built in the Netherlands, the sole *Piloto Pardo* (P45) was laid down in 1957 and entered service with the Chilean Navy in August 1958.
Notes: Designed to carry out essentially the same mission as that of the Royal Navy's HMS *Endurance*, the somewhat smaller *Piloto Pardo* has accommodation for up to 24 scientists and an expansive helipad aft for two utility helicopters, whose primary task is to resupply the shore-based research teams previously landed from the ship.

The Chilean Navy's Piloto Pardo *(P45) in Antarctic waters, 1977.*

Sentinel Type Patrol Vessel

Role: High endurance, ocean-going patrol.
Builder: Humsumer Schiftwerft, Federal Germany.
User: Royal Navy.
Basic data: 2353 tons full displacement, 203.7ft (62.1m) overall length; 42.6ft (13.0m) maximum beam.
Crew: 25.
Propulsion: 2 MaK 12M-45-3AK diesels (total 7760bhp); 2 controllable-pitch propellers.
Sensors: 1 Kelvin Hughes Type 1016 sea search and navigational radar; IFF.
Armament: 2 single 40mm Bofors 40/60 anti-aircraft guns; 3 single 7.26mm machine guns.
Top speed: 14 knots.
Range: 7000 nautical miles at 12 knots.
Programme: Built originally as the *Eda Sun* in 1975, the vessel subsequently became the *Seaforth Warrior* prior to its acquisition by the Royal Navy in February 1983. Following refit, the ship, now known as HMS *Sentinel* (P246), entered service towards the close of December 1983.
Notes: In the immediate post-Falklands conflict period, the Royal Navy were confronted with the need to provide economic-to-operate, high endurance ocean-going patrol ships for duties in the South Atlantic. Happily, for the Royal Navy, these requirements emerged at a time when the merchantile offshore supply vessel market was suffering a glut. Thus, the Royal Navy found itself in a position to acquire *Sentinel* and the two slightly smaller 'Protector' class vessels, all requiring minimun modification to meet their new task, at a fraction of the outlay needed to purchase new builds and bringing the bonus of providing earlier than new build delivery dates. Included in the crew is a seven-man team of Royal Marines deployable from the ship in two Pacific 22 rigid inflatables.

Beskytteren Type Patrol Vessel

Role: Fishery protection.
Builder: Aallborg, Denmark.
User: Royal Danish Navy.
Basic data: 1970 tons full displacement; 244ft (74.4m) overall length; 38.8ft (11.8m) maximum beam.
Crew: 59.
Propulsion: 4 B & W Alpha diesels (total 7440bhp); 1 controllable-pitch propeller.

HMS Sentinel *(P246) departing Rosythe in early 1984 for active duty in the south Atlantic. Note lack of external identification.*

Sensors: 1 CWS 2 sea search and navigational (to be replaced by Plessey AWS6) radar; 1 NWS 1 navigational radar; 1 Plessey MS 26 hull-mounted sonar.
Armament: 1 Alouette III helicopter; 1 single 76mm dual-purpose gun.
Top speed: 18 knots.
Range: 6000 nautical miles at 13 knots.
Programme: The *Beskytteren* (F340), an Improved Hvidbjornen type, is the sole example of its kind. The ship was laid down in 1970 and completed during 1975.
Notes: Despite its pennant number—which would indicate that the ship was a light frigate or corvette—the *Beskytteren* was built specifically as a fishery protection vessel, its large size being dictated by its need to operate in the waters around Greenland. The ship's single 76mm gun is mounted forward of the wheelhouse. Aft of the superstructure is a sizeable, elevated helicopter operating pad and hangar for the ship's Aerospatiale Alouette II. The *Bestytteren* is a much larger vessel than the preceding four ship 'Hvidbjornen' class that have a full load displacement of 1650 tons.

Protector Class Patrol Vessels

Role: High endurance, ocean-going patrol.
Builder: Cochrane & Sons, UK.
Users: Royal Navy.
Basic data: 1724 tons full displacement; 191.6ft (58.4m) overall length; 38.7ft (11.8m) maximum beam.
Crew: 24.
Propulsion: 2 Polar diesels (total 6160bhp); 2 controllable-pitch propellers.
Sensors: 1 Kelvin Hughes Type 1016 sea search and navigational radar; IFF.
Armament: 2 single 40mm Bofors 40/60 anti-aircraft guns; 3 single 7.26mm machine guns.
Top speed: 13.5 knots.
Range: 6000 nautical miles at 12 knots.
Programme: HMS *Protector* (P244) and HMS *Guardian* (P245) were built as merchantile offshore supply vessels in 1973 and 1974, being delivered as the *Seaforth Champion* and *Seaforth Saga*, respectively. Acquired for the Royal Navy in February 1983, both ships underwent refit prior to entering service later in 1983; *Protector* during late August and *Guardian* in mid-September.
Notes: The original design requirements of a North Sea-operating offshore supply vessel to which these ships were built matched almost perfectly with that of a high endurance, ocean-going patrol ship as sought by the

The Royal Danish Navy's Beskytteren *(F340).*

HMS Guardian *(P245) carrying no identification while on active duty. Clearly visible aft is one of her two Pacific 22 inflatables.*

Royal Navy for South Atlantic duties in the immediate post-Falklands conflict period. That this was so is evident from the minimum amount of conversion work required during the ships' pre-service entry refits, which centred around installing the gun armament and military communication equipment needed. Included in the ships' crew is a seven-man team of Royal Marines, who can operate as a boarding or landing party, deployable from the parent vessel in two Pacific 22 rigid inflatables.

Hvidbjornen Class Patrol Vessels

The Royal Danish Navy's Ingolf *(F350) with Alouette III aft.*

Role: Ocean patrol.
Builders: Aarhus, Aalborg an Svendborg, Denmark.
User: Royal Danish Navy.
Basic data: 1650 tons full displacement; 238.2ft (72.6m) overall length; 38.0ft (11.6m) maximum beam.
Crew: 70.
Propulsion: 4 General Motors 16-567C diesels (total 6400bhp); 1 controllable-pitch propeller.
Sensors: 1 CWS 1 (being replaced by Plessey AWS6) combined low-level air/sea search radar; 1 Scanter 009 sea search and navigational radar; 1 Plessey MS46 hull-mounted sonar.
Armament: 1 Lynx or Alouette III helicopter; 1 single 3in Mk 26 anti-ship gun; up to 2 lightweight anti-submarine torpedoes delivered by shipboard helicopters.
Top speed: 18 knots.
Range: 6000 nautical miles at 13 knots.
Programme: This four ship class comprises: *Hvidbjornen* (F348), *Vaedderen* (F349), *Ingolf* (F350) and *Fylla* (F351). Built in three different Danish shipyards, with Aarhus being responsible for the lead of class, all four vessels were laid down between June 1961 and June 1962; all launched between November 1961 and December 1962; the ships entering service between December 1962 and July 1963.
Notes: Far less warlike than their F for frigate pennant number prefix may suggest, the 'Hvidbjornen' class should, more properly, be considered as an early 1960s precursor to the latterday patrol vessels, such as the Royal Navy's 'Castle' class. The somewhat larger than normal size of these ships, relative to others of their kind, is dictated by their need to weather an often stormy North Atlantic in order to patrol the inhospitable waters off Greenland.

Castle Class Patrol Vessels

Role: Offshore protection.
Builder: Hall Russell, UK.
User: Royal Navy.
Basic data: 1450 tons full displacement; 265.75ft (81m) overall length; 37.75ft (11.5m) maximum beam.
Crew: 50.
Propulsion: 2 Ruston 12RKCM diesels (total 5640bhp); 2 propellers.
Sensors: 1 Kelvin Hughes Type 1006 sea search and navigational radar; 1 Decca CANE automatic plotter; 1 Kelvin Hughes Type 778A echo sounder.

Armament: Facility to operate 1 up to Sea King sized helicopter; 1 Bofors 40mm Mk 3 gun; 2 machine guns.
Top speed: 19.5 knots.
Range: 10,000 nautical miles at 12 knots.
Programme: Initially known as the Offshore Protection Vessel (OPV) Mk 2, the first order for two Royal Navy ships was placed in August 1980. These ships, HMS *Leeds Castle* (P258) and HMS *Dumbarton Castle* (P259), are now in service, having been accepted in August 1981 and March 1982, respectively.

HMS Leeds Castle *(P258), August 1981.*

Notes: The 'Castles' are the largest of a series of Hall Russell-developed OPVs to be built so far. As with the earlier 'Jura' and 'Island' class ships from the same yards, the 'Castles' are built to Lloyd's Register commercial standards, rather than to costlier naval practices. Beside the 'Castle' class, which can accommodate 25 marines in addition to the crew, armed variants of the OPV Mk 2 are on offer to meet anti-submarine, anti-air, anti-shipping or general purpose roles at significantly lower cost than comparatively armed vessels built to more expensive naval building standards.

Island Class Patrol Vessels

Role: Offshore protection.
Builder: Hall Russell, UK.
User: Royal Navy.
Basic data: 1280 tons full displacement; 195.2ft (59.5m) overall length; 36ft (11m) maximum beam.
Crew: 39.
Propulsion: 2 Ruston 12RKCM diesels (total 4380bhp); 1 controllable-pitch propeller.
Sensors: 1 Kelvin Hughes Type 1006 sea search and navigational radar; 1 Deccan CANE navigator/position fixer; 1 Kelvin Hughes MS45 echo sounder.

The Royal Navy's HMS Anglesey *(P277), 1978.*

Armament: 1 single Bofors 40mm Mk 3 anti-aircraft gun; 2 machine guns.
Top speed: 16.5 knots.
Range: 11,000 nautical miles at 12 knots.
Programme: The first of this seven ship class was laid down in late 1975, the ships and their commissioning dates being: HMS *Anglesey* (P277), May 1979; HMS *Alderney* (P278), November 1979; HMS *Jersey* (P295), October 1976; HMS *Guernsey* (P297), October 1977; HMS *Shetland* (P298), July 1977; HMS *Orkney* (P299), February 1977; and HMS *Lindisfarne* (P300), January 1978.
Notes: The 'Island' class vessels are a direct design development of the earlier *Jura* and *Westra* patrol vessels built for the Department of Agriculture and Fisheries for Scotland. Built to civil Lloyd's Register standards, these specialist offshore patrollers afford a much more economic means of policing the nation's waters than could be achieved using a conventional naval corvette or light frigate. The 'Island' class can accommodate an additional 25 Royal Marines.

Emer Class Patrol Vessels

Role: Fishery protection.
Builder: Verolme, Ireland.
User: Irish Navy.
Basic data: 1020 tons full displacement; 213.9ft (65.2m) overall length; 34.1ft (10.4m) maximum beam.
Crew: 46.
Propulsion: 2 SEMT-Pielstick 6 PA6L-280 diesels (total 4800bhp); 1 controllable-pitch propeller.
Sensors: 2 Decca sea search and navigational radars; 1 Decca Mk 21 Navigator; 1 Simrad SU hull-mounted sonar.
Armament: 1 single 40mm Bofors and 2 single 20mm Oerlikon anti-aircraft guns.
Top speed: 18 knots.

The Dutch-designed Irish Navy ship Emer *(P21), 1981.*

Range: 6750 nautical miles at 12 knots.
Programme: Based on the earlier *Deirdre* (FP20), the three ship 'Emer' class vessels consist of *Emer* (P21), *Aoife* (P22) and *Aisling* (P23), all of which were laid down between early 1977 and October 1979 and entered service in January 1978, October 1979 and May 1980, respectively.
Notes: Extremley seaworthy vessels, the handsomely proportioend 'Emer' class ships are a slightly larger and heavier development of the sole-of-class *Deirdre* (FP20), commissioned in May 1972 and which was the first Irish Navy vessels to be built in an Irish shipyard. Along with a planned new class of even larger helicopter-carrying patrol vessels, all of these ships are of Dutch design and have been, or will be fabricated in the Dutch-controlled Verolme dockyards in Cork.

Halcon Class Patrol Vessels

Mantilla (GC24), the lead of class, during 1982 sea trials.

Role: Offshore patrol.
Builder: Bazan, Spain.
Users: Argentinian coastguard and Mexican Navy.
Basic data: 910 tons full displacement; 220.0ft (67.0m) overall length; 34.4ft (10.5m) maximum beam.
Crew: 34.
Propulsion: 2 Bazan-built MTU MA 16V956 TB91 diesels (total 9000bhp); 2 propellers.
Sensors: 1 Decca AC 1226 navigational radar; 1 Kelvin Hughes MS-39 echo sounder; 1 Koden KS-508 VHF radio direction finder.
Armament: 1 Aerospatiale Alouette III helicopter; 1 single 40mm Breda/Bofors 40L/70 anti-aircraft gun; 2 single light machine guns.
Top speed: 22 knots.
Range: 4343 nautical miles at 18 knots.
Programme: The initial order for five ships of this class was placed by Argentina in March 1979, the lead ship, *Mantilla* (GC24), having been laid down in February 1981, launched on June 1981 and entered sea trails during 1982. The remaining Argentinian vessels comprise: *Azopardo* (GC25), *Thomson* (GC26), *Prefecto Fique* (GC27) and *Preffecto Derbes* (GC28). All were delivered in 1983. A further six of this class were ordered for service with the Mexican Navy in November 1980, the first, *Cadete Virgilio Uribe* (GH01), having been launched in November 1981 and completed in June 1982. The other Mexican vessels comprise: *Teniente Jose Azueta* (GH02), *Capitan de Fregata Pedro Sainz de Barranda* (GH03), *Contralmirante Castillo Breton* (GH04), *Vicealmirante Orthon P Blanc* (GH05) and *Contralmirante Angel Ortiz Monasterio* (GH06): all of which were completed between September and December 1982. All Argentinian ships were constructed at Bazan's El Ferrol yards, while the Mexican vessels were built at Bazan's San Fernando facilities.
Notes: This currently 11-ship programme is certainly impressive in industrial terms, with all vessels being completed within 45 months of receiving the first order. The 'Halcon' class, as Bazan refer to these ships, has been designed specifically for long range ocean patrol in rough sea conditions. Besides carrying out their primary role of fishery and offshore assets protection, these ships can double as salvage tugs and sea-spill pollution fighters.

Peacock Class Patrol Vessels

HMS Peacock *(P239), destined to serve with the Royal Navy's Hong Kong Patrol.*

Role: Offshore patrol.
Builder: Hall Russell, UK.
User: Royal Navy.
Basic data: 710 tons full displacement; 205.4ft (62.6m) overall length; 32.8ft (10.0m) maximum beam.
Crew: 42.
Propulsion: 2 APE Crossley Pielstick 18 PA6V280 diesels (total 14,400bhp); 1 propeller.
Sensors: 1 Kelvin Hughes Type 1006 sea search and navigational radar; 1 Kelvin Hughes Type MS45 Mk II echo sounder; 1 Sperry Sea Archer electro-optical fire control system.
Armament: 1 Single 76mm OTO-Melara compact dual-purpose gun; 4 single machine guns.
Top speed: 25 knots.
Endurance: 2500 nautical miles.
Programme: A five-ship class, ordered in July 1981, for use with the Royal Navy's Hong Kong Patrol. The class is led by HMS *Peacock* (P239), launched in December 1982. The remaining four vessesl are HMS *Plover* (P240), HMS *Starling* (P241), HMS *Swallow* (P242) and HMS *Swift* (P243), the whole class being accepted between October 1983 and March 1985.
Notes: The latest of a series of Hall Russell developed patrol vessels, the 'Peacock' class will replace the five 'Coniston' class former minesweepers used to patrol Hong Kong waters. More compact, but more heavily armed and faster than either of their 'Island' or 'Castle' class forebears, the 'Peacock' class is equipped to be replenished at sea and carry two Avon Searider outboard-powered inflatable boarding craft.

Pedro Teixeira Class Patrol Vessels

Role: River patrol.
Builder: Brazilian Naval Dockyards.
User: Brazilian Navy.
Basic data: 690 tons full displacement; 208.5ft (63.56m)

overall length; 31.85ft (9.71m) maximum beam.
Crew: 60.
Propulsion: 4 MAN V6V16/18 TLS diesels (total 3840bhp); 2 propellers.,
Sensors: 2 Decca 1216A sea search and navigational radars; 1 TACAN aircraft homer.
Armament: 1 Bell 206 Jetranger helicopter; 1 single 40mm Bofors anti-aircraft gun; 2 single 81mm mortars; 6 single 12.7mm machine guns.
Top speed: 16 knots. ·
Range: 5500 nautical miles at 10 knots.
Programme: Ordered in late 1970, this two ship class comprises: *Pedro Teixeira* (P20) and *Raposo Tavares* (P21). Both were launched simultaneously in early June 1972 and entered service in mid-December 1973.
Notes: Specifically designed to operate in very shallow waters and to have a high degree of slow speed manoeuvrability, these vessels carry out a multiplicity of duties, including assistance to the civil population. The ships can be used as troop and equipment transports or for river policing, and each is equipped with facilities, including a hangar, with which to operate a helicopter.

The Brazilian Navy's Raposo Tavares *(P21) with its Bell 206 Jetranger on the ship's helipad.*

Roraima Class Patrol Vessels

The Brazilian Navy's Amapa *(P32) navigating the Amazon.*

Role: River patrol.
Builders: Various, Brazil.
Users: Brazilian Navy and on order for the Paraguayan Navy.
Basic data: 340 tons full displacement; 151.9ft (46.3m) overall length; 27.7ft (8.45m) maximum beam.
Crew: 40.
Propulsion: 2 MAN V6V16/18 TL diesels (total 1824bhp); 2 propellers.
Sensors: 2 Decca 1216A sea search and navigation radars.
Armament: 1 single 40mm Bofors L70/40 anti-aircraft gun; 2 single 81mm mortars; 6 single 12.7mm machine guns.
Top speed: 14 knots.
Range: 6000 nautical miles at 8 knots.
Programme: Currently a four-ship class comprising the three Brazilian vessels: *Roraima* (P30), *Randonia* (P31) and *Amapa* (P32), along with the Paraguayna Navy's *Itaipu*, the construction of which is underway. Ordered in late 1970, the three Brazilian ships were built by Estaleiro McLaren and entered service in February 1975, December 1975 and January 1976, respectively. The *Itaipu*, laid down in March 1983, is being built at the Brazilian Naval Dockyards and will be delivered in March 1986.
Notes: As with the Brazilian Navy's larger 'Pedro Teixeira' class, the 'Roraima' class has little draught (depth of hull below the waterline) in order to operate in the frequently shallow waters of the Brazilian river network. The 'Roraima' class carries the same armament and most of the facilities found on its larger brethren, with the exception of having a helicopter. The recent Paraguayan Navy's order for one of these ships represents the first export contract for a Brazilian designed and developed warship.

Meghna Class Patrol Vessels

Role: Offshore patrol.
Builder: Vosper Group, Singapore.
User: Bangladeshi Navy.
Basic data: 234 tons full displacement; 152.5ft (46.5m) overall length; 24.6ft (7.5m) maximum beam.
Crew: 44.
Propulsion: 2 MTU 16V396 TB93 diesels (total 6000bhp); 2 propellers.
Sensors: 1 as yet undesignated combined low-level air and sea search radar; 1 Racal Decca TM1629C sea search and navigational radar; 1 as yet undesignated gun fire control system; 1 Jungner Instruments SAL ACCOR echo sounder and log.
Armament: 1 single 76mm OTO-Melara compact dual-purpose gun; 1 single 20mm Oerlikon anti-aircraft gun.
Top speed: 24 knots.
Range: 2000 nautical miles at 16 knots.
Programme: This two-vessel class comprising *Meghna* and her as yet unnamed sister were ordered by the Bangladesh government in late 1982. *Meghna* was launched in January 1984 and was delivered before the close of 1984, along with the second of class.
Notes: This Vosper Group patrol craft design employs a steel hull and light alloy superstructure. This 46-metre vessel's design deliberately sacrifices a high dash speed capability in order to gain the requisite rough water, long duration seaworthiness, coupled to crew habitability required to meet Bangladeshi operational needs. These vessels have a continuous cruising speed of 20 knots and carry accommodation for three trainees in addition to the normal crew complement of 44. For inspection and boarding puposes, each craft carries a six man Zodiac inflatible, powered by a 25bhp outboard engine.

A Vosper Group model of their 46 metre design, of which the two 'Meghna' class craft are the first examples.

Kingfisher Class Patrol Vessels

Role: Patrol/training.
Builder: Richard Dunston, UK.
User: Royal Navy.
Basic data: 230 tons full displacement; 118.1ft (36.0m) overall length; 23.0ft (7.0m) maximum beam.
Crew: 24.
Propulsion: 2 Ruston Paxman Ventura 16-YCJM diesels (total 4200bhp); 2 propellers.
Sensors: 1 Type 978 sea search and navigational radar; 1 Decca Hi-Fix precision position fixer.
Armament: 1 single 40mm Bofors L40/60 anti-aircraft gun; 3 single 7.6mm light machine guns.
Top speed: 20 knots.
Range: 1200 nautical miles at 15 knots.
Programme: Originally planned to have been a much larger class, only four of these vessels, comprising HMS *Kingfisher* (P260), HMS *Cygnet* (P261), HMS *Petrel* (P262) and HMS *Sandpiper* (P263) were to be completed. All laid down between July and December of 1973, the four craft entered service in October 1975, July 1976, July 1977 and September 1977, respectively.
Notes: Not popular with their crews, the 'Kingfisher' or 'Bird' class as the Royal Navy refer to them, represent an unsuccessful attempt to adopt the basic design of a Royal-Air Force air-sea rescue launch to that of the more ardous task of offshore patrol. Despite the incorporation of fin stabilisers, the class has a history of instability in certain sea conditions. The class is now largely relegated to inshore training duties.

HMS Cygnet (P261) differs from the others of her class in having a hull unbroken by the provision of portholes.

Kraljrvica Class Patrol Vessels

Role: Coastal patrol.
Builder: Tito Shipyards, Yugoslavia.
Users: Navies of Yugoslavia (5), Bangladesh (2) and Indonesia (5).
Basic data: 202 tons full displacement; 184.5ft (41.0m) overall length; 20.7ft (6.3m) maximum beam.
Crew: Up to 44.
Propulsion: 2 MAN W8V 30/38 diesels (total 3300bhp); 2 propellers.
Sensors: 1 Decca 44 sea search and navigational radar; 1 Tamir II or QCU-2 hull-mounted sonar.
Armament: 1 single 76mm dual-purpose gun and 1 40mm anti-aircraft gun (on Indonesian craft) or 1 twin 40mm anti-aircraft gun; 2 quintuple RBU-1200 anti-submarine rocket launchers (Yugoslavian only); 2 Mk 6 depth charge projectors; 2 depth charge rack.
Top speed: 18 knots.
Range: 1000 nautical miles at 12 knots.
Programme: Originally a 16-vessel class built during the 1957 to 1959 period, 12 remained in service by the end of 1982 comprising: Yugoslavia's *P510, 512, 519, 521* and *524*. Bangladesh's *P301* and *302*, along with Indonesia'a *P819, 820, 825, 829* and *830*.
Notes: Also referred to as the 'PPR-500' class by the Yugoslavians, craft of this class were also transferred to Ethiopia and Sudan, but are no longer operated by these navies.

Ford Class Patrol Vessels

Role: Coastal patrol.
Builders: Various, UK.
Users: Navies of Bangladesh (2), Nigeria (1) and South Africa (5).
Basic data: 160 tons full displacement; 117.3ft (35.76m) overall length; 20.0ft (6.1m) maximum beam.
Crew: Up to 26.
Propulsion: 2 Davet-Paxman YHAMX diesels (total 1000bhp); and 1 Foden FD-6 diesel (100bhp) cruising engine; 3 propellers.
Sensors: 1 of various sea search and navigational radars.
Armament: 1 single 40mm Bofors and 2 single 20mm Oerlik on anti-aircraft guns.
Top speed: 15 knots.
Range: 500 nautical miles at 12 knots.
Programme: A 21-vessel class of which 20 were built for the Royal Navy and delivered between January 1954 and July 1958, plus a later vessel, ordered by Nigeria and delivered during 1960. The remaining vessels in service in mid-1982 comprise: Nigeria's *Sapele* (P09), along with South Africa's *Gelderland* (P3105), *Nautilus* (P3120), *Rijger* (P3125), *Haerlem* (P3126) and *Oosterland* (P3127). All of these vessels were formerly Royal Navy craft. Bangladesh operates *Padua* (P201) and *Surma* (P202), both Indian-built versions of the 'Ford' class.
Notes: Referred to by the Royal Navy as Seaward Defence boats, the 'Ford' class vessels were generally held to be more seaworthy than their successors in the shape of the 'Kingfisher' class. However, as the 'Ford' class vessels' role was always considered something of a low priority within Royal Navy planning circles, the class was soon either transferred to other naval users, or relegated to the Royal Navy Reserve's university-based units for training duties.

SAS Rijger (P3125), one of this five-vessel South African Navy-operated class.

A beam aspect of one of the former Yugoslavian Navy craft.

The Royal New Zealand Navy vessel Pukaki

Brooke Marine 33 Metre Class Patrol Vessels

Role: Coastal patrol.
Builder: Brooke Marine, UK.
Users: Navies of Libya (4), New Zealand (4) Nigeria (4), plus 2 for the British Customs & Excise Service.
Basic data: 135 tons full displacement; 107.0ft (32.6m) overall length; 20.0ft (6.1m) maximum beam.
Crew: 21.
Propulsion: 2 Paxman 12 YJCM diesels (total 3000 bhp); 2 propellers.
Sensors: 1 Decca sea search and navigational radar.
Armament: 1 single 40mm Bofors and 1 single 20mm Oerlikon anti-aircraft guns (standard) or 2 twin 30mm Emerlec anti-aircraft guns (Nigerian craft).
Top speed: 23.5 knots.
Range: 2300 nautical miles at 11 knots.
Programme: An 18-craft class, deliveries of which started in 1965 with four to Pakistan (three of which were lost in the Indo-Pakistan War of 1971 and the craft no longer serves). Four more were delivered to Libya in the 1968/69 period comprising; *PC1, PC2, PC3* and *PC4*. Nigeria took delivery of a pair, *P167* and *P168* in 1974, along with *P171* and *P172* in 1977. The four Royal New Zealand Navy craft, *P3568, P3569, P3570* and *P3571* were all delivered during 1975.
Notes: Known as the 'Pukaki' class as operated by New Zealand, or as the 'Makurdi' class in Nigerian service, these craft share a common hull, but vary in considerable detail between vessels supplied to the varios users, especially in the profile of the forward deck housing. The retrofitting of the fore and aft-mounted twin Emerlec 30mm armed Nigerian craft commenced in 1981.

Azteca Class Patrol Vessels

Role: Offshore patrol.
Builder: Various, UK & Mexico.
User: Mexican Navy.
Basic data: 130 tons full displacement; 112ft (34.1m) overall length; 28.2ft (8.6m) maximum beam.
Crew: 25.
Propulsion: 2 Paxman 12 YJCM diesels (total 7200bhp); 2 propellers.
Sensors: 1 Decca sea search and navigational radar.
Armament: 1 single 40mm anti-aircraft gun; 1 twin 20mm anti-aircraft gun.
Top speed: 24 knots.

The fourth of the 'Azteca' class. Jose Maria Izazago (P-04).

Endurance: In excess of 2500 nautical miles.
Programme: Developed to the design of ABMTM, who undertook to act as overall programme co-ordinator, the Mexican Government placed an initial order for 21 of these craft in March 1973, subsequently contracting for a further 10 'Aztecas' in June 1975. The London-based ABMTM selected a grouping of Scottish boatbuilders, led by Ailsa of Troon, who built 11; James Lamont, who constructed five and Scott and Sons, who fabricated the remaining five. In Mexico, the Vera Cruz yards built seven, while the final three were the responsibility of Salina Cruz Pennant numbers of the 'Aztecas' are *P-01* through *P-31* and all entered service between October 1974 and January 1979.
Notes: Aimed at providing a robust, inexpensive craft, the 'Azteca' design breaks with conventional naval architectural practice by being some 30 per cent wider than comparable craft; a feature which provides the 'Aztecas' with excellent seaworthiness.

31.3 Metre Vosper Thornycroft Class Patrol Vessels

Role: Coastal patrol.
Builder: Vosper Thornycroft, UK.
Users: Navies of Guyana (1), Kenya (3), Malaysia (22), Trinidad (4) and Tunisia (2), plus the Panamanian National Guard (2) and Bahamas Police (1). *Note:* above were craft in service at mid-1982.
Basic data: 125 tons full displacement; 103.0ft (31.3m) overall length; 19.75ft (6.02m) maximum beam.

The Tunisian Navy's Menzel Bourguiba *(P206) during sea trials.*

Crew: Up to 24.
Propulsion: 2 of various type MTU (Malaysian and Tunisian) or Paxman Ventura (rest) diesels (totals between 2800 and 3500bhp) for Paxman and 3550 to 4000bhp for MTU); 2 propellers.
Sensors: Decca sea search and navigational radar.
Armament: 2 single 20mm Oerlikon anti-aircraft guns.
Top speed: From 23 knots up to 27 knots depending on engines fitted.
Range: 1500 nautical miles at 14 knots.
Programme: A total of 38 craft of this class were built between 1962 and 1978, 3 of which Bahamas (1) and Malaysia (2) have been lost. Remaining vessels comprise: Bahamas' *P01*, Guyana's *DF1010*, Kenya's *P3110*, *P3112* and *P3117*. Malaysia's *P34*, *P36* through *P48* and *P3139*, *P3140*, plus *P3142* through *P3147*, Panama's *GC10* and *CG11*. Trinidad's *CG1* through *CG4*, along with Tunisia's *P205* and *P206*. Deliveries of the Malaysian craft were made between 1962 and 1966, a pair each to Trinidad in 1965 and 1972, all four Kenyan in 1966, Panama's two in 1971, Tunisia's pair in 1977, as was the sole Guyanan craft, ending with the Bahaman pair in 1978.
Notes: Steel-hulled with aluminium superstructures, these seaworthy and inexpensive craft are very similar in general appearance, to their slightly larger 110ft (33m) 'Vosper Thornycroft' class brethren.

Piratini Class Patrol Vessels

Role: Coastal patrol.
Builder: Ilha das Crobras, Brazil.
User: Brazilian Navy.
Basic data: 105 tons full displacement; 95.0ft (28.95m) overall length; 20.0ft (6.1m) maximum beam.
Crew: 16.
Propulsion: 4 Cummins VT-12M diesels (total 2324bhp); 2 propellers.
Sensors: 1 unidentified sea search and navigational radar.
Armament: 1 single 81mm mortar; 3 single 12.7mm machine guns.
Top speed: 18 knots.
Range: 1700 nautical miles at 12 knots.
Programme: This six-vessel class comprises: *Piratini* (P10), *Piraja* (P11), *Pampeiro* (P12), *Parati* (P13), *Penedo* (P14) and *Poti* (P15). These craft entered service with the Brazilian Navy between November 1970 and October 1971.
Notes: Employing the design and propulsive machinery of

Parati (P13), fourth of a Brazilian-built six-vessel class.

the US Coast Guard's 'Cape' class cutter, these Brazilian-built craft are employed on both inshore and riverine patrol and policing duties.

Seeb Class Patrol Vessels

Role: Inshore patrol.
Builder: Vosper Group, Singapore.
User: Omani Navy.
Basic data: 90 tons full displacement; 82.8ft (25.24m) overall length; 19.0ft (5.8m) maximum beam.
Crew: 13.
Propulsion: 2 MTU 12V 331 diesels (total 3072bhp); 1 cummins diesel (200bhp); 2 propellers.
Sensors: 1 Decca sea search and navigational radar; 1 Kelvin Hughes echo sounder.

The Omani Navy's Seeb *(B20) seen during sea trials.*

Royal Navy Reserve's HMS Hunter *(P284) and HMS* Fencer *(P283).*

Armament: 2 single 20mm Oerlikon anti-aircraft guns.
Top speed: 25 knots.
Range: 750 nautical miles at 14 knots.
Programme: This four craft class comprises: *Seeb* (B20), *Shinas* (B21), *Sadah* (B22) and *Khasab* (B23). All four craft being delivered in the spring of 1981.
Notes: This design employs a steel hull and aluminium superstructure and is spacious enough to carry five extra above the normal compliment of 13. For long endurance patrol missions, the two engines are shut down and the craft operate on the smaller diesel, enabling the vessel to range out to 2000 nautical miles at 4 knots.

Fairey Tracker and Attacker Classes Patrol Vessels

Role: Patrol/rescue/fast dispatch.
Builder: Fairey Allday Marine, UK.
Users: Navies of Sierra Leone (1), South Africa (2), UK (5) and Yemen People's Republic (1), plus numerous non-naval operators.
Basic data: 34 tons full displacement; 65.6ft (20.0m) overall length; 17.0ft (5.15m) maximum beam.

Crew: Up to 11.
Propulsion: 2 Rolls-Royce DV8TCWM (total 1500bhp) on South African, or 2 MTU 8V331 TC82 (total 1800bhp) on Yemen or 2 General Motors 12V71TI diesels (total 1300bhp); 2 propellers.
Sensors: 1 of various sea search and navigational radars.
Armament: 1 single 20mm Oerlikon anti-aircraft gun; 2 single 12.7mm machine guns (no armament fitted to South African and UK craft).
Top speed: 29 knots (Yemen); 27 knots (South African); 24 knots (Sierra Leone and UK craft).
Range: 650 nautical miles at 20 knots.
Programme: Eight of these craft have been sold to four naval users by mid-1983 comprising South Africa's *P1554* and *P1555*, delivered in 1973; Yemen's craft, delivered in 1978; Sierra Leone's unit, delivered in 1982, plus the Royal Navy's HMS *Attacker* (P281), HMS *Chaser* (P282), HMS *Fencer* (P283), HMS *Hunter* (P284) and HMS *Stiker* (P285), all delivered in 1983.
Notes: Compact and seaworthy craft, all but the South African boats are built throughout from glass-reinforced plastic; the two early boats having the same hull material, married to wooden decks and aluminium superstructures.

Assault ships

Wasp Class Assault Ships

Role: Amphibious warfare.
Builder: Ingalls Shipbuilding, USA.
User: US Navy.
Basic data: 40,500 tons full displacement; 840.0ft (256.0m) overall length; 106.0ft (32.3m) maximum beam.
Crew: 1080.
Propulsion: 2 Westinghouse geared steam turbines (total 70,000shp); 2 propellers.
Sensors: 1 SPS-52B long-range air search and height finder (3-D) radar; SPS-49 long-range air search radar; 1 SPS-67 sea search and navigational radar; 1 Mk 86 and 2 Mk 115 fire control radars; TACAN aircraft homer; NTDS automated action information data processing system.
Armament: McDonnell AV-8 Harrier aircraft; Bell AH-1 helicopters; 2 Mk 25 octuple Sea Sparrow point air defence missile launchers; 2 single 5in Mk 45 dual-purpose guns; 3 Mk 15 Phalanx 20mm close-in weapons systems; 8 single .50 calibre machine guns.
Top speed: 24 knots.
Range: 10,000 nautical miles at 20 knots.
Programme: Authorised in late 1981, Ingalls

163

An artist's impression of this 'Tarawa' class derivative as completed.

Shipbuilding Division of Litton Industries received its first development contract in December 1981, the contract to proceed with construction of the lead, USS *Wasp* (LHD-1), of this five or more ship class being placed at the end of 1983. The lead ship should be in service by the close of 1986, with deliveries continuing into the early part of the 1990s.

Notes: While basically similar in both external appearance and internal layout to the earlier 'Tarawa' class, the 'Wasp' class design will vary considerably from its forebears in detail. In particular, there are changes to the flight deck, hangar deck, aircraft lifts and well deck. Designed to accommodate a 1902-man Marine Amphibious Unit (MAU) and its primary fighting equipment, the LHD-1's spacious immediately below flight deck hangars will be able to house up to 43 helicopters, or a mix of helicopters and fixed-wing, vertical-lift AV-8 Harriers.

Tarawa Class Assault Ships

Role: Amphibious warfare.
Builder: Ingalls Shipbuilding, USA.
User: US Navy.
Basic data: 39,300 tons full displacement; 820ft (249.9m) overall length; 106.6ft (32.5m) maximum beam.
Crew: 894.
Propulsion: 2 Westinghouse geared steam turbines (total 70,000shp); 2 propellers.
Sensors: Comprehensive suite of SPS-52B air search and height finder (3-D), SPS-40B air search and SPS-10F (sea search and navigational) radars; 1 Mk 86 and 2 Mk 115 fire control systems; TACAN aircraft homer; NTDS automated action information data processing system.
Armament: 2 octuple Mk 25 Sea Sparrow surface-to-air missile launchers; 3 Mk 45 dual-purpose 5in guns; 6 single 20mm Mk 67 anti-aircraft guns; 2 Phalanx 20mm close-in weapons systems (fitted from 1981 onwards).
Top speed: 24 knots.
Range: 10,000 nautical miles at 20 knots.
Programme: Originally planned to be a nine-ship class, the 'Tarawa' build was cut back to five ships in January 1971. All five ships, USS *Tarawa* (LHA1), USS *Saipan* (LHA2), USS *Belleau Wood* (LHA3), USS *Nassau* (LHA4) and USS *Peleliu* (LHA5), were ordered in a 36-month period between 1969 and 1971. US Navy acceptance of the respective ships took place in May 1976, October 1977, September 1978, July 1979 and May 1980.
Notes: While the detail planning and constructional phases of this programme, in company with virtually every other US major naval programme of the period, were best characterised as crisis-torn, the end result is an extremely impressive vessel. These 'Tarawa' class ships are the largest amphibious vessels built to date, being designed to combine the capabilities of no less than four

previous types of US Navy assault ship within the one vast hull. Thus the 'Tarawa' class ship can embark, transport over great distances, tactically deploy and stay to support a marine Amphibious Unit of around 1900 men, five M-60 tanks, six 105mm field howitzers, 11 large amphibious assault vehicles, mortars and various complements of anti-tank missiles and their supporting composite squadron of about 22 helicopters, ranging from the massive Sikorsky CH-53 Sea Stallion, through the Boeing Vertol CH-47 Sea Knight to the agile, anti-tank TOW missile equipped Bell AH-1T Hueycobra. Within the 'Tarawa's' stern well deck there is sufficient room to dock a pair of 390 ton tank-carrying landing craft, or up to 17 of the smaller LCM 6 craft of 62 tons displacement. Not only is there a need rapidly to disembark nearly 2000 men, but also several hundred tons of stores needed to support them. To meet this large cargo moving need, the ships incorporate an elaborate overhead conveyancing system, capable of handling up to 240 pallets per hour. Each ship is also equipped with very complete hospital facilities, including intensive care units for up to 90 people. Besides being routinely capable of operating both helicopters and the AV-8 Harrier, the spacious flight deck is ample from which to operate such short take-off and landing types as the North American OV-10 Bronco.

Iwo Jima Class Assault Ships

Role: Amphibious warfare.
Builders: Various, USA.
User: US Navy.
Basic data: 18,300 tons full displacement; 592.0ft (180.4m) overall length; 112.0ft (34.1m) maximum beam.
Crew: 652.
Propulsion: 1 Westinghouse geared steam turbine (22,000shp); 1 propeller.
Sensors: 1 SPS-40 air search radar; 1 SPS-10 sea search and navigational radar; 2 Mk 115 fire control radars for Sea Sparrow; 1 TACAN aircraft homer; NTDS automated action information data-processing system.
Armament: 2 octuple Sea Sparrow point air defence missile launchers; 2 twin 3in Mk 33 anti-aircraft guns; 2 Mk 15 Phalanx 20mm close-in weapons systems in course of installation.
Top speed: 23 knots.
Range: 6000 nautical miles at 14 knots.
Programme: This seven-ship class comprises: USS *Iwo Jima* (LPH2), USS *Okinawa* (LPH3), USS *Guadalcanal* (LPH7), USS *Guam* (LPH9), USS *Tripoli* (LPH10), USS *New Orleans* (LPH11) and USS *Inchon* (LPH12). Built in three separate shipyards, all seven ships were contracted between 1958 and 1966, with service entries between August 1961 and June 1970.
Notes: Similar in general appearance to the later types of US World War II escort carriers, these ships carried no deck catapults or aircraft arresting equipment and were thus confined to operating helicopters from the outset. The US Navy's first dedicated major assault ships, they can accommodate up to 25 helicopters, their main means of putting combat troops ashore, and have space for over 2000 US Marines. The ships carry extensive medical facilities for casualty treatment, including intensive care.

Austin Class Assault Ships

Role: Amphibious warfare.
Builders: Various, USA.
User: US Navy.
Basic data: 16,900 tons full displacement; 570ft (173.7m) overall length; 84ft (25.6m) maximum beam.

Crew: 447.

Propulsion: 2 De Laval geared steam turbines (total 24,000shp); 2 propellers.

Sensors: 1 SPS-40 air search radar; 1 SPS-10 sea search and navigational radar; 1 URN-20 TACAN aircraft homer.

Armament: 2 twin (reduced from 4 twin as originally fitted) 76mm MK 33 anti-aircraft guns; 2 Phalanx 20mm close-in weapons systems.

Top speed: 20 knots.

Range: In excess of 6000 nautical miles.

Programme: Laid down between February 1963 and October 1966, this 12-ship class consists of: USS *Austin* (LPD4), USS *Ogden* (LPD5), USS *Duluth* (LPD6), USS *Cleveland* (LPD7), USS *Dubuque* (LPD8), USS *Denver* (LPD9), USS *Juneau* (LPD10), USS *Coronado* (LPD11), USS *Shreveport* (LPD12), USS *Nashville* (LPD13), USS *Trenton* (LPD14) and USS *Ponce* (LPD15). The construction of these ships was shared between the US Navy Shipyard, New York (LPD4 to 6), Ingalls (LPD7 and 8) and Lockheed (LPD9 through 15). Commissioning of the class took place between February 1965 and July 1971.

Notes: An enlarged version of the slightly earlier 'Raleigh' class, the 'Austins' can carry up to 930 troops, their vehicles and supplies, who are taken ashore either by landing craft launched from the aft well deck, or by up to six Boeing Vertol CH-46 Sea Knight helicopters.

Whidbey Island Class Assault Ships

Role: Amphibious warfare.

Builder: Lockheed Shipbuilding and Avondale, USA.

User: US Navy.

Basic data: 15,775 tons full displacement; 609.0ft (185.6m) overall length; 84.0ft (25.6m) maximum beam.

Crew: 413.

Propulsion: 4 Fairbanks Morse-built SEMT Pielstick 16PC-2.5V400 diesels (total 41,600bhp); 2 controllable-pitch propellers.

Sensors: 1 SPS-40B air search radar; 1 SPS-67 sea search radar; 1 Litton LN66 navigational radar; 1 URN-25 TACAN aircraft homer; automated action information data processing system.

Armament: 2 Phalanx 20mm close-in weapons systems; 2 single 20mm Mk 67 anti-aircraft guns.

Top speed: 22 knots.

Endurance: In excess of 8000 nautical miles.

Programme: A planned ten-ship class (last two of modified design), the lead vessel, USS *Whidbey Island* (LSD41) was ordered in February 1981, laid down in August 1981, launched in July 1983 and delivered in January 1985. The second ship, USS *Germantown* LDS42, was laid down in August 1982, with delivery set for October 1985. By June 1985, the third ship, LSD43, had been ordered from Lockheed, while LSD44, 45 and 46 had been ordered from Avondale. All ten of this class should be ordered by the late 1980s and deliveries completed during the first half of the 1990s.

Notes: Planned by the US Navy to serve as replacements for their 'Thomason' class dock landing ships, built around the mid-1950s, the 'Whidbey Island' class programme became the focus of controversy between the Carter Administration and the US Congress during the late 1970s, resulting in several years' delay in the placing of the lead ship construction contract. Designed around an internal aft dock area measuring 440ft (134.1m) by 50ft (15.24m) capable of housing four Bell LCAC air cushion landing craft, the LSD41 class ships can each accommodate up to 440 US Marines and their fighting equipment. Up to two Sikorsky CH-53E Super Stallion helicopters can operate simultaneously from the aft flight deck, but no hangar facilities are carried. The US Navy has announced plans to exploit the basic LSD41 hull design

The 'Tarawa' class USS *Saipan (LHA2)* with a mix of Bell UH1 and Sikorsky CH53 helicopters on its flight deck.

USS Iwo Jima *(LPH2)* with nine CH-46 Sea Knight, four CH-53 Sea Stallion, one UH-1 and three AH-1 Hueycobra helicopters on deck.

USS Denver *(LPD9). The funnels are side-mounted (aft to port).*

An artist's impression of USS Whidbey Island *(LSD41) as completed and having just disembarked two of its four Bell LCAC air cushion landing craft.*

Ivan Rogov, *April 1980.*

with an envisaged procurement of a further two derivative classes totalling an additional 25 ships. While the construction programme for these follow-on classes is likely to be spread around a number of US shipyards, it is also highly probable that Lockheed Shipbuilding will participate in this work.

Ivan Rogov Class Assault Ships

Role: Amphibious warfare.
Builder: Kaliningrad, USSR.
User: Soviet Navy.
Basic data: 13,000 tons full displacement; 520ft (138m) overall length; 80ft (24m) maximum beam.
Crew: 200.
Propulsion: Gas turbines (total 40,000shp); 2 propellers.
Sensors: 2 air search radar/IFF; 2 sea search and navigational radars; 4 fire control radars (1 for missiles, 1 for 76mm and 2 for 30mm guns).
Armament: Facilities for up to 4 Kamov Ka-25 helicopters; 1 twin, SA-N-4 surface-to-air missile launcher; 1 twin 76mm gun; 4 single Gatling 30mm guns; 1 multiple 122mm bombardment rocket launcher.
Top speed: 20 knots.
Range: Not known.
Programme: *Ivan Rogov* was accepted during 1978 and one more of this class was in service by the end of 1983.
Notes: By far the biggest of the Soviet's assault ships, the *Ivan Rogov* can carry around 550 troops, 30 armoured personnel carriers and ten tanks. To speed boarding and unboarding, the ship has a floodable well deck aft long enough to house three Lebed class 85 ton air cushion landing craft. Forward, the ship has clam-shell bow doors and ramp, while the weather deck aft of the bow section can double as either a second helicopter pad or storage area for roll-on/roll-off equipment. The ship's helicopter hangar is located immediately forward of the main, stern helicopter pad. The range of the ship's SA-N-4 surface-to-air missiles is reported to be around 8 nautical miles.

Fearless Class Assault Ships

Role: Amphibious warfare.
Builders: Various, UK.
User: Royal Navy.
Basic data: 12,120 tons full displacement; 520ft (158.5m) overall length; 80ft (29.4m) maximum beam.
Crew: 447.
Propulsion: 2 English Electric geared steam turbines (22,000shp); 2 propellers.
Sensors: 1 Type 978 sea search and navigational radar; 1

Type 993 low-level air and surface search radar; CAAIS automated action information data-processing system.
Armament: 4 quadruple Seacat point air defence missile launchers; 2 single 40mm Bofors anti-aircraft guns.
Top speed: 21 knots.
Range: 5000 nautical miles at 20 knots.
Programme: This two-ship class comprises HMS *Fearless* (L10), built by Harland & Wolff, and HMS *Intrepid* (L11), by John Brown. The two ships were commissioned in November 1965 and March 1967.
Notes: Patterned very much on the lines of the US Navy's 'Raleigh' class assault ship, the 'Fearless' class can carry up to 1000 troops or a mix of fewer troops plus vehicles. As with other ships of this type, the 'Fearless' class incorporate a large docking well aft, which can accommodate up to four medium landing craft, while four 30-troop light landing craft can be carried on davits each side of the superstructure. The large flight deck aft can operate up to six Westland Wessex helicopters. Both ships operated with the UK Falklands Task Force, with *Intrepid*, at one point, known to have served as a refuelling station for Sea Harriers while anchored in Falkland Sound.

The Royal Navy's HMS Fearless *(L10).*

Ouragan Class Assault Ships

Role: Amphibious warfare.
Builder: DCAN Brest, France.
User: French Navy.
Basic data: 8500 tons full displacement; 488.85ft (149m) overall length; 70.5ft (21.5m) maximum beam.
Crew: 138.
Propulsion: 2 SEMT-Pielstick diesels (total 8640bhp); 2 propellers.
Sensors: 1 Decca/DRBN 32 sea search and navigational radar; 1 SQS-17 sonar on L9021 only.
Armament: 4 single Bofors 40mm anti-aircraft guns (on L9021 only).
Top speed: 17.3 knots.
Range: 4000 nautical miles at 15 knots.
Programme: A two-ship class, *Ouragan* (L9021), was ordered in 1960, followed by the contract for *Orage* (L9022) in 1965. *Ouragan* was laid down in June 1962, launched in November 1963 and accepted in June 1965. The keel laying of *Orage* took place in June 1966, with launch in April 1967 and acceptance in March 1968.
Notes: Designed primarily as a Landing Ship, Dock (LSD) with a floodable well deck astern, the ships can also be employed in the logistics support role. In the assault mission, the ships would typically carry around 350 troops, up to four Super Frelon or 13 Alouette helicopters, two EDIC 670 ton landing craft or 40 amphibious vehicles. In the logistics role, the ships can transport up to

Ouragan (L9021), 1966.

USS Newport *(LST1179) tank landing ship.*

1500 tons of equipment which could compromise 18 Super Frelon helicopters and all their supporting equipment, or 120 light tanks, or 340 jeeps, space being created by the use of two temporary deck sections, one measuring 295.25ft (90m), while the other is 118.1ft (36m) in length.

Newport Class Assault Ships

Role: Amphibious warfare.
Builders: Various, USA.
User: US Navy.
Basic data: 8342 tons full displacement; 562ft (171.3m) overall length; 69.5ft (21.2m) maximum beam.
Crew: 221.
Propulsion: 6 Alco diesels (total 16,500bhp); 2 controllable-pitch propellers.
Sensors: 1 SPS-10 sea search and navigational radar.
Armament: 2 twin 5in Mk 32 anti-aircraft guns to be replaced by 2 Phalanx 20mm close-in weapons systems as available.
Top speed: 20 knots.
Endurance: Over 6000 nautical miles.
Programme: The 20-ship 'Newport' class comprises: USS *Newport* (LST1179), USS *Manitowoc* (LST1180), USS *Sumter* (LST1181), USS *Fresno* (LST1182), USS *Peoria* (LST1183), USS *Frederick* (LST1184), USS *Schenectady* (LST1185), USS *Cayuga* (LST1186), USS *Tuscaloosa* (LST1187), USS *Saginaw* (LST1188), USS *San Bernardino* (LST1189), USS *Boulder* (LST1190), USS *Racine* (LST1191), USS *Spartanburg County* (LST1192), USS *Fairfax County* (LST1193), USS *La Moure County* (LST1194), USS *Barbour County* (LST1195), USS *Harlan County* (LST1196), USS *Barnstable County* (LST1197), USS *Bristol County* (LST1198). All ships were commissioned between June 1969 and August 1972.
Notes: The 'Newport' class stern-gated tank landing ships are the largest vessels capable of being beached. They can carry 300 Marines, plus 1800 metric tons of equipment.

LST1171/De Soto County Class Assault Ships

Role: Amphibious warfare.
Builders: Various, USA; AFNE, Argentina.
Users: Navies of Argentina (1), Brazil (1), Italy (2), Mexico (1) and US Navy Reserve (2).
Basic data: 8000 tons full displacement; 442.0ft (134.7m) overall length; 62.0ft (18.9m) maximum beam.
Crew: Up to 175.
Propulsion: 6 Fairbank-Morse diesels (total 13,700bhp); 2 controllable-pitch propellers. *Note:* Brazilian ship has 4 Nordberg diesels in place of the 6 US diesels fitted to all other ships.

The Brazilian ship Duque de Caxais *(G26) with two bridging pontoons slung from the ship's portside flank.*

Sensors: 1 of various types of air search radar; 1 of various types of sea search and navigational radar; 2 or 3 Mk 51 gun fire control radars.
Armament: 3 quadruple 40mm or 1 twin Mk 33 (Brazilian ship only) anti-aircraft guns; helipad (on Greek and Mexican ships).
Top speed: 16 knots.
Range: 6000 nautical miles at 12 knots.
Programme: This originally seven-ship, late 1950s-built US Navy class has been supplemented by the Argentinian-built vessel that entered service in November 1978. Known ships of this class in service at mid-1983 comprise: Argentina's *Cabo San Antonio* (Q42), Brazil's *Duque de Caxias* (G26), transferred in January 1973; Italy's *Grado* (L9890) and *Caorle* (L9891), both transferred in July 1972; Mexico's ex-USS *Lorain County* (LST1177), transferred in 1982 and the US Navy Reserve's *Suffolk County* (LST1173) and *Wood County* (LST1178), both of which had been scheduled for transfer to Greece in the 1982/83 period.
Notes: These tank landing ships can carry up to 700 troops, plus 23 medium-sized tanks and up to four medium landing craft or large bridging pontoons; the latter being used to facilitate vehicular transit from the ship's bow ramp to the beach.

San Giorgio Type Assault ship

Role: Amphibious warfare or roll-on/roll-off transport.
Builder: CNR Riva Trigoso, Italy.
Basic Data: 7665 tons full displacement; 437.3ft (133.3m) overall length; 67.3ft (20.5m) maximum beam.
Crew: 163.
Propulsion: 2 GMT A 420.12 diesels (total 10,390bhp).
Sensors: 1 Selenia RAN 105 air search radar; 1 sea search and navigational radar; 1 Elsag NA21 fire control system (76mm gun); 1 Elmer communications system.

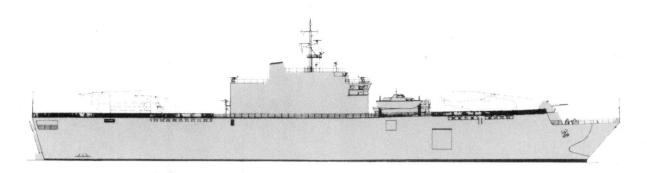

A side and plan view of this new Italian dock landing ship.

Armament: Facilities to operate 2 medium-sized helicopters simultaneously; 1 single 76mm OTO-Melara compact dual-purpose gun; 2 single 20mm Oerlikon anti-aircraft guns.

Top speed: 21 knots.

Range: 7500 nautical miles at 16 knots.

Programme: Ordered in November 1983, *San Giorgio* (L9892) was laid down in late September 1984.

Notes: The *San Giorgio* represents an interesting design exercise in producing a miniaturised version of the US Navy's 'Tarawa' class well-decked landing ship. Equipped with a floodable stern dock and near full length helicopter flight deck, the *San Giorgio* can accommodate around 400 troops, plus 36 tracked personnel carriers, three medium landing craft and three light landing craft. Alternatively, by omitting the three medium landing craft, up to 30 Leopard-sized main battle tanks can be carried in place of the tracked personnel carriers. The vessel's main vehicle deck runs the full length and is able to embark/disembark traffic through bow, stern and flank ramps.

Sir Bedivere Class Assault Ships

Role: Amphibious warfare.

Builder: Swan Hunter, UK.

User: Royal Fleet Auxiliary for the Royal Navy.

Basic data: 5674 tons full displacement; 413ft (125.9m) overall length; 58ft (17.7m) maximum beam.

Crew: 69.

Propulsion: 2 Mirrlees diesels (total 9400bhp); 2 propellers.

Sensors: 1 Type 1006 sea search and navigational radar.

Armament: Provisions for 2 single 40mm Bofors anti-aircraft guns.

Top speed: 17 knots.

Range: 8000 nautical miles at 15 knots.

Programme: The six ships in this class consisted of RFA *Sir Bedivere* (L3004), RFA *Sir Galahad* (L3005); RFA *Sir Geraint* (L3027), RFA *Sir Lancelot* (L3029), RFA *Sir Percivale* (L3036) and RFA *Sir Tristram* (L3505). Laid down between March 1962 and April 1966 in four shipyards (subsequently merged into the Swan Hunter group), the ships were launched between June 1963 and October 1967 and all entered service between January 1964 and March 1968. Victims of an Argentinian air strike on 8 June 1982, *Sir Galahad* and *Sir Tristram* were both damaged, the former irreparably.

RFA Sir Percivale (L3036) at speed.

Notes: The 'Sir Bedivere' class of multi-purpose logistic support and landing ship were designed as tank and other heavy vehicle carriers with aft section accommodation for around 340 military personnel. The ships have bow doors and ramp; a stern gate and light landing craft can replace the lifeboats abeam of the funnel, along with a large helicopter pad aft with support facilities. Military beaching lift capacity is quoted as being 340 tons.

Ropuchka Class Assault Ships

Role: Amphibious warfare.

Builder: Gdansk, Poland.

Users: Soviet Navy, South Yemen Navy.

Basic data: 3600 tons full displacement; 371ft (113m) overall length; 47.6ft (14.5m) maximum beam.

Crew: 70.

Propulsion: 4 diesels (total 10,000bhp); 2 propellers.

Sensors: 1 long-range air search radar; 1 IFF; 1 sea search and navigational radar; 1 fire control radar.

Armament: 2 twin 57mm anti-aircraft guns; some ships fitted with 1 quadruple SA-N-5 point air defence missile launcher.

Top speed: 17 knots.

Range: Not known.

Programme: A reported 12-ship class built by the Polish yards at Gdansk between 1975 and 1978.

Notes: Designed to carry a balanced force of around 230 troops, amphibious vehicles and supporting equipment, the 'Ropuchka' class have bow doors, stern gate and a covered vehicle deck forward. Ships of this class are often deployed with Soviet naval units operating in the Mediterranean, West African waters and the Indian Ocean region, where one was transferred to the South Yemen Navy during 1980. Although much smaller than the US Navy's 'Newport' class tank landing ship, the

'Ropuchka' class carry just over three quarters of the 'Newport' class's troop complement and appear to be better able to defend themselves against air attack, at least until such times as the 'Newports' receive their 2 Phalanx 20mm close-in weapons systems.

Miura Class Assault Ships

Role: Amphibious warfare.
Builder: Ishikawajima Heavy Industries, Japan.
User: Japanese Maritime Self-Defence Force.
Basic data: 3200 tons full displacement; 321.5ft (98.0m) overall length; 45.9ft (14.0m) maximum beam.
Crew: 115.
Propulsion: 2 Kawasaki-MAN V8V 22/30 AMTL diesels (total 4400bhp); 2 propellers.
Sensors: 1 OPS 14 air search radar; 1 OPS 16 combined low-level air/sea search and navigational radar; 1 GFCS 1 gun fire control radar (3in guns); Mk 51 fire control radar (40mm guns).
Armament: 1 twin 3in Mk 33 anti-aircraft gun; 1 twin 40mm anti-aircraft gun.
Top speed: 14 knots.
Endurance: Over 3000 nautical miles.
Programme: This three-ship class comprises: *Miura* (LST4151), *Ojika* (LST4152) and *Satsuma* (LST4153). All laid down between November 1973 and May 1975, the vessels were launched between August 1974 and May 1976, with the three vessels entering service in January 1975, March 1976 and February 1977, respectively.
Notes: The 'Miura' class tank landing ships can carry up to 1800 tons of cargo and have accommodation for 180 troops. Vehicular equipment is embarked and disembarked through the ships' twin-doored bow ramp. The vessels are equipped to carry two medium landing craft on the main deck, forward of the bridge and two light landing craft on davits just aft of the ship's funnel. The two larger landing craft are taken abroad and deployed using the gantry system (seen folded in the accompanying photograph), which, when in use, extends outboard; the actual gantry being able to handle one craft at a time.

Hengam Class Assault Ships

Role: Amphibious warfare.
Builder: Yarrow, UK.
User: Iranian Navy.
Basic data: 2540 tons full displacement; 305.1ft (93.0m) overall length; 48.9ft (14.9m) maximum beam.
Crew: 69.
Propulsion: 4 Paxman Ventura Mk II 12YJCM diesels (total 5600bhp); 2 controllable-pitch propellers.
Sensors: 1 Decca 1229 sea search and navigational radar; 1 URN-20 TACAN aircraft homer; 1 Cossor IFF radar; 1 Kelvin Hughes MS45 echo sounder.
Armament: Helipad (but no hangar) for Sea King helicopter operation; 4 single 40mm Bofors L40/60 anti-aircraft guns.
Top speed: 15 knots.
Range: 4000 nautical miles at 12 knots.
Programme: Initially planned as a six-ship class, only four vessels have been delivered comprising: *Hengam* (LST511), *Larak* (LST512), *Lavan* (LST513) and *Tonb* (LST514). The first two Iranian operated ships were launched in September 1973 and May 1974 and entered service in August 1974 and November 1974, respectively, followed by the latter two in early 1985.
Notes: The 'Hengam' class can carry a normal cargo capacity of 700 tons, including up to 300 tons of military vehicle fuel and up to six of the British heavyweight Chieftain main battle tanks. The ships are equipped with

The Soviet Navy's Polish-built 'Ropuchka' class LST, 1976.

Ojika (LST4152) underway. Note the twin 3in radar-directed anti-aircraft gun mounting on the bow section.

bow doors and ramp, along with a 10 ton load-lifting derrick forward of the bridge to handle the two deck-carried lighters and their containerised cargo when boarded. The ships can accommodate up to 168 troops, plus nine aircrew.

Brooke Marine 93 Metre Class Assault Ships

Role: Amphibious warfare.
Builder: Brooke Marine, UK.
Users: Algeria (2) and Oman (1).
Basic data: 2200 tons full displacement; 305.1ft (93.0m) overall length; 50.85ft (15.5m) maximum beam.
Crew: 81.
Propulsion: 2 MTU diesels (total 8000bhp); 2 propellers.
Sensors: 1 Decca TM 1226 sea search and navigational radar; 1 fire control radar and optronic fire director (customer choice); 1 Kelvin Hughes MS45 echo sounder.
Armament: 2 single 40mm Breda/Bofors L40/70 anti-aircraft guns; facilities to operate 1 Sea King-sized helicopter.
Top speed: 16 knots.
Range: 3000 nautical miles at 14 knots.
Programme: The initial order, for two ships, from Algeria was placed in June 1981, the vessel, *Klaat Benni Hammid* (L472) and *Klaat Benni Rached* (L473), (the construction of the latter ship being sub-contracted to Vosper Thorneycroft), to be delivered in December 1983 and August 1984. Oman ordered a single ship, *Nasr Al Bahr* (L2), in May 1982, reportedly scheduled for delivery before the close of 1984.

The Iranian Navy's Hengam *(LST511) seen wearing its original pennant number during its delivery voyage, 1974.*

The Omani ship *Nasr Al Bahr* (L2).

Notes: Described as a 93 metre Landing Ship, Logistics, this design is capable of transporting 380 tons of cargo right up to the beach. Beyond the normal crew complement, each ship can accommodate up to 240 troops and seven heavyweight main battle tanks plus a number of light and medium sized landing craft. Unlike the earlier Brooke Marine-developed 'Ardennes' class, the new 93 metre design dispenses with bow doors, employing a simple, winch-operated bow ramp. The ship incorporates a large helipad aft, capable of accepting a Sea King and carries the facilities to refuel the helicopter, but has no onboard hangarage.

Al Munassir Type Assault Ship

Role: Amphibious warfare.
Builder: Brooke Marine, UK.
User: Omani Navy.
Basic data: 2169 tons full displacement; 275.6ft (184m) overall length; 49.2ft (15m) maximum beam.
Crew: 47.
Propulsion: 2 Mirrlees Blackstone ES L8MGR diesels (total 2400bhp); 2 controllable-pitch propellers.
Sensors: 1 Decca TM 1229 sea search and navigational radar; 1 Kelvin Hughes MS45 echo sounder; 1 Redifon Omega navigator; 1 Ericsson laser range finder; 1 LSE optical fire director.

SNV Al Munassir *(L1) of the Omani Navy.*

HMAV Ardennes (L4001).

Armament: 1 OTO-Melara 76mm dual-purpose gun; facilities including fuel, for helicopters.
Top speed: 12 knots.
Range: 2000 nautical miles at 12 knots.
Programme: Ordered in 1977, the sole *Al Munassir* (L1) was laid down in July of that year, launched in July 1978 and entered into service during April 1979.
Notes: Equipped with bow doors and ramp for inshore beaching, the *Al Munassir* is a compact ship, with a particularly blunt bow section. The ship can carry up to 550 tons of cargo, or up to eight main battle tanks. There is accommodation for 188 embarked troops and the ship is equipped with an aft, elevated helicopter pad, capable of accepting a Westland Sea King/Commando-sized aircraft.

Ardennes Class Assault Ships

Role: Amphibious warfare.
Builder: Brooke Marine, UK.
User: British Army.
Basic data: 1650 tons full displacement; 235.3ft (71.7m) overall length; 49.3ft (15.0m) maximum beam.
Crew: 35.
Propulsion: 2 Mirrlees Blackstone ESL8MGR diesels (total 2440bhp); 2 propellers.
Sensors: 1 Decca TM1226 sea search and navigational radar; 1 Decca QM14 position fixer; 1 Kelvin Hughes MS45M echo sounder.
Armament: None fitted other than that of embarked troops.
Top speed: 10.2 knots loaded.
Range: 1200 nautical miles at 6 knots.
Programme: This two-ship class comprises: HMAV *Ardennes* (L4001) and HMAV *Arakan* (L4003). Built for

171

operation by the British Army, hence the HMAV or Her Majesty's Army Vessel prefixes, the two ships were delivered in late July 1977 and late February 1978, respectively.

Notes: The 'Ardennes' class can carry up to 350 tons of cargo, including up to five Chieftain main battle tanks. Besides the normal complement, the ships each carry additional accommodation for 34 officers and men.

Ambe Class/Type 502 Assault Ships

The Nigerian Ambe (LST1312) lead of class tank landing ship.

Role: Amphibious warfare.
Builder: Howaldtswerke, Federal Germany.
User: Nigerian Navy.
Basic data: 1625 tons full displacement; 285.5ft (87.0m) overall length; 45.9ft (14.0m) maximum beam.
Crew: 56.
Propulsion: 2 MTU 16V956 TB92 diesels (total 6694bhp); 4 propellers.
Sensors: 1 Decca TM1226 sea search and navigational radar.
Armament: 1 single 40mm Bofors L40/70 and 2 single 20mm Oerlikon anti-aircraft guns.
Top speed: 17 knots.
Range: 3000 nautical miles at 14 knots.
Programme: This two-ship class comprises: NNS *Ambe* (LST1312) and NNS *Ofiom* (LST1313). Ordered in early 1978, the two vessels were laid down in March and September 1978, launched in July and December 1978 and were delivered in May and July 1979.
Notes: Equipped with both bow and stern ramps, these vessels can each accommodate up to 540 troops in relative comfort, or 1080 men for short periods. With a cargo capacity of 400 tons, the Type 502 has space to transport up to five main battle tanks or seven light tanks. The 'Ambe' class has a distinctive, asymmetric, twin chimney-topped funnel that rises from the ship's port flank, positioned thus so as to leave sufficient maindeck space for unrestricted vehicle flow from end to end. Both the hull and much of the ship's superstructure, with the exception of the deckhouse, is built from steel. To add to the ship's firepower during its approach to an enemy-held beach, the port and starboard forward maindeck have reinforced, shock-absorbing stands from which to fire standard military 81mm mortars.

Champlain Class Assault Ships

Role: Amphibious warfare.
Builders: Various, France.
Users: Navies of France (6) and Morocco (3).
Basic data: 1330 tons full displacement; 262.5ft (80.0m)

overall length; 42.65ft (13.0m) maximum beam.
Crew: 39.
Propulsion: 2 SACM V12 diesels (total 1800bhp); 2 controllable-pitch propellers.
Sensors: 1 Decca TM1226 sea search and navigational radar; 1 echo sounder.
Armament: 2 single 40mm anti-aircraft guns; 2 single 81mm mortars; 2 single 12.7mm machine guns. *Note:* an aft helipad is installed.
Top speed: 16 knots.
Range: 4500 nautical miles at 13 knots.
Programme: Nine vessels of this class were known to have been ordered by mid-1983 comprising: *Champlain* (L9030), *Francis Garnier* (L9031), *Dumont D'Urville* (L9032), *Jacques Cartier* (L9033), plus L9034 and L9035 for France, along with *Daoud Ben Aicha* (LST42), *Ahmed Es Sakali* (LST43) and *Abou Abdallah El Ayachi* (LST44) for Morocco. The first two French vessels entered service in October and June 1974, respectively, followed by the second pair during 1983, at which time the fifth and sixth ships were fitting out. The three Moroccan vessels entered service in May 1977, September 1977 and December 1978, respectively. DCAN Brest built the first French pair, while the next two French ships were the responsibility of Constructions de Normandie, with Ateliers Français de l'Ouest constructing the fifth and sixth French vessels. All three Moroccan ships were built by Dubigeon.
Notes: Somewhat lighter and more attractive in appearance, thanks to their clipper bows, than their near contemporaries in the shape of the UK's 'Ardennes' class, the 'Champlain' class carry more cargo at a higher speed than that of the rival British design. The first pair of French, along with the three Moroccan vessels can transport up to 380 tons of cargo, including 133 troops and 12 vehicles, while all later French ships have an increased full displacement of 1400 tons, along with accommodation for up to 180 troops. Unlike the Nigerian-operated 'Ambe' class tank landing ships, the 'Champlain' class have no vehicular drive-through capability, everything having to be embarked and disembarked through the bow ramp.

The French Navy's Francis Garnier (L9031) with bow doors open.

LSM1 Class Assault Ships

Role: Amphibious warfare.
Builders: Various, USA.
Users: Navies of Ecuador (2), Greece (5), South Korea (10), Peru (2), Philippines (4), Taiwan (4), Turkey (5), Venezuela (1) and Vietnam (4).
Basic data: 1095 tons full displacement; 203.5ft (62.0m) overall length; 34.5ft (10.5m) maximum beam.
Crew: 50.
Propulsion: 2 General Motors 16-278A diesels (total

2800bhp); 2 propellers. *Note:* some ships have Fairbank-Morse diesels.

Sensors: 1 sea search and navigational radar (not fitted to all ships); 1 echo sounder.
Armament: 2 twin and 4 single 40mm anti-aircraft guns.
Top speed: 12.5 knots.
Range: 2500 nautical miles at 12 knots.
Programme: Originally a 494-ship class (excluding the 60 basic LSM1s converted to rocket-launching assault ships during construction), the class was built by four commercial and two navy shipyards and were delivered to the US Navy between 1944 and 1945. The 33 vessels known to remain in service at the end of 1984 comprise: Ecuador's *T51* and *T52*; Greece's *L161* through *L165*; South Korea's *LSM651* through *LSM662* (except 654 and 660); Peru's *LSM36* and *LSM37*; Philippine's *LP41*, *LP65*, *LP66* and *LP68*; Taiwan's *LSM637*, *LSM649*, *LSM659* and *LSM694*; Turkey's *N101* through *N105* (converted to minelayers); Venezuela's *Los Frailes* and Vietnam's four unidentified vessels that had passed through French and South Vietnamese hands.
Notes: Fitted with bow doors and ramp, the LSM1 class medium landing ship was a development of the smaller LCI(L)1 large infantry landing craft design. The LSM1 class has its bridge above a tall cylindrical structure, the whole of which is offset to starboard.

The Hellenic Navy's Ipopliarchos Grigorophoulos *(L161).*

Minelayers

Carlskrona Type Minelayers

Role: Minelaying/training.
Builder: Karlskronavarvet, Sweden.
User: Royal Swedish Navy.
Basic data: 3300 tons full displacement; 346.8ft (105.7m) overall length; 49.85ft (15.2m) maximum beam.
Crew: 118.
Propulsion: 4 Nohab Polar F212 D825 diesels (total 10,560bhp); 2 controllable-pitch propellers.
Sensors: The ship is equipped with a full Philips (Sweden) 9LV400 automated command and fire control system comprising: 1 long-range air search radar (Ericson Sea Giraffe); 1 combined low-level air/sea search radar; 2 Decca TM1226 sea search and navigational radars; 2 combined fire control radars and optronic fire directors; 1 SIMRAD SQ3D/SF hull-mounted sonar.
Armament: Helipad, but no hangar; 2 single 57mm Bofors SAK 57 Mk 1 dual-purpose guns; 2 single 40mm Bofors L70/40 anti-aircraft guns; 2 mine rails for up to 105 moored mines (more in the case of the lighter, new generation Bofors ground mines).
Top speed: 20 knots.
Endurance: Over 6000 nautical miles.
Programme: Ordered in November 1977, the *Carlskrona* (M04) was laid down in 1979, launched in May 1980 and entered service in January 1982.
Notes: Designed primarily to meet the peacetime role of training ship and the wartime role of minelayer, the *Carlskrona*, as with many latterday second line warships,

The Royal Swedish Navy's newest and largest ship, Carlskrona *(M04).*

has been built to merchant ship construction standard, rather than to those of the more stringent and, hence, expensive front line warship. Above and beyond the normal ship's complement, *Carlskrona* can accommodate 68 cadets.

Soya Type Minelayers

Role: Coastal minelayer.
Builder: Hitachi, Japan.
User: Japanese Maritime Self-Defence Force.

A frontal aspect of Soya *(N951) showing her aft helipad and outboard, starboard side mine-dispensing rail.*

Basic data: 3250 tons full displacement; 324.8ft (99.0m) overall length; 40.2ft (15.0m) maximum beam.
Crew: 185.
Propulsion: 4 Kawasaki-MAN V6V22/30 ATL diesels (total 6400bhp); 2 propellers.
Sensors: 1 OPS 14 long-range air search radar; 1 OPS 16 combined low-level air/sea search and navigational radar; 1 GFCS 1 gun control radar; 1 SQS-11A hull-mounted sonar.
Armament: Helipad to operate up to 1 Sea King sized helicopter, but no hangar; 1 twin 3in Mk 33 anti-aircraft gun; 2 single 20mm anti-aircraft guns 2 triple lightweight anti-submarine torpedo tubes; over 200 mines.
Top speed: 18 knots.
Range: Over 4000 nautical miles at 14 knots.
Programme: Ordered in 1970, the sole *Soya* (N951) was laid down in July 1970, launched in March 1971 and entered service at the end of September 1971.
Notes: A large ship by minelayer standards, the *Soya* has a spacious helipad aft, enabling it to operate a minesweeping helicopter, such as the Kawasaki-built Boeing Vertol KV-107 or Sea King. The ship's warload of mines is dispensed via four sets of dispensing rails, two of which straddle the flanks of the helipad.

Alvsborg Class Minelayers

Role: Minelaying.
Builder: Karlskronavarvet, Sweden.
User: Royal Swedish Navy.
Basic data: 2660 tons full displacement; 303.15ft (92.4m) overall length; 48.2ft (14.7m) maximum beam.
Crew: 97.
Propulsion: 2 Nohab-Polar 12-cylinder diesels (total 4200bhp); 1 controllable-pitch propeller.
Sensors: 1 surface search radar; 1 sea search and navigational radar.
Armament: 3 single Bofors 40mm anti-aircraft guns; 300 mines.

The Royal Swedish Navy's Alvsborg *(M02.)*

Top speed: 16 knots.
Range: Not known.
Programme: This two-ship class comprises *Alvsborg* (M02) and *Viborg* (M03). Laid down in November 1968 and October 1973, the ships entered service in April 1971 and February 1976, respectively.
Notes: These purpose-built minelayers (the Royal Swedish Navy also operates a converted merchantman as a minelayer) would, in times of crisis, be used to seed the waters of the Gulf of Bothnia and Western Baltic, thus denying access to enemy naval forces. In peacetime, the two 'Alvsborg' class ships double as submarine tender (M02) and Flag Ship. Coastal Fleet (M03). A larger, more powerful vessel, the *Carlskrona* (M04) has recently joined the Swedish fleet, where it doubles as the service's training ship. Both 'Alvsborgs' and the later *Carlskrona* have a helicopter landing deck immediately aft of the main superstructure.

Vidar Class Minelayers

Role: Minelayer.
Builder: Mjellem & Karlson, Norway.
User: Royal Norwegian Navy.
Basic data: 1722 tons full displacement; 212.6ft (64.8m) overall length; 39.4ft (12.0m) maximum beam.

The Royal Navy's HMS Abdiel *(N21) doubles as a minelayer and minehunter support tender.*

Crew: 50.
Propulsion: 2 Wichmann 7AX diesels (total 4200bhp); 2 propellers; 1 bow thruster.
Sensors: 2 Decca TM 1226 sea search and navigational radars; 1 Simrad SQ3D hull-mounted sonar.
Armament: Up to 320 mines; 2 single 40mm Bofors anti-aircraft guns; 2 triple lightweight anti-submarine torpedo tubes; 2 depth charge racks.
Top speed: 15 knots.
Range: Over 2400 nautical miles at 12 knots.
Programme: A two-ship class comprising *Vidar* (N52) and *Vale* (N53). Laid down in March 1976 and February

KNM Vale *(N53) which, with its sister ship, can also act as an anti-submarine escort or fishery protection vessel when not employed in its primary role.*

1976, respectively, *Vidar* was launched in March 1977, with *Vale* following in August 1977. The two ships entered service in October 1977 and February 1978, respectively.
Notes: As befits a navy saddled with the task of guarding numerous narrow water inlets, the Royal Norwegian Navy's 'Vidar' class ships are relatively large by European minelayer standards and can seed an impressively thick minefield when required, thanks to their modern automated transfer systems between the ships', three deck mine magazines and the three per ship mine jettisoning rails. When not needed for minelaying duties, the 'Vidar' class vessels can serve as transports, fishery patrol vessels, or anti-submarine convoy escorts. For the latter role, each ship carries two triple torpedo tubes immediately aft of the side-by-side ship's funnels, plus depth charge racks dispensing over the stern.

Abdiel Type Minelayer

Role: Minelayer/tender.
Builder: JI Thornycroft, UK.
User: Royal Navy.
Basic data: 1400 tons full displacement; 265.0ft (80.8m) overall length; 38.5ft (11.7m) maximum beam.
Crew: 96.
Propulsion: 2 Paxman Ventura 16-YSCM diesels (total 2690bhp); 2 propellers.
Sensors: 1 Type 978 sea search and navigational radar; 1 Decca Hi-Fix precision position fixer; 1 Kelvin Hughes MS45 echo sounder.
Armament: 1 single 40mm Mk 9 Bofors L40/60 anti-aircraft gun; up to 44 mines.
Top speed: 16 knots.
Range: 3200 nautical miles at 12 knots.
Programme: HMS *Abdiel* (N21), the Royal Navy's sole minelayer, started life as the second of a projected pair of mercantile car ferries planned to operate out of Malta. However, as the car ferry operator was compelled to cancel the contract for the second vessel, the Royal Navy stepped in, acquired the ship and had her modified to her present role. Laid down in May 1966 and launched in January 1967, HMS *Abdiel* entered service with the Royal Navy in October 1967.
Notes: Although employing none of the automated mine

Finland's single type Pohjanmaa *(N01), although a relatively compact ship, has the distinction of being the world's most powerfully armed minelayer, thanks to its 120mm Bofors gun.*

magazine-to-rail and dispensing systems to be found aboard the modern Scandinavian minelayers, HMS *Abdiel* still provides a useful platform both from which to train sailors in minelaying, as well as supplying vital experience for the crews of mine countermeasures ships. Of equal importance operationally is, *Abdiel*'s extensive capability to act as mother ship to a mine countermeasures squadron of, say, four ships, as she did during the Suez Canal clearance of 1974.

Pohjanmaa Type Minelayer

Role: Minelayer/training ship.
Builder: Wartsila, Finland.
User: Finnish Defence Force.
Basic data: 1350 tons full displacement; 256.6ft (78.2m) overall length; 38.0ft (11.6m) maximum beam.
Crew: 80.
Propulsion: 2 Wartsila-Vasa 16V22 diesels (total 5800bhp); 2 controllable-pitch propellers.
Sensors: 1 air search radar; 1 sea search and navigational radar; 1 Philips (Sweden) 9LV100 fire control radar and automated action information processing system; 1 Philips (Sweden) optronic fire director; 2 hull-mounted sonars.
Armament: 1 single 120mm Bofors TAK-120 dual-purpose gun; 2 single 40mm Bofors anti-aircraft guns; 4 twin; 23mm anti-aircraft guns; 2 five-barrelled 250mm RBU-1200 anti-submarine rocket launchers.
Top speed: 20 knots.
Range: 3000 nautical miles at 17 knots.
Programme: The single type *Pohjanmaa* (N01) was laid down in May 1978, launched in late August 1978 and entered service less than a year later in early 1979.
Notes: Constructed in a very short time at Wartsila's Helsinki yards, the *Pohjanmaa*'s design much more closely resembles that of a front line corvette than that of a typical minelayer. Powerfully sensored and armed for a ship of its size, *Pohjanmaa*, while not equipped with a helicopter hangar, has a helipad aft. Besides the normal complement, the ship can accommodate an additional 70 trainees housed in two readily portable container units mounted on the helipad, enabling the ship to quickly convert to or from its primary operational role. To facilitate precise positioning, the vessel is equipped with a bow thruster. The vessel can accommodate an additional 70 persons when operating in the training role.

Ex-LSM 1 Class Minelayer

Role: Minelaying.
Builders: Various, USA.
Users: Navies of Greece (2), South Korea (1) and Turkey (5).
Basic data: 1100 tons full displacement; 203.5ft (62.0m) overall length; 34.5ft (10.5m) maximum beam.
Crew: 65.
Propulsion: 2 General Motor 16-278A diesels (total 2800bhp); 2 propellers.
Sensors: Believed confined to communications equipment, although echo sounding equipment may be installed.
Armament: Up to 300 mines; 4 twin 40mm anti-aircraft guns; 6 single 20mm anti-aircraft guns.
Top speed: 12.5 knots.
Range: 3500 nautical miles at 12 knots.
Programme: Two of these former Landing Ship, Medium (LSM) are operated by the Hellenic Navy, *Aktion* (N04) and *Amvrakia* (N05). Constructed in 1943, the Greek vessels, along with others of the LSM 1 class, were converted to minelayers during 1952 under the US Military Aid Programme, prior to being handed over to various navies, but most are now out of service with the exception of South Korea's *Pung To* and Turkey's *Mordogan* (N101), *Meric* (N102), *Marmaris* (N103), *Mersin* (N104) and *Murefte* (N105).
Notes: These vessels are capable of carrying between 100

Amvrakia (N05), formerly LSM 303.

and 300 mines, depending upon type. The mines are winched aboard by the four derricks mounted in pairs fore and aft of the central wheelhouse. In operations, the mines are dispensed from the twin stern doors visible in the photograph. Interestingly, the current defensive armament fitted to these ships is greater than fitted to the original World War II LSMs.

Type 343 Class Minelayers

Role: Fast minelaying, minesweeping and minehunting.
Builders: Various, Federal Germany.
User: Federal German Navy.
Basic data: 570 tons full displacement; 180.4ft (55.0m) overall length; 29.9ft (9.1m) maximum beam.
Crew: 37.
Propulsion: 2 MTU 16V-538-TB91 diesels (total 6140bhp); 2 propellers.
Sensors: 1 low-level air and sea search/fire control radar; 1 sea search and navigational radar; IFF; 1 DSQS-11 hull-mounted sonar; 2 Penguin mine neutralization vehicles (when operating as minehunter).
Armament: 2 single 40mm Breda/Bofors L70/40 anti-aircraft guns; 60 mines.
Top speed: 24.5 knots.
Range: 1800 nautical miles at 22 knots.
Programme: Design studies on this planned ten-ship class were initiated in the early 1980s. As is becoming popular practice with the Federal German Navy, the programme is to be managed by a non-shipbuilding prime contractor, in this case Messerschmitt-Bolkow-Blohm (MBB), who will have responsibility for the ships' system integration. Along with this work, MBB, who will also supervise the vessels' construction, itself spread around the three Federal German constructors with minesweeper experience, Abeking und Rasmussen, Krogerwerft and Lurssen. The lead of class should be ordered in late 1985.
Notes: Required as replacements for the currently operated Type 340 and 341 'Schutz' class vessels, the projected Type 343 will employ special Federal German-developed non-magnetic steel as the primary hull material. The class will be subdivided into three groups depending upon their specialized equipment fit: the Type 343A having mechanical minesweeping gear; the Type 343B with diver and mine neutralization submersible and the Type 343C with equipment needed to operate unmanned Troika system slave craft. All Type 343s will be able to serve as minelayers.

Furusund Class Minelayers

Sweden's first of six 'Furusund' class.

An artist's impression of the multi-purpose Type 343 fast minelayer/minehunter.

Role: Coastal minelaying.
Builder: Asiverken of Amal, Sweden.
User: Royal Swedish Navy.
Basic data: 225 tons full displacement; 107.0ft (32.6m) overall length; 27.6ft (8.4m) maximum beam.
Crew: 24.
Propulsion: 2 Scania DSI 14 diesel-electric alternators (total 416bhp/310kW); 2 propellers. plus 1 electro-hydraulic bow thruster. (125bhp/93kW).
Sensors: 1 Racal Decca RM1226 sea search and navigational radar; 1 Racal Decca Navigator; 1 Simrad Skipper 607 echo sounder; 1 Racal Decca 450G autopilot and SAL24 log.
Armament: 1 single 20mm anti-aircraft gun; up to 22 tons of mines.
Top speed: 11 knots.
Range: 1200 nautical miles at 8 knots.
Programme: Constructed as the prototype of an ultimate six-vessel class, the *Furusund* (N20) was ordered in June 1981, launched mid-December 1982 and entered service in September 1983.
Notes: Built around an all-welded steel hull, the compact *Furusund* has been designed not only to lay mines, but also to retrieve them, along with their associated shore-to-sea control cables. To seed a minefield, the vessel is equipped with two stern-launching mine rails, while mine and cable retrieval is effected with the aid of the two foredeck-mounted, flank hydraulic hoists and the two HIAB 180 hydraulic cranes, positioned on the foredeck and afterdeck, respectively. The vessel carries a third Scania DN8 diesel-electric alternator, providing up to 73kW of power for other shipboard services. Interestingly, the designers have opted to exhaust the diesel efflux from the stern, eliminating the need for a view-obstructing funnel.

Minehunters

An artist's impression of USS Avenger *(MCM 1). The object being put over the starboard side is a deep-diving unmanned mine neutralisation vehicle (MNV), crucial to the task of countering the modern deep sea mine.*

Avenger Class Minehunters

Role: Oceangoing minehunter.
Builders: Peterson Builders and Marinetta Marine, USA.
User: US Navy.
Basic data: 1200 tons full displacement; 224.0ft (68.3m) overall length; 39.0ft (11.9m) maximum beam.
Crew: 81.
Propulsion: 2 Waukesha L-1616 diesels (total 2400bhp); 2 controllable-pitch propellers.
Sensors: 1 SPS-55 sea search and navigational radar; 1 SSN-2 precision position fixing system; 1 SQQ-30 hull-mounted sonar (to be replaced by SQQ-32).
Armament: 2 single 12.7mm machine guns.
Top speed: 14 knots.
Endurance: In excess of 4000 nautical miles.
Programme: In June 1982, the US Navy placed an initial $64 million contract with Peterson Builders to proceed with the construction of USS *Avenger* (MCM 1), the lead ship of a planned 14-ship class. Delivery of *Avenger* is scheduled for the late autumn of 1985, with the delivery programme building up rapidly thereafter to an annual four ships per year. The second of class, USS *Defender* (MCM2), is to be built by Marinetta Marine. Other known ships comprise: USS *Sentry* (MCM3) and USS *Champion* (MCM4).
Notes: Of conventional wooden-hulled construction, the MCM 1 design is the first new minehunting vessel to be developed for the US Navy in almost 30 years: an aspect that highlights the relative neglect into which US mine counter-measures operations had fallen. Somewhat larger and much heavier than either the Royal Navy's 'Hunt' class or the French-developed 'Eridan' class vessels, the 'Avenger' class requirement reflects the US Navy's revitalised concern for countering Soviet Bloc mine developments not just in the short term, but well on into

the early half of the next century. There has already been some European criticism concerning the design's somewhat conservative approach, but such criticism appears to overlook the fundamental point that, in a modern context, it is the ship's sensors and mine neutralisation vehicle that form the crucial elements and that the parent vessel is little more than a mobile platform from which to deploy them. This is particularly true in instances where the minehunter is called upon to deal with the highly complex, deep-sown mine or hybrid mine/torpedo combination employed against the current generation of deep-diving nuclear-powered submarines.

Waveney Class Minehunters

Role: Ocean minesweeping.
Builders: Richards Shipbuilders, UK.
User: Royal Navy Reserve.
Basic data: 900 tons full displacement; 154.2ft (47.0m) overall length; 34.4ft (10.5m) maximum beam.
Crew: 30.
Propulsion: 2 Ruston RKC diesels (total 3040bhp); 2 controllable-pitch propellers.
Sensors: 2 Racal-Decca Type 1226 sea search and navigational radars; 2 Kelvin Hughes MS28 echo sounders.
Armament: 1 single 40mm Bofors L40/60 anti-aircraft gun.
Top speed: 15.5 knots.
Range: Over 2000 nautical miles.
Programme: A 12-ship class, ordered on an incremental basis, from Richards Shipbuilders of Lowestoft. The lead of class, HMS *Waveney* (M2003), was ordered in September 1982, laid down in January 1983, launched in September 1983, followed by delivery in the spring of 1984. The rest of the class comprises HMS *Carron* (M2004), HMS *Dovey* (M2005), HMS *Helford* (M2006), HMS *Humber* (M2007), HMS *Blackwater* (M2008), HMS *Itchin* (M2009), HMS *Helmsdale* (M2010), HMS *Orwell* (M2011), HMS *Ribble* (M2012), HMS *Spey* (M2013), and HMS *Arun* (M2014). The first four were in service by the end of April 1985, the remaining for delivery by 1987.
Notes: The 'Waveney' class design is based on that of a commercial North Sea supply boat, thus, eliminating many of the problems associated with initiating a completely new development. Built to mercantile Lloyds Register standards, but with additional below-waterline compartments to minimise the effects of nearby detonations. The 'Waveney' class will operate in pairs, trailing a new, broader clearance lane and deeper-going minesweeping trawl, known as the WS Mk 9 system, devised jointly by UK's Admiralty Underwater Weapons Establishment and BAJ Vickers. Interestingly, because of the far less stringent operational requirements surrounding the design and construction of this class of ship compared with the 'Hunt' class, the fully equipped unit cost of the first four-ship batch was around £4.75 million in late 1982 values.

Natya Class Minehunters

Role: Ocean minesweeping.
Builder: Unknown, USSR.
Users: Soviet and Indian Navies.
Basic data: 750 tons full displacement; 200.1ft (61m) overall length; 31.5ft (9.6m) maximum beam.

Crew: 50.
Propulsion: 2 diesels (total 8000bhp); 2 propellers.
Sensors: 1 sea search and navigational radar; 3 IFF; 1 fire control radar.
Armament: 2 twin 30mm and 2 twin 25mm anti-aircraft guns; 2 five-barrel 250mm anti-submarine rocket launchers.
Top speed: 20 knots.
Endurance: In excess of 4000 nautical miles.
Programme: a reported 30-ship class for the Soviet Navy, built from 1970 through 1977, with an additional six ships built for the Indian Navy, delivered to that service at a rate of two per year between 1978 and 1980. These Indian Navy vessels carry the pennant numbers *M16* through *M66*.
Notes: Designed to operate as oceangoing minesweepers, the 'Natya' class can double as light anti-submarine escorts thanks to their exceptionally heavy armament for a minesweeper (raising questions over these ships' magnetic signature). Interestingly, even the quantitatively larger, if physically smaller, classes of Soviet minesweepers carry a much heavier anti-air armament than their Western counterparts. Here it should also be noted that the Soviet Navy has by far the largest minesweeper fleet numbering about 400.

Aggressive Class Minehunters

Role: Ocean minesweeping.
Builders: Various, USA.
Users: Navies of the USA and Spain.
Basic data: 750 tons full displacement; 172ft (52.4m) overall length; 35ft (10.7m) maximum beam.
Crew: 72.
Propulsion: 4 Packard or Waukesha diesels (total 2280bhp); 2 controllable-pitch propellers (4 US vessels, MSO428 to 431, have 4 General Motors diesels giving a total of 1520bhp).
Sensors: 1 SPS-5C or SPS-53E/L sea search and navigational radar; 1 UQS-1 or SQQ-14 sonar. (Spanish ships have Decca TM625 sea search and navigational radar.)
Armament: 1 single 20mm Mk 68 and 2 single 12.7mm anti-aircraft guns (some US Naval Reserve ships have 1 single 40mm Mk 3 gun).
Top speed: 15.5 knots.
Range: 3300 nautical miles at 10 knots.
Programme: Of an original 58-ship class built for the US Navy between 1951 and 1956, only 23 remained on US Navy inventory at the end of 1980. Of these US vessels, only three remain in active service (all with the Atlantic Fleet), the rest being employed by the US Naval Reserve. Spain operates a further four ships of this class. The seven ships in active operations comprise USS *Fidelity* (MSO443), USS *Illusive* (MSO448), USS *Leader* (MSO490), along with Spains' *Guadelete* (M41), *Guadalmedina* (M42), *Guadalquivir* (M43) and *Guardiana* (M44).
Notes: Of conventional wooden-hulled construction, these elderly ships are to be replaced in US Navy service by the 'Avenger' class vessels.

Hunt Class Minehunters

Role: Mine disposal.
Builders: Vosper Thornycroft & Yarrow, UK.
User: Royal Navy.
Basic data: 675 tons full displacement; 197ft (60m) overall length; 32.8ft (10m) maximum beam.
Crew: 45.
Propulsion: 2 Paxman Deltic 59K diesels (total 3540bhp) used for main propulsion; 2 propellers, plus a third Deltic

HMS Dovey (M2005), third of this 12-vessel class.

A Soviet Navy oceangoing 'Natya' class minesweeper.

Spain's oceangoing minesweeper Guadelete (M41).

HMS Ledbury (M30), the 2nd of the 'Hunt' class vessels.

diesel for low-speed operations and close manoeuvring involving a bow water jet thruster.

Sensors: 1 Type 1006 sea search and navigational radar; 1 Type 193M hull-mounted sonar.
Armament: 1 single 40mm Mk 9 Bofors anti-aircraft gun.
Top speed: 15 knots.
Range: Over 3500 nautical miles.
Programme: 13 'Hunt' class vessels had been ordered on an incremental basis by June 1985, comprising HMS *Brecon* (M29), HMS *Ledbury* (M30), HMS *Cattistock* (M31), HMS *Cottesmore* (M32), HMS *Brocklesby* (M33), HMS *Middleton* (M34), HMS *Dulverton* (M35), HMS *Chiddingfold* (M37), HMS *Hurworth* (M39), HMS *Bicester* (M36) and HMS *Atherstone* (M38). Vosper Thornycroft, as lead yard, have or are building the first, second third and sixth through 13th vessels, while Yarrow are responsible for the construction of the fourth and fifth ships. The lead ship, HMS *Brecon*, was ordered in May 1975, laid down in September 1975, launched in June 1978 and commissioned in December 1979. Seven further vessels have been commissioned by the beginning of May 1985 and the remainder should all have been commissioned by early 1987. It should be noted that the time taken to build these ships has been progressively reduced; HMS *Brecon* took 50 months, while HMS *Dulverton* was accepted in October 1983, or only 28 months from start.

Notes: While unquestionably expensive ships (a unit cost of £30 million being quoted for a fully equipped 'Hunt' class vessel in the 1981 UK Defence Estimates), the complexity of these ships and their equipment reflect the ever more arduous requirements associated with detecting and neutralising the many variety of modern mines. As with all minesweepers/hunters built since the introduction of the magnetically triggered mine, the 'Hunt' class vessels are designed to minimise magnetic influence. Unlike earlier generation wooden-hulled minesweepers/minehunters, the 'Hunt' class employ a hull built from glass-reinforced plastic, transverse frames being secured where necesary by titanium bolts to guarantee structural integrity. Many modern mines employ more than one method by which to trigger their detonation. They can be triggered by contact, magnetic influence, noise (of a ship's propellers) or pressure (of a ship's passage near the mine). So elaborate systems are needed by the 'Hunt' class minehunters, including noise reduction techniques and shallow draft, specifically contoured hull design to minimise pressure wave propagation. Unlike earlier minesweepers/hunters, the 'Hunt' class have been designed to operated singly rather than requiring several ships to work together. Thus each 'Hunt' class carries two PAP 104 wire-guided remotely controlled submersibles, along with a decompression chamber for use by human divers.

Lerici Class Minehunters

Role: Mine disposal.
Builder: Intermarine, Italy.
Users: Navies of Italy, Malaysia and Nigeria.
Basic data: 550 tons full displacement; 164.0ft (50.0m) overall length; 31.4ft (9.6m) maximum beam.
Crew: 39.
Propulsion: 1 GMT B-230-8M diesel (1840bhp) on Italian and Nigerian ships, or 2 MTU 12V652 TB81 diesels (total 2000bhp) on Malaysian ships. These drive one controllable-pitch propeller on Italian and Nigerian ships, or two propellers on Malaysian ships. For low speed minehunting operations, the Italian and Nigerian ships employ three hydraulically-driven auxiliary propulsors, while the Malaysian ships employ two such auxiliary propulsors.
Sensors: 1 SMA sea search and navigational radar; 1 SMA MM/SSM-714 precision fixing and plotting system; 1 FIAR AN/SQQ-14 variable depth sonar. For close-in mine location and neutralisation, Italian vessels are equipped with 2 MIN remotely-operated mini-submersible, while the Malaysian ships each carry 2 PAP-104 vehicles; the Nigerian ship carrying 2 Gay Marine Pluto submersibles.
Armament: 1 single 20mm (Italian and Nigerian) or 1 single 40mm Bofors anti-aircraft gun on Malaysian ships.
Top speed: 15 knots.
Range: 2500 nautical miles at 12 knots.
Programme: The initial Italian Navy order for four ships of a ten-ship class was placed in January 1978. Malaysia was the first export customer, placing an order for four vessels in February 1981, with an order for one ship being placed by Nigeria in early 1983. The first four Italian minehunters comprise: *Lerici* (M5550), *Sapri* (M5551), *Milazzo* (M5552) and *Vieste* (M5553), while the others are *Termoli* (M5554), *Alghero* (M5555), *Numana* (M5556), *Crotone* (M5557), *Viareggio* (M5558) and ----- (M5559). The Malaysian ships are *Mahamiru*, *Jerai*, *Ledang* and *Kinabalu*. Deliveries of the four Italian vessels should be completed in 1985, those for Malaysia by 1986, along with the single vessel for Nigeria. Late 1983 reports indicate that the Indonesian Navy intends to purchase up to eight additional stretched examples of this basic class.
Notes: Employing the same glass-reinforced plastic material as used in the construction of the 'Hunt' and 'Eridan' class minehunters, the 'Lerici' class carries the facilities to deploy either remotely controlled mine neutralisation vehicles or human divers during operation as a solo minehunter, or use minesweeping gear when operating in pairs. The protracted delay apparent in the originally scheduled delivery of early 'Lerici' class ships was, at least, in part caused by the existence of a low bridge to seaward of the yards, now opened, that had previously left the ships landlocked.

Lerici (M5550), lead of class, seen during fitting out and still to have her forward-mounted gun installed.

Eridan (Tripartite) Class Minehunters

Role: Mine disposal.
Builders: Various French, Belgian and Dutch.
Users: Navies of France, Netherlands and Belgium.
Basic data: 544 tons full displacement; 169.3ft (51.6m) overall length; 29.4ft (8.96m) maximum beam.
Crew: 55 in French, 34 in others.
Propulsion: 1 Brons-Werkspoor A-RUB 215 × 12 diesel (1900bhp); 1 controllable-pitch propeller, plus 2 electrically driven, rudder-mounted manoeuvring propellers and 1 bow thruster.
Sensors: 1 Racal-Decca 1229 sea search and navigational radar; 1 DUBM 21 hull-mounted sonar; 2 PAP-104 remotely-controlled mine locator submersibles; precision position fixing system.
Armament: 1 single 20mm anti-aircraft gun.
Top speed: 15 knots.
Range: 3000 nautical miles at 12 knots.
Programme: Following discussions between governmental and naval staffs of France, The Netherlands and Belgium initiated in April 1974, it was agreed that the programme would proceed on a work-sharing basis, with France taking overall technical leadership. The programme emerged as a 40 ship requirement for the three nations, comprising 15 each for France and The Netherlands, plus ten for Belgium. The lead ship, *Eridan* (M641) was ordered in 1976, followed by incremental orders for a further nine French ships by June 1983. *Eridan* had been completed by November 1981, with *Cassiopee* (M642), *Andromede* (M643) and *Pegase* (M644) being completed during 1984, with *Orion* (M645) and *Croix du Sud* (M646) in build. In all, five French vessels should be in service by the end of 1985, with the sixth through tenth ship accepted between 1986 and 1988. *Alkmaar* (M850), the lead of the Dutch class was ordered in 1977 and completed in February 1983, at which time, *Delfzijl* (M851) and *Dordrecht* (M852) had been launched, while *Haarlem* (M853), *Harlingen* (M854), *Helleevoetsluis* (M855), *Maasluis* (M856), *Makkum* (M857), *Middleburg* (M858) and *Scheveningen* (M859) were in build or on order. In all, seven Dutch vessels had been completed by the end of 1984. The lead ship for Belgium was ordered, after several false starts, in February 1983. The Belgium class comprises: *Aster* (M915), *Bellis* (M916), *Crocus* (M917), *Dianthus* (M918), *Fuchsia* (M919), *Iris* (M920), *Lobelia* (M921), *Myosotis* (M922), *Narchis* (M923) and *Primula* (M924). In terms of the construction programme DCAN Lorient are building all the French vessels, Van der Giesen de Noord are responsible for the Dutch build, while Beliard have responsibility for the Belgian ships.
Notes: Somewhat smaller than the Royal Navy's 'Hunt' class, these tripartite ships employ the same glass-reinforced plastic constructional technique and because they function in a similar manner, carry the same kinds of systems and equipment. However, in detail terms, the differences in design approach to particular facets is quite pronounced as, for example, in the more complex French design solution to the problem of low speed manoeuvring and stopped-on-the-water station-keeping. Here, the 'Eridan' class employs an electrically-driven propeller mounted on each of the ship's twin rudders, along with a forward-mounted, extending propeller-type thruster, compared with the conventional and simpler twin main propeller and bow water pump thruster combination of British ships.

Circe Class Minehunters

Role: Mine disposal.
Builder: CNM Normandy, France.
User: French Navy.

French Navy's Cassiopee *(M642) 'Eridan' class minehunter.*

The French Navy minehunter Clio *(M714) photographed in 1979.*

Basic data: 495 tons full displacement; 170.0ft (50.9m) overall length; 29.2ft (8.9m) maximum beam.
Crew: 47.
Propulsion: 1 MTU diesel (1800bhp); 1 propeller; or twin electrically driven, rudder-mounted propellers for operational quiet-running.
Sensors: 1 Decca 1229 sea search and navigational radar; 1 DUBM 20 sonar; EVEC automatic position plotting system; 2 PAP-104 remotely-controlled submersible.
Armament: 1 single 20mm anti-aircraft gun.
Top speed: 15 knots.
Range: 3000 nautical miles at 12 knots.
Programme: This five-ship class comprises: *Cybele* (M712), *Calliope* (M713), *Clio* (M714), *Circe* (M715), and *Ceres* (M716). The lead vessel, *Circe* was ordered and laid down in January 1969 and all five minehunters entered service between mid-May 1972 and early March 1973. Provisionally planned for retirement over 1991-1993 period.
Notes: Designed for very quiet running when operating in the minehunting mode, the 'Circe' class have wooden hulls and employ low magnetic material wherever possible in order to reduce the ship's overall magnetic signature. As with other minehunters, rather than minesweepers, the 'Circe' class carry both remotely-controlled mine neutralisation vehicles and a man diver team to deal with mines down to a depth of 197ft (60m).

Sandown Class Minehunters

Role: Coastal mine disposal.
Lead builder: Vosper Thornycroft, UK.
User: Selected for procurement by the Royal Navy.
Basic data: Around 480 tons full displacement; 172.25ft (52.5m) overall length; 34.5ft (10.5m) maximum beam.
Crew: Up to 40.
Propulsion: 2 Paxman diesels (total 3000bhp); 2 Voight Schneider cycloid propellers, plus 2 forward vectored thrust thrusters.

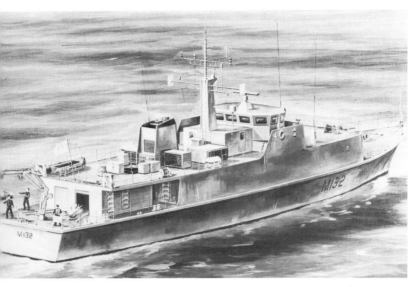

An impression of the Single Role Minehunter as completed.

Sensors: 1 Racal Decca Type 1229 sea search and navigational radar; 1 Plessey Type 193 hull-mounted sonar; 1 Racal Decca Hyperfix and Trisponder precision position fixing system: automated data-processing.
Armament: 1 single 40mm Bofors anti-aircraft gun.
Top speed: 15 knots.
Range: Over 2800 nautical miles at 12 knots.
Programme: The UK Ministry of Defence awarded Vosper Thornycroft a design contract for the Single Role Minehunter in January 1983 and announced that this design had been selected for ongoing development in mid-December 1983. With the detail design task scheduled to be completed by late 1984, a contract for the lead of class construction could be placed shortly afterwards, initiating a 12-or-more-ship programme for Royal Navy needs. Initial deployment is likely to occur no earlier than late 1988.
Notes: Being developed as a cheaper, more limited supplement to the Royal Navy's 'Hunt' class minehunters, the Single Role Minehunter employs many of the development fruits of its larger forebears, including their glass-reinforced plastic hull and superstructure. The Single Role Minehunter design is equipped to carry 2 PAP-104 mine neutralisation remotely-operated submersibles as standard equipment and can carry wire minesweeping gear if required. Vosper Thornycroft had commenced making initial presentations of an export version of the design as early as August 1983; a move pitched at countering export interest in the comparable French-developed 'Eridan' class and Italy's 'Lerici' class minehunters.

Hatsushima Class Minehunters

Role: Costal minesweeper.
Builders: Nippon Kokan and Hitachi, Japan.
User: Japanese Maritime Self-Defence Force.
Basic data: 440 tons full displacement; 180.4ft (55.0m) overall length; 30.8ft (9.4m) maximum beam.
Crew: 45.
Propulsion: 2 Mitsubishi YV12ZC-15/20 diesels (total 1440bhp); 2 controllable-pitch propellers.
Sensors: 1 OPS 9 sea search and navigational radar; 1 ZQS 2B hull-mounted sonar.
Armament: 1 single 20mm anti-aircraft gun or 20mm Phalanx on later ships.
Top speed: 14 knots.
Range: Over 2600 nautical miles at 8 knots.
Programme: A planned 19-ship class of which 15 had

been ordered by May 1984. The known ships comprise: *Hatsushima* (MSC649), *Ninoshima* (650), *Miyajima* (651), *Nenoshima* (652), *Ukishima* (653), *Ooshima* (654), *Niijima* (655), *Yukushima* (656), *Narushima* (657), along with the as yet unnamed 658 through 661. The lead of class was built by Nippon Kokan, being laid down in early December 1977, launched in October 1978 and entered service at the end of March 1979. The second of class was built by Hitachi, being laid down in May 1978 and entering service in mid-December 1979. Nippon Kokan were responsible for the construction of the third, fourth, seventh, eighth, 11th and 12th of class, while Hitachi built the second, fifth, sixth, ninth and tenth vessels. On the basis of current construction scheduling, all of this class should be delivered prior to the end of 1991.
Notes: These wooden construction vessels can operate in

Hatsushima (MSC649), the lead ship of this new Japanese coastal minesweeping class.

company as conventional minesweepers or singly as minehunters when deploying their Japanese-developed Type 54 mine neutralisation vehicle, an unmanned, remotely-operated submersible, similar in function to the French-developed PAP-104. Perhaps the most surprising, even if readily understandable, aspect of this programme is the decision to provide later ships with the 20mm Phalanx close-in weapons system, which, thanks to its lightweight, bolt-on nature would be readily retrofittable to the earlier vessels. Unquestionably, the incorporation of Phalanx will provide these ships with an unprecedented degree of protection from close-in air attack, either by manned aircraft or sea-skimming missile.

Sirius Class Minehunters

Role: Coastal mine disposal.
Builders: Various, France and Yugoslavia.
Users: Navies of France (10), Morocco (1) and Yugoslavia (4).
Basic data: 431 tons full displacement; 151.9ft (46.3m) overall length; 27.9ft (8.5m) maximum beam.
Crew: 40.
Propulsion: 2 SEMT-Pielstick 16 PA1-175 diesels (total 1600bhp); 2 propellers.
Sensors: 1 DRBN 31 sea search and navigational radar; 1 DUBA 1 (on French and Moroccan) or 1 Type 193 (on Yugoslavian) hull-mounted sonar.
Armament: 1 single 40mm Bofors or 1 single or 1 twin 20mm anti-aircraft gun.
Top speed: 15 knots.
Range: 3000 nautical miles at 10 knots.
Programme: Originally a 16 French-built ship programme completed between 1954 and 1957, plus one Yugoslavian-built ship, completed in 1960. Only 15 remained in service by mid-1985 comprising: France's *M737*, *M749*, *M755* through *757*, along with *A747* employed for sonar trials work and *P650*, *P656*, *P659* and *P660* now employed as patrol vessels. Morocco operates one example, *Tawific*, while Yugoslavia has four

A Yugoslavian operated French designed 'Sirius' class vessel.

consisting of *M151* through *M153* and the locally-built *M161*.

Notes: This French-developed equivalent of the Royal Navy's 'Coniston' class minesweeper employs a light alloy frame with wooden planking. As with other classes laid down in the earlier part of the 1950s, the 'Sirius' class was essentially built for minesweeping, as opposed to minehunting, but has proved reasonably adaptable in terms of being able to operate PAP-104 remotely-operated mine identification and disposal submersibles.

Coniston Class Minehunters

Role: Mine disposal.
Builders: Various, UK.
Users: Navies of Argentina, Australia, Ghana, India, Ireland, Malaysia, South Africa and UK.
Basic data: 427 tons full displacement; 153ft (46.6m) overall length; 28.6ft (8.7m) maximum beam.
Crew: 29 to 38.
Propulsion: 2 Napier Deltic diesels (total 3000bhp) or 2 Mirrlees JVSS 12 diesels (total 2500bhp); 2 propellers.
Sensors: 1 Type 978 sea search and navigational radar; 1 Type 193 hull-mounted sonar.
Armament: 1 single 40mm Bofors anti-aircraft gun.
Top speed: 16 knots.
Range: 3000 nautical miles at 8 knots.
Programme: Originally a 116-ship Royal Navy class, plus two export vessels for South Africa. Built between 1953 ad 1960, the 'Coniston' or 'Ton' class vessels now serve with a number of navies, a mid-1984 census indicating the following distribution: Argentina 6, Australia 3, Ireland 2, Malaysia 2, South Africa 10 and UK 34, including the rebuilt, plastic-hulled HMS *Wilton* (M1116). Refer to ship listing below.
Notes: Korean War experience with magnet and acoustic influence mines pointed up the shortcomings of existing minesweepers and led directly to the procurement of the 'Coniston' class, built in two versions, one suited to minesweeping, the other to minehunting. The minesweepers operate as a team, essentially trawling various cable-cutting, noisemaking or magnetic field generators through a sea area of conventional mines. The introduction of more complex mines led to the need for minehunters, which carry active sonar for detection, along with divers and other equipment to complete the task. Some of the class are now stripped of their mine clearing equipment and are employed on coastal patrol or fishery protection duties, including four South African and 12 Royal Navy vessels.

Royal Navy:

Minehunters;

HMS *Bildeston*	(M1110)
HMS *Brereton*	(M1113)
HMS *Brinton*	(M1114)
HMS *Bronington*	(M1115)
HMS *Wilton*	(M1116)
HMS *Bossington*	(M1133)
HMS *Gavinton*	(M1140)
HMS *Hubberston*	(M1147)
HMS *Iveston*	(M1151)
HMS *Kedleston*	(M1153)
HMS *Kellington*	(M1154)
HMS *Kirkliston*	(M1157)
HMS *Maxton*	(M1165)
HMS *Nurton*	(M1166)
HMS *Sheraton*	(M1181)

Minesweepers;

HMS *Alfriston*	(M1103)
HMS *Cuxton*	(M1125)
HMS *Hodgeston*	(M1146)
HMS *Shavington*	(M1180)
HMS *Upton*	(M1187)
HMS *Lewiston*	(M1208)
HMS *Crofton*	(M1216)

Fishery Protection;

HMS *Bickington*	(M1109)
HMS *Crichton*	(M1124)
HMS *Pollington*	(M1173)
HMS *Walkerton*	(M1188)
HMS *Wotton*	(M1195)
HMS *Soberton*	(M1200)
HMS *Stubbington*	(M1204)

Hong Kong Patrol;

HMS *Beachampton*	(P1007)
HMS *Monkton*	(P1055)
HMS *Wasperton*	(P1089)
HMS *Wolverton*	(P1093)
HMS *Yarnton*	(P1096)

Argentina:

Neuquen	(M1)
Rio Negro	(M2)
Chubut	(M3)
Tierra Del Fuego	(M4)
Chaco	(M5)
Formosa	(M6)

Australia:

Snipe	(M1102)
Curlew	(M1121)
Ibis	(M1183)

Ireland:

Grainne	(CM10)
Fola	(CM12)

Malaysia:

Tahan	(M1163)
Bringchang	(M1172)

South Africa:

Minesweepers;

Johannesburg	(M1207)
Kimberley	(M1210)
Port Elizabeth	(M1212)
Mosselbaai	(M1213)
East London	(M1215)
Windhoek	(M1498)

Patrol:

Pretoria	(P1556)
Kaapstad	(P1557)
Walvisbaai	(P1159)
Durban	(P1560)

The Royal Navy's HMS Gavington (M1140).

Type 331 Class Minehunters

Role: Mine disposal.
Builder: Burmester, Federal Germany.
User: Federal Germany Navy.
Basic data: 420 tons full displacement; 155.7ft (47.45m) overall length; 22.6ft (8.3m) maximum beam.
Crew: 46.
Propulsion: 2 Maybach diesels (total 4000bhp); 2 controllable-pitch propellers.
Sensors: 1 TRS-N sea search and navigational radar; 1 DSQS-11 towed variable depth sonar (fitted to all Type 331As), or 1 Plessey Type 193M hull-mounted sonar (fitted to Type 331Bs).
Armament: 1 single 40mm anti-aircraft gun.
Top speed: 17 knots.
Range: 3450 nautical miles at 9 knots.
Programme: Originally built as Type 320 'Lindau' class minesweepers and completed between 1957 and 1959, 12 of these vessels have been modified into Type 331 minehunters, commencing with the conversion of two craft into Type 331Bs. *Flensburg* (M1084) and *Fulda* (M1086), between 1968 and 1971. This was followed by the conversion to Type 331A, between 1975 and 1980, of the following: *Gottingen* (M1070), *Koblenz* (M1071), *Lindau* (M1072), *Tubingen* (M1074), *Wetzlar* (M1075), *Weilheim* (M1077), *Cuxhaven* (M1078), *Marburg* (M1080), *Minden* (M1085) and *Volklingen* (M1087).
Notes: Starting life as wooden-hulled minesweepers, the Type 331s form the central, manned element of the West German-devised Troika minehunting system. The Troika system employs drone, or operationally unmanned boats, along with the French-developed PAP-104 remote-controlled submersible to do the actual hunting; all of which is controlled from the Type 331s with 3 drones each.

Tubingen *(M1074), a Type 331A minehunter, 1978.*

Dokkum Class Minehunters

Role: Mine disposal.
Builders: Various, Netherlands.
User: Royal Netherlands Navy.
Basic data: 417 tons full displacement; 152.95ft (46.6m) overall length; 28.7ft (8.75m) maximum beam.
Crew: 31.
Propulsion: 2 Fijenoord-M.A.N. diesels (total 2500bhp); 2 propellers.
Sensors: 1 Decca 1229 sea search and navigational radar; 1 Type 193M hull-mounted sonar (fitted to M801, M818, M828 and M842 only).
Armament: 1 twin 40mm Bofors anti-aircraft gun.
Top speed: 14 knots.

The diver-carrying HNLMS Woeren *(M820).*

Range: 2500 nautical miles at 10 knots.
Programme: An 18-vessel class built between June 1953 and December 1958, the class comprises HNLMS *Dokkum* (M801), HNLMS *Drunen* (M818), HNLMS *Veere* (M842) and HNLMS *Staphorst* (M828) operated as minehunters; HNLMS *Roermond* (M806), HNLMS *Woeren* (M820) and HNLMS *Rhenen* (M844) operated as diver-carrying mine disposal vessels; HNLMS *Hooegezand* (M802), HNLMS *Naaldwijk* (M809), HNLMS *Abcoude* (M810), HNLMS *Drachten* (M812), HNLMS *Ommen* (M813), HNLMS *Giethoorn* (M815), HNLMS *Venlo* (M817), HNLMS *Naarden* (M823), HNLMS *Hoogeveen* (M827), HNLMS *Sittard* (M830) and HNLMS *Gemert* (M841) operated as minesweepers.
Notes: Comparable to the Royal Navy's 'Coniston' (Ton) class vessels, the 'Dokkums' curently form the deep-water going element of the Royal Netherland's Navy mine disposal service. The 'Dokkum' class is scheduled to be replaced by 15 'Alkmaar' class vessels during the 1980s and have been offered for resale in late 1984.

Bay Class Minehunters

Role: Mine disposal/patrol.
Builders: Various, Canada and France.
User: Various, Canada and France.
Users: Navies of Canada (6), France (4) and Turkey (4).
Basic data: 415 tons full displacement; 164.0ft (50.0m) overall length; 30.2ft (9.21m) maximum beam.
Crew: 33 to 38.
Propulsion: 2 General Motors 12-278A diesels (total 2500bhp); 2 propellers.
Sensors: 1 Sperry Mk 2 (original Canadian fit) or 1 DRBN 31 sea search and navigational radar.
Armament: 1 single 40mm Bofors and 1 or 2 single 20mm Oerlikon anti-aircraft guns. *Note:* the 40mm guns have been deleted from the Canadian vessels.
Top speed: 15 knots.
Range: 4500 nautical miles at 11 knots.
Programme: Only 14 ships of this large early 1950s Canadian and French construction programme remain in service comprising: the Royal Canadian Navy's *PFL 159* through *164* (employed as patrol training vessels for the Reserve), the French Navy's *P652* through *655* (again used as patrol craft) and Turkey's *M530* through *533* (the only examples of the class to retain their original role).
Notes: Very sturdy, seaworthy vessels, the 'Bay' class design employed a composite form of construction

comprising a steel hull framework sheathed with wooden planking (a technique, which even with electrical degaussing equipment raises questions in the context of minesweeping). The four French vessels currently in service were built in French shipyards, while the four Turkish Navy craft were transferred under the US Military Aid Programme during 1958.

MSC322/Addiriyah Class Minehunters

Role: Coastal minesweeping.
Builder: Peterson Builders, USA.
User: Royal Saudi Arabian Navy.
Basic data: 405 tons full displacement; 152.0ft (46.3m) overall length; 27.2ft (8.3m) maximum beam.
Crew: 39.
Propulsion: 2 Waukesha E1616 DSIN diesels (total 1200bhp); 2 propellers.
Sensors: 1 SPS-55 sea search and navigational radar; 1 SQQ-14 hull-mounted sonar.
Armament: 1 twin 20mm anti-aircraft gun.
Top speed: 14 knots.
Endurance: Over 2000 nautical miles.
Programme: Ordered by Saudi Arabia in September 1975, this four-ship class comprises: *Addiriyah* (MSC412), *Al Quysumah* (MSC414), *Al Wadecah* (MSC416) and *Safwa* (MSC418). Laid down between May 1976 and March 1977, all were launched in the December 1976 to December 1977 period and entered service from July 1978 through October 1978.
Notes: A longer and heavier development of the MSC289/'Adjutant' sub-class vessels, of which Peterson had built 21 examples, the 'Addiriyah' class retains the wooden hull construction and has the same external configuration as its forebears. These Royal Saudi Arabian Navy ships each carries a 1750kW sweep current generator, used to trigger seabed-laid magnetic mines.

Falcon Class Minehunters

Role: Coastal minesweeping.
Builders: Various, US and Norway.
Users: Navies of Greece (9), Iran (1), Norway (10) and Pakistan (4).
Basic data: 394 tons full displacement; 145.4ft (44.32m) overall length; 27.2ft (8.29m) maximum beam.
Crew: Up to 38.
Propulsion: 2 Waukesha L-1616 or General Motors 8-268A diesels (total 1200bhp); 2 propellers.
Sensors: 1 Decca (various models) sea search and navigational radar; 1 UQS-1 or Type 193 (Norway only) hull-mounted sonar.
Armament: 1 twin 20mm anti-aircraft gun (on Greek, Iranian and Pakistan ships) or 2 single 20mm Rheinmetall anti-aircraft guns (on Norwegian ships).
Top speed: 13 knots.
Range: 2500 nautical miles at 10 knots.
Programme: An original 34-vessel class of which all but the nine locally-built Norwegian craft were completed in US shipyards. All constructed during the first half of the 1950s, a known 24 of these minesweepers remain in service comprising: Greece's M211, 213, 214, 240, 241, 242, 246, 247 and 248; Iran's M301; Norway's M311 through 317, 331, 332 and 334, along with Pakistan's M160, 162, 164 and 165.
Notes: Of very similar design to the US Navy's 'Adjutant' and 'Redwing' classes of coastal minesweepers, the 'Falcon' class were always largely destined for the export market, being distributed to friendly navies under US

HMCS Thunder (P161) of the Royal Canadian Navy is now employed in the role of training vessel.

Addiriyah *(MSC412) of the Royal Saudi Arabian Navy.*

The Royal Norwegian Navy's KNM Tista (M331).

Military Aid Programmes. However, the US Navy did operate ten of these vessels for a while as *MSC190* through *199*. The Royal Norwegian Navy refer to their craft as 'Sauda' class vessels.

Landsort Class Minehunters

Role: Mine hunting/sweeping.
Builder: Karlsronavarvet, Sweden.
User: Royal Swedish Navy.
Basic data: 360 tons full displacement; 155.8ft (47.5m) overall length; 31.5ft (9.6m) maximum beam.
Crew: 22.
Propulsion: 2 SAAB-Scania diesels (total 5000bhp); 2 propellers.

Landsort (M71), lead ship of this new Swedish class.

Sensors: 1 Terma Electronic sea search and navigational radar; 1 Thomson-CSF TSM 2022 hull-mounted sonar; 1 Phillips (Sweden)-Racal Decca 9M3 400 integrated navigational and action information data-processing system; SAAB-Scania optronic fire control system.
Armament: 1 single 40mm Bofors multi-purpose gun (optronically laid); mines.
Top speed: 13 knots.
Endurance: In excess of 2000 nautical miles.
Programme: A planned six-ship class, the first two vessels were ordered in early 1981: comprising *Landsort* (M71) and *Arholma* (M72), these vessels being scheduled for delivery in 1984. Subsequent vessels comprise: *Kullen* (M73), *Koster* (M74), *Vinga* (M75) and *Ven* (M76).
Notes: Following the pattern of the UK's 'Hunt' class, France's 'Eridan' class and Italy's 'Lerici' class minehunters, the 'Landsort' class employs glass-reinforced plastic as its basic construction material. Each of the 'Landsort' class vessels will carry two remotely-controlled SUTEC Sea Owl mine neutralisation submersibles operating as a minehunter. In the minesweeping role, the 'Landsort' class vessels will each operate a number of Swedish-developed SAM unmanned, glass-reinforced plastic-hulled catamarans to carry out the actual lane sweeping in a fashion similar to that of the Federal German Navy's Troika system.

Cardinal Class Minehunters

Role: Coastal minesweeping and minehunting.
Builder: Bell Aerospace Halter, USA.
User: US Navy.
Basic data: 434 tons full displacement; 189.0ft (57.6m) overall length; 39.0ft (11.9m) maximum beam.
Crew: 43 to 51.
Propulsion: 4 Waukesha L1616 DSIN diesels (total 2400bhp) with 2 used to drive 2 lift fans and 2 used to drive 2 propellers, plus providing craft's electrical and electro-hydraulic power.
Sensors: 1 SPS-64 sea search and navigational radar; 1 LN-66 sea search and navigational radar; 1 SQS-32 variable-depth sonar; 1 Honeywell mine neutralisation vehicle.
Armament: None fitted.
Top speed: 25 knots.
Range: 1200 nautical miles at 12 knots.

An artist's impression of the air-cushion supported 'Cardinal' class coastal minehunter on order for the US Navy.

Programme: The lead of this planned 17-vessel class, USS *Cardinal* (MSH1) was ordered in November 1984 for a scheduled entry into service during 1987. A second of class is planned for 1989 delivery, followed by accelerating deliveries continuing well into the 1990s.
Notes: Employing the British-developed rigid side-wall, air-cushion principle taken up by Bell Halter family of SES-100 and -200 surface effect craft that originated during the latter 1970s, the 'Cardinal' class will be constructed primarily of glass-reinforced plastic/foam sandwich as developed by Karlskronavarct in Sweden. The 'Cardinal' class are primarily destined to be homeported at strategic bases around the US continental coastline from which it is assumed that they would be operating within friendly airspace, hence the lack of need for anti-air defences.

Arko Class Minehunters

The lead of class Arko (M57) seen firing its 40mm Bofors gun.

Role: Coastal minesweeping.
Builders: Karlskrona and Halsingborg, Sweden.
User: Royal Swedish Navy.
Basic data: 300 tons full displacement; 145.7ft (44.4m) overall length; 24.6ft (7.5m) maximum beam.
Crew: 25.
Propulsion: 2 MTU 12V493 diesels (total 1000bhp); 2 propellers.

Sensors: 1 Scanter 009 sea search and navigational radar; 1 SIMRAD hull-mounted sonar (not fitted to all vessels).
Armament: 1 single Bofors L70/40 anti-aircraft gun.
Top speed: 14.5 knots.
Endurance: Over 2400 nautical miles.
Programme: This 12-ship class comprises: *Arko* (M57), *Sparo* (M58), *Karlso* (M59), *Iggo* (M60), *Styrso* (M61), *Skafto* (M62), *Aspo* (M63), *Hasslo* (M64), *Vino* (M65), *Vallo* (M66), *Namdo* (M67) and *Blido* (M68). Karlskronavarvet were responsible for building the lead ship, plus the other five odd-numbered vessels, while Halsinborg built the six even-numbered ships. All entered service during the 1958 through 1964 period.
Notes: Destined to be replaced by the 'Landsort' class coastal minehunters, the 'Arko' class minesweepers were the first Swedish mine countermeasures vessel to employ wooden hull construction, as well as making maximum use of non-ferrous materials within their equipment in order to minimise their vulnerability to magnetically-triggered mines.

Schutze Class Minehunters

Role: Patrol/minesweeper.
Builder: Abeking & Rasmussen, Federal Germany.
Users: Navies of Federal Germany (21) and Brazil (6).
Basic data: 280 tons full displacement; 155.6ft (47.4m) overall length; 23.6ft (7.2m) maximum beam.
Crew: 30.
Propulsion: 2 Maybach diesels (total 4000bhp); on Type 340, or 2 Daimler-Benz diesels (total 4200bhp) on Type 341; 2 propellers.
Sensors: 1 TRS-N combined air/sea search and navigational radar.
Armament: 1 or 2 single 40mm anti-aircraft guns; mines.
Top speed: 24.5 knots.
Range: 1000 nautical miles at 18 knots.
Programme: Originally 32 of these vessels were built consisting of 26 for the Federal German Navy and six for Brazil. The Federal German Navy craft still in service by mid-1982 comprised eight Type 340: *Castor* (M1051), *Pollux* (M1054), *Sirius* (M1055), *Rigel* (M1056), *Regulus* (M1057), *Mars* (M1058), *Spica* (M1059) and *Skorpion* (M1060); along with 13 Type 341: *Schutze* (M1062), *Waage* (M1063), *Deneb* (M1064), *Jupiter* (M1065), *Atair* (M1067), *Wega* (M1069), *Perseus* (M1090), *Pluto* (M1092), *Neptun* (M1093), *Widder* (M1094), *Herkules* (M1095), *Fische* (M1096) and *Gemma* (M1097). *Stier*, the former M1092, has now been converted to a submarine rescue craft, carrying Y849 as its new identity. All of the Federal German craft were delivered between May 1958 and April 1963. Ordered in two batches of four and two craft each in April 1969 and November 1973, the Brazilian craft comprise: *Aratu* (M15), *Anhatomirim* (M16), *Atalaia* (M17), *Aracatuba* (M18), *Abrolhos* (M19) and *Albardao* (M20). All six Brazilian vessels entered service between May 1971 and July 1975.
Notes: These multi-purpose, wooden-hulled craft double as coastal patrollers and minesweepers. In the latter role, the 'Schutz' class is equipped to sweep for contact, acoustic and magnetic mines.

Van Straelan Class Minehunters

Role: Inshore minesweeping.
Builders: Various, Netherlands.
User: Royal Netherlands Navy.
Basic data: 171 tons full displacement; 108.5ft (33.1m) overall length; 22.5ft (6.9m) maximum beam.
Crew: 14.
Propulsion: 2 Werkspoor diesels (total 1000bhp); 2 propellers.

The Brazilian Navy's 'Schutze' class patrol minesweeper Aratu (M15).

Royal Netherlands Navy's HNLMS Bussenmaker (M869).

Sensors: 1 Decca sea search and navigational radar; precision position fixing and plotting systems.
Armament: 1 single 20mm Oerlikon anti-aircraft gun.
Top speed: 13 knots.
Range: 1000 nautical miles at 9 knots.
Programme: This 16-vessel class comprises: *Van Straelen* (M872), *Alblas* (M868), *Bussenmaker* (M869), *Lacombe* (M870), *Van Hamel* (M871), *Van Moppes* (M873), *Chompff* (M874), *Van Vell Groeneveld* (M875), *Schuiling* (M876), *Van Versendaal* (M877), *Van der Wel* (M878), *Van t'Hof* (M879), *Mahu* (M880), *Staverman* (M881), *Houtepen* (M882) and *Zomer* (M883). All were laid down between February 1958 and March 1961; with all entering service between March 1960 and October 1961. Of the three Dutch shipyards involved in the building programme, De Noord built six while De Vries-Lentsch and Arnhemse Scheepsbouw each built five vessels.
Notes: The 'Van Straelen' class are particularly well equipped vessels, carrying magnetic sweep generators for dealing with magnetically triggered mines, as well as cutting sweeps to deal with the elderly contact mine.

Rushcutter Class Minehunters

Role: Coastal mine disposal.
Builder: Ramsay Fibreglass Australasia, Australia.
User: Royal Australian Navy.
Basic data: 170 tons full displacement; 101.7ft (31.0m) overall length; 24.5ft (9.0m) maximum beam.
Crew: 14.

187

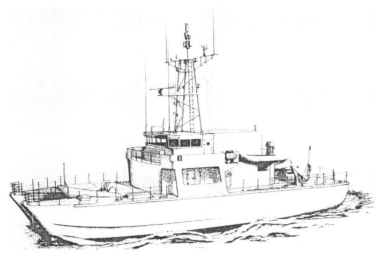

An impression of this Australian catamaran minehunter as completed.

The Yugoslavian Navy's Motajica *(M332) river minesweeper.*

Propulsion: 2 SACM-Poyond diesels (total 650bhp); electric drive; 2 propellers.
Sensors: 1 Kelvin Hughes Type 1006 sea search and navigational radar; 1 Krupp Atlas MWS80 weapons system incorporating 1 DSQS 11H sonar, 1 Deso 20 echo sounder, 1 DLO 3-2 doppler log and tactical action data-processing; 2 PAP-104 remote-controlled mine neutralisation vehicles.
Armament: 2 machine guns.

Top speed: 10 knots.
Range: 650 nautical miles at 9 knots.
Programme: Initial design work on this planned six-vessel class commenced during the spring of 1981. The lead catamaran, HMAS *Rushcutter* (M??) was ordered in August 1984 and should be delivered by February 1986. A second development vessel is under construction and should be completed by June 1986. Construction of the definitive third, fourth, fifth and sixth of class commences in June 1988 and continues at six-monthly intervals through to January 1990, with completions scheduled to occur between February 1990 through June 1991.
Notes: Employing a catamaran hull design of glass-reinforced plastic construction, the 'Rushcutter' class are optimized for relatively local inshore minehunting operations. Carrying an extensive electronics fit for a vessel of its size, the complete operational control equipment associated with the minehunting mission is housed within a readily removable container positioned immediately aft of the wheelhouse.

Nestin Class Minehunters

Role: River minesweeper/minelayer.
Builder: Brodotehnika, Yugoslavia.
Users: Navies of Yugoslavia and Iraq.
Basic data: 65 tons full displacement; 88.6ft (27.0m) overall length; 21.3ft (6.5m) maximum beam.
Crew: 17.
Propulsion: 2 diesels (total 520bhp); 2 propellers.
Sensors: 1 sea search and navigational radar.
Armament: 2 quadruple 20mm anti-aircraft guns.
Top speed: 11.9 knots.
Range: 863 nautical miles at 10.8 knots.
Programme: A known seven-craft class that entered Yugoslavian Navy service commencing in 1976, four of these vessels were reported to have been transferred to Iraq in the 1978/79 period. *Nestin*, the lead of class, carried the pennant number M331. Additional examples of this class may have been built.
Notes: Although primarily designed for mine clearance in rivers or lakes, the 'Nestin' class, or MS-50 design, can also operate in coastal salt water environments thanks to its corrosion-resistant light alloy hull construction. In addition to its primary function, the 'Nestin' class can also be employed as a minelayer, which, as a result of its greater deckweight, brings about some degradation in the above quoted performance characteristics.

Replenishers

Neosho Class Replenishers

Role: Underway replenishment.
Builders: Bethlehem Steel and New York Shipbuilding, USA.
Users: US Navy and Military Sealift Command.
Basic data: 40,000 tons full displacement; 655.0ft (199.6m) overall length; 86.0ft (26.2m) maximum beam.
Crew: 301 for US Navy and 105 in Military Sealift Command ships.
Propulsion: 2 General Electric geared steam turbines (total 28,000shp); 2 propellers.

Sensors: 1 Raytheon TM1650/6X low-level air/sea search radar; 1 SPS-10 sea search and navigational radar.
Armament: 4 twin 0.5in anti-aircraft machine guns (deleted from Military Sealift Command ships).
Top speed: 20 knots.
Range: 12,000 nautical miles at 18 knots.
Programme: This six-ship class comprises: USS *Neosho* (AO143), USS *Mississinewa* (AO144), USS *Hassayampa* (AO145), USS *Kawishwi* (AO146), USS *Truckee* (AO147) and USS *Ponchatoula* (AO148). All but the Bethlehem Steel-built lead of class were constructed by the New York Shipbuilding Corporation; all ships entering service between September 1954 and January 1956. All of this

Lead of class USS Neosho *(AO143) seen prior to joining Military Sealift Command in May 1978.*

class was subsequently transferred to the US Military Sealift Command between May 1978 and September 1980.

Notes: The 'Neosho' class ships can carry up to 23,600 tons of cargo in the form of 180,000 barrels of fuel. Three of the class, AO143, AO144 and AO145, were fitted with elevated stern platforms for vertical resupply operations by helicopters.

Berezina Type Replenishers

Role: Underway replenishment.
Builder: Kommuna, USSR.
User: Soviet Navy.
Basic data: 36,000 tons full displacement; 684.7ft (208.7m) overall length; 78.7ft (24.0m) maximum beam.
Crew: 600.
Propulsion: 2 diesels (total 54,000bhp); 2 propellers.
Sensors: 1 long-range air search radar; 2 of one and 1 of another type of sea search and navigational radar; 1 fire control radar (SA-N-4 missiles) and 2 fire control radars for 30mm guns, along with 1 separate type fire control radar for 57mm guns; hull-mounted sonar; automated action information data-processing system.
Armament: 2 Kamov Ka-26 helicopters; 1 twin SA-N-4 short-range air defence missile launcher; 2 twin 57mm dual-purpose guns; 4 sextuple 30mm Gatling type close-in weapons systems; 2 sextuple 300mm RBU-1000 anti-submarine rocket launchers.
Top speed: 22 knots.
Range: 12,000 nautical miles at 18 knots.
Programme: *Berezina* entered service with the Soviet Navy during 1978 and although no evidence existed in mid-1985 of Soviet plans to build further examples of this specific design, the need to build other ships of this size, or bigger, will continue to grow.
Notes: *Berezina* represents the largest and most capable of the Soviet Navy's replenishment ships yet built. Equipped to carry approximately 18,500 tons of liquid and solid cargo, the *Berezina* has the stores transfer systems to replenish up to three accompanying ships simultaneously; one on either side and one behind. While the bulk of the cargo, at around 16,000 tons, consists of fuel oil, the ship can also carry up to 3000 tons of missiles,

Berezina at anchor, with a 'Moma' class survey ship alongside.

ammunition and other naval provisions. The *Berezina*'s formidable three-tier anti-air and two-tier anti-submarine weapons fit reflects the Soviet Navy's philosophy of building ships that can readily form an integral part of a battle task group.

Olwen Class Replenishers

Role: Underway replenishment.
Builder: Hawthorn Leslie (Swan Hunter), UK.
User: Royal Fleet Auxiliary (for Royal Navy).
Basic data: 36,000 tons full displacement; 648.0ft (197.5m) overall length; 84.0ft (25.6m) maximum beam.
Crew: 94.
Propulsion: 1 Pametreda geared steam turbine (26,500shp); 1 propeller.
Sensors: 2 Kelvin Hughes Type 14 sea search and navigational radars; 1 MARISAT satellite-linked communications system.
Armament: Up to 2 Westland Sea King anti-submarine helicopters (1 normally carried); 2 single 20mm BMARC (Oerlikon) anti-aircraft guns.
Top speed: 20 knots.

RFA Olmeda (A124). Note the MARISAT satellite-link communications antenna above the ship's bridge.

Range: 10,000 nautical miles at 18 knots.
Programme: This three-ship class comprises: RFA *Olwen* (A122), RFA *Olmeda* (A124) and RFA *Olna* (A123). *Olwen* was launched in July 1964, *Olmeda* in November 1964 and *Olna* in October 1965. The class entered service in June 1965, October 1965 and April 1966, respectively.
Notes: The three 'Olwen' class fleet replenishers are the largest oilers in service with the Royal Fleet Auxiliary. Each ship can carry up to 25,000 tons of liquid cargo, including aviation turbine, diesel fuel and not forgetting its own fuel oil. The 'Olwen' class design incorporates a strengthened hull, suitable for operations in light sea icing conditions. The vessels are equipped with eight underway transfer stations (four either side), enabling them to re-supply two accompanying warships simultaneously. Both *Olmeda* and *Olna* played an active part in the necessary underway replenishment of the Royal Navy's South Atlantic Task Group dispatched to the Falklands and South Georgia in the spring of 1982. The above quoted crew complement of 94 includes seven naval aviation personnel associated with onboard helicopter operations and maintenance.

Ashtabula Class Replenishers

Role: Underway replenishment.
Builder: Bethlehem Steel, USA.
User: US Navy.
Basic data: 34,750 tons full displacement; 644ft (196.3m) overall length; 75ft (22.9m) maximum beam.
Crew: 345.

Propulsion: 2 geared steam turbines (total 13,500shp); 2 propellers.
Sensors: 1 SPS-10 sea search and navigational radar.
Armament: 2 single 3in Mk 26 anti-aircraft guns.
Top speed: 18 knots.
Endurance: In excess of 8000 nautical miles.
Programme: This three-ship class, comprising USS *Ashtabula* (AO51), USS *Caloosahatchee* (AO98) and USS *Canisteo* (AO99), are all that are left of an original 35-ships class delivered to the US Navy and Esso Oil Company between January 1939 and March 1946. In the mid-1960s, these 'Ashtabula' class ships underwent a major reconstruction, referred to as 'Jumboisation', during which an additional 91feet (27.7m) section was inserted amidships to increase both space for tankage and other stores.
Notes: These large US Navy oilers can carry 143,000 barrels of fuel oil, plus 175 tons of ammunition and 100 tons of general provisions. While the gun armament, along with its fire director systems, were removed in the late 1970s, the gun mounts have been retained. These ships carry no helicopter operating facilities, but have a small platform on the bow section on to which stores can be transferred to or from other ships by helicopter.

AOR (IIK) Class Replenishers

Role: Underway replenishment and helicopter maintenance support.
Builder: Awaiting late 1985 selection.
User: Royal Fleet Auxiliary.
Basic data: Around 30,000 tons full displacement; about 656.0ft (200m) overall length; about 85.0ft (25.9m) maximum beam.
Crew: Up to 250.
Propulsion: 2 unidentified medium speed diesels (total bhp); 2 (probably controllable-pitch) propellers.
Sensors: 1 unidentified long-range air search 3-D radar; 2 unidentified sea search and navigational radars; 2 Type 911 Sea Wolf fire control radars; 1 microwave satellite-fed position fixing system.
Armament: 2 Sea King anti-submarine helicopters; 1 multi-cell silo for vertically launched Sea Wolf point air defence missiles; 2 small calibre, rapid fire guns.
Top speed: Over 18 knots.
Range: Over 8000 nautical miles at 18 knots.
Programme: Invitations to submit competitive tenders for the lead of class, plus a second vessel were circulated to the British shipbuilding industry in September 1984. The contrast for the two ships is set to be placed at the end of 1985, with the first vessel planned to enter service in early 1990.

USS Caloosahatchee (AO98) with the US Atlantic Fleet, 1976.

The projected Royal Fleet AOR accompanied by a 'Duke' class frigate.

Notes: Referred to as the 'One Stop Auxiliary', the AOR design reflects the ever growing economic pressure to squeeze a quart into a pint pot. A truly multi-purpose support ship, the projected AOR follows the French philosophy, incorporated in the 'Boraida' class design, of providing an oiler, a stores ship, a mobile maintenance base and platform for active anti-submarine and local air defence all within the one hull. Features of the AOR include four dual-purpose transfer stations, capable of handling both liquid and solid stores, along with space to accommodate 141,264 cubic feet (12,000 cubic metres) of fuel, plus 70,632 cubic feet (6000 cubic metres) of solid cargo. Additionally, each AOR carries facilities to provide major maintenance for up to Sea King or EH101-sized helicopters carried by other ships within a task group.

Cimarron Class Replenishers

Role: Underway replenishment.
Builder: Avondale, USA.
Users: USA Navy and Military Sealift Command.
Basic data: 27,500 tons full displacement; 519.5ft (180.3m) overall length; 88.0ft (26.8m) maximum beam.
Crew: 181 on US Navy ships and 113 on Military Sealift Command ships.
Propulsion: 1 geared steam turbine (24,000shp); 1 propeller.
Sensors: 1 SPS-55 sea search and navigational radar; 1 Litton LN66 inertial navigator.
Armament: 2 Mk 15 Phalanx 20mm close-in weapons systems.
Top speed: 20 knots.
Range: Over 6000 nautical miles at 18 knots.
Programme: A five-ship class, all ordered by January 1983. The class comprises: USS Cimarron (AO177), USS Monongahela (AO178), USS Merrimack (AO179), USS Willamette (AO180), USS Platte (AO186). USS Cimarron entered service in January 1981, with all four of the following ships commissioned by December 1982. The break in these ships' pennant numbering sequence is explained by the fact that the designators AO181 through AO185 are allocated to 'Falcon' class vessels.
Notes: Capable of carrying up to 72,000 barrels of fuel oil, plus 48,000 barrels of aviation kerosene per ship, the 'Cimarron' class can off-load these liquids (sufficient to fully replenish two conventionally powered US carriers) while travelling at 15 knots. The ships are equipped with four transfer stations to port and three to starboard.

Tidespring Class Replenishers

Role: Underway replenishment.
Builder: Hawthorn Leslie (Swann Hunter), UK.
Users: Royal Fleet auxiliary and Chilean Navy.
Basic data: 27,400 tons full displacement, 582.7ft (177.6m) overall length; 71.0ft (21.6m) maximum beam.
Crew: 117.
Propulsion: 1 Pametreda geared steam turbine (15,000shp); 1 propeller.
Sensors: 2 Kelvin-Hughes Type 14 sea search and navigational radars.
Armament: 1 Westland Sea King anti-submarine helicopter; 2 single 20mm BMARC (Oerlikon) anti-aircraft guns (on Tidespring).
Top speed: 18 knots.
Range: 8500 nautical miles at 18 knots.
Programme: A two-ship class comprising FRA Tidespring (A75) and the former RFA Tidepool (A76), now in Chilean Navy service as Almirante Montt (AQR 52). The pair of replenishers were laid down in July and December of 1961, launched in May and December of 1962 and

USS Cimarron (AO177), lead ship of this Avondale-built class.

entered service in January and June of 1963, respectively. The former Tidepool was handed over to Chile in August 1982 and Tidespring entered into a refit in June 1985 which is scheduled to be completed in the autumn of 1985.
Notes: Smaller and lacking the degree of equipment automation to be found aboard the Royal Fleet Auxiliary's later 'Olwen' class replenishers, the 'Tidespring' class can carry up to 18,500 tons of liquid cargo, including that required for the ship's own propulsion. Unlike the larger 'Olwen' class, the 'Tidespring' class vessels are each equipped with only six underway transfer stations. Both Tidespring and the former Tidepool served with the Royal Navy's South Atlantic Task Group dispatched to the Falklands and South Georgia during the spring of 1982.

RFA Tidespring (A75) replenishing the Dutch 'Van Speijk' class frigate, Van Galen (F803) to starboard and a Canadian 'Annapolis' class frigate to port.

Supply Type Replenishers

Role: Underway replenishment.
Builder: Harland & Wolff, UK.
User: Royal Australian Navy.
Basic data: 26,500 tons full displacement; 583ft (177.7m) overall length; 70.85ft (21.6m) maximum beam.
Crew: 205.
Propulsion: 2 double reduction steam turbines (total 15,000bhp); 2 propellers.
Sensors: 1 Decca sea search and navigational radar.
Armament: 2 twin and 2 single Bofors 40mm anti-aircraft guns.

HMAS Supply *(AO195) showing her four forward-firing Bofors.*

Top speed: 17 knots.
Range: 8500 nautical miles at 13 knots.
Programme: HMAS *Supply* (AO195) was laid down as HMS *Tide Austral* in August 1952 and joined the Royal Navy in 1955, where it served until 1962, when it was transferred to the Royal Australian Navy in August of that year.
Notes: Although somewhat shorter than the aircraft carrier HMAS *Melbourne*, HMAS *Supply* (AO195) has been the heaviest ship to be operated by the Royal Australian Navy since being bought by that service in 1962. Capable of refuelling a destroyer in less than 30 minutes, the *Supply* will remain as the service's sole fleet oiler until the mid-1980s, when it will be replaced by the 'Durance' type oiler, HMAS *Success*. A big ship by any yardstick, *Supply* is quoted as being able to carry up to 17,600 metric tons of useful load.

Protecteur Class Replenishers

Role: Underway replenishment.
Builder: St John Shipbuilding, Canada.
User: Royal Canadian Navy.
Basic data: 24,700 tons full displacement; 564.3ft (172.0m) overall length; 76.0ft (23.16m) maximum beam.
Crew: 227.
Propulsion: 1 Canadian General Electric geared steam turbine (21,000shp); 1 propeller; 1 bow thruster.
Sensors: 1 Decca TM969 sea search and navigational

The Royal Canadian Navy's HMCS Preserver *(AOR510), 1978.*

radar; 1 Sperry Mk 2 gun fire control radar; 1 URN-20 TACAN aircraft homer; 1 SQS-506 hull-mounted sonar.
Armament: 3 Sea King helicopters; 1 twin 3in Mk 33 anti-aircraft gun.
Top speed: 21 knots.
Range: 4100 nautical miles at 20 knots.
Programme: This two-ship class comprises HMCS *Protecteur* (AOR509) and HMCS *Preserver* (AOR510). Both ships were laid down simultaneously in mid-October 1967, launched in July 1968 and May 1969; the ships entering service in August 1969 and July 1970, respectively.
Notes: Capable of carrying up to 13,250 tons of predominantly liquid cargo, each ship has the space to carry up to 12,000 tons of fuel oil, 600 tons of diesel oil, 400 tons of aviation kerosene and 250 tons of food, ammunition and spares. Each ship has four transfer points; two to port and two to starboard. The ships have accommodation for up to 57 people in addition to the normal crew. Both ships operate with the Royal Canadian Navy's Atlantic Coast forces.

Deepak Class Replenishers

Role: Underway replenishment.
Builder: Bremer Vulkan, Federal Germany.
User: Indian Navy.
Basic data: 22,000 tons full displacement; 552.6ft (168.4m) overall length; 75.5ft (23.0m) maximum beam.
Crew: 169.

Shakti (A57), the second of a two-ship Indian Navy class.

The South African Navy's SAS Tafelberg *(AO243) fleet oiler.*

Propulsion: 1 geared steam turbine (16,500shp); 1 propeller.
Sensors: 1 Decca sea search and navigational radar.
Armament: 3 single 40mm Bofors and 2 single 20mm Oerlikon anti-aircraft guns. Helipad and hangar for Sea King (not normally carried).
Top speed: 20 knots.
Range: 5500 nautical miles at 18.5 knots.
Programme: This two-ship Indian Navy class comprises: *Deepak* (A50) and *Shakti* (A57); the service entry dates for which were November 1972 and February 1976, respectively.
Notes: These ships can each carry up to 15,800 tons of cargo, of which 12,624 tons is fuel oil, 1280 tons of diesel fuel and 1495 tons of aviation kerosene, leaving 401 tons for solid stores and provisions. The 'Deepak' class is fitted with two liquid transfer stations per side, enabling them to replenish two accompanying ships simultaneously.

Tafelberg Type Replenisher

Role: Underway replenishment.
Builder: Nakskovs Skibsvaert, Denmark.
User: South African Navy.
Basic data: 18,890 tons full displacement; 559.7ft (170.6m) overall length; 71.85ft (21.9m) maximum beam.
Crew: 100.
Propulsion: 1 Burmeister and Wain diesel (8420bhp); 1 propeller.
Sensors: 1 SMA 3RM sea search and navigational radar.
Armament: Non fitted.
Top speed: 16 knots.
Range: 7000 nautical miles at 12 knots.
Programme: Launched in June 1958 as the Danish tanker *Annam*, the SAS *Tafelberg* (AO243) was purchased by South Africa in 1965 and refitted for her current role in Durban during the 1965 to 1967 period.
Notes: The *Tafelberg* can refuel two ships simultaneously, one on either side, from her two per side hose transfer and single solid store transfer stations. *Tafelberg* survived a collision with the 'South African' class frigate, SAS *President Kruger* at the beginning of 1982 during a replenishment mission; regrettably, the smaller ship was not so lucky and was lost with many hands.

Durance Class Replenishers

Role: Underway replenishment.
Builder: DCAN Brest, France and Vickers, Australia.
User: French Navy and on order for Royal Australian Navy.
Basic data: 17,800 tons full displacement; 515.1ft (157m) overall length; 68.9ft (21m) maximum beam.
Crew: 159.
Propulsion: 2 SEMT-Pielstick 16 PC 2.5V diesels (total 20,000bhp); 2 controllable-pitch propellers.
Sensors: 1 Decca 1226 sea search and navigational radar.
Armament: 1 Westland Lynx (lightweight anti-submarine torpedoes are stored aboard ship); 2 single Bofors 40mm anti-aircraft guns.
Top speed: 19 knots.
Range: 9000 nautical miles at 15 knots.
Programme: Ordered on an incremental basis, five 'Durance' class ships have been contracted for the French Navy, along with HMAS *Success* for the Royal Australian Navy. The first of class, *Durance* (A629), was laid down in December 1973, launched in September 1975 and entered service in December 1976. The second ship, *Meuse* (A607), was laid down in June 1977 and came into service in October 1980. *Var* (A608) was ordered in October 1977 and entered service in 1983, while *Marne* (A609) and the so far unnamed fifth vessels were ordered in March 1981 and 1984 for delivery in 1986 and 1989/90. HMAS *Success* (AOR304), launched in 1984, should be delivered during 1986.
Notes: Capable of remaining at sea for up to 30 days, the 'Durance' class ships can store up to 10,000 tons of cargo, around 95 per cent of which is fuel. Of this fuel load, 7500 tons is fuel oil, 1500 tons is diesel and 500 tons is aviation turbine fuel. This class can replenish up to three ships simultaneously. Up to 45 personnel can be accommodated besides the normal crew.

French Navy's Durance *(A629), 1976 the first of a five-class programme for underway replenishers.*

193

HNLMS Zuiderkruis (A832), 1981.

Improved Poolster Type Replenisher

Role: Underway replenishment.
Builder: Verolme, Netherlands.
User: Royal Netherlands Navy.
Basic data: 17,357 tons full displacement; 556.4ft (169.59m) overall length; 66.6ft (20.3m) maximum beam.
Crew: Around 200.
Propulsion: 2 Werkspoor TM410 diesels (total 22,500bhp); 2 propellers.
Sensors: 1 Decca 1226 sea search and navigational radar.
Armament: 2 Westland Lynx helicopters; 1 twin 20mm anti-aircraft gun. (*Note:* the ship carries a store of lightweight anti-submarine torpedoes, with which to arm the Lynx helicopters.)
Top speed: 21 knots.
Endurance: In excess of 6000 nautical miles.
Programme: HNLMS *Zuiderkruis* (A832) was laid down in July 1973, launched in October 1974 and entered service in June 1975.
Notes: Employing the same hull design and basic layout of its earlier sister ship HNLMS *Poolster* (A835), the *Zuiderkruis* differs principally in employing diesel rather than the geared steam turbines of its predecessor. Other differences include a lighter calibre gun armament (20mm rather than 40mm) and the deletion of the *Poolster*'s hull-mounted sonar equipment. Although marginally longer than its sister ship, *Zuiderkruis* carries a maximum of 9600 tons cargo, compared with the *Poolster*'s 10,300 tons. Of the latter's 9600 tons cargo capacity, 9000 tons is typically devoted to the carriage of fuel, used to refuel the other anti-submarine task group ships that the replenisher normally accompanies.

Sao Gabriel Replenishers

Role: Underway replenishment.
Builder: Navy Dockyards, Portugal.

The 14,200 ton Sao Gabriel (A5206) replenishment oiler.

User: Portuguese Navy.
Basic data: 14,200 tons full displacement; 479ft (146m) overall length; 59.75ft (18.2m) maximum beam.
Crew: 102.
Propulsion: 1 Pametrada geared steam turbine of 9500shp; 1 propeller.
Sensors: 1 MLN-1A air search radar; 1 Type 975 sea search and navigational radar.
Armament: None.
Top speed: 17 knots.
Range: 6000 nautical miles at 15 knots.
Programme: Launched in 1961, the sole example *Sao Gabriel* (A5206) entered service with the Portuguese Navy in March 1963.
Notes: Replacing the earlier and smaller Portuguese Navy oiler *Sam Bras* (A523), now used as an accommodation hulk, the *Sao Gabriel* can carry up to 9000 metric tons of cargo, predominantly fuel oil. The ship is equipped with two liquid and one solid store transfer stations on each side, enabling it to supply two ships simultaneously. The *Sao Gabriel* has no facilities or space from which to operate helicopters. The ship is unusual for a replenisher in mounting a relatively powerful if elderly air search radar atop the forward superstructure from which the ship is controlled.

Rover Class Replenishers

The small fast fleet tanker, RFA Grey Rover (A269).

Role: Underway replenishment.
Builder: Swan Hunter, UK.
User: Royal Fleet Auxiliary for the Royal Navy.
Basic data: 11,522 tons full displacement; 461ft (140.5m) overall length; 63ft (19.2m) maximum beam.
Crew: 47.
Propulsion: 2 SEMT-Pielstick 16PA4 diesels (total 16,000bhp); 1 controllable-pitch propeller.
Sensors: 1 sea search radar; 1 Type 1006 navigational radar.
Armament: Operating pad for up to Sea King-sized helicopter.
Top speed: 19 knots.
Range: 15,000 nautical miles at 15 knots.
Programme: The five ships of this class comprise RFA *Green Rover* (A268), RFA *Grey Rover* (A269), RFA *Blue Rover* (A270), RFA *Gold Rover* (A271) and RFA *Black Rover* (A273). Launched between mid-December 1968 and October 1973, the five ships entered service with the Royal Fleet Auxiliary (hence their RFA prefix) between August 1969 and August 1974.
Notes: These fast small fleet tankers are physically characterised by their relatively short main superstructure dominated by the single, very tall funnel. In operation, the 'Rover' class carry up to 6600 tons of fuel oil, fresh water, dry and refrigerated stores which can be transferred via the main pair of transfer stations at each side of the main gantry structure ahead of the bridge, plus another pair immediately aft of the funnel. While the ships incorporate a large elevated helicopter operating pad at their stern, no hangar or other facilities are carried. RFA

Blue Rover took part in the Falklands Campaign, one of 22 Royal Fleet Auxiliary ships so deployed.

Boraida Class Replenishers

Role: Underway replenishment, maintenance and training.
Builders: Chantiers Navals de la Crotat, France.
User: Ordered by the Royal Saudi Arabian Navy.
Basic data: 10,500 tons full displacement; 442.9ft (135.0m) overall length; 61.4ft (18.7m) maximum beam.
Crew: 195.
Propulsion: 2 SEMT-Pielstick PC2.5 diesels (total 18,200bhp); 2 controllable-pitch propellers.
Sensors: 2 Racal Decca TM 1229 sea search and navigational radars; 1 CSEE Naja optical gun fire control system.
Armament: 2 Aerospatiale AS 365 Dauphin helicopters; 2 twin 40mm Breda/Bofors L70 anti-aircraft guns.
Top speed: 20 knots.
Range: 7000 nautical miles at 15 knots.
Programme: This two-ship class was ordered in October 1980 as part of the Franco-Saudi Arabian arms sales package and comprises: *Boraida* (AO902) and *Yunbou* (AO903). *Boraida* was laid down in late 1981, launched in January 1982 and delivered prior to the end of 1984. Delivery of *Yunbou* is scheduled for approximately nine months later, during 1985.
Notes: Rather disparagingly described by some naval commentators as a truncated variant of the existing 'Durance' class replenishers, the DCN-designed 'Boraida' class is, in fact, a very versatile solution tailored to meet specific Royal Saudi Arabian Navy needs. Very much a modern, multi-role ship, the 'Boraida' class can carry up to 4350 tons of diesel and gas turbine fuel, plus a further 270 tons of food, ammunition and other stores. Besides acting as underway replenishers, these ships are equipped to act as floating maintenance bases. Further, the provision of the two armed helicopters per ship permits this class to also contribute to the total anti-ship/submarine punch of any surface naval group of which they may form a part. In their secondary training ship role, each ship carries sufficient accommodation to house around 30 trainees and their instructors.

Stromboli Class Replenishers

Role: Underway replenishment.
Builder: CNR, Italy.
User: Navies of Italy and Iraq.
Basic data: 8700 tons full displacement; 423.2ft (129.0m) overall length; 59.1ft (18.0m) maximum beam.
Crew: 115.
Propulsion: 4 GMT C 428 SS diesels (total 11,200bhp); 1 controllable-pitch propeller.
Sensors: 1 Selenia/SMA RAN-11L/X air/sea search radar; 1 Selenia/Elsag Orion 20X fire control radar; Selena IPN-10 automated action information data-processing system.
Armament: 1 single 76mm OTO-Melara dual-purpose gun; provision for 2 twin 40mm Breda/Bofors anti-aircraft guns (integrated within DARDO close-in weapons fire control system); helipad for up to Sea King-sized helicopter.
Top speed: 19.5 knots.
Range: 10,000 nautical miles at 16 knots.
Programme: Currently a two-ship class for the Italian Navy, a third ship was ordered by Iraq in February 1981. The Italian vessels comprise: *Stromboli* (A5327), which was launched in February 1975 and entered service in October 1975, while *Vesuvio* (A5329) was launched in June 1977 and joined the fleet in March 1979. The Iraqi

The Royal Saudi Arabian Navy's Boraida *(AO902).*

ship, *Agnadeen*, was delivered in 1984.
Notes: Capable of shipping a total of 4680 tons of various liquid fuels, plus 200 tons of munitions or other dry stores, the 'Stromboli' class also carries accommodation for up to 230 additional to crew. Two accompanying ships can be replenished simultaneously from the side transfer stations. The ships also carry a stern refuelling station for use in very high sea states or other emergency cases. Once equipped with their DARDO-directed, 40mm guns, these ships would mount a very respectable anti-air capability against both aircraft and incoming sea-skimming missiles, at least comparable to that found on many medium sized frigates.

Patapsco Class Replenishers

Role: Underway replenishment.
Builders: Various, USA.
Users: Navies of Chile (1), Columbia (1), Greece (2) and Taiwan (3).
Basic data: 4335 tons full displacement; 310.75ft (94.7m) overall length; 48.5ft (14.8m) maximum beam.
Crew: 46.
Propulsion: 2 General Motors 16-278A diesels (total 3300bhp); 2 propellers.

The Italian Navy's Stromboli *(A5327), lead of class.*

Ariadne (AO414) 'Patapsco' class oiler, one of two operated by Greece.

Sensors: 1 SPS-5 air search radar; 1 Decca sea search and navigational radar; 1 Mk 26 gunfire control radar.
Armament: 2 single 3in Mk 22 anti-aircraft guns; 2 single 40mm Bofors anti-aircraft guns (on some ships only).
Top speed: 13 knots.
Range: 4500 nautical miles at 10 knots.
Programme: Originally a 24-ship class built by Todd, Seattle and Cargill and Savage between 1943 and 1945, seven of these vessels are known to remain in service comprising: Chile's *Beagle* (AO54), Colombia's *Tumaco* (AO62), Greece's *Arethousa* (AO377) and *Ariadne* (AO414), plus Taiwan's *Long Chuan* (AO342), *Chang Pei* (AO378) and *Hsin Lung* (AO389).
Notes: Designed specifically to carry just over 2000 tons of aviation gasolene to replenish carrier-borne air group stocks, these ships are now used as general fleet oilers.

Lueneburg Class (Type 701) Replenishers

The lead of class, Lueneburg (A1411), built by Bremer Vulkan.

Role: Underway replenishment.
Builders: Bremer Vulkan and Blohm und Voss, Federal Germany.
User: Federal German Navy.
Basic data: 3700 tons full displacement; 341.8ft (104.2m) overall length; 43.3ft (13.2m) maximum beam.
Crew: 103.
Propulsion: 2 Maybach MD 872 diesels (total 5600bhp); 2 controllable-pitch propellers.
Sensors: 1 unidentified sea search and navigational radar.
Armament: 2 twin 40mm anti-aircraft guns.
Top speed: 17 knots.
Range: 3200 nautical miles at 14 knots.
Programme: In total an eight-ship class comprised of four Type 701As and four Type 710Cs. The Type 701As comprise: *Lueneburg* (A1411), *Freiburg* (A1413), *Nienburg* (A1416) and *Offenburg* (A1417), while the Type 701Cs comprise: *Coburg* (A1412), *Glucksburg* (A1414), *Saarburg* (A1415) and *Meersburg* (A1418). Five of the vessels were built by Flensburg (now Bremer Vulkan), while the remaining three, A1413, A1415 and A1417, were built by Blohm und Voss. All of this class were launched

between May 1965 and September 1966, entering service between January 1966 and August 1968.
Notes: The 'Lueneburg' class, or Type 701 ships were designed from the outset as multi-purpose vessels combining the replenisher and stores ship roles within the one hull. The Type 701s can carry some 1100 tons of cargo, of which around 650 tons was fuel oil, leaving 550 tons for ammunition, spare parts and other provisions, including fresh water. The A1415 has been lengthened by 37.7ft (11m) to more readily accommodate the carriage of Exocet missiles, while A1413 has been equipped with a platform to allow vertical replenishment helicopter operations.

Rimfaxe Class Replenishers

The Royal Danish Navy's Rimfaxe (A568). Note the gun mount aft of the ship's funnel.

Role: Coastal oiler.
Builder: Jeffersonville, USA.
User: Royal Danish Navy.
Basic data: 1390 tons full displacement; 173.9ft (53.0m) overall length; 31.4ft (9.75m) maximum beam.
Crew: 23.
Propulsion: 1 General Motors 8-278A diesel (640bhp); 1 propeller.
Sensors: 1 NWS3 sea search and navigational radar.
Armament: 1 single 20mm anti-aircraft gun.
Top speed: 10 knots.
Range: 2000 nautical miles at 8 knots.
Programme: This Danish-operated two-ship class comprises: *Rimfaxe* (A568) and *Skinfaxe* (A569). These vessels entered service with the US Navy in October and December of 1945, being transferred under the US Military Aid Programme to Denmark in August 1962.
Notes: The 'Rimfaxe' class are former US Navy YO65 class coastal oilers and can carry up to 900 tons of fuel oil, more than sufficient to fully refuel both of Denmark's 'Pedar Skram' class frigates.

Support ships

Cpl Louis J Haige Jr Class Support Ships

Role: Maritime pre-positioning stores ship.
Builder: Odense, Denmark, rebuilt by Bethlehem Steel Corporation, US.
User: US Military Sealift Command (under long-term charter from Maersk).
Basic data: 28,249 tons full displacement; 755.4ft (230.2m) overall length; 90.0ft (27.4m) maximum beam.
Crew: 65.
Propulsion: 1 Sulzer 7RND 76M diesel (16,800bhp); 1 propeller; 1 bow thruster.
Sensors: 2 Decca sea search and navigational radars; 1 LORAN C low frequency and 1 microwave satellite-fed position-fixing systems.
Armament: None fitted.
Top speed: 19 knots.
Range: 10,800 nautical miles at 17 knots.
Programme: These five former Maersk 'E' class roll-on/roll-off cargo carriers were selected for major conversion and stretching by Bethlehem Steel Corporation's Sparrow Point, Maryland and Beaumont, Texas yards in 1982. Originally delivered between April 1979 and April 1980, the class comprises *Cpl Louis J Haige Jr* (ex-*Estelle Maersk*), *PFC William B Baugh* (ex-*Eleo Maersk*), *PFC James Anderson Jr* (ex-*Emma Maersk*), *1st Lt Alexander Bonnyman Jr* (ex-*Emerlie Maersk*) and *Pvt Harry Fisher* (ex-*Evelyn Maersk*). Delivery of the ships to the US Military Sealift Command is scheduled to take place between August 1984 and September 1985.
Notes: Along with the five '2nd Lt John P Bobo' class and three 'Sgt Matey Kocak' class, this class forms the new US 13-ship force of mobile, long-term storage bases for vehicles, weapons, ammunition, fuel and other material used to resupply distant US Marine Corps amphibious operations; each ship carrying support for one Marine Amphibious Brigade. The Bethlehem Steel rebuild involved stretching each ship by 157ft (47.9m) and increasing the deck-to-keel depth by 16ft (4.9m) in order to add two further decks. Space exists to accommodate an additional 15-man team for surge loading and unloading.

Reliant Type Support Ship

Role: Helicopter support.
Builder: Gdansk Shipyards, Poland.
User: Royal Fleet Auxiliary (for Royal Navy).
Basic data: 27,867 tons full displacement; 670.0ft (204.2m) overall length; 101.7ft (31.0m) maximum beam.
Crew: 50.
Propulsion: 1 Ceglieski-built Sulzer 1ORND diesel (29,000bhp); 1 propeller.
Sensors: 1 Type 1229 sea search and navigational radar; 1 TACAN aircraft homer.
Armament: 5 Westland Sea King helicopters; 4 single 20mm Oerlikon anti-aircraft guns (2 fore, 2 aft).
Top speed: 22 knots.
Range: 12,000 nautical miles at 18 knots.
Programme: Completed as the merchant containership MV *Astronomer* in 1977, this British-registered vessel was chartered by the UK Ministry of Defence in May 1982 and after hurried conversion to act as helicopter operating and support platform was pressed into South Atlantic service. In early 1983, the ship was acquired by the Royal Fleet Auxiliary as RFA *Reliant* (A131) and following additional modification, including the provision of the quarter deck blockhouse, entered service in December 1983.

PFC James Anderson Jr, third of this five-ship US Military Sealift Command operated class, seen during her early 1985 sea trials.

Notes: As a large containership, RFA *Reliant*, as she is now, was readily suited for conversion to a helicopter support ship and was so converted for use in the Falklands Campaign. The modification centres around the US-developed modular Arapaho system of flight deck, maintenance hangar and associated fuel, lubrication, spares storage and naval aviation crew accommodation. These installations permit the ship to operate five Sea King anti-submarine helicopters. Besides her normal ship's crew complement, RAF *Reliant* houses up to 184 naval aviation personnel.

Fort Class Support Ships

Role: Ammunition and stores supply.
Builder: Scott-Lithgow, UK.
User: Royal Fleet Auxiliary for Royal Navy.
Basic data: 23,834 tons full displacement; 603.7ft (184.0m) overall length; 78.7ft (24.0m) maximum beam.
Crew: 204.
Propulsion: 1 Scott-Lithgow Sulzer 8 RND 90 diesel (23,200bhp); 1 propeller, plus 1 bow thruster.
Sensors: 1 Kelvin Hughes 21/16P navigational radar.
Armament: Nil, but large helipads aft (1 atop hangar roof) permit operation of up to 4 Sea King helicopters, with hangar space for 2.
Top speed: 20 knots.
Range: 10,000 nautical miles at 20 knots.
Programme: Ordered in November 1971 and April 1972, this two-ship class comprises: RFA *Fort Grange* (A385),

RFA Reliant (A131), showing her lengthy central helipad with helicopter hangar forward, December 1983.

RFA Fort Austin *(A386), second of a Scott-Lithgow built two-ship class.*

and RFA *Fort Austin* (A386). RFA *Fort Grange* was laid down in November 1973, launched in December 1976 and entered service in April 1978, while *Fort Austin* was laid down in December 1973, launched in March 1978 and entered service in May 1979.

Notes: Designed for long-range operations in any climate, along with the capability to transfer cargo ship-to-ship or by helicopter in higher sea states than previously permitted. In typical operation, the ships each carry around 3500 tons of cargo, comprising 1500 tons of ammunition, 1500 tons of victualling and 500 tons of naval stores. Besides this cargo, the ships can carry around 500 tons of fresh water, along with the means of distilling another 60 tons per day. Built to Lloyd's Register 100A1 standard, the ship's hulls have been reinforced to enable them to operate in light ice. To help fend off missile attacks, the ships are equipped with two chaff-dispensing 3in rocket launchers. Wartime complement is 298.

Emory S Land Class Support Ships

Role: Submarine support.
Builder: Lockhead Shipbuilding, USA.
User: US Navy.
Basic data: 23000 tons full displacement; 645.6ft (196.8m) overall length; 85ft (25.9m) maximum beam.
Crew: 1351.
Propulsion: 1 De Laval geared steam turbine (20,000shp); 1 propeller.
Sensors: 1 SPS-10 sea search and navigational radar.
Armament: 2 single 40mm Mk 19 and 4 single 20mm Mk 67 anti-aircraft guns.
Top speed: 18 knots.
Endurance: In excess of 6000 nautical miles.
Programme: A three-ship class, all were built by Lockhead Shipbuilding and comprise USS *Emory S Land* (AS39), USS *Frank Cable* (AS40) and USS *McKee* (AS41). These vessels were commissioned in 1979, 1980 and 1981.
Notes: A development of the preceding 'LY Spear' class of submarine tenders, the 'Land' class have been specifically designed to meet the needs of servicing 'Los Angeles' class submarines on extended operations away from their home port. Essentially floating maintenance bases, these large ships have more than 900 compartments on 13 different deck levels. Each ship can support 12 submarines, of which up to four can be handled simultaneously. The ships have a helicopter pad, but no hangar or aircraft of their own.

Resource Class Support Ships

Role: Ammunition and stores support.
Builders: Various, UK.
User: Royal Fleet Auxiliary.
Basic data: 22,800 ton full displacement; 640.0ft (195.1m) overall length; 77.0ft (23.5m) maximum beam.
Crew: 171.
Propulsion: 1 AEI geared steam turbine (20,000shp); 1 propeller.
Sensors: 1 Decca 707 sea search and navigational radar; 1 TACAN aircraft homer.
Armament: None fitted: helipad (no hangar) for 2 Sea King helicopters.
Top speed: 17 knots.
Range: 12,000 nautical miles at 14 knots.
Programme: This two-ship class comprises: RFA *Resource* (A480) and RFA *Regent* (A486). Built by Scotts of Greenock and Harland & Wolff of Belfast, respectively, the

USS McKee *(AS41) on sea trials, 1981.*

ships were launched in February and March of 1966 and entered service in May and June 1967.

Notes: With a cargo capacity of just under 4000 tons, each of these ships can transport around 2000 tons of ammunition and explosives. 1600 tons of victualling and nearly 400 tons of naval spares. The ships are each equipped with three transfer stations per side, with which to supply ships sailing alongside, or can resupply accompanying vessels by helicopter vertical replenishment (VERTREP).

2nd Lt John P Bobo Class Support Ships

Role: Stores pre-positioning.
Builder: General Dynamics Quincy Division, USA.
User: US Military Sealift Command.
Basic data: 22,700 tons full displacement; 671.1ft (204.6m) overall length; 105.5ft (32.2m) maximum beam.
Crew: 37.
Propulsion: 2 medium speed diesels (total 26,035bhp) feeding into a reduction gearbox and driving a single propeller; single 1000hp bow thruster.
Sensors: 1 long range sea search radar; 1 navigational radar; 1 TACAN aircraft homer.
Armament: None fitted but ship carries an aft-mounted helipad from which to operate an up to Sikorsky CH-53E Super Stallion-sized helicopter.
Top speed: 18 knots.
Range: 12,300 nautical miles at 18 knots.
Programme: Winner of a US Navy-sponsored design competition, General Dynamics' Quincy Division was awarded a contract for the construction of two of this new five-ship class in July 1982, followed by contracts for the other three in January 1983. With construction commencing in mid-1983, the ships are set to be delivered between February 1985 through March 1986. The class comprises: *2nd Lt John P Bobo*, *PFC Dewayne F Williams*, *1st Lt Baldomero Lopez*, *1st Lt Jack Lummus* and *Sgt William R Button*.
Notes: Veritable floating warehouses, these TAKX ships, as they were intitially known, have been designed to support the rapid deployment of US forces by providing mobile, long-term storage of both military equipment and supplies at forward bases close to potential trouble spots, or to act as the primary sustaining support link for the US Rapid Deployment Force (RDF) in times of crisis. Unlike their predecessors, a mixed fleet of dry cargo, roll-on/roll-off, container ships and tankers (known collectively as Near-Term Pre-Positioning Ships), these vessels will carry a balanced mix of vehicles, fuel, ammunition, rations and other supplies. Equipped with a swivelling vehicle ramp in the stern, and five 40-ton-lift pedestal cranes for hold and deck cargo handling, these ships can offload all the cargo within three days if pier-berthed, or in five days if necessarily unloaded at anchor away from the shore. Cost of this five-ship programme, including their chartering over a five-year period, totals $620.5 million.

Kikauea Class Support Ships

Role: Ammunition supply.
Builders: Various, USA.
Users: US Navy and US Military Sea Lift Command.
Basic data: 20,500 tons full displacement; 564.0ft (171.9m) overall length; 81.0ft (24.7m) maximum beam.
Crew: Around 350.
Propulsion: 1 General Electric geared steam turbine (22,000shp); 1 propeller.
Sensors: 1 SPS-10 sea search and navigational radar; 2 Mk 36 fire control radars (for Mk 33 guns).

RFA Resource (A480) employing Wessex helicopters vertically to replenish the accompanying carrier just visible over the stores ship's bow.

An artist's impression of two TAKX ships unloading. Note the total self-reliance on shipboard cargo handling capability.

USS Kiska (AE35) returning to San Diego, December 1982.

Armament: 2 twin 3in Mk 33 anti-aircraft guns (being replaced by 2 Mk 15 Phalanx 20mm close-in weapons systems; aft helipad and hangarage for up to 2 Boeing Vertol CH-46 Sea Knight helicopters.
Top speed: 22 knots.
Range: Over 10,000 nautical miles at 16 knots.
Programme: An eight-ship class comprising: USS *Kilauea* (AE26), USS *Butte* (AE27), USS *Santa Barbara* (AE28), USS *Mount Hood* (AE29), USS *Flint* (AE32), USS *Shasta* (AE33), USS *Mount Baker* (AE34) and USS *Kiska* (AE35). All were ordered between 1965 and 1968, launched between August 1967 and March 1972, with service entry dates spanning the period August 1968 and December 1972. Three shipyards built the class: AE26 and AE28 coming from General Dynamics' Quincy yards; AE28 and AE29 being constructed by Bethlehem Steel, while Ingalls Shipbuilding Division of Litton Industries were responsible for the remaining four ships.

USNS Observation Island *(T-AGM23), late 1981.*

Notes: The 'Kilauea' class vessels are each capable of accommodating more than 6000 tons of cargo, transferable to other vessels while underway. These ships represent a more specialised munitions carrier solution than could be afforded by less affluent navies, whose vessels have to carry a mix of ammunition, food and water, as exemplified by the British-operated 'Fort' class. The lead ship, *Kilauea*, has been transferred to the US Military Sea Lift Command, the equivalent of the UK's quasi-merchant Royal Fleet Auxiliary.

Mariner Class Support Ships

Role: Missile tracking.
Builder: New York Shipbuilding, USA.
User: US Military Sealift Command on behalf of US Air Force.
Basic data: 17,000 tons full displacement; 563.0ft (171.6m) overall length; 76.0ft (23.2m) maximum beam.
Crew: 78.
Propulsion: 1 General Electric geared steam turbine (22,000shp); 1 propeller.
Sensors: 1 Sperry sea search and navigational radar; 1 Raytheon SPQ-11 Cobra Judy phased-array radar and other dedicated sensor systems for the tracking of intercontinental missiles and their associated re-entry vehicles.
Armament: None fitted.
Top speed: 20 knots.
Range: 17,000 nautical miles at 13 knots.
Programme: USNS *Observation Island* (T-AGM23) is now the sole operating example of this two-ship US Navy class, acquired by them in 1956. Completed in February 1954 as the merchantman *Empire State Mariner*, the ship entered service with the US Navy in October 1958 and was subsequently progressively converted to undertake a number of missile test programmes prior to her latest 1977 through 1981 refit, involving the installation of the SPQ-11 Cobra Judy.
Notes: With her aft deck area dominated by the four-storey high, 250-ton turntable-mounted SPQ-11 Cobra Judy radar housing, *Observation Island* is based at Pearl Harbor. The ship carries accommodation for up to 65 US Air Force technicians besides the normal 78 civilian crew, and is used to monitor both US and Soviet missile tests carried out over the Pacific.

Stalwart Type Support Ship

Role: Destroyer support.
Builder: Cockatoo Dockyards, Australia.
User: Royal Australian Navy.
Basic data: 15,500 tons full displacement; 515.5ft (157.1m) overall length; 67.5ft (20.6m) maximum beam.
Crew: 396.

The Royal Australian Navy's HMAS Stalwart *(AD215), 1978.*

Propulsion: 2 Scott-Sulzer RD68 diesels (total 14,400bhp); 2 propellers.
Sensors: 1 unidentified combined low-level air/sea search radar; 1 Decca TM1226 sea search and navigational radar; 1 TACAN aircraft homer.
Armament: 2 Sea King helicopters; 2 twin 40mm anti-aircraft guns.
Top speed: 20 knots.
Range: 12,000 nautical miles at 12 knots.
Programme: The sole HMAS *Stalwart* (AD215) was laid down in June 1964, launched in early October 1966 and entered service early in February 1968.
Notes: HMAS *Stalwart* combined the function of stores support and mobile maintenance base for the Royal Australian Navy's destroyer and frigate forces. The ship's large complement is explained by the fact that *Stalwart* carries up to 200 machinists and other technicians, along with the storemen required to handle the ship's primarily dry cargo of missiles, ammunition and other provisions. *Stalwart* is equipped with two 6-ton lift derricks amidships, along with four 3-ton lift cranes, two forward and two aft of the main superstructure. *Stalwart* carries a large helipad aft, along with hangarage for up to two Sea Kings.

Zeus Type Support Ship

Role: Undersea cable laying and repair.
Builder: National Steel & Shipbuilding, USA.
User: US Military Sealift Command.
Basic data: 14,225 tons full displacement; 513.5ft (156.5m) overall length; 73.0ft (22.25m) maximum beam.
Crew: 126.
Propulsion: 5 General Motors EMD diesels, electric drive (total 10,000shp); 2 controllable-pitch propellers; 2 bow and 2 aft thrusters (total 4800hp).
Sensors: 2 sea search and navigational radars, plus precision position fixing equipment, including sonar systems.

RFA Engadine (KO8) underway with two Westland Wessex aft.

Engadine Type Support Ship

Role: Helicopter support/stores.
Builder: Henry Robb, UK.
User: Royal Fleet Auxiliary.
Basic data: 8690 tons full displacement; 420.0ft (128.0m) overall length; 58.0ft (17.7m) maximum beam.
Crew: 75.
Propulsion: 1 WSE-Sulzer 5RD68 diesel (4400bhp); 1 propeller.
Sensors: 1 Kelvin Hughes sea search and navigational radar; 1 TACAN aircraft homer.
Armament: No shipboard weapons installed, but ship can accommodate up to 4 Wessex, or 2 Sea King helicopters.
Top speed: 16 knots.
Endurance: Over 6000 nautical miles.
Programme: Ordered in August 1964, the sole example, RFA *Engadine* (KO8) was laid down in August 1965, launched in September 1966 and accepted into service in December 1967.
Notes: Designated a helicopter support ship, RFA *Engadine* was built to fulfil the dual roles of operational helicopter training ship, along with that of acting as a floating helicopter maintenance and repair base. Besides her normal crew, the ship has accommodation for an additional 29 officers and 84 seamen. The ship has a large helipad aft, plus a target drone aircraft launch facility above the helicopter hangar. The vessel carries sufficient spare parts in store to maintain up to six Wessex helicopters for a protracted period. RFA *Engadine* sailed with the South Atlantic Task Group to the Falklands in the spring of 1982.

IISNS Zeus (T-ARC7) photographed in December 1983 during initial sea trials.

Armament: None fitted.
Top speed: 16 knots.
Range: 10,000 nautical miles at 15 knots.
Programme: Ordered in August 1979, *Zeus* (T-ARC7) was laid down in June 1981, launched in October 1982 and entered service with Military Sealift Command in March 1984.
Notes: By far the largest US naval cable ship built to date, *Zeus* is also the first to be designed for this role from the outset (all previous US naval cable vessels being conversions). *Zeus* can carry in excess of 3100 tons of cable, along with being equipped to conduct such associated tasks as seabed trenching, hydrographic and bathymetric surveying. The five diesel engines installed, each with a rated output of 3600bhp, not only provide power for the ship's propulsion, but also for the other extensive onboard power demands, including the bow and stern cable handling platforms. The ship's peacetime crew consists of 88 officers and seamen, 32 technicians and eight US Navy communications specialists.

Challenger Type Support Ship

Role: Seabed rescue and salvage.
Builder: Scott Lithgow, UK.
User: Royal Navy.
Basic data: 7573 tons full displacement; 439.6ft (184m) overall length; 59.1ft (18m) maximum beam.
Crew: Up to 186.
Propulsion: 5 Ruston 16RK3ACZ diesel electric generators (total 17.150bhp); 1 cycloid propeller, plus 3 bow thrusters.
Sensors: 1 Kelvin Hughes Type 1006 navigational radar; 1 Marconi/Decca Hydroplot; 1 Type 162M and 193M hull-mounted sonars, plus 1 Type 2003 and 2013 towed array sonars.
Armament: Nil, but facilities to operate up to Sea King-sized helicopters.
Top speed: 15 knots.
Range: 8000 nautical miles at 15 knots.
Programme: Ordered in September 1979, HMS *Challenger* (KO7) was launched in May 1981 and commissioned in August 1984.
Notes: Built as a replacement for HMS *Reclaim*, HMS *Challenger* is one of the most capable seabed rescue and

HMS Challenger *(K07)*.

equipment recovery vessels extant. The ship has been designed to hold a precise position over a given point on the seabed in all but the worst weather, while deploying manned and unmanned deep diving systems best suited to the specific task. The ship is equipped with a large, two-element, unmanned tethered submersible system, capable of reconnoitering the seabed down to depths of around 950ft (300m) and out to ranges of over 26,000ft (7925m) over an area arcing aft of the vessel. In the case of rescue from a sunken submarine, the ship carries a large, three-man operated saturation (helium/oxygen breathing mix) diving bell, that can hold up to 12 survivors in its twin chambers. To handle heavy duty salvage work, such as recovering a downed aircraft, the ship carries a 25-ton lift crane just forward of its side-by-side funnels.

Smol'nyy Class Support Ships

Role: Training/patrol.
Builder: Warski Shipyards, Poland.
User: Soviet Navy.
Basic data: 6500 tons full displacement; 451.1ft (137.5m) overall length; 54.8ft (16.7m) maximum beam.
Crew: 210.
Propulsion: 4 diesels (total 16,000bhp); 2 propellers.
Sensors: 1 long-range air search radar; 4 sea search and navigational radars; 2 separate types of gun fire control radars (1 each); 1 hull-mounted sonar; automated action information data processing.

Smol'nyy, *the lead of this three-ship Soviet Navy class.*

Armament: 2 twin 76.2mm dual-purpose guns; 2 twin 30mm anti-aircraft guns; 2 twelve-barrelled 250mm RBU-2500 anti-submarine rocket launchers.
Top speed: 20 knots.
Range: Over 6000 nautical miles at 14 knots.
Programme: This three-ship class comprises: *Smol'nyy*, *Perekop* and *Khasan*. As with a number of Soviet Navy non-front line vessels, these ships were built in one of the Polish shipyards; the class entered service during 1976 through 1978 period.
Notes: Reportedly constructed to relieve the 'Sverdlov' class cruisers formerly employed as training ships for more active duties, these handsomely lined ships are believed to have accommodation for more than 270 cadets. Such is the standard of sensor and weapons fit installed aboard these ships that, in times of crisis, these vessels could readily be employed in active patrol duties, or alternatively as troop transports.

Sir Caradoc Type Support Ship

Role: Logistic support.
Builder: Trosvik Norway.
User: Royal Fleet Auxiliary.
Basic data: 5980 tons full displacement; 407.5ft (124.2m) overall length; 63.2ft (19.26m) maximum beam.
Crew: 24.
Propulsion: 4 Bergens-Normo LSM-9 diesels (total 10,080bhp); 2 controllable-pitch propellers.
Sensors: 1 Racal Decca TM 1226 sea search and navigational radar; 1 microwave satellite-fed precision position fixing system.
Armament: Nil fitted.
Top speed: 19 knots.
Range: 10,000 nautical miles at 18 knots.
Programme: Completed in 1973, this vessel, the former MV *Grey Master*, was chartered by the UK Ministry of Defence in February 1983. After a brief refit, carried out in Falmouth, the ship was renamed RFA *Sir Caradoc* (L3522) and entered Royal Fleet Auxiliary service towards the end of March 1983.
Notes: Chartered by the UK Ministry of Defence to help fill the gap left by the loss of RFA *Sir Galahad* and the major damage to RFA *Sir Tristram* (see 'Sir Bedivere' class), this

former merchant Roll-on/Roll-off (Ro-Ro) vehicle ferry operates a regular military vehicle and stores service for British forces in West Germany, plying between Marchwood and Amsterdam.

Sir Lamorak Type Support Ships

Role: Logistic support.
Builder: Ankerlokken, Norway.
User: Royal Fleet Auxiliary.
Basic data: 5230 tons full displacement; 355.3ft (108.3m) overall length; 69.0ft (21.04m) maximum beam.
Crew: 24.
Propulsion: 2 Lindholmen-Pielstick 8 PC 21 diesels (total 8000bhp); 2 controllable-pitch propellers.
Sensors: 1 Racal Decca TM1226 sea search and navigational radar; 1 microwave satellite-fed precision position fixing system.
Armament: Nil fitted.
Top speed: 18 knots.
Range: 8500 nautical miles at 16 knots.
Programme: Completed in 1972, the former MV *Lakespan Ontario* was chartered by the UK Ministry of Defence in February 1983 and after a short refit on the Clyde, entered service as RFA *Sir Lamorak* (L3532) in late March 1983.
Notes: This former merchant Roll-on, Roll-off (Ro-Ro) ferry was chartered, along with RFA *Sir Caradoc*, to fill the gap left by the loss of *Sir Galahad* and the major damage sustained by RFA *Sir Tristram* (refer to 'Sir Bedivere' class entry).

Sri Indera Sakti Class Support Ships

Role: Multi-purpose fleet support.
Builder: Bremer Vulkan, Federal Germany.
User: Malaysian Navy.
Basic data: 4300 tons full displacement; 328.1ft (100.0m) overall length; 49.2ft (15.0m) maximum beam.
Crew: Up to 215 (140 normally).
Propulsion: 2 Deutz S/BMV6 540 diesels (total 5986bhp); 2 propellers.
Sensors: 1 low level air and sea search radar; 1 navigational radar.
Armament: 1 single 40mm anti-aircraft gun; provision for 100mm gun.
Top speed: 20 knots.
Range: 7000 nautical miles at 16 knots.
Programme: The lead ship of this three-ship class, *Sri Indera Sakti* (A1503) was ordered in October 1979, laid down in February 1980, launched in July 1980 and delivered in October 1980. A follow-on order for a further example of this class was reportedly placed by Malaysia in February 1981. The ship *Mahawanga* (A1504) was completed in 1983. The status of the third ship was unknown at press time.
Notes: An extremely interesting and, in many ways, innovative design, this Bremer Vulkan developed class is capable of fulfilling a quite surprising range of tasks, stretching from acting as a task force command ship, through being a replenisher/tender for a fast attack craft squadron, to serving as the primary logistic support for an amphibious task group. Capable of carrying up to 1800 tons of cargo, these vessels have a vehicle bay aft, accessible by ramp from either port or starboard side of the stern section. Up to 10 standard 20ft containers can be accommodated on the maindeck amidships, handled by the prominent 15-ton lift derrick positioned forward of the funnel. The area aft of the rectilinear sectioned funnel has been reinforced to permit the installation of a helipad for up to Lynx-sized helicopters. Provision for a single 100mm gun mount is carried forward of the ship's bridge

Sir Caradoc (*L3522*): note sterngate, 1983.

RFA Sir Lamorak (L3532), showing her twin, flank-mounted funnels, so positioned to allow clear central deck areas at all levels.

The distinctly commercial-looking and as yet unarmed Sri Indera Sakti (*A1503*) *en route to Malaysia, October 1980.*

but the ship had no gun fitted when it left the constructor's yards.

Ingul Class Support Ships

Role: Salvage and rescue.
Builder: Admiralty Shipyard, USSR.
User: Soviet Navy.
Basic data: 4050 tons full displacement; 304.5ft (92.8m) overall length; 50.5ft (15.4m) maximum beam.
Crew: 120.
Propulsion: 2 Type 58D-4R diesels (total 9000bhp); 2 propellers.
Sensors: 2 sea search and navigational radars; 2 separate IFF radars.

Pamir, one of two Soviet Navy-operated 'Ingul' class salvage tugs.

Armament: No fixed armament installed.
Top speed: 20 knots.
Range: 9000 nautical miles at 18.5 knots.
Programme: This two-ship Soviet Navy class comprises: *Mashuk* and *Pamir*, another two of this class being operated by the Soviet merchant marine. Both of the Soviet Navy ships entered service during the mid-1970s.
Notes: Somewhat larger and heavier than the near contemporary US Navy's 'Edenton' class ocean-going salvage ships, the 'Ingul' class carries a comprehensive fit of heavy-duty pumping equipment, personnel rescue systems and fire fighting gear. Unlike the 'Edenton' class vessels, the 'Ingul' class ships carry little specific submarine rescue equipment, this task being met by the Soviet Navy's 10,000 ton full displacement Pioneer 'Moskvyy' class, of which there are two examples.

Primor'ye Class Support Ships

Role: Intelligence gathering.
Builder: Unidentified, USSR.
User: Soviet Navy.
Basic data: 3700 tons full displacement; 277.9ft (84.7m) overall length; 45.9ft (14.0m) maximum beam.
Crew: 100.
Propulsion: 2 diesels (total 1000bhp); 1 propeller.
Sensors: 2 sea search and navigational radars, plus an extensive set of electronic signal receivers covering a very broad frequency spectrum from low frequency communications to microwave radar transmissions.
Armament: None fixed, but ships are reported to carry shoulder-fired SA-N-7 'Grail' point air defence missile launchers.
Top speed: 12 knots.

A 'Primor'ye' class intelligence gatherer of the Soviet Navy.

Endurance: Over 10,000 nautical miles.
Programme: This six-ship class entered service with the Soviet Fleet during the early part of the 1970s and comprises of *Primor'ye*, *Krym*, *Kavkaz*, *Zaporozh'ye*, *Zakarpat'ye* and *Zabaykal'ye*.
Notes: A derivative of the 'Mayakovsky' class stern-haul factory trawlers, the 'Primor'ye' class vessels have been widely deployed to monitor naval events of interest as far afield as the North Pacific to the Falklands. The shoulder-fired 'Grail' missile has a maximum range of 5.4 nautical miles (10km) against low flying targets. Interestingly, the Soviet Navy appears to place far more emphasis upon the task of gathering electronic intelligence than the navies of the West, the Soviets having more than 50 of these so-called 'spy ships', headed by the new, larger than 'Primor'ye' class 4500 ton full displacement 'Bal'zam' class vessels.

Edenton Class Support Ships

Role: Salvage and rescue.
Builder: Brooke Marine, UK.
User: US Navy.
Basic data: 3117 tons full displacement; 287.7ft (86.1m) overall length; 50ft (15.2m) maximum beam.
Crew: 103.
Propulsion: 4 Paxman 12 YLCM diesels (total 6000bhp); 2 propellers, plus bow thruster.
Sensors: 1 SPS-53 sea search and navigational radar.
Armament: 2 single 20mm anti-aircraft guns.
Top speed: 16 knots.
Range: 12,000 nautical miles at 12 knots.
Programme: The first of this three-ship class was ordered in 1966, to be followed by contracts for the second and third vessels in 1967. The three ships, USS *Edenton* (ATS1), USS *Beaufort* (ATS2) and USS *Brunswick* (ATS3) entered service with the US Navy in January 1971, January 1972 and December 1972.
Notes: These powerful British-built ocean-going tugs can tow ships of over 50,000 tons displacement. The 'Edenton' class also carry the specialised equipment required for rescue and salvage diving operations associated with submarine recovery. To support such operations, the 'Edentons' carry high capacity compressed-air pumping equipment and hoisting gear, along with other facilities that enable divers to work at depths of up to 850ft below the surface. The ships carry two heavy duty cranes; a 10 ton forward and a 20 ton aft. The ships' bow thrusters aid precise positioning.

Anteo Type Support Ship

Role: Seabed rescue and salvage.
Builder: C.N. Breda, Italy.
User: Italian Navy.
Basic data: 3000 tons full displacement; 322.8ft (98.4m) overall length; 51.8ft (15.8m) maximum beam.
Crew: 130.
Propulsion: 3 GMT a230 12V diesels (total 12,150bhp) driving a single double-induction DC electric motor (5360shp); 1 propeller, plus 1 bow thruster.
Sensors: 1 Decca TM1226 navigational radar, plus high precision location-fixing systems and sonars.
Armament: Helipad for Agusta-Bell AB 212 helicopter; 2 single 20mm anti-aircraft guns.
Top speed: 18.3 knots.
Range: 4000 nautical miles at 14 knots.
Programme: Ordered in 1976, the *Anteo* (A5309) was laid down in 1977, launched in November 1978 and entered service in July 1980.
Notes: A smaller and, in some areas, less capable seabed

The British-built USS Edenton *(ATS1) ocean-going tug.*

rescue and recovery ship than the Royal Navy's HMS *Challenger*, the *Anteo*, nonetheless, is very well suited for Mediterranean operations. Amongst the equipment carried aboard is a 27-ton manned mini-submarine, capable of 4 knot speed and diving to depths of 1970ft (600m), along with a McCann diving bell, cleared for operations down to 492ft (150m). For operations in the case of a surface emergency, the ship carries four high pressure fire-fighting hoses.

The Italian Navy submarine rescue ship Anteo

Zinnia Type Support Ship

Zinnia *(A961) minehunter support. Belgium's largest naval vessel.*

Role: Minehunter tender.
Builder: Cockerill, Belgium.
User: Royal Belgian Navy.
Basic data: 2685 tons full displacement; 326.4ft (99.5m) overall length; 45.9ft (14.0m) maximum beam.
Crew: 123.
Propulsion: 2 Cockerill-Ougree V12 TR240 CO diesels (tota 5000bhp); 1 controllable-pitch propeller.
Sensors: 1 Decca 1216A sea search and navigational radar.
Armament: 1 Alouette III helicopter; 3 single 40mm Bofors anti-aircraft guns.
Top speed: 18 knots.
Range: 14,000 nautical miles at 12.5 knots.
Programme: Laid down in November 1966, the sole of type *Zinnia* (A961) was launched in May 1967 and entered service in early September 1967.
Notes: Designed expressly to act as a mine

KNM Horten *(A530) acting as tender to a mix of fast attack craft, comprising pairs of 'Snogg' (nearest ship) and 'Storm' classes, along with HMS* Cutlass *(P274) furthest away.*

countermeasures vessel support ship, *Zinnia* makes an interesting comparison with the contemporary HMS *Abdiel* and the more recent KNM *Horten*, both of which are multi-role ships. This said, it is interesting to note that *Zinnia* incorporates a telescoping helicopter hangar, similar to that subsequently adopted for such as the 'Lupo' class frigates. *Zinnia* is unique amongst Belgian warships in her ability to operate a helicopter.

Horten Type Support Ship

Role: Transport/tender.
Builder: Horton Shipyard, Norway.
User: Royal Norwegian Navy.

LNS Zeltin *(A711) showing its aft docking section.*

Basic data: 2500 tons full displacement; 285.4ft (87.0m) overall length; 44.9ft (13.7m) maximum beam.
Crew: 86.
Propulsion: 2 Wichman 7AX diesels (total 4200bhp); 2 propellers; 1 bow thruster.
Sensors: 2 Decca 1226 sea search and navigational radars.
Armament: 1 Westland Lynx helicopter; 2 single 40mm Bofors anti-aircraft guns.
Top speed: 16.5 knots.
Range: Over 3500 nautical miles at 12 knots.
Programme: Ordered at the end of March 1976, KNM *Horten* (A530) was laid down in late January 1977, launched in August 1977 and entered service in early June 1978.
Notes: Typical of the modern multi-purpose naval design, KNM *Horten* has a rather stark, tall, rectangular superstructure, topped by squat, staggered, side-mounted funnels. Although primarily designed as a support tender for the Royal Norwegian Navy's numerous submarines and fast attack craft, *Horten* can double as a troop and equipment transport, having accommodation for a further 190 personnel in addition to the normal ship's complement.

Zeltin Support Ships

Role: Maintenance and repair.
Builder: Vosper Thornycroft, UK.
User: Libyan Navy.
Basic data: 2470 tons full displacement; 324.0ft (98.75m) overall length; 48ft (14.6m) maximum beam.
Crew: 104.
Propulsion: 2 Paxman 16YSCM Ventura diesels (total 3500bhp); 2 propellers.
Sensors: 1 Decca 707 sea search and navigational radar.
Armament: 2 single 40mm Bofors anti-aircraft guns.
Top speed: 15 knots.
Range: 3000 nautical miles at 14 knots.
Programme: This sole ship LNS *Zeltin* (A711) was laid

down during 1967, launched in February 1968 and entered service in January 1969.

Notes: The primary function of this purpose-built ship is to provide a floating maintenance and repair base for the Libyan Navy's force of fast attack craft. The *Zeltin*'s whole aft section comprises a dock and stern gate through which can be sailed a craft of up to 120ft (36.6m) overall length and up to 30ft (9.1m) in beam, and to meet this requirement the ship can be ballasted down in the water very much as with submarines and dock landing ships. *Zeltin*'s dock, which measures 128ft (39m) by 33ft (10m), has a series of specially profiled blocks upon which the craft lies during its stay abroad. The ship also contains extensive accommodation for both fuel and other stores with which to support a fast attack flotilla at sea, including up to 200 tons of fuel out of the ship's total of 380 tons when operating out to 3000 nautical miles at 14 knots.

Cormorant Type Support Ship

Role: Deep submergence vehicle research.
Builder: Marelli, Italy.
User: Canadian Navy.
Basic data: 2350 tons full displacement; 245.8ft (74.6m) overall length; 39.0ft (11.9m) maximum beam.
Crew: 26.
Propulsion: 3 Marelli-Deutz ACR 12456 CV diesels/electric drive (2100shp); 1 controllable-pitch propeller.
Sensors: 2 Decca TM 1229 sea search and navigational radars; suite of specialised echo sounders and sonar systems.
Armament: None fitted.
Top speed: 15 knots.
Range: 13,000 nautical miles at 12 knots.
Programme: Built in Italy as the stern-haul trawler *Aspa Quarto* in 1971, the vessel was purchased by the Canadian Government in 1975 and put through a fairly major conversion to become HMCS *Cormorant* (A20), which entered service in November 1978.
Notes: Employed as an experimental vessel from which to launch both manned submersibles and divers, *Cormorant* carries a large structure just aft of amidships used to house submersibles. For launching such vessels, the submersible is rolled aft, attached to the stern-mounted 'A' frame, lifted and swung out aft of the ship's stern.

Piast Class Support Ships

Role: Salvage and rescue.
Builder: Polnocny Shipyard, Poland.
User: Navies of Poland and East Germany.
Basic data: 1750 tons full displacement; 240.2ft (73.2m) overall length; 35.4ft (10.8m) maximum beam.
Crew: 85.
Propulsion: 2 Cegielski-Sulzer 6TD48 diesels (total 3600bhp); 2 controllable-pitch propellers.
Sensors: 2 RN-231 sea search and navigational radars.
Armament: None fitted, but provision to mount 4 twin 25mm anti-aircraft guns.
Top speed: 16.5 knots.
Range: 3000 nautical miles at 12 knots.
Programme: This three-ship class comprises: *Piast* and *Lech* operated by the Polish Navy, along with the East German Navy's *Otto Von Guericke* (A46). The two Polish ships are reported to have entered service in the 1974/75 period, while the East German vessel joined the fleet in early 1978.
Notes: A derivative of the Soviet-developed 'Moma' class survey and electronic intelligence gathering ships, the 'Piast' class carries a submarine rescue diving bell

Canada's HMCS Cormorant *(A20) deep submergence experimental ship.*

A Polish Navy 'Piast' class salvage vessel photographed by the Royal Air Force in early May 1977.

deployed over the portside of the ship using a gantry that swings the bell out and clear of the vessel's flank just forward of the wheelhouse. The ships carry extensive heavy duty pumping and fire fighting equipment.

Spasilac Class Support Ships

Role: Subsea rescue and salvage.
Builder: Tito Shipyards, Yugoslavia.
Users: Navies of Yugoslavia and Iraq.
Basic data: 1590 tons full displacement; 183ft (55.5m) overall length; 40ft (12.0m) maximum beam.
Crew: 53 to 72.
Propulsion: 2 unidentified diesels (total 4340bhp); 2 controllable-pitch propellers; separate diesel-powered bow thruster.
Sensors: 1 Decca sea search and navigational radar.
Armament: 2 four-barrelled 20mm M75 and 2 single 20mm M71 anti-aircraft guns.
Top speed: 13.4 knots.
Range: 4000 nautical miles at 13.4 knots.
Programme: The first of this two-vessel class was delivered to the Yugoslavian Navy as *Spasilac* (PS12) in September 1976. The second ship, *Aka* (A51), was supplied to the Iraqi Navy during 1978.
Notes: Similar in its external appearance to an off-shore oil rig supply ship with the hull and main superstructure

The Yugoslavian Navy's latest submarine rescue and salvage vessel Spasilac (PS12).

Orion (A201), essentially a mobile electronic tracking/listening station and early warning command post.

The US Navy's Deep Submergence Rescue Vehicle Avalon (DSRV2), seen here cradled aboard HMS Repulse (S23) during 1980 Royal Navy trials in which submariners were successfully transferred underwater from HMS Odin (S10) to Repulse.

made of steel, only the wheelhouse employs light alloy in its construction. For submariner rescue, the vessel carries a small rescue submersible, diving bell and underwater cutting equipment. The vessel has a three-sectioned decompression chamber and can support diver operations to a depth of 985ft (300m). These ships can also transport up to 250 tons of deck cargo, giving them a useful secondary role as transports.

Orion Type Support Ship

Role: Intelligence gathering.
Builder: Karlskronevarvet, Sweden.
User: Royal Swedish Navy.
Basic data: 1340 tons full displacement; 201.0ft (61.25m) overall length; 38.4ft (11.7m) maximum beam.
Crew: 35.
Propulsion: 2 Hedemora V8A/135 diesels (total 1840bhp); 1 controllable-pitch propeller.
Sensors: 1 long-range air search and height finder (3-D) radar; 1 sea search and navigational radar; comprehensive suite of missile/aircraft tracking radar and receivers covering from very low frequencies to microwave.
Armament: None fitted.
Top speed: 12.5 knots.
Range: 1800 nautical miles of 10 knots.
Programme: The sole of type *Orion* (A201) was ordered in June 1981, laid down in August 1982 and launched in November 1983. Completed in the summer of 1984, the ship is now in service with the Royal Swedish Navy.
Notes: Literally bristling with electronic intelligence (ELINT)—gathering sensors, *Orion* would, in peacetime, be used to glean information on a variety of topics, ranging from monitoring Warsaw Pact naval communications around the Baltic area to tracking military aircraft and the periodic missile test firing. In times of crisis, *Orion* would act as part of the Swedish early warning network, along with serving as a floating tactical command, control and communications post.

Mystic Class Support Ships

Role: Deep-going submarine crew rescue.
Builder: Lockheed Missile & Space Company Inc, USA.
User: US Navy.
Basic data: 37.0 tons dived displacement; 49.3ft (15.0m) overall length; 8.1ft (2.47m) maximum beam.
Crew: 3.
Propulsion: Battery-powered DC electric motor (15shp) driving 1 ducted propeller, plus 4 DC electric motors (total 30shp) each driving a thruster (2 vertical, 2 horizontal).
Sensors: Active and passive sonars; low light level television and special optical sighting devices for DSRV-to-submarine lock docking.
Armament: Nil fitted.
Top speed: 4.5 knots dived.
Endurance: 5 hours at 4 knots dived.
Programme: The US Navy awarded Lockheed a 1966 contract to design and develop the Deep Submergence Rescue Vehicle (DSRV). As initially envisaged, the class was to comprise of 12 vehicles, each capable of accommodating up to 12 survivors. However, in the event only two larger 24 survivor-carrying boats were to be built: *Mystic* (DSRV1) and *Avalon* (DSRV2). Launched in January 1970 and May 1971, the two vehicles were completed in August 1971 and July 1972, respectively, but remained in development status until November 1977 and January 1978.
Notes: The subjects of a protracted and extremely costly development programme, reported to have cost in excess of $220 million, each of the vehicles can carry up to 24 survivors, rescued from waters as deep as 5000ft (1524m). To withstand such pressures, the vessel's primary structure comprises of three interconnected 7.5ft (2.3m) diameter steel spheres, all enclosed within a glass-reinforced plastic outer hull. The forward inner sphere houses the vehicle's two pilots, their controls and other equipment, while the centre sphere contains the third crewmember-operated air lock. All survivors are accommodated within the centre and aft spheres. Each DSRV is capable of being airlifted aboard a Lockheed C-141 Starlifter, with another two C-141 being required to fly the necessary support equipment. Alternatively, the DSRV can be shipped aboard a subsea rescue ship or transported 'piggy-back' by submarine at speeds of up to 15 knots dived.

Landing craft

Barbe Class Landing Craft

Role: Amphibious warfare.
Builder: Howaldtswerke, Federal Germany.
User: Federal German Navy.
Basic data: 403 tons full displacement; 131.4ft (44.0m) overall length; 28.9ft (8.8m) maximum beam.
Crew: 17.
Propulsion: 2 MWM diesels (total 1200bhp); 2 propellers.
Sensors: 1 Kelvin Hughes 14/9 sea search and navigational radar.
Armament: 1 twin 20mm Rheinmetall anti-aircraft gun.
Top speed: 11 knots loaded.
Range: 1200 nautical miles at 11 knots.
Programme: This 22-craft class comprises: *L760* through *L769* and *L788* through *L799*. Known as Type 520, or 'Barbe' class vessels, all units entering service between November 1965 and September 1966.
Notes: Based on the US Navy's LCU1646 class design, each of these craft can carry up to 141 tons of cargo in normal operation, but can carry up to 237 tons.

Plotze (L763), a Federal German 'Barbe' or Type 520 landing craft.

Arromanches Class Landing Craft

Role: Amphibious warfare.
Builder: Brooke Marine, UK.
User: British Army.
Basic data: 282 tons full displacement; 109.1ft (33.26m) overall length; 27.2ft (8.3m) maximum beam.
Crew: 6.
Propulsion: 2 Dorman 8JTCWM diesels (total 600bhp); 2 propellers.
Sensors: 1 Seaveyor sea search and navigational radar; 1 Kelvin Hughes MS 45 echo sounder.
Armament: Nil.
Top speed: 9.5 knots loaded; 10 knots unloaded.
Range: Limited.
Programme: Ordered for use with the British Army in March 1980, this currently two-boat class comprises *Arromanches* (L105) and *Antwerp* (L106), both of which were delivered during August 1981.
Notes: Unglamorous as these vessels may appear, their contribution in support of amphibious landings, such as that carried out by British forces to repossess the Falkland Islands, is vital. Carried as deck cargo to the theatre of action, these ramped landing craft (their official designation is Ramped Craft Landing, or RCL), are used to shuttle up to 96 tons of heavy vehicles or other necessary supplies ashore. Equipped with one heavy-duty kedge winch and two ramp winches, these vessels are manned by two NCOs and four soldiers.

The British Army's Arromanches (L105), 1981.

Aist Class Landing Craft

Role: Amphibious warfare.
Builder: Unknown, USSR.
User: Soviet Navy.
Basic data: 220 tons full displacement; 156.8ft (47.8m) overall length; 57.4ft (17.5m) maximum beam.
Crew: 8–10.
Propulsion: 4 gas turbine/turboprops (total about 16,000shp); 2 lift fans (driven from the gas turbines).
Sensors: 1 surface search and navigational radar; 1 fire control radar for 30mm guns; 3 IFF.
Armament: 2 twin 30mm anti-aircraft guns mounted side-by-side atop the bow section.

An 'Aist' class air cushion landing craft viewed from abeam, with its two twin fully automatic anti-aircraft guns clearly visible on the bow section.

Top speed: 65 knots.
Range: Not known.
Programme: The 'Aist' class air cushion landing craft entered service with the Soviet Navy at the beginning of the 1970s since when the type is reported to have remained in production at an increasing rate.
Notes: The 'Aist' class is the largest of three known Soviet

classes of air cushion landing craft (the other types being the 'Lebed' class and the even smaller 'Gus' class of 27 tons full displacement. The Soviet Navy is currently by far the world's largest single user of military air cushion vehicles, with the US Navy having relatively recently also having opted to procure this type of vehicle, first developed in Britain during the late 1950s. Besides its obvious speed advantage, the air cushion craft has the equally important advantage of being truly amphibious in itself and, hence, capable of continuing up over the beach area to disembark its troop and equipment load away from the natural 'killing ground' of a shoreline. The 'Aist' class can carry up to four light tanks and 150 troops, or one medium-sized tank plus 220 troops.

Bell Aerospace LCAC Class Landing Craft

An artist's impression of an LCAC departing USS Whidbey Island.

Role: Amphibious warfare.
Builder: Bell Aerospace/Halter, USA.
User: US Marine Corps.
Basic data: 147.3 tons full displacement; 87.0ft (26.5m) overall length (operating); 47.0ft (14.3m) maximum beam.
Crew: 3.
Propulsion: 4 AVCO-Lycoming TF40B gas turbines (total 17,600shp) driving 2 lift fans and 2 ducted propulsion propellers.
Sensors: 1 Litton LN-66 sea search and navigational radar.
Armament: None fitted on standard assault craft variant.
Top speed: 55 knots (loaded).
Range: 200 nautical miles at 50 knots.
Programme: In 1969, the US navy initiated the Amphibious Assault Landing Craft (AALC) programme, which led to the evaluation of several competitive designs. Amongst these craft was Bell Aerospace's Jeff (B) vehicle, which commenced a protracted period of service testing and evaluation in 1976. In June 1980, the US Navy requested bids for the Landing Craft Air Cushion (LCAC) production programme follow-on in the AALC, Bell Aerospace being selected as the design winner and given a full-scale development contract for six craft in June 1981. All six pilot production vehicles are to be delivered between 1984 and 1986. Over 100 LCACs are planned to be procured with large-scale production, reported to be 12 per year, commencing in 1985, with 66 scheduled to have been delivered by 1991.
Notes: Capable of carrying 53.6 tons (54,663kg) of cargo, or 70 tons (71,123kg) in overload conditions, the LCAC

can lift a main battle tank or a mix of lighter vehicles on its central deck section, plus up to 16 marines in portside accommodation. Bell Aerospace have enjoyed a long collaborative association with the British Hovercraft Corporation, some of whose designs have been licence-built by Bell. British Hovercraft have aided in the design of the LCAC's hull skirts and will act as a production programme sub-contractor.

Wellington Class Landing Craft

Role: Amphibious warfare.
Builder: British Hovercraft Corporation, UK.
Users: Royal Navy (1) and Iranian Navy (6).
Basic data: 55 tons full displacement; 78.3ft (23.9m) overall length; 45.5ft (13.9m) maximum beam.
Crew: 2 or 3.
Propulsion: 1 Rolls-Royce Proteus ISM549 (4250shp) or Gnome ISM541 (4750shp) gas turbine driving 1 lift fan and 1 propulsion propeller.
Sensors: 1 Decca sea search and navigational radar.
Armament: Provision for 2 anti-ship missiles, plus 1 twin 30mm anti-aircraft gun on fast attack craft variant.
Top speed: 60 knots.
Range: 450 nautical miles at 33.4 knots.
Programme: Designed and developed during the latter half of the 1960s, the prototype BH 7 'Wellington' class hovercraft made its maiden sortie in February 1970, being delivered to the Royal Navy as *P235* in April 1970. The first of six Iranian Navy craft, *LCH101*, was delivered later in 1970, delivery of three more assault craft, *LCH 102, 103* and *104* were followed by two combat craft, *P105* and *106*; Iranian deliveries being completed in 1975.
Notes: fitted with a clamshell bow door, the BH 7 carries up to a maximum of 29 tons disposable load, which can comprise up to 150 troops and military vehicles. The craft's rough water capability includes an ability to operate in wave heights of up to 14.8ft (4.5m) and mean wind speeds of 40 knots.

LCH101, the lead vessel of this Iranian Navy six-craft class.

Type 601 Landing Craft

Role: Amphibious warfare.
Builders: Various, Yugoslavia.
User: Yugoslavian Navy.
Basic data: 38 tons full displacement; 69.9ft (21.3m) overall length; 15.9ft (4.84m) maximum beam.

Crew: 7.
Propulsion: 1 MTU 12V 331 TC81 diesel (1360bhp); 1 propeller.
Sensors: 1 Decca RM 1216A sea search and navigational radar.
Armament: 1 single 20mm M71 anti-aircraft gun (720 ready-to-fire rounds).
Top speed: 24 knots.
Range: 320 nautical miles at 22 knots.
Programme: A known class of 12 that entered service with the Yugoslavian Navy during the 1976/77 period.
Notes: With its hull and superstructure made from glass-reinforced plastics, protected locally by armoured steel sheeting, the Type 601's overall lightweight structure provides the design with a very useful turn of speed. Capable of 24 knots when operated unloaded, the cruising range of the Type 601 is quoted by the constructors as being 400 nautical miles at 15 knots, indicating a performance more readily associated with a patrol boat than that of a landing craft. In terms of cargo, the Type 601 can carry up to 6 tons, which, in turn, translates into between 40 and 60 troops, or two jeeps, each with trailer, or one unloaded TAM 5000 heavy duty truck; all of which are embarked and disembarked through the craft's bow ramp.

The Yugoslavian-developed Type 601 is capable of a sustained 22 knots.

Winchester Class Landing Craft

Role: Amphibious warfare.
Builder: British Hovercraft Corporation, UK.
Users: Navies of Egypt (3), Iran (8), Iraq (6) and Saudi Arabia (16), plus numerous para-military and civilian operators.
Basic data: 16.7 tons full displacement; 60.0ft (18.3m) overall length; 28.0ft (8.5m) maximum beam.
Crew: 2.
Propulsion: 1 Rolls-Royce Gnome GN1301 gas turbine (1125shp), driving 1 lift fan and 1 propulsion propeller, except in the case of the Mk 6 which employs 2 propulsion propellers.
Sensors: 1 Decca sea search and navigational radar.
Armament: Provision to mount various weapons, ranging from 20mm to light machine guns.

Top speed: 60 knots.
Range: Around 120 nautical miles at 40 knots.
Programme: Developed from the SR N5 'Warden' class design, the first SR N6 'Winchester' class hovercraft made its debut in late 1967, this no longer operational example being delivered to the Royal Navy in December 1967. Iran was the first naval export customer, taking delivery of their first SR N6 in July 1968. In all, 33 naval models of the SR N6 had been sold to various Middle East customers by the end of 1983 comprising: eight for Iran (two Mk 3s and six Mk 4s), 16 for Saudi Arabia (eight Mk 1s and eight Mk 8s); six for Iraq (all Mk 6s) and three for Egypt (one Mk 1 and two Mk 2s). A further 51 SR N5 and N6s have been sold to para-military, customs and civilian users worldwide.
Notes: Capable of carrying up to 6 tons of stores, or a mix of stores and over 20 fully equipped troops, the SR N6 'Winchester' class has established itself as the best selling air cushion craft extant. Most examples of the 'Winchester' class employ a single propulsion propeller. However, a twin, side-by-side propeller arrangement, using power take-offs from the existing turbo-shaft to drive twin, transverse extension shafts, on the SR N6 Mk 6; a development that improves the craft's low-speed handling and reduces overall noise level.

One of 16 SR N6 'Winchester' class craft operated by the Royal Saudi Arabian Navy. A Mk 8 hovercraft is shown.

Survey ships

A stern aspect of HMNZS Monowai *(A06), showing her aft helipad and hanger.*

Monowai Type Survey Ship

Role: Hydrographic survey.
Builder: Grangemouth Dockyard, UK.
User: Royal New Zealand Navy.
Basic data: 4025 tons full displacement; 296.4ft (90.3m) overall length; 46.0ft (14.0m) maximum beam.
Crew: 126.
Propulsion: 2 Clark-Sulzer diesels (total 3640bhp); 2 controllable-pitch propellers; 1 bow thruster.
Sensors: 1 Decca sea search and navigational radar.
Armament: 1 Westland Wasp helicopter; 2 single 20mm anti-aircraft guns.
Top speed: 13.5 knots.
Range: 12,000 nautical miles at 13 knots.
Programme: HMNZS *Monowai* was launched in 1960 as the MV *Moana Roa* and served as a mixed passenger/cargo carrier until 1974. Converted to her present role by Scott Lithgow in Scotland, the *Monowai* entered service in her present form towards the close of 1977.
Notes: an extremely well-equipped ship in terms of the specialised requirement of precision position fixing and seabed scanning sensors, the *Monowai* had its light anti-aircraft armament fitted during 1980.

Tydeman Type Survey Ship

Role: Oceanographic research.
Builder: BV De Merwede, Netherlands.
User: Royal Netherlands Navy.
Basic data: 3000 tons full displacement; 295.8ft (90.15m) overall length; 47.2ft (14.4m) maximum beam.
Crew: 59.
Propulsion: 2 Stork-Werkspoor 8-FCHD-240 diesels (total 2800bhp) with electric drive to 1 propeller and 2 bow thrusters.
Sensors: 1 Decca TM 1226 sea search and navigational radar; 1 deep echo sounder; Omega and Satellite data link for precision position fixing.
Armament: Helipad and hangar for 1 Westland Wasp helicopter, but no shipboard armament carried.
Top speed: 15 knots.
Range: 15,700 nautical miles at 10 knots.
Programme: HMNLS *Tydeman* (A906) was laid down in April 1975, launched in December 1975 and entered service in November 1976.
Notes: Designed to carry out oceanographic and

The Royal Netherlands Navy oceanographic research ship, HMNLS Tydeman *(A906).*

meteorological research, HMNLS *Tydeman* is fitted with three similar diesel engines, any two, but not all three of which can be used to propel the ship at any given time; the other being used to provide ancillary power to the ship. The vessel has eight laboratories and carries 15 scientists in addition to the 59 crew required to operate the ship.

Hecla Class Survey Ships

Role: Hydrographic survey.
Builders: Yarrow and Robb Caledon, UK.
Users: Navies of UK and South Africa.
Basic data: 2750 tons full displacement; 260.0ft (79.25m) overall length; 49.0ft (14.9m) maximum beam.
Crew: Around 120.
Propulsion: 3 Paxman Ventura diesels (total 3840bhp) in Royal Navy ships, with a fourth Ventura fitted to South African ship (total 5120bhp), driving 2 electric motors; 1 controllable-pitch propeller.
Sensors: 1 Decca sea search and navigational radar; various sonar systems and precision position fixing equipment.
Armament: None fitted, but ships carry a helipad aft.
Top speed: 14.4 knots for Royal Navy ships; 16.6 knots (South Africa).
Range: 12,000 nautical miles at 12 knots.
Programme: This five-ship class comprises: HMS *Hecla* (A133), HMS *Hecate* (A137) and HMS *Hydra* (A144) along with the improved HMS *Herald* (A138) and South Africa's SAS *Protea* (A324). The initial three ships were all built by Yarrow, entering service between September 1965 and December 1966, while Robb Caledon built the fourth Royal Navy vessel, which entered service in October 1974. The sole South African ship was ordered in November 1969 and entered service in May 1972, having been built by Yarrow.
Notes: Designed for long duration voyaging in all weathers, these vessels have reinforced hulls that enable them to navigate through light ice. The Royal Navy ships carry Type 2004 hull-mounted, sidescanning active/passive sonar.

Quest Type Survey Ship

Role: Oceanographic research.
Builder: Burrard, Canada.
User: Canadian Navy.
Basic data: 2130 tons full displacement; 253.3ft (77.2m) overall length; 42.0ft (12.8m) maximum beam.
Crew: 37.
Propulsion: 2 Fairbanks-Morse 38D8 diesels/General Electric electric motor (2960shp); 2 propellers.
Sensors: 1 Decca 838 and 1 Decca 929 sea search and navigational radars.
Armament: None fitted.
Top speed: 15 knots.
Range: 10,000 nautical miles at 12 knots.
Programme: Ordered and laid down in 1967, HMCS *Quest* (A172) was launched in July 1968 and entered service in July 1969.
Notes: The larger of the two Canadian Navy operated oceanographic research vessels, *Quest* employs the same propulsive machinery as her sister, HMCS *Endeavour* (A171). *Quest* carries a clear upper deck area immediately aft of the ship's smack (combined mast/funnel structure), used for vertical replenishment from a hovering helicopter.

Naftlos Type Survey Ship

Role: Hydrographic survey.
Builder: Anastadiades, Greece.
User: Hellenic (Greek) Navy.
Basic data: 1480 tons full displacement; 207.0ft (63.1m) overall length; 38.1ft (11.6m) maximum beam.
Crew: 57.
Propulsion: 2 Burmeister & Wain SS28LH diesels (total 2640bhp); 2 propellers.
Sensors: 1 Decca sea search and navigational radar, plus unidentified precision position fixing systems, active sonar and echo sounder.
Armament: None fitted, but can operate helicopter from aft helipad.
Top speed: 15 knots.
Endurance: Over 4000 nautical miles.
Programme: The sole *Naftlos* (A478) was launched in November 1975 and entered service in April 1976.
Notes: Although primarily designed as a hydrographic survey ship, the large, forward deck-mounted derrick, with its associated loading platform suggests that the vessel could carry either a diving bell or mini-submersible, giving the ship a useful secondary role as a submarine rescue asset.

HMCS Quest *(A172), showing her combined funnel and mast structure.*

HMS Herald *(A138) photographed at the end of April 1982, when this 'Hecla' class ship was serving as a Falklands hospital ship.*

The Greek auxiliary, Naftlos *(A478) used for hydrographic work.*

Robert D Conrad Class Survey Ships

Role: Oceanographic research.
Builders: Various, USA.
Users: US Military Sea Lift Command; Brazilian and New Zealand navies.
Basic data: 1380 tons full displacement; 208.9ft (83.7m) overall length; 37.4ft (11.4m) maximum beam.
Crew: Around 26 + 16 scientists.
Propulsion: 2 Caterpillar Tractor D-378 diesels (total 1000bhp); 1 propeller, plus 175shp bow thruster.
Sensors: 1 RCA CRM-N1A sea search and navigational radar, plus precision position fixing systems and dedicated-to-task sonars.

Royal New Zealand Navy's HMNZS Tui (A2) modified for acoustic research.

Armament: None fitted.
Top speed: 13 knots.
Range: 12,000 nautical miles at 12 knots.
Programme: This nine-ship class comprises: *Robert D Conrad* (AGOR3), *James L Gillis* (AGOR4), *Lynch* (AGOR7), *Thomas G Thompson* (AGOR9), *De Steiguer* (AGOR12) and *Bartlett* (AGOR13), along with New Zealand's HMNZS *Tui* (A2) and Brazil's *Almirante Camara* (H41). All nine ships were delivered between November 1962 and April 1969 and are now operated by Military Sealift Command's civilian crews other than in the case of the two ships transferred to New Zealand and Brazil in 1970 and 1974, respectively.
Notes: While these ships vary in the detail of their superstructures, their disproportionately massive funnels stand out as a common characteristic; the size of these being dictated by the fact that they house a 620shp gas turbine, which is used to propel the ships at up to 6.6 knots during quiet running operations where the noise of the diesels could be detrimental to the task.

Bulldog Class Survey Ships

Role: Coastal hydrographic survey.
Builder: Brooke Marine, UK.
Users: Royal Navy, Nigerian Navy.
Basic data: 1080 tons full displacement; 189.3ft (57.7m) overall length; 37.4ft (11.4m) maximum beam.
Crew: 43.
Propulsion: 4 Lister Blackstone ERS8M diesels (total 2640bhp); 2 controllable-pitch propellers.
Sensors: 1 Decca TM626 navigational radar; 1 Decca Hi-

The Nigerian Navy's Lana (A498), built by Brooke Marine.

fix Type BM; 1 Kelvin Hughes Fisherman's Asdic Mk 11; 3 Kelvin Hughes MS26 echo sounders.
Equipment: 8.7m survey launch; 1.5 ton deck crane; 1 electronic Chernikeef log; 1 each heavy duty windlass and capstan.
Top speed: 15 knots.
Range: 4500 nautical miles at 12 knots.
Programme: Four Bulldog class vessels, HMS *Bulldog* (A317), HMS *Beagle* (A319), HMS *Fox* (A320) and HMS *Fawn* (A335), all entering service with the Royal Navy during 1968, commencing with *Bulldog* in March of that year. The Nigerian Government ordered a further example of this class in late 1973. This ship, NNS *Lana* (A498), laid down in April 1974 was launched in March 1976 and entered service in September 1976. An improved 'Bulldog' class, HMS *Roebuck* (A...), was ordered by the Royal Navy in May 1984.
Notes: although totally unarmed, these little ships carry out one of the most important, if unglamorous, peacetime naval tasks of all, namely, that of charting the ever-shifting contours of the seabed and its channels in coastal waters. In need of constant updating, such survey data are of vital importance to the conduct of safe maritime navigation worldwide.

Buykses Class Survey Ships

Role: Hydrographic survey.
Builder: Boele, Netherlands.
User: Royal Netherlands Navy.
Basic data: 1000 tons full displacement; 196.9ft (60.0m) overall length; 36.0ft (11.0m) maximum beam.
Crew: 43.
Propulsion: Any 2 of 3 diesels (total 1400bhp) powering an electric drive to 1 propeller.
Sensors: 1 Decca TM 1226 sea search and navigational radar; echo sounder; downward and side-scanning sonar systems; precision position fixing systems.
Armament: None fitted.
Top speed: 14 knots.
Range: 6000 nautical miles at 12 knots.
Programme: This two-ship class comprises: HMNLS *Buykses* (A904) and HMNLS *Blommendal* (A905). Both vessels were ordered in 1971, the lead ship *Buykses* being laid down in January 1972, launched in July 1972 and commissioned in March 1973, while the *Blommendal* was laid down in August 1972, launched in November 1972 and entered service in May 1973.
Notes: Employed primarily on North Sea hydrographic survey work, including the location and inspection of seabed wrecks. The ships are equipped with the Hydraut automated hydrographic survey system that records depth data on to magnetic tape, along with data on the ship's current position, time and data.

HMNLS Blommendal (A905), the second of this two-ship class operated by the Royal Netherlands Navy, photographed in 1980.

Naval aircraft

Airborne warning

Grumman E-2 Hawkeye Airborne Warning and Control

Type and role: 5-crew, twin turboprop engined, carrier-going tactical airborne early warning, command and control aircraft.
Makers: Grumman Aerospace Corporation, Bethpage, Long Island, USA.
Users: US Navy and the air forces of Egypt, Israel, Japan and Singapore.
Engines: 2 General Electric T56A-425 turboprop (total 9820shp) each driving 2 four-bladed, reversible-pitch fibre-glass propellers.
Dimensions: 57.6ft (17.5m) overall length; 80.6ft (24.6m) wingspan; 29.3ft (8.9m) wingspan folded; 700sq ft (65.03m²) wing area.
Weights: 37,945lb (17,212kg) empty; 51,817lb (23,503kg) maximum gross.
Performance: 325 knots/602km/h at 16,000ft/4877m maximum speed; 269 knots/498km/km/h at 27,000ft/8230m optimum cruise speed; 30,800ft/9388m service ceiling; 6.1 hours maximum endurance.
Armament: None fitted.
Programme: A direct fruit of the 1956 initiated US Navy requirement to develop its fully three-dimensional Naval Tactical Data System, Grumman won an industry-wide design competition for what was to emerge as the Hawkeye in March 1957, the prototype aircraft making its maiden flight in October 1960. Fifty-nine E-2A Hawkeyes were to be built, the first deployment being made in January 1964. Subsequently, 46 E-2As were modified to E-2B standard with much improved electronic data-processing capability. In 1968, the US Navy set out an operational requirement for a Hawkeye development that would have a much enhanced detection capability over land as well as water. This led to the E-2C, first flown in January 1971 and initially deployed in September 1974. Over 80 of the planned 101 E-2Cs earmarked for the US Navy had been delivered by early 1985. In late 1975, Israel ordered four E-2Cs, the first of which was delivered in 1977, followed by the remaining three in 1978. Japan placed its first order for eight in 1979, all of which will have been delivered between 1982 and 1984. Deliveries of four Egyptian E-2Cs, ordered at the end of 1982 (a fifth has been subsequently added), will commence in 1985. Singapore became the fifth customer, in January 1984, when it ordered four.
Notes: While being somewhat overshadowed in more recent years by the emergence of the much larger (and more expensive) Boeing E-3 Sentinel and British Aerospace Nimrod AEW 3, the E-2C Hawkeye's ability to 'see' great distances and then direct the appropriate responses has been more than borne out in its selection by both Israel and Japan: two customers renowned for their insistence on buying the best-value-for-money products available. Packed with a mass of passive electronic sensors as well as its vast radomed APS-125 primary radar system, all supported by advanced digital electronic data-processing, the E-2C can detect and track more than 600 small surface craft, vehicle or aircraft targets out to ranges of around 200 nautical miles (371km) even when operating in a hostile electronics warfare environment. Simultaneously, the E-2C can control over 40 friendly aircraft involved in interception or strike missions through its onboard data-link system, which also automatically updates the developing tactical situation to friendly surface ships in the area. Beyond this, such is the power of the E-2C's onboard data-processing capability, that the aircraft can actually compute the optimum means of vectoring friendly aircraft to their targets by the most economic and/or safe routing to avoid, for example, enemy surface-to-air missile (SAM) sites.

A characteristic view of Grumman's E-2C Hawkeye with its huge pylon-mounted dish radome.

Anti-submarine aircraft

An II-38 'May', the Soviet's counterpart to Lockheed's P-3 Orion and the British Aerospace Nimrod MR2.

Ilyushin IL-38 'May' Anti-Submarine Aircraft

Type and role: 12-crew, 4 turboprop engined, long-range ocean patrol and anti-submarine aircraft.
Maker: Ilyushin, USSR.
Users: Soviet Naval Aviation and Indian Navy.
Engines: 4 Ivchenko AM-20M turboprops (total 17,000shp) each driving a 4-bladed, reversible-pitch propeller.
Dimensions: 131.0ft (39.92m) overall length; 122.7ft (37.40m) wingspan; 1507sq ft (140.0m²) wing area.
Weights: 80,028lb (36,300kg) empty; 130,073lb (59,000kg) normal gross; 140,000lb (63,500kg) maximum gross.
Performance: 347 knots/643km/h at 14,764ft/4500m maximum speed; 321 knots/595km/h at 26,247ft/8000m economic cruise speed; 1549 nautical miles/2870km radius of action with 4409lb/2000kg warload.
Armament: Up to 4409lb (2000kg) of anti-submarine torpedoes, depth charges, mines and sonobuoys.
Programme: An aerodynamic prototype of the Il-38 is believed to have first flown in late 1965/early 1966, followed by the first system-equipped full-scale development aircraft in mid-1967. The aircraft was operationally deployed in 1968. Less than 100 Il-38s are believed to have been built, with production being reportedly completed during the latter half of the 1970s. Three refurbished ex-Soviet Il-38s were delivered to the Indian Navy during the 1977/1978 period.
Notes: In many ways directly comparable to the US Navy's P-3 Orion, the Il-38 'May' uses the same basic airframe/engine combination as that of the late 1950s Ilyushin Il-18 airliner. Unlike the Lockheed P-3, however, the Ilyushin design team chose to house all weaponry internally within a three-section weapons bay that accounts for almost 45 per cent of the aircraft's length, already extended to house a rear-mounted magnetic anomaly detection (MAD) boom. Again, unlike the P-3, the Il-38 carries its air-to-surface search radar in a forward, ventrally-mounted radome.

Lockheed P-3 Orion Anti-Submarine Aircraft

Type and role: 10-crew, 4 turboprop-engined long-range maritime patrol and anti-submarine warfare aircraft.
Maker: Lockheed-California Company, Burbank, California, USA, plus 42 Japanese-built aircraft manufactured under an industrial consortium led by Kawasaki Heavy Industries.
Users: Navies of the US and Netherlands, plus air forces of Australia, Canada, Iran, Japan, New Zealand, Norway and Spain (3 ex-US Navy P-3As).
Engines: 4 Allison T56A-114 turboprops (total 19,640shp) driving 4 four-bladed, reversible-pitch propellers.
Dimensions: 116.8ft (35.6m) overall length; 99.7ft (30.4m) wingspan; 1300sq ft (120.8m²) wing area.
Weights: 61,491lb (27,892kg) empty; 135,000lb (61,235kg) normal gross; 142,000lb (64,410kg) maximum gross.
Performance: 411 knots/761km/h at 15,000ft/4572m maximum speed; 206 knots/381km/h normal patrol speed at 1500ft/457m; 1346 nautical miles/2494km tactical radius of action including 3 hours patrolling.
Armament: Up to 19,252lb (8733kg) of weapons or sensors, including air-droppable lightweight, homing anti-submarine torpedoes, depth charges, sonobuoys, mines and Harpoon anti-ship missiles.
Programme: In August 1957, the US Navy issued a request for a Lockheed P-2 Neptune replacement, the contract for which was awarded to Lockheed in April 1958 for a derivative of their existing L-188 Electra

airliner. The first aerodynamic development Orion made its maiden flight in August 1958, followed by initial operational deployment in August 1962. In terms of quantities, the US Navy took 157 P-3As between 1962 and 1965, followed by 144 P-3Bs between 1966 and 1969, plus 235 P-3Cs up to the end of December 1984 out of a total of 247 scheduled to be completed by 1986. Additional deliveries include three P-3Ds to US Government agencies; ten P-3Bs and 11 P-3Cs to Australia; five each P-3Bs to New Zealand and Norway; 18 CP-140 Auroras to Canada; three P-3Cs to Japan, plus 42 locally built-aircraft; 13 P-3Cs to the Netherlands and six P-3Fs to Iran.

Notes: Despite the somewhat chequered history of its parent L-188 Electra airliner programme, the P-3 Orion has proven to be one of the finest maritime patrol aircraft yet built, both in operational and export market terms. The earliest of the current generation of land-based anti-submarine aircraft that includes the Dassault Breguet Atlantic and British Aerospace Nimrod, the P-3 Orion is yet a further example of the sustaining effects of evolving electronics on an aircraft's production life. As with all anti-submarine aircraft, the P-3's primary purpose is to act as a highly mobile means of transporting a set of sensor packages out to the suspected location of a hostile submarine. Once over the location, the aircraft will employ one or more of its sensor systems, including its rearward-projecting magnetic anomaly detector (MAD) which senses for unexpectedly large local variations in the earth's magnetic field introduced by the presence of a submarine's large ferrous metal mass (naturally, submarines such as the 'Alfa' class, with a non-ferrous titanium hull, tend to create problems for MAD operators). Another prime sensor employed is any one of a variety of air-droppable sonobuoys, with which the P-3 can picket a given area of sea, using the data received back from the sonobuoys to fix the submarine's position by triangulation techniques. Besides the various sensor packages carried, as with its European brethren, the P-3 carries an awesome mass of data-processing electronics pitched not only at the task of speeding up data handling, but also at providing much more discriminating target data, such as the specific class of submarine being hunted. In the case of the P-3 Orion in particular, it has been the refinement of the aircraft's data-processing that has been the pacing factor in the machine's continued development, the recent milestones of which have abandoned the practice of altering the variant suffix letter, as in the case of the P-3A, -3B and -3C, in favour of employing the term Update I, II and III: each of which reflects the status of the aircraft's data-processing capability. While it is easy to become preoccupied with the necessary complexity of the aircraft's sensor/processing systems, it must not be overlooked that machines such as the P-3 can carry a much larger load of weapons out to a much greater range and at much higher speeds than is within the capability of even the largest anti-submarine helicopter. Further, the advent of the air-launched Harpoon and Tomahawk missiles gives the P-3 Orion a very useful, stand-off anti-shipping punch.

Dassault-Breguet Atlantic Anti-Submarine Aircraft

Type and role: 12-crew, all-weather, twin turboprop-engined, land-based anti-submarine and anti-shipping aircraft.
Maker: Avions Dassault-Breguet, Vaucresson, France (prime contractor).
Users: Navies of France (37, plus 42 Generation 2 on order), Federal Germany (20), Italy (18), Netherlands (9) and Pakistan (3).
Engines: 2 Rolls-Royce Tyne Mk 21 turboprops (total

One of the 13 Royal Netherlands Navy Lockheed P-3C Orions, deliveries of which commenced in 1981 and end in 1984.

11,500shp), each driving a 4-bladed reversible-pitch propeller.
Dimensions: 104.2ft (31.75m) overall length 119.1ft (36.3m) for Atlantic or 122.6ft (37.36m) for Generation 2 aircraft's wingspan; 1295sq ft (120.34m²) for Atlantic or 1292sq ft (120.0m²) for Generation 2 aircraft's wing area.
Weights: 52,900lb (24,000kg) for Atlantic or 56,320lb (25,600kg) for Generation 2 aircraft's empty equipped; 95,900lb (43,500kg) maximum take-off for Atlantic or 97,230lb (44,200kg) for Generation 2 aircraft, which can operate in overload up to 111,640lb (46,200kg).
Performance: 355 knots/658km/h maximum speed at 18,000ft/5486m; 172 knots/320km/h maximum endurance cruising speed; 2450ft/747m/min initial rate of climb; 11 hours maximum time on station at 600 nautical miles from base with maximum load of 4409lb/2000kg and overload fuel.
Armament: Up to 4409lb (2000kg) of anti-submarine torpedoes and/or depth charges/sonobuoys; or 4 AM39 Exocet or 4 Martel anti-ship missiles carried on 4 underwing stores pylons.
Programme: As the winner of a 1957 NATO European industrial competition for a standard long-range, land-based anti-submarine aircraft, the first prototype Atlantic made its maiden flight in October 1961, the aircraft being initially deployed operationally in December 1965. Production of the total 87 Atlantics to be built under a multi-national work-sharing programme was completed in 1973. In February 1978, France launched the Atlantic Generation 2 programme, involving the building of a further 42 aircraft for the French Navy, the commencement of deliveries having recently been

Dassault-Breguet Atlantics serve with the Royal Netherlands Navy, Federal German Navy and French Navy.

brought forward from 1986 to around June 1984. To assist in the development of the Generation 2 variant, the French Navy have supplied two existing Atlantics for modification by the manufacturer; the first of these much improved machines flying for the first time in May 1981.
Notes: Developed to meet the same basic mission requirements as those of the US Navy's Lockheed P-3 Orion, the French-led multi-national Atlantic programme emerged later than that of the US aircraft and lacked the huge home-based market that the US Navy could promise. To compound Dassault-Breguet's problems, they had to develop a new aircraft in the Atlantic, whilst Lockheed's P-3 Orion was, in fact, a fairly straightforward adaptation of the company's existing L-188 Electra airliner; a factor that further adversely affected French market aspirations in terms of programme cost impact. Evidence of such factors was particularly apparent in the Dutch Government's December 1978 selection of the P-3 Orion in preference to the Atlantic Generation 2 bid; a choice predicated by the significantly lower price and earlier availability of the Lockheed contestant. Although the Generation 2 Atlantics vary little in their external shape from the earlier machines, the capability of their onboard sensors and level of automated data-processing systems have been greatly enhanced. Immediately visible external differences between the early and new model Atlantics are confined to the deletion of the fin-top radome and the incorporation of wing-tip passive electronic sensor nacelles, along with a chin-mounted forward-looking infra-red and low light-level television sensor package.

Beriev BE-12 'Mail' Anti-Submarine Aircraft

Type and role: 5-crew, twin turboprop-engined, high gull-winged amphibious anti-submarine and maritime patrol flying boat.
Maker: Beriev, USSR.
User: Soviet Navy.
Engines: 2 Ivchenko AI-20M turboprops (total 8500shp) driving 2 four-bladed, reversible-pitch propellers.
Dimensions: 105.7ft (32.22m) overall length; 97.3ft (29.67m) wingspan; 1030sq ft (95.7m²) wing area.
Weights: 42,990lb (19,500kg) empty; 65,255lb (29,599kg) maximum gross.
Performance: 230 knots/426km/h at 10,000ft/3280m

This view of a Be-12 displays the aircraft's gull-winged and twin fin and rudder configuration.

maximum speed; 173 knots/321km/h at 1000ft/328m normal patrol cruise speed; 2950ft/899m/min initial rate of climb; 26,900ft/8200m service ceiling; 538 nautical miles/998km maximum radius of action.
Armament: Up to 4400lb (2000kg) of anti-submarine torpedoes, depth charges, mines and sonobuoys.
Programme: Believed to have first flown in late 1960, between 100 and 120 production aircraft are reported to have been built during the 1963 to 1972 period. Of these, more than 70 were reported to remain in Soviet Navy service at the end of 1984.
Notes: An interesting aircraft from many viewpoints, the Be-12 follows the same general configuration as the earlier, piston-engined Beriev Be-6 'Madge', but exploits the fuel economy and speed of the turboprop engine (the even faster, but less economic twin jet Beriev Be-10 'Mallow' that preceded the Be-12 was only built in small numbers and never entered series production and service). Now largely superseded in front line operational terms by the Ilyushin Il-38 'May', the Be-12 continues to provide a useful, rapidly deployable anti-submarine or general surveillance capability for the Soviet's Northern, Pacific and Black Sea Fleets. Its ability to operate from both land and water also allows it to act as a useful senior naval staff or vitally needed equipment shuttle between shore establishments and fleet units at sea.

Lockheed S-3 Viking Anti-Submarine Aircraft

Type and role: 4-crew, 2 turbofan engined, medium-range carrier-going anti-submarine (S-3A) and 2-crew carrier-going transport aircraft (US-3A).
Maker: Lockheed-California Company, Burbank, California, USA.
User: US Navy.
Engines: 2 General Electric TF34-GE-400A turbofans (total 18,550lb/ 8414kg thrust).
Dimensions: 53.33ft (16.26m) overall length; 68.66ft (20.93m) wingspan; 29.5ft (8.99m) wings folded; 598sq ft (55.56m²) wing area.
Weights: 26,650lb (12,088kg) empty; 42,500lb (19,277kg) normal gross; 52,540lb (23.832kg) maximum gross.
Performance: 450 knots/834km/h (Mach 0.76) at 28,000ft/8534m; 159 knots/257km/h loiter speed at sea

level; 4200ft/1280m per minute initial rate of climb; more than 1150 nautical miles/2131km tactical radius of action without in-flight refuelling.

Armament: Up to 5000lb (2268kg) including up to 4 Mk 46 lightweight homing torpedoes carried internally, plus up to 3000lb (1361kg) of bombs or mines carried externally on underwing stores pylons.

Programme: The US Navy issued the requirement for what was to lead to the S-3 Viking during the latter half of 1967 and confirmed their selection of the Lockheed/Vought industrial team's design submission in August 1969. The maiden flight of the prototype S-3A was made in late January 1972 and the type entered operational service in February 1974. In all, 187 S-3 Vikings were built prior to production completion in June 1978; this figure including the 8 pre-series development aircraft and 3 aircraft converted to US-3A utility transport, or carrier onboard delivery (COD) standard.

Notes: Designed to replace the twin piston-engined Grumman S-2 Tracker carrier-going anti-submarine aircraft, the S-3A Viking, while carrying a generally comparable sensor and anti-submarine weapons fit to that of its bigger brother, the Lockheed P-3 Orion, can transit faster to the point where it is needed. More importantly, because of its carrier-going capability, the S-3 Viking can always be where the carrier-centred task group is, which can sometimes be well beyond the range of the shore-based P-3 Orion. In industrial terms, the S-3 programme is of interest inasmuch as most of the airframe was actually built by Vought, who produced the aircraft's wings, engine pods, rear fuselage tail unit and landing gear. In all, the US Navy operates 13 squadrons of S-3A Vikings, which are in the course of being brought up to S-3B standard as a result of being retrofitted with updated electronic processing equipment. Although production of the S-3 Viking was completed in mid-1978, all of the production tooling equipment for this aircraft has been retained awaiting a US Navy decision concerning the selection of a future carrier-going aerial tanker, for which the Viking remains a candidate.

An S-3A of anti-submarine Squadron 29 folded and parked away from the active flight deck area aboard USS Enterprise *(CVN65).*

Grumman S-2 Tracker Anti-Submarine Aircraft

Type and role: 4-crew, twin piston-engined, carrier-going anti-submarine aircraft (S-2) and carrier-going transport (C-1 Trader).

Maker: Grumman Aerospace Corporation, Bethpage, Long Island, USA.

Users: US Navy and the navies of Argentina (5), Australia (13), Japan (21), South Korea (23), Peru (9), Taiwan (9), Thailand (9), Turkey (8), Uruguay (3), Venezuela (6) and the air forces of Brazil (8) and Canada (15): *based on data available at the end of 1981.*

Engines: 2 Wright R-1820-82 radial pistons (total 3050hp).

Dimensions: 42.25ft (12.88m) overall length; 69.66ft (21.23m) wingspan; 27.0ft (8.23m) wings folded; 485sq ft (45.06m²) wing area: *data for S-2A.*

Weights: 18,750lb (8505kg) empty; 29,150lb (13,222kg) maximum gross.

Performance: 230 knots/426km/h maximum speed; 130 knots/241km/h at 1500ft/450m cruising speed; 1390ft/424m/min initial rate of climb; 21,000ft/6,400m service ceiling; 1129 nautical miles/2095km maximum range.

Armament: Up to 4810lb (2182kg) of homing torpedoes, depth charges, rockets or sonobuoys.

Programme: Born of a June 1950 US Navy requirement, the prototype S-2A made its maiden flight in December 1952 with the first production aircraft being deployed in February 1954. Including the two prototypes, Grumman built a total of 817 S-2 Trackers, the last of which was delivered in mid-January 1955. Grumman built a further

An S-2A Tracker coming aboard. Although only a few remain in service with the US Navy as training or utility aircraft, the type remains in active service with a number of other navies.

87 C-1 Traders between January 1955 and December 1958. An additional 99 Trackers were built by De Havilland Canada during the latter half of the 1950s and some of these remain in service as CP-121s.

Notes: Although superseded in US Navy service by the Lockheed S-3 Viking, the S-2 Tracker is likely to remain in service with a number of Latin American nations well into the 1990s.

Flight deck aspect of the Alize taken aboard the French carrier Clemenceau *(R98) in 1975.*

Breguet BR 1050 Alize Anti-Submarine Aircraft

Type and role: 3-crew, carrier-stowable, single turboprop-engined, all-weather anti-submarine and maritime patrol aircraft.
Maker: Dassault-Breguet Aviation, Vaucresson, France.
Users: Navies of France (36) and India (22) as of mid-1983.
Engine: 1 Rolls-Royce Dart R.Da 21 turboprop (2100shp).
Dimensions: 45.5ft (13.9m) overall length; 51.2ft (15.6m) wingspan; 23.0ft (7.0m) wingspan folded; 388sq ft (36m²) wing area.
Weights: 12,566lb (5700kg) empty equipped; 18,100lb (8200kg) maximum take-off.
Performance: 247 knots/460km/h at sea level rising to 254 knots/ 470km/h maximum speed at 10,000ft/3048m; 1380ft/421m/min initial rate of climb; 7 hours 40 minutes maximum endurance with 105 imperial gallon auxiliary fuel tank and flying at an altitude of 15,000ft/4572m.
Armament: Up to 1940lb (880kg) of weapons including 1 lightweight anti-submarine torpedo and 3 depth charges, plus 6 rocket projectiles.
Programme: In 1954, the French Navy drew up a requirement for a carrier-going, three-man, single-engined anti-submarine aircraft. Breguet, who had already developed and flown a naval strike design, the Br 960 Vultur, adapted this machine to meet the new requirement, the modified Vultur, known as the Br 965 making its maiden flight in March 1955, followed by the first flight of the prototype Alize in October 1956. Initial operational deployment of the Alize aboard French aircraft carriers occurred during the first half of 1959. In all, 92 Alizes were built, including development aircraft, production ending in 1962. Twenty eight of the French Navy's aircraft have been refurbished between 1980 and 1983, indicating that the type will remain in use for some years yet.
Notes: A solid, uncomplicated aircraft, the Breguet Alize was being operationally deployed at around the time the Royal Navy was phasing out its fleet of Fairey Gannet anti-submarine aircraft in favour of an all helicopter submarine-hunting force. Thus, it could be argued that the existence of the Alize helped shape both French and Indian naval policies towards the retention of conventional aircraft carriers; something that Britain sadly lacked during the Falklands War of 1982.

Anti-submarïne helicoptors

EH Industries EH101 Anti-Submarine Helicopters

Type and role: 3 or 4-crew, triple turboshaft-engined, single 5-bladed main rotor, all-weather, ship-stowable anti-submarine/ship helicopter. In its secondary logistics role, the EH101 can carry up to 24 troops or 10,000lb (4536kg) of externally-slung cargo.
Maker: EH Industries Limited, London, UK (a joint company formed by Westland Helicopters and Agusta).
Users: Under full development for the navies of Italy and UK.
Engines: 3 General Electric T700-401 turboshaft (total 5070shp).
Dimensions: 75.25ft (22.9m) overall length (rotors turning); 52.0ft (15.85m) overall length (rotors stowed); 61.0ft (18.59m) main rotor diameter.
Weights: 15,252lb (6917kg) empty; 28,665lb (13,413kg) maximum gross.
Performance: 160 knots/297km/h maximum speed at sea level; up to 5 hours endurance, including in excess of 2 hours hover/loiter time in the operational area.

A model of the all-weather, frigate-going EH101 naval variant.

Armament: Up to approximately 4000lb (1814kg) of weapons, including 2 Sea Eagle anti-ship missiles or 4 Stingray or other lightweight anti-submarine homing torpedoes, or a mix of 2 such torpedoes and depth charges.

Programme: In 1977, in response to a Royal Navy targeted need for a Sea King replacement, Westland Helicopters started studies on their WG 34. However, as soon became apparent, the cost estimates for the WG 34 indicated that the machine could not be developed on a single-nation basis and, in November 1979, the WG 34 became the EH101 in the wake of an Anglo-Italian government memorandum of understanding to progress the programme on a joint basis, around Westland and Agusta as the prime industrial partners. The EH101 entered full-scale development in January 1984. First flight of the naval prototype is set for late 1986, with initial operational deployment aboard ship to follow in the late 1989/90 period.

Notes: The EH101 venture, of which the navalised early variants comprise the main early thrust, represents an Anglo-Italian resolve to produce a helicopter at least comparable to the best of its US rivals. What is already evident, is that the naval variants of the EH101, differing in detail equipment fit for each of the two navies, should have a marked advantage in terms of true all-weather ship operability in comparison with existing shipboard anti-submarine helicopters. Similarly, although an unquestionably expensive aircraft, the EH101 will offer both sufficient reserves of engine power and the space to permit the carriage of multi-mission sensors and weapons loads not previously achievable. Military and civil models are also envisaged.

Aerospatiale SA321 Super Frelon Anti-Submarine Helicopters

Type and role: 2-crew, all-weather anti-ship/submarine or assault transport, 3-engined, 6-bladed single rotored, ship-stowable helicopter with accommodation for up to 27 troops.

Maker: Aerospatiale Helicopter Division, La Courneuve, France.

Users: French Navy (24) and the air forces of Chinese Peoples' Republic, Iraq, Israel, Libya and South Africa (all of whom operate the type as an assault transport).

Engines: 3 Turbomeca Turmo III CB turboshaft (total 3650shp).

Dimensions: 75.46ft (23.0m) overall length (rotors turning); 62.0ft (18.9m) main rotor diameter.

Weights: 15,130lb (6863kg) operating empty; 28,660lb (13,000kg) maximum take-off. *Note:* data for SA321G naval model.

Performance: 145 knots/268km/h maximum level speed at sea level; 1312ft/400m/min initial rate of climb; 365 nautical miles/679km maximum range with 5340lb/2450kg load, or 3 hour 30 minutes endurance.

Armament: Up to 2,866lb (1300kg) of offensive weaponry on naval version, including either 2 ASM39 anti-ship missiles or 4 Mk 46 lightweight anti-submarine torpedoes.

Programme: Derived from the smaller SA3200 Frelon of 1959, the first of two Super Frelon prototypes made its maiden flight in early December 1962. The first of the French Navy's SA321Gs flew initially at the end of November 1965. An all model total of 95 Super Frelons was officially quoted as being delivered by the end of 1982, at which time production had been completed.

Notes: With a fully watertight hull and floats on the SA321G naval model, these machines, unlike the military models, embody a foldable main rotor and tail boom for shipboard stowage aboard the French Navy's carriers and 'Ouragan' class assault ships. Recently re-equipped with a new and more discriminating ORB 32 Heracles II air-to-

A French Navy Super Frelon operating off the assault ship Ouragan.

surface radar, the SA321G almost begs comparison with its near US contemporary in the shape of the Sikorsky SH-3 Sea King.

Sikorsky SH-60 Seahawk Anti-Submarine Helicopters

Type and role: 4-crew, all-weather anti-submarine and anti-ship targeting, twin turbine engined, 4-bladed single rotor shipboard-stowable helicopter.

Maker: Sikorsky Aircraft Division of United Technology Corporation, Stratford, Connecticut, USA.

User: US Navy.

Engines: 2 General Electric T700-GE-401 turboshaft (total 3380shp).

Dimensions: 64.8ft (19.76m) overall length (rotors turning); 53.7ft (16.36m) main rotor diameter.

An SH-60B Seahawk about to be winched onboard USS McInerney *(FFG8) during aircraft/ship compatibility trials. Note the two Mk 46 torpedoes and magnetic anomaly detection drogue carried by the helicopter.*

Weights: 13,678lb (6204kg) empty 20,244lb (9183kg) normal gross; 21,884lb (9927kg) maximum gross.
Performance: 126 knots/234km/h at 5000ft/1524m maximum speed; 1192ft/363m/min initial rate of climb; 3hrs 52mins maximum duration on station at 50 nautical miles/93km from ship.
Armament: Approximately 1300lb (590kg), including 2 Mk 46 lightweight anti-submarine torpedoes and sonobuoys, or nuclear depth charges.
Programme: A navalised derivative of the US Army's UH-60 Black Hawk, the US Navy selected the Sikorsky SH-60B Seahawk to meet its Light Airborne Multi-purpose Ship/air System (LAMPS III) requirement at the beginning of March 1978, following extended evaluation of rival Sikorsky and Boeing Vertol designs. The first of five SH-60B prototypes made its maiden flight in December 1979 and by May 1983, the US Navy had placed orders for 45 machines, exclusive of prototypes, out of the originally planned procurement of 204 helicopters; a figure that could well be increased to 379 through the addition of 175 carrier-based SH-60Cs bought from 1987 onwards. Initial fleet deployment of the SH-60B Seahawk was planned to occur around mid-1984.
Notes: Bigger than the Kaman SH-2F Seasprite and heavier than the Sikorsky SH-3 Sea King, the SH-60B Seahawk seems at first sight to be a very expensive means of carrying no greater warload than that lofted by its much earlier forebears; its only immediately apparent advantage being its ability to remain on station for a respectable period of time. Such superficial comparisons, however, tend totally to overlook the operational pressures to provide more effective and farther ranged anti-submarine screening around a surface task force. To achieve these ends, the Seahawk not only carries a considerable amount of fuel, but, more importantly in some respects, is veritably stuffed with the necessary advanced electronics required rapidly and exhaustively to process the raw data obtained from combination of helicopter and friendly shipborne sensors. Indeed, such is the complexity of the Seahawk's electronic systems and data-links that it is easy to draw a ready analogy between the SH-60's function and that of the much bigger and far more expensive US Air Force's Boeing E-3 Sentinel; both aircraft providing the same Airborne Early Warning and Control System (AWACS) function, which is why IBM, as the electronics systems integrators on the Seahawk, act as prime contractor to the US Navy, rather than Sikorsky.

Sikorsky S-61/SH-3 Sea King Anti-Submarine Helicopters

Type and role: 4-crew, twin turboshaft-engined, 5-bladed single rotor, all-weather, ship-stowable anti-submarine (SH-3), utility transport with accommodation for up to 31 troops (CH-3) and long-range rescue (HH-3) helicopter.
Maker: Sikorsky Aircraft Division of United Technologies, Stratford, Connecticut, USA and licensee manufacturers in Italy, Japan and UK.
Users: US Navy and Marine Corps (330), plus the navies of Argentina (4), Brazil (4), Canada (41), Italy (54), Japan (62), Pakistan (4), Peru (4), Spain (15), UK (4, used to establish Westland Sea King programme, dealt with separately), along with over 300 models supplied to the US Air Force and the air forces of Italy, Japan and Malaysia. *Note:* the above figures reflect total orders not current inventory.
Engines: 2 General Electric T58-GE-10 turboshafts (total 2800shp).
Dimensions: 72.66ft (22.15m) overall length (rotors turning); 47.25ft (14.4m) overall length folded for stowage; 62.0ft (18.85m) main rotor diameter.
Weights: 11,865lb (5382kg) empty equipped; 20,500lb (9299kg) maximum take-off.

A Sikorsky SH-3D operated by the US Navy's anti-submarine Squadron 4, operating from the carrier USS Ranger *in November 1976.*

Performance: 137 knots/254km/h maximum speed at sea level; 117 knots/219km/h cruising speed at sea level; 2200ft/670m/min initial rate of climb; 161 nautical miles/300km radius of action with 2 torpedoes; 4.5 hours maximum endurance.
Armament: Up to 1200lb (544kg) of weapons and sonobuoys, including 2 Mk 46 lightweight anti-submarine torpedoes.
Programme: In December 1957, the US Navy awarded Sikorsky a non-competitive contract to develop a replacement for the earlier Sikorsky S-58/HSS-1 anti-submarine helicopter. The resultant S-61/H-3 design made its maiden flight in March 1959 and entered service with the US Navy in September 1961. In all, Sikorsky built 826 S-61s, including 136 civil S-61L or Ns. The S-61 was also licence-built by Mitsubishi in Japan, who produced a known 111 aircraft, while Agusta in Italy and Westlands in Britain are still manufacturing the machine; Sikorsky having delivered their last, a civil S-61N in June 1980. Currently, Sikorsky are developing a Service Life Extension Programme (SLEP) kit, 129 of which will be manufactured for installation aboard US Navy SH-3s commencing in 1986.
Notes: Quite a large helicopter for its time, the SH-3, with its unprecedented range/endurance capabilities, did more than any other machine to lift naval anti-submarine helicopter warfare capability out of its infancy. Ironically, because the US Navy had the carriers and large ships from which to operate the SH-3, it was left to the Royal Canadian Navy to pioneer the machine's operation from smaller warships. Besides carrying an extensive sensor fit of active/passive dipping sonar and sonobuoys, plus magnetic anomaly detection gear, the all-weather SH-3 can carry a useful weapons load of torpedoes or nuclear depth charges. The current US Navy SH-3 life extension programme virtually ensures that the machine will remain in front line service into the beginning of the next century.

Westland-Sikorsky Sea King Anti-Submarine Helicopters

Type and role: 3 or 4-crew, all-weather, twin turboshaft-engined, 5-bladed single rotor, ship-stowable anti-submarine helicopter.
Maker: Westland Helicopters, Yeovil, Somerset, England; under basic licence from Sikorsky (refer to separate Sikorsky SH-3 Sea King entry).
Users: (of Westland-built models); Royal Navy (106) and those of Australia (10), Federal Germany (22), India (14) and Norway (10), plus Royal Air Force (18).
Engines: 2 Rolls-Royce Gnome 1400 turboshafts (total

3000shp on early models or 3320shp on later machines).
Dimensions: 72.66ft (22.15m) overall length (rotors turning); 47.25ft (14.4m) overall length folded for stowage; 62.0ft (18.85m) main rotor diameter.
Weights: 15,816lb (7176kg) empty equipped; 21,000lb (9525kg) normal gross; 21,400lb (9707kg) maximum gross.
Performance: 124 knots/230km/h maximum speed at sea level; 114 knots/ 211km/h cruising speed at sea level; 1805ft/550m/min maximum initial rate of climb at sea level and normal gross. 2 hours on station at 86 nautical miles from ship with 4 torpedoes, including 30 minutes hover while on station.
Armament: Up to 3520lb (1597kg) of weapons, including up to 4 Mk 44 or Stingray lightweight anti-submarine torpedoes, or Mk 11 depth charges in addition to fixed sonar, radar and doppler systems.
Programme: By the mid-1960s, the Royal Navy had drawn up a requirement for a more capable replacement for the Westand-Sikorsky Wessex anti-submarine helicopter and had settled on an Anglicised variant of the Sikorsky S-61/SH-3 Sea King. In early 1967, Sikorsky delivered four SH-3Ds to Westlands; these aircraft serving as production pilot models. The first Westland-built Sea King HAS Mk 1 made its maiden flight in May 1969 and the type was initially deployed in February 1970. Subsequently, Westland evolved the basic S-61 design into a family of anti-submarine, air sea rescue and troop transport models, the latter being known as the Commando or Sea King HC Mk 4, dealt with separately as the Commando. By June 1984, Westland held orders for over 222 Sea Kings, plus 74 Commandos, for a total of over 296 aircraft. Just over 254 had been delivered.
Notes: Although following the parent S-61/SH-3's general external lines, with the exception of the Westland machine's prominent dorsal radome, the British variant differs considerably in interior detail, with more power and a UK-developed sensor fit. As often happens, when an American aircraft is adapted for European and, in particular, British use, a subtle shift in payload/range capability occurs and the Sikorsky versus Westland variants of the Sea King highlight this aspect. Whereas the Sikorsky SH-3 emphasises long-range or loiter capability, the Westland Sea King exchanges range for a heavier sensor and weapons load. Royal Navy Mk 1 Sea Kings are now operated from Royal Fleet Auxiliary ships, while all remaining Mk 2s have been retrofitted up to Mk 5 standard. The Royal Air Force operated Sea Kings are a specialised variant specifically equipped to carry out air sea rescue duties.

Typifying the numerous export models of the Sea King is this Mk 43 of the Royal Norwegian Navy.

A 'Hormone A' basic anti-submarine variant.

Kamov KA-25 'Hormone' Anti-Submarine Helicopters

Type and role: 4-crew, ship-stowable, twin turboshaft-engined, 3-bladed counter-rotating rotor anti-submarine ('Hormone A') or anti-submarine/anti-ship targeting ('Hormone B') or utility transport ('Hormone C') helicopter, with accommodation for up to 12 troops.
Maker: Kamov, USSR.
Users: Soviet Navy and those of India, Syria and Yugoslavia.
Engines: 2 Glushenkov GTD-3 turboshafts (total 1800shp).
Dimensions: 52.0ft (15.85m) overall length (rotors turning); 35.5ft (10.8m) overall length folded for stowage; 52.0ft (15.85m) rotor diameter.
Weights: 10,500lb (4765kg) empty equipped; 16,500lb (7494kg) maximum take-off.
Performance: 130 knots/241km/h maximum speed at sea level; 104 knots/ 193km/h cruising speed at sea level; 108 nautical miles/200km maximum radius of action with weapons.

Armament: Up to 3968lb (1800kg) of anti-submarine torpedoes, depth charges and sonobuoys all stowed in internal ventral weapons bay or main cabin area.
Programme: First flown in the 1966/67 period, the Kamov Ka-25 is a derivative of the earlier Ka-20 'Harp' (no longer in service). The Ka-25 'Hormone' was initially deployed with the Soviet Fleet during late 1969. An estimated 450 Ka-25s were produced between 1966 and 1975 when production was reported to have ended. Over 200 Ka-25 'Hormones' are reported to currently serve with the Soviet Navy, plus small numbers with the navies of India (around 5), Syria (4) and Yugoslavia (12).
Notes: Although not the first helicopter to employ the counter-rotating rotor system that eliminates the need for an anti-torque tail rotor, the Kamov Ka-20 and 25s were the first shipboard-going machines to use this technique. While the counter-rotating rotor system does little to reduce the necessarily high complexity of the helicopter's rotor design, it does have one major advantage from a naval viewpoint, in that it offers operators a machine of smaller overall length when folded for stowage by obviating the need to provide a machine with a lengthy moment-armed tail rotor. The Kamov Ka-25 makes an

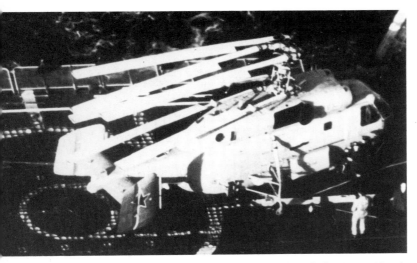

This Kamov 'Helix' was photographed aboard the Soviet Navy's Udaloy *while the ship was operating off Norway in October 1981.*

interesting comparison with its two US Navy contemporaries in the shape of the Kaman SH-2 Seasprite and Sikorsky SH-3 Sea King, lacking the range of either, but having the ability to loft a heavier load of sensors and weapons.

Kamov KA-27 'Helix' Anti-Submarine Helicopters

Type and role: 4 or 5-crew, all-weather, ship-stowable, twin turboshaft-engined, 3-bladed counter-rotating rotor anti-submarine and anti-ship targeting helicopter.
Maker: Kamov, USSR.
User: Soviet Navy.
Engines: 2 Glushenkov turboshafts (total approximately 3200shp).
Dimensions: 54.95ft (16.75m) overall length (rotors turning); 38.45ft (11.72m) overall length folded for stowage; 54.95ft (16.75m) rotor diameter.
Weights (estimated): 11,023lb (5000kg) empty equipped; 21,000lb (9525kg) maximum take-off.
Performance (estimated): 130 knots/241km/h maximum speed at sea level; 313 nautical miles/580km maximum tactical radius of action with weapons.
Armament: At least 3968lb (1800kg) of anti-submarine torpedoes; nuclear or conventional depth charges; sonobuoys carried in internal weapons bay.
Programme: Flown in prototype form during the latter part of the 1970s, this more powerful and heavier derivative of the Kamov Ka-25 'Hormone' was first spotted by Western observers in the autumn of 1981 and has since been seen in sufficient numbers to conclude that the 'Helix' is being series produced as a replacement for 'Hormone'.
Notes: While similar in general configuration to the earlier Ka-25 'Hormone', the Helix has a twin-finned tailplane, compared with the triple fins of its forebear. Similarly, the 'Helix' exhausts its efflux gases from its engines via short, side-mounted jetpipes, rather than via a long, common jetpipe as on the Ka-25.

Agusta-Bell AB-212ASW Anti-Submarine Helicopters

Type and role: 4-crew, all-weather, anti-submarine and anti-ship targeting, shipboard-stowable, coupled turboshaft-engined, single 2-bladed rotor helicopter.

Maker: Agusta Costruzioni Aeronautiche, Milan, Italy.
Users: Navies of Italy (28), Greece (20), Iran (7), Peru (6), Spain (12), Turkey (9) and Venezuela (12).
Engine: 1 Pratt & Whitney Canada PT6T-3B Turbo Twin Pac coupled turboshaft (1800shp).
Dimensions: 57.25ft (17.45m) overall length (rotors turning); 48.2ft (14.0m) main rotor diameter.
Weights: 7540lb (3420kg) empty equipped; 11,200lb (5080kg) maximum take-off.
Performance: 140 knots/259km/h maximum speed at sea level; 100 knots/185km/h cruising speed at sea level; 1320ft/402m/min initial rate of climb; 1.63 hours on station at a distance of 72 nautical miles/133km from parent ship maximum endurance with no weapon load.
Armament: Up to 988lb (448kg) of weaponry, including 2 Mk 44 or other lightweight anti-submarine homing torpedoes.
Programme: A derivative of the Bell Model 212/UH-1N, this exclusively Agusta-built machine made its first flight during the first quarter of 1972 and was initially operationally deployed with the Italian Navy during early 1974. Identified orders for this helicopter stood at 94 by the end of 1984, distributed as set out above in the Users column. The current production of the AB-212ASW is likely to continue for at least four to five years.
Notes: Designed to operate off and onto the decks of ships down to corvette size, the Agusta-Bell AB-212ASW carries a team of two pilots, plus two tactical anti-submarine systems operators. The AB-212ASW can carry a broad range of sensors, including dipping sonars and magnetic anomaly detection equipment, along with its permanently-mounted Italian-developed air-to-surface search radar, sited above the cabin.

An Italian Navy-operated AB-212ASW. Note the slightly bent sausage-shaped objects fitted to the helicopter's skid undercarriage – buoyancy bags, which inflate to keep the aircraft afloat in the event of an emergency ditching.

Kaman SH-2F Seasprite Anti-Submarine Helicopters

Type and role: 3-crew, all-weather anti-submarine anti-ship targeting, twin turbine-engined, 4-bladed single rotor, ship-stowable helicopter.
Maker: Kaman Aerospace Corporation, Bloomfield, Connecticut, USA.
User: US Navy.
Engines: 2 General Electric T58-GE-8F turboshaft (total 2700shp).
Dimensions: 52.6ft (16.0m) overall length (rotors turning); 44.0ft (13.4m) main rotor diameter.

Weights: 7040lb (3193kg) empty; 12,800lb (5806kg) normal gross; 13,500lb (6124kg) maximum gross.
Performance: 143 knots/266km/h maximum speed; 130 knots/241km/h cruise speed; 2440ft/744m/min maximum rate of climb; 366 nautical miles/ 679km maximum range.
Armament: 2 Mk 46 lightweight anti-submarine torpedoes out to 35 nautical miles (65km) with 1.2 hours loiter on station, or 1 Mk 46 out to 70 nautical miles (130km) with 1.1 hours on station.
Programme: The Kaman 20, as it was initially known, was born out of a 1956 US Navy requirement for a compact, long-range utility helicopter, capable of operations from larger ships and carriers. First flown in July 1959, the US Navy were to order 190 UH-2, delivered between 1961 and 1966. These were single-engined machines, but all were converted to twin-engined aircraft between 1967 and 1970. Following the failure of the US Navy's DASH unmanned anti-submarine torpedo-carrying helicopter programme in the latter part of the 1960s, the Navy turned to the existing H-2 Seasprite as an alternative. 105 of the remaining UH-2s were converted into SH-2Ds or Fs (all Ds being subsequently modified to F standard between 1980 and 1982). Initially deployed aboard 'Knox' class frigates commencing December 1971, a further 72 SH-2F Seasprites are to be built for the US Navy, with deliveries commencing in 1984 and continuing at 18 a year through 1986.
Notes: The Kaman Seasprite, some quarter of a century after its maiden flight, is still one of the most capable small ship-going anti-submarine helicopters extant, as evidenced by the US Navy's decision to acquire a further 72 new-build examples of the type. A large part of the Seasprite's underlying success stems from the initial sizing of the airframe, which proved sufficiently large to permit both the re-engining to be carried out, along with the parallel enhancement of its primary dynamics and sensor/weapons fit.

Westland Lynx Anti-submarine Helicopters

Type and role: 3 crew, shipboard-stowable, twin turboshaft-engined, single 4-bladed rotor, all-weather anti-submarine, anti-ship and ship-targeting helicopter.
Maker: Westland Helicopters, Yeovil, Somerset, UK.
Users: Royal Navy (91), plus the navies of Argentina (2), Brazil (9), Denmark (8), France (40), Federal Germany (12), Netherlands (24), Nigeria (6), and Norway (6). Another 124 military models had been ordered or delivered by early July 1985, making a total of 322 known sales.
Engines: 2 Rolls-Royce Gem 2 (total 1800shp) on early aircraft, or Gem 4 (total 2240shp) turboshafts on later models.
Dimensions: 49.75ft (15.16m) overall length (rotors turning); 42.0ft (12.8m) main rotor diameter; 34.8ft (10.62m) folded length ready for stowage.
Weights: 7311lb (3316kg) empty weight equipped for anti-submarine mission; 9500lb (4309kg) for early aircraft or 10,500lb (4763kg) maximum take off weight for later aircraft.
Performance: 146 knots/271km/h maximum speed at sea level; 70 knots/130km/h optimum cruising speed at sea level; 2175ft/663m/min initial rate of climb; 1 hour on station at 61 nautical miles/113km from parent ship maximum endurance with 2 Mk 44 torpedoes and flying at 120 knots/222km/h on station.
Armament: Up to 1800lb (816kg) when operating in the anti-ship role and equipped with 4 Sea Skua missiles (later aircraft only).
Programme: The origins of the Westland WG 13 Lynx stem from the Anglo-French Government Memorandum of Understanding concerning the joint industrial

A Kaman SH-2F Seasprite; the shuttlecock-like device under the starboard stores pylon is a magnetic anomaly detection (MAD) drogue, which, in operation, is deployed rearwards.

A Lynx HAS Mk 88 of the Federal German Navy.

development of three military helicopter programmes (the other two being the Gazelle and Puma), signed in February 1967. The Lynx programme, in which Westland were the team leaders working in collaboration with Aerospatiale Helicopters, was formally launched at the beginning of April 1968. The first flight of the prototype Lynx, a military utility model, took place in March 1971, followed by that of the first naval prototype in May 1972. The first naval Lynx to be delivered joined the Royal Navy's Fleet Air Arm in September 1976, followed by the type's initial operational deployment (aboard HMS *Sirius*, a 'Leander' class frigate) in December 1977. The uprated 10,500lb (4763kg) model (delivered to the Netherlands) entered service during 1979. The mid-1985 listing of naval users and their orders is set out above in the Users column.
Notes: Very few aircraft ever advance from the drawing board stage to operational service without encountering fairly major problems in one form or another and, in retrospect, the Lynx can be seen to have had more than its fair share, ranging from major cutbacks to the proposed numbers to be procured, to engine problems. Despite these setbacks, few of which were of Westland's making, the Lynx has emerged as a formidable anti-submarine/anti-

ship weapons platform. Battle-proven during the Falklands conflict in the spring and early summer of 1982, the Royal Navy operated Lynx had little opportunity to demonstrate its submarine hunter/killer capability, but, in combination with the Sea Skua missile, gave a good account of itself in terms of its anti-ship potential by sinking one Argentinian vessel and seriously damaging three others. In September 1983, Westland Helicopters formally announced that they were developing an improved range/load carrying capability model known as the Naval Lynx 3, powered by two Rolls-Royce Gem 60 turboshaft engines, each developing a rated output of 1263shp.

Westland Wasp Anti-submarine Helicopters

One of four ex-Royal Netherlands Navy Wasps recently refurbished by Westland Helicopters prior to delivery to the Indonesian Navy.

Type and role: 2 crew, shipboard-stowable single engined, single 4-bladed rotor, anti-submarine helicopter with provision to carry up to 3 in addition to crew.
Maker: Westland Helicopters Limited, Yeovil, Somerset, UK.
Users: Navies of Brazil, Indonesia, New Zealand, South Africa and UK.
Engine: 1 Rolls-Royce Nimbus Mk 503 turboshaft (710shp).
Dimensions: 40.33ft (12.3m) overall length (rotors turning); 32.25ft (9.83m) main rotor diameter.
Weights: 3452lb (1566kg) empty; 5500lb (2495kg) maximum gross.
Performance: 105 knots/194km/h maximum speed; 1440ft/439m/min initial rate of climb; 263 nautical miles/487km maximum range with standard fuel; 8800ft/2682m hover ceiling over water.
Armament: Up to 988lb (448kg) of weaponry including 2 Mk 44 or 46 lightweight anti-submarine homing torpedoes over a short radius of action.
Programme: Designed to meet a late-1950s Royal Navy requirement for an all-weather, shipboard anti-submarine helicopter, the Wasp was a navalised variant of the P.531 Scout. The Wasp made its maiden flight in late October 1962 and remained in production from 1962 through 1970, during which time a total of 126 Wasps were built including 30 direct exports. Deployed in 1964.
Notes: The Westland Wasp, although antedated by early models of the US Navy's Kaman SH-2 Seasprite, can still claim a place in the annals of naval development as being the first successful anti-submarine helicopter to be operated off frigate-sized warships anywhere in the world; beating the SH-2 Seasprite by seven years in terms of operational deployment. Testament to the basic durability of the Wasp has been evidenced in recent years by the supply of fully refurbished examples to the navies of Brazil,

Indonesia and New Zealand, while within the Royal Navy, Wasps were still providing almost 50 percent of the service's frigate-going airborne anti-submarine capability in the spring of 1983.

Aerospatiale AS 365F Dauphin 2 Anti-submarine Helicopters

Type and role: 2/3 crew, all-weather anti-ship/submarine and missile targeting, twin-engined, 4-bladed single rotored, ship-stowable helicopter.
Makers: Aerospatiale Helicopter Division, La Courneuve, France.
User: Royal Saudi Arabian Navy.

The prototype AS 365 F showing its complement of four AS 15T anti-ship missiles and chin-mounted radar.

Engines: 2 Turbomeca Arriel 1M turboshaft (total 1498shp).
Dimensions: 44.15ft (13.46m) overall length (rotors turning); 39.13ft (11.93m) main rotor diameter.
Weights: 4776lb (2166kg) empty; 8820lb (4000kg) maximum gross.
Performance: 164 knots/305km/h maximum speed at sea level; 136 knots/260km/h cruising speed at sea level; 1440ft/440m/min maximum rate of climb; 472 nautical miles/875km maximum range at sea level at 111 knots/206km/h.
Armament: Up to 1058lb (480kg) of mainly externally-mounted stores, including 4 AS 15TT anti-ship missiles, 2 lightweight anti-submarine torpedoes; magnetic anomaly detection (MAD) equipment; sonar/sonobuoy systems or rescue equipment.
Programme: A specialised naval variant of the Aerospatiale AS 365N, the AS 365F development was launched with the Saudi Arabian Government's major naval equipment contract placed with France in October 1980. The maiden flight of the parent AS 365N took place in March 1979, while the first flight of the AS 365F occurred at the beginning of July 1982, with deliveries of the initial batch of Saudi Arabian machines scheduled to be made in late 1984. In all, 31 AS 365Fs were on order by June 1985, along with 96 of the associated AS 366Gs in course of delivery to the US Coast Guard, plus 233 AS 365Ns to other users.
Notes: The AS 365F Dauphin 2 represents Aerospatiale's next-generation successor to the navalised variants of the Alouette II and III family of helicopters that did so well in terms of sales during the 1960s and early 1970s. A key element of the AS 365F is its lightweight, low drag, chin-mounted Thompson-CSF Agrion 15 air-to-surface radar, which allows sea-skimming missiles such as the AS 15TT to be launched against specific targets even in narrow and crowded seaways.

Aerospatiale Alouette Anti-submarine Helicopters

Type and role: 1 or 2 crew, anti-submarine/ship or utility, single turbine-engined, 3-bladed single rotored, ship-stowable helicopter.
Maker: Aerospatiale Helicopter Division, La Courneuve, France.
Users: Navies of Argentina, Belgium, Chile, Denmark, Ecuador, France, India, Indonesia, South Korea, Libya, Mexico, Pakistan, Peru and Sweden.
Engine: 1 Turbomeca Artouste IIIB turboshaft (858shp) on Alouette III.
Dimensions: 42.1ft (12.84m) overall length, rotors turning; 36.15ft (11.0m) main rotor diameter.
Weights: 2519lb (1143kg) empty for basic Alouette III; 4850lb (2200kg) maximum gross for Alouette III.
Performance: 113 knots/209km/h maximum speed at sea level; 100 knots/185km/h cruise speed at sea level; 846ft/258m/min maximum rate of climb; 267 nautical miles/495km maximum range at sea level. *This data applies to Alouette III.*
Armament: Up to 1102lb (500kg) of sensors and weapons including air-to-surface radar, magnetic anomaly detection (MAD) equipment, or up to 2 lightweight anti-submarine torpedoes.
Programme: Flown initially in March 1955, the SA 313 Alouette II was followed, in late February 1959, by the maiden flight of the SA 316 Alouette III. In all, Sud Aviation and its successor, Aerospatiale, produced or licensed the building of more than 2730 Alouettes, of which more than 110 naval models remained in service at the end of 1984, out of a known total of 186 naval models sold.
Notes: Very much a contemporary of the Westland Wasp, the Alouette family of helicopters have benefited, perhaps more than most, from staying in production for more than 20 years. This aspect is clearly visible in the evolution of the naval series of Alouette IIs and IIIs, which started life as simple shipgoing four/five seat utility helicopters that, with the passage of time, grew into quite useful, somewhat range-limited, anti-submarine/ship aircraft. In French naval service, the Alouette has been replaced operationally by the Lynx, but remains available for training and utility tasks.

Hughes Models 369/500 Defender Anti-submarine Helicopters

Type and role: 2 crew, single turboshaft-engined, single 4- or 5-bladed rotor anti-submarine and surveillance helicopter.
Maker: Hughes Helicopters, Culver City, California, USA and licensees in Italy and South Korea.
Users: Navies of Argentina (6), Iceland (1), South Korea (18), Mexico (5), Spain (11) and Taiwan (12), plus numerous others with military users throughout the world.
Engine: 1 Allison T63-A-5A turboshaft (317shp) on Model 369 or Allison 250-C20B turboshaft (375shp) on Model 500.
Dimensions: 30.84ft (9.4m) overall length (rotors turning); 26.25ft (8.0m) main rotor diameter. *Note:* data for Model 500.
Weights: 1496lb (679kg) empty; 3000lb (1360kg) maximum take-off. *Note:* data for Model 500MD/ASW.
Performance: 130 knots/241km/h maximum speed at sea level; 115 knots/213km/h maximum speed at sea level with external stores; 1650ft/503m/min initial rate of climb; 200 nautical miles/370km maximum range at sea level and carrying no external stores. *Note:* data for Model 500MD/ASW.

This submarine-hunting Alouette III carried a nose-mounted radar, a magnetic anomaly detector (MAD) drogue under its port pylon and a lightweight homing torpedo to starboard.

Armament: 1 Mk 44 or 46 lightweight anti-submarine homing torpedo.
Programme: The origins of this family date back to the US Army's 1962/63 competition held to select a replacement Light Observation Helicopter (LOH) for the existing Bell Model 47/H-13 Sioux, which was won by the Hughes Model 369/OH-6 Cayuse, first flown in late February 1963. In all, the US Army were to eventually buy 1434 OH-6s, few of which remain in service. Seeing their opportunity, Hughes Helicopters developed the Model 369 for civil and military export markets, along with the more powerful Model 500. Production of the Model 500 continued at around eight or ten ship sets per month in late 1984, with the dominant share going to civil markets.
Notes: As an anti-submarine weapons platform, the

Hughes Model 500MD/ASW with nose-mounted air-to-surface search radar, magnetic anomaly detection gear and lightweight anti-submarine torpedo.

Three Spanish Navy AH-1Gs, photographed prior to delivery and yet to be equipped with their cannon.

Hughes Model 500MD/ASW represents the lowest cost solution available. It also represents about the minimal solution in terms of operational effectiveness, particularly in terms of range when carrying a torpedo. This said, the machine could prove useful for shallow water operations, or where directed into the area by shipborne sonars.

Bell AH-1 Hueycobra Attack Helicopters

Type and role: 2 crew, armed and armoured, single or twin turboshaft-engined, 2-bladed single rotor helicopter used to suppress enemy ground fire.
Maker: Textron Bell Helicopters, Fort Worth, Texas, USA and Japanese licensee.
Users: US Marine Corps (364, plus 44 ordered), Spanish Navy (4), US Army (1,212), Iranian Army (202, Israel (6), Spanish Army (16). *Note:* Japan is to license-build 54 AH-1Ss, manufactured by Fuji.
Engine/s: 1 Avco-Lycoming T53-L-13 turboshaft (1100shp) on AH-1G, or T53-L-703 (1800shp) on AH-1S, or 1 Pratt & Whitney Canada T400-WV-402 coupled turboshaft (2050shp) on AH-1J and T.
Dimensions: 59.7ft (18.2m) overall length (rotors turning): 48.0ft (14.6m) main rotor diameter. *Note:* data for AH-1T.
Weights: 8014lb (3635kg) empty; 14,000lb (6350kg) maximum take-off. *Note:* data for AH-1T.
Performance: 157 knots/291km/h maximum speed at sea level; 2880ft/878m/min initial rate of climb; 113 nautical miles/209km combat radius with weapons. *Note:* data for AH-1T.

Armament: Various chin-mounted gun fits ranging from 7.62mm miniguns to Hughes Aircraft 30mm cannon, plus anti-tank rocket pods or missiles carried on port and starboard weapons sponsons.
Programme: The US Army had first mooted the idea of procuring a dedicated attack helicopter in 1962, but it was not until April 1966 that Bell was to receive the contract that formally launched their Model 209/AH-1 programme. In fact, Bell had such faith in this requirement from the start, that they privately funded their initial development work, flying a semi-definitive prototype (Bell Model 207) in July 1963; the prototype Model 209/AH-1 making its maiden flight in early September 1965, some seven months before the receipt of their first US Army production contract. Deployment of the initial AH-1G aircraft occurred during 1967. Production of new AH-1 helicopters, along with the modernisation of existing machines is scheduled to continue for some years, both within the US and Japan.
Notes: Although overshadowed during its early years by the larger Lockheed AH-56 Cheyenne (abandoned in 1969) and latterly by the Hughes AH-64 Apache, the Bell AH-1 family have long since proven their ruggedness under fire in places as far afield as South East Asia and the Middle East. Perhaps even more significantly, the AH-1 design has emerged as a very flexible and adaptable vehicle, ready to accept either one or two engines and more power, which, in turn, permits the designers to pack in both more weaponry and the vital additional sensors, necessary to permit round-the-clock, all-weather operation.

228

Bombers

Tupolev Tu-22 'Blinder' Bombers

Type and role: 3 crew, twin reheated turbojet-engined supersonic medium-range bomber and reconnaissance aircraft with 4 crew operational trainer variant.
Maker: Tupolev, Kazan, USSR.
Users: Soviet Naval Aviation and the air forces of USSR, Iraq and Libya.
Engines: 2 Koliesov VD-7 reheated turbojets (total 62,000lb/28,123kg thrust).
Dimensions: 134.25ft (40.92m) overall length; 81.1ft (24.72m) wingspan; 2023sq ft (188m²) wing area.
Weights: 185,000lb (83,915kg) estimated maximum gross.
Performance: 860 knots/1595km/h (Mach 1.5) at 36,000ft/10,973m reducing to 595 knots/1103km/h (Mach 0.9) at sea level maximum speed; 54,000ft/16,460m service ceiling; 1670 nautical miles/3095km maximum radius of action.
Armament: Up to 17,637lb (8000kg) of weapons and ammunition for the defensive single 23mm tail-mounted, radar controlled NR-23 cannon.
Programme: Believed to have first flown in prototype form during 1959, the aircraft entered series production around 1965 and was initially operationally deployed at the turn of 1966/67. Around 250 'Blinders' were reported to have been built in four basic versions before production was completed in the early 1970s to make way for the 'Backfire'. Currently, around 40 'Blinders' are reported to be in service with Soviet Naval Aviation.
Notes: Designed as a replacement for the strictly subsonic Tupolev Tu-16 'Badger', the Tu-22 'Blinder' has sometimes been described as a failure as a result of the latter's inferior warload/range capability compared with the slower Tu-16. While there is clearly some substance in such criticism, it does largely ignore the very positive speed advantage of the Tu-22, which in theatres such as the Mediterranean could mean the difference between survival and extinction. Further, it is equally worth remembering that the Tu-22 'Blinder' development formed a fundamental stepping stone in the evolution of the variable geometry winged Tu-22M 'Backfire'. Of extremely clean lines, the 'Blinder' is characterised by its two aft-mounted engines that straddle the base of the aircraft's fin and rudder. 'Blinder A' is the initial bomber-reconnaissance version; 'Blinder B' has a modified underside to carry missiles; 'Blinder C' is a navalised conventional bomb-carrier, while 'Blinder D' is the four-crew operational trainer variant.

Tupolev Tu-22M 'Backfire' Bombers

Type and role: 4 or 5 crew, twin-turbojet-engined, supersonic variable wing geometry bomber and reconnaissance aircraft.
Maker: Tupolev, Kazan, USSR.
Users: Soviet Naval Aviation and Soviet Air Force.
Engines: 2 Kuznetsov NK-144 reheated turbojets (total 92,594lb/42,000kg thrust).
Dimensions: 131.9ft (40.20m) overall length; 86.0/112.9ft (26.2/34.4m) swept/unswept wingspan; 1830sq ft (170m²) unswept wing area.
Weights: 103,617lb (47,000kg) empty; 270,066lb (122,500kg) maximum gross.
Performance: 1147 knots/2126km/h (Mach 2.0) at 36,090ft/11,000m reducing to 595 knots/1103km/h (Mach 0.9) at sea level maximum speed; 27,500ft/8382m/min initial rate of climb; over

This 'Blinder B' carries a 'Kitchen' long ranged anti-ship missile semi-recessed into the lower fuselage centre section.

59,000ft/17,983m service ceiling; up to 3238 nautical miles/6000km unrefuelled maximum radius of action extending to 4695 nautical miles/8700km with one mid-air refuelling.
Armament: Up to 17,637lb (8000kg) of weapons and ammunition for the defensive twin 23mm tail-mounted, radar-controlled NR-23 cannons. 'Backfire' can carry a 13,288lb (6000kg) 'Kitchen' or the lighter and smaller 'Kingfisher' air-launched, long range anti-ship missiles semi-recessed into the lower fuselage centre section.
Programme: Thanks to US Air Force reconnaissance satellite photography, it has been established that both prototype Tu-22M 'Backfires' had entered flight testing by the latter part of 1970. These machines were followed by ten to 12 pre-series 'Backfire As' built in the 1972 to 1973 period, before the definitive 'Backfire B' emerged to enter series production in 1975 at a rate of around 40 aircraft per year. Subsequently, according to Soviet sources this high initial production rate was cut back to 30 aircraft per year in the latter 1970s as a result of the never-ratified Strategic Arms Limitations Talks (SALT II) held between the US and USSR. Official US sources put the number of 'Backfires' in operation with the Soviet military and naval airarms as 130 each as at the end of 1984 with production continuing at 30 a year.
Notes: Despite the need for extensive redesign associated with the aircraft's landing gear early on, the definitive

The Soviet Navy's potent 'Backfire B' seen with its wings in the maximum lift-producing unswept configuration.

A Soviet Naval Aviation 'Badger F' photographed while shadowing US naval movements in the Pacific during the early 1960s. A substantial number of these elderly missile carriers still and will continue to operate over the North Western Pacific for some years to come.

machine has emerged as one of the most formidable weapons carriers in the Soviet's arsenal. Subject to some greatly exaggerated early US claims, such as having a Mach 2.5 speed capability, coupled with a virtually global range, the Tu-22M's downward-revised range still brings most US Navy sea-going operations under its operational flight coverage, or 'footprint'.

Tupolev Tu-16 'Badger' Bombers

Type and role: 6 to 9 crew, twin turbojet-engined subsonic, air-refuellable bomber reconnaissance type, plus aerial tanker version.
Makers: Tupolev, Kazan, USSR and Xian, China.
Users: Soviet Naval Aviation and Air Force, plus air forces of China and Egypt.
Engines: 2 Mikulin AM-3M turbojet (total 38,581lb/17,500kg thrust).
Dimensions: 114.2ft (34.80m) overall length; 108.0ft (32.93m) wingspan; 1772sq ft (164.65m²) wing area.
Weights: 88,185lb (40,000kg) empty; 115,742lb (52,500kg) normal gross; 169,756lb (77,000kg) maximum gross.
Performance: 508 knots/941km per hour (Mach 0.885) at 36,090ft/11,000m increasing to 542 knots/1005km/h at sea level maximum speed; 40,026ft/12,200m service ceiling; up to 1562 nautical miles/2895km radius of action with 19,842lb/9000kg warload unrefuelled.
Armament: Up to 19,842lb (9000kg) of weapons including ammunition for 3 twin 23mm, radar-controlled NR-23 cannons. 'Badger F' can carry 1 AS-6 'Kingfish' or 2 AS-5 'Kelt' long range anti-ship missiles.
Programme: First flown in prototype form during 1952, the Tu-16 entered service in 1955. Production of approximately 2000 Soviet-built Tu-16s came to an end in 1964, to be followed by the licence-building of the aircraft in China, where it is designated B-6; still, according to US official sources, being manufactured in limited numbers. In all, around 350 of the Chinese-built aircraft are believed to have been completed by the end of 1982. Fourteen ex-Soviet Tu-16s were reported to still be operational with the Egyptian Air Force at the end of 1982.
Notes: Despite its age, the Tu-16 'Badger' still forms the backbone of the Soviet Naval Aviation bomber force, only gradually being replaced by the Tu-22M 'Backfire'. The 'Badger' has been built or converted into ten different versions (A through K, with I being omitted). The A model was a conventional bomber; B, C and G variants are

missile carriers; D, E, F, and K 'Badgers' are used for reconnaissance or electronic intelligence gathering, while H and J models are specialised electronics warfare types. Out of around 830 still active Soviet Tu-16s, 280 are naval aircraft.

Grumman A-6 Intruder & Prowler Bombers

Type and role: 2-seat, twin turbojet-engined, all-weather, high subsonic strike aircraft (A-6 series) and 4-seat electronics warfare aircraft (EA-6B).
Maker: Grumman Aerospace Corporation, Bethpage, Long Island, USA.
Users: US Navy and US Marine Corps.
Engines: 2 Pratt & Whitney J52-P-8B turbojets (total 18,600lb/8437kg thrust) in A-6E and 2 Pratt & Whitney J52-P-40B turbojets (total 22,400lb/10,160kg thrust) in EA-6B.
Dimensions: 54.75ft (16.7m) for A-6E and 59.25ft (18.1m) for EA-6B's overall length; 53.0ft (16.15m) wingspan; 25.3ft (7.7m) for A-6E and 25.9ft (7.8m) for EA-6B's wingspan folded; 529sq ft (49.15m²) wing area.
Weights: 26,456lb (12,00kg) for A-6E and 32,162lb (14,589kg) for EA-6B empty; 60,395lb (27,395kg) for A-6E and 60,610lb (27,493kg) for EA-6B maximum gross.
Performance: 560 knots/1038km/h (Mach 0.85) at sea level for A-6E and 541 knots/1002km/h (Mach 0.82) at sea level for EA-6B's maximum speed; 42,500ft/12,954m for A-6E and 38,000ft/11,582m for EA-6B's service ceiling; 321 nautical miles/595km tactical radius of action unrefuelled with 28 Mk 81 bombs (A-6E).
Armament: Up to 18,000lb of externally-carried weapons including Tomahawk cruise and Harpoon anti-ship missiles. No provision for the carriage of internal cannons or other weaponry (A-6E); up to 5 Raytheon ALQ-99 high powered electronic jammers can be carried plus extensive internally-mounted electronics warfare equipment (EA-6B).
Programme: Born from a 1956 US Navy requirement for a low-level, all-weather carrier-going bomber, the development award for the A-6 went to Grumman in December 1957. The prototype A-6A made its maiden flight in April 1960, the A-6 being initially deployed in February 1963. Subsequent milestone dates in the programme include May 1966 as the first flight date of the KA-6D tanker, the first of which was delivered to the Fleet in April 1970. The EA-6B (developed to replace the interim 2-seat EA-6A) made its maiden flight in May 1968 and was operationally deployed in January 1971, to be followed by the first flight of the A-6E in February 1970, its deployment being made in the latter half of 1971. In all, excluding the many conversions to EA-6A (78), EA-6B (12) and A-6E (192), total identified orders at the end of 1982 amounted to 740, comprising: 488 A-6As, 15 EA-6As, 91 EA-6Bs and 146 A-6Es. Of this total, 608 are for the US Navy and 80 are Marine aircraft and both the A-6E and EA-6B remain in current production.
Notes: The rugged A-6 family is destined to remain in front line carrier service through the year 2000. To help understand the underlying success of this family of aircraft it is pertinent to go back to the original US Navy requirement that led to their birth. In calling for an all-weather, low-level high subsonic speed carrier-borne bomber, the Navy specification tied Grumman down to having to build a bulky aircraft simply in order to house a second man, needed to handle numerous electronic sensors. Simultaneously, the Navy's need to operate at relatively high speed *and* low-level predicated that the aircraft's structure and particularly its wings be built as strongly as possible, in order to absorb the frequent gusting air loads encountered when flying at minimum altitude. Thus, Grumman were, in fact, compelled to produce a big and heavy machine, which, in turn, meant

An EA-6B Prowler, readily identified by its large fin top-mounted electronics housing and additional canopy for the two additional crew members. Note the recently-adopted low visibility paint scheme.

that the Grumman A-6 family started off with a robust, long life airframe and one that had sufficient internal volume to be able to take advantage of advances in sensor and associated electronics processing technology. Perhaps nowhere better than in the case of the A-6 family is the old aviation axiom that 'Big is Beautiful' seen to be borne out, as evidenced by the ready ability to stretch the basic design to take a four-man crew plus up to around 25,000lb (11,340kg) of high-powered electronics warfare equipment in the case of the EA-6B Prowler. A similar story of evolving operational flexibility can be seen

with the evolution of the standard A-6 bombers, the A-6E crews now being able to attack targets using the hybrid TRAM or Target Recognition Attack Multisensor system, which, because it incorporates forward looking infra-red sensors, can be used to approach the target without radiating tell-tale radar emissions. Similarly, today's A-6E can carry more than 30 different types of missiles, bombs, mines, rockets and fuel tanks to aid its mission capability; a far cry indeed from the limited variety of weaponry carried by the original A-6As.

Missile directors

Tupolev Tu-142 'Bear D to G' Missile Director

Type and role: 11 to 13 crew, 4 turboprop-engined, subsonic long-range anti-ship missile director and reconnaissance aircraft.
User: Soviet Naval Aviation.
Engines: 4 Kuznetsov NK-12MV turboprops (total 59,000shp) each driving 4-bladed, contra-rotating, reversible-pitch propellers.
Dimensions: 162.5ft (49.53m) overall length; 167.5ft

(51.05m) wingspan; 3150sq ft (292.6m²) wing area.
Weight: Up to 414,469lb (188,000kg) maximum gross.
Performance: 484 knots/897km/h (Mach 0.82) at 29,528ft/9000m maximum speed; 384 knots/711km/h (Mach 0.67) at 36,089ft/11,000m economic cruise speed; 44,290ft/13,500m service ceiling; 6253 nautical miles/11,587km maximum unrefuelled range with 25,000lb/11,340kg warload.
Armament: Up to 66,189lb (30,000kg) of weaponry

A Tupolev Tu-142 'Bear D' seen being escorted by a US Navy A-7E Corsair II while operating in the vicinity of the A-7E's parent carrier, the USS Nimitz (CVN68).

including ammunition for 1 or 2 twin 23mm radar-controlled NR-23 cannons.

Programme: A direct derivative of the Tupolev Tu-95 'Bear A to C' designs that first flew in mid-1954, the Tu-142 derivatives were initially deployed in early 1967. Around 70 Tu-142s are thought to be in current service with Soviet Naval Aviation units and low-scale production of these aircraft is reported to be continuing.

Notes: With the exception of the Tu-142 'Bear D', which has a lengthened fuselage, all Tu-142 variants are virtually indistinguishable from the earlier Tu-95 in every feature, except that all Tu-142s carry electronic support measures (ESM) antenna fairings at the tips of their tailplanes. Although ancient in appearance, the Tu-142 continues to fill a vital function in terms of Soviet naval operations by providing almost global-ranging over-water surveillance. With the exception of the 'Bear E' specialised electronics intelligence gatherer, all Tu-142 variants are equipped with the sensors and data links necessary to guide the various Soviet long ranged ship and air-launched anti-ship missiles against their distant targets; primary target and missile tracking being carried out using their massive 'Puff Ball' air-to-surface radar that is ventrally-mounted in the fuselage centre section.

Fighters

With its wings in the fully swept position, this Grumman F-14A of the 32nd Fighter Squadron aboard USS John F Kennedy *(CV67) is carrying six long-range Phoenix air-to-air missiles.*

Grumman F-14 Tomcat Fighters

Type and role: 2-seat, variable-geometry winged, supersonic all-weather carrier-going fighter.

Maker: Grumman Aerospace Corporation, Bethpage, Long Island, USA.

Users: US Navy and Iranian Air Force.

Engines: 2 Pratt & Whitney TF30-P-412A turbofans with reheat (total 41,800lb/18,960kg trust).

Dimensions: 62.7ft (19.1m) overall length; 64.1ft (19.6m) wingspan unswept; 38.2ft (11.7m) wingspan swept; 565sq ft (52.5m²) wing area.

Weights: 39,762lb (18,036kg) empty; 59.372lb (26,931kg) normal gross; 70,426lb (31,945kg) maximum gross.

Performance: Approximately 1348 knots/2498km/h (Mach 2.35) at 37,000ft/11,276m reducing to around 860 knots/1593km/h (Mach 1.3) at sea level maximum speed; 550 knots/1019km/h (Mach 0.96) optimum cruising speed at 37,000ft/11,276m; 60,000ft/18,288m in 2.1 minutes time-to-climb; 665 nautical miles/1232km tactical radius of action for unrefuelled mission with 6 AIM-7 Sparrows and 4 AIM-9 Sidewinders.

Armament: Up to 6423lb (2913kg) of externally-mounted missiles comprising 6 AIM-54 Phoenix and 2 AIM-9 Sidewinder, plus 676 rounds of ammunition for the internally-mounted 20mm General Electric M61 six-barrelled Vulcan cannon. *Note:* the aircraft is capable of lifting a considerably greater warload and/or externally carried additional fuel which is only limited by the missile mix available.

Programme: Following the failure of the largely politically inspired and overweight F-111B, the US Navy issued an industry-wide request in July 1968 for a new fighter, known as VFX, the development contract for which was awarded to Grumman in January 1969. As Grumman had been working on what was to become the F-14 since January 1968, coupled to a post-award engineering effort of gargantuan proportions, the company was in a position to put the first of 12 pre-series aircraft into the air at the end of December 1970. The first production aircraft were delivered to the US Navy in June 1972 and the first F-14 carrier deployment followed in September 1974 aboard USS *Enterprise* (CVN65). Original US Navy planning foresaw the purchase of 463 excluding development aircraft, but this figure, which has 'yo-yoed' alarmingly over the aircraft's history, now looks set to reach 835 when production closes in the mid-1990s. By the beginning of 1985, just under 500 Tomcats were scheduled to have been delivered to the US Navy, including the 12 pre-series machines. In January 1974, Iran placed its first order for 30 F-14As, subsequently increased to a total of 80 aircraft. Delivery of these Iranian F-14s commenced in January 1976 and all but one had been delivered at the time of the Iranian Revolution.

Notes: Built as a replacement for the McDonnell F-4 Phantom II, the real-life chronology of the F-14A Tomcat programme would pale most television dramas into insignificance. To set out just a few of the more salient highlights, the F-14 Tomcat, all in relatively quick succession, crashed on it second flight, nearly bankrupted Grumman and proved to have a critically unreliable engine during its earlier service life. All this notwithstanding, the total weapons system concept around which the F-14 had been designed had always held out much promise to the US Navy already facing ever further ranging potential adversaries, many of which were equipped with potent, stand-off missile capability. Once in service, the F-14, despite all of its shortfalls (related to the decision to stay with what had always been considered an interim engine fit), soon provided practical proof of the US Navy's underlying confidence in its abilities. To summarise these intrinsic F-14 advantages would require far more space than is available here. However, suffice it to note that with its powerful track-while-scan AWG-9 radar capable of tracking up to 20 targets and simultaneously controlling up to 6 AIM-54 Phoenix missiles, the US Navy, for the first time ever, found itself in possession of a truly all-weather fighter whose sensor/weapons fit and airframe were actually well matched for both long ranged, often head-on interception and the rough-and-tumble of close-in air combat.

Vought F-8 Crusader Fighters

Type and role: Single-seat, supersonic, carrier-going, single turbojet tactical fighter and photographic reconnaissance aircraft.
Maker: Vought Corporation, Dallas, Texas, USA.
Users: US Navy (1219, of which a handful of RF-8Gs remain in use), French Navy (42) and Philippine Air Force (25 ex-US Navy F-8H).
Engine: 1 Pratt & Whitney J57-P-12 or -20 turbojet (16,000 or 18,000lb thrust with reheat. *Note:* P-12 fitted to RF-8G; P-20 to F-8E/H.
Dimensions: 54.2ft (16.5m) overall length; 35.7ft (10.9m) wingspan; 22.5ft (6.9m) wingspan folded for stowage; 375sq ft (34.8m²) wing area.
Weights: 19,750lb (8960kg) empty equipped; 27,550lb (12,496kg) normal gross; 34,000lb (15,420kg) maximum gross.
Performance: 973 knots/1802km/h (Mach 1.7) maximum speed at 40,000ft/12,192m; 6 minutes to 57,000ft/17,374, rate of climb; 521 nautical miles/ 966km maximum tactical radius of action for F-8E or -8H.
Armament: 4 internally-mounted 30mm cannons, plus up to 5000lb (2268kg) of externally carried weaponry, including 4 short-range air-to-air missiles on 4 fuselage-mounted pylons and underwing bombs. *Note:* RF-8G carries no armament.
Programme: Designed against a 1952 US Navy supersonic air-superiority fighter requirement, the prototype F-8 Crusader made its maiden flight in March

A US Navy camera-equipped RF-8G.

1955 and was to be followed by another 1260 Crusaders before production came to an end in 1968. The F-8A was first deployed operationally aboard ship in late 1957.
Notes: A veteran of the 1962 Cuban-US missile crisis, the F-8 Crusader went on to provide the backbone of US Navy fighter force during the earlier years of their South East Asian campaign; the Crusader being favoured in preference to the McDonnell F-4 Phantom II as a fighter-on-fighter dogfighting mount. Although taken out of front-line US Navy service in the late 1960s, an ever diminishing number of the specialised RF-8G have remained operational. Similarly, while scheduled to be replaced by the Super Etendard in French naval service, the F-8E (FN) is likely to remain operational with them through the mid-1980s.

Strike fighters

McDonnell F/A-18 Hornet Strike Fighters

Type and role: Single-seat, twin turbofan-engined, supersonic carrier-going strike fighter (F-18A); two seat operational trainer (TF-18A) and two seat tactical fighter (CF-18).
Maker: McDonnell Aircraft Company, St Louis, Missouri, USA.
Users: US Navy/Marines, Canadian Armed Forces and on order for the air forces of Australia and Spain.
Engines: 2 General Electric F404-GE-400 turbofans (total 32,000lb/14,515kg thrust).
Dimensions: 56.0ft (17.1m) overall length 36.5ft (11.4m) wingspan; 27.5ft (8.4m) wingspan folded; 400sq ft (37.16m²) wing area.
Weights: 28,000lb (12,700kg) empty; 35,800lb (16,239kg) normal gross; 56,000lb (25,401kg) maximum gross.
Performance: 786 knots/1457km/h (Mach 1.18) at sea

Three F-18A Hornets of US Marine Fighter Squadron 314 making a climbing turn to port shows the aircraft's planform to advantage.

level rising to 1033 knots/1914km/h (Mach 1.8) at above 36,000ft/10,973m maximum speed; in excess of 50,000ft/15,240m service ceiling; 399 nautical miles/740km tactical radius of action with 2 Sparrow and 2 Sidewinder air-to-air missiles and no externally carried fuel.

Armament: Up to in excess of 17,000lb (7711kg) of weapons including a typical fighter mission mix of 4 Sparrow and 2 Sidewinder missiles plus 1 internally-mounted General Electric six-barrelled 20mm M61 Vulcan cannon with 570 rounds of ammunition.

Programme: During 1973, when the Grumman F-14 programme looked close to failure (largely as a result of cost escalation), the US Navy issued a requirement for a lower cost tactical fighter, the VFAX. In October 1974, the US Congress intervened in the VFAX builder selection process to insist that the US Navy consider only navalised derivatives of the existing single-engined General Dynamics F-16 and the twin-engined Northrop F-17 lightweight fighters. Not unexpectedly in May 1975, the US Navy selected the McDonnell/Northrop F-18 (a derivitive of the F-17 in which Northrop had to relinquish programme leadership to McDonnell as the former company lacked experience in designing and building carrier-going aircraft). The first flight of the F-18A took place in mid-November 1978, followed by that of the two-seat TF-18A in late October 1979. In all, the US Navy plans to buy a total of 1377 F/A-18s for itself and the Marines, of which the initial aircraft were deployed by a land-based Marines unit in January 1983. The first carrier-going deployment of a US Navy F-18 squadron is scheduled to take place during 1985. In early March 1980, Canada announced its decision to purchase 138 Hornets, the first of which were delivered in late 1982. This was followed, in October 1981, by the Australian announcement that it was to buy 75 Hornets, the first of which would be delivered in late 1984. The latest customer to select the F-18 is Spain, which announced its intention to buy 84 during 1982. By the end of 1984, a total of 198 Hornets, including the 11 pre-series aircraft, had been delivered.

Notes: Designed as a truly multi-mission aircraft capable of replacing the McDonnell F-4 Phantom II fighter and the Douglas A-4 Skyhawk and Vought A-7 Corsair II light strike types, much controversy has surrounded the development of the F-18 programme primarily concerned with cost considerations, but with some earlier anxieties also being expressed about the aircraft's ability to meet the US Navy specifications in the attack, or strike mission mode. While costing questions had not totally vanished by early 1983 and may well continue partly as a result of a broader dialogue concerning the proper mix of US Navy heavy and light fighter and attack aircraft levels to be established through the end of the century, the Hornet, itself, appears to be emerging as an admirable fighting or attack platform both in terms of pilot handling and

An F-4J of the USS Independence *(CV62) seen on HMS* Ark Royal's *flight deck during a visit to the British carrier in April 1975.*

weapons delivery. In the fighter role, the F-18 can accelerate faster than an F-4J by around 20 per cent and outrange the same machine also by some 20 per cent, while the turning performance is approaching 40 per cent in favour of the F-18. Designed for ease of single pilot operation, the aircraft's Hughes APG-65 multi-mode radar is readily reprogrammable in order to keep pace with developments in electronics warfare, and provides the sensor means by which the Hornet can meet most airborne threats, including the Soviet Navy's 'Backfire' and its air-launched stand-off anti-ship missiles.

McDonnell F-4 Phantom II Strike Fighters

Type and role: 2-seat, twin turbojet-engined, supersonic carrier-going all-weather tactical fighter and photographic reconnaissance aircraft.

Makers: McDonnell Aircraft Company, St Louis, Missouri, USA (5057 built) and Mitsubishi, Tokyo, Japan (138 licence-built).

Users: US Navy/Marine Corps and the air forces of Australia, Federal Germany, Greece, Iran, Israel, Japan, South Korea, Spain, Turkey, UK and USA.

Engines: 2 General Electric J79-GE-10 turbojets with reheat (total 35,800lb/16,239kg thrust) in F-4J. *Note:* all F-4s are GE J79 powered, other than RAF Phantoms, which have 2 Rolls-Royce Spey 202 turbofans with reheat (total 40,630lb/18,429kg thrust).

Dimensions: 58.25ft (17.75m) overall length; 38.4ft (11.7m) wingspan; 27.55ft (8.4m) wingspan folded; 530sq ft (49.2m²) wing area: *data for 4J.*

Weights: 28,000lb (12,701kg) empty; 46,000lb (20,865kg) normal gross; 54,600lb (24,766kg) maximum gross: *data for 4J.*

Performance: 754 knots/1397km/h (Mach 1.14) at sea level rising to 1193 knots/2211km/h (Mach 2.08) at 37,500ft/11,430m maximum speed; 1.2 minutes to climb to 36,000ft/10,973m; 57,000/17,374m combat ceiling; 532 nautical miles/986km typical radius of action with 4 AIM-7 Sparrows: *data for 4J.*

Armament: Up to 8300lb (3765kg) of weapons including typical combat air patrol (CAP) fit of 4 AIM-7 Sparrow and 2 AIM-9 Sidewinder missiles.

Programme: In June 1954, the US Navy verbally informed three US manufacturers of a need for a new all-weather strike fighter, a development contract for which was placed with McDonnell Aircraft in October 1954. The first of five prototype F-4As made its maiden flight in May 1958, followed by initial deployment (with the US Navy) in June 1961; the aircraft being cleared for carrier operations in October 1961. Of the total 5195 Phantom IIs built during the aircraft's 24-year production life, the US Navy and Marine Corps took 1205 machines comprising 637 F-4Bs, 46 RF-4Bs and 522 F-4Js. Of these naval F-4s, 228 F-4Bs were converted into F-4Ns between 1972 and 1978, with a further 265 former F-4Js being converted to F-4S standard more recently. As the 'Midway' class carriers cannot accept the Grumman F-14 Tomcat, coupled with the knowledge that the US Marine Corps hold priority for F-18 Hornet deliveries, it would appear that the F-4 is destined to remain in US Navy service well into the 1990s.

Notes: Very much a legend in its own time, the US Navy-sponsored F-4 Phantom II, like the Grumman A-6 Intruder, always enjoyed the benefits of size and internal volume: factors that permitted the incorporation from inception of a powerful, long-range radar and other sensors, along with a second crew member to reduce pilot workload by operating the aircraft's onboard electronics. Under the thrust of its two General Electric J79s, the F-4 set about demonstrating its vivid performance capabilities quite early in its career, setting two altitude, five speed and eight time-to-climb records between December 1959 and

April 1962. During this period, the joint US Navy and McDonnell team's efforts were centred not on setting new records, but on the more serious business of developing the aircraft's multi-mission capabilities, which ranged from all-weather interceptor to bomb-hauler. So impressive were the results of this effort that for the first time since the late 1920s, the US Air Force, who were ultimately to buy 2712 F-4s, placed its first order for this naval fighter in April 1962. In US Navy service, the F-4 served primarily in the fleet air defence role, while the US Marine Corps employed the type as a close air support (strike) aircraft. The Phantom II's baptism of fire came in August 1964, when F-4Bs of two navy squadrons aboard USS *Constellation* struck at North Vietnamese torpedo boat shore facilities, to be followed by the first US Air Force South East Asian deployment of the F-4 in April 1965. From that point on, the Phantom II was given the opportunity to demonstrate its mission flexibility on an ever increasing scale. As was only to be expected, the type's employment in action showed up areas of weakness, such as the vulnerability of the aircraft's hydraulic system to ground fire, and the limited effectiveness of having an all-missile armament, particularly when engaged in dogfights. Much of the fruit of this experience can be found incorporated in later models of the F-4 developed for both the US Navy and US Air Force.

In-flight aspects of the Federal German Navy's Panavia Tornado. The aircraft is seen equipped with Kormoran stand-off ranged anti-ship missiles.

Panavia Tornado Strike Fighters

Type and role: 2-seat, twin turbofan-engined, land-based, all-weather supersonic (at all altitudes) strike fighter and reconnaissance aircraft, incorporating in-flight refuelling capability.
Maker: Panavia GmbH, Munich, Federal Germany.
Users: Federal German Navy (112) and the air forces of Federal Germany (212), Italy (100) and the UK (220 strike and 165 fighters).
Engines: 2 Turbo-Union RB199 Mk 101 turbofans (total 18,000lb/8165kg without reheat, or 32,000lb/14,515kg thrust with reheat).
Dimensions: 54.8ft (16.7m) overall length; 45.6ft (13.9m) wingspan unswept; 28.2ft (8.6m) wingspan swept; 322.9sq ft (30.0m²) wing area.
Weights: 23,000lb (10,433kg) empty; 58,400lb (26,490kg) maximum gross.
Performance: Approximately 1262 knots/2339km/h (Mach 2.2) above 36,000ft without external stores reducing to around 800 knots/1483km/h (Mach 1.2) at 500ft in clean configuration; under 2 mins to climb to 30,000ft/9144m; 573 nautical miles/1062km typical high-low-high tactical radius of action unrefuelled.
Armament: Up to 16,000lb (7257kg) of weaponry, including 4 Kormoran or Sea Eagle stand-off anti-ship missiles and 2 internally-mounted 27mm Mauser cannons.
Programme: The aircraft that was to become the Tornado was first drawn up by British Aerospace's Warton Division in the 1967/1968 period, in the wake of the cancellation of the Anglo-French Variable Geometry combat aircraft project. After an initially industrially turbulent period of around four years during which the envisaged numbers to be procured fell from 1185 to 809 aircraft, coupled to a significant slippage in programme timescales, the jointly Anglo-German-Italian developed and built Tornado made its first flight in mid-August 1974. The first production aircraft (a two-seat operational trainer) flew for the first time in early July 1979. Initial operational deployment of the strike variant of Tornado took place during the summer of 1982 with both the Federal German Navy and Royal Air Force squadrons. Although each of the three participating nations has responsibility for the manufacture of various elements of the Tornado airframe,

engines and systems for all aircraft, each nation retains control over the final assembly and testing of its own aircraft. By the end of 1984, just over 410 Tornadoes had been built and delivered to their respective user services.
Notes: Despite the apparent protracted nature of the Tornado's development, compared with such as the US Navy's Grumman F-14A Tomcat, this tripartite variable geometry-winged machine has emerged as a very credible, long-range strike aircraft, capable of operating in a contour-hugging mode at speeds of up to 600 knots/1112km/h with external stores in any kind of weather. Although not destined for naval user operation, it is pertinent to note that the air defence version, known as the Tornado F-2, being developed for the Royal Air Force is destined to spend a significant portion of its useful life over the hostile waters of the Greenland-Iceland-UK gap, where it will fly, accompanied by tanker aircraft, acting as a missile-carrying, airborne radar picket against incursions by aircraft of the Soviet's Northern Fleet.

Vought A-7 Corsair II Strike Fighters

Type and role: Single seat, limited all-weather carrier-going high subsonic strike fighter (A-7A, B and E: D, H and P versions being land-based) and 2 seat operational trainer (TA-7C, H and K).
Maker: Vought Corporation, Dallas, Texas, USA (1606 built).
Users: US Navy/Marines (A-7A, B, E and TA-7C); US Air Force/Air National Guard (A-7D and K) and the air forces of Greece (A-7H) and Portugal (ex-US Navy aircraft refurbished as A-7P).
Engine: 1 Allison/Rolls-Royce TF41-A-2 turbofan (15,000lb/6804kg thrust) on A-7D and subsequent models; A-7A, B and C had 1 Pratt & Whitney TF30 of 11,350lb/5148kg (A-7A) or 12,200lb/5534kg thrust (A-7B and C).
Dimensions: 46.1ft (14.1m) overall length; 38.7ft (11.8m) wingspan; 23.8ft (7.25m) wingspan folded; 375sq ft (34.8m²) wing area.
Weights: 18,546lb (8412kg) empty; 38,000lb (17,237kg) normal gross; 42,000lb (19,051kg) maximum gross.
Performance: 572 knots/1060km/h (Mach 0.86) at sea level reducing to 520 knots/964km/h (Mach 0.91) at

An A-7E awaits its catapult launch in this dramatic picture taken on the USS Forrestal's *forward flight deck.*

36,000ft/10,973m maximum speed with 2 Sidewinders; 38,000ft/11,582m in 11 minutes time-to-climb with 2 Sidewinders; 490 nautical miles/908km tactical radius of action with 12 Mk 86 bombs and 2 Sidewinders.

Armament: Up to 15,000lb (6804kg) of externally-carried weapons, plus 1 internally-mounted General Electric 20mm Mk 61 Vulcan six-barrelled cannon with 1000 rounds of ammunition (selectable to fire 6000 or 4000 rounds per minute).

Programme: In May 1963, the US Navy issued an industry-wide requirement for a new attack aircraft which Vought won in November 1963, the prototype A-7A making its first flight one month ahead of schedule in September 1965. The A-7A was first operationally deployed in February 1967 with the much uprated TF41 powered A-7D making its maiden flight in September 1968. In all, Vought will have built 1606 A-7s when deliveries are completed in 1983, comprising 1051 for the US Navy/Marines, 495 for the US Air Force/Air National Guard and 60 for Greece, the 20 Portuguese aircraft being refurbished US Navy machines.

Notes: Designed to serve as a replacement for the US Navy's carrier-going Douglas A-4 Skyhawk, the Vought A-7, along with the heavier Grumman A-6, still provides the US Navy with its total carrier-going attack aircraft punch and the A-7 is expected to remain in service for some years before its total replacement by the McDonnell Douglas A-18 Hornet.

Dassault Breguet Super Etendard Strike Fighters

Type and role: Single seat, single engined transonic shipboard strike fighter and reconnaissance aircraft.
Maker: Dassault Breguet Aviation, Vaucresson, France.
Users: Navies of France and Argentina, plus Iraqi Air Force.
Engine: 1 SNECMA 8K50 turbojet (11,023lb/5000kg thrust).

Three French Navy Super Etendards, two of which are demonstrating their air refuelling capability.

Dimensions: 46.9ft (14.31m) overall length; 31.5ft (9.6m) wingspan; 307sq ft (28.4m²) wing area.
Weights: 13,780lb (6250kg) empty; 20,283lb (9200kg) normal gross; 25,350lb (11,500kg) maximum gross.
Performance: 591 knots/1095km/h (Mach 1.03) at 36,090ft/11,000m or 628 knots/1164km/h (Mach 0.95) maximum speed at sea level; 19,685ft/6000m/min initial rate of climb; 350 nautical miles/649km maximum radius of action with 1 Exocet.
Armament: Up to 4600lb (2087kg) of externally-mounted weapons, including 2 anti-ship AM39 Exocet missiles, plus 2 internally-mounted 30mm DEFA cannons, each with 125 rounds of ammunition.
Programme: A 1973 contracted development of the mid-1950s Etendard IV, from which the prototype super Etendards were converted, the first of which made its maiden flight in October 1974. The first production Super Etendard flew for the first time just over three years later in November 1977, followed by initial operational deployment of the type during 1979. Originally, 100 Super Etendards had been ordered for use with the French Navy, but general economic factors acting on the French defence budget brought the number down to 71, plus another 14 ordered for the Argentine Navy in 1979. Deliveries of the French Navy aircraft should, by now, be complete, while six were reported to have been delivered

to Argentina prior to April 1982 and the commencement of the Falklands hostilities during which none were lost in combat, according to official British sources. Deliveries of a reported five machines commenced by Iraq in late 1983.
Notes: Generally similar in external appearance to the earlier Etendard IV series, the Super Etendard incorporates a more powerful and fuel efficient engine, an improved higher-lift-at-low-speed wing and a far more comprehensive electronics fit that includes a Thomson-CSF multi-mode Agave primary radar. Another important improvement in the aircraft's electronics is the embodiment of a Kearfott-ETNA inertial nav-attack system. Previously largely overlooked, especially in the UK, the Super Etendard/Exocet combination leapt into instant prominence in the wake of the loss of HMS *Sheffield* on 4 May 1982. While this event represents the first recorded occasion in which a major warship was totally disabled by the action of an aircraft-launched anti-ship missile, it is even more sobering to recall the fact that the parent Super Etendard was operating not from a relatively nearby aircraft carrier's flight deck, but from a far distant airfield, thanks to their ability to take on additional fuel in flight.

A formating pilot's eye view of an Indian Navy Sea Harrier FRS 51.

British Aerospace Sea Harrier Strike Fighters

Type and role: Single seat, single vectoring thrust engined transonic shipboard strike fighter and reconnaissance aircraft.
Maker: British Aerospace, Kingston Division, UK.
Users: Royal Navy and Indian Navy.
Engine: 1 Rolls-Royce Pegasus 104 vectored thrust turbofan (21,500lb/9752kg thrust).
Dimensions: 47.6ft (14.5m) overall length; 25.25ft (7.7m) wingspan; 201.1sq ft (18.68m²) wing area.
Weights: 13,000lb (5897kg) empty; 21,700lb (9840kg) normal gross; 25,600lb (11,612kg) maximum gross with rolling take-off.
Performance: 628 knots/1271km/h (Mach 0.95) at sea level reducing to 528 knots/978km/h (Mach 0.92) at 36,000ft/10,973m maximum speed; over 50,000ft/15,240m service ceiling; 252 nautical miles/467km maximum tactical radius of action with combat air patrol weapons and 2 drop tanks.
Armament: Up to 5000lb (2268kg) of externally carried weapons, including 2 AIM-9 Sidewinder air-to-air missiles and 2 podded 30mm Aden cannons as a typical combat air patrol warload.
Programme: Approval to proceed with the development of a specialised naval derivative of the existing Harrier was received by the then Hawker Siddeley Aviation Group in May 1975, the first flight of the Sea Harrier taking place in August 1978, followed by the acceptance of the first Royal Navy aircraft in June 1979. The original Royal Navy order was for 34 Sea Harriers, of which six were lost during action in the Falklands. To make good these losses and bolster Britain's sea-going fighter cover, a follow-on order for a further 14 Royal Navy aircraft was placed in July 1982. An order for six Sea Harrier FRS 51s for the Indian Navy was received in December 1979 with the first aircraft delivered in January 1983. Production of the Sea Harrier is expected to continue for some years.
Notes: In reality, the Sea Harrier represents a quite radical departure from the previously slowly evolving family of ground attack Harriers and this is readily visible in any comparison of the aircraft's outlines. One of the primary differences centres on the two aircraft's nose radomes, the Sea Harrier's being much larger because it needed to house the multi-mode Ferranti 'Blue Fox' airborne interception radar. Equally necessary in the case of a fighter aircraft is the need to provide the pilot with the maximum all-round visibility, hence, the Sea Harrier's adoption of a whole new front fuselage section, within which the cockpit was raised and topped by a prominent

An excellent air-to-air view of the AV-8B showing the aircraft's new wing of greater area, underwing stores stations and two fuselage-mounted 25mm gun pods.

bubble canopy. Much non-visible redesign of the aircraft's structure and systems was also required in order to meet the changed mission stipulations. Put to the acid test of providing the vital air cover for the British South Atlantic Task Force during the spring of 1982, the Sea Harrier acquitted itself with honour in and around the Falklands, accounting for the downing of a confirmed 20 enemy aircraft, plus another probable; all for the loss of only two to enemy action, plus four more to non-directly hostile causes. Indeed, it is interesting to note that both of the Sea Harriers lost in action were downed by enemy ground fire while in the execution of strike missions, thus, none were lost in air combat, where the aircraft often found themselves pitted against agile Skyhawks and the much faster Mirage delta-winged fighters. Existing Sea Harriers will undergo a mid-life update to convert them to FRS 2 standard.

McDonnell AV-8B Harrier II Strike Fighters

Type and role: Single seat, single vectored thrust turbofan-engined, high subsonic, land and ship-going vertical and short take-off strike fighter.
Maker: McDonnell Aircraft Company, St. Louis, Missouri, USA.
Users: US Marine Corps and on order for the Royal Air Force and Spanish Navy.
Engine: 1 Rolls-Royce F402-RR-406 Pegasus 11 vectored thrust turbofan (21,180lb/9607kg thrust).
Dimensions: 46.3ft (14.1m) overall length; 30.3ft (9.25m) wingspan; 230sq ft (21.36m²) wing area.
Weights: 12,750lb (5783kg) empty; 19,185lb (8702kg) normal gross; 29,750lb (13,494kg) maximum gross with rolling take-off.

Performance: 582 knots/1078km/h (Mach 0.88) at sea level reducing to 534 knots/989km/h (Mach 0.93) at 36,000ft/10,973m maximum speed; 601 nautical miles/1114km tactical radius of action with a warload of 7 Mk 82 bombs.

Armament: Up to 9200lb (4173kg) of weaponry; a typical fit consisting of 4 Maverick air-to-ground missiles along with 2 Sidewinder air-to-air missiles and 2 externally-mounted 25mm gun pods.

Programme: Following the 1969 US Marine Corps' decision to buy the Harrier (which they designated AV-8A), Hawker Siddeley Aviation as they then were and McDonnell Aircraft, who were to support the AV-8A in the USA, set about the development of an Advanced Harrier, known as the AV-16. Although cancelled in May 1976 on cost grounds, some of the high transonic AV-16's aerodynamic and structural technology was salvaged to be incorporated into the less expensive AV-8B development: the AV-8B being formally launched in July 1976. From this point work proceeded on the conversion of two existing AV-8As into aerodynamic prototype YAV-8Bs, the first of which made its maiden flight in early November 1978, followed by the first of four full-scale development AV-8Bs in early November 1981. Delivery of the first of 12 pre-series AV-8Bs to the US Marines was made in late 1983 and the first of a planned 384 production aircraft should be initially deployed during 1986. In July 1981, the UK Government announced an initial order for 62 Harrier IIs (or Mk GR 5s), deliveries of which will commence to the Royal Air Force in late 1986. In March 1983, McDonnell Aircraft revealed the Spanish Government's intention to buy 12 AV-8Bs for delivery to its Navy, also commencing in late 1986. A total of 17 AV-8Bs had been delivered by the end of 1984.

Notes: employing a US-developed Supercritical-sectioned wing of 14 per cent greater wing area than that of the standard Harrier, the AV-8B's design has been optimised around achieving the maximum load-carrying/range trade-offs, rather than pushing the boundaries of pure flight performance, as in the case of the Sea Harrier. Indeed, while having a somewhat lower maximum level speed than either of its British brethren, the AV-8B carries nearly 58 per cent more weaponry or, conversely, can fly almost three times as far as the earlier AV-8A or Harrier GR 3. In industrial terms, the Harrier II programme is a US-led collaborative venture in which both British Aerospace and Rolls-Royce act as major subcontractors and which, in total, involves some 67 US and 27 UK suppliers.

Yakolev Yak-36mp 'Forger' Strike Fighters

One of Kiev's *'Forger As' about to land on board.*

Type and role: Single seat (Forger A) transonic vertical take-off and landing strike fighter and 2 seat (Forger B) operational trainer.

Maker: Yakolev, USSR.

User: Soviet Navy.

Engines: 1 possibly Lyulka vectored thrust cruise turbojet (18,078lb/8200kg thrust); 2 Koliesov lift turbojets (total 18,078lb/8200kg thrust).

Dimensions: 52.5ft (16.0m) overall length; 24.6ft (7.5m) wingspan; 167sq ft (15.50m²) wing area.

Weights: 12,125lb (5500kg) empty; 22,002lb (9980kg) maximum gross.

Performance: 631 knots/1169km/h (Mach 1.1) at 36,000ft/10,973m or 628 knots/1164km/h (Mach 0.95) maximum speed at sea level; 39,000ft/11,887m service ceiling; 200 nautical miles/371km maximum radius of action.

Armament: Up to 2205lb (1000kg) of externally-carried weapons, including 2 'Atoll' air-to-air missiles or other warloads on 4 underwing pylons.

Programme: The prototype Yak-36 is believed to have first flown during 1971 and was first operationally deployed at sea in mid-1976. As each of the four ship 'Kiev' class carriers can accommodate up to 25 'Forgers', production of the type is likely to exceed 150 aircraft when reserve and training requirments are taken into consideration. Thus, it is likely that production of the type is continuing at a relatively low rate of around 20 aircraft per year.

Notes: While the Yak-36 'Forger' is, by the nature of its compound cruise/lift plus lift-only engine system, incapable of making the warload-enhancing, forward rolling take-offs similar to those of the Harrier/Sea Harrier family, its emergence as a carrier deployable aircraft marked a significant advance for Soviet Naval Aviation. While no match for the speed and agility of the US Navy's essentially conventional carrier fighters (all of which require large, heavy ships from which to operate), the Yak-36 could well provide a useful, beyond stand-off missile ranged defence against incoming attacking aircraft. However, the Soviet Navy probably sees 'Forger's' primary role as being that of anti-shipping strike rather than air defence.

Douglas A-4 Skyhawk Strike Fighters

Type and role: Single seat, single turbojet-engined, carrier-going high subsonic strike fighter (A-4 models) and 2 seat operational trainer (TA-4 models).

Maker: Douglas Aircraft Company, Long Beach, California, USA.

Users: US Navy/Marine Corps, Argentinian Navy and the air forces of Australia, Indonesia, Israel, Kuwait, Malaysia, New Zealand and Singapore.

Engine: 1 Pratt & Whitney J52-P408A turbojet (11,200lb/5080kg thrust) in A-4M. *Note:* A-4A, B and C models used the Wright J65 turbojet (up to 8500lb/3856kg thrust) while all subsequent models employed variants of the Pratt & Whitney J52.

Dimensions: 42.8ft (13.0m) overall length; 27.5ft (8.38m) wingspan; 260sq ft (24.16m²) wing area. *Note:* A-4M data, other models show slight variations in overall length.

Weights: 10,465lb (4747kg) empty; 24,500lb (11,113kg) maximum gross.

Performance: 582 knots/1079km/h (Mach 0.88) at sea level or 563 knots/1044km/h (Mach 0.94) at 26,000ft/7925m maximum speed; 8440ft/2573m/min initial rate of climb; 295 nautical miles/547km tactical radius of action with a 4000lb/1814kg warload and without aerial refuelling. *Data for A-4M.*

Armament: Up to 9100lb (4128kg) of weaponry including 2 internally-mounted 20mm Mk 12 cannons plus various combinations of missiles, bombs and additional fuel tanks.

Programme: Conceived on a company-funded basis in January 1952, the US Navy placed its first contract for the aircraft in June 1952. The first and only prototype made its maiden flight in June 1954, followed by initial operational deployment of the A-4A in October 1956. In all, Douglas produced 2960 Skyhawks comprising: 2405 single seat A-4s and 555 of the two seat TA-4 variant by the time the Skyhawk production programme was completed in late February 1979; some 26 years after first metal was cut. Of the 2683 A-4 Skyhawk ordered for service with the US Navy/Marine Corps, 175 A-4F or Ms, plus another 75 reserve aircraft remained in service with the Marine Corps, along with around 60 Navy TA-4F or Js at the beginning of the 1980s. Between late 1966 and 1971, Argentina acquired a total of 91 refurbished A-4s: 75 for its Air Force and 16 for its Navy. Of these Argentinian machines, official British estimates indicate that 45 were lost during the Falklands fighting.

Notes: Essentially the brainchild of Douglas's then chief military aircraft engineer, Edward Heinemann, the A-4 Skyhawk was the product of private venture studies into ways of reducing the complexity, weight and cost elements involved in the design of a successor to the carrier-going, piston engined Douglas A-1 Skyraider; all within the context of producing a faster, jet-powered solution. Just how well Heinemann and his team succeeded in their task is now part of aviation history. Blooded in action in South East Asia, the Middle East and more recently over the Falklands, the A-4 Skyhawk proved to be capable of withstanding severe battle damage and still getting home. On more than one occasion, Skyhawks have returned to their carriers, to fly again,

A US Navy A-4M used for trials with the AGM-65E Laser Maverick.

even after suffering anti-aircraft fire that tore open up to 20 per cent of their wing skinning. As to be expected, the A-4 Skyhawk external appearance has undergone a series of changes over the years, with the aircraft sprouting in-flight refuelling probes, a second seat for training purposes and a saddle-humped fuselage housing for additional electronics in the A-4F and subsequent models. Commencing with the A-4H for Israel, some export models have had their internally-mounted 20mm cannons replaced by two 30mm DEFA weapons.

Maritime patrol

Fokker F27 Maritime Maritime Patrol Aircraft

Type and role: 6 crew, all-weather, twin turboprop-engined, land-based, medium-range maritime patrol or 38-seat transport aircraft.

Maker: Fokker BV, Schipol, Amsterdam, The Netherlands.

Users: Navies of Peru (2), Philippines (3) and Spain (3), along with the air forces or governments of Angola (1), Netherlands (2), Nigeria (2) and Thailand (3), plus over 700 other airline and military variants.

Engines: 2 Rolls-Royce Dart RDa7 turboprops (total 4740shp), each driving a 4-bladed, reversible-pitch propeller.

Dimensions: 77.3ft (23.56m) overall length; 95.15ft (29.0m) wingspan; 754sq ft (70.0m²) wing area.

Weights: 29,352lb (13,314kg) empty equipped; 45,000lb (20,412kg) normal gross; 47,500lb (21,547kg) overload gross.

Performance: 256 knots/474km/h maximum speed at 20,000ft/6098m; 160 knots/297km/h typical patrol cruise speed at 2000ft/610m; 2400ft/732m/min initial rate of climb; 9 hours maximum endurance on station

This F27 Maritime, is operated by the Angolan Government for fishery protection, search and rescue operations and coastal surveillance.

200 nautical miles/371km from base from a take-off weight of 47,500lb/21,547kg; 810 nautical miles/1500km maximum range with 10,000lb/4536kg load.

Armament: None fitted to standard model.

Programme: A maritime patrol variant of the Fokker F27 Friendship airliner, first flown in November 1955, the F27M made its maiden flight in February 1976. A total of

One of two CL-215s delivered to the Royal Thai Navy in 1978.

16 F27Ms had been ordered by June 1985, of which 14 had been delivered.

Notes: The requirement for the maritime patrol aircraft emerged from the so-called series of cod wars between Britain and Iceland and the subsequent implementation of the 200-nautical-mile (371km) offshore Exclusive Economic Zone (EEZ) around the coastlines of maritime countries. The maritime aircraft is an unarmed machine, packed with precision position-fixing equipment, separate air-to-surface and weather radars, along with camera and electronic recording equipment with precise time and position read-out capability. Although not the largest or fastest of this new breed of dedicated maritime patrol aircraft (which currently are variants of the Lockheed Hercules and Boeing 737, respectively) the F27M appears to have been amongst the most successful in commercial terms to date. As with other maritime patrol types, the F27M doubles as a fast response air-sea rescue machine.

Canadair CL-215 Maritime Patrol

Type and role: 2 or 3 crew, twin piston-engined amphibious utility.
Maker: Canadair Limited, Montreal, Quebec, Canada.
Users: Royal Thai Navy, air forces of Greece and Spain plus civil agencies.
Engines: 2 Pratt & Whitney R-2800-23AM piston radials (total 4200hp).
Dimensions: 60.02ft (18.29m) overall length; 93.83ft (28.60m) wingspan; 1080sq ft (100m²) wing area.
Weights: 27,740lb (12,585kg) empty; 43,500lb (19,728kg) maximum gross.
Performance: 157 knots/291km/h at 10,000ft/3048m maximum cruising speed; 970 nautical miles/1798km maximum range with 4500lb/2041kg payload.
Armament: None fitted to standard aircraft.
Programme: First flown in October 1967, the production of this 80 aircraft programme is approaching completion.

Notes: Designed as a specialised forest fire-fighting aerial water tanker, the ability of the CL-215 to operate from both land and water provided the aircraft with a useful secondary function as both a sea search and rescue (SAR) and maritime patrol type. In the context of the two latter roles, the air forces of Greece and Spain operate 11 and 17, respectively, while the Royal Thai Navy operates two radar-equipped aircraft as maritime patrollers. In the rescue role, the CL-215 can seat up to 29 people or 12 stretcher cases.

Dassault Guardian Maritime Patrol

Type and role: 4 to 6 crew, twin turbofan-engined, land-based, high subsonic maritime patrol and senior personnel transport.
Maker: Dassault Breguet Aviation, Vaucresson, France.
Users: French Navy and US Coast Guard.
Engines: 2 Garrett ATF3-6A-3C turbofans (total 10,880lb/4935kg thrust).
Dimensions: 56.25ft (17.15m) overall length; 53.5ft (16.30m) wingspan; 440sq ft (40.87m²) wing area.
Weights: 18,190lb (8258kg) equipped empty; 32,000lb (14,528kg) maximum gross.
Performance: 572 knots/1060km/h (Mach 0.865) maximum speed at 36,000ft/10,972m; 476 knots/882km/h optimum cruising speed at 36,000ft/10,972m; 2500 nautical miles/4633km maximum range.
Armament: None fitted as standard.
Programme: A specialised maritime surveillance and re-engined derivative of the 1963 Dassault Mystere/Falcon 20 business jet, the Guardian (Gardian in French service) was selected for development by the US Coast Guard in January 1977; the prototype flying in late November 1977. All 41 US Coast Guard aircraft, designated HU-25A, had been delivered by the end of 1983. Subsequently, the French Navy placed an initial contract

for five Gardians, all five of which are to be delivered prior to the close of 1984.

Notes: The Guardian carries a comprehensive suite of precision position fixing and recording equipment in addition to its primary air-to-surface VARAN radar. The forward cabin window on either side of the aircraft have been enlarged to permit improved lookout visibility, while a large ventral bay has been built into the aircraft's fuselage, enabling it to drop fairly bulky loads such as large inflatable lifeboats. Dassault claim that the Guardian could be readily adapted to carry up to 7716lb (3500kg) of weaponry, carried externally on four underwing pylons.

Embraer EMB-111 Maritime Patrol

Type and role: 4 crew, twin turboprop-engined, land-based, medium-range, armed maritime patrol and light transport aircraft.
Maker: EMBRAER, Sao Jose dos Campos, Brazil.
Users: Chilean Navy (6), plus the air forces of Brazil (12) and Gabon (1).
Engines: 2 Pratt & Whitney Canada PT6A-34 turboprops (total 1500shp), each driving a 3-bladed, reversible-pitch propeller.
Dimensions: 48.95ft (14.91m) overall length; 52.4ft (15.95m) wingspan; 313sq ft (29.1m^2) wing area.
Weights: 8269lb (3760kg) equipped empty; 15,432lb (7000kg) maximum gross.
Performance: 207 knots/385km/h maximum speed at 10,000ft/3048m; 172 knots/318km/h typical patrol cruise speed at 2000ft/610m; 1190ft/363m/min rate of climb at sea level; 1589 nautical miles/2945km maximum range with no load and full fuel.
Armament: Up to approximately 1653lb (750kg) of wing pylon-mounted stores, including 4 pairs of 127mm rocket projectiles.
Programme: A highly militarised derivative of the very successful EMB-110 Bandeirante feederliner, first flown in August 1972, the prototype EMB-111 made its maiden flight in July 1977. Initial deliveries of the EMB-111, to the Brazilian Air Force, commenced in 1979. Chile accepted the first of its EMB-111s in 1979, the Gabonese machine being handed over in 1980.
Notes: Readily differentiated from the EMB-110 Bandeirante by its prominent nose-mounted radome and wingtip fuel tanks, the EMB-111 employs a Litton air-to-surface radar, position fixing sensors, plus photographic and precision timing equipment. Unlike most maritime patrol aircraft, the EMB-111 is armed and is capable of delivering up to eight 5in (127mm) unguided rocket projectiles, or 28 2.75in (70mm) rockets.

GAF Searchmaster Maritime Patrol

Type and role: 2 crew, twin turboprop-engined, land-based, short field-capable maritime patrol and utility transport aircraft.
Maker: Government Aircraft Factories, Canberra, Australia.
Users: Indonesian Navy (16), plus other military and civil users.
Engines: 2 Allison 250-B-17B turboprop (total 800shp), each driving a 3-bladed, reversible-pitch propeller.
Dimensions: 41.2ft (12.56m) overall length; 54.1ft (61.52m) wingspan; 324sq ft (30.1m^2) wing area.
Weights: 4741lb (2150kg) empty; 8500lb (3855kg) maximum gross.
Performance: 167 knots/311km/h maximum speed at sea level; 1460ft/445m/min rate of climb at sea level; 580 nautical miles/1074km maximum range at sea level.

Dassault's Guardian demonstrator aircraft overflying a coaster.

An EMB-111, this particular aircraft belonging to the Brazilian Air Force.

Two GAF N22B Searchmasters of the Indonesian Navy.

Armament: None fitted as standard, however, Indonesian aircraft are equipped with underwing pylons for the carriage of external stores.
Programme: An air-to-surface radar equipped maritime patrol variant of the 1971 GAF N22 Nomad, the N22B Searchmaster was ordered by Indonesia shortly after its first flight in 1975. At least 145 Nomads and Seamaster/Missionmasters were known to have been ordered or delivered by the end of 1983.
Notes: The original N22B Searchmaster is equipped with the Bendix RDR 1400 radar, ventrally-mounted immediately below the cockpit. A more recent variant, the Searchmaster L, employs a chin-mounted Litton LASR 2 radar.

An air-to-surface radar equipped MBB Bo 105 of the Mexican Navy.

MBB Bo 105 Maritime Patrol Helicopters

Type and role: 2 crew, all-weather anti-ship/maritime surveillance, twin-engined, 4-bladed single rotor, shipboard-stowable helicopter.
Maker: Messerschmitt Bolkow Blohm GmbH, Munich, Federal Germany.
Users: Navies of Columbia, Indonesia, Mexico and Philippines.
Engines: 2 Allison 250-C20B turboshaft (total 840shp).
Dimensions: 38.9ft (11.86m) overall length (rotors turning); 32.3ft (9.84m) main rotor diameter.
Weights: 3060lb (1388kg) empty; 4296lb (1944kg) normal gross; 5291lb (2400kg) maximum gross.
Performance: 145 knots/270km/h maximum speed at sea level; 1575ft/480m/min maximum initial rate of climb; 310 nautical miles/575km maximum range with 441lb/200kg load.
Armament: Up to 995lb (451kg) of weapons or sensors over short mission distances, with the capability to carry air-to-surface missiles.
Programme: The Bo 105 design origins date back to mid-1962, the machine initially being conceived for purely civilian operations. The prototype Bo 105 made its maiden flight in mid-February 1967. During the earlier half of the 1970s, the Federal German Government funded the development of a military variant of the Bo 105 as an anti-tank helicopter, several hundred of which have subsequently been ordered by Federal Germany and Spain. The emergence of the navalised Bo 105 occurred at the beginning of the 1980s. By mid-1985, a total of 22 navalised Bo 105s had been ordered, comprising four for Indonesia, six for Mexico and ten for the Philippines, out of cumulative Bo 105 sales exceeding 1060 aircraft.
Notes: The navalised Bo 105 is, perhaps, typical of the modern practice of adopting a basically civilian design for more warlike purposes. Although less capable than such dedicated naval solutions as the Westland Lynx and Sikorsky Seahawk, the Bo 105 provides a relatively inexpensive platform upon which to mount various mixes of sensors and weapons. Indonesia employs the type as a veritable mini-Airborne Early Warning & Control System (AWACS), while the Mexican version represents a closer to mainstream naval model, likely to find more sales in places such as Argentina and other parts of Latin America as well as the Far East.

Transports

Lockheed C-130 Hercules Tanker/Transports

Type and role: 4 crew, 4 turboprop-engined, land-based, short or rough field-capable, bulk cargo or up to 92 troop carrier and aerial tanker.
Maker: Lockheed Georgia Corporation, Marietta, Georgia, USA.
Users: US Navy, US Marine Corps, US and Japanese Coast Guards, plus over 45 air forces and numerous civilian agencies and operators.
Engines: 4 Allison T56-A-7 turboprops (total 20,200shp), each driving a 4-bladed, reversible-pitch propeller.
Dimensions: 97.75ft (29.8m) overall length; 132.6ft (40.4m) wingspan; 1745sq ft (162.1m²) wing area.
Weights: 75,832lb (34,397kg) empty; 155,000lb (70,310kg) normal gross; 175,000lb (79,380kg) maximum gross.
Performance: 335 knots/621km/h maximum speed at 12,000ft/3658m; 1900ft/579m/min rate of climb at sea level; 3995 nautical miles/7410km maximum range with additional wing tank-carried fuel and 20,000lb/9070kg of cargo.
Armament: None fitted.
Programme: Developed initially to a January 1951 US Air Force requirement, the first of two prototype C-130s made its maiden flight in August 1954. Initial US Navy orders for the aircraft were placed in 1958 and led to a cumulative procurement of 46 KC-130F, plus 14 KC-130H for the US Marine Corps, along with 11 KC-130F and 6 KC-130H for the US Navy, itself. Another 25 of various C-130 models have been bought for use with the US Coast Guard, while the equivalent Japanese service operates 1 C-130HMP model.
Notes: Designed as an assault transport from the outset, the C-130 Hercules is equipped with an in-flight operable rear loading ramp. The primary operational role for the C-130 in both US Navy and US Marine Corps service is to act as an in-flight tanker aircraft, capable of refuelling two aircraft simultaneously from its underslung, outboard wing-mounted fuel pods. A number of naval C-130s have been equipped with ski landing gear to enable them to resupply US polar and Antarctic bases. Overall, a total of 1735 Hercules had been delivered by the end of 1984. Certainly, the Hercules has proven to be the best-selling and most widely operated multi-propeller driven transport since the Douglas DC-3 family and is likely to remain in production for some years to come.

Douglas C-9B Skytrain II Transports

Type and role: 3 crew, twin turbofan-engined, land-based, pressurised, high subsonic combination cargo or up to 50 passenger transport.
Maker: Douglas Aircraft Company, Long Beach, California, USA.
Users: US Navy, US Marine Corps, plus Italian and Kuwaiti air forces and numerous airlines.
Engines: 2 Pratt & Whitney JT8D-9 turbofan (total 28,930lb/13,122kg thrust).
Dimensions: 119.3ft (36.4m) overall length; 93.4ft (28.5m) wingspan; 1000sq ft (93.0m²) wing area.
Weights: 62,247lb (28,235kg) empty; 108,000lb (48,990kg) maximum gross.
Performance: 505 knots/935km/h (Mach 0.83) maximum speed at 23,000ft/7010m; 912 nautical miles/1690km maximum range with a full payload of 24,750lb/11,226kg.
Armament: None fitted.

A US Marine Corps KC-130F seen at lift-off.

Programme: A derivative of the Douglas DC-9 twin jet airliner first flown in February 1965, the US Navy ordered its first batch of C-9Bs in 1972, with first deliveries commencing in May 1973. Subsequent incremental orders for US Navy and US Marine aircraft took the total navalised model procurement to 23; all of which had been delivered by the end of 1983.
Notes: The C-9B Skytrain II, along with the 23 US Air Force C-9A Nightingales, are essentially modified cabin variants of the otherwise 'off the shelf' Douglas DC-9-32 wide freight doored cargo carrier developed for the Italian airline, Alitalia. By the end of 1983, Douglas had delivered a total of 976 DC-9s, by when production had been switched to the re-engined MD-80 series.

Grumman C-2 Greyhound Transports

Type and role: 2 crew, twin turboprop-engined carrier-going short- to medium-range transport.
Maker: Grumman Aerospace Corporation, Bethpage, Long Island, USA.
User: US Navy.
Engines: 2 General Electric T56-A-426 turboprops (total 8100shp) each driving a 4-bladed reversible-pitch propeller.
Dimensions: 56.6ft (17.26m) overall length; 80.6ft (24.6m) wingspan; 29.3ft (8.9m) wings folded; 700sq ft (65.03m²) wing area.
Weights: 31,369lb (14,229kg) empty; 54,354lb (24,655kg) carrier launch gross; 55,000lb (24,948kg) maximum gross from airfield.

A US Navy Douglas-C-9B derivative of the DC-9-32 airliner.

One of the two development YC-2As folded up and on flight deck elevator.

A US Navy RH-53D hovering near USS Illusive *during joint air/sea mineclearing exercises held in the Mediterranean during 1981.*

Performance: 343 knots/636km/h maximum speed; 260 knots/484km/h cruising speed; 2330ft/710m/min initial rate of climb; 1300 nautical miles/2409km maximum unrefuelled range with 10,000lb/4536kg payload.

Armament: Nil.

Programme: Designed and developed to a 1963 US Navy requirement for a carrier onboard delivery (COD) aircraft, the two deployment YC-2As were converted from E-2As; the maiden flight of the YC-2A being made in November 1964. Production of 17 C-2As commenced in 1965 with deliveries taking place between 1966 and 1968. Initial deployment of the C-2A took place in December 1966. Following protracted evaluation of their future COD needs, the US Navy decided to buy 39 more C-2 Greyhounds in 1981, manufacture of which commenced in 1982, with deliveries being made between 1985 and 1989. Meanwhile, existing C-2As are undergoing a Service Life Extension Programme (SLEP) refurbishment that includes the incorporation of a flight refuelling capability to extend the aircraft's range.

Notes: A derivative of the Grumman E-2A Hawkeye, the C-2 Greyhound has a distinctly bulkier fuselage and a horizontal tailplane. A rear loading ramp is incorporated to facilitate the loading and unloading of bulky cargo, such as aero engines. Alternatively, the C-2 Greyhound can carry up to 39 fully equipped Marines or up to 20 litter-carried casualties. The possibility exists that additional C-2s could yet be procured to augment the US Navy's existing force of Grumman KA-6D carrier-based aerial tanker aircraft.

Sikorsky S-65/H-53 Sea Stallion Transport Helicopters

Type and roles: 3 crew, all-weather, ship-stowable, twin turboshaft-engined, 6-bladed, single main rotor helicopter employed as assault transports with accommodation for vehicles or 55 troops (CH-53A, C, D); long-range search and rescue (HH-53B, C, H); airborne minesweepers (RH-53A, D).

Maker: Sikorsky Aircraft Division of United Technologies, Stratford, Connecticut, USA (404 built); VFW-Fokker, Bremen (110 built).

Users: US Marine Corps (287); US Navy (30); Federal German Army (112); Iranian Navy (6); Israeli Air Force (25); US Air Force (52); Austrian Air Force (2).

Engines: 2 General Electric T-64-GE-6 (total 5700shp) (CH-53A), through 6870shp-16s (CH-53C), to 7850shp-413s (CH/RH-53D).

Dimensions: 88.2ft (26.9m) overall length (rotors turning); 72.2ft (22.0m) rotor diameter; 24.9ft (7.6m) height (rotors turning).

Weights: 23,485lb (10,650kg) empty; 36,400lb (16,507kg) normal gross; 42,000lb (19,047kg) maximum gross; 12,915lb (5857kg) useful load. *Note:* all data quoted is for CH-53D.

Performance: 170 knots/315km/h maximum speed at sea level; 150 knots/278km/h cruising speed at sea level; 2180ft/664m/min initial rate of climb; 21,000ft/6400m service ceiling; 223 nautical miles range from normal gross take-off weight. *Note:* all data is for CH-53D.

Armament: None.

Programme: The first of two YCH-53A made its maiden flight 16 October 1964. Production deliveries commenced in September 1966 with the first of 139 US Marine Corps' CH-53As. These were followed by eight HH-53Bs for the USAF, 20 CH-53Cs for the USMC, 44 HH-53Cs for the USAF, two CH-53D/Gs for Germany (another 110 being built in Bremen), two S-65-Oes for Austria, 25 S-65Ds for Israel, 30 RH-53Ds for the USN and 6 RH-53D for Iran; production being completed with the 514th aircraft in 1976.

Notes: Currently providing the backbone of the US Marine

Corps' airborne assault heavy lift capability, along with furnishing the greater part of the US Navy's total minesweeping assets. Sikorsky's S-65 Sea Stallion and its Super Stallion derivative (dealt with separately below) have been and will continue for some years yet to be the largest operational helicopter in service outside the Eastern bloc. From a design viewpoint, the S-65 family, along with Bell's AH-1 Hueycobra gunship helicopters, demonstrate an often overlooked aspect of rotary-winged development; namely, that having stumbled upon a successful 'dynamic raft' design (this term embraces the rotor systems and the associated power transmission and gearing), the helicopter designer is then left a virtually free hand to hang just about anything he desires in the way of suspended structure beneath. In the case of the S-65 Sea Stallion, which uses the same basic dynamic systems as that of the earlier S-64 Skycrane, the Sikorsky design team by simply changing the shape of the helicopter's airframe, brought about a dramatic shift in the aircraft's payload/range capability. By incorporating an aerodynamically much cleaner airframe with greater internal fuel capacity. Sikorsky transformed what had been a limited-range weight lifter into a far more flexible vehicle in operational terms. Just how robust is the S-65 Sea Stallion was graphically demonstrated in October 1968, when a US Marine Corps' CH-53A displayed its ability to carry out full loops and rolls, something previously undreamt of being within the capability of such a large helicopter. Another often overlooked aspect of the Sea Stallion is its ability to operate as a very effective airborne minesweeper, a role pioneered by the US Marine Corps in 1971 and later adopted by the US Navy. Such was the success of this development that, today, the Sea Stallion provides a major part of the US Navy's minesweeping capability.

Sikorsky S-65A/H-53E Super Stallion Transport Helicopters

Type and roles: 3 crew, all-weather, ship-stowable, three turboshaft-engined, 7-bladed single rotor helicopter employed as a vehicle and troop carrying assault (CH-53E) or aerial minesweeper (MH-53E) type; all being air-refuellable.
Maker: Sikorsky Aircraft Division of United Technologies, Stratford, Connecticut, USA.
Users: US Marine Corps (CH-53E) and US Navy (CH-53E and MH-53E).
Engines: 3 General Electric T64-GE-415 turboshafts (total 13,140shp).
Dimensions: 99.5ft (30.48m) overall length (rotors turning); 79.0ft (24.08m) main rotor diameter; 60.5ft (18.44m) length folded for shipboard stowage.
Weights: 33,226lb (15,071kg) for CH-53E or 33,336lb (16,482kg) for MH-53E empty equipped; 69,750lb (31,631kg) normal gross; 73,500lb (33,339kg) maximum gross with external load.
Performance: 170 knots/315km/h maximum speed at sea level; 150 knots/278km/h cruising speed at sea level; 2500ft/762m/min initial rate of climb; 50 nautical miles/93km range with 16 ton load (CH-53E) or 820 nautical miles/1520km with 7500lb/3402kg load (MH-53E), without refuelling.
Armament: None fitted to CH-53E; MH-53E hauls mine detonating magnetic, acoustic and pressure-generating equipment.
Programme: The genesis of the super Stallion family can be traced back to October 1967, when the US Navy drew up a requirement for a heavy lift helicopter, capable of lifting up to 16 tons of cargo. During the next four years, two companies, Boeing Vertol, with their 20-ton lift XCH-62 design (favoured by the US Army) and Sikorsky, with an uprated derivative of the existing CH-53, both bid for

A US Marine Corps Sikorsky CH-53E lifting a heavy truck.

this development award. In November 1971, Sikorsky gained a decided edge in the competition, with the receipt of a contract to produce two development YCH-53E aircraft; the final mould being cast in May 1973, when the US Navy elected to continue with the Super Stallion programme. The maiden flight of the YCH-53E followed in March 1974. In January 1975, Sikorsky were authorised to proceed with the construction of two pre-series aircraft, the first of which initially took to the air in December 1975. Sikorsky received its next milestone award, a contract for six production machines, in February 1978, the first of which was to make its maiden flight in December 1980. The initial operational deployment of the type, with the US Marines, came about in June 1981. By December 1984, Sikorsky had delivered over 80 CH-53Es and were scheduled to deliver a further ten during 1985. Future planned procurement of the type could take the aggregate US Marine Corps/US Navy requirment to 139 aircraft by the end of 1988, with production scheduled to continue well into the 1990s; a conclusion borne out by US Navy plans to buy more than 50 of the MH-53E minesweeping version, production of which will not commence prior to 1986.
Notes: Thanks to the incorporation of a third engine immediately aft of the main rotor head, the Super Stallion gains just over 40 per cent additional installed power for just less than 30 per cent increase in empty equipped weight for the basic transport version. While the majority of the CH-53Es will go to US Marine Corps units, a number of this model will be operated by the US Navy for ship-to-ship or ship-to-shore vertical onboard delivery (VOD). The

US Navy MH-53E variant is readily identifiable by its enlarged sponsons that protrude from the fuselage mid-section, increased in size to carry additional fuel.

Bell-Boeing V-22 Osprey (JVX) Transport Helicopters

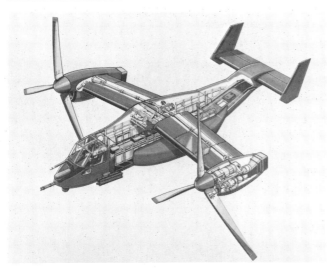

A cut-away impression of the assault transport version of the V-22 Osprey.

Type and role: 2 crew, all-weather, twin tilting-turboshaft-engined assault transport and combat area search and rescue ultra-short landing and take-off aircraft with accommodation for up to 24 troops; all versions being foldable for ship stowage or air-portability.
Makers: Bell Helicopters, Fort Worth, Texas and Boeing-Vertol, Philadelphia, Pennsylvania, USA.
Users: US Navy, US Marines, US Army and US Air Force, planned procurement for the four services being 50, 552, 231 and 80 aircraft, respectively.
Engines: 2 General Electric T64-717 turboshaft (total 9636shp approximately).
Dimensions: 56.75ft (17.3m) overall length; 84.5ft (25.75m) wingspan (rotors turning).
Weights: 25,800lb (11,703kg) estimated operating empty; 55,000lb (24,948kg) maximum take-off.
Performance: 350 knots/649km/h maximum level speed at 17,500ft/5334m or 310 knots/574km per hour at sea level; 34,000ft/10,363m absolute ceiling; 2000 nautical miles 3706km maximum range with 8000lb/3629lb payload without recourse to in-flight refuelling (fitted as standard equipment).
Armament: 1 multi-barrelled 0.5in calibre rapid fire gun turret, plus externally-mounted air-to-ground missile launcher pods.
Programme: Based on the in-flight proven tilt-engine/rotor technology provided by the NASA-funded Bell XV-15, first flown in May 1977, the current US joint service programme was put underway in December 1981 with request for industry design proposals for a Joint-service Vertical support experimental (JVX) aircraft. In what looked to be an almost foregone conclusion, the US Department of Defense selected the Bell-Boeing industrial team to proceed with the preliminary design of the V-22 Osprey in early 1983. At press time, the full-scale development launch was set for mid-1985, to be followed by the V-22's first flight in May 1987 and initial service deliveries (to the US Marine Corps) in mid 1991. Initial US Navy deliveries should commence in late 1992, followed by those to the US Air Force in early 1993 and those to the US Army in mid-1993 for a projected total build for some 913 aircraft.

Notes: Research and development effort on this hybrid helicopter-cum-high speed fixed winged aircraft commenced as for back as 1951 and has evolved via a series of aircraft and system design and demonstrator programmes that included tilting rotors only, tilting wing/engines/rotors before arriving at the definitive V-22's tilt rotor configuration. The economically-driven decision to launch the development of the V-22 Osprey on an all four US armed forces basis allows the type to replace a number of existing machines, including the US Marines' CH-46 Sea Knight and UH-1 helicopters, part of the US Army's CH-47 Chinook mission needs and virtually all of the US Air Force existing special missions helicopter fleet.

Boeing Vertol CH-46 Sea Knight Transport Helicopters

Type and role: 3 crew, twin turboshaft-engined, twin 3-bladed rotored, vehicle and troop transport helicopter, with accommodation for up to 26 troops, or 4200lb (1905kg) of internal cargo.
Maker: Boeing Vertol Company, Philadelphia, Pennsylvania, USA and license-built by Kawasaki, Japan.
Users: US Navy (201 UH-46s), US Marine Corps (426 CH-46), Canada (16), Swedish Navy (20, including 8 Japanese-built), plus 12 civil models for a total Boeing build of 666 aircraft, plus 110 Japanese-built aircraft. *Note:* these figures are for total production and do not represent current inventories, which will have been reduced by attrition.
Engines: 2 General Electric T58-GE-16 turboshafts (total 2800shp) on CH-46E; some Japanese-built engines derated to 2500shp.
Dimensions: 84.3ft (25.7m) overall length (rotors turning); 51.0ft (15.54m) main rotors diameter.
Weights: 13,342lb (6057kg) empty; 23,000lb (10,442kg) gross.
Performance: 144 knots/267km/h maximum speed at sea level; 133 knots/248km/h cruising speed at sea level; 1715ft/523m/min initial rate of climb; 206 nautical miles/382km maximum range with 4000lb/1815kg load.
Armament: None fitted to US aircraft, but Swedish and some Japanese Maritime Self-Defence Force aircraft carry depth charges.
Programme: A derivative of the Boeing Vertol Model 107/YHC-1A, first flown in April 1958, the CH-46, or Model 107-II was selected for development by the US Navy, Canada and Sweden in 1961; the first CH-46A making its maiden flight in mid-October 1962. Boeing Vertol production of the CH-46 ended in 1971, but Kawasaki, who commenced license-built production in 1965, was still building the aircraft in small numbers in mid-1983. In December 1980, Boeing Vertol were awarded a US Government contract to modernise and extend the life of 355 Sea Knights; kit manufacture for which will commence in 1985 and extend through 1988, ensuring that these aircraft will continue in service well into the 1990s, if not beyond.
Notes: Equipped with a vehicle-loading rear ramp, this rugged workhorse has seen service from places as far afield as South East Asia during the 1960s, to helping chase Soviet submarines from Swedish waters in 1983. The US Navy UH-46s are used extensively for vertical replenishment of stores to ships at sea.

Westland-Sikorsky Commando Transport Helicopters

Type and role: 3 crew, all-weather, twin turboshaft-engined, 5-bladed single rotor, ship-stowable transport

A CH-46E, one of the modernised Sea Knights operated by the US Marine Corps.

helicopter with accommodation for up to 27 troops.
Maker: Westland Helicopters, Yeovil, Somerset, England; under licence from Sikorsky.
Users: Royal Navy/Marines (34), Egyptian Air Force (28), Qatar (12).
Engines: 2 Rolls-Royce Gnome 1400 turboshafts (total 3320shp).
Dimensions: 72.66ft (22.15m) overall length (rotors turning); 47.25ft (14.4m) overall length folded for stowage; 62.0ft (18.85m) main rotor diameter.
Weights: 11,174lb (5069kg) empty equipped; 21,000lb (9526kg) maximum gross.
Performance: 121 knots/225km/h maximum speed at sea level; 112 knots/207km/h cruising speed at sea level; 2020ft/616m/min initial rate of climb; 240 nautical miles/445km maximum range at sea level with 27 troops.
Armanent: Can carry armour-piercing rocket pods or anti-armour missiles.
Programme: A parallel Westland development to the Sikorsky S-61L/CH-3A, the Commando made its maiden flight in September 1972 and was initially deployed during the autumn of 1973. The Sea King/Commando HC Mk 4, the latest version being initially deployed in November 1979. Orders for this machine totalled 74 by August 1984, of which over 63 had been delivered.

A Royal Marines' Commando HC Mk 4 demonstrating its load-lifting capability.

A Royal Navy Wessex HUR Mk 5 of No 848 Squadron.

Notes: Although retaining the hull-form fuselage of the basic S-61 Sea King design, the Commando/Sea King HC Mk 4 dispenses with the retractable main wheels of the outboard float-equipped anti-submarine aircraft, these being replaced by simple, robust, non-retractable main legs.

Westland-Sikorsky Wessex HUR Mk 5 Transport Helicopters

Type and role: 2 or 3 crew, all-weather, twin turboshaft-engined, 4-bladed single rotor, ship-stowable transport helicopter with accommodation for up to 16 troops.
Maker: Westland Helicopters, Yeovil, Somerset, England; under licence from Sikorsky.

Users: Royal Navy/Marines (35), Royal Australian Navy (4).
Engines: 2 Rolls-Royce Gnome 2000 series turboshafts (total 2500shp).
Dimensions: 65.9ft (20.1m) overall length (rotors turning); 38.5ft (11.7m) overall length folded for stowage; 56.0ft (17.06m) main rotor diameter.
Weights: 7925lb (3595kg) empty equipped; 13,500lb (6124kg) maximum take-off.
Performance: 115 knots/213km/h maximum speed at sea level; 110 knots/204km/h cruising speed at sea level 230 nautical miles/426km maximum range at sea level with 16 troops.
Armament: Can be equipped to carry rocket pods or anti-armour missiles.
Programme: A much modified and re-engined variant of the basic Sikorsky S-58/HSS-1 design, Westlands built a total of 399 Wessex helicopters, comprising 222 Gnome-powered and 177 Gazelle-powered models between late 1956 and the close of 1969 when production ended. The maiden flight of the Mk 5 version happened in May 1963, the type being initially deployed in October 1964. Thanks to the decision to respar the rotors and refurbish a number of these machines, the type should remain in limited service with Royal Navy and Royal Marine units well into the 1980s, if not beyond.
Notes: Built in numerous versions, ranging from air sea rescue, through troop transports, to anti-submarine machines, the Wessex has served as one of the prime workhorse helicopters of the Royal Navy and Royal Marines since the early 1960s. The British Government-backed Westland decision to re-engine the basic piston engined S-58 design with turboshaft engines gave the Wessex a much enhanced payload/range capability, compared with its US forebear, which could only carry a crew of two, plus 12 troops over a much more limited distance.

Trainers

Bell UH-1 Iroquois Utility Helicopters

Type and role: Single pilot, plus up to 14-troop single UH-1L) or twin turboshaft-engined (UH-1N), single 2-bladed utility transport (UH-1s) and training (TH-1L) helicopter.
Maker: Textron Bell Helicopters, Fort Worth, Texas, USA and licensee manufacturers in Federal Germany, Italy, Japan and Taiwan.
Users: US Navy and Marine Corps (289 +), plus the navies of Australia (6), Brazil (17), Chile (4), Iran (19), Italy (24), Mexico (2), Norway (20), Peru (20), Sweden (10), Thailand (3) and Turkey (3), plus many of the world's air arms. *Note:* these figures exclude Agusta-built AB-212 ASWs covered separately.
Engines: 1 Avoc-Lycoming T53 various marks turboshaft (up to 1400shp) on all models up to UH/TH-1L or 1 Pratt & Whitney Canada PT6T-3B Turbo Twin Pac coupled turboshaft (1800shp).

A US Marine Corps' Bell UH-1N, deliveries of which started in February 1970.

Dimensions: 57.25ft (17.45m) overall length (rotors turning); 48.2ft (14.0m) main rotor diameter. *Note:* data for UH-1N.
Weights: 5549lb (2517kg) empty; 11,200lb (5085kg) maximum take-off. *Note:* data for UH-1N.
Performance: 123 knots/229km/h maximum speed at sea level; 1745ft/532m/min initial rate of climb; 237 nautical miles/439km maximum range at sea level. *Note:* data for UH-1N.
Armament: Capable of carrying wire-guided air-to-surface missiles.
Programme: In February 1955, Bell Helicopters won a US helicopter industry-wide competition for a US Army turbine-powered utility helicopter that was to become the UH-1 family, but initially known as the XH-40 (prototype) and YH-40 (six development aircraft). The XH-40 first flew in late October 1956, followed by the first operational deployment of the UH-1 during 1958. Since that time and up to the beginning of July 1982, Bell had produced 10,111 examples of this family, plus the several hundred additional military helicopters produced by their licensees. Of this total number, 417 plus were identified as having been ordered by the various navies listed above in the Users column, which also cites known numbers of helicopters delivered to the individual services.
Notes: The Bell UH-1 Iroquios family, or 'Huey' as it has become affectionately known over the years, is and will continue to be the most widely used military helicopter for many years yet. The first military utility transport helicopter to enter large-scale production for the US Army, who were its prime sponsor, the UH-1 series, more than any other helicopter, made possible the US Army and Marine Corps credo of vertical assault, used with such effect in South East Asia during the latter 1960s and early 1970s. Although neither the US Government nor Bell saw fit to develop a dedicated naval version of the UH-1, the Italians did, leading to the development of a semi-naval variant, built by Agusta and operated by the Italian Navy from the late 1960s on. With the advent of the more powerful UH-1N, Italy again took the initiative in terms of exploiting naval market potential, with the result that Agusta was encouraged to develop the fully anti-submarine warfare capable Agusta-Bell AB212 ASW variant, of which they hold the exclusive world manufacturing rights; the machine being covered under a separate entry elsewhere in this section.

Bell Model 206/TH-57 and OH-58 Kiowa Utility Helicopters

Type and role: 2 crew, single turboshaft-engined, 2-bladed single rotor utility/observation/training helicopter with accommodation for up to 3 people additional to crew.
Maker: Textron Bell Helicopters, Fort Worth, Texas, USA and licensees Commonwealth Aircraft Corporation, Australia and Agusta, Italy.
Users: Navies of the US (102), Australia (2), Brazil (17), Chile (4), Iran (14), Israel (4), Peru (10) and Sweden (10), along with numerous army and airforce users, plus worldwide civilian operators.
Engine: 1 Allison 250-C18 or 20 turboshaft (total 375 or 420shp).
Dimensions: 38.8ft (11.82m) overall length (rotors turning); 33.3ft (10.15m) main rotor diameter.
Weights: 1500lb (680kg) empty; 3200lb (1451kg) gross.
Performance: 121 knots/225km/h maximum speed at sea level; 115 knots/214km/h cruising speed at sea level; 1780ft.543m/min initial rate of climb; 194 nautical miles/360km maximum tactical radius of action with no load and no fuel reserves.
Armament: Up to 540lb (245kg), including 1 Mk 44 or other lightweight anti-submarine torpedo, or one or more rocket projectile pods.

Three Chilean Navy Model 206As, each carrying a single Mk 44 lightweight anti-submarine torpedo.

Programme: The Bell Model 206, designed against the 1961 US Army Light Observation Helicopter (LOH) requirement, first flew in late 1962 as the OH-4, losing out in this initial stage to the Hughes Model 369/OH-6. Undismayed, Bell revamped the OH-4's fuselage to create the enormously successful civilian Jet Ranger helicopter, first flown in January 1966. The low unit cost and ready availability of this type has subsequently made it very attractive to many armed forces, including the US Army and those of Australia and Canada (OH-58), along with the US Navy (TH-57), who operate the type as their basic rotary-winged training aircraft. Well over 7000 Model 206s have been built since production commenced in 1965.
Notes: Although primarily a civilian machine, the low capital cost and general flexibility of this machine makes it look quite attractive for a range of light military and naval roles. While most navies employ the Model 206 as a communications aircraft, it is interesting to note that Chile employs it in the anti-submarine role, while Israel uses the type for over-the-horizon missile launch targeting, when operating from the 'Aliyah' or 'Saar' 4.5 class vessels.

Hawker Hunter Trainers

Type and role: Shore-based single seat (GA11) and two seat (T8) single turbojet-engined transonic pilot trainers.
Maker: British Aerospace, Kingston Division, Surrey, UK.
User: Royal Navy. *Note:* numerous other Hunters continue in service with various air forces as strike fighters, along with the 2 seat trainers.
Engine: 1 Rolls-Royce RA28 Avon 207 reheated turbojet (10,500lb/4763kg thrust) in GA11 or Avon 122 (7550lb/3425kg thrust) in T8.

The Hunter T8 two seater used for high speed fixed wing pilot instruction.

Dimensions: 45.9ft (13.98m) for GA11 or 48.9ft (14.9m) for T8's overall length; 33.66ft (10.26m) wingspan; 349sq ft (32.43m²) wing area.
Weights: 12,543lb (5689kg) for GA11 or 13,360lb (6060kg) for T8 empty; 17,100lb (7756kg) for GA11 or 17,750lb (8051kg) for T8 normal gross; 24,000lb (10,886kg) maximum gross.
Performance: 621 knots/1151km/h (Mach 0.94) for GA11 or 603 knots/1117km/h (Mach 0.92) for T8 maximum speed at sea level; 8100ft/2469m/min initial rate of climb for GA11; 426 nautical miles/789km maximum range for GA11 without extra fuel tanks.
Armament: Internally-mounted gun armament deleted from Royal Navy aircraft, but GA11 has provision to mount 8 underwing rocket projectiles.
Programme: Deliveries totalling 41 Hunter T8s to the Royal Navy commenced in July 1958, followed by a total of 40 Hunter GA11s starting in June 1962. Twenty single seat GA11s, plus 16T8 trainers remained in service by June 1983.
Notes: Although initially conceived in the closing months of 1947 as a high altitude interceptor, Sir Sidney Camm's Hawker Hunter remains in relatively widespread use as a strike aircraft some 39 years on, thanks largely to its robust structure combined with admirable low-level handling characteristics. Besides the T8s and GA11s mentioned above, the Royal Navy had seven Hunter T7s and 1 Hunter PR9, along with another 11 Hunters in storage, all available for use in mid-1983.

Dassault Mystere 10MER Trainers

Type and role: 2 crew, twin turbofan-engined, land-based, high subsonic speed advanced trainer, target facility and senior personnel transport for 4 to 8 passengers.
Maker: Dassault Breguet Aviation, Vaucresson, France.
Users: French Navy, plus numerous civilian operators.
Engines: 2 Garrett TFE721-2 turbofan (total 6460lb/2930kg thrust).
Dimensions: 46.0ft (13.1m) overall length; 42.95ft (13.86m) wingspan; 259.4sq ft (24.0m²) wing area.
Weights: 11,145lb (5060kg) equipped empty; 19,300lb (8,760kg) maximum gross.
Performance: 575 knots/1066km/h (Mach 0.87) maximum speed at 28,000ft/8534m, reducing to 350 knots/649km/h at sea level; 1870 nautical miles/3465km maximum range with full payload of 2855lb/1295kg.
Armament: None fitted.
Programme: A minimum modification of the 1970 Dassault Mystere/Falcon 10 business jet, four of these navalised Mystere 10MERs were acquired by the French Navy during the mid-1970s.
Notes: The Mystere 10MER purchase represents yet another example of a so-called 'off-the-shelf' buy: a progressively growing practice, popular with naval and military procurement agencies everywhere as a means of avoiding the need to fund the development of a new specialist trainer. Beside being used as a pilot instrument trainer, the Mystere 10MER doubles as a target facility type by acting as a 'live' target upon which French Navy fighter pilots can practice interception techniques. When needed, the machine, with its essentially intact business jet cabin interior, can be operated as a high speed transport for very important people (VIPs).

Douglas T-45 Trainers

Type and role: 2-crew, single turbofan-engined, carrier-going high subsonic, advanced pilot trainer.
Makers: Douglas Aircraft Company, Long Beach, California (prime contractor); British Aerospace, Kingston, UK (principle subcontractor).
User: Under development for the US Navy.
Engines: 1 Rolls-Royce Adour 861 turbofan (5700lb/2585kg thrust).
Dimensions: 38.9ft (11.9m) overall length; 30.8ft (9.4m) wingspan; 179sq ft (16.7m²) wing area.
Weights: 8756lb (3972kg) empty; 12,440lb (5643kg) maximum gross; including 3000lb (1361kg) of internal fuel.

One of four Mystere 10MERs operated by the French Navy.

Performance: 488 knots/904km/h (Mach 0.85) maximum speed at 36,000ft/10,973m/min; 9300ft/2835m/min rate of climb at sea level; 375 nautical miles/695km radius of action with 2 hours loiter on internal fuel only.

Armament: None fitted as standard on US Navy aircraft, but the T-45 will have wing hardpoints for pylon mounted weapons incorporated.

Programme: Selected by the US Navy in November 1981, following evaluation of the Hawk, Alpha Jet and MB 339, the T-45 is, in essence, a navalised and Americanised variant of the British Aerospace Hawk strike trainer. Full-scale development of the T-45 was set underway during 1984, followed by initial deliveries to the US Navy commencing in 1989, against a planned need for 309 aircraft.

Notes: Now known under the programme title Strike Trainer System, of which the T-45 forms the major element, the aircraft is particularly thrifty in terms of fuel consumption. Using only 1370lb (621kg) of fuel per hour on a typical training mission, the T-45 will bring about 65 per cent annual fuel saving, compared to that used by existing US Navy advanced trainers. Capable of climbing to 40,000ft (12,191m) in 20 minutes from a standing start, the T-45s radio/navigational equipment and cockpit instrumentation will have a high degree of commonality with that of the McDonnel F-18 Hornet, the type onto which T-45 student pilots will pass on completion of their training.

British Aerospace Jetstream T.2/3 Trainer Aircraft

Type and role: 5-crew, twin turboprop-engined radar observer trainer.

Maker: British Aerospace Scottish Division, Prestwick, Ayrshire, UK.

User: Royal Navy.

Engines: 2 Turbomeca Astazou 16D turboprops (total 1,992shp) on T2s, or Garrett TPE 331-10 turboprops (total 1800shp) on T.3s.

Dimensions: 26.92ft (8.2m) overall length; 52.0ft (15.85m) wingspan; 270sq ft (25.0m^2) wing area.

Weights: 8741lb (3965kg) empty; 12,500lb (5670kg) maximum gross.

Performance: 245 knots/454km/h at 10,000ft/3048m maximum speed; 25,000ft/7620m service ceiling; 1198 nautical miles maximum range.

Armament: Nil.

Programme: 14 former Royal Air Force operated Jetstream T1s were converted to T2 standard, delivery of which commenced in October 1978 and completed the following year. In April 1984, British Aerospace announced that the Royal Navy had placed an order for 4 of the Garrett TPE 331-powered Jetstream 31s, also to be used as trainers and designated Jetstream T3s.

Notes: Based at RNAS Culdrose and operated by 750 Squadron, the Jetstream T2 is employed for radar observer training and as such carries a more extensive electronics fit, including a nose radome-housed cloud and collision avoidance radar which sets the T2 apart from all other Jetstream variants. Other onboard electronics include a Decca doppler navigational radar and tactical navigation system (TANS) which processes data being supplied to the two trainee observers and two instructors in the cabin as well as to the aircraft's flight deck.

A retouched photograph of a British Aerospace Hawk, depicting the modified twin nose wheels and fuselage-side airbrakes of the T-45 carrier-going advanced trainer.

The Royal Navy's Jetstream T2 displaying its prominent nose radome that sets it apart from all other Jetstream variants.

Rockwell North American T-2 Buckeye Trainers

Type and role: 2 seat, twin turbojet-engined, high-subsonic intermediate and advanced trainer/light strike aircraft.

Maker: Rockwell North American, Columbus Division, Ohio, USA.

Users: US Navy (T-2B and C) and air forces of Greece (T-2E) and Venezuela (T-2D).

Engines: 2 Pratt & Whitney J60-P-6 turbojets (total 6000lb/2720kg thrust on T-2B or 2 General Electric J85-GE-4 turbojets (total 5900lb/2676kg thrust) on T-2C.

Dimensions: 38.33 ft (11.7m) overall length; 38.2ft (11.6m) wingspan; 255sq ft (23.7m^2) wing area.

Weights: 8115lb (3681kg) empty; 13,179lb (5978kg) maximum take-off.

Performance: 453 knots/840km/h maximum level at 25,000ft/7620m; 6100ft/1859m/min initial rate of climb; 909 nautical miles maximum range with no external stores.

Armament: Up to 640lb (290kg) of bombs or rocket projectiles carried externally on 2 underwing stores pylons.

Programme: A twin-engined derivative of the earlier T-2A, the first T-2B (a converted T-2A) flew initially in August 1962, followed by the maiden flight of the first production T-2B in May 1965. This was succeeded by the first flight of the prototype T-2C in April 1968. In all, the US Navy received 217 T-2As, 97 T-2Bs and 231 T-2Cs, of

A T-2B Buckeye operated by the US Navy's 4th Training Squadron.

which around 200 T-2Cs remain in service. In addition, aircraft, Venezuela took 24 T-2Ds and Greece 40 T-2Es.
Notes: Destined to be replaced by the Douglas T-45 in the early 1990s, the T-2 Buckeye and its single-engined predecessor, the T-2A, have provided stalwart service in US Navy training squadrons since the end of the 1950s. When operated as an intermediate trainer, the T-2 is used to introduce student pilots, fresh from the Beech T-34C turboprop primary trainer, to jet aircraft handling. In the advanced training mission, the Buckeye is employed to introduce trainee pilots to advanced instrument flying, carrier flight operations and weapons delivery, before they pass on to the more advanced Douglas TA-4J Skyhawk.

Beechcraft T-34C Turbo Mentor Trainers/Light Strike

Type and role: 2 seat, single turboprop-engined basic pilot trainer and light strike/close support aircraft.
Maker: Beechcraft Aircraft Corporation, Wichita, Kansas, USA.
Users: US Navy (450 planned), Argentine Navy (15), Peruvian Navy (6) and the air forces of Ecuador (23), Gabon (4), Indonesia (25), Morocco (12) and Uruguay (3), plus Algerian Government (6).
Engine: 1 Pratt & Whitney Canada PT6A-25 turboprop (derated to 400shp for US Navy or 550shp in export models) driving a 3-bladed reversible-pitch propeller.

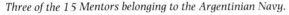

Three of the 15 Mentors belonging to the Argentinian Navy.

Dimensions: 28.75ft (8.76m) overall length; 33.4ft (10.18m) wingspan; 180sq ft (16.7m^2) wing area.
Weights: 3150lb (1429kg) empty; 4300lb (1950kg) normal gross for US Navy; 5500lb (2495kg) maximum gross for export.
Performance: 214 knots/396km/h at 17,500ft/5334m maximum speed; 1350ft/411m/min initial rate of climb; 300 nautical miles/555km tactical radius of action.
Armament: Up to 1369lb (620kg) of external weapons or fuel tanks.
Programme: A derivative of the late 1940s piston-engined T-34, development of the turboprop-powered T-34C was initiated by the US Navy in 1972, with the T-34C's first flight being made in September 1973. Deliveries of the US Navy T-34Cs commenced in November 1977. By early April 1983, Beechcraft had delivered 184 US Navy aircraft out of a planned total service procurement of 450 machines, plus 86 out of 94 known export orders.
Notes: Intended as a minimum-cost uprated performance development of the 1948 T-34A, the T-34C and export Turbo Mentor had to pass through a fraught period of massive cost escalation, a fatal development flight crash and subsequent curbs on the aircraft's flight performance envelope, prior to emerging as the current best selling single-engined turboprop trainer.

Pilatus PC-7 Turbo Trainer Trainer/Light Strike

Type and role: 2 seat, single turboprop-engined basic/intermediate trainer and light strike aircraft.
Maker: Pilatus Aircraft Limited, Stans, Switzerland.
Users: Chilean Navy (10), plus more than 320 in service or on order for 11 air forces and 3 civilian operators.
Engine: 1 Pratt & Whitney Canada PT6A-25A turboprop (derated to 550shp at take-off) driving a 3-bladed controllable-pitch propeller.
Dimensions: 32.1ft (9.78m) overall length; 34.1ft (10.4m) wingspan; 178.7sq ft (16.60m^2) wing area.
Weights: 2932lb (1130kg) empty; 4169lb (1900kg) normal gross; 5950lb (2700kg) maximum gross.
Performance: 222 knots/411km/h maximum speed at sea level; 175 knots/324km/h typical cruise at sea level; 2000ft/610m/min rate of climb at sea level; 730 nautical miles/1350km maximum range with no load; 4.22 hours maximum endurance.
Armament: Up to 1791lb (800kg) of externally carried weaponry, including bombs or pod-mounted rocket projectiles or cannon.

Programme: Developed directly from the piston-engined Pilatus P-3 of 1953, the re-engined, but otherwise minimally-modified PC-7 prototype first flew in April 1966. Following a lengthy hiatus, the first production deliveries, to Burma, commenced in February 1979. By mid-1983, total PC-7 orders exceeded 330 aircraft, of which approximately 250 had been delivered.

Notes: The design evolution of the robust PC-7 Turbo Trainer very much parallels that of the Beech T-34C Turbo Mentor in that both aircraft are essentially more powerful turboprop-engined variants of established trainer designs. The popularity of both aircraft in terms of their exportability owes as much to the price increase and growing scarcity of aviation gasoline in the post-1973 era as to the significant performance enhancements brought about by fitting the turboprop engine.

Aerospatiale SA 341 Gazelle Training Helicopters

Type and role: 2 crew, single turboshaft-engined, 3-bladed single rotor, training and light communications helicopter.

Maker Aerospatiale Helicopter Division, La Courneuve, France.

Users: Royal Navy, Royal Marines, plus numerous military and para-military users.

Engine: 1 Turbomeca Astazou III turboshaft (592shp).

Dimensions: 36.3ft (11.97m) overall length (rotors turning); 34.5ft (10.5m) main rotor diameter.

Weights: 1873lb (850kg) equipped empty; 3747lb (1700kg) maximum gross.

Performance: 143 knots/265km/h maximum speed at sea level; 1214ft/370m/min maximum rate of climb at sea level; 350 nautical miles/650km maximum range with no weapons.

One of ten Chilean Navy PC-7s at Stans, prior to delivery.

Armament: Provision to fit up to 4 Aerospatiale AS 11 or AS 12 wire guided missiles on Royal Navy aircraft.

Programme: Along with the Lynx and Puma, the SA 341 Gazelle was one of the three Anglo-French helicopters built collaboratively by Aerospatiale and Westland. The prototype SA340 made its maiden flight in April 1967, followed by the flight debut of the first production SA 341 in August 1971. Deliveries of 36 Gazelles for the Royal Navy and Royal Marines commenced in December 1974. In all, 1100 orders had been placed for the SA 341 and SA 342 by the end of April 1983, including aircraft built under licence in Egypt and Yugoslavia.

Notes: Developed as a replacement for the earlier Alouette family of helicopters, the Gazelle has proven equally successful in its export market penetration. Deliveries of the higher powered SA 342 employing a 858shp Astazou XIV turboshaft engine, commenced in 1980.

A Gazelle HT2 of 706 Squadron, Royal Naval Air Station Culdrose.

Naval missiles and guns

Strategic Missiles

SS-N-8 'Sawfly Mod 3' Strategic Missiles

A pair of SSN6 Sawfly Mod 1 seen on their transporters are slightly smaller, but similar in shape, to the SSN8.

Role: Submerged submarine-launched, intercontinental ballistic missile.
Prime contractor: Soviet Union.
Mode of operation: Once activated, the missile's inertial guidance system is fed with positional data of both the target and the launch point. Once launched, the missile boosts away on its ballistic trajectory employing its stellar sensor inputs to update its onboard inertial guidance system's knowledge of its whereabouts. Unlike the earlier SS-N-6, which carried a single nuclear warhead, the SS-N-8 carries three manoeuvrable independent re-entry vehicle (MIRV) nuclear warheads.
User: Soviet Navy.

Basic data:	SS-N-6	SS-N-8 (Estimated)
Overall Length:	42.7ft (13.0m)	45.9ft (14.0m)
Diameter:	5.9ft (1.8m)	5.4ft (1.65m)
Launch weight:	41,888lb	
	(19,000kg)	72,752lb
		(33,000kg)

Propulsion: Two-stage liquid propellant rocket motor.
Sensors: Inertial navigational guidance system with stellar sensing data updating capability.
Warheads: 3 nuclear manoeuvrable independent re-entry vehicles, each carrying a charge reported to be in the megaton range.
Speed: High hypersonic.
Range: Up to 4948 nautical miles (9170km) for SS-N-8; up to 1619 nautical miles (3000km) for SS-N-6.
Programme: The SS-N-8 was first deployed aboard 'Delta' class submarines during the 1977/78 period, having been first tested in 1971. The SS-N-8 appears to be a much improved derivative of the SS-N-6 series of missiles, first deployed aboard 'Yankee' class submarines in 1968. Around 1000 SS-N-6s were estimated to have been built, followed by approximately 500 SS-N-8s up to the close of 1981.
Notes: Very much a contemporary rival to the US Navy's Trident I strategic missile, the SS-N-8 'Sawfly Mod 3' has a longer range than its American counterpart, carrying fewer, but more powerful yield manoeuvrable independent re-entry vehicled warheads, whose circular error position accuracy has been quoted as around 4265ft (1300m), making the SS-N-8 a most formidable weapon.

Lockheed UGM-93 Trident I Strategic Missiles

Role: Submerged submarine-launched, intercontinental ballistic missile.
Prime contractor: Lockheed Missile & Space Company, Sunnyvale, California, USA.
Mode of operation: Current launch position and target data is fed to the missile's guidance sensors on a continuing basis, during high alert states from the submarine's Mk 98 on 'Ohio' class, or Mk 88 for 'Franklin' class boats. Missile launch is subject to dual-key authority after which the missile is expelled from its vertical launch tube by pressure of expanding gases, followed by first stage rocket motor ignition and subsequent ballistic trajectory. Corrections for errors in launch position and re-entry manoeuvres can be made by the missile's onboard inertial sensors and integral Post-Boost Vehicle (PBV) until all eight independently targetable nuclear warheads or decoy re-entry vehicles have separated to go their own way.
User: US Navy and on order for the Royal Navy.
Basic data: 34.1ft (10.4m) overall length; 6.2ft (1.9m) diameter; no wings or fins; 73,000lb (33,112kg) weight.
Propulsion: Thiokol/Hercules 3-stage solid propellant rocket motor.
Sensors: General Dynamics/MIT/Hughes/Raytheon Mk 5 self-contained inertial guidance system incorporating stellar-sensing cross-check inputs.
Warheads: Up to 8 Mk 4 re-entry vehicles each carrying a 100 kiloton nuclear weapon or a mix of Mk 4 and decoy re-entry vehicles.
Speed: High hypersonic.
Range: Up to 4168 nautical miles (7725km).
Programme: In 1973, Lockheed received a $2 billion cumulatively valued contract covering the development and production of the first 52 Trident I missiles. Initial test firings of the missile commenced in January 1977, this test firing phase being completed in 1979 with 25 launches rather than the originally planned 30. The first at-sea deployment of the Trident I was made aboard USS *Francis Scott Key*, a 'Franklin' class submarine in October 1979, exactly to schedule as laid down in 1976. In July 1980, the UK Government announced its intention to purchase Trident for deployment in the early 1990s.
Notes: The basic US Navy requirements for this fifth generation submarine-launched ballistic missile included the stipulation that its range be increased by some 60 per cent over that of its Poseidon predecessor, along with significant enhancements to the missile's warhead delivery accuracy. To achieve these stringent specifications, Lockheed and its team of subcontractor companies embarked upon a multi-thrusted series of major technical developments in such seemingly disparate fields as micro-electronics, graphite/epoxy composite materials and solid fuel rocket engine technology. A 636-missile programme, including the 25 development models, the Trident I total cost element of the overall Trident System was quoted as $12.139 billion in 1981 terms. In 1978, Lockheed received the first US Navy design contract to commence work on a longer, improved model, referred to as the UGM-96 Trident II and work is progressing on this variant, which is scheduled to be initially deployed aboard US Navy submarines during

These views of a Trident I missile each highlight a salient aspect of the programme; the launch photograph conveying something of the missile's awesome power, while the dockside loading of the containerised missile helps lend perspective to the overall costs involved.

1989. The cost of the Royal Navy's Trident System procurement, which includes the building of four modified 'Ohio' class submarines, base facilities and other support equipment was estimated to amount to some £7.5 billion in 1981 values, based on the Trident II missile, but excluding the cost of a fifth submarine. Incidentally, the Royal Navy's Trident II submarine, which will be British-built, will only carry 16 missiles, as opposed to the 'Ohio' class submarine's complement of 24.

Aerospatiale MSBS Strategic Missiles

Role: Submerged submarine-launched, transcontinental ballistic missile.
Prime contractor: Aerospatiale, Divisions Systemes Balistiques & Spatiaux, Les Mureaux Cedex, France.
Mode of operation: Prior to launch, the activated missile's inertial navigation system is fed with positional information of both the parent submarine and its target. The actual launch is subject to onboard dual-key authority. After launch, the missile boosts away along its hypersonic ballistic trajectory, the maximum height of which is a function of the target distance. All missiles in this family carry nuclear warheads: the M-2 and M-20 having single warheads of 0.5 and 1 megaton equivalence, respectively, while the M-4 will carry a reported six or seven warheads of 150 kilotons each; all of which have manoeuvrable independent re-entry capability (MIRV).

The launching of a development model of the latest French submarine-launched M-4 missile to be operational in 1985.

User: French Navy.

Basic data:	M-20	M-4
Overall length:	34.1ft (10.4m)	37.7ft (11.5m)
Diameter:	4.9ft (1.5m)	6.3ft (1.93m)
Launch weight:	19,684lb	
	(20,000kg)	33,747lb
		(35,000kg)

Propulsion: GZP two-stage (M-20) or three-stage (M-4) solid-propellant rocket motors.

Sensors: SAGEM inertial guidance system; Electronique Marcel Dassault Sagittaire digital computer.

Warhead/s: 1 single 1 megaton equivalence nuclear warhead in M-20; reported up to 6 or 7 manoeuvrable independent re-entry vehicles, some or all of which each carry a 150-kiloton nuclear charge.

Speed: High hypersonic.

Range: Over 1619 nautical miles (3000km) for M-20; 2,158 nautical miles (4000km) for M-4.

Programme: The first of the French-developed submarine-launched ballistic missiles, the M-1, went into service in 1971, these weapons being replaced by the M-2 from 1974; the M-2, in turn, being replaced by the M-20 from 1977 onwards. The current M-20 missile is scheduled to be replaced by the higher capability M-4 commencing in 1985. Estimates of missiles built indicate 60 of the M-1, 60 M-2s and 100 M-20s. The M-4 was first successfully test-launched in November 1980.

Notes: The Mer-Sol-Balistique-Strategique (MSBS) family of missiles represents the spearhead of French strategic forces. The new M-4 will be deployed aboard *L'Inflexible,* sixth of the French missile submarines.

General Dynamics BGM-109 Tomahawk Strategic Missiles

One of the development BGM-109A nuclear-warheaded missiles seen over the Mojave Desert during a 1980 trials flight that commenced with a vertical launch in southern California and terminated at a test site in Dugway, Utah.

Role: Submarine or ship-launched (BGM-109A, B and C) long-range strategic (BGM-109A) or tactical (BGM-109B and C) or air-launched BGM-109L long-range tactical high subsonic cruise missiles. Other versions under development for the US Air Force include the ground-launched AGM-109G and air-launched AGM-109H.

Prime contractor: General Dynamics Convair Division, San Diego, California, USA.

Mode of operation: Prior to launch, the missile needs to be provided with pre-programmed navigational instructions which can include non-direct routeing to decoy or evade enemy defences. After launch, which is rocket-boosted in the case of sea or ground-based launching, the missile settles into a low-level cruise mode, flying a contour-hugging flight profile in the case of those attacking land targets. Cruise guidance is provided by inertial system updated by a terrain comparison (TERCOM) processor when overflying land. In the terminal phase, the missiles are guided to their target by digital scene-matching area correlation (DSMAC) system for land targets, or active radar seeker when operating against ship targets.

Users: US Navy and US Air Force.

Basic data: 2650lb/1202kg (BGM-109A), 2700lb/1225kg (BGM-109B) or 2800lb/1270kg (BGM-109C) weight; 18.2ft/5.55m overall missile length or 20.5ft/6.25m including booster; 8.6ft/2.62m wingspan.

Propulsion: 1 Atlantic Research solid propellant booster rocket motor (7000lb/3175kg thrust); 1 Williams Research F107 turbofan (around 600lb/272kg thrust).

Sensors: Litton Industries inertial navigation system; Honeywell radar altimeter; McDonnell Douglas terrain comparison system; digital scene matching area correlation system or Texas Instruments active radar seeker; impact (land targets) or delayed impact (ship) fuzing system.

Warhead weight: 1 W-80 nuclear warhead of 200 kiloton yield on BGM-109A or 992lb (450kg) of high explosive on BGM-109B and C.

Speed: High subsonic (around Mach 0.72 or 478 knots/885km/h at 500ft altitude).

Range: Up to 1349 nautical miles (2500km) for BGM-109A; up to 248 nautical miles (460km) for BGM-109B and up to 701 nautical miles (1300km) for BGM-109C.

Programme: US Navy studies into the development of submarine or ship-launched long-range cruise missiles which had lapsed after the Vought Regulus and Northrop Snark programmes of the 1950s were reactivated in 1972. From this point on until early 1976, developments continued on a competitive basis between General Dynamics and Vought, with their BGM-110, until March 1976, when General Dynamics won the full-scale development contract. The first flight of a full-scale development BGM-109A occurred in February 1977, followed 12 months later by the missile's first submarine launch. Operational deployment of the BGM-109A was set for mid-1984, followed by that of the BGM-109B and C prior to March 1985. Currently, the US Navy are planning a total procurement of nearly 4000 Tomahawks.

Notes: As with the McDonnell Douglas Harpoon, the Tomahawk is stowed within a 21in (533mm) diameter capsule for submarine launching via existing torpedo tubes. However, a vertical launch system for both submarine and shipboard installation is currently under development by the Martin Marietta Corporation. Operational deployment of the US Navy's air-launched BGM-109L is planned to take place during 1986. The estimated average unit cost of the Tomahawk was quoted as around $2 million in 1982 values.

Anti-ship Missiles

SS-N-3 'Shaddrock' Anti-Ship Missiles

Role Ship- and submarine-launched, long-range cruise anti-ship or anti-shore missile.
Prime contractor: Soviet.
Mode of operation: Shipboard target position data is fed to the missile's guidance system for programming and the launcher elevated prior to launch. After launch, the missile is controlled by its pre-programmed autopilot and radar altimeter, both of which are capable of being passed updated mid-course correction data via a radio frequency command data link. During the terminal flight phase, the missile homes on to its target using either active radar or infra-red (passive) onboard seekers depending on variant.
User: Soviet Navy.
Basic data: 37.5ft (11.43m) overall length; 3.0ft (910mm) diameter; 10.0ft (3.05m) wingspan; 26,500lb (12,020kg) weight including booster rockets.
Propulsion: 2 jettisonable solid propellant rocket motors; 1 integral turbojet or ramjet engine for sustained cruise.
Sensors: Pre-programmable onboard guidance system, readily updated via radio frequency command data link; impact, delayed impact or proximity fuzing systems.
Warhead weight: Up to 2205lb (1000kg) of kiloton range nuclear charge or high explosive.
Speed: High subsonic (around Mach 0.8) for turbojet-powered versions or low supersonic (around Mach 1.2) for the reduced ranged ramjet-powered models.
Range: Up to 434 nautical miles (805km).
Programme: Initially operationally deployed aboard 'Echo' and 'Juliet' class submarines at the beginning of the 1960s, the SS-N-3 is also installed aboard 'Kynda' and both 'Kresta' I and II class cruisers. Over 3000 of these missiles were reported to be held in the Soviet Navy's active inventory at the beginning of 1982.
Notes: The largest of the known Soviet Navy shipboard missiles, the SS-N-3 'Shaddrock' is a logical evolution of the earlier SS-N-2 'Styx' missile. Terminal cruise is at sea skimming height.

The combined container/launcher for the winged and ventral finned 'Shaddrock' missile, whose flying surfaces fold down against the forward end of the missile's twin underslung booster rocket motors until leaving the launcher. This installation of two launchers to starboard and two to port belongs to a Soviet Navy 'Kresta' I class cruiser photographed in 1970.

AS-4 'Kitchen' Anti-Ship Missiles

Role: Air-launched, 'fire-and-forget', long-range, high supersonic anti-ship (when fitted with conventional warhead) or anti-surface task group missile (when fitted with nuclear warhead).
Prime contractor: Soviet.
Mode of operation: Prior to launching, the missile requires to be activated and its inertial guidance fed with target position data. On release from the parent aircraft, depending upon the pre-selected flight profile chosen by the launch controller, the missile either climbs away for maximum-range strikes, or descends towards the target on shorter-range attacks. On longer-range strikes, the missile ascends in a constant Mach 1.8 speed mode to a maximum altitude of up to 88,600ft (27,000m), prior to making a high supersonic descent on to the target, commencing at Mach 2.5 and rising to as much as Mach 3.5 on impact or predetermined detonation point. In the shorter-range profile, the missile initially descends quite rapidly along a progressively shallower curving flight path towards its target, reaching a maximum speed not exceeding Mach 1.2 in the denser, low-level air. For optimum range using either flight profiles, the missile requires to be launched at around just over 39,000ft (12,000m) and at a parent aircraft speed of Mach 0.9.
User: Soviet Naval Aviation and Air Force.

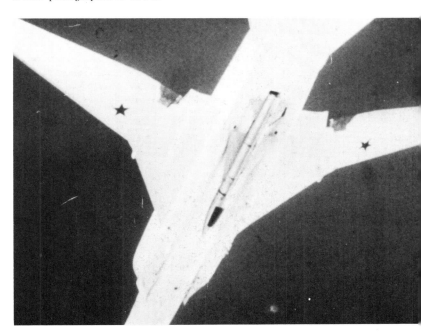

A Soviet AS-4 'Kitchen' slung semi-recessed beneath a Tupolev Tu-22M 'Backfire'.

Basic data: 37.1ft (11.3m) overall length; 2.95ft (900mm) diameter; 9.5ft (2.9m) wingspan; 13,228lb (6000kg) weight at launch.
Propulsion: 1 rocket motor (probably liquid fuelled).
Sensors: 1 inertial guidance system; 1 autopilot system; 1 radar; 1 passive infra-red homing system; impact and proximity fuzing system.
Warhead weight: 2205lb (1000kg) nuclear or high explosive.
Speed: Supersonic to high supersonic (Mach 1.2 to Mach 3.5 at target).

Range: Up to 388.5 nautical miles (720km) when using optimum climb cruise technique, or 162 nautical miles (300km) using descending approach.

Programme: The AS-4 'Kitchen' was first identified by Western sources as early as 1961 and was subsequently reported as being first operationally deployed around 1967. AS-4 missiles are known to have been carried by Tupolev Tu-95 'Bear', Tu-22 'Blinder' and Tu-22M 'Backfire' bombers.

Notes: Developed at around the same time as the Soviet's SS-N-2 'Styx' ship-to-ship missile, the AS-4 was and remains an awesome weapon and virtually begs performance comparisons with the range of much more recently introduced Western naval air-launched 'stand-off' missiles, such as the US Navy's AGM-84 Harpoon and the French-developed MM 39 Exocet. While remarkably little substantial data is available on, for example, the AS-4's onboard guidance systems, the presence of dielectric antenna fairings at the trailing edges of the missile's wingtips would suggest that, if not originally inbuilt, 'Kitchen' now carries the capability to receive and act upon mid-course information concerning target track and position: a technique in which the Soviets appear to have done much pioneering development, particularly during the 1960s, when compared with the US Navy's rival three-dimensional tactical command and control system known as Naval Tactical Data System (NTDS).

OTO-Melara/Matra Otomat Mk 2 Anti-Ship Missiles

Role: Ship-launched, high subsonic, medium-range, sea-skimming anti-ship missile.

Prime contractor: OTO-Melara SpA, La Spezia, Italy.

Mode of operation: The launch sequence is initiated manually by the missile launch controller, who, when satisfied concerning the target data, activates the missile's systems and turbojet. Target data can be derived from shipboard radar, optronics or from external-to-ship data links. As the missile has a pre-programmable autopilot system and the ability to manoeuvre through 360 degrees in azimuth on to the target bearing, the missile can be launched irrespective of the relative headings of the launch and target vessels. After launch, the missile climbs away, reaching its cruising speed and booster separation at around 3000ft (915m), prior to descending into cruise phase flight under the guidance of its autopilot and radar altimeter. At a predetermined point along the flight path, the missile's active homing radar is activated and, upon radar lock-on to the target, the missile descends from its

An Otomat anti-ship cruise missile climbs away under the combined thrust of its twin booster rocket motors and turbojet.

final cruise height of around 65ft (19.8m) into the terminal attack phase, the height of which is determined by the radar altimeter-sensed sea state.

Users: Navies of Italy, Egypt, Iraq, Libya, Nigeria, Peru, Philippines, Saudi Arabia and Venezuela.

Basic data: 14.64ft (4.642m) overall length; 1.3ft (400mm) diameter; 4.43ft (1.35m) wingspan; 1720lb (780kg) weight, including boosters.

Propulsion: 2 Hotchkiss/SNPE solid propellant rocket booster motors, plus 1 Trubomeca Arbizin IIIB turbojet cruise engine.

Sensors: Pre-programmable autopilot system; radar altimeter; active homing radar equipment (all from Thomson-CSF in Mk 1 radar homer by SMA in Mk 2); OTO-Melara delayed impact fuzing system.

Warhead weight: 551lb (250kg) of semi-armour piercing high explosive and incendiary charge.

Speed: High subsonic (Mach 0.9, or approximately 595 knots).

Range: Up to 97 nautical miles (180km) maximum; 3.2 nautical miles (6km) minimum. *Note:* data applies to Mk 2 missiles.

Programme: The design and development of this joint industrial venture between French and Italian companies was commenced at the close of the 1960s, with the first live firing taking place around the middle of 1972. Initial operational deployment of the Otomat Mk 1 occurred in 1977 and by the beginning of 1983, total orders stood at 750 missiles, destined to equip some 83 vessels, ranging from the 13,370 ton 'Garibaldi' type aircraft carrier to the 60.5 ton 'Sparviero' class fast attack hydrofoils.

Notes: As with Exocet and Harpoon, the Otomat missile owes its existence directly to Western naval needs to find an effective counter to the Soviet-developed SS-N-2 'Styx'. The Mk 1 missile had a maximum range of around 35 nautical miles (65km) and needed to make a 'pop-up' manoeuvre during its terminal flight phase, rendering it more vulnerable to detection and, hence, enemy fire. These operational disadvantages have been eliminated from the Mk 2 version, which also enjoys a much enhanced maximum range capability.

McDonnell Douglas AGM/RGM-84 Harpoon Anti-Ship Missiles

Role: Air-launched (AGM-84A) or ship/submarine-launched (RGM-84A) medium-range, sea-skimming anti-ship missile.

Prime contractor: McDonnell Douglas, St Charles, Missouri, USA.

Mode of operation: Prior to launch, the missile's systems are primed and fed with target position and vector data. After launch, the air-launched version drops away as its turbojet is started up, whereas both ship and submarine-launched versions climb away in a low ballistic trajectory, driven by a booster rocket motor which has to be jettisoned prior to ignition of the missile's sustaining turbojet. From this point, both air and sea-launched versions descend to a sea-skimming altitude, continuing towards the target under the guidance of the missile's onboard inertial navigation and radar altimeter systems. Terminal phase homing is provided by Harpoon's active radar seeker.

Users: Navies of Australia, Denmark, Federal Germany, Greece, Israel, Japan, South Korea, Netherlands, Saudi Arabia, Spain, Turkey, UK and US.

Basic data: 1168lb (530kg) weight for AGM-84; 1470lb (667kg) weight for ship-launched version; 1530lb (694kg) for encapsulated submarine-launched version; 12.6ft (3.84m) for AGM-84 and 15.0ft (4.58m) for RGM-84A overall lengths; 1.1ft (340mm) diameter; 2.98ft (910mm) wingspan.

Propulsion: 1 Teledyne CAE J402 turbojet (600lb/272kg

thrust), plus 1 Aerojet General solid propellant rocket booster motor (14,550lb/6600kg thrust) on RGM-84A.

Sensors: Lear/Norden inertial guidance system; Honeywell radar altimeter; Texas Instrument active radar seeker; delayed-action impact and back-up proximity fuzing systems.

Warhead weight: 570lb (259kg) high explosive.

Speed: High subsonic (around Mach 0.9).

Range: Up to 86 nautical miles (160km) for AGM-84A and 44 nautical miles (82km) for RGM-84A.

Programme: In January 1971, the US Navy requested industry bids for a new all-weather anti-ship missile system, the development contract for which was awarded to McDonnell Douglas in June 1971. Initial launch trials involving aircraft and submarine capsule separation trials commenced in May and July 1972, respectively, the first fully guided live firing following in December of the same year. In July 1975 came the first US Navy production contract for 282 Harpoons, followed during the next 18 months by its selection for use by several overseas navies. Operational deployment of the ship and submarine-launched Harpoon had been achieved by 1978, followed by deployment of the AGM-84A in the spring of 1979. By the end of 1984, Harpoon firm orders stood at 3880, of which 3170 had been delivered.

Notes: Always benefiting from the support and, hence, massive home-based market provided by the US Navy, Harpoon has clearly emerged not only as the most operationally flexible of the modern Western World anti-ship missiles, but also as the best selling of this breed. Besides being supplied in its own container/launcher for shipboard use, the Harpoon can also be launched from the standard US Navy Tartar and ASROC launchers. In the encapsulated submarine-launched version, the missile's aerodynamic surfaces are foldable to facilitate stowage within the 21in (533mm) diameter and 20.5ft (6.35m)-long capsule.

British Aerospace Dynamics Sea Eagle Anti-ship Missiles

Role: Air-launched (P3T) or boosted ship-launched (P5T) long range high subsonic, sea-skimming anti-ship missile.

Prime contractor: British Aerospace Dynamics, Stevenage, Herts, UK.

Mode of operation: Prior to launch, the missile's systems are activated and target's position relative to launch platform is fed into missile's onboard guidance, which can be programmed to incorporate decoying 'dog leg' tracking or to overfly a lower priority en route to its designated prey. On launch, the missile drops away from the aircraft, or is rocket-boosted away from the ship, airflow through the now exposed air intake being used to spin up the missile's turbojet engine prior to ignition. The missile then settles into a sea-skimming cruise mode at an altitude barely above the wave spray zone in order to minimise its detectability. During the terminal flight phase, which may be up to 8 nautical miles (15km), the missile makes a momentary climb so that its active radar homing head can positively acquire the target in order to update the onboard inertial navigation system prior to continuing on to the target, which it is capable of hitting close to the waterline.

Users: On order for the Royal Navy, Indian Navy and Royal Air Force (for use with Sea Harrier, Buccaneer, Tornado and Sea King).

Basic data: 1826lb (828kg) weight for air-launched P3T; 13.1ft (3.99m) overall length; 1.3ft (400mm) diameter; 3.9ft (1.19m) wingspan.

Propulsion: 1 Turbomeca TRI 60 turbojet only on air-launced P3T, plus 2 solid propellant rocket booster motors on ship-launched P5T.

Sensors: British Aerospace Dynamics inertial guidance;

A Harpoon boosting away from one of the two midships quadruple launchers aboard USS Fletcher *(DDG992), a 'Spruance' class destroyer. Note how the launchers positioning ensures that blast effects are dumped overboard away from ship's crew.*

Plessey J-band radar altimeter; GEC-Marconi active radar seeker; Impact fuzing system.

Warhead weight: 441lb (200kg) high explosive (aluminised RDX-TNT).

Speed: High subsonic (Mach 0.85).

Range: Up to in excess of 54 nautical miles (100km). *Note:* the missile also has a very short minimum range and can be launched from as low as 98ft (30m) altitude.

Programme: Studies for this Martel replacement commenced during the latter 1970s as the air-launched P3T, the first UK Ministry of Defence engineering development contract being announced in July 1979. Initial air-launched firing trials commenced during the summer of 1981, the trials aircraft being a Buccaneer.

Sea Eagles being carried by a Sea Harrier FRS 1 provides a ready means of gauging the missile's size.

The full production was authorised in early February 1982 and the air-launched P3T Sea Eagle should be operationally deployed by late 1984 or early 1985. Meanwhile, in October 1981, British Aerospace Dynamics announced that it had completed studies into a twin rocket motor-boosted ship-launched variant, referred to as the P5T Sea Eagle.

Notes: A truly 'fire and forget' weapon, the Sea Eagle meets the same mission requirements as that of the MBB Kormoran, Aerospatiale's AM 39 Exocet and the McDonnell Douglas AGM-84 Harpoon. Incorporating some of the most advanced digital electronics and signal processing capability, Sea Eagle is claimed to be far less susceptible to enemy electronics and other countermeasures than earlier missiles. Similarly, its cleverly faceted warhead shaping, developed by the Royal Armament Research and Development Establishment, ensures the maximum explosive penetration of the target hull even if the missile strikes at a grazing angle. The ship-launched P5T version is designed to be carried on its own combined container/launcher box, the external fitting of which allows it to be readily mated to the already developed Lightweight Sea Dart quadruple launcher.

Aerospatiale MM38/AM39/MM40 Exocet Anti-ship Missiles

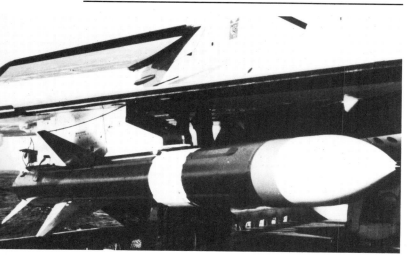

The AM39 air-launched Exocet mounted on a Dassault Super Etendard.

Role: Medium ranged ship or air-launched, sea skimming anti-ship missile.

Prime contractor: Aerospatiale, Division Engins Tactiques, Chatillon Sous Bagneux, France.

Mode of operation: Prior to launch, the missile's inertial guidance system and radar altimeter are fed the necessary data input from the parent ship or aircraft sensors. Following launch, the missile tracks towards target steered by its own inertial guidance until such time as the missile's own active radar seeker acquires the target to commence the terminal homing phase.

Users: Navies of France, Argentina, Bahrain, Belgium, Brazil, Brunei, Chile, Colombia, Ecuador, Federal Germany, Greece, Indonesia, Libya, Malaysia, Morocco, Oman, Peru, Thailand, United Arab Emirates and United Kingdom, plus 8 air forces.

Basic data:

	MM38 (ship)	AM39 (air)	MM40 (ship)
Overall length:	17.1ft/5.2m	15.4ft/4.7m	18.5ft/5.7m
Diameter:	1.1ft/350mm	1.1ft/350mm	1.1ft/350mm
Span:	3.3ft/1.0m	3.3ft/1.0m	3.3ft/1.0m
Weight:	1620lb/ 735kg	1442lb/ 654kg	1841lb 835kg

Propulsion: SNEP/Aerospatiale 2-stage (booster/sustainer) solid-propellant rocket motor.

Sensors: EMD inertial guidance system; TRT radar altimeter; EMD active radar seeker; delayed impact and proximity fuzing systems.

Warhead weight: 364lb (165kg) high explosive.

Speed: High subsonic (Mach 0.93 or 615 knots/ 1140km/h).

Range: MM38, up to 22.7 nautical miles (42km); AM39, between 37.8 and 27.0 nautical miles (70 and 50km); MM40, up to 37.8 nautical miles (70km).

Programme: Development work on the Exocet was initiated during the latter half of the 1960s, with test firings of the missile commencing in July 1970, followed by the first French Navy firing in November 1972. The initial MM38 shipboard model became operational in 1974, while the first AM39 air-launched missiles entered service during 1977, the improved ranged MM40 shipboard version entering operational use in 1981. Currently, development of a submarine-launched variant, the SM39 is progressing as production continues against a total Exocet order book reported to exceed 2250 by the close of May 1985, of which 2100 had been delivered.

Notes: Developed as a direct counterweapon to the Soviet 'Styx'-equipped missile craft, Exocet has contributed significantly to the continuing story of French defence equipment export successes, being simple to operate and requiring minimal maintenance. Indeed, protected as the shipboard MM38 and MM40 versions are by their individual hermetically sealed container/launcher canisters, no onboard periodic inspection is required while the vessel remains at sea. Another important operational aspect of the Exocet centres on its 'fire and forget' capability, which frees the launch vessel/aircraft from continuing to 'illuminate' the target during missile transit; a need that gives the potential prey more warning time and may even render the missile-launcher vulnerable to counter-missile attack. Deployed by both of the belligerents in the Falklands conflict, the basic efficacy of the air-launched AM39 was twice demonstrated in strikes that led to the subsequent loss of both HMS *Sheffield* and the container ship, *Atlantic Conveyor*. In terms of shipboard application, Exocet can and has been fitted to quite small-displacement vessels, such as the Royal Thai Navy's 270-ton 'Racharit' class missile craft, while the air-launched AM39 variant has been deployed on a variety of aircraft, ranging from the Super Etendard through Atlantic NG fixed wing types to the Super Puma and Super Frelon medium-sized helicopters.

SS-N-2 'Styx' Anti-ship Missiles

Role: High subsonic cruise, medium-range anti-ship missile.

Prime contractor: Soviet.

Mode of operation: Missile's auto pilot can be programmed from shipboard sensors prior to launch. Alternatively, the missile can be fired in the general direction of the target and subjected to mid-course track correction via a data link system. Basically, the missile follows a constant altitude cruise path which is at sea-skimming level in later models. Terminal flight phase guidance is supplied by the missile's own onboard sensors, which can be active radar, semi-active radar or infra-red radar seeker depending on version employed.

Users: Navies of USSR, China, India, Warsaw Pact, Cuba, Yugoslavia, North Korea and radical Arab nations.

Basic data: 21.3ft (6.3m) overall length; 2.5ft (750mm) diameter; 8.9ft (2.7m) wingspan; 5000 to 6600lb (2250 to 3000kg) weight dependent upon version.

Propulsion: 1 solid propellant rocket booster motor plus 1 turbojet cruise engine.

Sensors: Radio frequency detector; infra-red seeker or

tracking radar head; impact and proximity fuzing systems.

Warhead weight: 1100lb (500kg).

Speed: High subsonic (Mach 0.9, or approximately 595 knots).

Range: 21.7 nautical miles (40.2km) for early models; 40 nautical miles (74km) for later models.

Programme: First deployed operationally during the 1959–60 period on 'Komar' and subsequently 'Osa' and 'Nanuchka' class fast attack craft, the 'Styx' has been built in many versions, including a locally-built Chinese model for fitment aboard China's 'Luta' class destroyers.

Notes: Although long obsolescent, the 'Styx', to give it its NATO code name, will always have a place in the annals of naval development by virtue of being not only the first operationally deployed ship-to-ship cruise missile, but also the first to demonstrate its effectiveness with its sinking of the Israeli destroyer, *Eilat*, in late 1967. Deployed more than a decade ahead of any Western ship-to-ship cruise missile to enter large-scale production, the existence of 'Styx' arguably had more impact on the course of Western naval development in the late 1960s onwards through the 1970s than that of any other single Soviet weapon, including the emergence of the 'Kiev' class aircraft carriers. Certainly, the presence of 'Styx' added impetus to the development of Exocet, Otomat, Harpoon and Tomahawk in terms of Western ship-to-ship missiles; while similarly, it was the demonstrable effectiveness of 'Styx' that brought the need for more effective shipboard anti-missile defences into sharper focus: a development that spurred work on missiles such as Phalanx in the US and Seawolf in Britain.

SAAB Bofors RBS 15 Anti-ship Missiles

Role: Ship and air-launched, medium-range, sea-skimming anti-ship missile.

Prime contractor: SAAB Bofors Missile Corporation, Stockholm, Sweden.

Mode of operation: Prior to launch, the missile's onboard inertial guidance system is fed with target range and bearing data derived from either ship-board or data-linked sensors. Following shipboard launch, which can be at offset angles exceeding 90 degrees from target track, the missile ascends under rocket boost prior to commencing a pre-programmable or mid-course corrected three phase cruise mode. During cruise, the missile progressively descends under the control of its radar altimeter until it is sea-skimming, prior to making a terminal 'pop-up' to enable it to dive into its prey.

Users: On order for the Royal Swedish Navy and Finnish naval forces.

Basic data: 14.27ft (4.35m) overall length; 1.64ft (0.50m) diameter; 4.59ft (1.40m) span; 1698lb (770kg) launch weight with boosters or 1318lb (598kg) without boosters.

Propulsion: 2 solid propellant booster rocket (under 5 second firing duration); 1 Microturbo TR 160-1-077 turbojet cruise engine.

Sensors: Philips (Sweden) provide both the onboard inertial guidance/radar altimeter system and active radar seeker; impact fuzing.

Warhead: Approximately 496lb (225kg) high explosive.

Speed: Up to more than 529 knots/980km/h (Mach 0.8) at sea level.

Range: Over 38 nautical miles (70km) effective from ship launch.

Programme: The RBS 15 was selected for full-scale development by the Swedish Government in 1979 after a round of competing missile evaluations. The first sea-going development rounds were delivered before the close of 1982 and initial shipboard firing trials had been completed prior to mid-1983. The RBS 15 is scheduled to

This view of a 'Styx' being lowered aboard ship emphasises its distinctly aircraft-like appearance.

be initially operationally deployed aboard Swedish 'Spica' II and 'Stockholm' class vessels during 1985. In 1983, Finland placed initial orders for the RBS 15 for installation aboard new 'Helsinki' class fast attack craft.

Notes: Derived from the earlier SAAB RB 05A air-launched anti-ship missile, the canister-launched RBS 15 employs a very refined monopulse active radar seeker that not only can cope with modern electronics jamming, but also has the ability to discriminate between its target and, say, a small, nearby island.

An impression of the RBS 15 shown in its sea-skimming mode.

Two Martel anti-radiation missiles slung beneath the wing pylons of a French Navy operated Dassault-Breguet Atlantic.

Matra AS 37 Martel Anti-ship Missiles

Role: Air-launched, medium-range, anti-radiation/anti-ship missile.
Prime contractor: Engins Matra Military Division, Velizy-Villacoublay, France.
Mode of operation: Prior to launch, the missile's systems are activated and the missile's broad band radar homer must have acquired lock-on to the target, either by specific frequency identification or, where the frequency is not known, by broad band direction finding techniques. After launch, the missile homes on to the target, even if the target's radiation is frequency agile. A television headed version of Martel is employed as an anti-ship weapon by the Royal Air Force.
Users: French Navy and Air Force (anti-radiation version), along with the Royal Air Force (television version).
Basic data: 13.5ft (4.12m) overall length; 1.3ft (400mm) diameter; 3.9ft (1.19m) wingspan; 1173lb (532kg) weight at launch.
Propulsion: Hotchkiss Brandt/Aerospatiale dual thrust (2.4 seconds boost, 22.2 seconds sustainer) composite solid propellant rocket motor.
Sensors: Electronique Marcel Dassault passive broad band radiation seeker; autopilot system; Thomson-CSF impact and proximity fuzing system.
Warhead weight: 331lb (150kg) blast fragmentation high explosive.
Speed: High subsonic (around Mach 0.85).
Range: Up to 32.4 nautical miles (60km) dependent upon launch altitude and parent aircraft's speed.
Programme: In the early 1960s, the Royal Navy and Royal Air Force initiated joint studies around an air-to-surface missile for use on both maritime and tactical strike aircraft. This work culminated in the issue of (Royal) Naval Air Staff Requirement 1168 in January 1963. As the French foresaw a similar need, it was agreed that the programme proceed on a joint Anglo-French basis; a decision that was to be ratified in September 1964. Initial live missile launches took place in the autumn of 1967 and the missile was first operationally deployed by both France and Britain during 1972. Around 2000 of these missiles are believed to have been built for both customer nations.
Notes: Deployed aboard French Navy maritime patrol Atlantics, French Air Force Mirage IIIE and Jaguar strike fighters and Royal Air Force (former Fleet Air Arm) Buccaneers, the Martel's protracted gestation between concept and deployment was, at least, in part due to British procurement policy vaccilation during the mid-1960s; a period during which the Royal Air Force saw the relatively close cancellation of, first, the BAC TSR-2, followed by the General Dynamics F-111K (both of which

were to have employed Martel). Despite these setbacks, Martel has demonstrated its ability to operate effectively in heavy electronics countermeasures conditions; its airframe subsequently serving as the basis for the P3T Sea Eagle turbojet-powered, sea-skimming anti-ship missile.

MBB Kormoran Anti-ship Missiles

Role: Air-launched, medium-range, high subsonic, sea-skimming (in terminal flight phase) anti-ship missile.
Prime contractor: Messerschmitt-Bolkow-Blohm, Munich, Federal Germany.
Mode of operation: Prior to launch, the missile is activated and fed with processed target position data from the launch aircraft's navigational system. After release, the missile descends to its pre-programmed low-level cruise altitude under the direction of its onboard inertial navigational and radar altimeter systems. At a predetermined distance from the target, the missile's navigation system automatically switches on the weapon's active radar seeker, which, once it has acquired lock-on to the target, assumes directional control. Shortly before impact, the missile descends further into a sea-skimming mode, so as to add to the enemy's threat detection problems.
User: Federal German Navy.
Basic data: 14.44ft (4.4m) overall length; 1.13ft (341mm) diameter; 3.28ft (1.0m) wingspan; 1323lb (600kg) launch weight.
Propulsion: Two stage solid propellant rocket motor (SNPE producing the boost stage and Aerospatiale the sustainer stage).
Sensors: BBG inertial system; TRT radar altimeter; Thomson-CSF active radar seeker; delayed impact fuzing system.
Warhead weight: 353lb (160kg) triple ignition high explosive.
Speed: High subsonic (Mach 0.95 or 628 knots at sea level).
Range: 21 nautical miles (40km maximum; reported 13 nautical miles (21km) maximum effective.
Programme: Development work on the Kormoran was initiated during the latter part of the 1960s by MBB (acting as prime contractor in collaboration with Aerospatiale). Trial firing of the Kormoran commenced in early 1972 and had been completed by 1975. Initial operational deployment of the missile occurred during 1977, with around 500 Mk 1 missiles having been produced for the Federal German Navy's then current fleet of Lockheed F-104 Starfighters, each capable of carrying two missiles. These Mk 1 missiles are currently being fitted

to the Federal German Navy's Panavia Tornado, which can loft up to four Kormorans. However, this is considered to be an interim measure and MBB are currently under contract to develop an enhanced capability Mk 2 version of the missile which should be built in greater numbers than the Mk 1.

Notes: The Kormoran, as with the earlier Matra Martel anti-radiation and later Aerospatiale MM 39 air-launched anti-ship missile, is a stand-off range weapon, enabling the launch aircraft's crew to launch the missile well beyond the range of most shipboard anti-air defences. Once launched, Kormoran navigates its own way to the target, relieving the launch aircraft's need to stay in the area and illuminate the target with its onboard radar. One of the most salient weaknesses of this fire-and-forget weapon when compared with its contemporaries in the shape of MM 39 Exocet, AGM-84 Harpoon and Sea Eagle is its relatively poor range performance. This aspect is, no doubt, being currently addressed during the development of the Kormoran Mk 2, but is not likely to prove a decisive factor in comparison with the overriding consideration of ensuring that Federal Germany maintains its ability to produce such missiles.

British Aerospace Dynamics Sea Skua Anti-ship Missiles

Role: Air-launched, short/medium-range, sea-skimming missile.
Prime contractor: British Aerospace Dynamics, Filton, UK.
Mode of operation: Target is acquired by the launch helicopter's radar, passive electronics support system or from stabilised optical sighting device and is then processed by the helicopter's onboard digital nav-attack system prior to being passed to the missile's navigational sensors. After launch, the missile descends to one of four pre-programmable sea-skimming altitudes (depending on local wave height) and closes onto target using data inputs from its semi-active radar seeker and/or data link with launch helicopter.
User: Royal Navy.
Basic data: 8.2ft (2.50m) overall length; 0.9ft (280mm) diameter; 2.0ft (610mm) span; 450lb (205kg) weight.
Propulsion: IMI 2-stage (boost and sustainer) solid propellant rocket motor.
Sensors: GEC-Marconi semi-active radar seeker; TRT radar altimeter; contact fuzing system.
Warhead weight: About 66lb (30kg) of high explosive.
Speed: High subsonic (around Mach 0.93 or 615 knots/1140km/h).
Range: Up to 13 nautical miles (24.1km) maximum; 1.7 nautical miles (3.2km) minimum.
Programme: Development of the Sea Skua, then known as CL834 commenced in early 1972, with the first fully-guided air launch of the missile taking place in November 1979. Around 250 examples of Sea Skua were reported to have been built by the beginning of 1982, with full-scale production just getting underway at that time.
Notes: A relatively simple and inexpensive missile, Sea Skua was conceived as a means of extending the defensive range of the Royal Navy's modern breed of expensive helicopter-carrying destroyers and frigates against attack by fast and agile missile-equipped craft. Deployed with the South Atlantic Task Force, the Lynx-launched, sea-skimming Sea Skua graphically demonstrated its beyond-ship-horizon capabilities early in the campaign, when eight out of eight Sea Skuas launched all hit their targets, destroying one patrol craft and seriously damaging three other Argentinian ships. Requiring no shipboard pre-launch check-out, up to four Sea Skuas can be carried externally aboard a Lynx and, if necessary, ripple fired against their target.

A Panavia Tornado of the Federal German Navy service carrying four Kormorans.

Aerospatiale AS 15 TT Anti-Ship Missiles

Role: All-weather, air-launched short-range anti-ship missile.
Prime contractor: Aerospatiale Division Engin Tactiques, Chatillon-sous-Bagneaux, France.
Mode of operation: Prior to launch, the missile's systems are activated and data from the launch aircraft is fed in to provide target's bearing and the predetermined low-level cruise altitude to be flown. After launch, the missile is directed on to the target by means of the parent aircraft's search radar monitoring the position of the target and missile and feeding directions via an aircraft-to-missile data link. Within around 985ft (300m) of the missile run-in, the launch aircraft sends a command instruction for the missile to make its terminal phase dive on to the target.
User: Saudi Arabian Navy and planned for deployment with units of the French Navy.
Basic data: 7.55ft (2.3m) overall length; 0.62ft (188mm) diameter; 1.85ft (564mm) wingspan; 220lb (100kg) launch weight.
Propulsion: Aerospatiale dual-thrust, solid propellant rocket motor of around 54 seconds duration.
Sensors: TRT radar altimeter; Thomson-CSF data link receiver; impact fuzing system.
Warhead weight: 66lb (30kg) high explosive.
Speed: High subsonic (over Mach 0.9 or 595 knots/1103km/h).
Range: More than 8 nautical miles (15km) maximum.
Programme: Development work on the Aerospatiale AS

Sea Skua, seen here mounted aboard a Lynx, can effectively extend a modern frigate's ability to defend itself out to ranges far beyond the reach of all but the most expensive air-launched anti-ship missiles.

A view of two of the missiles mounted on an Aerospatiale AS365N Dauphin 2.

15 for use in clear daylight conditions and the all-weather, radar-directed AS 15 TT commenced at the end of 1979, with trials being initiated during the summer of 1982. The first live firings of the missile from a helicopter took place in June 1983 and the type is scheduled for initial delivery to Saudi Arabia in 1984. The initial order for the AS 15 TT came from Saudi Arabia and covers sufficient rounds to arm 20 AS 365N Dauphin 2 helicopters (allowing for four missiles per aircraft, plus reloads and spares, this should amount to a minimum of 500 missiles). France plans to procure the missile and reports indicate that Federal Germany is considering procuring the AS 15 and AS 15 TT for its services.

Notes: Designed as a replacement for the 1950s Aerospatiale-developed AS 12 wire-guided anti-ship missile, the AS 15 anti-armour and AS 15 TT anti-ship missiles are being promoted as a lightweight, low-cost weapon suitable for use with the smaller, ship-going helicopter, mounting aboard fast attack craft or employment as a coastal defence system. In many ways, the AS 15 TT meets the same mission requirements as that of the British Aerospace Dynamics' Sea Skua, but lacking the British missile's semi-active radar seeker should cost less to produce, at the possible expense of terminal phase hit accuracy.

Aerospatiale SS/AS 11 Anti-Ship Missiles

Role: Ship (SS), and air-launched (AS), short-range, wire-guided anti-ship missile.
Prime contractor: Aerospatiale, Division Engins Tactiques, Chatillon-Sous-Bagneux, France.
Mode of operation: Prior to launch, the target must be optically acquired by the ship or aircraft missile controller, who then launches the missile and directs it on to the target by control commands, fed directly to the missile via a twin wire link.
Users: Navies of France, Belgium, Brazil, Libya, Portugal, Senegal, South Africa and UK.
Basic data: 3.97ft (1.21m) overall length; 0.54ft (164mm) diameter; 1.64ft (0.5m) span; 66lb (29.9kg) launch weight.
Propulsion: 1 SNPE dual stage solid propellant rocket (1.2 second boost, 20 second cruise).
Sensors: External guidance; impact fuzing.

Warhead: Up to 17.6lb (8kg) shaped high explosive charge.
Speed: Average of 291 knots/540km per hour.
Range: Effective up to 1.62 nautical miles (3km).
Programme: Developed during the latter 1950s from the smaller SS 10 missile, the SS/AS 11 weapon was initially operationally deployed in 1962. More than 200,000 of these missiles had been built before production came to an end in the mid-1970s.
Notes: A simple, rugged missile, the SS/AS 11, despite its limited range and effectiveness against other than lightly armoured targets, proved to be very successful in export terms, having sold to no less than 35 countries. The missile controller's effectiveness can be significantly improved if he employs a gyroscopically stabilised sighting system as adopted by the Royal Navy and a number of other services. The basic sighting system is referred to as line-of-sight and involves the controller keeping the image of the missile superimposed over that of the target, aided by a missile-mounted flare to help tracking in poorer visibility conditions.

A pair of AS 11 missiles mounted aboard a Royal Navy Westland Wasp helicopter.

Anti-submarine missiles

Australian Government Ikara Missile Anti-Submarine Missiles

Role: Shipboard short/medium-range anti-submarine missile.

Prime contractor: Australian Government Department of Productivity, Canberra, Australian Capital Territory, Australia.

Mode of operation: Prior to launch, the missile launcher is trained and elevated under the control of shipboard systems employing sonar or radar derived data (which can be supplied via data linked inputs from accompanying ships or helicopters). Once launched, the missile radiates radio frequency signals which are tracked by the launch vessel's tracking radar; this data being constantly compared with the range and bearing data of the hostile submarine and the missile's path constantly directed to bring the missile as close over the target as possible. At the closest point of positional coincidence, the missile is commanded to release its lightweight homing torpedo, which descends to the surface under parachute retardation and then proceeds to home on to its submerged prey.

Users: Navies of Australia, Brazil, New Zealand and UK.

Basic data: 11.2ft (3.4m) overall length; 1.2ft (350mm) width; 5.0ft (1.52m) wingspan, 1213lb (550kg) weight including torpedo.

Propulsion: 1 Australian Government Explosive & Ordnance Factory 2-stage (boost/sustainer) solid propellant rocket motor.

Sensors: EMI radio frequency command tracking and guidance transceiver system controlling onboard autopilot and responsible for release of the torpedo at the optimum point above the target.

Warhead weight: Related to the type of lightweight homing torpedo employed.

Speed: Subsonic (around Mach 0.75).

Range: Up to 9.7 nautical miles (18km).

Programme: Developed by the then Australian Government Department of Supply in collaboration with the Royal Australian Navy during the early 1960s, the Ikara was initially deployed in 1964 when it was retrofitted to Australia's six 'River' class frigates (one system per ship). Subsequently, Ikara was fitted to the Royal Australian Navy's three 'Perth' class destroyers (two systems per ship), the Royal Navy's sole Type 82 destroyer and retrofitted to eight 'Leander' class frigates, along with being installed aboard four of the Brazilian Navy's 'Niteroi' class frigates (all Royal Navy and Brazilian ships having only one system each). About 1200 Ikaras had been produced by the end of 1981.

Notes: Although dissimilar in its chosen aerodynamic configuration and considerably lighter than its parallel French-developed Latecoere Malafon, Ikara and, for that matter, Malafon, both represent the first successful attempts to considerably extend the range of homing anti-submarine torpedoes by the simple expedient of marrying them to a rocket propelled airframe and, as such, owe their genesis to the earlier World War II German missile development work undertaken with the Blohm und Voss Bv 143 and LT-950B hybrid torpedo/airframe combinations. That both post-war solutions succeeded where the Blohm und Voss designs failed essentially centres on the pace of electronic guidance developments during the intervening years, coupled to the fact that both the Australian and French designs elected to go down the physically softer route of going for shipboard-launched missiles, as opposed to the German aim to produce an air-launched weapon. By going down the shipboard route,

The two crew members preparing this Ikara for launch help give scale to this lightweight homing torpedo armed missile.

both post-war systems could afford to employ the relatively weight and space insensitive environment of a warship's hull around which to spread the mass of vital-to-task sensors and control electronics, rather than the highly weight and space constrained confines of an aircraft. Just how difficult this control problem remained in the late 1950s (the time at which the Ikara system was fixed) can be perceived when it is realised that to function at all, the Australian missile required no less than 13 fairly sizeable shipboard electronics units (11 of which were Ikara-dedicated elements), while the missile, itself, carried eight units, excluding the umbilical connector, used to 'power up' the missile from shipboard supplies prior to launch. While the system fundamentals remain the same, the shipboard Ikara system layouts vary considerably from ship class to ship class. As part of the UK-Australian agreement by which the Royal Navy acquired the Ikara in the late 1960s, Hawker Siddeley Dynamics, now British Aerospace Dynamics, acquired the international sales agency for this missile. Ikara can carry a variety of lightweight homing torpedoes, including the US-developed Mk 44 and 46, the British-developed Stingray, along with Italian and Swedish developed weapons.

Latecoere Malafon Anti-Submarine Missiles

Role: Shipboard short-range anti-submarine missile.

Prime contractor: Société Industrielle d'Aviation Latecoere, Paris, France.

Mode of operation: Prior to launch, the missile's launcher mount is trained and elevated under the control of shipboard sonar or radar derived data. Once launched, the missile is tracked by shipboard sensors (which can include optical sighting on missile carried flares) and its track corrected via a radio frequency shipboard command link to head it towards its submerged target. After launch, the Malafon is propelled under boost for 2.8 seconds reaching a maximum speed of around 447 knots/828km per hour after which the missile continues unpowered at a sea-skimming altitude employing its variable-incidence wing

A close-up view of the Malafon on its launcher aboard a French Navy Type T-47 ASW 'D'Estrees' class destroyer.

to trade forward speed for increasing aerodynamic lift. When within range of its submarine target, the parachute retarded homing torpedo is released by radio command and continues on its homing course towards its prey.

User: French Navy.

Basic data: 20.18ft (6.15m) overall length; 2.1ft (650mm) diameter; 10.83ft (3.3m) wingspan; 3307lb (1500kg) weight including torpedo.

Propulsion: 2 SNPE solid propellant booster rocket motors which burn simultaneously for 2.8 seconds.

Sensors: SFENA/Thomson-CSF radio frequency command/
guidance system; TRT radar altimeter.

Warhead weight: Related to the type of homing torpedo employed.

Speed: 447 knots/828km/h maximum and constantly decreasing as missile progresses beyond 'burn-out' of its booster rockets.

Range: Up to 7 nautical miles (13km).

Programme: Development of the Malafon system was initiated in 1956, followed by the first sea-going trial launches in 1962 and operational deployment during 1965. Malafon is installed aboard the two 'Suffren' class, three 'Tourville' class, the sole 'Aconit', one Type 56 and five 'D'Estrees' class destroyers.

Notes: Designed to carry a heavier and more powerful anti-submarine homing torpedo than the Australian-developed Ikara, the combined tactical radius of action of the French missile/torpedo combination is likely to be much closer to that of the Ikara than a simple comparison of missile ranges would suggest. Malafon can carry either of the French-developed E14 or E15 heavyweight torpedoes, the former weighing some 1984lb (900kg).

Anti-air missiles

This, the first of 15 engineering development AIM-54Cs, being loaded aboard a Grumman F-14A Tomcat.

Hughes AIM-54 Phoenix Anti-Air Missiles

Role: Long-range air-to-air combat against multiple targets.

Prime contractor: Hughes Aircraft Company, Conoga Park, California, USA.

Mode of operation: The target must be acquired by the parent aircraft's AWG-9 radar prior to missile launch. After launch, the AIM-54 heads towards its prey under the guidance of its own semi-active radar homing with target illuminated by parent aircrafts AWG-9 radar, switching to active homing by missile's own radar during final closure phase of flight.

Users: US Navy and Iranian Air Force (AIM-54A only).

Basic data:	AIM-54A	AIM-54C
Overall length:	13.0ft (3.96m)	13.0ft (3.96m)
Diameter:	1.0ft (0.30m)	1.25ft (0.38m)
Span:	3.0ft (0.91m)	3.0ft (0.91m)
Loaded weight:	975lb (442.7kg)	1008lb (447.6kg)

Propulsion: 1 Rocketdyne Mk 47 single-stage, solid propellant rocket.

Sensors: Tracking radar; impact and proximity fuses.

Warhead weight: 133lb (59.9kg) high explosive.

Speed: Hypersonic (maximum duration 3 minutes).

Range: Approximately 86.8 nautical miles (160.9km).

Programme: With development initiated in 1962 Hughes built 2509 of the AIM-54A version between 1972 and 1980 when production terminated in favour of the improved AIM-54C model. Deliveries of the AIM-54C commenced in 1977 with the first of 15 development missiles, followed in October 1981 with the handover of the first of 30 pre-series production missiles, this batch being completed by mid-1982. Initial production, involving 60 more Phoenix, is underway, with series production commencing in 1983, with another 1064 missiles being built through early 1987.

Notes: The largest air-to-air missile yet to be operationally deployed within the non-Eastern bloc world, the Phoenix and its associated Hughes AWG-9 long-range pulse doppler radar are fitted only aboard Grumman's swing-wing F-14A Tomcat, making that aircraft one of the most potent adversaries extant. The AIM-54/AWG-9 combination provides the F-14 with the ability to combat up to six enemy aircraft simultaneously, even in conditions of severe electronic countermeasures. One hundred and fifty five Phoenix had been test fired between May 1972 and December 1981, of which 92 per cent are adjudged to have killed or disabled their prey had they all been armed. One Phoenix scored a hit on a target 110 nautical miles (204km) distant from the point of launch.

General Dynamics RIM-65/66 and AGM-78 Standard Anti-Air Missiles

Role: Shipboard medium/long-range air defence missile (RIM-65) and air- or ship-launched medium-range anti-radiation missile (AGM-78).
Prime contractor: General Dynamics Pomona Division, California, USA.
Modes of operation: In the case of RIM-65, the target is detected and tracked by shipboard radar whose inputs are used to train the launcher and update the missile's guidance sensors (including inertial platform in the SM-2). After launch, the missiles home on to target by use of their semi-active radar seekers and target returns from the shipboard illuminating radar with additional mid-course correction available in the SM-2. With the AGM-78 version, the missile is fired in the predetermined direction of the radiating target source, using its passive broad-band radar seeker to home on to the hostile radio frequency radiation source.
Users: Navies of US, Australia, France, Federal Germany, Iran, Italy, Japan, South Korea and Netherlands.

Basic data:

	RIM-65 (ER)	RIM-66 (MR)
Overall length:	27.0ft (8.2m)	14.7ft (4.5m)
Missile diameter:	1.1ft (340mm)	1.1ft (340mm)
Booster diameter:	1.5ft (460mm)	No booster
Maximum span:	5.3ft (1.6m)	3.0ft (980mm)
Loaded weight:	2920lb/1325kg	1350lb/613kg

AGM-78
Overall length: 15.0ft (4.57m)
Missile diameter: 1.1ft (340mm)
Booster diameter: No booster
Maximum span: 3.0ft (980mm)
Loaded weight: 1350lb/613kg

Propulsion: 1 Atlantic Research solid propellant rocket booster motor plus 1 Aerojet single-burn solid propellant rocket sustainer motor on RIM-65; 1 Aerojet or other Mk 56 dual thrust solid propellant rocket motor on RIM-66 and AGM-78.
Sensors: General Dynamics semi-active radar seeker on RIM-65 and -66; General Dynamics passive radar seeker on AGM-78; Motorola Mk 45 contact or proximity fuzing system on RIM-65 and -66; proximity fuzing system on AGM-78.
Warhead weight: Approximately 90lb (40.8kg) high explosive.
Speed: Supersonic; Mach 2.5 plus for RIM-65 and air-launched AGM-78; Mach 2 plus for RIM-66 and ship-launched AGM-78.
Range: Up to 65.1 nautical miles (121km) and altitude of 65,000-plus ft (19,812-plus m) for RIM-65; up to 30.4 nautical miles (56km) and altitude of 65,000ft (19,812m) for RIM-66; up to 30.4 nautical miles (56km) air-launched reducing to 13.5 nautical miles sea-launched for AGM-78.
Programme: Development of the RIM-65 ER (for Extended-Range), RIM-66 MR (for Medium-Range) and the AGM-78 ARM (for Anti-Radiation Missile) all commenced during 1964, the shipboard RIM-65 and -66 models being designed to replace the earlier General Dynamics developed Terrier and Tartar missiles,

A RIM-65B Standard SM-2ER launched from the US Navy 'Belknap' class cruiser, USS Wainwright (CG28).

respectively. Initial deployment of the RIM-66 and AGM-78 took place in 1969, while the RIM-65 entered service in 1978. By the beginning of 1983, production of all Standard missiles had exceeded 10,000; comprising more than 4000 RIM-65, well over 5000 RIM-66 and around 700 AGM-78. By the end of 1982, over 80 ships were equipped with Standard, while another 80 are scheduled to receive the weapon, thus ensuring continuing production well into the 1990s.
Notes: Standard certainly lives up to its name, being adopted by not only the US Navy but also by several other major navies as their standard shipboard area air defence missile. The RIM-65B forms an integral part of the US Navy's Aegis fleet area air defence system fitted to the CG47 'Ticonderoga' class cruisers coming into service. The AGM-78 anti-radiation missile, employed by both the US Navy and South Korean Navy was developed for use against hostile radiators of radio frequency energy, which includes not only attacking ships and aircraft, but also the shore-based radar and radio networks used in the tactical control of enemy forces. Thus one of the AGM-78's primary functions is to destroy or suppress enemy missile control and guidance systems, such as target illuminating radars. The AGM-78 can be air-launched from the Grumman A-6 Intruder and is installed as part of the Standard missile complement of all US Navy cruisers. This missile is also carried on some of the South Korean Navy's PSMM-1 'Paek Ku' class fast attack craft on which it is stern-mounted in a bin-type container/launcher. The 1982 unit cost of RIM-65 is quoted at around $500,000, while that of the RIM-66 is put at approximately $200,000. While production of the AGM-78 missile is now complete, annual deliveries of RIM-65s and RIM-66s continue to climb, with nearly 700 in total being delivered during 1982.

A Sea Dart blasts away from its foredeck launcher aboard a Royal Navy Type 42 'Sheffield' class destroyer.

British Aerospace Dynamic Sea Dart Anti-Air Missile

Role: Shipboard medium/long-range air defence missile.
Prime contractor: British Aerospace Dynamics, Filton, UK.
Mode of operation: Initial target detection and tracking data derived from shipboard radars. After launch, the missile homes on to target using its continuous wave (CW), K band semi-active radar seeker detecting target reflections from the shipboard illuminating radar.
Users: Navies of UK and Argentina.
Basic data: 14.3ft (4.36m) overall length; 1.4ft (420mm) diameter; 3.0ft (910mm) span; 1210lb (550kg) loaded weight including booster.
Propulsion: 1 Rolls-Royce Odin ramjet sustainer engine; 1 IMI solid propellant rocket booster (2-5 second burn duration).
Sensors: Semi-active GEC-Marconi continuous wave (CW), K band radar detection; 1 EMI proximity fuse.
Warhead weight: Reportedly around 60lb (27.2kg).
Speed: Supersonic (Mach 3.0).
Range: Up to 54 nautical miles (80km) and altitudes up to 82,000ft (24,994m).
Programme: Development of the Sea Dart was initiated in August 1962 as a replacement for the then yet to enter service Seaslug missile; the early design work being carried out at Whitley, where the same Armstrong Whitworth design team had drawn up Seaslug. Test firings of the first development models commenced in 1965. This phase was followed by the award of the initial production contract in late 1967, the missile being declared operational during 1968 (around four years in advance of its going to sea aboard HMS *Bristol*, the first ship purpose-built to deploy Sea Dart). According to reports, around 1000 Sea Darts had been produced by the beginning of 1982 and production of the missile is set to continue through the 1980s.
Notes: The British equivalent of the US Navy's Standard area air defence missile, the Sea Dart provides the lethal element of the Royal Navy's GWS 30 systems package that includes not only the missile, but other associated equipment, such as the shipboard Type 909 target illuminating radar, the Vickers-built twin missile launcher and vertically-loaded missile magazine-to-launcher mechanisms. Sea Dart and its associated GWS 30 equipment has been fitted into the Royal Navy's 'Bristol' type and 'Sheffield' class destroyers and 'Invincible' carriers, the same system being used in the

two Argentinian Type 42 destroyers. More recently, during the latter half of the 1970s, British Aerospace Dynamics developed a lighter weight and more flexible Sea Dart system funded from company sources. In this Lightweight Sea Dart system, the same missile is employed, but is mounted in a non-reloadable Exocet-type sealed box container and launcher, and the customer has the choice of buying the associated sensor package or simply integrating the missiles and containers into some existing shipboard sensor net. Used in anger for the first time during the Falklands campaign, the Sea Dart is officially credited with downing eight enemy aircraft: no mean feat when it is remembered that most of the air attacks were carried out at very low level, just above fairly turbulent water. As with the US Navy's Standard area air defence missile, Sea Dart has a limited secondary capability as an anti-surface ship weapon, although this is likely to be confined to relatively light displacement and lightly armoured craft.

Raytheon AIM-7 Sparrow Anti-air Missiles

Role: Medium/long-range all-weather air-to-air combat missile.
Prime contractor: Raytheon Company, Lexington, Massachusetts, USA.
Mode of operation: Parent aircraft's radar acquires target and transmits steering data to missile as a prerequisite to launch, after which the Sparrow homes on to target using its own semi-active radar seeker sensing target signal returns from the launch aircraft's illuminating radar.
Users: US Navy/Marine Corps and 13 other national air forces, including the Royal Air Force, who operate an anglicised variant known as Sky Flash.
Basic data: 12.0ft (3.65m) overall length; 0.58ft (200mm) diameter; 3.3ft (1.0m) span; 503lb (228kg) for AIM-7F and M models and 450lb (204.5kg) for AIM-7E model weight.
Propulsion: 1 Hercules Mk 58 dual thrust, solid propellant rocket motor in AIM-7F and M models, or Mk 38 dual thrust motor in AIM-7E and Sky Flash.
Sensors: Raytheon monopulse semi-active radar seeker in AIM-7M or GEC Marconi J band continuous wave semi-active radar seeker in Sky Flash; all models employ both proximity and impact fuzing systems.
Warhead weight: 88lb (40kg) in AIM-7F and M; 66lb (30kg) in AIM-7E.
Speed: Hypersonic (around Mach 4.0) in all models.
Range: Up to 52.1 nautical miles (96km) for AIM-7F and M or up to 26.1 nautical miles (48km) for AIM-7E.
Programme: Based on the initial US Navy Ordnance Centre's development work of the early 1950s, Raytheon delivered the first production Sparrows in 1956; these being operationally deployed in August 1958 on McDonnell F3H-2M Demon fighters of the US Navy's 6th Fleet. Since that time, more than 32,000 Sparrows or derivatives of this missile have been produced, including over 3000 of the shipboard RIM-7 Sea Sparrow. Besides the US-built models produced by Raytheon and its second-source contractor, General Dynamics Ponoma Division, more than 1500 examples of the Italian derivative, and the Selenia-built Aspide, and over 3000 of the British Aerospace Dynamics-built Sky Flash have been produced.
Notes: Very much paralleling the similarly US Navy developed Sidewinder short-range air-to-air missile programme, the Sparrow and its derivatives have become the standard medium/long-range air-to-air missile with many of the major air arms outside the Eastern Bloc. Employed extensively by both the US Navy and US Air Force in South East Asia, early Sparrows proved to have a disappointingly low kill rate; a factor that led to the fairly rapid development of the later AIM-7E and F models and more recently the AIM-7M which has improved 'look

An AIM-7E Sparrow seen boosting away from a McDonnell F-4 Phantom II.

down' capability and is less vulnerable to electronic countermeasures in comparision with earlier models. Sparrow is scheduled to be progressively superseded in the all-weather air-to-air combat role within the three US services and the majority of NATO air forces by the Hughes Aircraft-developed AMRAAM (Advanced Medium Ranged Air-to-Air Missile) from mid-1986 onwards. However, as many of the 24,000 AIM-7E models still remain in service as front line weapons, it is doubtful if the Sparrow will disappear from use until past the end of this century.

British Aerospace Dynamics Seaslug Anti-air Missiles

Role: Shipboard area air defence missile.
Prime contractor: British Aerospace Dynamics, Filton, UK.
Mode of operation: Target acquisition is made by shipboard radar, whose data is used to train and elevate launcher. After launch, the missile is guided towards the target by radio frequency command guidance signals derived from data inputs from the shipboard illuminating radar.
User: Royal Navy (not employed on Chilean and Pakistani purchased 'County' class destroyers).
Basic data: 19.7ft (6.00m) overall length; 1.3ft (400mm) diameter; 4.7ft (1.43m) wingspan; 1984lb (900kg) missile alone or 4409lb (2000kg) missile plus booster weight.
Propulsion: 4 IMI jettisonable solid propellant booster rocket motors plus 1 ICI solid propellant sustainer rocket motor.
Sensors: Radio frequency command guidance; EMI proximity fuzing system.
Warhead weight: Around 200lb (90.7kg) high explosive.
Speed: Supersonic (Mach 1.8).
Range: Up to 24.3 nautical miles (45km) and altitudes of 50,000ft (15,240m).
Programme: Developed by the then Armstrong Siddeley organisation to a Royal Navy requirement, work on the Seaslug started during the latter half of the 1950s, the missile being operationally deployed aboard the first of the 'County' class destroyers in November 1962. Prior trial firings having been made for HMS *Girdle Ness*. A longer-

A Seaslug seen boosting away from the quarterdeck of a Royal Navy 'County' class destroyer, the only ships to be equipped with this now elderly area air defence missile.

range Mk 2 version of the missile also embodied an improved capability against incoming low-level targets, while remaining fully compatible with the rest of the supporting missile systemry, including the twin missile launcher.
Notes: Seaslug represents the Royal Navy's first attempt to produce a shipboard air defence missile, having been preceded into service by the US Navy's Terrier and Soviet Navy's Goa area air defence missiles. While the Seaslug system may have proven to have been as operationally effective, there is clear evidence that the British solution was far bulkier, not only in terms of its launcher, but also where magazine space is concerned.

SA-N-1 'Goa' Anti-air Missiles

Role: Shipboard short/medium-range air defence missile.
Prime contractor: USSR.
Mode of operation: Initial target acquisition and tracking data derived from shipboard radar, with post-launch radio command guidance supplied by the ship. The missile is believed to be equipped with its own semi-active radar homing head for use in the terminal phase of its flight.
Users: Navies of USSR, Poland and India.

An SA-N-1 boosting away from a Soviet Navy 'Kashin' class destroyer.

Basic data: 22.0ft (6.7m) overall length; 2.0ft (600mm) diameter; 4.0ft (1.2m) span; 1320lb (600kg) weight inclusive of booster.
Propulsion: 2 stage boost/sustain solid-propellant rocket motors.
Sensors: Radio frequency detectors; possible semi-active tracking radar; no information available on fusing system/employed.
Warhead weight: Approximately 22.0lb (10kg).
Speed: High supersonic (around Mach 3.5).
Range: Up to 16.5 nautical miles (30.6km) and altitudes up to 60,000feet (18,300m).
Programme: A naval adaptation of the land-based SA-3, with which it was first operationally deployed in parallel during the 1961–62 period. 'Goa' is installed aboard 'Kresta' I and 'Kynda' cruisers, along with 'Kanin', 'Kashin' and 'Kotlin' class destroyers.
Notes: An almost true contemporary of the US Navy's Tartar shipboard air defence missile, the SA-N-1 'Goa' appears to have a superior performance envelope in terms of both speed and hemispheric radius of action. Aboard ship, 'Goa' is launched from a roll-stabilised twin launcher mounted immediately above its reload missile magazine, from which the weapons are vertically loaded to the launcher, as with the Royal Navy's far more recent Sea Dart system. Very advanced for its time, the SA-N-1 'Goa' must still be considered a formidable weapon, particularly when operated in a relatively benign electronics countermeasures environment.

Raytheon/Ford AIM-9 Sidewinder Anti-air Missiles

Role: Short to medium-range air-to-air combat.
Prime contractors: Raytheon Company, Lexington, Massachusetts, USA (AIM-9C, G, H, L. M. models); Ford Aerospace, Newport Beach, California, USA (AIM-9B, D, E, H, J, N, P models).
Mode of operation: Infra-red homing, with initial acquisition being made by the missile which provides launch aircraft with release signal.
Users: US Navy, Marines, Air Force; NATO forces and recipients of US Military assistance and US Foreign Military Sales programmes (all models).

Basic data:	AIM-9B	AIM-9L
Overall length:	9.4ft (2.87m)	9.4ft (2.87m
Diameter:	0.4ft (0.13m)	0.4ft (0.13m)
Span:	2.1ft (0.64m)	2.1ft (0.64m)
Loaded weight:	195lb (88.8kg)	18.75lb (85.2kg)
Warhead weight:	20lb (9.1kg)	25lb (10.2kg)

Propulsion: 1 Mk 36 single-stage, solid propellant rocket motor in AIM-9L, Mk 17 or SR116 motor alternatives in other models.
Sensors: Infra-red, conical scan homing head; active

An AIM-9L Sidewinder aboard a Grumman F14A Tomcat.

optical laser proximity and contact fuzes (data for AIM-9L).
Speed: Mach 2.5 to Mach 3.0 (related to launch aircraft's speed).
Range: 1.7 nautical miles (3km) for short-range B and E models; up to 9.6 nautical miles (18km) for other models, including L.
Programme: Initially developed by the US Naval Weapons Centre during the early 1950s and first operationally deployed in 1956, approximately 121,000 Sidewinders had been produced by the end of 1982, at which time production was continuing on the current AIM-9L and M models. Of this total, around 100,000 are B through E Models, just under 10,000 G through J variants, along with over 11,000 of the L (US Navy) and M (US Air Force) versions. At least 21,000 earlier B and J models have been modified into the improved AIM-9N and P variants. Of the total Sidewinders built to date, around 10,000 have been produced by the West German company, Boden-seewerk, who, along with Dornier, have contributed several significant improvements to the missile's guidance

system. Initial deployment of the much improved AIM-9L took place in 1978.

Notes: Without question the most widely used guided missile yet developed, the Sidewinder currently serves as the standard short-range air-to-air missile with over 40 different user forces. First fired in anger during 1958, the Sidewinder has seen action in virtually every war zone since, ranging from South East Asia, through the Sinai to the Falklands. The current production L and M models offer a greatly improved target acquisition capability over earlier versions, which needed to be pointed relatively precisely at the target prior to missile lock-on. However, both the L and M models incorporate a new infra-red seeker head employing the Dornier-developed conical scan technique, which enables the missile to acquire a lock on to the target even if it is approaching the launch aircraft head on, the worst case in terms of detecting the prey's hot engine exhaust gases on to which the Sidewinder homes.

General Dynamics RIM-116 RAM Anti-air Missiles

Role: Shipboard, rapid-response, short-range air defence missile.

Prime contractor: General Dynamics Pomona Division, California, USA.

Mode of operation: Compatible with existing shipboard sensors (either electronic or optical) from which the missile would normally require minimal assistance in acquiring its target. Usually launched on a 'fire-and-forget' basis, employing the missile's own passive infra-red seeker to acquire the target, the missile's own guidance incorporates a passive radio frequency detector, enabling it to act on mid-course corrections transmitted from the parent ship.

Users: Under joint development by the US, Danish and Federal German navies.

Basic data: 4.5 tons overall weight per 24-cell launcher system; 9.17ft (2.8m) overall length; 5in (130mm) diameter; 1.4ft (430mm) unfolded span; 156lb (70.8kg) weight.

Propulsion: Bermite/Herculese Modified Mk 36 single-stage, solid propellant rocket motor.

Sensors: General Dynamics passive infra-red seeker plus broad-band radio frequency detector; Raytheon DSU-15A/B proximity/impact fuzing system.

Warhead weight: 25lb (10.2km) high explosive.

Speed: Supersonic (around Mach 2 or 1323 knots/2451km/h at sea level).

Range: Up to 8.5 nautical miles (15.75km).

Programme: Designated RIM-116A, the General Dynamics RAM (for Rolling Airframe Missile) development was initiated under a joint US-Danish-Federal German naval agreement of the mid 1970s. The first successful RAM interception of a drone aircraft was announced in May 1982, with three more successful interceptions being recorded by December 1982 as missile testing progressed from the land-based to over-water phase trials. Initial operational deployment is planned for 1984.

Notes: Designed to provide a low cost anti-missile point air defence supplement to existing shipboard defences, or as a stand-alone system for smaller craft, the RAM design makes the maximum use of existing and, hence, proven components. RAM employs the passive infra-red seeker from General Dynamics' Stinger infantry missile, the fuzing system and rocket motor from the US Navy's AIM-9L Sidewinder, to which has been married a new autopilot, radio frequency detector and fold-away aerodynamic control surfaces. The specially designed 24-cell EX144 launcher owes much to the existing Phalanx launcher, being trainable through 360 degrees in

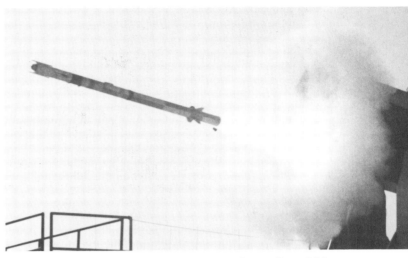

A RAM missile leaving its specially developed 24-cell EX144 launcher.

azimuth and between + 80 and − 25 degrees in elevation. RAM is also compatible with the standard NATO Sea Sparrow launcher, which can house ten RAMs (five each in its two inboard cells).

Thomson-CSF Crotale Naval Anti-air Missiles

Role: Shipboard short-range anti-air defence missile.

Prime contractor: Thomson-CSF, Paris, France.

Mode of operation: Target acquisition is made by shipboard radar, whose data are used to train the octuple launcher mount at the target area. Subsequent to launch, the missile or missiles (two can be launched simultaneously) home on to the target using shipboard data-linked supplied guidance directions, derived from the mount's integral sensor tracking of the missile and target.

Users: Navies of France and Saudi Arabia.

Basic data: 9.5ft (2.9m) overall length; 1.6ft (515mm) wingspan; 0.5ft (150mm) diameter.

Propulsion: 1 SNPE single-stage solid propellant rocket motor.

Sensors: Thomson-CSF radio frequency data-link for shipboard command guidance; infra-red proximity fuzing system.

Weight: 183lb (93kg) at launch.

Warhead weight: 33.1lb (15kg) high explosive with directed burst.

Speed: Supersonic (Mach 2.5 or 1653 knots at sea level).

The Crotale Naval launcher and its associated radar and optronic fire directors mounted above the central plinth.

Range: Up to 4.6 nautical miles (8.5km) and effective between altitudes of 164ft (50m) and 11,483ft (3500m).
Programme: During the mid-1960s, Thomson-CSF commenced work on the development of a second generation short ranged, rapid-response air defence missile system, initially envisaged for the protection of mobile land forces. This system, known as Crotale was initially deployed with the French Army during 1972. At about this time, the French Navy, realizing the comparative ease of adopting the system for naval application, commenced development of the Crotale Naval. The naval version of the system was initially installed and tested aboard the French trials ship *Ille d'Oleron* in mid-1977 and first deployed operationally aboard the lead of class destroyer *Georges Leygues* (D640) in December 1979. Crotale Naval had been retrofitted to the 'Tourville' class destroyers and is being installed aboard the Saudi Arabian frigates of the 'Madina' class. In excess of 3000 Crotale and Crotale Naval missiles had been produced by early 1983.
Notes: Designed to meet the same set of basic mission requirements as the UK's Sea Wolf missile, the dart-like Crotale and Crotale Naval missile programme benefits from a broad-based export market demand (mainly for the mobile land-based system), which should have a favourable impact in terms of system and unit pricing.

British Aerospace Dynamics Sea-Wolf Anti-air Missiles

Seawolf being loaded into its sextuple launcher, with crewmen of HMS Penelope, *a 'Leander' class frigate, to lend scale to this readily manhandleable rapid response missile.*

Role: Shipboard rapid response point air defence missile.
Prime contractor: British Aerospace Dynamics, Filton, UK.
Mode of operation: Initial target detection and tracking data derived from shipboard sensors (normally radar with electro-optical sighting back-up) and used to elevate and train GWS25 launcher (or capable of being 'gathered' back on to director beam if employing the new vertical launch system). After launch, the missile is directed towards coincidence with the target by radio frequency command signals derived from the shipboard tracking radar, via a data processing system.

User: Royal Navy.
Basic data: 6.42ft (1.96m) overall length; 0.5ft (150mm) diameter; 2.25ft (686mm) wingspan; 176lb (79.8kg) weight exclusive of the booster rocket employed with the vertical launch version.
Propulsion: 1 IMI solid propellant rocket motor.
Sensors: GEC-Marconi radio frequency command data link; EMI impact and proximity fuzing system.
Warhead weight: 31.3lb (14.2kg) high explosive fragmentation.
Speed: High supersonic (above Mach 2).
Range: Out to 3 nautical miles (5.6km).
Programme: Born of a 1964 Royal Navy Staff target requirement, initial firing trials were conducted at Woomera and Aberporth in early 1975, followed later in the year by the first sea-going trials aboard HMS *Penelope* (F127). In June 1977, Seawolf demonstrated its ability to shoot down an incoming 4.5in (114mm) shell. Seawolf was operationally deployed in May 1979 with the commissioning of the first of the Type 22 or 'Broadsword' class frigates and is to be installed on the Royal Navy's broad-beamed 'Leander' class frigates, of which HMS *Andromeda*, and *Charybdis* were already so equipped, while HMS *Scylla*, *Hermione* and *Jupiter* were being retrofitted in the spring of 1983.
Notes: Designed as the lethal element of the Royal Navy's GWS25 rapid response, all-weather short-range weapons system, the Seawolf is the first Western World shipborne missile to have a proven anti-missile capability. Although the weight of the overall GWS25 system limits Seawolf's application to vessels of over 2500 tons displacement, British Aerospace have successfully demonstrated that the missile is fully compatible with a much lighter supporting system that would allow its installation in corvettes of around 800 tons displacement. Early in 1982, British Aerospace Dynamics revealed that they had initiated the development of a vertically launched Seawolf with an additional booster rocket motor stage and thrust vector control system that promises to provide the missile with more hemispherical radius of effective action. This system has been adopted for the Royal Navy's 'Duke' class or Type 23 frigates. Used in anger during the Falklands action of May and June 1982, the Seawolf is officially credited with downing five enemy aircraft: a figure that assumes greater significance, compared with the eight each confirmed kills attributed to the Sea Dart and Sea Cat, when it is remembered that Seawolf was only installed aboard three of the South Atlantic Task Group ships, as opposed to seven Sea Dart and 16 Seacat-equipped warships.

Shorts Seacat Anti-air Missiles

Role: Shipboard point air defence missile.
Prime contractor: Short Brothers Limited, Missile Division, Belfast, UK.
Mode of operation: Initial target detection and tracking has to be carried out by shipboard sensors (optical, electro-optical or radar), data that are then used to train and elevate launcher. On launching, the missile is gathered into the required heading by optical (binocular), electro-optical (television) or tracking radar inputs that are processed and transmitted to the misssile via a radio frequency guidance command link. The gathering and subsequent guidance process, when working in the manual (optical) or semi-manual (television) modes, is aided by tail fin flares mounted on the missile to achieve line-of-sight guidance on to the target.
Users: Navies of Argentina, Australia, Brazil, Chile, India, Iran, Jordan, Libya, Malaysia, New Zealand, Nigeria, Qatar, Thailand and UK (Federal Germany, Sweden and Venezuela no longer use Seacat).
Basic data: 4.9ft (1.49m) overall length; 0.6ft (180mm)

diameter; 2.1ft (640mm) wingspan; 139lb (63kg) weight.
Propulsion: IMI dual thrust solid propellant rocket motor.
Sensors: Radio frequency command guidance links; impact and proximity fuzing system.
Warhead weight: Around 12lb (5.44kg) high explosive.
Speed: High subsonic (around Mach 0.85).
Range: Up to 2.8 nautical miles (5.2km) and altitudes of 15,000ft (4572m).
Programme: The development of this Royal Navy-sponsored missile began in the late 1950s, the first operational rounds being deployed as part of the GWS20 system aboard the eight 'Daring' class destroyers in 1962 (GWS20 being subsequently installed aboard 'Rothesay' class frigates and 'Fearless' class assault ships). Further refinements led to the GWS21, GWS22 and GWS24 systems and the Seacat remains in production, with well in excess of 4000 missiles built so far.
Notes: Amongst the earliest of shipboard missiles to be deployed, the Seacat airframe is about the only element of the evolving Seacat systems not subject to change. In 1972, Shorts announced a lightweight Seacat system, with a triple missile launcher, capable of installation aboard fast attack craft-sized vessels and, in 1980, announced a new sea-skimming guidance system to give the missile a more effective secondary all-weather capability against lightly armoured surface craft and shore targets. Used operationally during the Falklands conflict, the Seacat is officially credited with eight confirmed kills against enemy aircraft. Ongoing Royal Navy orders for Seacat, the latest of which was announced

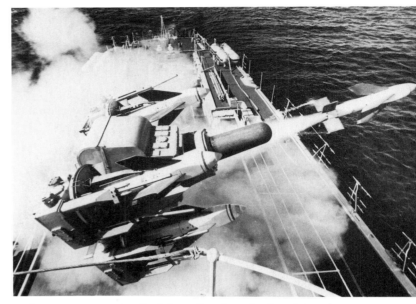

A dynamic yet exceptionally informative view of a Seacat launch showing not only the relatively squat missile, but also its rapidly trainable, hydraulically powered quadruple launcher used aboard Royal Navy warships.

in September 1982, ensure that this missile will remain in service into the 1990s.

Naval guns

US Navy 16 In Mk 7 Naval Guns

Role: Primary anti-ship and long-range shore bombardment battleship gun system.
Prime contractor: US Navy's Naval Ordnance Centre, USA.
Mode of operation: These triple-barrelled turrets are hydraulically actuated and take their aiming instructions from radar, optronic or optical sensors, via the human agency of the turret fire control officer. The guns are manually loaded and each turret requires a gun crew of 79.
User: US Navy.
Basic data: 1700 tons per turret including the armoured ammunition lift from below deck magazine to turret, but excluding ammunition.
Calbire: 16in (406mm) 66.7ft (20.32m) barrel length.
Rate of fire: 2 rounds per minute each barrel, or 6 rounds per minute each turret, with capability of firing all 3 barrels in salvo.
Ammunition on turret: Believed confined to 1 round per barrel.
Ammunition type: 16in armour-piercing or high (range) capacity.
Arcs of fire: 270 degrees in azimuth: +45 to 0 degrees in elevation.
Range: UP to 20.5 nautical miles (28km) for high capacity ammunition, or up to 19.8 nautical miles (36.7km) for armour-piercing ammunition.

An impressive close-up aspect of the angry end of battleship USS New Jersey's triple-barrelled 'B' turret.

Programme: Six ship-sets, each of three triple-barrelled turrets, were ordered during the first half of 1940 for installation aboard the originally six-ship 'Iowa' class battleship. Fabrication of these turrets commenced in late 1940 and work on the four ship-sets actually built was completed by late 1943. The original three turret primary gun armament designed for the 'Iowa' class has been retained on the four ships undergoing reactivation and modernisation during the first half of the 1980s.
Notes: Despite the fact that the 16in naval gun first made

its operational debut as long ago as 1919, its shells still provide one of the most potent shipboard-launched weapons extant, thanks to their having a combined impact force/warhead energy release level at least comparable to that of the modern medium-range anti-ship missile, such as Harpoon or Exocet. The penetrative power of the 12 ton armour-piercing projectile is sufficient to bore through 29.5ft (9m) of concrete; the round having left the gun barrel at around twice the speed of sound, or approximately 1320 knots.

Soviet New Model Twin 130mm Mount Naval Guns

The aft new model twin 130mm turret of the Soviet Navy's lead of class destroyer Sovremennyy, *photographed in March 1985.*

Role: Dual-purpose gun for use against both surface and air targets.
Prime contractor: Soviet.
Mode of operation: Fully automatically loaded and stabilized, radar-directed dual-purpose twin-barrelled mount. The normal 'Kite Screech' radar gun laying is supplemented by an unidentified optronic fire director system mounted on the turret.
User: Soviet Navy.
Basic data: No verifiable information available at press time.
Calibre: 130mm; 29.9ft (9.1m) barrel length.
Rate of fire: Over 30 rounds per minute per barrel, or more than 60 per turret.
Ammunition on gun: No information available at press time.
Ammunition type: Proximity or impact fuzed, fragmentation or armour piercing.
Arcs of fire: Limited only by ship's superstructure in azimuth; +85 to −15 degrees in elevation.
Range: 15.1 nautical miles (28km) maximum against surface targets.
Programme: Developed during the latter half of the 1970s, the new model 130mm turret made its operational debut during 1981 aboard the Soviet Navy's lead of class destroyer *Sovremennyy*, which carries fore and aft

mounted turrets. Subsequently, the turret has been installed on the new 'Slava' class cruisers and *Fruze*, the second of the 'Kirov' class battle cruisers; each class carrying one turret only.
Notes: Almost certainly hydraulically operated, this new model twin 130mm turret has a combined rate of fire, at least three times as great as the US Navy's slightly smaller calibre Mk 45 single-barrelled turret. Considering the gun's long-range and high overall ammunition 'throw weight', this new 130mm turret looks to be useful not only against well-armoured surface/hardened shore targets, but also against incoming air threats and, in particular, manned aircraft.

FMC Single 5in Mk 45 Naval Guns

Role: Dual-purpose (anti-ship/shore and anti-air).
Prime contractor: FMC Corporation, Northern Ordinance Division, Minneapolis, Minnesota, USA.
Mode of operation: This fully automatic, single-barrelled gun takes its sighting and firing instruction from shipboard radar, via the Mk 86 fire control system.
User: US Navy.
Basic data: 25 tons (25,401kg) total installation weight, exclusive of ammunition, but including associated below deck ammunition hoist.
Calibre: 5in (127mm); 22.5ft (6.86m) barrel length.
Rate of fire: Up to 20 rounds per minute.
Ammunition types: Proximity fuzed (anti-air); impact or delayed impact fuzed (anti-ship/shore).
Ammunition on gun: Up to 20 rounds ready to fire.
Arcs of fire: Limited only by ship's superstructure in azimuth; +65 degress to −5 degrees in elevation.
Range: Up to 24 nautical miles (44.5km) maximum or 12.8 nautical miles (23.7km) effective range against ship/shore targets or 8 nautical miles (14.8km) maximum range against medium/low altitude air targets.

The Mk 45 naval mount seen aboard the 'Spruance' class destroyer. USS Merrill *(DDG976).*

Programme: Development of the Mk 45 naval mount commenced in the early 1960s, the US Navy awarding the initial design contract to the FMC Corporation in 1964. The Mk 45 mount first went to sea in 1968 aboard the US Navy's weapons trail ship USS *Norton Sount* (AVM1). Operational deployment of the Mk 45 occurred in February 1974 aboard the cruiser USS *California* (CGN36). The Mk 45 is installed aboard 'California', 'Virginia' and 'Ticonderoga' class cruisers, plus 'Spruance' and 'Kidd' class destroyers (two guns per ship), along with the 'Tarawa' class assault ships (three guns each). By mid-1983, a total of 95 Mk 45 mounts were operational, with production continuing for the 'Ticonderoga' class construction programme.

Notes: Already longer ranging than the US Navy's big 16in guns, the Mk 45's range is likely to be doubled if the service adopts the Deadeye laser guided, rocket-boosted 5in shell under development by Martin Marietta Corporation's Orlanda Aerospace Division. Clearly, from the Mk 45's low maximum rate of fire, the US Navy, like the Royal Navy with its Mk 8 mount, places primary emphasis on the gun's ability to engage ship or shore targets, rather than incoming air threats.

The 127mm OTO-Melara Compact naval mount aboard the Italian lead of class frigate Lupo *(F564).*

OTO-Melara 127mm 127/54 Compact Naval Guns

Role: Primary dual-purpose (anti-ship/shore and anti-aircraft) gun for cruisers, destroyers and frigate sized warships.
Prime contractor: OTO-Melara SpA, La Spezia, Italy.
Mode of operation: Radar or optronically directed, electrically driven automatic naval mount.
Users: Navies of Italy, Canada, Iraq, Peru and Venezuela.
Basic data: 39.97 tons (40,614kg) total installation weight inclusive of ammunition on gun.
Calibre 127mm (5in); 22.5ft (6.86m) barrel length.
Rate of fire: From a maximum of 40 down to 10 rounds per minute selectable, along with single shot.
Ammunition on gun: 66, comprising 3 loader drums of 22 rounds each.
Ammunition types: Readily selectable impact, delayed impact or proximity fuzed ammunition.
Arcs of fire: 350 degrees in azimuth; +85 to −15 degrees in elevation.
Range: 8.1 nautical miles (15km) maximum effective range against surface targets; 3.8 nautical miles (7km) maximum effective range against aerial targets.
Programme: During the mid-1960s, the Italian Navy and OTO-Melara carried out extensive studies into a new medium calibre naval mount, which, in turn, led to OTO-Melara receiving a contract to design and develop the 127/54 Compact mount in March 1966. Selected by both Italy and Canada for their 'Audace' class and 'Iroquois' class destroyers, the 127/54 mount was initially deployed in 1972 and has subsequently been selected and deployed as the primary gun armament for the 'Lupo' class frigates.
Notes: The OTO-Melara 127/54 Compact is one of the only two 127mm (5in) gun mounts currently in production throughout the Non-Eastern Bloc world, the other weapon in this category being the US Navy's Mk 45 mount. Compared with its US rival, the 127/54 has a heavier total mount weight, along with somewhat shorter maximum range. However, in comparison with the Mk 45, the Italian mount has a maximum rate of fire double that of the US weapon, coupled to which it carries over double (at 44) the number of ready to fire rounds per gun; giving the 127/54 Compact a distinct edge in terms of total ammunition 'throw weight'.

A Bofors TAK 120 mount in action aboard one of the two Finnish-built and operated 'Turunmaa' class corvettes.

Bofors TAK 120 Naval Guns

Role: Primary dual-purpose gun armament for frigate sized ships, down to vessels of around 600 tons.
Prime contractor: AB Bofors Ordnance, Bofors, Sweden.
Mode of operation: Single-barrelled automatic anti-air or surface target mount laid by shipboard sensor and driven electrohydraulically. In emergency, the mount can be laid manually.
Users: Navies of Sweden, Finland and Indonesia.
Basic data: 28.5 tons (28,960kg) total installation weight exclusive of ammunition.
Calibre: 4.72in (120mm).
Rate of fire: 80 rounds per minute selectable down to single shot.
Ammunition on gun: Up to 48 rounds and up to 16 ready to fire.
Ammunition types: Readily selectable impact or proximity fuzed rounds.
Arcs of fire: 360 degrees in azimuth; +80 to −10 degrees in elevation.
Range: 3.2 nautical miles (6km) for effective anti-air fire; 7.8 nautical miles (14.5km) for effective anti-surface fire; 12.4 nautical miles (23km) for maximum range fire against surface/shore targets.
Programme: Initially deployed aboard the Royal Swedish

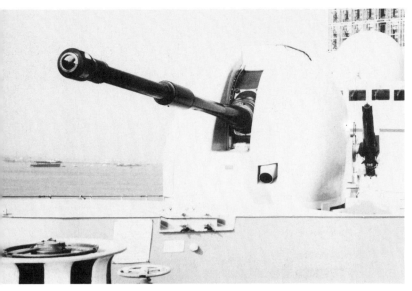

A frontal aspect of the Vickers Mk 8 single 4.5in naval gun mount seen fitted aboard a Type 42 Batch I 'Sheffield' class destroyer.

The Model 1968 mount as fitted to the French 'Georges Leygues' class destroyers and 'D'Estienne D'Orves' class corvettes.

Navy's 'Halland' class destroyers, the Bofor TAK 120 has subsequently been installed on the 2 Finnish-built 'Turunmaa' class corvettes and Indonesia's three 'Fatahillah' class corvettes.

Vickers Mk 8 Naval Guns

Role: Dual-purpose (anti-shipping/shore bombardment and anti-air).
Prime contractor: Vickers Shipbuilding& Engineering Limited, Barrow-in-Furness, Cumbria, UK.
Mode of operation: This single-barrelled fully automatic dual-purpose gun normally takes its sighting and firing instructions from shipboard radar, via the fire control system. However, in emergency, the gun can be laid and fired from deck-mounted optical sighting systems.
Users: Navies of Argentina, Brazil, Iran, Libya, Malaysia, Thailand and UK.
Basic data: 25.75 tons (26,162kg) total installation weight exclusive of ammunition.
Calibre: 4.5in (114mm).
Rate of fire: 25 rounds per minute.
Ammunition type: Compatible with all types of 4.5in (114mm) ammunition.
Ammunition on gun: 16 rounds ready to fire.
Arcs of fire: 340 degrees in azimuth; + 55 to − 10 degrees in elevation.
Range: Up to 7 nautical miles (13km) for effective ship-shore fire; up to 3.2 nautical miles (6km) for effective anti-air fire.
Programme: Based on the gun system design of the British Army's Abbott self-propelled 105mm gun, the Vickers-built Mk 8 naval mount was developed during the 1960s by the Royal Armament Research and Development Establishment on behalf of the Royal Navy. By the late 1960s, the Mk 8 had been selected as the primary gun armament for the Royal Navy's Type 82 and Type 42 destroyers and Type 21 frigates. Subsequently, this gun was to be fitted to a number of Vosper Thornycroft export frigates, including the Brazilian 'Niteroi' class, along with the two Yarrow Light Frigates exported to the Far East. The Mk 8 naval mount is to be fitted to the three Royal Navy Type 22 Batch III frigates and will, in all probability, be specified for incorporation aboard the Royal Navy's planned Type 23 frigates.
Notes: Battle-tested aboard Royal Navy warships serving with the British South Atlantic Task Force, the Vickers Mk

8 gun mount is electrically driven and incorporates a hydraulically powered ammunition feed system. Interestingly, although the Mk 8 gun has, in the past, been criticised for its low rate of fire (an important aspect in countering airborne threats), it appears to have stood up well to the rigours of being employed in sustained naval bombardment of on-shore targets during the critical phase of the Falklands campaign. Maximum range against surface targets is 11.8 nautical miles (21.9km).

DTCN Single 100mm Model 1968 Naval Guns

Role: Automatic dual-purpose (anti-ship/shore and anti-air).
Prime contractors: Cresuot-Loire, Paris, France and ECAN (Naval Arsenal), Ruelle, France.
Mode of operation: Fully automatic, electrically driven, single-barrelled mount, directed at the target with aiming data supplied by shipboard radar/optronic sensors via a fire control system.
Users: Navies of France, Argentina, Belgium, Malaysia and Portugal.
Basic data: 22 tons (22,353kg) total installation weight, exclusive of ammunition.
Calibre: 100mm; 18.0ft (5.5m) barrel length.
Rate of fire: Up to 60 rounds per minute or single shot.
Ammunition type: Proximity or impact/delayed impact fuzed; fragmentation or armour-piercing.
Ammunition on gun: Up to 90 rounds with ready selectability of type.
Arcs of fire: 350 degrees in azimuth; + 80 to − 15 degrees in elevation.
Range: 9.2 nautical miles (17km) maximum or 6.5 nautical miles (12km) effective against ship/shore targets; 4.3 nautical miles (8km) maximum or 3.2 nautical miles (6km) effective against air targets.
Programme: A refined version of the earlier 100mm Model 1953 and Model 1964 mounts, the Model 1968 was initially deployed aboard the French destroyer *Aconit* (D609) in March 1973. The Model 1968 has subsequently been installed aboard the 'Tourville' and 'Georges Leygues' classes of destroyers and 'D'Estienne D'Orves' class corvettes. The weapon has also been selected for installation aboard the 'Wielingen' class Belgium frigates. Portugal's 'Baptiste de Andrade' class frigates and to be retrofitted to Malaysia's two British-built

frigates. Production continuing for French new-builds.
Notes: The Model 1968 has a respectable rate of fire, along with a barrel life of around 3000 rounds. The Model 1968 mount will remain in production until completion of existing French destroyer and corvette programes, alongside assembly of the new 100mm Compact gun mount that weighs 16.73 tons (17,000kg) exclusive of ammunition. With an increased rage of fire quoted as up to 90 rounds per minute, the new 100mm Compact has already been selected by Saudi Arabia for installation aboard their 'Madina' class frigates.

OTO-Melara 76mm 76/72 Compact Naval Guns

Role: Dual-purpose (anti-ship/shore and anti-aircraft/missile).
Prime contractor: SpA OTO-Melara, La Spezia, Italy and licencees.
Mode of operation: Fully automatic, lightwieght mount that takes its target tracking and firing instructions from any of a large variety of radar-controlled or optronic fire control systems. The mount is electrically actuated.
Users: Navies of Algeria, Argentina, Australia, Brazil, Canada, Denmark, Ecuador, Egypt, Federal Germany, Greece, Iran, Iraq, Ireland, Israel, Italy, Japan, South Korea, Kuwait, Libya, Malaysia, Morocco, Netherlands, Nigeria, Oman, Peru, Qatar, Senegal, Singapore, South Africa, Spain, Taiwan, Thailand, Turkey, United Arab Emirates, US and Venezuela (as of mid 1985).
Basic data: 7.38 tons (7500kg) total installation weight, exclusive of ammunition (each round weighing up to 28.7lb (13kg).
Calibre: 76mm (3in): 12.95ft (5.47m) barrel length.
Rate of fire: From 85 round per minute maximum to single shot.
Ammunition types: Proximity and impact fuzed ammunition.
Ammunition on gun: 80 rounds ready to fire.
Arc of fore: Limited only to ship installation in azimuth; +85 to −15 degrees in elevation.
Range: Up to 8.8 nautical miles (16.3km) maximum horizontal range; maximum effective range against aerial targets reported as 2.7 nautical miles (5km).
Programme: Developed during thelatter half of the 1960s, this mount has rapidly established itself as the world's premier naval gun, thanks to a confluence of factors ranging from technical excellence, to the timing of its availability that, in turn, coincided with one of the major growth swings in the somewhat cyclic market for fast attack craft to frigate-sized warships. By mid-1983, known deliveries and orders for the 76/72 Compact mount had exceeded the 300 mark.
Notes: Unquestionably the best selling naval mount to be produced by any country in the post-World War II period, much of the success of this weapon must be attributed to the Italian Government's farsighted armament marketing policy of supporting areas of specific interest, such as naval guns and propulsive machinery, rather than dissipating its development effort and funding over too wide a spectrum of programmes. Another major factor underlying this export success story centres on the fact that this lightweight mount can be installed aboard craft having a displacement of as low as 100 tons.

Bofors SAK 57 Mk 1 Naval Guns

Role: Primary dual-purpose gun armament for frigates, patrol vessels and fast attack craft.
Prime contractor: AB Bofors Ordnance, Bofors, Sweden.
Mode of operation: single-barrelled automatic anti-air or

The 76mm OTO-Melara compact here seen mounted aboard the Venezuelan 'Constitucion' class craft Idependencia (P-13).

surface target mount normally laid by inputs from shipboard radar or electro-optical sensors. Electro-hydraulically driven, the mount can be laid and loaded manually if needs be, involving a 1 to 3 man mount crew in addition to the 2 hoist-bottom ammunition loaders normally required for protracted firing.
Users: Navies of Sweden, Finland, Indonesia, Iraq, Malaysia, Norway and Yugoslavia.
Basic data: 6.2 tons (6300kg) total installation weight exclusive of ammunition.
Calibre: 2.25in (57mm).
Rate of fire: 200 rounds per minute, normally involving four 10 round bursts against air targets down to single round fire against surface target.
Ammunition on gun: 128 rounds, with 40 rounds ready to fire.
Ammunition types: Readily selectable delayed-action impact or proximity fuzed rounds.
Arcs of fire: 360 degrees in Azimuth; +75 to −10 degrees in elevation.
Range: Up to 7.0 nautical miles (13km) for effective anti-surface target fire and 2.7 nautical miles (5km) for effective anti-air; 9.7 nautical miles (18km) maximum range against surface targets.
Programme: Developed out of earlier Bofors 57mm L/60 naval and military gun, the SAK 57 Mk 1 was first deployed aboard Sweden's six 'Spica' class during the latter half of the 1960s. Since then the mount has been

The Bofors 57mm SAK 57 Mk 1 naval mount installed aboard a Royal Swedish Navy's 'Spica' class fast attack craft.

selected for Sweden's 12 'Spica' II and 17 'Hugin' classes, Finland's eight 'Helsinki' class, Indonesia's 8 PSK class, Malayia's six 'Jerong', four 'Combattante' II and eight 'Handalan' classes, along with two mounts each for Yugoslavia's 'Rade Koncar' class (all the preceeding being fast attack craft). Other ships employing this gun are Norway's three 'Nordcapp' patrol vesels and the two Yugoslavian frigates under construction, plus the single examples of this basic design already sold to Indonesia and Iraq.

Notes: One of the most successful recent naval gun programmes, the Bofors SAK 57 Mk 1 owes much of this success not simply to its exceptionally high rate of fire, but to Bofors' philosophy of maintaining total control over the development not only of their guns, but also of the ammunition that they use. This 'double-footed' capability allows Bofors more flexibility than most in optimizing the effectiveness of the system. For example, the pre-fragmented, proximity fused anti-sea skimming misisle round employed on the SAK 57 embodies a wealth of earlier Bofors anti-air experience gained during the development of their highly effective 40mm proximity fused ammunition. Similarly, the enhanced lethalness of the SAK 57 Mk 1 gun against surface targets benefits from Bofors' associated development work into delayed-action impact fused rounds, which ensure that the shell explodes inside the target vessel rather than against its side where some of the blast would be dissipated.

Bofors SAK 57 Mk 2 Naval Guns

A Model of the SAK 57 Mk 2.

Role: Primary dual-purpose gun armament for frigates, patrol vessels, corvettes and fast attack craft.
Prime contractor: AB Bofors Ordnance, Bofors, Sweden.
Mode of operation: Single-barrelled fully automatic anti-air or surface target mount laid by shipboard sensors and electrically driven. In a back-up mode, the gun can be laid using a simple optical sight.
Users: Royal Swedish Navy and the navies of Canada and the Netherlands.
Basic data: 6 tons (6096kg) total installation weight exclusive of ammunition.
Calibre: 2.25in (57mm).
Rate of fire: 220 to 230 rounds per minute depending on ammunition type.
Ammunition on gun: 120 rounds of which up to 40 are ready to fire.

Ammunition types: As with SAK 57 Mk 1, plus new High Capacity Extended Range (HCER) round for use against surface targets.
Arcs of fire: 360 degrees in azimuth; +85 to −10 degrees in elevation.
Range: 8.6 nautical miles (16km) for effective anti-surface fire and 2.7 nautical miles (5km) for effective anti-air fire. 11.3 nautical miles (21km) maximum range against surface targets.
Programme: A much more automated and accurate derivative of the SAK 57 Mk 1, this gun has been ordered for the new Stockholm (Spica III) class of fast attack craft, plus Canada's Halifax class and the Dutch M class frigates.
Notes: Externally readily identifiable from its forebear, the SAK 57 Mk 2 mount is physically much smaller and slimmer. The Mk 2 mount benefits from an improved autostabilisation system for enchanced firing accuracy, an even higher rate of fire compared with the Mk 1, along with a new twin ammunition cassette feed system which enables the ready selection of varying ammunition types, including the new, longer ranged, higher explosive power HCER delayed-action, impact fuzed round.

Breda/Bofors Twin 40L70 Compact Naval Guns

Role: Twin-barrelled short-range anti-air and lightly armoured surface vessel weapon.
Prime contractor: Breda Meccanica Bresciana SpA, Brescia, Italy.

The Breda/Bofors twin 40mm mount seen aboard a 'Lupo' class frigate.

Mode of operation: electrically driven, unmanned mount that takes its target tracking and firing instrucitons from shipboard sensors, via a fire control system.
Users: Navies of Argentina, Bahrain, Colombia, Ecuador, Egypt, Iraq, Italy, Kuwait, Libya, Nigeria, Oman, Peru, Qatar, Saudi Arabia, Thailand, Tunisia, Turkey United Arab Emirates and Venezuela.

Basic data:	Type A	Type B
Total weight less ammunition:	12,125lb/ 5500kg	11,684lb/ 5300kg
Total weight with ammunition:	16,094lb/ 7300kg	13,889lb/ 6300kg

Calibre: 40mm; 9.19ft (2.8m) barrel length.
Rate of Fire: Twice 300 for a total 600 rounds per minute.
Ammunition Types: Proximity or impact/delayed impact fuzed; fragmentation or armour-piercing.

Ammunition on gun: 736 rounds on Type A; 444 rounds on Type B mount.

Arcs of fire: Limited only by superstructure in azimuth; +85 to −13 degrees in elevation.

Range: Over 2.4 nautical miles (4.5km) maximum against low-level air target; over 1.35 nautical miles (2.5km) demonstrated effective 98 per cent kill probability against sea-skimming or diving target.

Programme: Development of this mount was initiated in the mid-1960s as part of the Italian Navy DARDO radar-directed shipboard close-in weapons system. Firing trials with the mount were completed in early 1976, the mounting, as part of the DARDO system, being initially deployed aboard the *Lupo*, lead of class Italian frigate in 1977. Production of this mount continues at a relatively high rate.

Notes: This lightweight weapon with its minimum demands in terms of encroaching on shipboard space has proven popular with many navies. Even when operated in a single mount context, the demonstrated high kill probability of this weapon and its proximity fused ammunition at ranges beyond which missile debris could continue into its potential target does much to enchance its attractiveness over smaller calibre mounts; a factor that can only be strengthened with the inevitable deployment of next-generation supersonic sea-skimming,anti-ship missiles, whose debris could carry over substantially greater distances than the up to 0.49 nautical mile (900m) currently possible.

Oerlikon Type GDM-A Naval Gun

Role: Short-Range, rapid fire air defence.

Prime contractor: Oerlikon Buhrle, Zurich, Switzerland.

Mode of operation: This twin-barrelled gun can be operated either in a fully automatic mode taking its sighting instruction from any of a range of shipboard sensors such as radars, electro-optical or optical sighting devices via a suitable aiming processor. Alternatively, it can be controlled manually from within the mount by a gunner employing a lead angle computing sight and steering the guns by means of a stabilised sighting joystick control.

Users: Navies of Ecuador, Greece, Iran and Libya.

Basic data: Approximately 5.86 tons (5950kg) excluding ammunition rising to around 6.2 tons (6300kg) with 336 rouns carried.

Calibre: 35mm.

Rate of fire: 2 × 550 rounds per minute = 1100 rounds per minute.

Ammunition type: Impact and proximity fized 35mm.

Ammunition on gun: 336 rounds.

Arcs of fire: 360 degrees in azimuth; +85 to −15 degrees in elevation.

Range: From approximatley 1 nautical mile downwards.

Programme: Developed during the 1960s, Oerlikon has supplied small batches of these naval gun mounts to British, French and Federal German shipbuilders during the early and mid-1970s. The gun was fitted as original equipment aboard the following vessels: Iran's four British-built 'Saam' class frigates; Greece's four 'La Combattante' II fast attack craft; Libya's sole British-built Mark 7 frigate and the three West German-built 'Quito' class fast attack craft supplied to Ecuador.

Notes: The twin-barrelled gun element of this electrically-driven naval gun owes much to Oerlikon's earlier army field air defence weapon. OTO-Melara, the Italian armament manufacturer, has taken out a licence to employ this twin-barrelled gun system in a somewhat lighter gun mounting of their own design, in which the individual gun barrels are more widely separated, being positioned on the flanks of the turret.

The twin 35mm Oerlikon Type GDM-A seen installed aboard a Hellenic (Greek) Navy 'La Combattante' II class fast attack craft.

Emerlec-30 Naval Guns

Role: Power-operated, twin-barrelled, short-range anti-aircraft weapon.

Prime contractor: Emerson Electric Company, St Louis, Missouri, USA.

Mode of operation: This lightweight, twin-barrelled mount is electrically power-operated, with on-mount standby battery power and capability to revert to manual handcranking when all else fails. The mount can be trained and sighted by a gunner from within or directed remotely from a shipboard fire control system.

Users: Navies of Ecuador, Greece, South Korea, Malaysia, Nigeria and Philippines.

Basic data: 4200lb (1905kg) total installation weight including below deck ammnition bin, but excluding ammunition.

Calibre: 30mm.

Rate of fire: Twice 600 for a total of 1200 rounds per minute.

Ammunition: Impact-fuzed armour-piercing or fragmentation shells.

Ammunition on gun: 1970 rounds ready to fire.

Arcs of fire: Limited only by superstructure in azimuth; +80 to −15 degrees in elevation.

Range: Up to 2.37 nautical miles (4.4km) effective against sea-level targets or 14,760ft (4500m) effective against higher-level targets.

Programme: Developed during the first half of the 1970s, under contract to the US Navy for the EX-74 gun development programme, the first production of these units was put underway during 1976. Emerlec delivered the 100th example of this mount in early 1982.

Notes: This lightweight, all-weather Emerlec-30 mount employs the same twin Oerlikon 30mm KCB cannon as those fitted to the Royal Navy's BMARC-built GMC-A03-2 mount being retrofitted to 'Broadsword' class frigates.

The Emerlec-30 power-driven mount with its twin Oerlikon 30mm cannons.

Contraves 25mm Seaguard Naval Guns

Role; 25mm four-barrelled, radar directed, automatically aimed rapid rate of fire close-in weapons system for use against aircraft and missile (both sea-skimming and diving).
Prime contractor: Contraves AG, Zurich, Switzerland.

A close-up of the Contraves 25mm four-barrelled Seaguard close-in weapons system mount.

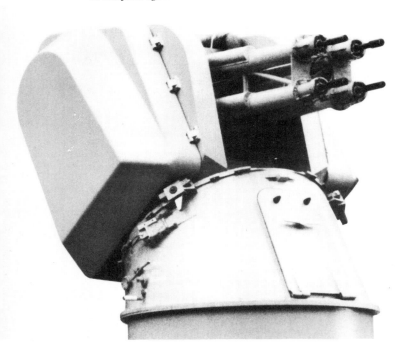

Mode of operation: Target detection and designation is derived from the Plessey Radar-developed Dolphin C-band search radar, the data being passed to the Seaguard multi-sensor (Ku-band radar infra-red and laser) tracking unit, which, in turn directs the aiming of the high agility gun mount. Each gun mount is remotely controlled from a one man tactical control console.
Users: Selected by several unidentified NATO navies, including Turkey.
Basic data: 4.3 tons (4500kg) for mount, exclusive of ammunition, plus another 4.3 tons (4500kg) of associated sensors and console, along with 1.18 tons (1200kg) of ammunition (1600 rounds).
Calibre: 25mm.
Rate of fire: $4 \times 50 = 3400$ rounds per minute total.
Ammunition on gun: 1600 rounds, comprising 400 rounds each in ammunition feed systems, each feeding one of the four independent gun barrels.
Ammunition type: Impact only (Anti-missile Discarding Sabot Shell).
Arcs of fire: 180 degrees in azimuth; + 127 to a maximum of − 40 degrees in elevation.
Range: Up to 1.08 nautical miles (2km) for high kill probability.
Programme: Work on the Seaguard system was initiated as a private venture by Contraves, a member of the Oerlikon-Buhrle Group, at the close of 1977. Live firing tests with the system's Sea Zenith gun mount commenced during the latter half of 1981 and by mid-1983, the Seaguard system had been selected by Turkey for incorporation aboard their new construction MEKO 200 frigates.
Notes: As with the US Navy's Phalanx and other close-in weapons systems employing smaller than 40mm ammunition, the Seaguard system depends on its fired rounds actually hitting the incoming threat. This prerequisite, in turn, infers that the threat must either be hit at a distance sufficient for its debris not to carry on into

its intended target, or that Seaguard can destroy the threat missile by detonating its warhead if hit at closer range. Unlike Phalanx, Seaguard is not dependent upon a common ammunition feeds system to maintain firing.

General Dynamics Mk 15 Phalanx Naval Guns

Role: Fully automatic, rapid firing short-range anti-aircraft/missile weapons system.
Prime contractor: General Dynamics' Ponoma Division, Ponoma, California, USA.
Mode of operation: The system incoporates the means with which to search, detect and track incoming targets in any weather, while evaluating and setting threat-countering priorities in the case of detecting multiple hostiles (this function being subject to human over-ride). Once within effective firing range, the system's integral multi-barrelled gun lays down a stream of fire, whose track is compared by the system's closed loop processor with that of the target, the processor driving the gun laying mechanism so that the two tracks are brought into coincidence.
Users: Navies of the US, Saudi Arabia, UK and Japan.
Basic data: Less than 5.85 tons per overall system package, exclusive of ammunition.
Calibre: 20mm employing special rounds (see **Ammunition** below).
Rate of fire: 6 × 500 rounds per minute = 3000 rounds per minute.
Ammunition type: Special-to-system saboted 12.5mm heavy metal bullet mated to 20mm shell.
Ammunition on gun: 1100 rounds.
Arcs of fire: 360 degrees in azimuth; + 90 to − 35 degrees in elevation.
Range: Effective from 0.9 nautical miles downwards.
Programme: General Dynamics received the initial feasibility study contract in 1969 and were given the go-ahead to proceed with the full-scale engineering develoment of the system during 1970. By late 1973, a seagoing prototype Phalanx system had been installed aboard the 'Coontz' class destroyer USS *King* (DDG41). Initial production contract award for the system was received in 1977, with the first production system being delivered in 1979 (the first of these to go to sea being installed aboard the aircraft carrier USS *America* (CV66) in 1980). General Dynamics delivered the 100th system during April 1982 and 171 systems by the end of 1982, with the current order book extending deliveries into 1988.
Notes: Development under the guidance of the US Naval Sea Systems Command, the Phalanx system employs the General Electric six-barrel Gatling-type Vulcan gun around which have been fitted separate search and tracking radars, fire control processing electronics and gun training mechanism all assembled ina single, simple bolt-on package (only the gunnery control console being built as a separate unit). During Operational Test and Evaluation (OPEVAL) trials, conducted between 1974 and 1977, the Phalanx system demonstrated its ability to hit all types of targets flown against it, including supersonic drones, sea-skimming missiles and streamed multiple target attacks. The US Navy currently plans to install or refit Phalanx aboard 35 ship classes, representing more than 270 indivudual vessels. The system is also fitted to the Saudi Arabian PCG612 and PGG 511 classes, along with having been retrofitted to both of the Royal Navy's 'Invincible' class carriers in the wake of the Falklands air attack experience. Japan has placed large-scale production contracts for Phalanx, which is to be retrofitted to existing ships as well as being installed aboard new build ship programmes.

The US Navy's Mk 15 Phalanx close-in weapons system seen in action.

Oerlikon single 20mm Type GAM-B01 Naval Guns

Role: Manually operated, short-range anti-air lightly armoured surface craft weapon.
Prime contractor: Oerlikon-Buhrle Ltd, Zurich, Switzerland and its UK subsidiary: British Manufacture & Research Ltd, Grantham, Lincolnshire, UK.
Mode of operation: This lightweight, single-barrelled gun mount is trained and elevated manually by its gunner, who sights the weapon with bead sight or, optionally, with a low light/night vision sight as fitted on recent Royal Navy mounts (see accompanying photograph).
Users: Navies of Spain and UK.
Basic data: 1102lb (500kg) total installation weight, including 198lb (90kg) of ammunition.
Calibre: 20mm 5.58ft (1.7m) barrel length.
Rate of fire: Approximately 1000 rounds per minute, or single shot.
Ammunition type: Impact-fused only.
Ammunitin on gun: Belt-fed ammunition box containing 200 rounds.
Arcs of fire: Limited only by superstructure in azimuth; + 60 degrees to − 15 degrees in elevation.
Range: 3.7 nautical miles (6.8km) range against surface target; 2.4 nautical miles (4.5km) maximum range against air targets.
Programme: Developed during the mid-1970s as a replacement for the earlier Oerlikon 20/80 single gun mount, the GAM-B01 mount has been ordered by the Royal Navy for installation aboard its 'Sheffield' class destroyers as an interim short ranged anti-air weapon pending selection and installation of a close-in weapons gun system.
Notes: The Oerlikon Type GAM-B01 mount employs the Oerlikon KAA belt-fed automatic firing cannon. Beautifully engineered as this weapon is, its overall

281

The carefully balanced design of the GAM-BO1 relieves the gunner of much of the physical effort involved in tracking the target with this purely manually operated weapon.

The Creusot-Loire 100mm Compact.

accuracy, dependent as it is upon manual tracking, is very much reliant upon the competence and temperament of the gunner, particularly when attempting to his such a low frontal area targets as an oncoming sea-skimming missile.

Creusot-Loire 100mm Compact Naval Guns

Role: Single-barrelled fully automatic dual-purpose mount for fire against surface or air-threat targets.
Prime contractor: Creusot-Loire, Division Mecanique Specialisee, Paris, France.
Mode of operation: Fully automatic ammunition loading, hydraulically actuated and electricaly trained and elevated mount. The mount takes its aiming data from shipboard sensors in the form of radar, optronic or optical fire control systems via the mount's remotely-positioned main control processor. In an emergency, the mount can be hand-cranked into position and fired so long as the correct interlocks are set and electrical and compressed air are available on mount.
Users: Navies of Saudi Arabia and Malaysia; the mount is also on order for future French warships.
Basic data: 13.287 tons (13,500kg) total mount weight, exclusive of ammunition.
Calibre: 100mm; 18.0ft (5.5m) barrel length.

Rate of fire: 90 rounds per minute, or selectable in 40 rounds per minute, 10 round per minute or single shot steps.
Ammunition on turret: Up to 18 rounds, with a further 48 automatically transferred from magazine without need to reload by a 2 or 3 man crew.
Ammunition type: High explosive or fragmentation with impact, delayed impact or variable proximity fuzing.
Arcs of fire: Up to 350 degrees in azimuth; +80 degrees to −15 degrees in elevation.
Range: 9.4 nautical miles (17.5km) maximum range against surface targets; 5.4 nautical miles (10km) against surface or 4.3 nautical miles (8km) against air targets effective range.
Programme: Design work on this mount was initiated towards the end of the 1970s. All phases of the mount's firing trials had been completed by the autumn of 1984. This gun has been chosen for installation aboard the Saudi Arabian four-ship 'Madina' class frigates and Malaysia's two-ship 'Howaldtswerke' FS1500 class frigates. The mount is also scheduled to be installed on future French frigates and destroyers.
Notes: With a barrel life of over 3000 rounds, this water-cooled gun mount's low total installed weight permits it to be fitted to vessels with a full load displacement as low as 786 tons. The mount's high maximum rate of fire should contribute significantly to the weapon's 'kill' potency against fast moving incoming air threats.

Addenda

Fairey Loadmaster 33 Class Landing Craft

Role: Amphibious warfare.
Builder: Fairey Marine, UK.
User: Kuwaiti Navy.
Basic data: 350 tons full displacement; 108.3ft (33.0m) overall length: 33.5ft (10.2m) maximum beam.
Propulsion: 2 Caterpillar 3412 DITA 12 diesels (total 1214bhp): 2 propellers.
Sensors: 1 Racal Decca 150 sea search and navigational radar.
Armament: 2 single machine guns on bridge deck flanks.
Top speed: 10.5 knots.
Range: 1000 nautical miles at 10 knots.
Programme: Ordered in March 1983, as a final part of a larger naval support craft contract undertaken for the Kuwaiti Ministry of Defence, the first of this four-craft class was launched in September 1983. The lead craft was delivered in July 1984, with deliveries of the remaining craft being completed by August 1985.
Notes: The Loadmaster 33 design derives from the smaller Cheverton Loadmaster (Cheverton having been acquired by Fairey Marine in 1982). However, unlike the earlier Loadmaster, the new 33 metre model incorporates a totally new hull, much more boat-like than the traditional flat-bottomed shape associated with landing craft. This new, double-chined hull, combined with its twin tunnel located and Kort-nozzled propellers improve the craft's performance considerably, especially in terms of going astern, general seaworthiness and manoeuvrability. In terms of load-carrying, the Loadmaster 33 can accommodate up to 150 tons of cargo, including up to two 60 ton main battle tanks embarked and off-loaded via a 14.8ft (4.5m) power winch operated bow ramp.

A Loadmaster 33 on trials carrying a Chieftain main battle tank, along with another piece of heavy earth-moving equipment.

Rockwell North American OV-10 Bronco Light Strike Aircraft

Type and role: 2-crew, twin turbo prop-engined, land or carrier-going, poor weather-capable close air support and observation aircraft.
Maker: Rockwell North American, Columbus Division, Ohio, USA.
Users: US Marine Corps, US Navy and the air forces of the US, Federal Germany, Indonesia, Morocco, Philippines, Thailand and Venezuela.
Engines: 2 Garrett T76-G-420/1 turboprops (total 2080shp) each driving a 3-bladed reversible-pitch propellers on OV-10D (earlier models had less power).
Dimensions: 41.6ft (12.7m) overall length; 40.0ft (12.2m) wingspan; 291sq ft (27.0m²) wing area.
Weights: 7190lb (3261kg) operating empty; 14,444lb (6552kg) maximum gross. *Note*: data for OV-10D.
Performance: 244 knots/452km/h maximum level speed at sea level; 2380ft/725m/min initial rate of climb; 28,800ft/8778m service ceiling; 270 nautical miles/500km radius of action with internal fuel only.
Armament: Up to 3800lb (1724kg) of externally-carried bombs, rocket pods and/or 20mm multi-barrelled gun,

including ammunition for the two 7.62mm internally mounted guns.
Programmes: In late 1963, the US Marine Corps drew up their Light Armed Reconnaissance Airplane (LARA) requirement, full-scale development of which, including seven development aircraft, being awarded to North American's OV-10 design in August 1964. The first YOV-10A prototype made its maiden flight in July 1965, by which time the programme was being pursued as a joint US Marine, Navy and Air Force venture. The first production contract, covering 185 aircraft (109 USAF and 76 USMC) was placed in October 1966, followed by the Bronco's initial operational deployment in Vietnam in July 1968. Including export models, Rockwell North

This US Marine Corps' OV-10D, caught in a characteristic pose, displays its unlovely, but highly functional form. Note the externally carried stores.

The single 100mm automatic loading dual-purpose turret, two of which are seen mounted forward on the 'Udaloy' class destroyer Vitse Admiral Kulakov.

American were to build a total of 384 OV-10s prior to the programme's completion.

Notes: Similar in its basic configuration to the earlier French-developed Potez 75 counter-insurgency (COIN) design, the OV-10 Bronco is capable of operating out of rough fields or from the deck of a 'Tarawa' class assault ship. The US Marine Corps and Air Force operated OV-10Ds are re-engined conversions of existing OV-10As, the noses of which have been rebuilt to house an infra-red night sight/laser target designator turret. Besides these modifications, the OV-10D has provision to mount a 20mm triple-barrelled M-97 gun pod further aft beneath the fuselage. These night-capable OV-10Ds were developed for South East Asian operations under the US Air Force-led 'Pave Nail' programme introduced operationally during early 1972.

Soviet Single 100mm Dual-Purpose Naval Guns

Role: Primary dual-purpose (against air or surface targets) gun armament for destroyer and frigate-sized ships.
Prime contractor: Soviet.
Mode of operation: Single-barrelled, automatically-loaded anti-surface or air mounting normally radar directed. However, in emergency the gun's fire can be directed manually from the gun mount.
User: Soviet Navy.
Basic data: No verifiable information available.
Calibre: 100mm; 15.24ft (5.0m) barrel length.
Rate of fire: 80 rounds per minute maximum, selectable down to single shot firing.
Ammunition on turret: No verifiable information available.
Ammunition type: Armour-piercing or fragmentation warhead with relevant impact or proximity fuzing.
Arcs of fire: No verifiable information available.
Range: Estimated 8.1 nautical miles (15km) maximum range against surface targets; 4.3 nautical mies (8km) effective range against surface or air targets.
Programme: Developed during the earlier half of the 1970s, this gun made its operational debut aboard the 'Krival' II class frigates, each of which carries two mounts, as does the 'Udaloy' class destroyers. Two of these single 100mm guns are fitted aboard the lead of class battle cruiser *Kirov*, but have been replaced by the new Soviet twin 130mm mounting aboard *Frunze* and later ships of this class.
Notes: The Soviet single 100mm gun makes an interesting comparison with the French-developed 100mm Model 1968, with the Soviet gun trading a somewhat shorter maximum range for a higher rate of fire.

CASA C-212 Aviocar Maritime Patrol

Type and role: 2 to 6-crew, twin turbo prop-engined, rough-field-capable landbased maritime surveillance and transport aircraft.
Maker: Construcciones Aeronauticas SA, Madrid, Spain and Indonesian licensee.
Users: Navies of Indonesia (6) and Mexico (10), plus the air forces of Indonesia, Jordan, Portugal, Spain and Uruguay, along with numerous civilian operators.
Engines: 2 Garrett TPE-331-1OR turboprop (total 1800shp) each driving a 4-bladed reversible-pitch propeller.
Dimensions: 49.75ft (15.2m) overall length; 62.3ft (19.0m) wingspan; 430.5sq ft (40.0m^2) wing area.
Weights: 9072lb (4115kg) empty unequipped for role; 16,975lb (7700kg) maximum take-off.
Performance: 194 knots/360km/hour maximum level speed at 1000ft/305m; 1555ft/474m/min initial rate of climb.
Armament: Optional underwing pylons for up to 2 lightweight anti-submarine torpedoes or 2 Sea Skua-sized anti-ship missiles.
Programme: Designed to a 1965 Spanish Air Force requirement for a light, short/rough airfield-capable transport, the first of two CASA C-212 prototypes made its maiden flight in late March 1971. Subsequently to be built both in Spain and under licence by PT Nurtanio in Indonesia, the CASA C-212 Aviocar has proven popular with military and civilian operators alike, with more than 370 aircraft sold in total by the end of May 1985.
Notes: An extremely rugged and readily maintainable aircraft, the military/naval models of the C-212 Aviocar embody a rear fuselage loading ramp. The Spanish Air Force were the first to exploit the Aviocar's maritime surveillance capability by equipping the machine with a nose-mounted air-to-surface radar, plus, in their case, the equipment necessary to carry out search and rescue missions at sea. The incorporation of the nose radome adds 2.5ft (0.76m) to the standard overall length of the C-212 quoted above.

A CASA C-212 Aviocar passing abeam the container ship MS Sea Land Pioneer; *this particular aircraft belonging to the Spanish Air Force.*

Index of warships

Index of naval aircraft

Index of naval missiles

Index of naval guns

Index of navies